BODY AND SOUL

Body and Soul

ESSAYS ON ARISTOTLE'S HYLOMORPHISM

Jennifer Whiting

OXFORD
UNIVERSITY PRESS

Oxford University Press is a department of the University of Oxford. It furthers
the University's objective of excellence in research, scholarship, and education
by publishing worldwide. Oxford is a registered trade mark of Oxford University
Press in the UK and certain other countries.

Published in the United States of America by Oxford University Press
198 Madison Avenue, New York, NY 10016, United States of America.

© Oxford University Press 2023

All rights reserved. No part of this publication may be reproduced, stored in
a retrieval system, or transmitted, in any form or by any means, without the
prior permission in writing of Oxford University Press, or as expressly permitted
by law, by license, or under terms agreed with the appropriate reproduction
rights organization. Inquiries concerning reproduction outside the scope of the
above should be sent to the Rights Department, Oxford University Press, at the
address above.

You must not circulate this work in any other form
and you must impose this same condition on any acquirer.

Library of Congress Cataloging-in-Publication Data
Names: Whiting, Jennifer, author.
Title: Body and soul : essays on Aristotle's hylomorphism / Jennifer Whiting.
Description: New York, NY, United States of America : Oxford University Press, [2023] |
Includes bibliographical references and index. |
Contents: v. 1. Body and soul—v. 2. Living together |
Identifiers: LCCN 2023004938 (print) | LCCN 2023004939 (ebook) |
ISBN 9780197666005 (v. 1 ; hb) | ISBN 9780199969678 (v. 2 ; hb) |
ISBN 9780197666029 (v. 1 ; epub) | ISBN 9780197666036 |
ISBN 9780197682708 (v. 2 ; epub) | ISBN 9780190063160
Subjects: LCSH: Hylomorphism. | Aristotle.
Classification: LCC BD648 .W45 2023 (print) | LCC BD648 (ebook) |
DDC 128/.1—dc23/eng/20230501
LC record available at https://lccn.loc.gov/2023004938
LC ebook record available at https://lccn.loc.gov/2023004939

DOI: 10.1093/oso/9780197666005.001.0001

Printed by Integrated Books International, United States of America

To the August Company of
Martin, Fabienne, and Tom
... and Ethan

Contents

Preface ix
Acknowledgments xiii

Introduction 1

1. Form and Individuation in Aristotle 17

2. Form and Generation in Aristotle 35

3. Living Bodies 58

4. Metasubstance: Critical Notice of Frede-Patzig and Furth 77

5. Locomotive Soul: The Parts of Soul in Aristotle's Scientific Works 102

6. Hylomorphic Virtue: Cosmology, Embryology, and Moral Development in Aristotle 151

7. *Nicomachean Ethics* VII.3 on Akratic Ignorance (with Martin Pickavé) 177

8. The Lockeanism of Aristotle 216

9. The Mover(s) of Rational Animals: *De Anima* III.11 in context 261

REPRINT INFORMATION 283
INDEX LOCORUM 285
GENERAL INDEX 299

Preface

THIS IS THE third of three volumes that collect essays drafted, with one exception, between 1980 and 2011. (The exception is Chapter 9 in this volume, drafted in 2016 and recently added because its contents are closely related to those of Chapters 5 and 6.) I have made small changes here and there, especially in punctuation, so as to make individual sentences easier to read. And I have added, in square brackets, cross-references to essays in the other volumes, along with a few notes. But the essays are otherwise unchanged. I have arranged the essays within each volume in the order in which they were drafted, rather than that in which they were published, since this best displays the evolution of my thought. But I have assigned the essays to their respective volumes more or less along thematic lines.

The essays in Volume I present my attempts to come to grips with the philosophical questions that have been of most interest to me since my first encounter with philosophy, reading Plato's *Apology* and *Crito* in my early teens and being immediately captivated by the character of Socrates: questions about our nature as persons, our knowledge of ourselves and one another, and the prima facie tension between what justice sometimes requires of us and what we owe—or are at least permitted to grant—to those to whom we stand in special relations such as friendship and kinship. Though Plato's *Euthyphro* remains the most brilliant treatment I know of these last questions, my own positive views owe more to Aristotle than to Plato, with whose works I am only recently, and very gradually, starting to find my footing.

The single most important idea in Volume I—the one that ties most of the essays together—is Aristotle's conception of the ideal sort of friend as an "other self." It is from this that my title, *First, Second, and Other Selves*, derives. But the essays in that volume, though generally inspired by my reading of Aristotle, are not directly concerned with what Aristotle himself thought. The precarious task of forming hypotheses about that is reserved for essays collected in the second and third volumes, where I pursue questions about what might be called, borrowing from Terence Irwin's title, "the metaphysical and psychological basis of Aristotle's ethics."

The first two essays in Volume II are relics of the dissertation I was writing on this topic when I first met Rogers Albritton and had two relatively brief but remarkably fruitful conversations with him about the material in "Form and Individuation in Aristotle" (Volume III, Chapter 1; henceforth III.1). He said—rightly, I then thought and still do think—that what I had to say about Aristotle's metaphysics was more interesting than what I had to say about the connection between Aristotle's metaphysics and his ethics. So eight months later I submitted a dissertation—*Individual Forms in Aristotle* (Cornell 1984)—whose central arguments are presented in Chapters 1 to 4 of the present volume (on which more in the introduction that follows). The remaining essays back in Volume II explore questions at the heart of my original project: questions about Aristotle's conception of eudaimonia and the extent to which it is grounded in his account of the human essence or what John McDowell calls "first" as distinct from "second" nature; and questions about the roles played in that conception by the activities of theoretical and practical intellect and by the quality of our relationships with one another. Special attention is paid to Aristotle's account of "character-friendship," which inspired most of the essays on friendship and personal identity that appear in Volume I.

The first step there was to defend neo-Lockean accounts of personal identity against the charge that they make our future selves numerically distinct from our present selves and so undermine the common-sense view that each of us has special reasons to care about our own futures selves, reasons commonly called "prudential" and taken to be different in kind from those we have to care about other folks' present or future selves. I recommended that neo-Lockeans assimilate the special concern we are supposed to have for our own (as distinct from others') future selves to the special concern we are supposed to have for our own (as distinct from others') friends. This allows neo-Lockeans to concede (at least for the sake of argument) the numerical distinctness of our present and future selves without having to give up on the idea that each of us is justified in having special concern for her own (as distinct from others') future selves. The key is to see that just as concern for another is part of what makes the other one's friend in the first place, so too concern for a future self is part of what makes a future self one's own in the first place. Special concern is in each case part of what *constitutes* the relationship: just as concern for another is part and parcel of the friendship relation, so too concern for our future selves is part and parcel of the sort of psychological continuity that serves (according to neo-Lockeans) to bind us to our future selves.

I support this by comparison with the Buddhist ideal of self-dissolution. Absent common patterns of concern, there is no persisting self in play. But it does not follow that the appearance of persisting selves is illusory. Common patterns of concern are partly constitutive of the existence of such selves. And preventing their existence may be well-nigh impossible, especially if evolution favors them, which is why I speak of the Buddhist "ideal." But this ideal is compatible with the point at the heart of my argument—namely, that such concerns play a causal-cum-constitutive role in the existence and persistence over time of what we call "selves." I return to these questions in Chapter 8 of the present volume, where I situate neo-Lockean accounts of personal identity in broader historical context, starting with Aristotle's views about the nature of substance, to which much of the present volume is devoted.

Acknowledgments

I HAVE OFTEN been tempted to curse Rogers Albritton and Sydney Shoemaker: Rogers for having rerouted my dissertation through Aristotle's *Metaphysics* and Sydney for encouraging me so long to turn the product into a book that I decided in the end not to publish (referred to, alas, in published notes, as "*Aristotelian Individuals*, forthcoming"). But I could never bring myself to curse them. I have learned too much from them and have, more importantly, been blessed over the years by their friendship. I am grateful to Rogers for the role he played in leading me to develop the argument that spans Chapters 1–4 below. What I owe to Sydney is perhaps clearest in the essays on personal identity collected in Volume I. But all of that came long after the independent study in which Kristin Guyot and I worked with him through David Wiggins's *Sameness and Substance*. And after countless discussions prompted by Sydney's written comments, as constructive as they were critical, on the dissertation material included in the present volume. It was only after an exceptionally fruitful year in Oxford that I turned, under the influence of Derek Parfit, to the topic of personal identity as such and so, once again, to Sydney.

Thanks to the generosity of Lesley Brown (who hosted me at Sommerville College) and the Woodrow Wilson Foundation (which awarded me a Charlotte W. Newcombe Fellowship for the academic year 1982–1983), I wrote most of the dissertation in Oxford, where I benefited from hours of lively conversation with Michael Woods and David Charles. I was warmly welcomed by the members of David's reading group on the *Posterior Analytics*—Paula Gottlieb, Lindsey Judson, Gavin Lawrence, Penelope Mackie, Chris Megone, and Michael Morris—and thus acquired a taste for their spirit of collaborative (but not necessarily unanimous) attention to detail, something I have continued to enjoy over the years, these days in the *Parva Naturalia* reading group hosted by Verity Harte, Brad Inwood (with whom I worked closely in Toronto), and again David (with whom I have been in dialogue for nearly forty years). I was also fortunate during the year in Oxford to attend the London reading group that was then working its way through *Metaphysics* Z. I was rendered mute by the august company but had countless conversations in private with Bob Heinaman. His work on Aristotle's commitment to individual forms served as a model for my own and he hosted me repeatedly throughout that year and in the years that followed, even when he moved from London to the Lake District.

But being less interested in metaphysics as such than in the metaphysical and psychological bases of ethical views, I was inspired by Derek Parfit's lectures on personal identity and began during the year in Oxford to correspond with him about the potential connections between psychological continuity theories of personal identity and theories of rationality (both prudential and moral). His untimely death is a serious loss—if not (given his views) to himself, at least to those of us nourished by his intellectual and personal generosity. Most of the fruits of my conversations with him are presented in Volume I, but I followed up in recent years with the historical background presented in Chapter 8 below, "The Lockeanism of Aristotle" (on which I received helpful comments from another dear, departed friend: Sarah Broadie).

That chapter was completed during the year I spent as an Adenauer Prize Fellow at the Humboldt University in Berlin: I am grateful to the Royal Society of Canada and the Humboldt Stiftung for that opportunity, to Christof Rapp and Dominik Perler for their superb hospitality, and to Marta Jimenez for research assistance above and beyond the call of duty. My work on Chapter 8 benefited most from conversations with Sebastian Rödl and the members of his seminar in Basel, who spent weeks in advance of my visit preparing to discuss it. The same group later spent weeks preparing to discuss "Locomotive Soul" together with other articles on Aristotle's *De Anima* by Hendrik Lorenz and Aryeh Kosman, who were also present and to whom I owe much over many years. I am grateful to all who participated in those conversations, especially Matt Boyle and Matthias Haase; and to those who continued some of these conversations in Leipzig, especially Andrea Kern, whose work on rational capacities plays (together with Boyle's work) an increasingly prominent role in my thoughts about personal identity. I have recently been rethinking my views in conversations with Erica Shumener and the members of our graduate seminar, trying to develop a version of animalism that applies to rational animals as such, thus incorporating key insights of the Lockean account of persons. I call this "Rational-animalism" (with 'rational' modifying 'animal' and the '-ism' applying to the whole) and I distinguish this view from what I call "dumb Animalism" (with 'dumb' modifying the name of the philosophical position). Erica's departure for Syracuse is a real blow to the Pitt department, but I look forward to continuing conversations with her high above Cayuga's waters.

It was also during the year in Oxford that I first encountered John McDowell, whose early papers on Aristotle I had read but not yet begun to fathom. Fortune favored me when I landed in Pittsburgh simultaneously with John, without whose moral support I would not have survived the early years there. His influence on my reading of Aristotle is manifest in Chapters 5–9 of this volume. But I am no less indebted to Steve Engstrom and to the experience of co-teaching with him, which sparked the transition from the relatively scattershot method employed in Chapters 1–4 to the more dialectical approach to individual texts employed in the later chapters. Of course I could not have grown into this approach had I not enjoyed years of conversation with significant others—especially Gisela Striker, Charles Brittain, and Michael Thompson, for whose friendship over many years I am profoundly grateful.

Many other friends have made this work and its appearance in these volumes possible: Anil Gupta, who suggested the "three state solution," and Peter Ohlin, whose confidence in the project made it possible. Anil's comments on the Introduction that follows also helped me to clarify its highly compressed argument. Larkin Philpot has assisted from day one of the work on Volume I (and still keeps track of important things, like reprint permissions); Max Tegtmeyer has helped me edit Volumes II and III; and Victor Gonçalves de Sousa has served as proof reader extraordinaire. Thanks to him I have even improved some of the translations. But these things are small compared to what I have learned from them both in the classroom and in discussions about their dissertations and much else. Aristotle's hylomorphism plays a central role in Max's work and Victor is a living, breathing critical apparatus of the texts featured in this volume. For a note about Larkin's thesis on Aristotle's assimilation of the primary form of friendship to virtue, see the Introduction that follows here.

Last but not least, my collaboration with Martin Pickavé—first in co-teaching Aristotle and his medieval commentators on akrasia, then in co-authoring and much else—was the greatest, but one, windfall of my years in Toronto. It is exceeded only by his and Fabienne's friendship with me and Tom, who routinely enjoys much deserved breaks from the superhero demands placed on him at home when he visits Fabienne and Martin in Switzerland for hiking, wining, and dining. (Tom cannot altogether escape the superhero thing, so he adds mountain races, placing right up there with people who train year round at altitude.) I dedicate this volume, with love and admiration, to my crystal gems: Martin, Fabienne, and Tom . . . and Ethan (who spices up my life on a daily basis).

Introduction

THESE ESSAYS DEAL for the most part with Aristotle's protean conception of the relationship between form [*morphê*] and matter [*hulê*]. They are grounded in the "hylomorphism" of *De Anima* II.I, where Aristotle describes an animal's soul as the form and the essence [*to ti ên einai*] of its organic body. I discuss this view at length in "Living Bodies" (Chapter 3). But as I argue in "Hylomorphic Virtue" (Chapter 6), Aristotle also adopts a hylomorphic account of the relationship between practical intellect and the desiring part [*to orektikon*] of a human soul. On this account, moral development recapitulates (so to speak) the coming-to-be of the organism. Just as menstrual fluid must be "mastered" by the form carried in the movements of the father's semen, so too a child's desires must be "mastered" by the form embodied in the habits and customs established by its father and/or other pedagogues. If all goes well, the child acquires *phronêsis*, which is the central virtue of practical intellect and the proper form of the *orektikon*.

The emphasis here is on "proper," since, as with bodily parts, things can go wrong. Just as there can be blind eyes and paralytic limbs, so too human desire can fail to develop in appropriate ways. Its subjects may end up vicious or akratic. Chapter 7 ("*Nicomachean Ethics* VII.3 on Akratic Ignorance," co-authored with Martin Pickavé) is focused on the case of *akrasia*, where the *orektikon* is only partially mastered by practical intellect, with the result that recalcitrant desires sometimes lead an agent to act in ways opposed to those recommended by her own intellect [*nous*]. Pickavé and I rely on the sort of explanatory asymmetries afforded by Aristotle's teleology, asymmetries

I explain in Chapter 6 ("Hylomorphic Virtue") and exploit in Chapter 9 ("The Movers of Rational Animals").

In nature as in craft, the generator somehow embodies the form that comes to be in what is generated and the generator imparts that form (via movements in some medium) to matter suitable for receiving it. When the elements are (so to speak) aligned, and present in whatever proportions are required to realize the relevant form, then formal causes dominate the explanatory scene and matter plays a supporting role in something like the way suggested by Socrates in the "autobiographical" passage of Plato's *Phaedo*: form is the true cause and matter is that without which form could not function as cause.

Aristotle is with Socrates in spirit if not in letter: when the elements are suitably aligned, formal causes dominate and matter plays a supporting role. But Aristotle wants to recognize matter's status as a genuine cause, and not simply some sine qua non, for at least two reasons. First, even when things go well and the relevant form is completely realized, features of the matter in which the form is realized are responsible for many accidents of the hylomorphic compound: its qualities, for example, such as the color of its skin or hair, and its size. Second, when things go (teleologically speaking) wrong, Aristotle tends to trace the flaws to matter's capacity to interfere in efficient-causal ways with the operation of formal causes. Just as a knife is blunted by that which it cuts, so too form-imparting movements can be affected by the matter they strive to "master." When the matter is recalcitrant—when, for example, the menstrual fluid is too great in quantity and/or too cold—the result is an incomplete realization of the father's form: a daughter, for example, or a son who resembles his mother and her ancestors. And even in the case of "natural" death, Aristotle treats the decline of the animal's body as due to the ways in which the elements of which its parts are composed act in accordance with *their* respective natures—vital heat escaping as fire moves up and out, bones shrinking as earth moves down, etc. For more on this, see "Living Bodies" (Chapter 3), which prepares the way for "Hylomorphic Virtue: Cosmology, Embryology, and Moral Development" (Chapter 6).

Chapters 6 and 7 take up one of the ideas prominent in Volume I, the idea of what I call "psychic contingency." There are two thoughts here: first, that the psychological structures characteristic of human beings may in fact vary, not just from one cultural (or socio-historical) context to another, but even within relatively unified cultural and socio-historical contexts from one *individual* to another; and second, that such variation may be legitimate in ways that are not always recognized. In "Friends and Future Selves" (I.1), I stress the potential legitimacy of such variation by appeal to Buddhist views opposing the forms of attachment to our future selves that cultivate the illusion (as Buddhists see it) and the existence (as I see it) of selves that persist over time. I consider other possible forms of legitimate variation in I.4 ("Back to 'The Self and the Future'") and I.6 ("One is not Born but Becomes a Person"). But in I.7, "Psychic Contingency in the *Republic*," I turn to ways in which variations in psychic structure can be pathological.

That essay rejects the standard reading according to which Plato's Socrates takes each and every human soul to have exactly three and only three parts (the rational, the spirited, and the appetitive) and sees contingency only in the ways in which these parts are *related* to one another in this or that individual soul. On my account, Plato has Socrates speak of the so-called appetitive part in two different ways. In the well-ordered souls discussed in *Republic* II–IV, where musical and medical models prevail, *to epithumêtikon* is simply a class [*genos*] of individual appetites, each natural, moderate, and doing its own job. In corrupt souls of the sort discussed in *Republic* VIII and IX, where political models prevail, *to epithumêtikon* is a distinct part [*meros*] of soul: it is an organized unit making demands against other such units in ways analogous to those in which one political faction [again, *meros*] makes demands against others. And just as there should be no factions in a well-ordered state, so too there should be no appetitive *part*, as distinct from class of individual appetites, in a well-ordered soul. But these are norms departures from which are all too common. So Plato recognizes a form of "radical psychic contingency" in which corrupt human souls have "parts" rather than well-ordered ones.

I defend a similar reading of Aristotle—especially in connection with akratic and enkratic agents—in "Hylomorphic Virtue." Following John McDowell, I read Aristotle as taking *phronêsis* to be the proper form of the human *orektikon*.[1] When practical intellect fully masters the *orektikon*, there is—as in the *proper* soul-body relation—only one thing there: an essentially desiderative form of thought analogous to the essentially embodied soul of *De Anima* II; or, to put it the other way round, an essentially rational form of desire analogous to the essentially ensouled body of that book. For—as Aristotle says in connection with the relation between the body qua matter (or potentiality) and the soul qua form (or actuality)—the actualization of a potentiality is the strictest form of unity there is [*De Anima* II.1, 412b6–9].

Still, as in reproduction and physical development, so in moral development things can go wrong. Just as the father's semen may be too cold or the movements in it too weak, so too the parent's practical intellect may be deficient. It may be too soft, giving in to the child's demands in ways that are not good for the child and perhaps even rationalizing its actions in ways that lead to its own corruption. Or the manner in which its perfectly reasonable contents are conveyed to the child may be too detached and cold for the child to trust that the parent has beneficent reasons the child herself is not yet in a position to understand.[2] An unruly child may, like that which blunts the knife that cuts it, weaken her parent's practical intellect: think, for example, of the overindulgent parent, whose own psychic needs interfere with his imposing on a

---

[1] The relevant works of McDowell are discussed in Chapters 5 and 6 below. For more on McDowell's views, see "Strong Dialectic, Neurathian Reflection, and the Ascent of Desire: Irwin and McDowell on Aristotle's Methods of Ethics" (II.5).

[2] I develop this point in "See the Right Thing: 'Paternal' Reason, Love, and *Phronêsis*," in M. Boyle and E. Mylonaki (eds.), *Reason in Nature: Essays in Honor of John McDowell* (Cambridge, MA: Harvard University Press, 2021), 243–384. That essay defends the unorthodox reading of *EN* I.13 that I sketch toward the end of this Introduction.

willful child the sort of discipline she needs. Furthermore, just as the matter provided by the menstrual fluid may be too cold or too great in quantity to be fully mastered, so the autonomous desires of the child may be too weak or too strong—as, for example, in the case of a congenitally lethargic or unresponsive child or the case of an excessively willful one.

Things can also go wrong due to the interference of outside forces, both efficient-causal and formal. On the efficient-causal (or relatively "mechanical") front, the embryo's development may be impeded by (for example) its mother's excessive drinking or its father's beating of her. On the formal-causal (or what might be called the "aspirational") front, an adolescent's development may be impeded by (for example) peer pressure or bad role models at home and elsewhere. There is nothing mysterious here. A child acquires practical wisdom by imitating the actions—and not simply the behavior—of practically wise adults. Such imitation is not mindless and is often explicitly reason-involving. The child must, in addition to *trusting* the model, repeatedly ask not simply how the model would *behave* in various situations but how the model would *act* in these situations, where this involves reflecting on the model's reasons for behaving as he does. If the child imitates only the behavior, without coming to appreciate the model's reasons for behaving as he does, she will not engage in the sort of repetition, involving *proper* motivation, that results in genuine virtue, which is a settled disposition to decide on virtuous actions *for themselves*.[3]

If, for example, the child takes the model to behave as he does primarily for the sake of honor and she seeks to follow in his footsteps, she may often behave in ways that *seem* virtuous. But she will not be *acting virtuously*. Furthermore, behaving in the relevant ways for "extrinsic" reasons, such as the honors bestowed or punishments avoided, will leave the agent open to temptation: she may sometimes behave akratically. And that—given the all too human tendency to rationalize one's own behavior—could lead in the end to various forms of vice. Still, the fact that Aristotle recognized these forms of corruption is compatible with his having seen in the fully *phronimos* individual an intrinsic unity of reason and desire analogous to the intrinsic unity of form and matter that is exemplified in his conception of an animal's soul as the form and essence of its organic body.

---

[3] For this point, see II.3: "*Eudaimonia*, External Results, and Choosing Virtuous Actions for Themselves." That chapter reads Aristotle's conception of virtuous action as parallel to his conception of "character" friendship insofar as the "for themselves" requirement serves in each case to make the nature of the relevant object—as distinct from any benefits or pleasures that might accrue to the agent—central. Just as a genuinely virtuous agent chooses to perform virtuous actions on account of the features that make them virtuous (e.g., their tendency to promote the welfare of others or fair distributions of the benefits and burdens of living together), so "character" friends wish and do well to one another on account of the virtuous characters that make them who they are (on which, see II.6: The Nicomachean Account of *Philia*"). But Aristotle treats these phenomena as parallel in other respects as well: he sees each as a stable disposition to make certain kinds of decisions [a *hexis prohairetikê*]. On this point, I have learned much from Larkin Philpot. See his Ph.D. thesis, *The Elements of Aristotelian Philia* (University of Pittsburgh, 2021).

It is worth pausing to note that the term 'intrinsic unity' is potentially misleading insofar as it seems to indicate the presence of two components each of which is separable, at least in thought, from the other. But I use the term to refer to a single thing with two aspects neither of which can be understood, let alone exist, apart from the other. So, as I explain in what follows, an animal can on Aristotle's account be described in either of two, ultimately equivalent ways: as an *essentially ensouled body* or as an *essentially embodied soul*. And since I used the term 'intrinsic unity' in Chapters 1–4, I shall continue to use it here. But we should keep in mind, especially when we turn to moral psychology, that 'essentially' does not entail 'perfectly' or 'completely': just as an essentially embodied soul can be more or less perfectly embodied (think infants born without limbs or non-vital organs proper to their kind), so too an essentially ensouled body can be more or less perfectly ensouled (think anencephalic infants, who are arguably missing an important part of the human soul).

Commentators tend to be happier with the idea of essentially embodied souls than with that of essentially ensouled bodies. For the idea of essentially embodied souls tends to go with the thought that bodily organs are involved in the actualization of most psychic capacities, from reproduction through perception and locomotion. Bodily organs may even be involved in the actualization of human (as distinct from divine) forms of thought if human thought involves the use of images that come about through perceptual activity. But whatever (if anything) Aristotle concludes about thought, the idea of essentially ensouled bodies seems to conflict both with common sense and with his own theoretical commitments. Let's start with the latter.

Aristotle often describes an animal's body as standing to its soul as "matter" to "form." So given his general conception of matter as potentiality—as what, in generation and corruption, can acquire and then lose form—it seems that he *should* treat an animal's body as what first acquires and later loses the animal's form. And this seems to fit common sense, at least about what happens at the end of an animal's life: both we and Aristotle's contemporaries seem to think that animal bodies can—and usually do—become corpses. So the idea of an essentially ensouled animal body seems to conflict both with common sense and with Aristotle's official conception of matter as what underlies and persists throughout the coming-to-be and passing-away of individual substances. How then can Aristotle be entitled to speak of an animal's soul as the form *and the essence* of its body? And why does he want to speak this way?

The former question, famously posed by J. L. Ackrill, sets the agenda for "Living Bodies," where I argue that Aristotle works with two distinct conceptions of matter, one "functional" and the other "compositional." What Aristotle calls the "organic" body is comprised of organs that are defined by their respective functions: the capacity to see is essential to the existence of an eye, the capacity to fly essential to the existence of a wing, and so on. More importantly, the organic body, taken as a whole, is also functionally defined: just as a detached eye is only homonymously an eye, a corpse is only homonymously a body of the relevant kind. So the organic body *is* essentially ensouled. But when it comes to the stuffs out of which organic bodies and their functionally defined parts are composed, these stuffs—primarily, earth, air, fire, and water—are *not* essentially ensouled.[4]

But what *motivates* Aristotle's commitment to the existence of essentially ensouled bodies? My answer is ultimately that he takes such bodies to be required if we are to account for what he sees as the real (and not merely conventional) distinction between the coming-to-be and passing-away of an individual substance and the mere alterations of persisting portions of matter. The basic argument is as follows.

If there is only one form for each infima species—an eternal form that constantly comes and ceases to be embodied in various portions of persisting stuff but does not itself come to be or pass away—then the product of any given species form's coming or ceasing to be embodied in any particular portion of matter is an *accidental unity*. On this account, the persisting matter's coming or ceasing to embody a species form seems to be a mere alteration or rearrangement of it; so what we call the 'coming-to-be' and 'passing-away' of an individual substance does not differ in any fundamental way from alteration or rearrangement.[5] In other words, we can explain the coming-to-be of a genuinely new entity and the ceasing-to-be of an existing entity only if we recognize *intrinsic* unities of form and matter—i.e., unities such that an entity's form can no more exist apart from *its* matter than *its* matter can exist apart from *it*.

An animal is precisely such a unity: an intrinsic unity of *its* individual soul with *its* organic body. It is this body that no longer exists once an animal dies, not even if the stuffs that once constituted it then constitute (at least for a while) an intact corpse. The substratum of coming-to-be and passing-away is thus "compositional" matter. But if the only forms that such matter comes and ceases to embody are species forms, then such matter's coming and ceasing to embody these forms seems no different in kind from the alteration or rearrangement of persisting stuffs. A genuinely new substance comes to be only with the coming-to-be of an individual soul as the form and essence of some particular organic body, which body can no more exist apart from its soul than its soul can exist apart from it.

---

[4] What Aristotle calls '*pneuma*' is another matter, but animal parts cannot live on that alone. And Aristotle's conception of *pneuma* and the ways in which it differs from the four elements is simply grist for my claim that he distinguishes among kinds of matter some that *are* essentially ensouled and some that *are not*.

[5] "Portion of stuff" is meant to be neutral between a portion of divisible stuff and a collection of indivisible atoms (which do not themselves come-to-be or pass away). And references to "rearrangement" are a nod to atomist views, according to which (as Democritus put it) "by convention [*nomos*] sweet, by convention bitter . . . by convention color, in reality atoms and void" [B25]. The crucial point is that moving from atoms to divisible stuffs does not eliminate the accidental relation Aristotle sees between an eternal species form and any given portion of matter to which it belongs: I can easily imagine Aristotle echoing Democritus as follows: "by nomos coming-to-be and passing-away, by nomos mere alteration . . . in reality elements coming and ceasing to embody eternal forms." There are complications here to do with transformations of the elements into and out of one another: I address some (but not all) of these in Chapter 2 ("Form and Generation in Aristotle").

There are of course complications, especially to do with theoretical intellect, that I cannot go into here.[6] But the cumulative case for ascribing this view to Aristotle is presented in Chapters 1–4 below. The basic argument is presented in Chapter 2 ("Form and Generation in Aristotle"), which builds on Chapter 1's argument against the traditional view that Aristotle takes matter to be the "principle of individuation" in the sense that matter is what distinguishes conspecific individuals from one another. Chapter 1 ("Form and Individuation in Aristotle") argues by appeal to what Aristotle says about conjoined twins that he does not view compositional matter, simply as such, as up to this individuative task. What he says in the case of blooded animals is that where there is a single spatiotemporally cohesive animal body with what appear to be extra limbs or organs, we should look to see whether the body has one or two hearts. If there is only one such "principle" [*archê*], then we should say that there is only one animal; if there are two such principles, then we should say there are two animals [*Generation of Animals* IV.4, 773a1–12].[7]

Aristotle speaks here from a cardio-centric point of view. Unlike his cephalo-centric opponents—whom we can easily imagine engaging in the sort of thought experiments I discuss in Volume I—he treats the heart as the primary locus of an animal's form insofar as that form is responsible not just for vital activities but also for cognitive ones. Were he to engage in thought experiments comparable to those current among neo-Lockeans, he would no doubt ask his readers to imagine bodies swapping hearts, not brains. It is controversial whether (and if so how) such localization can be reconciled with Aristotle's hylomorphism. But I am inclined to reject developmental hypotheses according to which Aristotle abandoned localization for hylomorphism: I think he sought to combine the two. So I read the *Generation of Animals* (*GA*) passage as suggesting that in the case of blooded animals, we can tell how many individual animals there are in a spatiotemporally cohesive body only by determining how many *individual* forms, each associated with its own numerically distinct heart, are present in that body.

In sum, Aristotle seems to take individual forms, each "one in number" with the organic body whose form it is, to play an important role not just in determining whether (or not) one and the same animal persists *over* time, but also in determining how many individual animals of a given species exist *at* a time. Matter plays important roles here, but it plays these roles only qua enformed: form is what *unifies* matter in ways such that the matter of an animal is not simply a portion of stuff but a living body that can persist throughout changes in the identity of the various portions of stuff that constitute it at different times. And form is what determines how many members of a species are present at any given time. For what appears to be a single body may, in unusual circumstances, house numerically distinct forms of the same species.

---

[6] For more on this, see II.2: "Human Nature and Intellectualism in Aristotle."
[7] I assume that Aristotle take the claims made here to apply only to organisms that have reached a certain level of complexity.

Chapters 3 and 4 approach this "intrinsic unity" argument from different points of view. Chapter 3 ("Living Bodies") is focused on Ackrill's question and argues that Aristotle recognizes the existence of essentially enformed matter as part of his solution to the pre-Socratic conundrum concerning how to distinguish the coming-to-be and passing-away of individual substances from the mere alteration of persisting stuffs. Chapter 4 ("Metasubstance") is focused on the forms of natural substances, which are (according to Aristotle) the only substances that come-to-be and pass-away.[8] According to the account I give there, Aristotle distinguishes the forms of natural substances from the forms of mathematical entities by taking the forms of natural substances to be essentially (and not simply necessarily) enmattered.

"Metasubstance" is a heavily revised version of the corresponding dissertation chapter, reframed so as to present my views in relation to those of two important works that appeared, more or less simultaneously, a few years after I submitted the dissertation. One—Montgomery Furth's *Substance, Form, and Psychê*—offered a defense, grounded in Aristotle's biological works, of the traditional view according to which Aristotle recognizes only one form for each infima species, a form common to each (and every) individual member of its species. The other—a new edition of *Metaphysics* Z, with German translation and commentary by Michael Frede and Günther Patzig—concurred with me in taking Aristotle to recognize a numerically distinct form for each individual member of an infima species. But Frede and Patzig differ from me on Aristotle's conception of the relation between individual forms and their matter.

As I read *Metaphysics* VII.10–11, Aristotle takes the definition of a natural substance—i.e., the account of its form or essence—to involve reference to the sort of matter proper to members of an infima species in something like the way the definition of 'snub' involves reference to a nose. Snubness is not concavity that *simply happens* to be in a nose: it is *essentially* concavity-in-a-nose. Similarly, to paraphrase Aristotle's point, Man [*ho anthrôpos*] is not a practically rational agent that *simply happens* to be in a human body: it is *essentially* a practically-rational-agent-in-that-sort-of-body, where the body plays a role in determining what *kind* of rational agent it is. In this respect, the definitions of natural substances differ from the definitions of mathematical entities like circles, which can be defined without reference to what Aristotle calls "perceptible" (as distinct from "intelligible") matter.[9]

---

[8] Aristotle does not allow that these forms are themselves subject to coming-to-be and passing-away. But if, as in the paradigm case of an individual animal, the form of a natural substance is peculiar to an individual body whose "essence" it is, then the form of a natural substance will exist when and only when that individual (and essentially alive) body exists. It seems plausible to suppose that such forms are among the entities that Aristotle says "are and are not without coming-to-be and passing away." For this idea, see section 7 of Chapter 4 below.

[9] Even if there can be no "disembodied" circles, there is no specific kind of stuff in which a circle, in order to exist, must be embodied: a circle may be engraved in gold, silver, or some other receptive stuff; drawn in crayon, chalk, or even air; wrapped around a pole in string, rubber, or whatnot. In other words, the kind of matter in which a circle or any other mathematical entity is embodied is not part of that entity's essence. The same goes for numbers, not the abstract numbers "with which we count" but the numbers counted [*Physics* 220b9–10]. There can be two or three or four, etc. of *anything*: Calling birds, French

Frede and Patzig read *Metaphysics* VII.10–11 in a different way. On their account, no individual form of a given kind can exist apart from the relevant sort of matter, but such matter is not itself part of the form or essence of any member of that kind. It may of course be the case that facts about the sorts of matter required for the realization of a given form *follow from* the nature of the form in question together with facts about the sorts of matter there are: it may be that only certain sorts of matter can play the functional roles definitive of the form in question. But this does not mean that the requisite sorts of matter are themselves part of the form or essence of any member of the relevant kind. They are simply, as Aristotle might say, "hypothetically necessary" for the existence of any form of that kind.

There are difficult questions here whose resolution, should any be in the cards, would depend both on working out Aristotle's conceptions of definition and on determining the roles he takes the sort of differentiae identified in his biological works to play in the definitions of natural substances. I have not reached anything approaching reflective equilibrium on these questions and want to thank Myles Burnyeat for having encouraged me, when I was struggling to turn Chapter 1–4 into *Aristotelian Individuals*, to return to questions nearer and dearer to me, especially questions about psychic contingency. The remaining chapters of this volume are thus addressed to questions more closely connected with the ethical questions discussed in Volumes I and II. But they are firmly grounded in the conception of hylomorphism developed in "Living Bodies."

That essay first appeared in *Essays on Aristotle's "De Anima,"* edited by Martha Nussbaum and Amelie Rorty. I had originally been asked to contribute a piece on the account of animal motion in *De Anima* III.9–11 and had started to work on that, taking *DA* III.7's apparent identification of the desiring part of soul [*to orektikon*] with the perceiving part of soul [*to aisthêtikon*] as my point of departure. But I had not made sufficient progress by the time the deadline rolled round, and the editors graciously agreed to take "Living Bodies." I resumed work on *DA* III.7–11 when I was invited to present a paper at Princeton's annual Classical Philosophy Colloquium. But once again I bit off more than I could chew: the paper I presented there had eventually to be split into two. There is thus an intimate connection between Chapters 5 ("Locomotive Soul") and 6 ("Hylomorphic Virtue"): they are, in a way, fraternal twins. "The Mover(s) of Rational Animals" (Chapter 9) is, as it were, a younger sibling but no accident: the conception was arduous.

"Locomotive Soul" is focused on another significant unity in Aristotle's account of soul—the unity of the desiring part of soul [*to orektikon*] with the perceiving and imagining parts [*to aisthêtikon* and *to phantastikon*]. This chapter seeks to explain the conjunction of two claims: first, that *to orektikon* is "not different" from *to aisthêtikon*, though the being of each (i.e., *what it is to be capable of desiring* and *what it is to be*

Hens, Turtledoves, and so on. But there must be twosomes, threesomes, and foursomes of *some* things in order for there to be numbers in *this* sense. If monism were true, there would be no such numbers and so none of the kind "with which we count" (which *Physics* IV.11 seems to view as depending for their existence on the presence of soul).

capable of perceiving) is different [431a12–14]; and second, that *to aisthêtikon* is "the same" as *to phantastikon*, though the being of each (*what it is to be capable of perceiving* and *what it is to be capable of imagining*) are again different [459a15–17]. The idea seems to be that it is one and the same part of soul—what I call the "locomotive" part—that engages in each of these three, definitionally distinct forms of activity: one and the same part that perceives and desires (or not) to pursue what it perceives, and one and the same part that imagines and desires (or not) to bring about the imagined end. And as I argue in "Locomotive Soul," Aristotle thinks such unity is required in order to account for the voluntary (as distinct from the autonomic) movements of animals: if it were the case that one part perceived or imagined the object of desire and a numerically distinct part desired that object, then we could not account for the animal's pursuit of the relevant object.[10]

Aristotle's reasons for endorsing the unity of the locomotive part are on my account parallel to the reasons he gives for positing a single "common" sense with definitionally distinct capacities: to see, to hear, to taste, and so on. Just as he worries that taking the various senses to be distinct in number from one another will make it impossible to explain how a perceiving subject can judge of one and the same object that it is (for example) both white and sweet, so I think he worries that taking *to orektikon* to be distinct in number from *to aisthêtikon* and *to phantastikon* will make it impossible to explain the voluntary motions of animals. And just as he thinks that the capacity to judge of a single object that it is both white and sweet presupposes a single sense in which sight and taste are unified, so, I submit, he thinks the voluntary motions of animals presuppose a single subject in which desire is unified with perception and imagination. This move—namely, taking Aristotle's reasons for endorsing the numerical unity of *to orektikon* with both *to aisthêtikon* and *to phantastikon* to be parallel to his reasons for endorsing the unity of the special senses in the "common" sense—is admittedly speculative. But it is supported both by the coherence of the view it affords and by the fact that Aristotle uses the same locutions and the same analogies in each case: in the latter case, he speaks of something that is indivisible in number but divisible in being, and he compares its divided operation to the way in which (as in the former case) a single point or boundary can serve as two (i.e., as the end of one segment or field and the beginning of another).

On this account, Aristotle takes the unity of *to orektikon* with *to aisthêtikon* and *to phantastikon* to be the *norm* throughout the animal world. Animals tend for the most part to move more or less immediately when they perceive or imagine means to achieving what they (most) desire. Even rational animals do this. But rationality complicates the picture. As I explain in "The Mover(s) of Rational Animals," the *phantastikon* of a rational animal is more complex than that of a non-rational one. For the possession of *logos* gives rise to a distinct form of *phantasia*—what Aristotle calls "deliberative" (as

---

[10] For perspicuous discussion of the Platonic origins of this view, see Myles Burnyeat, "Plato on the Grammar of Perceiving," *Classical Quarterly* NS 26 (1976): 29–51; reprinted in Volume 2 of Burnyeat, *Explorations in Ancient and Modern Philosophy* (Cambridge: Cambridge University Press, 2012), 70–98.

opposed to "perceptual") *phantasia*. The *phantasmata* that come about in and through thought may differ in content from those that come about in and through perception, and each sort of *phantasma* is inseparable from its own form of *orexis*.[11] Perceptual *phantasia* may present x as pleasant and thus to-be-pursued, while deliberative *phantasia* presents x as unhealthy and thus to-be-avoided. So a creature with both forms of *phantasia* may be subject to conflicting *orexeis*. For example, perceptual *phantasia* may dispose a subject to go for some object that deliberative *phantasia* disposes her to reject; or perceptual *phantasia* may dispose her to flee some object that deliberative *phantasia* disposes her to pursue.

Such discrepancies give rise to two forms of pathology to which non-rational animals are apparently immune: first, *akrasia*, in which an agent pursues pleasure or some other apparent good in spite of believing that she ought not do so; and second, *enkrateia*, in which an agent does what she believes she ought to do, in spite of being strongly tempted to pursue pleasure or some other apparent good (such as revenge). Aristotle struggles to account for these possibilities, especially the possibility of *akrasia*, to which *EN* VII.3 [aka *EE* VI.3] is devoted. Chapter 7, co-authored with Martin Pickavé, is essentially a commentary on that text. But before turning to that, let me recall the brief account, given above, of what goes on in "Hylomorphic Virtue," the fraternal twin (so to speak) of "Locomotive Soul."

At the center of "Hylomorphic Virtue" are the sort of explanatory asymmetries Aristotle sees between cases where things go as they should (teleologically speaking) go and cases where things go (teleologically speaking) wrong. When things go as they should go, the material conditions and processes that are "hypothetically necessary" for the formal causes to do their jobs are in place and facilitate the dominance of formal-causal explanation. When things go wrong, it is often (though not always) because the requisite conditions and processes are suboptimal in ways such that they interfere with formal causal operations and in some cases even allow the subject's activity to be hijacked. This, Pickavé and I argue, is why Aristotle's account of *akrasia* assimilates the condition of the *akratês* to that of a subject who, like the sleeping geometer of *GA* 735a9–11, has knowledge but fails on account of her physiological condition to make use of it.[12] As Aristotle puts it in *EN* VII.3, the *akratês* is like someone

---

[11] Whence Aristotle's conception of *prohairesis* (on which more below) as a kind of "deliberative desire." The contrast is with merely perceptual forms of desire associated with the sort of *phantasmata* characteristic of non-rational animals.

[12] Please note that I say "fails to make use," not "cannot make use": a sleeping geometer might well dream up a new (and legitimate) proof in a way that a non-geometer could never do. The point here concerns physiological conditions that tend for the most part to interfere with the *normal* operations of thought, conditions that tend to interfere with a subject's bringing her first actuality knowledge into second actuality use in circumstances where its use is called for, circumstances in which (absent the physiological disturbance) she would *normally* use it. So pace David Charles, from whom I have learned much: Aristotle is not assimilating the condition of the *akratês* to the condition of "learners," who are still in the process of acquiring "first actuality" knowledge. Aristotle's point is simply that the condition of the *akratês* is in *one* respect like that of the learner: during an akratic episode, she can "say the words" that ordinarily express knowledge. But her saying these words does not count, then and there, as an

mad, drunk, or asleep: her condition may well interfere with her making the sort of use she normally makes of knowledge she really does have. That's why, if we want to know how this temporary "ignorance" is resolved and the *akratês* returns to her normal condition, Aristotle says we should consult the *phusiologoi*.

These folk are not, as Pickavé and I read Aristotle, the same as the *phusikoi* Aristotle applauds for seeking to explain what we today would call psychological phenomena in psychological (as distinct from physiological) terms.[13] Aristotle uses '*phusiologoi*' here to refer to a specific group of natural scientists, those concerned with the material-efficient causal mechanisms (such as heating, evaporating, and settling) that are involved in phenomena like digestion, sleep, and waking. It should come as no surprise that Aristotle allows malfunctions at the level of such mechanisms to interfere with the proper functioning of the sort of formal causes involved in perception, thought, and desire. Even thinkers who do not adopt his teleological framework can allow that all sorts of efficient-causal processes—from those associated with lack of sleep to those associated with ingesting hallucinogenic substances—can disturb the "normal" operations of perception and thought. For the fact that the "normal" operations presuppose the presence of certain material conditions and processes does not entail that such operations can be fully explained by appeal to material conditions and efficient causal processes simply as such. Even if (for example) thirst facilitates hallucinations and/or wishful thinking, our hallucinations and wishful thoughts can, in virtue of their contents, give rise to propositional attitudes whose existence and effects cannot be explained in purely efficient-causal terms—as, for example, when garden varieties of wishful thinking lead us to overestimate favorable odds and underestimate unfavorable ones. In other words, the sort of asymmetries recognized by Aristotle are relatively commonplace even if the teleological framework in which he situates them is not.

What is controversial—and central to my reading of Aristotle—is the way in which such asymmetries give rise to the sort of radical psychic contingency I see in Plato's *Republic,* contingency not just in the way the parts of this or that individual human soul are *related* to one another but also in *how many* parts this or that human soul has in the first place. My appreciation of Aristotle's commitment to such contingency was a long time coming. I used to puzzle over McDowell's Socratic reading of Aristotle: how could Aristotle *identify* (ethical) virtue with *phronêsis*? For Aristotle divides the human soul primarily into two parts, one that has reason and one that does not, and he assigns virtue and *phronêsis* to different parts: *phronêsis* belongs of course to the part that has reason, but virtue belongs to the non-rational part. This we know—for the canon tells us so.

---

expression of the knowledge that she (unlike someone still learning) actually has. For more on this, including reference to the Charles paper, see section 5 of Chapter 7.

[13] Aristotle makes parallel claims about the need to account for *philia* by appeal to principles appropriate [*oikeion*] to the nature of the explanandum. For more on this, see sec. 8 of "The Nicomachean Account of *Philia*" [II.6].

Here, however, it pays take a closer look at the canonical texts: *EN* I.13 and *EN* VI.1. The former is usually read as dividing the human soul into the four parts that are more or less explicitly present in the latter: the part that has reason is subdivided into theoretical and practical intellect and the part that lacks reason is subdivided into the nutritive and desiderative parts.[14] And the latter is usually read as following suit. But the arguments of these two chapters are markedly different. VI.1 divides the part of soul that has reason into theoretical and practical subparts directly by appeal to a difference in kind between their respective objects: the objects of the former are necessary, the objects of the latter contingent. But there is little sign of this distinction in I.13. I think it is implicitly there, but not in a way that preserves the canonical view.

After dividing the part of soul that lacks reason into nutritive and desiderative subparts, Aristotle says in I.13 that the desiderative subpart has reason "in a way" [*pôs*]: *to orektikon* "has reason" in the sense that it is "attentive to it and disposed to obey <it>." Aristotle assimilates the way in which this subpart "has reason" to the way in which we say we "have" the reason of our fathers and he contrasts this with the way in which we "have" the reason of mathematicians. He then says *immediately* that if we say *to orektikon* "has reason" in the former way, then we must also divide the part of soul that has reason into two parts, one that has reason "strictly and in itself" and one that has reason in the way that someone disposed to listen to her father does. In other words, he goes on immediately to describe one of the subparts of the part that has *reason* in the *same* way he has just described the desiderative subpart of the *non-rational* part of soul.

This is puzzling in ways to which commentators have not done justice. But this move makes perfectly good sense if we read the argument of I.13 on its own terms and not in the light of VI.1. For the argument in I.13 is that taking desire to partake of reason in whatever way it does *entails* taking the part that has reason to have two parts. And the easiest way to make sense of the entailment is to read Aristotle as saying that the way in which the desiring part has reason is sufficient for saying that it is *itself* a subpart of the so-called rational part and *so* requires us to divide the rational part. But this yields (at least so far) only three parts: (1) a nutritive part (which is purely non-rational); (2) a theoretical part (which is purely rational); and (3) a desiring part (which has both rational and non-rational aspects).

This reading of I.13 has two clear advantages. First, it yields a division that approximates more closely the three-part division found in the *De Anima* and other scientific works. Second, it honors Aristotle's objection to those who divide the soul primarily along the rational/non-rational axis. His objection is that they "break up" the *orektikon*,

---

[14] *EN* VI.1 subdivides *to logon echon* into *to epistêmonikon* (whose characteristic activity is clearly theoretical) and *to logistikon* (whose characteristic activity is to deliberate about contingent matters). VI.3 speaks of the latter as *to doxastikon*, which is presumably the most general term for a subpart that engages in various ways—some deliberative, some not—with contingent matters. I plan to say more about this in future work, for which Ben Morison's "Aristotle on the Distinction between What Is Understood and What Is Believed" (unpublished) prepares the ground.

as this reading of I.13 does not: it treats *to orektikon* as a single part with two aspects, one rational and the other not.

But this reading has one at least apparent disadvantage: it seems to contradict VI.12's reference to the nutritive part as the "fourth" part of soul [1144a9–10]. Here, however, I think we should privilege the tripartite account found in the scientific works by taking it to express the norm, while taking Aristotle's reference to a "fourth" part, which appears in an ethical context, to reflect his commitment to the sort of psychic contingency described above. Even if *phronêsis* is the *proper* form of the *orektikon*, practical intellect and desire can and do come apart, as in the *akratês* and *enkratês*. But when moral development goes as it should (teleologically speaking) go, practical intellect and desire form a unified part with two aspects, one rational and the other non-rational. This is what I call the "locomotive" part, also known (according to the argument of Chapter 5) as *to orektikon, to aisthêtikon,* and *to phantastikon*. On this account, the norm is three parts: nutritive, locomotive, and theoretical. That's what one would find in the soul of a fully virtuous (aka *phronimos*) agent. But the locomotive part is vulnerable to the sort of division characteristic of akratic and enkratic agents, who may thus be said to have four parts.

I set aside for now difficulties to do with the souls of vicious agents. The point here is this: if Aristotle embraces the sort of radical psychic contingency voiced by Plato's Socrates, then we can read him as identifying virtue (in the "strict" or "authoritative" sense) with *phronêsis*. For given such contingency, it does not follow from the distinctness of the *orektikon* and practical intellect in an akratic or enkratic agent that the *orektikon* and practical intellect of a fully virtuous agent must be distinct: *phronêsis* can be the proper form of the *orektikon*, which, when things go as they should (teleologically speaking) go, is a single part that can be described in different ways and has both rational and non-rational aspects. But this is a *norm:* in non-virtuous subjects the *orektikon* is divided into a more and a less rational subpart, each speaking in a different voice.

This requires us to read I.13 in the way sketched here. I defend this reading at greater length in "See the Right Thing: 'Paternal' Reason, Love, and *Phronêsis*." The basic idea there is as follows.

Mathematicians can give proofs, so a part of soul has reason in the way a mathematician does when *it* can generate proofs—i.e., when its *hexis* is *apodeiktikê*. But our fathers are not expected to give proofs about the sorts of things we learn from them qua fathers—i.e., practical [I should perhaps have said "ethical"] matters. For such things tend not to admit of proof. So a part of soul can have reason in the way a father does *without* being able to generate proofs. To have reason in the way a (decent) father does, a part of soul must be such as to generate (decent) *prohaireseis*. But *prohairesis*, unlike *apodeixis*, involves desire. Aristotle in fact characterizes *prohairesis* as a form of desire: it is *nous orektikos* or (in other words) *orexis dianoêtikê* [1139b4–5]. So exercises of practical intellect involve desire in a way that exercises of theoretical intellect do not.[15]

This is why Aristotle distinguishes *phronêsis*, qua *hexis* involving *logos*, from *epistêmê* and *technê*, which are also *hexeis* involving *logos*, by saying that *phronêsis* is "not a *hexis* with *logos* alone" [1140b27]. Proper desires and affections (those, roughly speaking, lying in the relevant means) are essentially involved in (and not just hypothetically necessary for) *phronêsis*.

Aristotle's conception of *prohairesis* plays various important roles in these essays. I take his identification of it (at 1139a31–b5) as "either desiderative thought [*orektikos nous*] or thinking desire [*orexis dianoêtikê*]" to support a hylomorphic conception of the relation between practical intellect and desire. When, as in this passage, Aristotle uses '*prohairesis*' to refer to a propositional attitude as distinct from its contents, he is not referring (as Irwin's translation "thought *combined with* desire or desire *combined with* thought" suggests) to a combination of two distinct attitudes. His point is that there is a *single* attitude which is *both* a form of thought *and* a form of desire. And to the extent that he takes both enkratic and akratic agents to reach the right *prohairesis*, he uses '*prohairesis*' in a different way: he is using it as we often use 'belief' to refer to the *content* of some belief as distinct from the propositional *attitude* of belief. Aristotle's point is that these agents have propositional attitudes whose contents *approximate* those that belong to the *prohaireseis* of the *phronimos*.

Aristotle may think that the physiological conditions associated with strong desire interfere with beliefs playing in an agent's behavior the sort of role they *normally* play. In spite of a strong desire to do something else, an agent may *believe* that she ought to do what (more or less) the *phronimos* wholeheartedly decides [*prohairetai*] to do. And differences in physiological states may make it easier for the relevant belief to prevail in some agents than in others, or even in the same agent at some times but not others. There is likely a continuum here such that one and the same agent sometimes behaves enkratically and sometimes akratically, and differences in physiological dispositions probably render some subjects closer to and others further from the enkratic end of the spectrum. These differences may in fact be subject to various forms of modification, including those recognized today: for example, biofeedback, meditation, and cognitive-behavioral therapy—all practices that make good sense in a hylomorphic context.

In sum, if we grant psychic contingency, there is no conflict between what Aristotle says about these subjects and his treatment of the *prohairesis* of the *phronimos* as the product of a state in which practical reason stands to desire in a way like that in which the soul of an organism stands to its properly developed body.[16] Aristotle's conception

---

[15] I quote here from the paper cited in note 2 above.
[16] I take myself to be agreeing here the "third way" reading that David Charles develops in a series of important papers starting with "Aristotle's Desire," which shares its point of departure in *De Anima* III.7 with "Locomotive Soul" (Chapter 4 below). The main difference, I think, is that Charles does not stress

of *prohairesis* also plays an important role in connecting his views, via those of Stoic, neo-Platonic, and other thinkers, to Locke's account of personal identity. Or so I argue in Chapter 8, "The Lockeanism of Aristotle," which returns to the questions explored in detail in Volume I.

---

explanatory asymmetries in quite the way I do. See "Aristotle's Desire," in V. Hirvonen, T. Holopainen, and M. Tuominen (eds.), *Mind and Modality: Studies in the History of Philosophy in Honour of Simo Knutilla* (Leiden: Brill, 2006), 19–40. See also Charles' "Aristotle on Practical and Theoretical Knowledge," in D. Henry and K. Nielsen (eds.), *Bridging the Gap between Aristotle's Science and Ethics* (Cambridge: Cambridge University Press, 2015), 71–79; and "Practical Truth: An Interpretation of Parts of Nicomachean Ethics VI," in D. Brink, S. Meyer, and C. Shields (eds.), *Virtue, Happiness, and Knowledge: Themes from the Work of Gail Fine and Terence Irwin* (Oxford: Oxford University Press: 2018), 149–68.

1
Form and Individuation in Aristotle

THERE IS A traditional interpretation of Aristotle according to which matter is the principle of synchronic individuation—that is, matter is what individuates two simultaneously existing members of the same *infima species*.[1] This traditional view—hereafter the TV—is usually supported by appeal to Aristotle's claim that Socrates and Callias are the same in form, but different on account of their matter (*Metaphysics* [*Met.*] 1034a5–8). The main tasks of this essay are to argue (1) that matter cannot be the principle of individuation and (2) that Aristotle must introduce individual forms if he is to provide principles of individuation.[2]

---

[1] See Eduard Zeller, *Aristotle and the Earlier Peripatetics* (London: Longmans Publishers, 1897), 83–96; G. E. M. Anscombe and K. Popper, "The Principle of Individuation," *Proceedings of the Aristotelian Society* 27 (1953): 83–96, 97–120; A. C. Lloyd, "Aristotle's Principle of Individuation," *Mind* 79 (1970): 519–29; Montgomery Furth, "Transtemporal Stability in Aristotelian Substances," *Journal of Philosophy* 75 (1978): 624–46. I follow these commentators in discussing primarily the individuation of sensible substances. But one virtue of my account over theirs is that making form the principle of individuation allows us to give an univocal account of the individuation of sensible and non-sensible substances.

[2] The view that individual form is the principle of individuation is defended by W. Charlton, "Aristotle and the Principle of Individuation," *Phronesis* 17 (1973): 239–49. The primary purpose of this essay is to argue that Aristotle *must* admit individual forms if he is to provide principles of individuation. I have argued at length elsewhere ("Individual Forms in Aristotle," Ph.D. Thesis, Cornell University, 1984) that Aristotle does in fact acknowledge the existence of individual forms. My arguments there include the following: (1) Aristotle explicitly says that forms are *tode ti* [*Metaphysics* (*Met.*) 1017b24–26, 1042a28–29, 1049a35–36, 1070a11–12; *Generation and Corruption* (*GC*) 318b32] and he believes that being one in number and a particular are necessary for being *tode ti* [*Categories* (*Cat.*) 3b13–18; *Met.* 999b34–35, 1038b35–1039a1]. (2) Aristotle's criteria for being a (primary) substance, especially the *tode ti* and separability requirements, require substances to be individuals, and this—in conjunction with Aristotle's repeated claims that form is (primary) substance [*Met.* 1017b24–25, 1032b1–2, 1033b17, 1037a28–29, 1041b7–9,

1

The claim that matter is the principle of individuation can be interpreted either as an epistemological, or as a metaphysical, thesis.[3] As an epistemological thesis its point might be that matter is what enables us to distinguish one individual from another of the same species. In other words, material differences enable us to tell Callias and Socrates apart; one has brown, the other blue, eyes. But because Aristotle does not rule out the possibility that there are two simultaneously existing conspecific individuals whose matter is the same in the sense that it is qualitatively indistinguishable, matter is not very well suited to serve this epistemological function. So if matter is supposed to answer an epistemological question, it must be the question of how we can tell when there are two (or more) simultaneously existing members of the same species.

In this case, matter might provide us with a primarily ostensive way of distinguishing two individuals. We might be able to distinguish *this* man here from *that* one over there, and so to say that there are two numerically distinct individuals, even if we cannot tell them apart in some non-ostensive way. Here, however, we would presumably be relying on a metaphysical claim that matter is what *makes* two individuals to be numerically distinct in the sense that certain material characteristics (e.g., being composed of non-overlapping portions of matter) are somehow sufficient[4] (either causally or logically) for the numerical distinctness of two simultaneously existing conspecific individuals. This justifies taking the TV to be committed to the metaphysical thesis that matter is what makes two simultaneously existing members of the same species to be distinct.

Like the epistemological version of this thesis, the metaphysical version can be interpreted as referring either to qualitative or to numerical distinctness. But here

---

1050b1–2]—shows that at least some forms (i.e., whichever ones are substances) must be individuals. Furthermore, the consistency of Aristotle's most mature work on the substance (i.e., the middle books of the *Metaphysics*) depends on his accepting the conclusion that substantial forms are individuals. (3) Aristotle's criticisms of Plato require (on pain of inconsistency) that substantial forms be individuals. (4) Aristotle is explicitly committed not only to the general claim that the cause of something's being F must itself be F [*Met.* 999b24–28], but also to the specific claim that the principles of particulars must themselves be particulars [*Met.* 1071a20–21]; and the latter appears in a passage where Aristotle refers to forms that are numerically distinct but the same in species [*Met.* 1071a18–29]. In addition to these arguments, I present an extended argument that Aristotle needs individual forms in order to defend a genuine and not purely conventional distinction between generation (or destruction) *simpliciter* and mere alteration. The purpose of this essay is to elucidate a further, but related, philosophical motivation for Aristotle's commitment to individual forms.

[3] See Charlton 1973, 239–40.

[4] There is some question about whether Aristotle thinks that being composed of different matter is also necessary (as well as sufficient) for the existence of numerically distinct individuals. It is sufficient because he rejects the notion of a scattered particular [*Topics* (*Top.*) 103a7–25]. But the question whether it is also necessary depends upon whether Aristotle allows the possibility of two things, each of which is constituted by the same matter, existing in the same place at the same time; and on whether Aristotle admits the existence of "kooky objects" that are individuated by descriptions such as "pale Socrates" and "Socrates sitting." See G. Matthews, "Accidental Unities," in M. Schofield and M. Nussbaum (eds.), *Language and Logos* (Cambridge: Cambridge University Press, 1982), 223–40.

too, the qualitative version suffers from the possibility that there might be two numerically distinct individuals whose matter is qualitatively indistinguishable. So the metaphysical thesis is best interpreted as claiming that matter is what makes Socrates numerically (rather than qualitatively) distinct from Callias. For although Aristotle believes that material differences often result in qualitative ones, there is no evidence that he thinks this must always be so. The idea is that even if there are no qualitative differences between Callias and Socrates, they would still be numerically distinct on account of their matter. In what follows, then, both the traditional view (that matter is the principle of individuation) and the alternative view (that form is the principle of individuation) will be interpreted as metaphysical rather than epistemological theses.

At this point it is worth noting a prima facie objection that applies to each of these views—namely, that each only shifts the location of the problem. For just as we can ask the TV to account for the differences of matter that are themselves supposed to individuate Callias and Socrates, so we can also ask the alternative view to account for the differences between individual forms that are themselves supposed to individuate.[5] And if (as I argue in sections 2–4) proponents of the TV must appeal to form to account for the requisite material differences, and (as they might argue) I must appeal to matter in order to account for the requisite formal differences, then perhaps we ought to conclude that each must help to individuate the other. But there is a conception of individual forms that offers Aristotle a way out of this circle; if individual form somehow includes the matter that is necessary for individuation, then it can be sufficient for (and hence *the* principle of) individuation.[6]

2

Perhaps the best way to understand the TV is to ask why it maintains that matter must be the principle of individuation. The first thing to notice is that the TV does not regard matter as the principle of individuation in all cases. Matter is called on to individuate only *simultaneously* existing members of the *same species*. But I think that it is the restriction to conspecificity, not to simultaneity, that does most of the work. Let me explain.

Proponents of the TV think there is a special problem with the individuation of conspecific individuals primarily because they think Aristotle recognizes the existence of only one form for each infima species.[7] So Socrates and Callias are the same in form not in the sense that each of them possesses a numerically distinct form of

---

[5] See Anscomb and Popper 1953, 97–120.
[6] See note 22 below.
[7] There are various formulations of the TV and not all distinguish (as I do here) the species (which is something like a set or class) from the species-form (which is something like a property in virtue of which things belong to a species). I argue against the species-form view because I believe that it represents the most plausible version of the TV.

the same type, but rather in the sense that there is only one form for the species Man, which form is said of many individuals at the same time and is thus a universal.[8] On this view, Socrates and Callias have the very same form, so any differences between them, including their numerical distinctness, must be explained by appeal to their matter.

This appeal to matter is not necessary in individuating members of different species. A man and a horse have different forms and this, at least when they exist simultaneously, is sufficient for their being distinct individuals. Furthermore, given certain essentialist claims to which Aristotle is committed, having different species-forms will be sufficient for the distinctness of two individuals existing at different times.[9] So according to the TV, form is the principle of individuation for members of different species and this is true both at and across times. This supports my claim that it is conspecificity rather than simultaneity that does most of the work.

That claim receives further support from the fact that the problem the TV has with the synchronic individuation of conspecific individuals arises equally for their diachronic individuation. The parallel between synchronic and diachronic individuation emerges from the following consideration. If form is to be the metaphysical principle of individuation, then having a certain form must be what makes an individual existing at t_1 to be the same as (or distinct from) an individual existing at t_2. But because the TV recognizes only one form for each species, Socrates' form at t_1 cannot be what makes him the same individual as Socrates at t_2 and distinct from Callias at t_3. For not only do Socrates at t_1 and Socrates at t_2 have the same form, but each of them also shares that form with Callias at any t at which he exists, with Coriscus at any t at which he exists and so on.

This is simply another version of the problem that arose in trying to individuate *simultaneously* existing members of the same species. Just as in accounting for synchronic diversity within a species, so also in accounting for diachronic identity, the

---

[8] J. A. Driscoll, "*Eidē* in Aristotle's Earlier and Later Theories of Substance," in D. O'Meara (ed.), *Studies in Aristotle* (Washington DC: Catholic University Press, 1981), 125–59, argues that there is a sense in which the species-form is an individual because he wants to explain how it can be a substance without violating the *Met.* VII.13 requirement that no universal be a substance. But the sense in which a species-form is an individual is the broad sense in which it is the referent of a singular referring expression, which is not sufficient for its not being a universal. This does not suffice for its being an individual in the sense in which Aristotle contrasts individuals with universals at *De Interpretatione* (*De Int.*) 17a39–40.

[9] Essential properties are those which an individual cannot lose without ceasing to exist; the species gives the *ti esti* or essence of a subject [*Cat.* 2b8–10]. An individual cannot cease to belong to its species without ceasing to exist; the same animal cannot be at one time a man and at another time not a man. [*Top.* 125b25–30]. [This requires qualification in light of the asymmetries afforded by Aristotle's teleology discussed in "Hylomorphic Virtue" (Chapter 6 below). For Aristotle's teleologically grounded essentialism differs from many forms of contemporary essentialism in that it allows for the possibility that individual members of a species may lose (or even fail ever to acquire) properties that are part of the essence of its kind (e.g., sight and the capacity to walk in the case of the human kind). It is in this sense contingent, but non-accidental, that an individual has the properties associated with membership in its species, and an individual can cease to have one or more of these properties (or simply fail to acquire them) without ceasing to exist (or without failing to belong to the relevant species).]

inadequacy of species-form forces the TV to appeal to matter. It must account for synchronic diversity by picking out one and the same species-form in *different pieces of matter*, and for diachronic identity by picking out the same species-form in the *same piece of matter*.[10] To trace Socrates' career is to trace the form of Man as it occurs in "the particular piece of matter that constitutes Socrates' body."[11] To trace Callias' career is to trace the *very same form* in a different piece of matter—namely, the one that constitutes Callias' body.

So just as the TV must explain synchronic individuation (within a species) by appeal to matter, it must also appeal to matter in order to explain diachronic individuation. The main problem for this view is to explain the requisite sameness and difference of matter without introducing form. This is precisely what I argue the TV cannot do.

3

The main problem with the TV can be explained clearly in terms of Lloyd's distinction between a *principle of unity* (i.e., what makes this *one* thing rather than so many limbs, organs, and bits of flesh) and a *principle of individuation* (i.e., what makes this man the same as or different from that one). Lloyd claims that form is the principle of unity and that unity is "prior to and implied by individuation." "The flesh and the bones have to have made one man, the metal one penny, before either can be or not be the same man or penny as another."[12]

Lloyd's point, that unity is prior to individuation, can be applied both to synchronic and to diachronic individuation. This matter has to make up one thing before it can be the same as (or different from) another individual at a time. It also has to make up one thing at each of t_1 and t_2 in order for it to be the same (or a different) thing at each of t_1 and t_2. In a way, this priority of unity should be obvious. For we are asking when one individual (i.e., a unity) is the same as or different from other individuals (i.e., other unities) both at and across times. There is thus a conceptual connection between unity and individuation; being an individual (and hence being the same individual as this one or a different individual from that one) is conceptually tied to having or embodying a certain form.

This priority of unity threatens the view that matter is *the* principle of individuation; if form is the principle of unity, and if individuation presupposes unity, then individuation presupposes form. This suggests that only informed matter can individuate and thus that form is at least a necessary condition for individuation.

---

[10] This does not require that we have the same set of particles and this, as we shall see, is part of the problem. For what enables us to think of it as the same piece of stuff throughout the displacement of its constituent particles is that we think of it as a whole having a certain shape and form.

[11] M. J. Woods, "Substance and Essence in Aristotle," *Proceedings of the Aristotelian Society* 75 (1974–1975): 179.

[12] See Lloyd 1970, 519.

4

Someone might defend the TV by conceding that unity is prior to individuation and then denying that form is the requisite principle of unity. He might argue instead that something like spatiotemporal continuity is the principle of unity. If he thinks that spatiotemporal continuity is purely a function of material characteristics and does not involve form, he may conclude that matter (by way of spatiotemporal continuity) is the principle of individuation.

This strategy for defending the TV is recommended both by the difficulty of denying the conceptual priority of unity and by Aristotle's claim that things of which the matter is one are themselves one [*Met.* 1016b31–32]. This passage suggests that Aristotle does appeal to some sort of unity of matter in order to account for something's being one in number or an individual. The problem is to see what this unity of matter involves and whether it does not belong to matter in virtue of that matter's relation to some form.

There is a prima facie case for thinking that this unity of matter does in fact depend upon matter's relation to form. The case rests on two general Aristotelian views. First, Aristotle repeatedly claims that matter is not in itself an individual or a particular sort of thing [*De Anima (DA)* 412a7–8; *Met.* 1029a20–21, 1042a27–28]. Matter is precisely what stands in need of individuation (or unification). Second, when matter is individuated (or unified) Aristotle says that form is that by which matter is some one thing (i.e., a unity or an individual) [*Met.* 1041b4–9]. So Aristotle appears to say explicitly that form is the requisite principle of unity for matter. But perhaps the defender of the TV can defeat this prima facie case by showing that form is not the *only* principle of unity for matter. If he can show that there is another principle of unity for matter (for instance, spatiotemporal continuity), then he can argue that it is *not necessary* to appeal to form as the principle of unity for matter.

Aristotle distinguishes simple continuity from continuity by nature and not by touch and binding [*Met.* 1052a19–20]. Simple continuity, unlike natural continuity, is roughly equivalent to spatial continuity plus some sort of dynamic cohesiveness.[13] Since form is necessary for natural continuity,[14] we need to know whether Aristotle can account for the oneness (and hence for the numerical distinctness) of different

---

[13] I borrow the term "dynamic cohesiveness" from E. Hirsch, *The Concept of Identity* (Oxford: Oxford University Press, 1982), 108. Hirsch describes this as an object's capacity "to hang together when subjected to various strains" and claims that it is related (as a necessary but not a sufficient condition) to separate movability. These points tie dynamic cohesiveness to Aristotle's notion of indivisibility of motion. The idea is roughly that a sugar cube, but not a heap of granulated sugar, would satisfy Aristotle's requirements for simple continuity.

[14] In *Met.* X.1, Aristotle distinguishes (1) simple from natural continuity and (2) natural from artificial wholes. Since he allows that natural wholes are continuous in a way stronger than that afforded by the requirements of simple continuity (i.e., touch and binding), it seems that the fundamental contrast is between simple continuity on the one hand, and wholeness (either natural or artificial) on the other. And what distinguishes wholes is that they have a certain shape and form. So form is necessary for natural continuity.

pieces of matter by appealing only to the requirements of simple continuity. First let's consider whether this is possible in the easiest case—that of synchronic individuation.

A proponent of the TV might argue that Aristotle thinks that Socrates' matter is one thing and Callias' matter is another, simply because each is a piece of a certain sort of stuff, a piece whose constituents are spatially continuous but is not itself continuous with any other stuff of this kind that is not a part of it. But what would he (or Aristotle) say if he came upon Socrates and Callias wrestling and hence entangled with one another, or worse yet, if they were Siamese twins?

Aristotle sometimes explains the continuity involved in numerical oneness in terms of indivisibility of motion [*Met.* 1052a25–27]. So he might say that although they are spatially continuous, Socrates and Callias each embodies an indivisibility of motion distinct from that embodied in the other. Socrates can pull this way without determining which way Callias will pull; Callias can give Socrates the slip and so on.[15] That this is how Aristotle would in fact respond is suggested by his discussion of Siamese twins in *Generation of Animals* (*GA*) IV.4, where he says that it is the principle [or *archê*] that determines whether we count a monstrosity (where embryos have grown together) as one or as several. If it has one heart (where the heart is an efficient cause and so presumably a principle of motion) we count it as one; if it has more than one heart, as more than one. Furthermore, Aristotle sometimes suggests that the form of a living thing resides primarily in its heart and so that there is an important connection between the formal cause of an individual and his heart. So Aristotle may be saying that we need to count forms in order to determine how many individuals of a given kind there are.

The problem is that Aristotle generally associates the indivisibility of motion characteristic of individuality with natural continuity [*Met.* 1052a25] and this introduces the forms we are trying to do without. In general, Aristotle will have trouble saying that the individual cars of a train (or lakes that are connected by rivers and channels) are numerically distinct because their matters are different, if he must explain this difference of matter by appealing exclusively to simple continuity. The problem is that simple continuity may be necessary, but is not sufficient, for oneness of matter.[16] So it must be supplemented by sortal criteria—that is, by appealing to the forms that the matter embodies or instantiates.

This is not to deny that there is a sense in which simple continuity is sufficient for the oneness and hence for the numerical distinctness of matter. The matter of all the cars of a train (or of a car and the trailer it pulls) constitutes an individual or one big piece of stuff. But this is not sufficient to show that these pieces are not further

---

[15] The reference to motion introduces questions of diachronic identity that reinforce my point that we cannot separate questions of synchronic and diachronic individuation. If we must individuate Socrates and Callias *at a time* by appeal to indivisibility of motion, then we must invoke *diachronic* considerations. And if these require reference to individual forms, then *synchronic* individuation must also involve reference to individual forms.

[16] See note 4 above.

divisible into smaller pieces, each of which is one and indivisible in the sense that it embodies an indivisibility of motion conferred upon it by form: for instance, the individual cars of the train or the car and the trailer. Relying exclusively on simple continuity does not provide us with adequate principles for counting objects and will often lead us to make deviant identity judgments.[17] For it would have us count the car and the trailer it pulls as one object in much the same way as we count the car and its bumpers as constituting one thing. This reveals the sense in which simple continuity is not sufficient and must be supplemented by sortal criteria. And this supports my claim that the traditional view can account for the differences of matter necessary for synchronic individuation only by appealing to form. Socrates and Callias are different on account of their having different matters. But it is a necessary condition of their having different matters that each of these matters is or constitutes a unity—i.e., that each embodies some form.

5

I deliberately stated the foregoing conclusion so as to leave open the question whether Socrates' and Callias' matters each embodies the very same form (i.e., the species-form of Man) or whether each embodies its own numerically distinct form (i.e., Socrates' soul and Callias' soul). Someone who defends the TV probably won't be too worried by the need to appeal to sortal criteria or forms, for that is a relatively uncontroversial thesis accepted both by advocates of individual forms and by proponents of the TV. And the latter may be able to concede that only informed matter can individuate (and hence that form is a necessary condition for individuation), without also conceding that this commits Aristotle to the existence of numerically distinct individual forms. But he will succeed only if he can show that species-form and matter are jointly sufficient for individuation and so, that there is no need for *individual* forms.

The defender of the TV will presumably argue that there is one species-form of Man and that this specifies the criteria for the existence (and the persistence) of individual men and is thus relevant to synchronic (and to diachronic) individuation. He can then argue that we can tell how many individuals there are at (and across) times by counting how many pieces of matter instantiate the form of Man at (and across) times.[18] This is supposed to show that species-form and matter are jointly sufficient for individuation and so that there is no need for individual forms.

Now we may wonder what these various instances of the species-form are, if not individual forms. But as long as proponents of the TV can deny that individual

---

[17] See Hirsch 1982, 27.
[18] This works across times in the following way: We can ask how many pieces of matter embody this form from t_1 to t_2. But if we individuate pieces of matter by their constituent particles, then we will have to say that each change of particles brings about the existence of a numerically distinct piece of matter. And this will yield deviant identity judgments. So, as I shall argue below, Aristotle needs alternative criteria for sameness and difference of matter.

instances of the species-form are themselves individual forms, or agree to adopt the greatest impossibility view of the *Parmenides* (i.e., that the form as a whole, while being one thing, is in each of the many), then it looks as though they can allow that only informed matter individuates without also conceding the existence of individual forms. But this appearance results largely from concentrating primarily on the problem of synchronic individuation, and this narrow focus is unwarranted. For the problem the TV finds with the synchronic individuation of conspecific individuals arises equally for their diachronic individuation. And it is the problem of diachronic individuation that most clearly reveals the need for individual forms. Let me explain.

6

If the TV were correct, then we could conclude that having the *same species-form* in the *same matter* from t_1 to t_2 would be sufficient for having the same individual from t_1 to t_2. Again, the problem is to explain the requisite sameness of matter without appealing to form. Suppose that in order to avoid individuating matter by appeal to form, we identify this matter as a piece of certain sort of stuff (e.g., bronze) with the following strict but apparently form-independent identity conditions: (a) it is identified in terms of its constituent particles and (b) these particles must be spatiotemporally continuous and dynamically cohesive with one another. It is like a Lockean body, which need not have the shape or form that it actually has (John Locke, *Essay Concerning Human Understanding*, II. 27.3).

On the TV, as long as this piece of bronze continues to instantiate the species-form Statue, we must conclude that it is the same individual statue. But couldn't this piece of bronze constitute a statue of Hermes at t_1 and then (by being gradually reshaped but without ever losing a single particle or ceasing to embody the statue form) come to constitute a statue of the Discobolus at t_2? Shouldn't we be able to say that although we have the same species-form in the same piece of matter, we nevertheless have a new statue, the Discobolus, which is a different individual and is thus numerically distinct from the original statue of Hermes? But if sameness of matter is explained as above, then it cannot be a difference of matter that accounts for their numerical distinctness. Nor, by hypothesis, can it be a difference of species-form that explains this difference. This suggests that diachronic individuation requires an appeal to individual forms.[19]

There seem to be three ways of defending the TV against the proposed counterexample. If the defender of that view accepts our intuition that the statue of Hermes and that of the Discobolus are two distinct individuals, he can try to account for this

---

[19] Michael Woods objects (in conversation) to this counterexample roughly that since there is no evidence that this sort of problem ever occurred to Aristotle, we cannot take the counterexample as evidence against the traditional view. But Aristotle's discussion (in *Physics* [*Ph.*] V.4) of an individual's health and whether it is the same before and after an illness, or even whether it is the same from morning to night, shows that Aristotle was concerned with these problems in the case of non-substance particulars. So there is no reason for saying that the general problem never occurred to him.

without abandoning the TV in either of two ways. (1) He can deny that the two statues have the same species-form. Or (2), he can deny that they have the same matter. If, on the other hand, he rejects our intuition, he will (3) simply deny that the statue of Hermes and that of the Discobolus are distinct individuals.

If anyone adopts the third alternative, we might attempt to get him to accept our intuition by asking him to consider modern abstract art rather than statues of Hermes and of the Discobolus. Suppose that Calder has decided that the large orange statue that he made for the city of Chicago ten years ago is really hideous. So he takes the piece of metal (i.e., the Lockean body) that constitutes the statue and twists and bangs it around in extreme ways. When he is finally satisfied and stands back to appreciate his work, he would presumably have some reason for saying that this is a much better statue than the other one was. And if the defender of the TV objects to these artificial examples on the grounds that they rely implicitly on our willingness to recognize individual essences for works of art, we can ask him to consider whether it is inconceivable that the same living body should continuously embody the species-form of Man while undergoing changes (of personality and experience memories) so radical that we may be justified in saying that it no longer is or constitutes the same person. For the artificial examples were introduced only as the simplest way of fixing the sameness of matter. But we can imagine an alternative case in which it seems reasonable to say that we have the same species-form continuously realized in the same matter from t_1 to t_2, but numerically distinct individuals at t_1 and t_2.

Suppose that instead of receiving Brown's brain (for that would involve a change of matter), Robinson retains his own brain while his memory traces are systematically erased and replaced by those of Brown. Let's also suppose that through some process of brain state transfer, he is caused to acquire all of Brown's character traits and dispositions.[20] Leaving aside the question of whether the resulting individual is Brown, let's simply ask whether he is still Robinson. In other words, do we still have the same individual? Now even if proponents of the TV do not agree, Robinson would surely have some reason for viewing this outcome as tantamount to his destruction. And this supports the intuition that here (as in the Hermes-Discobolus case) there are two distinct individuals involved. So we should consider the other two replies to the proposed counterexample.

First, someone might object that we do not have the same species-form continuously realized from t_1 to t_2 because the relevant species is not at the level of Statue but rather at the level of Statue-of-Hermes and Statue-of-the-Discobolus. In other words, Statue would be to Statue-of-Hermes and to Statue-of-the-Discobolus roughly as a genus is to its various species. For Statue-of-Hermes is clearly a type of which there can be a plurality of tokens.

This objection raises a number of important questions about Aristotle's criteria for being a universal, but I doubt that it will serve proponents of the TV. For it is not clearly

---

[20] See S. Shoemaker, *Self-Knowledge and Self-Identity* (Ithaca NY: Cornell University Press, 1963), 23–25.

consistent with Aristotle's conception of species-forms. In *Metaphysics* X.9 Aristotle argues that not every qualitative difference entails a difference in species, for some qualitative differences belong to matter rather than to form. But let's suppose (for the sake of argument) that qualitative differences do entail specific ones, so that pace Aristotle, black and white man, and male and female, along with Statue-of-Hermes and Statue-of-the-Discobolus, all constitute subspecies. This leads toward the conclusion that even more refined qualitative differences constitute subspecies, and so that there might be distinct forms for Callias and Socrates that, although logically repeatable, may in fact be uniquely instantiated.[21] On this account, it seems that as long as there are qualitative differences between them, we individuate Socrates and Callias by appeal to their forms in much the same way that we can individuate dogs from men by appeal to standard Aristotelian species-forms. For having different forms in this sense will be sufficient (even if not necessary) for the existence of numerically distinct individuals. So, given Aristotle's conception of species-form, the Hermes-Discobolus case raises a genuine problem.

At this point, someone might suspect that it is the qualitative differences between the statues of Hermes and of Discobolus (and between Robinson and the person with his body and Brown's psychological traits) that account for our intuition that we have (in each of these cases) numerically distinct individuals at t_1 and at t_2. If so, and if (as I am arguing) it is the presence of numerically distinct individual forms that accounts for the presence of numerically distinct individuals, then it may seem that I am relying on a conception of individual forms according to which such forms are qualitatively distinct. Moreover, it may seem that these forms must be *essentially* qualitatively distinct, if they are to serve as principles of individuation. However, although I am willing to allow that individual forms may be accidentally qualitatively distinct in virtue of differences in the matter that belongs (accidentally) to them,[22] I do not suppose (nor do I wish to suppose) that my argument depends upon essential qualitative differences between numerically distinct individual forms. For I think we can imagine cases in which we have the same species-form continuously realized in the same matter from

---

[21] Actual unique instantiation is not necessary to the argument. Even if Socrates' form is multiply instantiated and is thus a universal, it could still be sufficient to individuate him from Callias as long as Callias' form was qualitatively distinguishable from Socrates'. For the fact that the form of Dog is multiply instantiated does not show that we cannot individuate dogs from men by appeal to form. The issue about unique instantiation has more to do with the ontological status of these forms—i.e., whether they are universals or particulars.

[22] In "Individual Forms in Aristotle" (cited in note 2 above) I argue (by appeal to *Met.* VII.10–11) that the individual forms of natural (as opposed to mathematical) objects *essentially* contain or include their proximate matter. I also allow that such forms *accidentally* contain the non-proximate matter that accounts for the qualitative differences between numerically distinct individuals belonging to the same *infima species*. So in this sense, I allow that individual forms are accidentally qualitatively distinct in virtue of the qualitative differences arising from differences in the non-proximate matter that belongs accidentally to such forms. [Some of this argument appears in "Metasubstance" (Chapter 4, this volume).]

t_1 to t_2 and numerically distinct but qualitatively indistinguishable individuals in that matter at t_1 and t_2.[23]

There remains one further response to my proposed counterexample. That is (2), to deny not that we have the same species-form, but rather that we have the same matter in the relevant sense. Proponents of the TV might object that the appeal to Lockean bodies in the artificial examples is unwarranted because this is not how Aristotle understands sameness of matter. For in speaking of the body as matter, Aristotle admits different criteria. These criteria presumably allow for the displacement of the matter's constituent particles.

I agree that these criteria (rather than those for Lockean bodies) provide the correct account of sameness of matter, but they are not going to help the TV. For what enables us to think of the body as one thing that persists throughout the displacement of its constituent particles is that we think of it as a whole having certain shape and form. We think of it as a thing constituted, rather than as constituent stuff.

At this point it is worth noting Aristotle's distinction between the body as proximate matter (i.e., the ensouled body) and the body as non-proximate matter (i.e., the heap of flesh and bones or perhaps the heap of elements that constitute the flesh and bones). The body as non-proximate matter is what underlies and survives the loss of soul. But it is a mere heap and not an individual or a unity in the sense required for individuation [*Met.* 1040b5–10]. Because non-proximate matter is not a unity and so is not strictly an individual that survives material displacement, we must turn instead to proximate matter for the requisite account of sameness of matter. But proximate matter (or the ensouled body) is individuated by form (or soul) and so survives only as long as it is informed (or ensouled). This is the body of which the soul is the form or the essence [*DA* 412b11, 415b11]. The body as proximate matter is the same at t_1 to t_2 only insofar as it embodies the same form (or soul) continuously from t_1 to t_2.[24]

Once again proponents of the TV might concede that only informed matter can individuate, but attempt to deny that this requires the existence of numerically distinct individual forms. The real issue is how to interpret the claim that the body remains (numerically) the same only insofar as it continuously embodies the same

---

[23] Suppose, e.g., that someone wishes to dispose of me without running the risk of being charged with (bodily) murder and so decides to use a brain-state transfer device to transfer gradually the states of someone else's brain into mine (and my brain states into her brain) without actually transferring any matter. The person whose brain states he chooses to transfer happens to be my twin sister and further, unbeknownst to him and by some fluke, she and I happen also to be psychological twins; we have qualitatively indistinguishable memories, personalities, and so on. In this case, when the brain state transfer is completed, it seems that my original body and hers each embody an individual form that is numerically distinct not only from that embodied by the other, but also from the one it originally embodied. My body now has her numerically distinct but qualitatively indistinguishable form and her body now has mine. So in the case of each of these bodies, we have the same species-form continuously realized in the same matter from t_1 to t_2 and numerically distinct individuals in that matter at t_1 to t_2. This possibility supports the claim that my original counterexample and argument do not depend on essential qualitative differences between numerically distinct individual forms.

[24] For more on this, see "Living Bodies" (Chapter 3, this volume).

species-form. Is a body (numerically) the same because it continuously embodies the same species-form? Or is it the same because it embodies the same individual form (or soul)?[25]

Proponents of the TV will presumably say that a body is (numerically) the same insofar as it continuously realizes the same species-form. But this leaves them unable to distinguish the statue of Hermes from that of the Discobolus, or Robinson from the successive person with his body and all of Brown's character traits and experience memories. Here too, deviant identity judgments result from attempting to operate without adequate criteria of identity. For although species-form and spatiotemporal continuity of matter may seem to be jointly sufficient for synchronic individuation, they are not clearly adequate for diachronic individuation. Unless we are prepared to deny that the statue of Hermes and that of the Discobolus are numerically distinct, and to deny that the same body might successively embody two distinct persons, we must concede that the problem of diachronic individuation calls for numerically distinct individual forms. Once we have ruled out the three foregoing replies, it seems natural to say that the statue of Hermes at t_1 and that of the Discobolus at t_2 are numerically distinct because each of them has or embodies a numerically distinct individual form. Similarly, Socrates at t_1 is numerically the same as Socrates at t_2 because each embodies the same individual form or soul.

We could also apply this solution to synchronic individuation and say that Socrates and Callias are distinct (at a time) because each of them has or embodies a numerically distinct individual form or soul. The question is whether we ought to do so, for species-form and matter did seem to be jointly sufficient for synchronic individuation. But I suspect that this appearance is due to the fact that the embodiment or realization of a species-form in matter is sufficient for the existence of an individual form at a time. We can even say that the realization or embodiment of a species-form in matter *is* an individual form.[26] But if we fail to recognize that they are the same, then we may

---

[25] Sydney Shoemaker asks why we should take these two alternatives as exhaustive. In particular, he asks, why not appeal instead to a causal criterion of identity across time? I have two replies. First, I limit myself to these alternatives because I think that Aristotle assumes that he must solve the problem of individuation by appeal to form or to matter (or to some relationship between form and matter). Second, I do not think that these alternatives exclude causal considerations. We might allow that the appeal to individual forms resembles (or even involves) a causal criterion in the following way: x at t_1 and y at t_2 are numerically the same if and only if they have (numerically) the same individual form and the individual form of y at t_2 is numerically the same as that of x at t_1 if and only if the individual form of x at t_1 is causally responsible (in the appropriate ways) for the existence of the individual form of y at t_2. These causal connections may of course be mediated by the matter that (as I argue elsewhere) belongs to these forms. The idea is roughly that if the form in this matter (i.e., this individual form) at t_1 is causally responsible (in the appropriate ways) for the existence of the form in that matter (i.e., that individual form) at t_2, then these forms are numerically the same and so serve to make the individuals to which they belong numerically the same.

[26] Someone may object that the realization or embodiment of species-form in matter (i.e., an instance of species-form) is not an individual form, but rather a compound. But in "Individual Forms in Aristotle," I argue that there is a sense in which compounds are identical to individual forms, and so, that compounds and forms are simply the same things considered or described in different ways. If this is so, then the realization or embodiment of a species-form in matter *is* an individual form if it is a compound.

think that species-form and matter are jointly sufficient for synchronic individuation. But we would be wrong to conclude that individual forms are not necessary, for that's just what realizations of the species-form in matter are.

First, the bare existence of a species-form and some appropriate matter is not sufficient for the existence of any given individual; it is also necessary that the species-form and the matter be related in certain ways; the species-form must be embodied in a piece of matter or the matter must make up or constitute an instance of the species-form. And on my view, this is just to say that species-form and matter must be related in ways sufficient for the existence of an individual form.[27] So there is a sense in which species-form and matter are jointly sufficient for synchronic individuation; species-form and matter related to each other in certain ways are sufficient for synchronic individuation. But the ways in which they must be related (i.e., realizing or constituting individual forms) will not comfort proponents of the TV.

Second, it is unlikely that we can isolate principles of synchronic from principles of diachronic individuation.[28] If the problem of diachronic individuation reveals that what makes an individual to be the same as (or different from) an individual existing at another time is their embodying or constituting the same (or different) individual forms, then it is reasonable to suppose that embodying or constituting the same (or different) individual forms is what makes simultaneously existing individuals to be numerically the same or different.[29] But this is a claim only about a metaphysical principle of individuation and is consistent with the claim that species-form and matter are in some sense epistemologically sufficient for synchronic individuation. The previous paragraph suggests that someone could successfully count simultaneously existing conspecific individuals by counting embodiments or realizations of the species-form in matter without realizing that he was, ipso facto, counting individual forms. This intentional aspect of epistemological individuation does not show that individual form is not the metaphysical principle of individuation. Furthermore, it (along with

---

In conversation, Michael Woods allows that there are instances of the species-form and even concedes that speaking of these as being (in some sense) individual forms would allow proponents of the TV to explain much of what appears to be evidence that Aristotle admits the existence of individual forms without having to radically alter their views. In general, he thinks that there is less difference between my alternative and the TV than I often suggest. The difference comes not in admitting individual forms (for the TV can accommodate individual forms as instances or realizations of the species-form in matter), but rather in admitting a particular conception of individual forms according to which they either include (or are constituted by) their matter. (See note 22 above.)

[27] The idea here is roughly that the matter should either constitute or be identified with an instance of the species-form, which instance I take to be an individual form. (See below.) I cannot now say which of these two alternatives Aristotle would prefer. That would require further investigation of his application of the form-matter analysis to the relationship between soul and body.

[28] M. J. Woods, "Identity and Individuation," in R. J. Butler (ed.), *Analytical Philosophy* (Oxford: Blackwell 1962), 120–30.

[29] This reintroduces the question of whether it is not really individual form that individuates animals of different species. Here too, embodying different species-forms may provide an epistemological principle of individuation simply because it is sufficient for the existence of different individual forms that are themselves the metaphysical principles of individuation.

the tendency to focus primarily on synchronic rather than diachronic individuation) helps to explain how the flaws of the TV have so often gone unnoticed. Although it explains why commentators have often denied the conclusion that (individual) form is the metaphysical principle of both synchronic and diachronic individuation, it provides no reason or justification for that denial.

7

There is, however, an objection to the foregoing conclusion that individual form is the principle of both synchronic and diachronic individuation. If Aristotle really thinks that (individual) form is the principle of individuation, then why does he say that Socrates and Callias are the same in form and different on account of their matter?

The answer to this objection has two parts. First, we must show that Aristotle's claim that Socrates and Callias are the same in form is consistent with each having his own numerically distinct form. Second, we must recognize that having (or being realized in) some matter is at least a necessary condition for the existence of an individual form and furthermore, that this matter plays an important role in the form's capacity to individuate. This reveals a sense in which Socrates and Callias are different on account of their matter, but one that is compatible with the claim that form is the principle of individuation.

First then, we must read Aristotle as claiming that Socrates and Callias are the same in species (or species-form) and that this is indivisible.[30] But this does not rule out the possibility that each also has his own individual form and that this is what individuates him from the other. For Aristotle apparently recognizes the existence of numerically distinct forms that are the same in species [*Met.* 1071a26–29]. Each of these—the individual and the species-form—is one and indivisible. But only the individual form is one and indivisible in a way that can account for the numerical distinctness of Callias and Socrates.

The species (form) is one and indivisible not in number (for that would be Platonism), but because there is no contrariety in its account.[31] It is not further divisible into subspecies. But the individual form must be one and indivisible in a different way—namely, by being one and indivisible in place and time [*Met.* 1052a25–26]. And a plurality of such individual forms can be the same in species because the account of what it is for each of them to be is the same. But the important point here—and this brings us to the second part of our answer—is that once we see what is necessary in order for individual forms to be one in movement and indivisible in place and time, it will be clear that matter too plays an important role in their capacity to individuate.

---

[30] Aristotle clearly uses '*eidos*' to refer both to individual forms and to species (or to species-forms).
[31] This is the point of *Met.* X.9. By "one in number" here I mean being an individual in the sense in which Aristotle characterizes individuals in *De Int.* 17a38–40, i.e., being something that cannot be in many things (or places) at the same time and so, something that cannot be spatially scattered.

Initially we might wonder how an individual form can be one in movement and indivisible in place and time. For Aristotle says that movement is not in the form, but rather in the thing being moved [*Ph.* 224b25]. Furthermore, spatiotemporal characteristics are generally associated with material bodies, and Aristotelian forms are supposed to be immaterial. But this supposition is open to challenge. Ultimately, I think, it must be qualified.[32] First, it is important to note what Aristotle says about soul in the *De Anima*. For as *Metaphysics* 1042a25–26 reveals, it applies equally to the forms of other sensible objects. He says that soul is neither without a body nor a certain kind of body, but that it is something that belongs in a certain sort of body [*DA* 414a20–22]. The general point is that the (individual) form of a sensible object cannot exist apart from some matter. And this matter plays a fundamental role in explaining how these forms can be one in movement and indivisible in place and time.

Aristotle allows that something can be moved in either of two ways—owing to another or owing to itself [*DA* 406a4–5]. Something is moved owing to another (or accidentally) when it is in the thing being moved—for instance, as sailors in a ship are moved. So Aristotle can say that the soul in particular (and individual forms in general) are accidentally one in movement and indivisible in place and time—that is, that forms are one in this way on account of the spatiotemporal continuity of the matter in which they are embodied [*DA* 408a30–35].[33] But this just means that individual forms will be one in number and thus individuals on account of the matter in which they are embodied. This in turn explains why Aristotle says that Socrates and Callias are different on account of their matter.

In order for Socrates and Callias to be numerically distinct, each of them must be some one thing—i.e., an individual. But form is the principle of unity and the spatiotemporal continuity of matter is a necessary condition for a form's being one in number. So there is a sense in which each of Socrates and Callias is an individual and hence numerically distinct from the other on account of the spatiotemporal continuity of his matter.

At this point, someone might object that if form is one and indivisible on account of the spatiotemporal continuity of its matter, then it is matter that ultimately deserves to be called the principle of individuation. But here it is important to remember that mere spatiotemporal continuity of matter is not always sufficient for individuation. It would have us count the statue of Hermes at t_1 and that of the Discobolus at t_2 as one and the same thing—and worse yet, as one and the same as the puddle of bronze into which either statue might be melted. So spatiotemporal considerations must at least be supplemented by sortal or formal criteria. But if we concede this point, our objector

---

[32] See note 22 above.

[33] In "Individual Forms in Aristotle," I argue that some of Aristotle's claims that certain properties (e.g., perishability and the capacity for movement) do not belong to forms *must* (on pain of inconsistency) be elliptical for claims that these properties do not belong essentially to forms. These properties may, however, belong to forms accidentally and in virtue of the matter in which they are embodied. (On the movability of the soul, compare *DA* 408b30–32 with 408a29–31.)

may argue that this is not sufficient to show that form is *the* principle of individuation. He may object that the only warranted conclusion is that each of form and matter is a necessary condition for individuation (i.e., for the existence of something sensible that is one in number). So although each of form and matter is *a* principle of individuation, neither is *the* principle of individuation.

This objection combines two arguments—first, the TV's argument that matter individuates (or accounts for the plurality of instances of) form, and second, my argument that it is the form that unifies and thus individuates matter. It then concludes that neither form nor matter can be *the* principle of individuation. But this conclusion rests on a conception of form that must be challenged.[34] This is the traditional conception of form as something abstract and immaterial that, even if it must be realized or embodied in some matter in order to exist, does not itself contain or include any matter. On this account, form and matter are apparently two distinct things—one a universal and the other some sort of stuff—each standing in certain relations to the other. But, Aristotle challenges this when he says that the proximate matter and the form are the same and one, the one potentially what the other is actually [*Met.* 1045b18–19]. This suggests that form, because it is somehow the same and the one with its proximate matter, includes the matter necessary for individuation. On this account, form can be sufficient for, and hence, *the* principle of individuation.

This raises difficult questions about Aristotle's conception of the relationship between form and matter and what exactly he means by saying that the form and the proximate matter are one and the same. There are two salient possibilities. One is that Aristotle identifies the form with its proximate matter and that they are simply the same thing under two different descriptions.[35] Another is that the relationship between form and matter is one between a thing constituted and its constituent stuff.[36] On either account, we must think of form not as something abstract and immaterial (or more precisely, not as a universal realized in a particular piece of matter), but rather as a concrete thing constituted by or identified with some matter.

These alternatives are not exclusive. If we adopt Aristotle's distinction between proximate and non-proximate matter, then we can generally interpret the relationship between form and matter as that between a thing constituted and its constituent stuff, and so generally refuse to identify a form with constituent matter. But this leaves open the possibility that there is a special case of the form-matter relationship in which the form or thing constituted is identified with its constituent matter. This is the relationship between a form and its proximate matter.

---

[34] Here, as elsewhere, a particular conception of what Aristotelian forms must be can lead commentators to reject apparent evidence for the existence of individual forms. In this case, a conception of Aristotelian forms as abstract and immaterial may lead to the conclusion that form *cannot* be *the* principle of individuation. But if this conception of form is mistaken, then the argument fails.

[35] See W. Sellars, *Philosophical Perspectives* (Charles C. Thomas Publishers, 1976), 73–124; E. Hartman, *Substance, Body and Soul* (Princeton University Press, 1977).

[36] See D. Wiggins, *Identity and Spatio-Temporal Continuity* (Oxford University Press, 1967), 48; W. Charlton, *Aristotle's Physics* (Oxford University Press 1970), 70–79.

Determining the exact nature of Aristotle's form-matter relationship requires further consideration of his application of the form-matter analysis to the relationship between soul and body, a project that I cannot now undertake. For now, the important point is that whether Aristotle identifies a form with its proximate matter or simply regards it as constituted by its proximate (or non-proximate) matter, he does suggest an account of form that allows it to include the matter necessary for individuation. And this allows him to argue that form is the principle of individuation.

There remains one further objection to this account of form as the principle of individuation. This is that individual forms don't explain anything, but simply presuppose what (i.e., individuality) they are supposed to explain. In a sense this is obviously true, but how much it should concern Aristotle depends upon how he conceives his project and what he thinks a principle of individuation is.

"Principles of Individuation" is Scholastic, but the closest Aristotelian equivalent to 'principle' is '*archê*,' which Aristotle often uses interchangeably with '*aitia*' ('cause'). And when we recall Aristotle's four causes I think we can see how he might deal with this objection. Form is not what makes something to be an individual in the sense that it is something distinct from that individual. Form is the formal cause—*the what it is to be* or *the essence*—of an individual. To be an individual is simply to be a certain form. And this is just what we should expect, given Aristotle's identification of each thing with its form or essence.[37]

---

[37] I should like to thank Gail Fine, Terry Irwin, Elijah Millgram, Sydney Shoemaker, and Michael Woods for discussing previous drafts of this essay with me.

2

Form and Generation in Aristotle

THERE ARE TWO basic families of views about the nature and distribution of Aristotle's substantial forms.[1]

The members of the first family agree that Aristotle recognizes only one form for each *infima species*. On their view, each individual member of an *infima species* (e.g., each individual man) has the very same form—not only qualitatively but also numerically. This form, often referred to as the "species-form," can belong to many individuals at the same time.[2] So it is usually thought to satisfy Aristotle's

---

[1] This essay presents a brief and simplified overview of the central argument of my *Aristotelian Individuals* (unpublished). It was written—and can be read—without the notes, which have been added to supply further clarification and justification, along with references to relevant literature.

[2] "Species-form" is due to commentators and not to Aristotle, who generally uses the same noun 'εἶδος' to refer both to the *form* (as opposed to the matter) of a thing and to the *species* (as opposed to the genus) to which its bearer belongs. Members of the first family assume that when Aristotle uses 'εἶδος' to refer to the form (as distinct from the species), he takes himself to be referring to a unique form common to each and every member of the species to which that thing belongs. (The same goes for 'μορφή' and 'λόγος,' which Aristotle also uses to refer to forms.) Such commentators would presumably explain the (non-chance) homonymy of '*form*' and '*species*' by claiming that the form of a thing is the set of characteristics or capacities the possession of which makes its bearer a thing of its respective species or kind. On the distinction between 'εἶδος' as "form" and 'εἶδος' as "species," see Driscoll 1981, 141–48, especially n. 54.

criteria for being a universal.³ Views of this sort have been standard in recent years.⁴

The members of the second family take Aristotle to recognize a plurality of numerically distinct forms for each *infima species*. On their view, each individual man has his own numerically distinct form, which may or may not differ qualitatively from the numerically distinct forms of other individual men.⁵ This form is peculiar to him in the sense that it *cannot* belong, one and the same in number, to any other individual. So it is *not* a universal; it is an "individual form."⁶ Views of this sort were favored by the

---

³ Aristotle takes a universal to be what is by nature such as to be predicated of (or to belong to) more than one thing: *De Interpretatione (De Int.)* 17a38–b1, *Metaphysics (Met.)* 1038b11–12. This leaves a question (discussed in Irwin 1988) about whether a universal is simply what *can be* predicated of more than one thing or rather what *is actually* predicated of more than one. But we can ignore this dispute here, since Aristotle in fact takes species-forms to satisfy the stronger requirement of being *actually* predicated of many. The important point here is that not all commentators who take Aristotle to recognize only one form for each *infima species* take such forms to be universals. Some—e.g., Woods 1967 and Code 1986—have denied that species-forms are universals on the grounds that the species-form is predicated only of matter that, prior to form's being predicated of it, is not a countable thing. On this view the species-form, being predicated only of matter, is not predicated of *any* individual and so, ipso facto, is not predicated of *many* individuals. Thus it is not a universal.

⁴ Balme 1980 traces this view back to Porphyry. For more recent adherents, see Ross 1924, Owen 1965b, Woods 1967 and 1974–1975, and Furth 1988.

⁵ There are different versions of this basic view, some according to which there are qualitative differences among individual form belonging to one and the same species and some according to which there are no such qualitative differences. Note that the former versions do not (as it is sometimes supposed) require us to deny that individual forms are tokens of a type; we can allow qualitatively distinct tokens of a type as long as we allow that there is more to a token than its type. A token of a given type may have characteristics in addition to those that belong to it qua token of that type and it is even possible that some of these additional features are essential to it not qua token of that type but rather qua this or that particular token of the relevant type. I remain, for present purposes at least, neutral on these issues.

⁶ Although such forms have often been referred to as "particular forms," *I* call them "individual forms" because I take 'particular' to best represent 'καθ' ἕκαστον' and I know of no passage (apart from *De Caelo* 278a1o, which is ambiguous) where Aristotle clearly refers to a form as 'καθ' ἕκαστον.' I take 'individual' to represent 'ἓν ἀριθμῷ' or "one in number" used as a one-place predicate. [See note 6 of "Metasubstance" (Chapter 4, this volume)]. Since Aristotle says that substance forms are τόδε τι, substance forms will be one in number if (as suggested below) whatever is τόδε τι is one in number. And although *Met.* 999b33–1000a1 appears to say that something is an individual if and only if it is a particular, Aristotle suggests a distinction between what is one in number and what is particular when he allows that the prime mover (which is immaterial and imperishable) is one in number [*Met.* 1074a36–37] but says *both* that place [τόπος] is proper ([Ἴδιος) to particulars [*Met.* 1092a18–20] *and* that all (sublunary) particulars are perishable [*Met.* 1039b30–31]. (I take the restriction to sublunary particulars to be indicated by the 'αὐτῶν' at 1039b31. And although the authenticity of 1074a36–37 has been disputed, I accept the arguments of Owens (1978, 447–50) for taking it to be authentic.) These passages suggest that Aristotle denies that immaterial individuals are particulars, and instead takes particulars to be *material* individuals. This need not conflict with *Met.* 999b33–1000a1 if the universe of discourse there is restricted to *sensible* substances. The distinction between individuals and particulars is important because (as I argue in an unpublished paper presented at a conference at Oriel College, Oxford in 1989) Aristotle argues only against knowledge of particulars and not (as usually supposed) against knowledge of individuals. Note, however, that Ross and others often render 'καθ' ἕκαστον' as "individual" rather than "particular," so one cannot count on existing translations to mark the distinction as I do. [Code 1986 sees a distinction here, but not the one I see: see note 12 below.]

Greek commentators and have become increasingly popular since Sellars and Albritton revived the debate back in 1957.[7] But they are still (as far as I can tell) minority views.

Recent discussions of the question whether Aristotle is committed to the existence of individual forms have tended to be relatively atomistic, focusing on scattered passages where Aristotle seems to be directly concerned with the ontological status of forms—for example, passages where he says that every substance form is τόδε τι (roughly "some this") and passages where he *argues* that forms are substances and that substances cannot be universals. Very little attention has been paid to the fundamental question of *why*, *if* at all, Aristotle thinks he needs to introduce individual forms in the first place. That is the question I propose to address here. I shall argue that *one* of Aristotle's reasons for introducing individual forms is that he thinks that they are needed in order to account of the distinction between, on the one hand, generation and destruction *simpliciter*, and, on the other hand, alteration and other sorts of accidental change (such as growth and locomotion). Like Aristotle, I shall focus primarily on the distinction between generation and destruction *simpliciter*, on the one hand, and mere alteration on the other.[8]

The existence of some such distinction seems to be assumed in the ordinary language not only of ancient Greeks but also of contemporary speakers of English.[9] For example, when someone has a child, we ordinarily say that she becomes a mother rather than that a mother comes to be. And when someone dies, we ordinarily say that he ceases to exist rather than that he becomes a corpse. Aristotle believes that these practices are not simply linguistic conventions. He believes that they reflect a genuine distinction between something's coming into (or going out of) existence, and an existing thing's undergoing (and so surviving) certain changes.

But some of Aristotle's predecessors—namely, monists like Thales and Anaximenes—seemed to him to deny the existence of a distinction between generation and destruction *simpliciter* and mere alteration. Because they took everything to come to be from (and to perish into) a single underlying matter, Aristotle concludes that they were committed to treating *all* changes—including those ordinarily called "generations and destructions"—simply as alterations of this single underlying matter.[10]

---

[7] On the views of the Greek commentators, see Lloyd 1981. The controversy was revived by Sellars 1957 and Albritton 1957. Since then, Aristotle's commitment to individual forms has been defended further by Sellars 1967 and by Hartman 1977, Frede 1978, Heinaman 1979, Whiting 1986 [Chapter 1, this volume], Irwin 1988, Frede and Patzig 1988, and Witt 1989.

[8] Helen Cartwright rightly objected, in her comments, to my previous assimilation of other kinds of accidental change (such as growth and locomotion) to alteration. Aristotle is of course concerned to distinguish generation and destruction *simpliciter* not only from alteration but also from growth, decline, and locomotion. But he focused, as I myself focus, primarily on the case of alteration (perhaps because his opponents assimilated these other kinds of accidental change to it).

[9] There is an ambiguity in 'γίγνεσθαι,' generally used *with a complement* to indicate non-substantial change, and *without a complement* to indicate substantial change. But Aristotle often disambiguates by supplying 'ἁπλῶς' when referring to coming-to-be *simpliciter*. See Williams 1982, chapters X–XI.

[10] *Generation and Corruption* (*GC*) 314a8–11; *Met.* 983b6–18; on Thales, see DK 11 B 3; on Anaximenes, see DK 13 A 5.

But many of Aristotle's predecessors sought to avoid this conclusion by positing a plurality of basic elements the association and dissociation of which they took to constitute generation and destruction *simpliciter*.[11] On their view, the association of earth and water to form a clay bowl is generation, and the dissociation of this earth and water is destruction. But Aristotle, though sympathetic to this project, objects that these pluralists are unable to give an adequate account *of alteration*.

Aristotle's own view is that we can give an adequate account of the distinction between generation *simpliciter* and mere alteration only if we appeal to what he calls "form" [εἶδος or μορφή]. And I argue here that Aristotle's view requires an appeal not simply to species-forms common to each of the members of their respective species, but also to individual forms that are peculiar to the individual substances (like Socrates and Callias) that come to be and pass away.[12]

1

Before proceeding, it is important to note that Aristotle assumes that an adequate account of the distinction between generation and destruction *simpliciter* and alteration must satisfy two criteria. First, not just any distinction will do. The distinction must coincide roughly with our ordinary ways of describing and classifying changes. A man's death cannot be simply an alteration of his body or matter. Nor can what we would ordinarily describe as his coming to be musical turn out to be the destruction of an unmusical man and the generation of a musical one. Let's call this the "common-sense criterion."[13]

Second, this distinction cannot be simply a matter of convention or how we choose to describe things. There is no genuine distinction if *any* change can be described *either* as a generation or destruction *or* as an alteration and it is simply a matter of convention which descriptions we decide to use. Let's call this the "anti-conventionalist criterion." We can see these assumptions at work if we examine the

---

[11] This may have been truer of atomists (like Democritus and Leucippus) than of other pluralists, some of whom (e.g., Anaxagoras) appeared (in identifying generation and destruction *simpliciter* with alteration) to deny the distinction. (On this issue, see Barnes 1982, 441.) But Aristotle suggests that Anaxagoras was simply mistaken about the consequences of his own view, and he may have thought the same of Empedocles. (See *GC* 314a13–15 and Joachim 1922 ad loc.) On Anaxagoras, see DK 59 A 52; 59 B 17. On Empedocles, see DK 31 B 8; 31 B 11; 31 B 17. And on the atomists, see DK 67 A 7; 67 A 14; 68 A 37.

[12] Except for Irwin and Code, most commentators view the alternatives of species-form and individual forms within a species as exclusive. But I argue (in Whiting, unpublished) that Aristotle believes that there must be *both* species-forms *and* individual forms if sensible substances are to be both separate and knowable. My view differs from Irwin's insofar as our accounts of species-forms differ; it differs from Code's view insofar as I take Aristotle's view to require that individual forms (or what Code calls "particular forms") be *tokens* or *instances* of their respective species-forms. Code denies this because he (unlike me) denies that species-forms are universals. On this issue, see notes 3 and 5 above.

[13] For some discussion of the methodology supporting this criterion, see Owen 1961, Nussbaum 1982, and especially (in connection with its apparently problematic relationship with the sort of realism I attribute to Aristotle) Irwin 1988.

arguments Aristotle gives in *Generation and Corruption* against his monist and pluralist predecessors.

Let's take the monists first. As we have seen, Aristotle thinks they are committed to taking *all* changes simply as alterations of a single underlying stuff. Like a man who is first pale and then dark, this stuff can be first airy and then watery, or first human and then equine. If the monists are correct, then most if not all of our ordinary substantival expressions (like 'man' and 'horse') ought to be replaced by adjectival ones (like 'human' and 'equine').

Nevertheless, a monist may continue to use misleading substantival expressions primarily for the sake of convenience. Suppose, for example, that bronze is his primary stuff. He might argue that when this bronze becomes statuesque, we can (for convenience sake) choose to regard this statuesque bronze as *itself* a subject. We can call it a "statue" and talk as if it were an independent substance rather than bronze characterized in certain ways. We can then say that the *statue* has various properties and undergoes certain changes: we can say, for example, that *it* is a representation of Socrates or that *it* loses a limb. And when this statuesque bronze is melted down, we can say that there is a destruction of the statue as well as an alteration of this bronze. On this view, we speak as if there were generations and destructions *simpliciter*, but these (like the living substances and medium-size dry goods that we say come to be and pass away) are simply convenient logical fictions.

Here, however, it is important to note that the monist can regard anything at all as a subject; statues are no more privileged than large-statues, musical-statues, or statues-in-the-Metropolitan.[14] So what we would ordinarily regard as locomotion (e.g., a statue's being transported from the Metropolitan to the Smithsonian) may equally be regarded as the destruction of one thing and the generation of another (i.e., as the destruction of a statue-in-the-Metropolitan and the generation of a statue-in-the-Smithsonian). And the same goes for growth and alteration: the former can be regarded as the destruction of a small thing and the generation of a large one, and the latter can be regarded as the destruction of a non-F (e.g., an unmusical thing) and the generation of an F (e.g., a musical thing). In fact, *any* change, suitably described, can be regarded as a generation or destruction *simpliciter*. So this move fails to isolate a proper subset of changes that are generations and destructions *simpliciter* and thus fails to satisfy Aristotle's first, common-sense criterion. Furthermore, all of the descriptions that admit generation and destruction are purely conventional. So this move also fails to satisfy Aristotle's second, anti-conventionalist criterion.

Let us turn then to the pluralists. Since the arguments Aristotle actually gives against the pluralists in *Generation and Corruption* are bad arguments, I shall not

---

[14] I use the hyphenated expressions to designate accidental unities or what Matthews 1982 calls "kooky objects." These objects are individuated by their hyphenated descriptions in the sense that satisfying (and continuing to satisfy) these descriptions is a necessary condition for their existence (and persistence). So a musical-man is essentially both a man and musical, and ceases to exist if the man by which it is partially constituted ceases to be musical.

waste time on them now.¹⁵ What I want to do instead is to consider a somewhat more charitable account of pluralism than the one Aristotle actually presents and then to show that Aristotle has good reasons for objecting that the pluralists still cannot satisfy the common-sense and anti-conventionalist criteria without introducing form.

First, I shall assume (as Aristotle does not) that the pluralist view need not be atomistic. This allows the pluralist to claim that generation is the association of divisible (but actually undivided) magnitudes, and that destruction is the dissociation of divisible (but actually undivided) magnitudes (and perhaps also the division of previously undivided magnitudes). The pluralist can then claim that alteration and other sorts of accidental change are simply *rearrangements* of associations of divisible (but actually undivided) magnitudes.

Note that *given this account* of the distinction between generation and destruction *simpliciter* and accidental change, the pluralist's decision whether to call any particular change a generation (or destruction) *simpliciter* or an accidental change is *not* simply a matter of convention. Any change involving the continuous association of a certain set (or quantity) of magnitudes *must* be called an accidental change.¹⁶ And this applies not only to a certain quantity of bronze's change from hot to cold but also to that quantity of bronze's change from constituting a statue to constituting a shield. So if we have any temptation to call the latter change the destruction of a statue and the generation of a shield, we may object that the pluralist requires *too many* (rather than too few) changes to count as accidental.

On the other hand, we may find that the pluralist sometimes requires *too many* changes to count as generations (or destructions) *simpliciter*. Every time a statue loses or acquires a particle of bronze, we must say that this is generation or destruction rather than growth or diminution. The problem is much worse for living organisms, which regularly suffer the displacement of their material constituents. On this view, what we would ordinarily call a persisting man is really a succession of distinct entities each of which is destroyed simultaneously with the generation of its successor.

We can now see that the fundamental problem with this crude pluralism is *not* that it is unable to draw *any* distinction between generation and destruction *simpliciter*, on the one hand, and alteration and other sorts of accidental change on the other, but rather that it locates that distinction in the wrong places. What we would ordinarily call the generation of a statue may be treated simply as an alteration of some

---

¹⁵ I describe these arguments in somewhat more detail in Whiting, unpublished.
¹⁶ I am using 'quantity' here in the technical sense explained in Cartwright 1970, 25–42. According to this sense, a quantity is like a set the identity of which is determined by the identity of its members: the identity of a quantity is determined by the identity of its constituent particles, and quantities (like sets) can exist even if their constituents are scattered (or spatiotemporally discontinuous with one another). Aristotle's denial of atomism raises problems with such individuation from the "bottom up," but I must for present purposes set these problems aside.

bronze. And entire species of accidental change (such as growth and diminution) must be assimilated to generation and destruction *simpliciter*.

At this point, the pluralist might defend himself by arguing that associations are like heaps; they can perhaps tolerate some small and gradual changes in their material constituents. This is true, for example, of political associations and their members. This defense requires the pluralist to deny that *every* association (or dissociation) is generation (or destruction) *simpliciter*. But that is not to say that *no* association (or dissociation) is generation (or destruction) *simpliciter*. The pluralist's problem is to provide some criterion for determining which associations or dissociations *are*, and which *are not*, generations and destructions *simpliciter*.

Aristotle's objection is that the pluralist cannot provide a plausible and nonarbitrary criterion without appealing to form. To say that any association can survive the replacement of up to forty-nine (or any other) percent of its matter seems arbitrary. Why not forty-eight or fifty-one (or some other) percent? Furthermore, why should the replacement of some arbitrary percent of my matter constitute my destruction while my death (as long as my body remains intact) counts simply as an *alteration*? Aristotle can reasonably object that this (or any other) purely quantitative criterion is not only arbitrary but implausible.

Aristotle can raise a similar objection to the pluralist's account of alteration as the rearrangement of a continuous association of elements. For he believes that *some* changes in a fixed association of elements are sufficient for the destruction of one thing and the generation of another. Just as a tragic chorus may differ from a comic one composed of the very same elements, so too a πόλις may not survive a change in the form [εἶδος] of its government even if its citizens remain the same [*Politics* 1276b1–9]. Some changes in arrangement—namely, those which involve changes in a thing's form—are sufficient for the destruction of one thing (e.g., a democracy) and the generation of another (e.g., a tyranny). Aristotle's objection is that unless the pluralist introduces form, he cannot distinguish these changes in rearrangement from relatively minor changes such as the reapportionment of electoral districts or the passing of new sanitation laws.[17] Worse yet, the pluralist may be forced to count the change from democracy to tyranny as an alteration of a πόλις while—at the very same time—counting the emigration of some of its citizens as its demise.

In summary then, the crude pluralist criterion (which identifies *all* association and dissociation with generation and destruction *simpliciter* and *all* rearrangement with alteration) clearly fails to satisfy Aristotle's first, common-sense criterion. But if the pluralist attempts to revise his criterion by isolating some proper subset of associations and dissociations that are to count as generations or destructions *simpliciter*, he risks running afoul of Aristotle's second, anti-conventionalist criterion; purely quantitative distinctions seem arbitrary and conventional. Furthermore, they often fail to

---

[17] [I should not, in 1983, have been so cavalier about the reapportionment of electoral districts!]

line up even roughly with our ordinary ways of describing and classifying changes and so still fail to satisfy the common-sense criterion. Aristotle thinks that we can satisfy *both* criteria only if we introduce form.[18]

2

Let me pause at this point to explain roughly how Aristotle conceives of form. Although Aristotle's distinction between form and matter is intended to apply primarily to living organisms, he often illustrates this distinction by appeal to artifacts. Take, for example, a statue. The form of a statue is roughly its shape and this—its shape or form—is what *makes* something a statue. Aristotle distinguishes this form from the matter in which it is embodied by asking us to imagine that the form can be embodied in different kinds of matter—e.g., in bronze or stone or wood [*Met.* 1036a31–34]. We can also imagine that the particular portion of matter in which some form is embodied is gradually replaced by different portions of the same kind of matter—as in the case of living organisms.[19] Take, e.g., the form of a human being, which is not its external shape (which it may share with corpses and statues) but rather the more complicated set of capacities that makes something a human being—the capacities to reason, perceive, move, and act. Aristotle calls this set of capacities constituting the form of a living thing its soul [ψυχή] [*De Anima* (*DA*) II.1–3]. We can easily imagine that the matter in which this set of capacities is embodied is gradually replaced so that this set of capacities (or soul) is embodied in different quantities or portions of the same kind of matter at different times. In this case, the form is what persists throughout changes in the organism's matter and the form is what makes the organism what it is (namely, a human being) throughout these changes.[20]

It is this characteristic of forms—namely, that *they make their subjects what they are*—that explains why Aristotle identifies forms with essences [*Met.* 1032b1–2] and so why he thinks form is crucial to distinguishing generation and destruction *simpliciter*

---

[18] There is no commitment yet as to whether the requisite forms are individual or species-forms; the arguments for that come elsewhere.

[19] In order to leave open the possibility of a non-atomistic treatment of such matter, I shall henceforth use "portion" in place of "quantity" (explained in note 16 above).

[20] Aristotle explicitly treats the form as such a subject, persisting throughout changes in the matter in which it is embodied, at *GC* 321b25–28 and 322a28–33; this explains how form can (as it must if it is to be primary substance) satisfy the subject criterion, which is endorsed both in the *Categories* (*Cat.*) and in *Metaphysics* VII.3. Please note that I reject the view that *Metaphysics* VII.3 presents a reductio ad absurdum of the subject criterion, for Metaphysics VII.13 explicitly appeals to the subject criterion in arguing (at *Met.* 1038b15–16) that no universal is a substance. *Metaphysics* VII.3 should rather be taken as arguing that the subject criterion must be applied (or interpreted) in conjunction with the other criteria for being a substance—in particular, those requiring that every (primary) substance be τόδε τι and separable [χωριστόν]. This means that (primary) substances must be subjects that are both separable and τόδε τι. Aristotle's requirements for being τόδε τι are discussed below. On separability, see Fine 1984 and 1985, and Morrison 1985a and 1985b.

from alteration and other sorts of accidental change. But Aristotle's own criterion for distinguishing generation and destruction *simpliciter* from alteration does not explicitly mention form. He says (at *GC* 319b10–16) that generation occurs "whenever a whole changes, there remaining nothing perceptible as the same subject" and that alteration occurs "whenever the subject, remaining something perceptible, changes in its properties" [or affections, πάθη]. But the lack of explicit reference to form here is misleading. For as we shall see, we cannot distinguish subjects from their properties or affections, and so cannot apply this criterion, without appealing to form.

But first let me note that there are good reasons for thinking that Aristotle's references to perceptibility are superfluous and can for present purposes be ignored.[21] The reasons are complicated, so I shall support this only by noting that immediately after presenting his criterion for generation and destruction *simpliciter* from alteration at *Generation and Corruption* 319b10–16, Aristotle considers the case in which water comes to be from air. In this case, Aristotle thinks that the wet-transparent (or wet-cold) comes to be out of the dry-transparent (or dry-cold) and that the transparent (or cold) remains.[22] Aristotle denies that this is an alteration of the transparent (or cold) on the grounds that the terminus of the change is not an affection [πάθος] of what persists. Water is not an affection of the transparent or cold; if anything, they are affections (first of air and then) of *it*. But Aristotle thinks that the transparent and cold *are* perceptible; the transparent is visible (not in itself but on account of the color of something else) and the cold is tangible [*DA* 418b4–6; 422b25–27]. This suggests that perceptibility is irrelevant and that the terminus ad quem's not being an affection [πάθος] of what persists is sufficient to distinguish generation and destruction *simpliciter* from mere alteration.

---

[21] It is possible that Aristotle takes the perceptibility of the persisting subject to be relevant because he is focusing on a special case of generation and destruction *simpliciter*—namely, that of the four elements. Aristotle thinks that he must allow that *something* persists in all cases of generation and destruction *simpliciter*, since he would otherwise have to admit generation *ex nihilo* and destruction *in nihil*. In most cases, what persists is perceptible but Aristotle denies that it is the subject of the relevant change; it is an affection (first of one thing then of another) so the change is not an alteration of *it*. But in the special case of the generation and destruction of the four elements, he may think that what persists (i.e., prime matter) is the subject of the relevant change; so he may *add* the requirement that what persists not be a *perceptible* subject in order to protect his view that transformations of the elements are really generations and destructions *simpliciter* and not simply alterations of prime matter. This may seem ad hoc, but Aristotle could have avoided the problem by arguing (as suggested by the example I go on to discuss) that it is a *sufficient* condition for generation and destruction *simpliciter* that the terminus ad quem is not an affection or an accident of what persists and then denying that earth and water are affections or accidents of prime matter.

[22] There is no need to delete 'ἡ ψυχρά' from the text on the grounds that Aristotle took air to be composed of the fundamental contraries, the *hot* and the *wet*, and so could not have supposed the *cold* to remain throughout the change from air to water. Aristotle may (as Joachim suggests) add this alternative to accommodate views other than his own. Or, as seems more likely, Aristotle may be relying on a distinction between attributive adjectives (used elsewhere as substantives to refer to the four fundamental contraries) and predicate adjectives (used here to characterize water and air, both of which can be either hot or cold).

This, however, is not quite right. For the terminus ad quem's not being an affection of what persists is sufficient for generation and destruction *simpliciter* only if (as in the foregoing passage, *GC* 319b6–31) Aristotle is focusing only on alteration and ignoring other sorts of accidental change. In order to distinguish generation and destruction *simpliciter* not only from alteration but also from other sorts of accidental change (e.g., growth, diminution, and locomotion) Aristotle must *generalize* the requirement that the terminus not be an affection of what persists, as he proceeds to do at *Generation and Corruption* 320a1–2, where he says that generation and destruction occur "whenever *nothing* remains of which the other <contrary> [i.e., the *terminus ad quem*] is an affection *or an accident generally* [συμβεβηκός ὅλως]"[23] This, then, is Aristotle's general criterion for distinguishing generation and destruction *simpliciter* from alteration and other sorts of accidental change. The fact that he formulates it without reference to the perceptibility of the persisting subject confirms my claim that the initial reference to perceptibility is superfluous and can for present purposes be ignored.

If this is correct, then the crucial question is this: what are the subjects and what are their accidents? And Aristotle indicates in his preliminary account of the criterion (at *GC* 317a20–27) that we cannot answer this question without appealing to form when he says that generation and destruction *simpliciter* occur "whenever a whole changes from this to this" and elaborates as follows:

> ... in the subject there is one <thing> corresponding to the λόγος and one to the matter, and whenever the change is in *these*, there is generation and destruction, but whenever <the change is> in the affections [ἐν τοῖς πάθησι] and accidentally (κατὰ συμβεβηκός) < there is> alteration. [*GC* 317a20–27]

For 'λόγος' is used here (as elsewhere) to refer to form. So this passage indicates that we cannot distinguish subjects from their affections and accidents, and so cannot apply Aristotle's criterion, without appealing to form.

3

Here it is worth pausing to note the central problem facing Aristotle—namely, that his criterion seems to leave open the possibility that what we would ordinarily regard as a single change can be regarded either as a generation or destruction *simpliciter* or as an alteration—or as both—depending on what we take the relevant subjects and their accidents to be. Take, for example, what we would ordinarily regard as a man's death. If the subject is the man and it is part of his λόγος (or essence) and not simply one of his accidents to be alive, then this change will be a destruction *simpliciter* of the man. If, on the other hand, the subject is the pale thing and being a man and being a

---

[23] Affections [παθή] are accidents in the category of quality, but there are accidents in other categories as well.

corpse (or being alive and being dead) are properties of *it*, then this change will be an alteration of the pale thing. And if *anything* can be a subject and *anything* an accident, then any change can be regarded either as a generation (or destruction) *simpliciter* or as an alteration, depending on what we take the subjects and their accidents to be.[24] So Aristotle needs to restrict the number of proper subjects if his criterion for distinguishing generation and destruction *simpliciter* from alteration and other sorts of accidental change is going to satisfy the common-sense and anti-conventionalist criteria that he imposed on his monist and pluralist opponents.

In the *Categories*, which is probably an early work, Aristotle restricts the class of subjects by taking substance individuals (like a certain man or a certain horse)[25] to be the only proper subjects of alteration, or as he says, the only things that "can receive contraries while remaining the same and one in number" [*Cat.* 4b10]. Alteration occurs when these things change in quality [κατὰ τὸ ποῖον, 15b11–12] and this cannot occur without change in their properties [*De Caelo* 270a28]. And although the *Categories* does not explicitly discuss generation and destruction *simpliciter*, it is reasonable to assume that the *Categories* takes the subjects of generation and destruction and the subjects of alteration to be the same.[26] For Aristotle's preliminary account of the criterion for distinguishing generation and destruction *simpliciter* from alteration and other sorts of accidental change takes them to be the same: alteration is change in the πάθη of these subjects, and generation and destruction *simpliciter* are changes in these subjects themselves, particularly with respect to their λόγος (or form) and matter.[27]

---

[24] At this point, someone might object (as Helen Cartwright 1990 does) that there is not *one* subject here that can be described either as a man or as a pale thing, but rather two subjects (one a man and one a pale thing) each of which has different conditions of identity and persistence. (There are presumably also many other subjects.) In this case, we should also say that there is not *one* change here that can be described as either a man's death or as an alteration of a pale thing, but rather that there are two (or more) changes—one a generation-cum-destruction *simpliciter* and the other an alteration (and so on)—each having a different subject but *coinciding* with one another. Here I agree with Cartwright that Aristotle would say that there are as many changes as there are subjects. But I doubt that he would be willing to allow so many subjects that there are generations and destructions *simpliciter* coinciding with *every* accidental change and *vice versa*; and I doubt this not simply because the effect of this would be practically the same as that of taking every change to be *both* a generation-cum-destruction *simpliciter* and an alteration (or some other sort of accidental change). For Aristotle wants to deny that something that is a παθός [affection] can also be a subject of other παθή [affections]. See, e.g., *Posterior Analytics* 83b20–22 and *Met.* 1007b2–5.

[25] Although I do not think it inappropriate to render the indefinite 'τις' in phrases like 'ὁ τις ἄνθρωπος' as "an individual" (as Ackrill 1963 renders it) or as "a particular," I choose to render it as "a certain . . ." so as not to presuppose any connection with Aristotle's use of 'καθ' ἕκαστον' (which I render "particular") or 'ἓν ἀριθμῷ' (which I render "individual"); for more on this, see note 6 above). 'Certain' has the right sort of indefiniteness insofar as it allows phrases like "a certain animal" or "a certain color" to refer to a *kind* of animal or color (e.g., to Man or to Red) as distinct from individual instances of these kinds, while still allowing "a certain man" and even perhaps "a certain red" to refer to *individual instances* of these kinds.

[26] See *GC* 317a20–22. In the subject there is λόγος and matter: change in these is generation and destruction, but change in the accidents <of this subject> is alteration.

[27] It will become clear from my account of the distinction between functional and compositional matter, that παθή are here associated with compositional matter and that the matter with respect to which a subject undergoes generation and destruction *simpliciter* is functional matter.

The *Categories* distinguishes (a) substance individuals not only from (b) their species and genera (e.g., the species Man and Horse and the genus Animal) but also from (c) non-substance individuals (e.g., the individual qualities and quantities that are *in* substance individuals) and (d) the species and genera to which these non-substance individuals belong (e.g., the species White and Red and the genus Color).[28] So taking substance individuals as the *only* proper subjects of generation, destruction, and alteration rules out the generation, destruction, and alteration of (b) substance species and genera; (c) non-substance individuals; and (d) non-substance species and genera. On this view, no species or genus (whether substance or non-substance) comes to be, passes away, or suffers alteration. And individual men and horses come to be, pass away, and suffer alteration, in a way in which the non-substance individuals in them (e.g., their sizes, and their colors and other qualities) do not.

It should by now be clear roughly how this view is supposed to satisfy the commonsense criterion. On this view, a man is a subject in a way in which the pale in him is not. So when a man dies, we say that he ceases to exist rather than that a particular pale—or a certain pale thing—becomes a corpse. Here, however, it is important to note that it is qua man (and not qua pale, qua animal, or qua anything else) that an individual man is a subject of substantial and non-substantial change. In other words, the *Categories* takes the proper subjects of alteration (and implicitly of generation and destruction *simpliciter*) to be not simply individuals, but individuals that are essentially members of the *infimae species*: that is, particulars that are essentially men, horses, and so on, and that cannot cease to be men, horses, and so on without ceasing to exist.[29]

I believe that this is part of Aristotle's point when he says of the *Categories*' primary substances that they are each τόδε τι—or some this (e.g., some man or some horse).[30] For Aristotle claims in the *Metaphysics* that only things that are members of the *infimae species* count as τόδε τι [*Met.* VII.4, 1030a2–14]. But in order to see how

---

[28] At this point I am not assuming either the traditional account of non-substance individuals (as peculiar to the numerically distinct subjects to which they belong) or the alternative account (defended by Owen 1965a and Frede 1978) according to which non-substance individuals are fully determinate and hence indivisible forms capable of belonging to a plurality of numerically distinct subjects at the same time. See section 4 below. [I discuss this issue in "Non-substance Individuals in Aristotle's *Categories*," forthcoming in an OUP Festschrift for David Charles, edited by D. Bronstein, T. Johansen, and M. Peramatzis.]

[29] For, as Aristotle says at *Categories* 2a29–37, substance species (along with their concomitant genera) give the τί ἐστι [or *what it is*] of each of the subjects of which they are said. And this, as Aristotle claims elsewhere, is the essence [τὸ τί ἦν εἶναι] of its subject. Moreover, the *Topics* (*Top.*)—which (like the *Categories*) forms part of the early *Organon*—explicitly claims that "it is not possible for the same <thing> to remain if it is wholly changed from its εἶδος, just as the same animal cannot be at one time a man and at another time not <a man>" [*Top.* 125b37–40]. Furthermore, there is no indication in the *Categories* (apart from two isolated references to material items, one to a log at 8a23 and one to honey at 9a33) that the substance species include anything other than the biological species that Aristotle takes to be indivisible. Artifacts—whose status as substances is elsewhere dubious—have not yet entered the picture. And Aristotle does not mention musicians or slaves or any other such things, except (as in the case of slaves) as falling in some non-substance category (in this case, that of relatives).

[30] At *Categories* 3b10–18, I take 'τόδε' as demonstrative and 'τι' as performing the function of an indefinite article so that the expression as a whole is parallel to phrases like 'ὁ τις ἄνθρωπος' (discussed in note 24 above). An alternative, more natural in some contexts, is to take 'τόδε' again as demonstrative but to

restricting the class of proper subjects to things that are τόδε τι enables Aristotle to satisfy the common-sense criterion, we need to examine what is involved in being τόδε τι. Aristotle suggests different (but cosatisfiable) criteria in different passages.[31]

(1) *The Numerical Unity Requirement*
What is common [τὸ κοινόν], or predicated in common, is not τόδε τι [*Topics* 178b38–179a10]. What is τόδε τι must be indivisible [ἄτομον] and one in number [*Cat.* 3b10–14].
(2) *The Complete Subject Requirement*
Whatever is *just what it is* [ὅπερ ἐστι] by being (or belonging to) something different—as, e.g., a pale <thing> is just what it is by being (or belonging to) a surface or a body—is not τόδε τι. What is τόδε τι must be just what it is (e.g., a man), not being (or belonging to) something different [*Posterior Analytics* (*A.Po.*) 73b8–9].
(3) *The Intrinsic Unity Requirement*
Whenever one thing is predicated of another [ἄλλο κατ' ἄλλου λέγηται] the product is not τόδε τι. E.g., a pale-man is not τόδε τι, for being τόδε τι belongs only to substances [*Met.* 1030a3–6].

The *numerical unity requirement* has the effect of ruling out species and genera (both substance and non-substance species and genera) as proper subjects of generation, destruction, and alteration. It is most often cited as evidence that Aristotelian forms are individual, for Aristotle repeatedly says that forms are τόδε τι. For this reason, I propose to ignore (1) and see how far we can get without it.[32] The important points for our purposes are (2) and (3).

The *complete subject requirement* rules out taking non-substance individuals as subjects of generation, destruction, and alteration, for they are essentially dependent on being or belonging to something else: there is no paleness or size that is not the paleness or size of some surface or body. Similarly the *intrinsic unity requirement* rules out taking accidental compounds (like pale-men and musical-men) as such subjects, for they are essentially the product of one thing (e.g., the musical or the pale) being

---

take 'τι' as an indefinite pronoun so as to yield "this something" as, e.g., in "this man" or "this horse." The alternative suggests (in a way in which "some this" does not) that primary substances are individual members of species or kinds. Since it is not only possible but also plausible that this pair of words functions differently in different contexts, I generally leave it untranslated and indicate (as above) when I think a particular context favors one alternative over the other. This should encourage the reader to determine autonomously what any given context requires or permits.

[31] Note that (3)—unlike (1) and (2)—is taken not from the *Organon* but from the *Metaphysics*. Aristotle may have introduced it only later, after encountering the problems of unity raised by his analysis of the primary substances of the *Categories* into their form and matter.
[32] It is worth noting that controversies about what Aristotle requires for numerical unity render controversial the claim that (1) requires individual forms. That is one reason for seeing how far we can get without appealing to it. For some discussion of these controversies, see "Form and Individuation in Aristotle" [Chapter 1, this volume].

predicated of another (i.e., the man). Aristotle believes that only members of the *infimae species* are *both* complete subjects *and* intrinsic unities.

4

Here, however, we must pause to ask not only why Aristotle denies that non-substance individuals are proper subjects of accidental change, but also why Aristotle takes the species whose members are proper subjects of change to include *only* kinds like Man, Horse, and Cow, and *not* kinds either *more general* (like Fish, Bird, or Mammal) or *more specific* (like Pale-man and Dark-man, Musician and Athlete, or Smith and Jones). For Aristotle needs to provide some argument for these restrictions if his account of the distinction between generation and destruction *simpliciter*, on the one hand, and alteration and other sorts of accidental change, on the other, is to satisfy not only the commonsense but also the anti-conventionalist criterion. By "independent argument," I mean argument that does not depend simply on intuitions about the very distinction that Aristotle seeks to defend.[33]

Aristotle clearly thinks that the inseparability of properties (or affections) places some independent constraints on the class of proper subjects: non-substance items like color and knowledge are essentially dependent and cannot exist except by being or belonging to something else. And Aristotle takes this to show that non-substance items cannot be the ultimate subjects of any of the properties or changes that might appear to be predicable of them. Take, e.g., the case of a pale ‹thing› that is first unmusical and then musical. Because "this pale" is not itself a complete subject but exists by being or belonging to something else (e.g., a man), Aristotle believes that the musical and the unmusical should not be predicated of it but must instead be predicated of the ultimate subject to which it belongs—i.e., the man. So changes that might appear to be predicable of "the pale" are strictly predicated only of the complete subject to which "the pale" belongs: i.e., the man who is pale. And the man is a complete subject in a way in which the pale is not because *he* does not exist by being or belonging to something else.

There are many difficulties here not only about Aristotle's actual arguments but also about the nature of these non-substance items, especially about whether any of them are peculiar to the individual subjects to which they belong. But it is not necessary to resolve these difficulties for the purposes of the present argument.[34] For these purposes it is sufficient to note that Aristotle's actual arguments for the inseparability of properties (or affections) occur in contexts where he is not especially concerned with change. The argument in *Metaphysics* IV.4 is part of a dialectical argument against

---

[33] Note that the requirements for being τόδε τι—to the extent that they are independently motivated—may provide some of the requisite independence.

[34] [This issue is discussed at length in my contribution to the Festschrift for David Charles, cited in note 28 above.]

someone who purports to deny the Principle of Non-Contradiction.[35] And the argument of *Posterior Analytics* is concerned to establish the possibility of knowledge and definition. Each appeals to the impossibility of an infinite series of predications. This is important because it suggests that Aristotle takes himself to be armed with some independent support for his claim that non-substance items are not proper subjects of change.

Similarly, *Metaphysics* I.9 illustrates the sort of independent argument Aristotle invokes for locating the *infimae species* at the level of Man and Horse rather than at some level either more general or more specific. In *Metaphysics* I.9, Aristotle asks why the differences between male and female and between pale-man and dark-man are not differences in species [εἴδει]. He replies that some differences are due to the form [λόγος] and some to matter, and that only those differences which are due to the form yield different species. He then claims that the differences between male and female and between pale-man and dark-man are due to matter rather than form.[36] So he concludes that they do not yield different species.

Note that Aristotle does not simply stipulate which differences do, and which do not, yield different species. He appeals to the fact (in his view) that male and female come from the *same seed* to support his claim that the difference between male and female is due to matter rather than form [*Met.* 1058b23–24]. This suggests that he takes what we would call "genetic" considerations to be primary. These considerations are also relevant to deciding whether pale-men and dark-men constitute different species. If there were a tendency to reproductive isolation among different races (as there is among animal species), then Aristotle might have to conclude that pale-men and dark-men do constitute different species.[37] And if humans sometimes gave birth to calves and horses to puppies, or if it appeared that men sometimes turned into wolves and wolves into lambs, then Aristotle might have to locate intrinsic unities at some more generic level.

The important point here is that Aristotle ties his identification of the subjects of generation and destruction *simpliciter* to independently plausible biological theories. He takes these theories (which introduce formal and final causes) to be independently plausible insofar as they enable him to explain natural phenomena that he claims his reductionist opponents cannot adequately explain.[38] And he believes that forms and

---

[35] On this argument see Irwin 1988, chap. 9.
[36] Aristotle clearly sees an important difference between these pairs of contraries, male and female belonging καθ' αὑτό to animal in a way which pale and dark do not. So he may think that these pairs are due to matter in different ways—the former (i.e., male-female) belonging to functional matter and the latter (i.e., pale-dark) belonging to compositional matter. For this distinction see below (section 5).
[37] Note that this claim, like other scientific claims about what happens in the sublunary sphere, holds only "for the most part" (ὡς ἐπὶ τὸ πολύ); it is not an exceptionless generalization. Aristotle allows limited interbreeding between members of different species if certain conditions are satisfied. E.g., the species must be συγγενές and their gestation periods similar enough in length, while the catamenial matter must be the right temperature. See *Generation of Animals* (GA) 738b27–30 and 746a29–b11.
[38] See, e.g., his criticism of Empedocles in *Physics* (Ph.) II.8.

essences of men and horses are required by these biological theories in a way in which forms and essences of musical-men and pale-men are not. In this respect, he has independent reasons for believing that there is an important difference between musical-men and men as such—i.e., reasons that are independent of his views about which changes are, and which are not, generations and destructions *simpliciter*.[39]

It should by now be clear how Aristotle's account of the distinction between generation and destruction *simpliciter* and alteration (along with other sorts of accidental change) requires an appeal to form, and how this appeal to form renders his account both better able than the pluralist's crude account of generation as mere association, and better able than the pluralist's revised quantitative account, to satisfy the common-sense and anti-conventionalist criteria. Form isolates the common-sense subjects of generation, destruction, and accidental change; and the existence of such form is a matter of biological fact and not simply a matter of convention or of how we choose to describe things.

5

So far, I think the opponent of individual forms can agree. It is hardly controversial that Aristotle thinks he needs to introduce form in order to give an adequate account of the distinction between generation *simpliciter* and accidental change. But the opponent of individual forms will deny that this essentialism requires *individual* forms. On his account, generation (or destruction) *simpliciter* is simply some matter's coming (or ceasing) to embody a species-form (or essence), which can belong to a plurality of numerically distinct subjects at the same time. On this account, Socrates comes to be when the species-form Man comes to be embodied in *Socrates'* matter, and Callias comes to be when the very same species-form comes to be embodied in *his* numerically distinct matter. And similarly, Socrates ceases to exist when *his* matter ceases to embody the human species-form, while Callias ceases to be when *his* numerically distinct matter ceases to embody the very same species-form.

In order to see what is wrong with this account and why Aristotle must invoke *individual* forms, we must recall two things—first, that the subjects of generation and destruction *simpliciter* must be τόδε τι and so must be intrinsic unities; and second, that generation and destruction *simpliciter* occur if and only if the terminus of change is not an accident (or affection) of what persists. So if generation *simpliciter* is to consist in some species-form's coming to be embodied in some matter, we need to ask two things. First, is what comes to be—i.e., the compound of species-form and matter—an intrinsic unity? And second, is the terminus of this change an accident (or affection) of the persisting matter?

---

[39] Pace Cartwright (1990), I do not think that Aristotle's view is in principle incompatible with the mutability of biological species. Such mutability would mean only that there are different subjects of generation and destruction *simpliciter* at different stages of an evolutionary sequence.

Aristotle believes that A is an accident of B if A does not belong to B either necessarily or for the most part and if A can belong or not belong to B.[40] So if the matter in which species-forms come and cease to be embodied persists throughout the acquisition and loss of species-form, then it seems clear that the termini of such changes (i.e., the embodied form and its privation) are accidents of the persisting matter, and that these changes are simply alterations of the underlying matter. But this is precisely the result that Aristotle wants to avoid.

For this reason, some commentators have denied that Aristotle allows matter to persist throughout substantial change.[41] On their view, Socrates' matter is individuated in roughly the same way that his height and weight are: like his height and weight, Socrates' matter comes and ceases to be when Socrates comes and ceases to be.

These commentators are right insofar as Aristotle believes that there *is* a kind of matter that does not persist through substantial change. But they are wrong insofar as Aristotle thinks that there must be *another* kind of matter that persists through substantial change, if generation *ex nihilo* and destruction *in nihil* are to be avoided. Aristotle recognizes *both* types of matter in the *De Anima*, where he introduces the organic body, which is essentially ensouled and so cannot survive the loss of soul. This body is a functionally defined continuant and can be constituted by different portions or quantities of stuff at different times. But this stuff—which I call "compositional matter"—is not essentially ensouled, so it can survive the loss of soul. It is what can first have, and then lack, soul. The organic body is thus a functionally defined continuant that can be constituted by different portions or quantities of stuff at different times. But this stuff—the compositional matter—is not essentially ensouled. Nor is it essentially enformed in other ways (e.g., essentially bronze, or essentially earth or wine): it is what *Generation and Corruption* calls the "substratum of coming to be and passing away" [320a2–5] Now it is often claimed that Aristotle's commitment to functionally defined matter that is incapable of persisting through substantial change conflicts with this conception of matter as the substratum of generation and destruction.[42] But there is no conflict here if Aristotle takes the compositional matter (which persists through substantial change) to *constitute* the organic (or functionally defined) bodies that come to be and pass away simultaneously with their "owners." What I am suggesting is that Aristotle's commitment to a kind of matter that does not persist through substantial change is not a *problem*, but rather part of Aristotle's *solution* to the problem of distinguishing generation and destruction *simpliciter* from alteration and other sorts of accidental change.

---

[40] See *Top.* 102b4–10, 102b34–35; *Met.* V 30.

[41] See Charlton 1970, 75–77, and Jones 1974, many of whose claims (criticized in Code 1976) are unobjectionable if taken as claims about the organic body and its functionally defined parts rather than as claims about the matter constituting the organic body and its functionally defined parts (on which more below).

[42] See Ackrill 1972–1973, criticized in Whiting 1991 [Chapter 3, this volume].

We can see this if we recall the problem with the traditional account of generation (or destruction) *simpliciter* as a species-form's coming (or ceasing) to be embodied in some matter. If this matter persists throughout these changes and the species-form is an accident of it, then these changes are simply alterations of that matter and the compound of species-form and matter is only an accidental unity. In order to solve this problem, Aristotle must show how a form's coming to be embodied in some matter can yield a product that is not an accident of what persists and that is itself an intrinsic unity. And as we shall see, both individual forms and organic bodies play an important role in Aristotle's solution.

We must begin by attempting to identify the subject of generation and destruction *simpliciter*. In the generation of a man, this subject must be something that is *essentially* a man. This subject cannot be the species-form, since that is supposed to be eternal. Nor can it be the persisting matter since that preexists and is (if at all) only accidentally a man. There remain two obvious candidates—one an individual form and the other the compound of form and matter. So the opponent of individual forms will presumably argue that the compound (which is essentially a man) is the proper subject of generation and destruction *simpliciter*. But this will not do. For as we shall see, compounds can be the subjects of generation and destruction *simpliciter* only if they have or are identified with individual forms.

To see this, we must first note that Aristotle's distinction between two types of matter yields a distinction between two types of compound. The first, which I call the "thin compound," is a compound of form (or soul) and the organic (or functionally defined) body. It essentially includes the organic body, but only accidentally (if at all) includes the particular portion of compositional matter that constitutes its organic body at any given time. So a thin compound can survive as long as it has the same organic body, even if that body is successively constituted by different quantities of compositional matter.

The thin compound is to be distinguished from what I call the "thick compound," which is a compound of a form (or soul) and the particular portion of matter that constitutes its organic body at a given time. Because the thick compound essentially includes at any given time the particular portion of compositional matter that constitutes the organic body of the soul to which it belongs, the thick compound cannot be constituted by different portions of compositional matter at different times: different compositional matter yields a different thick compound. This explains why (at *GC* 322a28–33) Aristotle treats form (rather than matter) as the subject that persists throughout the loss and acquisition of matter.

But it is important to note that the matter here is compositional and not functional matter. For the functionally defined organic body is coextensive with the soul which Aristotle says (at *DA* 412b11) is its form and essence, and *it* (i.e., the organic body) is what is successively constituted by different portions of compositional matter. But because there is no particular portion of compositional matter that must constitute an organic body at any particular time, Aristotle regards the particular portion of compositional matter constituting an organic body at any given time as an accident of that body and so as an accident of the thin compound consisting of that organic body and the soul which is its form or essence. The same goes for all those properties that belong to a thin compound (or its organic body) at any given time because they belong to the particular portion of compositional matter constituting it at that time: they are all accidents of the thin compound (or its organic body) and this explains the sense in which matter is the cause of what is accidental [*Met.* 1027a13–15]. It also explains Aristotle's assimilation of matter to properties at *Metaphysics* 1049b36–37: compositional matter, like the properties that supervene on it, is only an accident of the subject it constitutes. In this respect it differs from functional matter, which must be mentioned in the account—and so belongs to the form or essence—of the subject to which it belongs.[43]

We are now in a position to see that the thick compound is an accidental unity in much the same way that a musical man is: just as the musical is predicated of the man as one thing of another insofar as the man is an independent subject capable of existing apart from the musical and apart from that unity, so too the particular portion of compositional matter constituting an organic body is predicated of that body (or of the soul that is its essence) as one thing of another. For that body (along with the soul that is its essence) is an independent subject capable of existing apart from that particular portion of compositional matter and apart from that unity.[44] It is thus easy to see that the thick compound cannot be the proper subject of generation and destruction *simpliciter*. For if it were, Aristotle would then have to say that a new subject comes to be (and an old one passes away) every time an organic body loses or acquires matter. This account, because it attends to the compositional matter rather than to the functionally defined organic body, suffers deficiencies similar to those of the pluralist's purely quantitative attempts to distinguish generation and destruction *simpliciter* from alteration and other sorts of accidental change. On this account, entire species of accidental change (e.g., growth and diminution) are assimilated to generation and destruction *simpliciter*.

So the thick compound cannot be the proper subject of generation and destruction *simpliciter*. If any compound is such a subject, it must be the thin compound. But this requires Aristotle to show that the thin compound does not fall prey to the same objection as that to which the thick compound fell. In other words, Aristotle must show that the thin compound (unlike the thick one) is not simply an accidental unity of form and

---

[43] For Aristotle's defense of this view, see my account of *Met.* VII.10–11 in Whiting, unpublished). [See also section 6 of "Metasubstance: Critical Notice of Frede-Patzig and Furth," Chapter 4, this volume).] On this view, *GC* 317a20–27 (quoted at the end of section 2 above) analyzes the subjects of generation, destruction, and alteration into form and functional (as distinct from compositional) matter; so it is functional (rather than compositional) matter that is there opposed to the properties or affections belonging to those subjects.

[44] Note that insofar as the soul is the essence of this body, it is potentially misleading (since Aristotle identifies things with their essences) to speak of taking the organic body "together with" the soul that is its essence as if the body were an independently existing entity to which such a soul could be added: there would be no such body without that soul. In this respect the organic body differs from the matter constituting it at any particular time; that matter (unlike the organic body) can exist apart from that soul.

matter: the form of the thin compound cannot be predicated of its matter—nor can its matter be predicated of it—as one thing of another (i.e., in a sense that takes *either* to be an independent subject capable of existing apart from that unity).

Socrates' thin compound is a unity of his soul and his organic body. So if Socrates' soul is essentially related to his organic body and Socrates' body is essentially related to his soul in ways such that neither can exist apart from the other, then Aristotle can claim that Socrates' thin compound is an intrinsic unity. This will allow him to say that the thin compound is the proper subject of generation and destruction *simpliciter*. So Aristotle's task falls into two parts—one to show that the organic body is essentially ensouled, the other to show that the soul is essentially embodied (by the organic body).

Aristotle performs the first part of this task in the *De Anima*, where he argues that organic bodies are essentially alive and cannot survive the loss of soul: for the soul is the essence (τὸ τί ἦν εἶναι) of such a body [*DA* 412b10–12]. You should now be able to see why I think that this is *not a problem* for Aristotle, but rather part of his *solution* to the problem of distinguishing generation and destruction *simpliciter* from alteration and other sorts of accidental change.

Aristotle performs the second part of this task in *Metaphysics* VII.10–11, where he argues that the forms of natural (as distinct from mathematical) objects are essentially embodied. This, in conjunction with the *De Anima*'s argument that organic bodies are essentially ensouled, supports the conclusion that the thin compound (of a soul and its *organic* body) is an intrinsic unity neither component of which is separable from the other. This in turn supports the conclusion that thin compounds are the proper subjects of generation and destruction *simpliciter*.

Now *one* way to understand the intrinsic unity of the thin compound is to argue that each of its "components" is the same thing considered or described in a different way. On this account, the form of a thin compound is really an embodied soul, the matter of a thin compound is really an ensouled body, and each of these is in turn the same (in some sense) with the thin compound itself.[45] This account will explain why Aristotle argues that each (presumably compound) thing is the same as its essence or form [*Met.* 1031b19–20] and that the form and the proximate matter are the same and one [*Met.*1035a18–19].

Nevertheless, this identification of thin compounds with individual forms is *not necessary* for the conclusion that thin compounds require individual forms. For Aristotle's general belief that the cause of something's having a certain characteristic must itself

---

[45] As Pelletier 1979 argues, it is not entirely clear to what in (if anything) in Aristotle our contemporary notion of identity (as involving Leibniz's Law) corresponds. It is not clear, e.g., whether Aristotle would say that the road-up and the road-down, which he says (at *Ph.* 202a 19–21) are the same although their λόγος is not one, satisfy this conception of identity or whether he would take this conception of identity to require sameness in λόγος. But the proposed sameness of form and (functional) matter must involve more than being one in number, which involves sharing (compositional) matter; it must involve at least necessary coexistence (where this involves roughly having the same conditions of identity and persistence) even if not sameness in λόγος. I discuss this matter further in Whiting, unpublished. [See also "Locomotive Soul: The Parts of Soul in Aristotle's Scientific Works" [Chapter 5, this volume]; and "Hylomorphic Virtue" [Chapter 6, this volume].

have that characteristic provides a direct argument for that conclusion.[46] For it is a consequence of this general belief that the cause of something's being an individual or τόδε τι must itself be individual or τόδε τι. And Aristotle explicitly endorses this consequence in a number of ways: by saying that the principles of particulars (which are one in number) must themselves be particulars and so one in number [*Met.* 1071a20–21]; by saying that if the principles were one only in species [εἴδει] then nothing would be one in number [*Met.* 999b24–25]; and by saying that those things are one in number whose substance is one in number [*Met.* 1040b17].

So Aristotle is committed to the following argument:

(1) The subject of generation and destruction *simpliciter* must be τόδε τι.
(2) (Thin) compounds are the subjects of generation and destruction *simpliciter*.
(3) The cause of something's being τόδε τι (and so individual) must itself be τόδε τι (and so individual).[47]
(4) Its form is the cause of a (thin) compound's being τόδε τι.[48]
(5) Therefore, the form of a (thin) compound is itself τόδε τι.
(6) Therefore, the proper subjects of generation and destruction *simpliciter* have individual forms.

Either way then—whether or not we *identify* thin compounds with individual forms—thin compounds must have individual forms. So if the proper subjects of generation and destruction *simpliciter* are thin compounds, the existence of generation and destruction *simpliciter* requires individual forms.[49]

BIBLIOGRAPHY

Ackrill, J. L. 1963. *Aristotle Categories and De Interpretatione.* Oxford: Clarendon Press.
Ackrill, J. L. 1972–1973. "Aristotle's Definitions of 'Psuchê.'" *Proceedings of the Aristotelian Society* 73: 119–33; reprinted in J. Barnes, M. Schofield, and R. Sorabji (eds.) 1979. *Articles on Aristotle: Volume 4: Psychology and Aesthetics.* London: Duckworth, 65–75.
Albritton, R. G. 1957. "Forms of Particular Substances in Aristotle's *Metaphysics.*" *Journal of Philosophy* 54: 699–708.
Aristotle. 1922. *De Generatione et Corruptione.* H. H. Joachim (trans.) Oxford: Clarendon Press.

---

[46] See *Met.* 993b24–26. There are, of course, exceptions to this principle. But Aristotle explicitly applies it to the cause of something's being an individual in the three passages cited below. So the exceptions, whatever their rationale and degree of justification, need not be taken as obstacles to the present argument.
[47] Note that this involves appeal to the first (numerical unity) requirement for being τόδε τι.
[48] See *DA* 412a8–9 and *Met.* VII.17.
[49] This essay has benefited from discussion with audiences at the Boston Colloquium for Ancient Philosophy; Columbia, Duke, and the University of Arizona. I am especially grateful to Helen Cartwright, whose comments in Boston helped me to avoid some fundamental errors. I should also like to thank Terry Irwin for years of discussion of these issues; those of my claims he still regards as errors are at least—thanks to him—well considered.

Aristotle. 1924. *Metaphysics*. W. D. Ross (trans.) Oxford: Clarendon Press.
Balme, D. M. 1980. "Aristotle's Biology Was Not Essentialist." *Archiv für Geschichte der Philosophie* 62, no. 1: 1–12.
Barnes, J. 1982. *The Presocratic Philosophers*. London: Routledge and Kegan Paul.
Cartwright, H. 1970. "Quantities" *Philosophical Review* 79, no. 1: 25–49.
Cartwright, H. 1990. "Commentary on Whiting." *Proceedings of the Boston Area Colloquium of Ancient Philosophy* 64–78.
Charlton, W. 1970. *Aristotle: Physics Books I and II*. Oxford: Clarendon Press.
Code, A. D. 1976. "The Persistence of Aristotelian Matter" *Philosophical Studies* 29 (6): 357–67.
Code, A. D. 1986. "Aristotle: Essence and Accident." In R. Grandy and R. Warner (eds.), *Philosophical Grounds of Rationality: Intentions, Categories, Ends*. Oxford: Oxford University Press, 411–39.
Driscoll, J. 1981 "*Eidē* in Aristotle's Earlier and Later Theories of Substance." In D. J. O'Meara (ed.), *Studies in Aristotle*. Washington, DC: Catholic University of America Press, 129–59.
Fine, G. 1984. "Separation." *Oxford Studies in Ancient Philosophy* 3: 31–87.
Fine, G. 1985. "Separation: A Reply to Morrison." *Oxford Studies in Ancient Philosophy* 3: 159–65.
Frede, M. 1978. "Individuals in Aristotle." In M. Frede (ed.), *Essays in Ancient Philosophy*. Minneapolis: University of Minnesota Press, 49–71.
Frede, M. and Patzig, G. 1988. *Aristoteles Metaphysik Z*. Munich: C. H. Beck.
Furth, M. 1988. *Substance, Form, and Psyche: An Aristotelian Metaphysics*. Cambridge: Cambridge University Press.
Hartman, E. 1977. *Substance, Body, and Soul: Aristotelian Investigations*. Princeton, NJ: Princeton University Press.
Heinaman, R. 1979. "Aristotle's Tenth *Aporia*." *Archiv für Geschichte der Philosophie* 57: 1–20.
Irwin, T. H. 1988. *Aristotle's First Principles*. Oxford: Oxford University Press.
Jones, B. 1974 "Aristotle's Introduction of Matter." *Philosophical Review* 83, no. 4: 474–500.
Lloyd, A. C. 1981. *Form and Universal in Aristotle*. Liverpool: Francis Cairns.
Matthews, G. B. 1982. "Accidental Unities." In M. C. Nussbaum and M. Schofield (eds.), *Language and Logos*. Cambridge: Cambridge University Press, 223–40.
Morrison, D. 1985a. "Separation in Aristotle." *Oxford Studies in Ancient Philosophy* 3: 125–57.
Morrison, D. 1985b. "Separation: A Reply to Fine." *Oxford Studies in Ancient Philosophy* 3:167–73.
Nussbaum, M. C. 1982. "Saving Aristotle's Appearances." In M. C. Nussbaum and M. Schofield (eds.), *Language and Logos*. Cambridge: Cambridge University Press, 267–93.
Owen, G. E. L. 1961. "τιθέναι τὰ φαινόμενα." In S. Mansion (ed.), *Aristote et les problèmes de method*. Louvain: Publications Universitaires, 83–103.
Owen, G. E. L. 1965a. "Inherence." *Phronesis* 10: 97–105.
Owen, G. E. L. 1965b. "The Platonism of Aristotle." *Proceedings of the British Academy* 51: 125–50.
Owens, J. 1978. *The Doctrine of Being in Aristotelian Metaphysics: A Study in the Greek Background of Mediaeval Thought*. Toronto: Pontifical Institute of Mediaeval Studies.
Pelletier, F. J. 1979. "Sameness and Referential Opacity in Aristotle." *Nous* 13: 283–311.
Ross, W. D. 1924. *Aristotle's Metaphysics*. Oxford: Clarendon Press.
Sellars, W. 1957. "Counterfactuals, Dispositions, and the Causal Modalities." In H. Feigl, M. Scriven, and G. Maxwell (eds.), *Minnesota Studies in the Philosophy of Science*, II. Minneapolis: University of Minnesota Press, 225–308.
Sellars, W. 1967. *Philosophical Perspectives*. Springfield, IL: Charles C. Thomas. Reprinted in two volumes, 1977. *Philosophical Perspectives: History of Philosophy and Philosophical Perspective: Metaphysics and Epistemology*. Atascadero, CA: Ridgeview Publishing.

Whiting, J. 1986. "Form and Individuation in Aristotle." *History of Philosophy Quarterly* 3, no. 4: 359–77. [Chapter 1, this volume]

Whiting, J. 1991. "Metasubstance: Critical Notice of Frede-Patzig and Furth." *The Philosophical Review* C, no. 4: 607–39. [Chapter 4, this volume]

Whiting, J. unpublished. *Individual Forms in Aristotle*. Ph.D. thesis, Cornell University, 1984.

Williams, C. F. J. 1982. *Aristotle's "De Generatione et Corruptione."* Oxford: Clarendon Press.

Witt, C. 1989. *Substance and Essence in Aristotle: An Interpretation of Metaphysics VII–IX*. Ithaca, NY: Cornell University Press.

Woods, M. J. 1967. "Problems in *Metaphysics* Z, Chapter 13." In J. M. E. Morvcsik (ed.), *Aristotle*. London: Palgrave Macmillan, 215–38.

Woods, M. J. 1974–1975. "Substance and Essence in Aristotle." *Proceedings of the Aristotelian Society* 75, no. 1: 167–80.

3

Living Bodies

THE DE ANIMA'S commitment to the existence of essentially ensouled bodies has long been regarded as something of a problem for Aristotle. Because Aristotle says that such a body is the matter of an animal, the standard objection—at least since the publication of Ackrill's influential article[1]—is that this commitment conflicts with Aristotle's primary conception of matter as potentiality (to embody different forms) and as the substratum of generation and destruction [*Generation and Corruption* (*GC*) 320a1–4]. For matter so conceived is supposed to persist through substantial change and to be what (in substantial change) loses and acquires form—in the case of living things, what loses and acquires soul. But if a body is essentially ensouled, then *it* cannot lose and acquire soul. So Aristotle seems to require of one thing both that it can, and that it cannot, lose and acquire soul.

Aristotle's commitment to the existence of essentially ensouled matter has more recently been taken by Burnyeat to show that Aristotle's philosophy of mind is no longer credible and must be "junked" because he does not share our post-Cartesian conception of matter, which leaves the emergence of life and mind in need of explanation.[2]

---

[1] Ackrill 1972–1973.

[2] See Burnyeat 1992. It is an oddity of Burnyeat's view that he seems to take Aristotle's Platonist and Democritean contemporaries to be committed to the problematic post-Cartesian conception of matter (though this may not be so odd if, as Steve Strange suggests in personal communication, Descartes derives his account of the physical world from the *Timaeus*, which is itself indebted to Democritus on this point). In any case, Burnyeat's idea must be that Aristotle's reaction is distinct from the contemporary functionalist reaction because it is free from assumptions about matter that the contemporary functionalist cannot escape.

According to Burnyeat, Aristotle takes as primitive the fact that certain kinds of matter, such as flesh and blood, are *essentially* alive and *essentially* capable of awareness, and so takes the emergence of life and awareness as something for which no explanation can or need be given. Burnyeat thinks this debunks the increasingly popular portrait of Aristotle as the father of contemporary functionalism[3] because Burnyeat takes functionalism to assume that the relation between matter and form is *contingent* in a way in which Aristotle's hylomorphism does not. Furthermore, Burnyeat thinks it would be a mistake for Aristotle (or his apologists) to try to solve Ackrill's problem by showing that there is a sense in which the matter of an animal *is* only contingently related to its form or soul. For then Aristotle would be "abandoning his project of beating the Platonists and the Democriteans at one blow by stopping the question "What makes this a living thing?" before it can arise."[4]

I doubt, however, that we need take the concern to avoid having to explain the emergence of life and awareness as the dominant motivation for Aristotle's commitment to the existence of essentially ensouled matter. For it is also possible to interpret this commitment as part of Aristotle's solution to the problem of distinguishing generation and destruction *simpliciter* from alteration and other sorts of accidental change (such as growth and locomotion).[5] The main project of this essay is thus to argue that we can solve Ackrill's problem by allowing that there *is* a sense in which the matter of an animal is only contingently related to its form and that we can do so without undermining Aristotle's arguments for introducing essentially ensouled bodies in the first place. The plan is roughly as follows.

Section 1 solves Ackrill's problem by arguing that there are two distinct things Aristotle calls "the matter" [*hê hulê*] of an animal: one (the organic body) is essentially ensouled, while the other (the quantity of elements that constitutes the organic body at any given time) is only accidentally ensouled. Since the relation between form (or soul) and the quantity of elements that constitutes the organic body at any given time is contingent in a way in which that between form (or soul) and the organic body itself is not, this allows for the sort of contingency required by functionalism without requiring us to deny that Aristotle is committed to the existence of essentially ensouled bodies.[6]

Section 2 argues that we can interpret Aristotle's commitment to the existence of essentially ensouled matter as part of his *solution* to the problem of distinguishing generation and destruction *simpliciter* from alteration and other sorts of non-substantial

---

[3] See Nussbaum and Putnam 1992; Cohen 1992. See also Putnam 1975; Nussbaum 1978; essay 1; Modrak 1987; chaps. 1–2 of Shields 1999; and Irwin 1991.
[4] Burnyeat 1992, 26.
[5] This view is defended in more detail in Whiting 1990 [Chapter 2, this volume].
[6] Here it is worth noting that I aim only to show that functionalist interpretations of Aristotle are not vulnerable to this objection. I do not pretend to provide positive arguments for such interpretations, references to which are provided in note 3 above. Furthermore, I take the solution to Ackrill's problem in section 1 to be self-contained and independent of my claims (in section 2) about Aristotle's reasons for introducing essentially ensouled bodies in the first place.

change, and so need not suppose that this commitment is intended primarily to forestall Platonic and Democritean worries about the emergence of life and awareness.[7]

Finally, since Aristotle's commitment to the existence of essentially ensouled bodies has also been thought problematic because he says of such bodies that they are "potentially alive"—thus suggesting that they are not necessarily alive—section 3 will explain briefly the sense in which Aristotle takes essentially ensouled bodies to be potentially alive.

1

It is relatively uncontroversial that Aristotle is committed to the existence of organic bodies that are essentially ensouled. For Aristotle says not only that the soul is the essence [*to ti ên einai*] of a certain sort of body [*De Anima* (*DA*) 412b11–12], but also that this body is *organikon* [*DA* 412a29–b1]. This means that the relevant body has organs that are defined by their functions, and so that it cannot exist in the absence of soul (without which these organs could not perform their functions). For Aristotle says of all things defined by their functions that

> each is in reality the thing capable of performing its function, such as an eye when it sees, while the one not capable <of performing its function> is *homonymously* <that thing>, such as one dead or one made of stone. [*Meteorologica* (*Meteor.*) IV, 390a10–12][8]

[T]here is no face not having soul, nor flesh, but when these have perished the one will be called <a> face and the other flesh *homonymously*, just as if they had been made of stone or wood. [*GA*, 734b24–27][9]

---

[7] I claim only that my story renders Burnyeat's hypothesis *unnecessary*. Someone could argue that my story about Aristotle's reasons for introducing organic bodies is compatible with Burnyeat's: for it is possible that Aristotle is concerned *both* (a) to defend the distinction between substantial and nonsubstantial change *and* (b) to avoid having to explain the emergence of life and awareness, *and, moreover*, that he takes essentially ensouled bodies to play an important role in the explanation of *each*. This is especially plausible if Aristotle takes the primary subjects of generation and destruction *simpliciter* to be living organisms. But the details of such an account would presumably differ from those of my account in so far as mine is intended to avoid the sort of mysteriousness that Burnyeat ascribes to essentially ensouled matter.

[8] For *some* defense of the authenticity of *Meteor.* IV, see Furley 1983. Since the view expressed in this passage is also expressed elsewhere (as evidenced in the next note), my appeal to the *Meteorologica* here is relatively unproblematic.

[9] These passages—along with *Parts of Animals* (*PA*) 640b34–641a34; *Generation of Animals* (*GA*) 734b24–735a9; and *Politics* (*Pol.*) 1253a19–25)—illustrate what Ackrill calls the "homonymy principle." The idea (explained at *Categories* 1a1–4) is that an '*F*' that is not (or no longer) capable of performing the function of an *F* is an *F* only *in name*: it does not satisfy the account of the being (or essence) of an *F*. For two alternative accounts of homonymy—an extreme account according to which the definitions of homonyms are unrelated, and a moderate account according to which the definitions may or may not be related—see Irwin 1981. As Shields (unpublished) notes, the moderate account allows Aristotle to treat corpses (along with detached organs and limbs) as extreme homonyms. But (pace Shields) this does not seem to

And although Aristotle illustrates the homonymy principle with an eye (both here and at *DA* 412b21–23) and with a finger [at *Metaphysics* (*Met.*) 1035b24], his claim [at *DA* 412b22–23] that we should treat the whole body as we have treated its parts licenses applying this principle to the body as a whole. (So does his reference to natural bodies as the organs of the soul at *DA* 415b18–19.) So just as a dead or detached eye is only homonymously an eye, a "body" having lost its soul is only homonymously a body.

But because of Aristotle's commitment to the homonymy principle and its application to the body (or matter) of a living organism as a whole, it is more controversial to claim that Aristotle takes each living organism to have some matter that is only accidentally ensouled. Part of the problem is that Aristotle seems to treat nearly all of the parts of animals—including *homoiomerous* parts such as flesh and blood—as defined by their functions and so as essentially ensouled.[10] So if the *anhomoiomerous* parts (like eyes, limbs, and hearts) are ultimately composed of functionally defined *homoiomerous* parts, it seems that organic bodies cannot be constituted by any matter that is only accidentally ensouled.

For this reason some commentators have denied that *any* of an animal's matter can survive the loss of soul. On their view, Socrates' corpse is not composed of *any* of the same matter as was its living ancestor: when Socrates dies, his matter (namely, the flesh and blood that constitute his bodily parts) is destroyed and is immediately replaced by the matter of his corpse. The latter is presumably some compound of the four elements, which these commentators believe can never constitute a living organism or any of its parts.[11]

This interpretation rests on two common beliefs about Aristotle's account of the matter of an animal. The first is that Aristotle takes the *homoiomerous* parts (like flesh and blood) to be the *ultimate* matter of living organisms and so denies that the four elements are part of the matter of a living thing. The second is that Aristotle believes that the *homoiomerous* parts, being functionally defined, cannot survive the loss of soul. From these two beliefs it follows that the living body, being composed of flesh

---

me to be required by Aristotle's commitment to functional definitions. Nor does it seem *required* by my view. For clarification, see note 20 below.

[10] *Homoiomerous* parts are uniform parts (like flesh and blood) any proper part of which is the same both in form and in name with the whole. This is not true of *anhomoiomerous* parts: the proper parts of hands and hearts are not themselves hands and hearts. (See *History of Animals* 486a5–9.) Note, however, that Aristotle recognizes [at *PA* 647b17–21] that in the case of some *homoiomerous* parts there is *a* sense in which the proper parts are not the same both in form and name with the whole: while any proper part of blood is itself blood, it is not true that any proper part of *a* vein (or *a* bone), which is of course composed entirely of vein (or bone), is *itself a* vein (or *a* bone). This may escape notice more easily in Greek, where the absence of an indefinite article complicates marking the distinction between mass- and count-nouns.

[11] Burnyeat expressed this view (while defending the views expressed in Burnyeat 1992) in a lecture at Cornell University in 1982. See also Charlton 1970, 75–77; and Jones 1974, many of whose claims about matter, criticized in Code 1976, are unobjectionable if taken as claims about the organic body and its functionally defined parts rather than as claims about the matter constituting the organic body and its parts.

and blood, cannot share any of its matter with its corpse, which, given the homonymy principle, cannot be composed of flesh and blood.

Here, however, it is important to note what Aristotle says at *DA* 412b18–27:

> If the eye were an animal, sight would be its soul. For this is the being [*ousia*] of an eye according to its account [*logos*]. But the eye is the matter [*hulē*] of sight, which [sight] taking leave it is no longer an eye, except homonymously, like the one made of stone or painted. And it is necessary to take what is said of the part <to apply> to the whole living body, for as part is to part so perception as a whole is to the whole perceptive body as such. But it is not the <body>[12] having lost its soul [*to apobeblēkos tēn psuchēn*] that is potentially such as to live, but the one having <soul>; and the seed and the fruit are potentially such a body [i.e., the seed and the fruit are *potentially* bodies that are *potentially* such as to live].

This passage is important both because it suggests that Aristotle believes that there is some matter that once was but is no longer [*ouketi*] an eye when sight is removed and because Aristotle's use of the perfect participle in his reference to the thing having lost its soul shows that he takes *something* to survive the loss of soul. This suggests that there is something wrong with the interpretation according to which Aristotle holds the remarkable view that Socrates and his corpse have nothing in common except for their uncanny similarity. We can see what is wrong with this interpretation if we see how each of the two common beliefs on which it is based is open to challenge.

Against the second belief, *Meteorologica* IV.12 seems to allow that flesh and blood survive (at least for a while) in a corpse. For although Aristotle says that flesh and the other *homoiomerous* parts have functions, he acknowledges that it is not always easy to tell what their functions are or when they are still capable of performing them. His example is instructive.

> The function of it [sc., flesh] is less clear than that of the tongue. Similarly also with fire, but <its function> is probably even less clear naturally than the function of flesh. And similarly also with plants and inanimate things such as bronze and silver. For all these are <what they are> by some potentiality to act or to be affected, just like flesh and sinew. But the accounts [*logoi*][13] of these are not precise. So it is not easy to discern when they exist [*huparchei*] and when they do not,[14] unless a thing is very far gone and the shapes alone remain, as when the bodies of very old corpses suddenly turn to ashes in their coffins. [*Meteor.* 390a14–24]

---

[12] 'Body' is suggested (but not required) by the neuter, and is supported by *to dunamei toiondi sōma* at the end of the passage.
[13] The *logoi* here may be the proportions of elements involved.
[14] This can also be translated as "when they belong <to a subject> and when they do not."

This suggests that Aristotle takes the *homoiomerous* parts of animals (like flesh and blood) to differ from *anhomoiomerous* parts (like hands and eyes) in so far as the *homoiomerous* parts do not perish simultaneously with the animal itself. He seems to think that there is some indeterminacy about just when such parts perish: it is clear that they are no longer there in the case of very old corpses, but not so clear in the case of fresher ones.[15] And this suggests that he thinks it possible that flesh survives (at least for a while) in a fresh corpse and is what decomposes. Furthermore, taking this as a serious expression of Aristotle's own view allows us to explain his otherwise curious remark [at *Met.* 1035a31–34] that Callias perishes *into flesh and bones*.[16]

But can we reconcile this with Aristotle's view that flesh and the other *homoiomerous* parts are functionally defined and so cannot survive the loss of soul? I think we can, *if* we recognize that Aristotle admits two accounts of flesh—one functional and the other compositional.[17]

Flesh plays an important functional role as the medium of touch and in this sense it perishes with the animal itself. This is reasonable since the ability of flesh to perform its function depends on its being related in certain ways to the other functionally defined parts of the organism as a whole—especially to the heart, which Aristotle takes to be central not only to touch but also to the other senses. When flesh no longer stands in the right relation to a functioning heart it can no longer perform its function. And since death occurs when the heart ceases to function, flesh can no longer perform its function once death has occurred.[18] The same applies to blood, which (by heating and cooling) contributes both to physiological processes (such as nourishment) and to psychophysical processes (such as anger). The important point here is that the ability of a part (whether *homoiomerous* or not) to perform its function depends on its standing in the right relations to the other functionally defined parts of the organism as a whole.

But immediately after pointing out that the *homoiomerous* parts have functions, Aristotle acknowledges that it is *also* possible to speak of the homoiomeries not as parts of a functional whole but rather in terms of differentiae (such as tension,

---

[15] Someone might object that Aristotle's point here is simply the epistemological point that it is not easy to tell when flesh and such parts still exist and when they do not, and so that we cannot take this passage as showing that he allows that flesh and such parts in fact survive the death of an animal. But the epistemological point is sufficient to show that Aristotle does not take it to follow simply from the fact that flesh and such parts are functionally defined that they perish simultaneously with animal itself. For a similar account, see Cohen 1984.

[16] See also *Met.* 1035a17–22. These passages provide some support for appealing to *Meteorologica* 390a14–24 (in spite of the doubt cited in note 8 above about its authenticity).

[17] For my original account of the distinction between functional and compositional matter, there taken as equivalent to the distinction between proximate and non-proximate matter, see Whiting 1984, especially chap. 4, sec. III and chap. 5, sec. I. (I have since abandoned the terms 'proximate' and 'non-proximate' because different commentators use them in so many different ways.) I was pleased to find that my conclusions about matter, arrived at primarily through an investigation of form, were complemented by those reached by M. L. Gill 1989 (especially chap. 4) in her investigation of matter as such.

[18] See *De Juventute* 469a7–22, 469b1–20.

ductility, brittleness, hardness, and softness) that are produced by hot and cold and their combined motions [*Meteor.* 390b2–10]. And it is not clear that flesh and blood cease to exist simultaneously with the whole living organism when defined in this way. When Socrates dies, his corpse may still be constituted by flesh and blood in the sense that the contraries are still present in roughly those proportions causally necessary (but not sufficient) for the existence of functional flesh and blood. As the flesh decomposes and the proportions of these contraries change owing to the loss of heat and moisture, this gradually ceases to be true [*Meteor.* 379a17–26].[19]

There is further evidence of Aristotle's commitment to the distinction between functional and compositional flesh in *Generation and Corruption* where he says that "flesh, bone, and each of the parts like these are twofold [*ditton*] . . . *for both the matter and the form are called flesh or bone*" [*GC* 321b19–22]. Here Aristotle is talking about two things (the form and the matter) each of which is called 'flesh,' and not about one thing capable of being considered or described in two different ways. This is clear not only from the fact that Aristotle goes on to ascribe different properties (and implicitly different criteria of identity) to the form and the matter—the form is what persists as matter flows in and out of the whole—but also from his claim that this phenomenon is clearer in the case of the *anhomoiomerous* parts because it is clearer there (than in the case of the *homoiomerous* parts) that the matter is different from the form [*GC* 321b22–32].

Aristotle's view seems to be that functional flesh (the form) and compositional flesh (the matter) are homonyms; they share the same name, but the accounts of their being (or essence) are different.[20] Compositional flesh is only homonymous with functional

---

[19] Just as we distinguish bronze as a certain kind of stuff from particular portions or pieces of bronze, we can also distinguish compositional flesh as a certain kind of stuff (e.g., the stuff composed of these elements standing in such-and-such proportions to one another) from particular portions or pieces of compositional flesh. Any particular bit of functional flesh must always be constituted by compositional flesh, but it may be constituted by different portions of compositional flesh at different times in so far as its compositional flesh can (as a result of material displacement) be constituted by different portions of the elements (in roughly the same proportions) at different times. For a further question about compositional flesh, see the next note.

[20] On homonymy, see note 9 above. If we take "compositional flesh" to refer to any portion of the elements standing in such-and-such proportions to one another, we can still distinguish two ways of specifying compositional flesh. We can specify it *purely quantitatively*—as in "4 parts of earth to 3 parts of water, etc."—in which case it seems reasonable to say that the definition of compositional flesh, insofar as it has a definition, is not related to that of functional flesh. Or we can specify it *causally*—as in "earth and water, etc., in whatever proportions are (hypothetically) necessary for functional flesh"—in which case it seems reasonable to say that the definition of compositional flesh, in so far as it has a definition, is related to that of functional flesh. But even in this case the relationship between compositional flesh and functional flesh will be contingent insofar as compositional flesh *need not* constitute functional flesh, since it must (if it is to constitute functional flesh) also stand in the right relation to the functionally defined organic body as a whole and it will be contingent whether or not any particular portion of compositional flesh does so. Our decision about which way to specify compositional flesh and bone, etc., will affect what we say about the issue of compositional plasticity, though the issue here is complicated by Aristotle's view that everything must (in some sense) ultimately be composed of the four elements. If we adopt the *causal* account, then functional flesh cannot be realized in anything except compositional flesh, though this still leaves open the possibility of variation in the proportions of elements capable of constituting functional flesh. If we adopt the *quantitative* account, then it seems at

flesh and so can survive the loss of soul. But that does not mean that compositional flesh cannot *constitute* functional flesh. This is important because a proper account of compositional flesh will also help to show what is wrong with the first belief that is used to support the view that a living body cannot have any matter in common with its corpse—i.e., the belief that Aristotle denies that the elements are part of the matter of a living organism.

This belief rests primarily on two passages. The first occurs in *Metaphysics* VIII.4, where Aristotle says that in stating the material cause of man, we must not name fire or earth but must state the peculiar matter [*tên idion* <*hulên*>, *Met.* 1044b1–2]. The second occurs in *Metaphysics* IX.7, where Aristotle asks whether earth is potentially a man and then suggests that it is not earth, but rather the seed (or perhaps even the fertilized egg or embryo) that is potentially a man [*Met.* 1049a1–3].

But neither of these passages shows that the elements are not the matter of a man, and the first actually suggests that the elements *are* in some sense the matter of a man. For it excludes earth on the grounds that we ought to state the nearest or most proximate [*engutata*] causes. Aristotle's use of the superlative here suggests that he thinks that earth *is* in some sense the matter of a man and that his point is simply that it is not the most proximate matter of a man.

The second passage also fails to show that the elements are not the matter of a man. But this has gone unnoticed largely, I suspect, because commentators have not paid adequate attention to Aristotle's use of temporal adverbs. Aristotle begins this chapter by asking whether earth is "potentially a man or not, but rather only when it has already become sperm and not even then perhaps" [*Met.* 1049a1–3]. And Aristotle picks up this reservation again at 1049a14–16, where he says that "the sperm is *not yet* [*oupô*] <potentially a man> for it needs to be in another and to change" and then concludes that the sperm is potentially a man "whenever it is already on account of its own principle such"—that is, whenever it is able to develop into a man *on its own*.

I take this passage to show only that Aristotle thinks that sperm and earth, taken by themselves and before they are in developing embryos or ensouled bodies, are *not yet* potentially men.[21] But this leaves open the possibility that earth and sperm *are* potentially men when they are *already* in developing embryos or ensouled bodies. Note, however, that the sperm in an embryo and the earth in an ensouled body may be potentially men in *different* ways. The sperm is potentially a man in the sense that it *can become* a man, and Aristotle believes that this is true even though the sperm itself does not survive as a constituent of the final human product.[22] But there is evidence

---

least logically (even if not physically) possible that functional flesh should be realized in something other than compositional flesh as we know it. But since these issues are not central to my argument I leave them aside for now, noting only the relevance of *PA* 649b22–28 (on the sense in which blood is hot) to their resolution.

[21] The distinction between proximate and remote potentialities developed in Irwin 1988 (chap. 11, §124) shows how *x* can be the matter of *y* without being potentially *y* insofar as *x* can be the *non-proximate* matter of *y* without being *proximately* potentially *y*.

[22] See *GA* I.21.

that Aristotle thinks that earth and the other elements are potentially men in a different way, one that allows them not only to survive as constituents of the final human product but also to have (in some sense) the characteristics that belong primarily to that product.

First, Aristotle argues in *GC* I.10 that the elements in a mixture can neither survive without being altered (for that is mere synthesis and not mixture) nor be destroyed. The elements are *actually* the new compound but *potentially* what they were before being mixed; their potentiality [*dunamis*] is preserved [*GC* 327b22–31]. This point is confirmed by the following passage from *Parts of Animals* II.3:

> earth and ashes and such things having been mixed with liquid are actually and accidentally liquid [*energeiai men hugra kai kata sumbebêkos*] but in themselves and potentially dry [*kath' hauta de kai dunamei xêra*]. But when these have been separated, the watery, anaplestic <components> are both actually and potentially liquid [*kai energeiai kai dunamei hugra*] while the earthy <components> are dry. . . . [*PA* 649b14–19]

This passage is important for several reasons. First, it shows that earth dissolved in water somehow survives in that mixture. Second, it shows that this earth accidentally has characteristics (like that of being liquid) that belong to the mixture as a whole. And third, it says that the water (taken by itself) is both (at one and the same time) potentially and actually liquid. The importance of the third point will become clear in section 3 below. The important points for now are the first two. Since Aristotle believes that the *homoiomerous* parts of an organism are mixtures of the elements, this passage suggests first, that the elements somehow survive in the *homoiomerous* parts, and second, that these elements then have accidentally the characteristics that belong primarily and essentially to the *homoiomerous* parts themselves.

The first suggestion is confirmed not only by the fact that Aristotle regularly appeals to the elements in order to explain the characteristics of animal parts, but also by his view that animals age and perish because they are composed of materials (namely, the elements) that differ with respect to their natural places and because the elements in them are not in their natural places [*De Caelo* 288b15–19]. The idea is that living bodies age and corpses decay because the elements that constitute them tend to move toward their natural places—fire up and earth down—with the result that the elements gradually become separated from one another and cease to be present in the proportions necessary for the existence of the (functionally defined) *homoiomerous* parts.[23] Furthermore, the nature of nails, hoofs, horns, and beaks is explained by their earthy composition and man is said to have the smallest nails in proportion to his size because he has the least earthy residue [*PA* 655b12–13; *GA* 745a15–20]. The coagulation of blood (which *PA* 651a14 says is the matter of the whole body) is due to the presence

---

[23] See *DA* 415b28–416a8.

of earthy fibers, and watery blood is associated with greater intellect [*PA* II.4]. There are countless such claims scattered throughout the biological works, all of which suggest that the elements somehow persist in the organic body.

In these passages scattered throughout the corpus, Aristotle consistently uses adjectival or paronymous expressions derived from the names of the elements to characterize the parts of animals that are composed of these elements: parts composed of or dominated by earth [*hê gê*] are said to be "earthy" [*geôdês*] and parts composed of or dominated by water [*to hudōr*] are said to be "watery" [*hudatôdês*]. Here Aristotle treats animal parts such as nails and blood as the subjects of which *being earthy* and *being watery* are predicated. This exemplifies his general view that whenever y comes to be from x (where x is matter that persists and comes to constitute y) we should say not that y is x but rather that y is x-en. For example, when a statue or a shield comes to be from bronze (where the bronze is matter that persists and comes to constitute the statue or the shield) we should say not that the statue or the shield is bronze, but rather that the statue or the shield is *brazen*. Similarly, when wood or flesh comes to be from earth (where the earth is matter that persists and comes to constitute the wood or flesh) we should say not that the wood or flesh is earth, but rather that the wood or flesh is *earthen*. The use of the paronymous expression 'x-en' indicates *both* that the product is not strictly identical with its matter (but only composed of it) *and* that the matter of which the product is composed must undergo change in the course of generation; its predicate position indicates that as a result of such change, the matter is now the matter *of a different subject*.[24]

Aristotle's reasons for treating constitutive matter as a predicate are complicated and will be explained more fully in section 2 below. At this point let me say simply that one of Aristotle's primary reasons is to avoid having to treat the apparent subjects of generation and destruction *simpliciter* merely as mere accidents of their constitutive matter and so to avoid having to treat generations and destructions *simpliciter* merely as alterations of the persisting matter. For this threatens to eliminate the distinction between generation and destruction *simpliciter* on the one hand, and alteration and other sorts of accidental change on the other. We shall return to these issues shortly.

But first let me note that treating constitutive matter on a par with properties and other accidents such as size and location allows us to explain how Aristotle might come to say that the matter constituting a subject can have *accidentally* characteristics that belong primarily and *essentially* to the subject this matter constitutes—as in the foregoing example (from *PA* II.3) of the earth in a liquid mixture. For although Aristotle

---

[24] See *Metaphysics* 1033a5–23 (where Aristotle takes the expression 'x-en' to indicate that the matter undergoes change in generation), 1049a19–b1, and *Physics* (*Ph.*) 245b7–17. The *Physics* passage shows that although generation and destruction *simpliciter* cannot (according to Aristotle) *be* alterations of matter, they can *involve* alterations of matter: although the coming to be of a statue is not an alteration of some bronze, because the form of the statue and its privation are not strictly properties of the bronze, the coming to be of a statue may involve alterations (e.g., the heating and cooling) of that bronze as a result of which the bronze ceases to constitute (or belong to) one subject and comes to constitute (or belong to) another.

denies [at *Met.* 1007b2–5] that one accidental entity can serve as the proper subject of another, he allows that we sometimes speak as if one accidental entity (e.g., the musical) is subject to another (e.g., the white) insofar as both (i.e., the musical and the white) belong to one and the same subject (e.g., Socrates). And Aristotle may allow in a similar way that we sometimes speak as if the matter that is predicated of some subject is itself a subject of those properties that belong to the subject of which it is predicated insofar as both (the matter and those properties) belong to one and the same subject. He may allow, for example, that the earth that is predicated of flesh is itself a subject (albeit only accidentally) of whatever belongs to the flesh itself and so, for example, that the earth is accidentally alive (or ensouled) insofar as one and the same thing (the flesh or the organic body) is the proper subject to which both the earth and being alive (or being ensouled) belong.

This concludes my argument that Aristotle allows that the elements survive in the *homoiomerous* parts and that these elements have *accidentally* characteristics that belong primarily and *essentially* to the organic body and its functionally defined parts—in particular, the characteristic of being alive or ensouled. We are now in a position to see how Aristotle can consistently claim *both* that the matter of an animal is essentially ensouled *and* that the matter of an animal is only accidentally or contingently ensouled. For Aristotle is talking about different things, each with different criteria of identity and persistence—one, the organic body, with its functionally defined parts (including the *homoiomerous* ones); the other, the elements constituting the *homoiomerous* parts. And the organic body and its functionally defined parts (both *homoiomerous* and *anhomoiomerous*) are essentially ensouled but constituted by portions of the elements that (when they constitute an organic body) are (in virtue of constituting that body) accidentally ensouled. So there is (as the functionalist interpretation requires) *a* sense in which the matter of an animal is *only contingently* related to its form or soul, but not (pace Burnyeat) one that Aristotle takes to be incompatible with the sense in which the matter of an animal is *essentially* ensouled.

2

Here, however, we need to ask why Aristotle introduces essentially ensouled matter in the first place. In this section, I argue that Aristotle introduces essentially ensouled matter as part of his solution to the problem of distinguishing generation and destruction *simpliciter* from alteration and other sorts of accidental change, and so that we need not adopt Burnyeat's hypothesis that Aristotle takes such matter as primitive in order to avoid having to explain the emergence of life and awareness.

Note first that it is an important part of Aristotle's view that the elements can constitute different things at different times, some of which (e.g., organic bodies) are essentially ensouled and some of which (e.g., clay pots) are not. For this explains the sense in which the elements are matter and potentiality as well as the way in which matter can serve as the substratum of generation and destruction *simpliciter*, which is something that Aristotle takes to be necessary if he is to avoid generation *ex nihilo* and destruction *in nihilum*. It also explains the continuity of certain properties throughout substantial change; it explains why, for example, Socrates' corpse has so much in common with his living body. But this raises a problem for Aristotle. For it suggests that *all* changes are simply alterations of the underlying elements, and so threatens to do away entirely with generation and destruction *simpliciter*.[25] For it suggests that being a man and being a corpse are simply accidents of the underlying matter, and so that Socrates' death is simply an alteration of this matter (which is first a man and then a corpse).

But Aristotle rejects this suggestion. For he believes (i) that generation and destruction *simpliciter* occur whenever the termini of a change are not properties or accidents of what persists throughout the change [*GC* 320a1–2], and (ii) that the persisting matter is not the subject of which the things generated and destroyed (e.g., individual organisms) are properties; the matter is rather an accident of the things it comes and ceases to constitute [*GC* 322a28–33].[26] Take, for example, the case in which some earth constitutes Socrates' flesh at t_1 and then (when Socrates' flesh decomposes) a pot at t_2. In this case, Aristotle thinks we would say not that the earth is first flesh and then a pot, but rather that the flesh (which is earthen) is destroyed and a pot (which is earthen) comes to be. The case for treating matter as an accident is clearest with growth and decline, which Aristotle treats as processes in which a persisting subject changes by having matter added to or taken away from it [*GC* 321b23–322a4, 322a28–34].

We can see why it is important for Aristotle to take the persisting matter as an accident of the things that come to be and pass away if we recall that he takes generation and destruction *simpliciter* to consist in a form's coming to be embodied in some preexisting matter. For since that matter can exist whether or not it embodies that form, it looks as though embodying that form is simply an accident of it, in which case the compound of form and matter seems to be an accidental unity on a par with a musical man. But if the compound is an accidental unity on a par with a musical man, then the dissolution of the compound (i.e., the matter's ceasing to embody that form) would no more constitute destruction *simpliciter* than would a man's ceasing to be musical.[27]

In order to solve this problem Aristotle needs to show how a form's coming to be embodied in some matter can yield a product that is not a property of what persists

---

[25] See *GC* 314a8–11; *Met.* 983b6–18.
[26] The claim that matter is not the subject of which the things generated and destroyed are properties is controversial and I defend it in more detail in Whiting (unpublished). The general line of argument—sketched in Whiting 1990 [Chapter 2, this volume]—receives some support from the way in which Aristotle explains accidental differences as due to matter. On my view, these differences are differences in compositional and not functional matter. And functional matter, being the same for all members of a kind, is thus knowable and definable in a way in which compositional matter is not.
[27] But taking the persisting matter as an accident of the subjects of generation, destruction, and alteration will not by itself solve this problem. For a similar problem arises if Aristotle takes the form to be a species-form, which preexists and then (in generation and destruction) comes and ceases to be embodied in different portions of matter. For since the species-form can exist whether or not it is embodied in any particular portion of matter (as long as it is embodied in some portion of matter or other) it looks as though the compound of form and matter is still an accidental unity.

and that is itself an *intrinsic unity*—i.e., a unity neither component of which is separable from the other *in a way such that it <u>could</u> serve as subject in some <u>other</u> unity*, as, for example, a man (in the unity pale-man) is separable from his paleness and so can stand as subject in the unity dark-man. This product, qua product of a form's coming to be embodied in some matter, is presumably a compound of form and matter neither of which is separable from the other: the form is essentially the form of this matter, and the matter essentially the matter of this form. Thus, when Socrates comes (or ceases) to be, there comes (or ceases) to be a compound that is an intrinsic unity of form and matter—the form (or soul) of *his* (as opposed to any other man's) body and the body of which *this* soul (and no other) is the form and the essence.

We are now in a position to see how Aristotle might have introduced functionally defined organic bodies (along with individual forms) as part of his solution to the problem of distinguishing generation and destruction *simpliciter* from alteration and other sorts of accidental change. The compound that comes (and ceases) to be when Socrates comes (and ceases) to be is a compound of *his* individual form or soul and *his* organic body. And although the organic body must be constituted by some compositional matter at any time at which it exists, it can, insofar as it is functionally defined, be constituted by different portions of compositional matter at different times. But insofar as it is functionally defined, the organic body (unlike its constituent matter) cannot exist apart from the soul, which is the set of capacities in virtue of which the organic body is capable of performing its defining functions. In other words, this body is *essentially* ensouled and so comes and ceases to exist simultaneously with the soul, which is its form and essence.[28]

Assuming that Aristotle takes the product of a form's coming to be embodied in some matter to be some sort of compound, we can see why Aristotle should take it to be a compound of form and an *organic* body if we examine the alternative. The distinction between the organic body and the matter constituting it at any given time yields a distinction between two kinds of compound. One, the "thin compound," is a compound of form and an *organic body*. The other, the "thick compound," is a compound of form and *the portion of compositional matter constituting that compound at a given time*.[29] This distinction is important for the following reason. If we take the subjects of generation, destruction, and alteration to be thick compounds, then there will be generation and destruction every time what we would ordinarily call a man loses or acquires matter: entire species of what we would ordinarily take to be accidental change (like growth and decline) will (if they involve *any* acquisition or loss of matter) be assimilated to generation and destruction *simpliciter*.

---

[28] I defend the view that individual form is the principle of individuation both of the compound and of its functionally defined organic body (or proximate matter, explained in n. 18) in Whiting 1986 [Chapter 1, this volume]. See also Gill 1989, 4. 4. 1.

[29] See Irwin 1988, chap. 11, § 132 on the distinction between *formal* and *material* compounds. His material compounds differ from my thick compounds insofar as thick compounds (unlike his material compounds) cannot be constituted by different portions of matter at different times.

But Aristotle can save the appearances if he takes the subjects of generation, destruction, and alteration to be thin compounds. For the thin compound (of soul and an organic body) can be constituted by different portions of matter at different times and so can grow and decline without ceasing to exist. The thin compound will cease to exist if and only if its organic body ceases to embody the set of functionally defined capacities that constitute its soul—that is, if and only if its soul, and hence its organic body, ceases to exist.

This concludes my argument that Aristotle's introduction of essentially ensouled bodies is not (as Ackrill claims) a problem, but rather part of Aristotle's solution to the problem of distinguishing generation and destruction *simpliciter* from alteration and other sorts of accidental change. If this is correct, then there is no need to appeal to Burnyeat's hypothesis that Aristotle introduces such bodies in order to avoid having to explain the emergence of life and awareness. The non-contingency of the relation between a soul and its organic body (along with that body's functionally defined parts, both *homoiomerous* and *anhomoiomerous*) need not involve any sort of primitively or mysteriously alive or sentient matter. It is simply a matter of the functional relations among the (functionally defined) parts and the system as a whole.[30] Because the identity of each of these parts is dependent on its relation to the system as a whole in a way in which the identity of their constituent matters (which can survive in the absence of these functional relations) is not, these parts are essentially related to the system as a whole whereas their constituent matter is only contingently related to that system. Once again, the contingent relation between matter and form that is required by the functionalist interpretation is preserved, but not at the expense of essentially ensouled bodies.

3

I should like to conclude by considering a common objection to Aristotle's account of essentially ensouled bodies.[31] The problem arises because Aristotle says of such bodies that they are potentially [*dunamei*] alive [*DA* 412a19–21, 27–28]. But these bodies are,

---

[30] On the relation to the whole, see *Politics* 1253a20ff. The functioning of the whole need not depend on the functioning of each and every part, but the functioning of each of the parts will depend on that of the whole. Thus, the system as a whole might survive in the absence of functioning eyes, but the eyes cannot survive in the absence of the functioning whole (which is a matter of the functional relations between some critical subset of its parts, starting with its heart).

[31] This objection is raised by Ackrill 1972–1973), 124–27. He assimilates it to the objection raised in section 1, this chapter, because he accepts Aristotle's identification of matter with potentiality and of form with actuality, and he does not distinguish the organic body from its compositional matter in the way that I suggest. But someone might object that there is a problem here even if we accept that distinction. For it is clearly the organic body and not simply its compositional matter that Aristotle says is potentially alive. And this seems odd if (as Ackrill suggests) the concept of potentiality depends on the idea that what is actually the case might not have been the case. For it is never true of the organic body at any time at which it exists that *it* (as opposed to its compositional matter) might not have been alive.

as we have seen, *essentially* alive. So they are *necessarily actually* alive. But this makes it difficult to understand the sense in which they are *potentially* alive. For we ordinarily say that something is potentially F only when it is not actually F. And even if we allow that something can at one time be both potentially and actually F, the distinction between potentiality and actuality seems to require that what is actually F might not have been F. But this is just what, in the case of the organic body, Aristotle denies: the organic body, unlike its constituent matter, could not have lacked soul.

Parts of Animals 649b14–19 (quoted in section 1 above) shows clearly that Aristotle allows something to be at one and the same time both potentially and actually F: water in a liquid state is both potentially and actually liquid. But Ackrill, in pressing his objection, claims that this is possible only where the relevant potentiality is a capacity (like sight) that can be distinguished from its actualization (namely, seeing), and not where the relevant potentiality is the matter of some object. The idea is apparently that although I am able to play squash (or am potentially a squash player) even when I am actually playing, clay is not able to be (or potentially) a statue when it actually is (or constitutes) a statue. But this is not Aristotle's view.

First, Aristotle does not distinguish potentiality as capacity from potentiality as matter in the way that Ackrill suggests.[32] Because Aristotle takes actuality [*energeia*] to be prior to potentiality [*dunamis*], his distinction between two kinds of potentiality is based on a distinction between two types of actuality—one called '*kinêsis*' (or 'change') and the other called '*energeia*' in a strict sense. Here, as elsewhere, Aristotle uses the same term, in this case '*energeia*,' to refer to a genus and to one of its species. For the sake of clarity, I shall use '*energeia*' only when referring to the species that is being distinguished from the species *kinesis*; when referring to the genus that includes both species (i.e., *energeia* and *kinesis*) I use 'actuality'.

Aristotle explains the distinction between *energeiai* proper and *kinêseis* as follows:

> Of these, then, <it is necessary> to call some *kinêseis* and some *energeiai*. For every *kinêsis* is incomplete—reducing, learning, walking, building. These are changes and incomplete. For it is not the case that at the same time one walks and has walked, or builds and has built, or that <something> comes to be and has come to be or is changed and has been changed, but these are different. But the same <subject> at the same time has seen and sees, and thinks and has thought. [*Met.* 1048b28–35][33]

Part of the point of saying that a *kinêsis* is incomplete is that it is defined by an end the completion of which spells the end of the *kinêsis*: when the house has been built, the buildable no longer exists. For as Aristotle claims, "the *energeia* of the buildable, qua buildable, is the <activity of> building" [*Met.* 1066a2–3]. In this case, the actualization

---

[32] See *Metaphysics* 1048a25–b9.
[33] Following Jaeger 1957, who took *kai kinei kai kekinêken* in l.33 as an interpolation.

of the sort of potentiality Aristotle associates with *kinêsis* cannot exist simultaneously with the potentiality itself. Here, actualization and potentiality are temporally incompatible.

This suggests that the sort of potentiality that Aristotle associates with *energeia* proper *can* exist simultaneously with its own actualization. That this is at least part of Aristotle's point when he claims that "the same <subject> at the same time sees and has seen" is confirmed by the fact that he goes on after listing several cases in which *x* at the same time *F*s and has *F*-ed to say,

> if this were not the case, it would have been necessary to stop at some time, just as whenever <someone> reduces; but in fact <one does> not <stop> but rather one <at the same time> lives and has lived. [*Met.* 1048b26–27]

In other words, if "*x* has lived" were not temporally compatible with "*x* lives," then just as one cannot be building a house that has already been built, "*x* lives" could not be true at any time at which "*x* has lived" was true. But as Ackrill himself recognizes, Aristotle is so far from thinking that "*x* lives" is temporally incompatible with "*x* has lived" that he thinks that "*x* lives (at *t*)" actually *entails* "*x* has lived (at *t*)."[34] This suggests that Aristotle takes living and other *energeiai* not simply as compatible with, but as implying, the existence of the potentialities whose actualizations they are. And this would explain why he says that only a body that is actually alive is potentially alive: living is the actualization of one of the body's potentialities, an actualization that could not occur in the absence of that potentiality.

It should not surprise us if Aristotle claims that *energeiai* entail (and, as we shall see below, are entailed by) their correlative potentialities. For Aristotle introduces the distinction between two kinds of actualization immediately after claiming that taking form as actualization and matter as potentiality will solve the problem about the unity of substance by showing that "the last matter and the form are the same and one, the one in potentiality, the other in actuality" [*Met.* 1045b18–19]. The point of introducing this distinction is to show that it is form as *energeia* (and not as *kinêsis*) that is in some way the same and one with the *dunamis* of which it is the actualization. The *dunamis* here is matter that is "last" in the sense of being closest to the form: it is that of which the form (or soul) is the actualization—i.e., the organic body rather than its constituent matter.[35] So the role played by the organic body here in Aristotle's account of the unity of substance supports section 2's claim above that Aristotle takes the organic body (of which the soul is the actualization and essence) to play an important role in providing intrinsic unities of the sort required if Aristotle is to distinguish generation and destruction *simpliciter* from alteration and other sorts of accidental change.

---

[34] Ackrill 1965, 120–25.
[35] On the closeness of matter to form, see *Metaphysics* 1035a11–14.

But Aristotle has reasons for saying not only that there is a sense of 'potentiality' in which any body that is actually alive is potentially alive, but also that there is a sense of 'potentiality' in which any body that is potentially alive is actually alive. The reasons lie in what Aristotle takes to be two important facts about living bodies. First, living bodies are natural rather than artificial. This means that they have internal sources of motion and rest [*Ph.* 192b8–15]. Second, the soul is not only the formal and final cause of something's being an animal; it is also the efficient cause (i.e., an internal source of motion and rest: *DA* 415b8–28). These two facts work together in the following way: Aristotle argues that for any *natural* object x, the presence of an internal efficient cause of x's being (or coming to be) F is a necessary condition for saying that x is potentially F. So if the soul is the efficient cause of a body's being (or coming to be) alive, then a body will be potentially alive only if and when it is ensouled.

The primary evidence for this interpretation appears in *Metaphysics* IX.7, where Aristotle distinguishes natural from artificial generation in the following way: x is potentially some artifact (e.g., a house) whenever, *if* the agent has willed, it comes to be <a house> if nothing internal or external prevents it [1049a5–12]. But in the case of *natural* objects, x is potentially "whatever it will be through itself [*di' hautou*] if nothing external interferes" [1049a13–14].

There is some question here about whether Aristotle's account of artificial generation is merely conditional or whether the antecedent must be fulfilled—that is, about whether or not the external efficient cause (e.g., the willing agent) must be present (and active) if x is to be potentially some artifact. Aristotle's claim that matter is potentially a house whenever nothing must be added, removed, or changed might seem to suggest that the presence of an external efficient cause is necessary for some matter to be potentially a house. This would make the artificial case more like that natural case in which some matter is potentially alive (or an animal) only when it is actually alive (or an animal). But Aristotle's apparent belief that earth is potentially a statue when it has become bronze and whether or not a sculptor is present [*Met.* 1049a17–18] suggests that he does not assimilate artificial to natural generation in this way. Furthermore, taking the contrast between artificial and natural potentiality as I have suggested is supported not only by Aristotle's claim that "actuality is not said similarly of all things, but by analogy" [*Met.* 1048b6–7] but also by the fact that it helps to make sense of Aristotle's appeal to axes in *DA* II.1.

In that chapter, Aristotle asks us to imagine what would happen if an ax were a natural body. He then says that being-an-ax would be the substance and the soul of it and that if this were removed, it would no longer be an ax except homonymously. Now being-an-ax is presumably something like being-capable-of-chopping and it would seem that if this were removed, an ax would no longer be an axe and that this follows *whether or not an axe is a natural body*. What the hypothesis that the ax is a *natural* body adds is the requirement that the ax be capable of chopping *on its own*. This requirement is needed to explain why Aristotle thinks that his subsequent point about eyes is similar to the one about axes: if an eye were an animal, sight would be its soul and it would be able to see on its own rather than by depending (as in fact it must) on its relation to the soul of the whole living animal. This passage requires us to suppose that the relevant similarity between eyes and artificial objects like axes is that they do not have their own internal efficient causes of motion and rest: they cannot see or chop by themselves. This distinguishes them from living bodies, which have their own internal efficient causes of motion and rest.

It is important to notice this difference between natural and artificial potentiality because failure to do so will prevent us from seeing why Aristotle's view (that a natural body is potentially alive only if it is ensouled) is not as odd as it may initially sound. Aristotle believes that an ax is capable of chopping (or potentially chops) because it can chop *if* there is an external efficient cause around to chop with it. (The antecedent need not even be fulfilled.) But when Aristotle says that a body is capable of living (or potentially alive) he does not mean that it *can* live *if* there is some external efficient cause around to make it live: a natural body is potentially alive only given the presence of an *internal* efficient cause of its being alive—that is, only given the presence of its soul.[36]

REFERENCES

Ackrill, J. L. 1965 "Aristotle's Distinction between *Energeia* and *Kinesis*." In Bambrough 1965, 121–41; reprinted in Ackrill 1997.

Ackrill, J. L. 1972–1973. "Aristotle's Definitions of 'Psuchê.'" *Proceedings of the Aristotelian Society* 73: 119–233; reprinted in Barnes et al. 1979, 65–75; and Ackrill 1997.

Ackrill, J. L. 1997. *Essays on Plato and Aristotle*. Oxford: Clarendon Press.

Bambrough, R. (ed.) 1965. *New Essays on Plato and Aristotle*. New York: Humanities Press.

Barnes, J., Schofield, M., and Sorabji, R. (eds.) 1979. *Articles on Aristotle: Volume IV: Psychology and Aesthetics*. London: Duckworth.

Burnyeat, M. F. 1992. "Is an Aristotelian Philosophy of Mind Still Credible? (A Draft)." In Nussbaum and Rorty (eds.) 1992, 15–26.

Charlton, W. 1970. *Aristotle's Physics I–II*. Oxford: Clarendon Press.

Code, A. 1976. "The Persistence of Aristotelian Matter." *Philosophical Studies* 29: 356–67.

Cohen, S. M. 1984. "Aristotle's Doctrine of the Material Substrate." *Philosophical Review* 93: 171–94.

Cohen, S. M. 1992. "Hylomorphism and Functionalism." In Nussbaum and Rorty (eds.) 1992, 57–74.

Everson, S. (ed.) 1991. *Psychology*. Companion to Ancient Thought. Cambridge: Cambridge University Press.

Furley, D. J. 1983. "The Mechanics of *Meteorologica* IV: A Prolegomenon to Biology." In P. Moraux and J. Weisner (eds.), *Zweifelhaftes im Corpus Aristotelicum: Studien zu einigen Dubia. Akten des 9. Symposium Aristotelicum*. Berlin: de Gruyter, 73–93; reprinted in Furley, D. J. 1989. *Cosmic Problems*. Cambridge: Cambridge University Press, 132–48.

---

[36] I should like to thank Paul Hoffman, Paul Matthewson, Philip Mitsis, Martha Nussbaum, Amélie Rorty, and Steve Strange for comments on an early draft of this essay, and Helen Cartwright, whose comments on another paper led to significant improvements here. Terry Irwin, as always, deserves special thanks.

Gill, M. L. 1989. *Aristotle on Substance: The Paradox of Unity*. Princeton, NJ: Princeton University Press.
Irwin, T. H. 1981. "Homonymy in Aristotle." *Review of Metaphysics* 34: 523–44.
Irwin, T. H. 1988. *Aristotle's First Principles*. Oxford: Oxford University Press.
Irwin, T. H. 1991. "Aristotle's Philosophy of Mind." In Everson (ed.) 1991, 56–83.
Jaeger, W. 1957. *Aristotelis Metaphysica*. Oxford: Clarendon Press.
Jones, B. 1974. "Aristotle's Introduction of Matter." *Philosophical Review* 83: 474–500.
Modrak, D. 1987. *Aristotle: The Power of Perception*. Chicago: University of Chicago Press.
Nussbaum, M. C. 1978. *Aristotle's "De Motu Animalium."* Princeton, NJ: Princeton University Press.
Nussbaum, M. and Putnam, H. 1992. "Changing Aristotle's Mind." In Nussbaum and Rorty (eds.) 1992, 27–56.
Nussbaum, M. C. and Rorty, A. (eds.) 1992. *Essays on Aristotle's "De Anima."* Oxford: Oxford University Press.
Nussbaum, M. C. 1992. "Introduction, (A) The Text of Aristotle's De Anima." In Nussbaum and Rorty (eds.) 1992, 1–6.
Putnam, H. 1975. "Philosophy and Our Mental Life." In H. Putnam (ed.), *Mind, Language, and Reality: Philosophical Papers, Volume II*. Cambridge Cambridge University Press, 291–303.
Shields, C. J. 1989. "The First Functionalist." In J. C. Smith (ed.), *The Historical Foundations of Cognitive Science*. Dordrecht: Kluwer Academic Publishers, 19–33.
Shields, C. J. 1999. *Order in Multiplicity: Homonymy the Philosophy of Aristotle*. Oxford: Oxford University Press.
Shields, C. J. Unpublished. "The Homonymy of the Body in Aristotle." See now chap. 5 of Shields 1999.
Whiting, J. 1984. "Individual Forms in Aristotle." Ph.D. Thesis, Cornell University.
Whiting, J. 1986. "Form and Individuation in Aristotle." *History of Philosophy Quarterly* 3: 359–77. [Chapter 1, this volume]
Whiting, J. 1990. "Aristotle on Form and Generation. *Proceedings of the Boston Area Colloquium of Ancient Philosophy* 6: 35–63. [Chapter 2, this volume]
Whiting, J. unpublished. *Aristotelian Individuals*.

4

Metasubstance

CRITICAL NOTICE OF FREDE-PATZIG AND FURTH

METAPHYSICS (MET.) Z, generally regarded as presenting Aristotle's most considered (if not conclusive) views about substance, is the focus of numerous recent publications, among which Frede and Patzig's two-volume translation and commentary is one of the few required readings for anyone with a serious interest in the subject.[1] More detailed than the chapter length commentaries by Ross and Bonitz or the more recent *Notes on Zeta*,[2] it aims—as many have despaired of doing—at presenting a consistent reading of Z based not on a general conception of Aristotle's thought, but on an exhaustive and critical examination of Z *itself*. In this respect it differs from Montgomery Furth's stimulating and provocative *Substance, Form and Psyche*, which aims to explain and motivate the *Metaphysics'* mature theory of substance by appeal to Aristotle's biology.[3]

Furth, who suggests that Aristotle invented "our Western philosophical concept of a material individual" [p. 60], explicitly distinguishes his unorthodox method, which promises something "markedly different from what we are used to" from "the usual

---

[1] Michael Frede and Günther Patzig, *Aristoteles Metaphysik Z* (Munich: C. H. Beck, 1988).
[2] W. D. Ross, *Aristotle's Metaphysics*, Volume II (Oxford: Clarendon Press, 1924); H. Bonitz, *Aristotelis Metaphysica Commentarius* (Hildesheim: G. Olms Verlag, 1960); M. Burnyeat et al., *Notes on Zeta of Aristotle's Metaphysics, Being the Record of a Seminar Held in London, 1974–1975* (Oxford: Sub-faculty of Philosophy, 1979).
[3] Montgomery Furth, *Substance, Form, and Psyche: An Aristotelian Metaphysics* (Cambridge: Cambridge University Press, 1988).

approach to a historical philosopher—that of working from his text to his meaning." Furth aims

> to recreate in imagination the world the philosopher saw ... and to do this so completely and so vividly that ... it becomes possible to "*deduce* the text," to validate a reaction that goes: "But someone who assumed *that* ... would quite naturally say things like *this*"—where this is some characteristic verbal behavior ... which has discouraged, if not outright baffled, standardly cautious essays at picking out a plausible meaning directly *ex ipsissimis verbis*. [p. 1]

The results are ironic. What Furth ends up with is more or less the traditional view that Frede and Patzig—working unabashedly from Aristotle's text to his meaning—find unacceptable.

Although subject to some variation, the traditional view is, roughly, (1) that Aristotle recognizes only one substantial form for each *infima species*; (2) that these species-forms are the primary substances of *Metaphysics* Z; (3) that species-forms, being common to each individual member of their respective species, are universals; and (4) that matter is the principle of individuation (or pluralization) in the sense that it is what distinguishes co-specific individuals (which share one and the same form) from one another.

Furth adopts each of these views except for (3).[4] On his view, an individual is essentially a *compound* of species-form (which it shares with other co-specific individuals) and some matter (not necessarily the same over time) that distinguishes it numerically (and perhaps also qualitatively) from other co-specific individuals. It comes to be only gradually as the species-form comes to be embodied, via movements transported in the father's semen, in the particular mass of menstrual fluid provided by the mother [p. 123]. Furth's defense of the traditional view by appeal to the biological works is distinctive, and the familiarity of his conclusions nothing to hide: it would be a significant achievement to show that the biological works provide unequivocal support for the traditional view.

Frede and Patzig make no pretense that their alternative to the traditional view originated with them. Their alternative—variations of which date back to Alexander of Aphrodisias and have recently been proposed by Lloyd, Sellars, Heinaman, and

---

[4] Point (3) has always been the Achilles' heel of the traditional view because Aristotle argues in *Metaphysics* Z 13 that no universal is a substance. But (3) has recently been abandoned by some proponents of the traditional view who argue that matter (prior to form's being predicated of it) is not a countable thing, so that the species-form (being predicated of matter) is not predicated of *any* individual, and so ipso facto not predicated of *many*. On this view, the species-form does not satisfy the definition of a universal [at *Met*. 999b34–1000a1] as what is predicable of (many) *individuals* (or particulars). For this view (which is not, however, Furth's) see Michael Woods, "Problems in *Metaphysics* Z, Chapter 13," in J. Moravcsik (ed.), *Aristotle: A Collection of Critical Essays* (South Bend, IN: University of Notre Dame Press, 1968), 213–38 [esp. pp. 237–38]; and Alan Code, "An Aporematic Approach to Primary Being in *Metaphysics* Z," *Canadian Journal of Philosophy*, supp. vol. 10 (1984): 1–20 [esp. p. 18]. The Woods-Code line presents the strongest case in the literature for rejecting (3), so it surprises me that Furth, whose own case is considerably weaker, does not adopt their line—especially given its affinity with his emphasis on the mass-logical character of the matter of which form is predicated. (I discuss Furth's case in section 4 below.)

Irwin[5]—is, very roughly, (1′) that Aristotle recognizes within each species a plurality of numerically distinct individual forms, each peculiar to the compound to which it belongs;[6] (2′) that these individual forms are the primary substances of *Metaphysics* Z; (3′) that Z rejects the existence of substantial universals common to each and every member of their respective species;[7] and (4′) that the (individual) forms of natural substances, though themselves immaterial in the sense that they do not have any material *parts*, are nevertheless *necessarily enmattered*. Frede and Patzig take (3′) to represent a nominalist departure from the realism about substance universals that they see in the early *Categories* (*Cat.*). So they see Aristotle as finally, in his *Metaphysics*, escaping the grip of the Platonic picture.

Each of these works contains a wealth of material to which I cannot do justice within the limits defined here. So I am going to focus primarily on the points of difference (enumerated above) between Furth's version of the traditional view and Frede and Patzig's alternative view. For these are precisely the points on which Frede and Patzig's commentary is itself focused. I want to suggest that the truth is something of a *synthesis* according to which Aristotle recognizes for each species *both* a unique species-form *and* a plurality of numerically distinct individual forms of which the species-form (itself a universal) is predicated. The result closely resembles Frede and Patzig's alternative, but without the nominalism of (3′). For Aristotle clearly thinks that universals are necessary for knowledge.

---

[5] On Alexander's testimony, see A. C. Lloyd, *Form and Universal in Aristotle* (Liverpool: Francis Cairns, 1981). Contemporary defenses include W. Sellars, "Substance and Form in Aristotle," *The Journal of Philosophy* 54 (1957): 688–99; R. Heinaman, "Aristotle's Tenth *Aporia*," *Archiv für Geschichte der Philosophie* 57 (1979): 1–20; and T. H. Irwin, *Aristotle's First Principles* (Oxford: Oxford University Press, 1988), especially chap. 12. See also M. Frede, "Substance in Aristotle's *Metaphysics*," in A. Gotthelf (ed.), *Aristotle on Nature and Living Things* (Pittsburgh, PA: Mathesis Publications, 1985), 7–26, reprinted in M. Frede, *Essays in Ancient Philosophy* (Minneapolis: University of Minnesota Press, 1987), 72–80.

[6] As Frede and Patzig note, Anglophone commentators have generally designated such forms "particular." But I call them "individual" because I use 'particular' to render '*kath' hekaston*' and I know of no passage (apart from *De Caelo* 278a10, which is ambiguous) where Aristotle clearly refers to a form as '*kath' hekaston*'; and I use 'individual' to represent Aristotle's use of '*hen arithmô(i)*' (literally 'one in number') as a one-place predicate. Aristotle suggests some such distinction between what is *individual* (or one in number) and what is *particular* when he allows that the Prime Mover (which is immaterial and imperishable) is one in number [*Met.* 1074a36–37] but says that place is proper or peculiar [*idios*] to particulars [1092a18–20], thus suggesting that a *particular* is a *kind of individual*—namely, a *material* one. This explains why [at 1039b30–31] he treats particulars (at least sublunary ones, as indicated by *autôn*) as perishable in a way in which immaterial individuals (like the Prime Mover) are not. It also explains the connection between particularity and perceptibility (as, e.g., at *Prior Analytics* 43a27 and in *De Caelo* I.9). On this view, Aristotle admits the existence of immaterial individuals, but denies that they are particulars. So 'individual' and 'particular' cannot generally be used interchangeably, even though Aristotle sometimes appears to use them this way (as, e.g., at *Met.* 999b33–34, presumably because he is thinking there primarily of *material* substances). For further discussion of this and other aspects of my own view, see my *Aristotelian Individuals* (unpublished).

[7] (1′) and (2′) form the core of the alternative view, common to all varieties of it. (3′) is distinctive of (though not peculiar to) Frede and Patzig. See Lloyd, *Form and Universal in Aristotle*, which combines (1′) with a conceptualist account of universal forms [p. 3]; and Irwin, *Aristotle's First Principles*, which combines (1′) with a realist account of substance universals [pp. 265–68].

I also want to recommend that Frede and Patzig abandon (4′) in favor of the view that the individual forms of *natural substances, being essentially (and not just necessarily) enmattered, are themselves* material in the sense that they have material parts. For (4′) shares the traditional view's assumption that forms are themselves immaterial, even if they are necessarily enmattered. But allowing that forms are themselves material strengthens the case for taking individual forms to be independent in the way required if they are to be—as (2′) asserts they are—*primary substances.*

First let me say a few words about Frede and Patzig's text and translation.[8]

1. THE FREDE-PATZIG TEXT AND TRANSLATION

The text on which Frede and Patzig's interpretation is based departs from Jaeger's in over 130 places and is printed alongside their German translation. Because Frede and Patzig relied on the critical apparatus of Christ, Ross, and Jaeger, checking only the conjectured readings of Asclepius and Pseudo-Alexander, Frede and Patzig provide no apparatus but simply note their departures from Jaeger's text.[9] This is unfortunate because the commentary does not always describe the relevant variants and so must be used in conjunction with another editor's apparatus.

Although some of Frede and Patzig's deviations from Jaeger are based on the testimony of ancient commentators, especially Asclepius, most are based on a general preference (supported by the Greek commentators and medieval translations) for the authority of manuscripts E (Paris, tenth century) and J (Vienna, ninth century), representing one manuscript tradition, over that of Ab (Florence, twelfth century), representing another such tradition. Frede and Patzig believe that Ab (the text of which is often smoother than those of E and J) is the product of an editor who altered the text by deleting grammatical irregularities and unintelligible or misunderstood expressions, and by glossing in view of perceived substantive difficulties. So they strengthen Ross's principle of following EJ except where the evidence of the commentators, grammar or sense favors Ab: they aim to follow EJ wherever it provides an *acceptable* (even if not better) reading. For the "better" reading may be the result of editorial "correction" [Vol. 1. pp. 13–17].[10]

---

[8] Nonspecialists may prefer to skip the next section as well as those footnotes in which I comment on details of interest primarily to specialists.

[9] W. Jaeger, *Aristotelis Metaphysica* (Oxford: Clarendon Press, 1957).

[10] Noteworthy features of Frede and Patzig's text include (1) their persuasive case for bracketing '*kai to ek toutôn*' at 1038b3; (2) the somewhat weak appeal to '*eti*' [at 1038b15, 23, 29 (*not* 24) and 1039a3] to justify reading '*prôton*' with Ab at 1038b9, even though EJ's '*prôte*' seems "acceptable" despite its suggestion that Z may implicitly retain the distinction between primary and secondary substance—weak not only because not every series of '*eti*'s begins with a '*prôton*,' but also because retaining the distinction between primary and secondary substance would actually serve to *solve* some problems (e.g., the one raised by the reference to the universal *logos* as '*ousia*' at 1039b20); (3) the attractive interpretation of the traditional text at 1037b5–7—taking '*oude*' to mean "*not simply*"—so that Aristotle claims that accidental compounds (like musical-men) are *neither* identical with their essences *nor simply* accidentally one with them (thus obviating the need for Ross's emendation); (4) the deletion at 1037a1–2 of Ab's '*kai pantos gar*

Frede and Patzig's translation, which is intended to be used in conjunction with their commentary, explicitly aims (1) to preserve ambiguities of the Greek in their German; (2) to render Greek expressions uniformly in German wherever possible; and (3) to capture the force and vivacity, as well as the simplicity and naturalness, of Aristotle's Greek *without* relying on the sort of clarificatory and interpretive interpolation that is characteristic of Ross [Vol. 1, pp. 18–19]. I shall at various points comment on the extent to which Frede and Patzig have succeeded in realizing these aims.

2. TYPOLOGICAL ESSENTIALISM, SUBSTANCE, AND *TODE TI*

One point on which Furth and Frede-Patzig seem to agree is this: individual substances, at least sublunary ones, come in species. Each *species* is associated with some set of characteristics (i.e., its form or essence) the possession of which is (generally) necessary and sufficient for membership in it. Each *individual* is essentially constituted by some such set of characteristics (whether individual or shared) the continuous realization of which is both necessary and sufficient for its continued existence.[11] Let's call this "typological essentialism."[12]

Frede and Patzig take Aristotle's requirement that a substance be *tode ti* to reflect his typological essentialism and they translate accordingly—taking '*tode*' as demonstrative and '*ti*' as representing *what* (as in what *kind* of thing) the thing demonstrated is. This yields "*ein Dies von der Art*" [roughly, "a this of that kind"].[13] This is certainly no less interpretive than Ross's "this" (adopted by Furth) or Bonitz's "*ein einzelnes Etwas*"

---

hulē tis estin ho mē esti ti ēn einai kai eidos auto kath' hauto alla tode ti,' the motivation for which deletion (i.e., the apparent and unexpected distinction between the form and what is *tode ti*) may be undermined by the way in which *De Caelo* I.9 (cited in note 59 below) supports taking the distinction between "the form itself in itself" and "the form mixed with the matter" as one between a universal and a particular (or individual), thus allowing us to read this passage as distinguishing the universal form (which is *not* *tode ti*) from the individual form (which *is tode ti* and, as my view explains, has matter).

[11] "Characteristic" is potentially misleading insofar as it suggests an independent subject to which characteristics belong, but the language of constitution is supposed to mitigate this. "Necessary" may also mislead, since Aristotle suggests (at *Topics* 134b6–8) that a defective organism may lack some of the characteristics of its species without failing to be a member of that species. [For more on this issue, see my "Hylomorphic Virtue" (Chapter 6, this volume).] Finally, there are problems not adequately represented by Frede and Patzig [Vol. 1, pp. 43–47] about whether the persistence of specific characteristics is *sufficient* for the persistence of the same *individual*. I discuss these problems in "Form and Individuation in Aristotle," *History of Philosophy Quarterly* 3 (1986): 359–77 [Chapter 1, this volume], where I challenge the traditional view's claim that matter is the principle of individuation (or pluralization) within species.

[12] The label is from J. Lennox, 'Kinds, Forms of Kinds, and the More and Less in Aristotle's Biology," in A. Gotthelf and J. Lennox (eds.), *Philosophical Issues in Aristotle's Biology* (Cambridge: Cambridge University Press, 1987), 340, n. 4. On Furth's ambivalence about the *Categories*' commitment to typological essentialism, see note 23 below.

[13] Frede and Patzig (ad 1028a12) cite '*poion ti tode*' at 1028a15 in support of this. Johanna Seibt (personal communication) conjectured that Frede and Patzig used the somewhat artificial "*von der Art*" (which given its standard use with a relative clause would not naturally be taken to introduce a sortal) rather than the more acceptable "*von einer Art*" in order to indicate that Aristotle is referring to a this of *some definite kind* and not simply *of some kind or other*.

["an individual something"], which, insofar as they do not explicitly introduce kinds, better preserve the vagueness of the Greek.[14] This seems desirable, since a necessarily unique substance that is not a specimen of any kind (like, e.g., the Prime Mover) should be *tode ti* if Aristotle takes being *tode ti* to be a requirement for being a substance.[15]

This desideratum can, however, be satisfied either by (a) "this something" or by (b) "some this" (which takes '*ti*' to play the role of an indefinite article as in "*anthrôpos tis*" or "some man").[16] Each has the advantage that it (like the Greek) is compatible with typological essentialism but does not require it. And since there are parallels in different passages for each construction, we ought to follow the suggestion that Frede and Patzig make without implementing and allow that Aristotle uses '*tode ti*' both ways—meaning "this something" in some contexts and "some this" in others. This, however, leaves us with the task of deciding on independent grounds what Aristotle requires when he says that a substance must be *tode ti*. Is he—as "some this" seems to suggest—requiring that substances be *individuals*? Or is he—as "this something" (understood as "this F-thing") suggests—emphasizing the role that *kinds* play in the identity and individuation of substances?[17]

Categories 3b10–18 associates being *tode ti* with being indivisible and one in number in the way that primary substances (like individual men and horses) are, and then argues that a secondary substance like Man or Animal, because it is said of many things, is not *tode ti* [or "some this"] but rather *poion ti* [or "some such"]. This suggests that Aristotle associates being *tode ti* with being indivisible and one in number in a way in which universals, which are said of many things, are not. Like Frede and Patzig, many commentators have thus taken the *Metaphysics*' requirement that a substance be *tode ti* as requiring that substances be individual rather than species-forms. The standard objection to this has been that it leaves primary substances unable to satisfy the requirement that substances be knowable and definable, since Aristotle denies that individuals are proper objects of knowledge and definition.[18]

---

[14] I do not understand Frede and Patzig's claim [Vol. 1, p. 20] that Bonitz emphasizes only the demonstrative component, for this seems to me to be the one thing he fails to capture. Perhaps Frede and Patzig are conflating individuality with demonstrability, possibly on the Aristotelian grounds that one cannot point to a universal [see *Posterior Analytics* 87b28–33]. Another passage (besides the one discussed in section 5 below) where Frede and Patzig's translation seems both unnecessarily interpretive (even for their own purposes) and controversial is Met. 1028a36–1028b2, where they render "*hotan ti esti ho anthrôpos gnômen ê to pur*" as "wenn wir wissen, was z.B. *ein bestimmter Mensch ist* oder was *ein bestimmtes Feuer ist*," thus representing Aristotle as asking explicitly about some particular man or fire rather than—as the Greek permits—about Man or Fire in general; and "*hotan ti esti to poson ê to poion gnômen*" as "wenn wir wissen, was das so Bemessene oder das so Beschaffene ist."

[15] It is, however, possible that Aristotle takes the requirement that a substance be *tode ti* only as the *specific* version (i.e., the version applying to *perceptible* substances) of some more *general* requirement (applying to *all* substances) of oneness or indivisibility.

[16] The German would be either (a) 'dieses Etwas' or (b) 'ein Dies' (or perhaps 'ein gewisses Dies').

[17] These are salient (not exclusive) options. I return to this issue in section 8 below; see especially note 58.

[18] I think this objection mistaken, since Aristotle argues [in *Metaphysics* Z 15 and at *Rhetoric* 1356b29–33] only against knowledge of *particulars* (i.e., *material* individuals) and not against knowledge of individuals as such. For this distinction, see note 4 above.

A common alternative, intended to escape this objection, is to deny that the *Metaphysics* retains the *Categories*' commitment to the priority of individual substances to the kinds to which they belong. Some commentators even suggest that the *Metaphysics* reverses this priority, taking species or species-forms—insofar as they provide criteria for the identity and individuation of their individual members—as prior to these individuals. Such commentators tend to view Aristotle's development as a gradual return to the Platonism against which the youthful *Categories* rebelled.[19] But this makes it difficult to explain Z's extended argument that no universal is a substance—an argument that (according to Frede and Patzig) makes Z look more (rather than less) anti-Platonic than the *Categories*. For the *Categories* allows that Man and Animal are substances, even if only secondary ones.[20]

3. THE CLOSET PLATONISM OF FURTH'S *CATEGORIES*

One of the most interesting and distinctive parts of Furth's book is his chapter on the *Categories*, where he presents a novel alternative to the two common pictures of the mature Aristotle: either as returning to Platonism (Owen) or as finally escaping the grip of the Platonic picture (Frede-Patzig). Furth begins by comparing the task of reconstructing the views expressed in Aristotle's various works on logic, method, nature, and metaphysics with that of reconstructing a colossal ancient statue, parts of which are clearly missing and parts of which are clearly duplicated because the sculptor experimented with various alternatives in the course of construction. Furth takes the *Categories* as a relatively perfect miniature, which served as a model for the larger work: a sort of *Prolegomenon* to the *Metaphysics* that deliberately avoids the complexities associated with form and matter.

What is surprising is that Furth, taking the *Categories* as his model, reconstructs a traditional and relatively Platonic *Metaphysics* according to which species-forms (rather than individual forms or compounds) are the primary substances. This is surprising because the salient feature of the *Categories* is surely its commitment to the primacy of individuals, and Aristotle could no doubt have avoided this commitment without having to introduce form and matter had he been writing the *Categories* with the *Metaphysics* up his sleeve. It makes more sense to view the *Categories* as a miniature *Metaphysics* if (like Frede and Patzig) one takes the primary substances of the *Metaphysics* to be individual forms. For that allows one to view the *Metaphysics*' identification of each thing with its essence as identifying each individual substance (i.e., each primary substance of the *Categories*) with its *individual form*. On this eminently

---

[19] See G. E. L. Owen, "The Platonism of Aristotle," *Proceedings of the British Academy* 51 (1966): 125–50; reprinted in Owen, *Logic, Science and Dialectic* (Ithaca, NY: Cornell University Press, 1986).

[20] See (2) in note 9 above for some evidence that the *Metaphysics* may at least implicitly retain the distinction between primary and secondary substance, thus allowing us to interpret Z 13 as arguing that no universal is a *primary* substance.

plausible view, the primary substances of the *Metaphysics* are simply the individual forms with which the primary substances of the *Categories* come to be identified, and it is easy to imagine Aristotle ignoring this complication had he intended the *Categories* as an introductory work.[21]

But Furth does not view the *Metaphysics* as continuous with the *Categories* in this way. He attempts to minimize the apparent distance between the *Categories* (which explicitly denies that species are each *tode ti*) and the *Metaphysics* (which Furth reads as taking species-forms to be each *tode ti*) by arguing that, even in the *Categories*, Aristotle is trying—admittedly obscurely—to express the view that "there is something 'thislike' about the substantial species" [p. 31]. On this view, the *Metaphysics* represents a sort of coming out for the closet Platonism of the *Categories*.

Furth begins with what he sees as the *Categories*' technical account of an individual as what is *not said* (or *essentially* predicated) of anything more determinate than itself in the way in which, for example, Color *is said* (or *essentially* predicated) of determinate colors like Red and White (insofar as Red and White are each *essentially* colors). Here Furth simply endorses the view, shared by Owen and Frede, that Aristotle recognizes non-substance individuals (such as a particular *shade* of white) that can be *in* (or *accidentally* predicated of) a plurality of subjects (but *not said* of them) in cases where a plurality of numerically distinct subjects (e.g., a plurality of men or horses) are indistinguishable *in color* (or whiteness) from one another.[22]

Furth then assimilates the indivisibility of substantial species (as distinct from genera) to the indivisibility of non-substance individuals: Man is indivisible in the sense that it (like a particular *shade* of white) is "a fully differentiated and not further differentiable species" [p. 31]. The idea is apparently that the individual men of which Man is said are not determinations *of Man* in the way in which particular colors are determinations *of Color*: the differences between individual men are differences not *of Man* but, for example, *of size, color, and location* (just as the differences between the "instances" of a particular shade of red are differences not *of Color* but, for example, *of size, shape, and location*).

Furth then claims that "in some way that is related to [this], Man (the species) . . . divides what it is said-of . . . into 'thises' in the sense that is 'true and beyond dispute' [*Cat.* 3b11]—in this case, the discrete individual men" [p. 31]. The point, as I understand it, is that Man divides what it is said-of *not* into "suches" (like Whiteman and Black-man) of which there might be a plurality of instances, *but rather* into non-repeatable "thises" (like Socrates and Callias). In this respect, indivisible species (like Man) differ from higher genera (like Animal), which divide what they are said-of

---

[21] Note, however, that the nominalism of Frede and Patzig's *Metaphysics* is not represented in the *Categories*. So taking the *Categories* as a miniature *Metaphysics* is more plausible if we resist their tendency to see the transition from the *Categories* to the *Metaphysics* as one from realism to nominalism.

[22] See G. E. L. Owen, "Inherence," *Phronesis* 10 (1965): 97–105 (reprinted in Owen, *Logic, Science and Dialectic*); and M. Frede "Individuen bei Aristoteles," *Antike und Abendland* 24 (1978): 16–31 (reprinted in translation in Frede, *Essays in Ancient Philosophy*, 49–71).

into "suches" (like Man and Horse) of which there might be a plurality of instances. Furth concludes that Aristotle's point is that Man is "not an individual but *a kind of individual*, in the sense of a kind in which individuals come" [p. 32].[23]

But since there is a sense in which least divisible species in non-substance categories are (on Furth's view) also kinds in which individuals come, Furth must—in order to distinguish species dividing what they are said-of into substance individuals from species dividing what they are said-of into non-substance individuals—assume that the individuals of which substantial species are said are individuals in a more fundamental way than that in which non-substance individuals are individuals. That, I take it, is the point of appealing to the "true and indisputable way" in which primary substances are said to be *tode ti* at *Categories* 3b11. Now the most important difference between primary substances and non-substance individuals as conceived by Furth is that primary substances are spatiotemporally unified in a way in which non-substance individuals are not. For a particular shade of white can be spatially scattered and can suffer temporal gaps in its existence in a way in which Socrates cannot. So on Furth's view, Man divides what it is said-of into spatiotemporally unified entities in a way in which least divisible species in non-substance categories do not. So Man is a "kind of individual" in the sense that it is a kind in which *spatiotemporally unified* beings come.

If this is the correct way to interpret the admittedly obscure view that Furth attributes to Aristotle, then Furth represents Aristotle as shifting from the technical account of an individual (as what is not said-of anything more determinate than itself) to a more familiar account involving spatiotemporal continuity under a substance sortal. This presumably expresses the "Western-philosophical concept of a material individual," which, according to Furth, Aristotle invented. But there is surprisingly little discussion here about just what this concept involves. This is unfortunate because of the general interest of Furth's account of the *Categories*.

4. FURTH: FROM SUBSTANCE *AS SUBJECT* TO SUBSTANCE *AS CAUSE*?

Furth views the *Metaphysics*' relocation of primary substance as a consequence of Aristotle's having replaced the *Categories*' subject criterion with a causal criterion according to which a substance is primarily that which causes an individual "to be what [it] is and a 'this'" [pp. 185--86]. Furth claims that once Aristotle has acknowledged the dependence (not explicit in the *Categories*) of individuals on the species to which they belong, he must admit that species (or species-forms) are the primary substances.[24]

---

[23] This sort of play on words is characteristic of Furth.
[24] There seems to be some tension in Furth's views about the *Categories*. Although he takes substance species to be the substances of individual men and horses [p. 232], he suggests on pp. 33–34 that the *Categories* is not explicitly committed to essentialism but is "compatible with a deviant interpretation under which some or all of the substantial individuals may be 'bare particulars' capable of retaining their numerical identities through arbitrary migrations between substantial kinds or out of the kinds altogether."

Their individual members (i.e., the *Metaphysics*' compounds) are still substances and have essences, but only in a derivative sense: because the essence of an individual compound is strictly identical with the essence of any other co-specific compound, its essence belongs strictly only to the species itself [pp. 235–36].[25]

This move would allow Furth to satisfy Z 13's explicit requirement that each essence be peculiar to that of which it is strictly the essence, as taking a species-form to be the essence of the individual members of its species would not. Furth aims similarly to respect Z 13's claim that no universal is a substance by defining a universal as "that whose nature is to belong to more than one substance in the sense of substantial specific kind," thus restricting universals in the category of substance to *generic* kinds [pp. 247–48]. But this definition is not only ad hoc (and question-begging against an opponent who counts the claim that no universal is a substance as evidence against the traditional view that species-forms are substances); it is also inconsistent with Aristotle's account of universals both in the *Organon* and in the *Metaphysics*.[26]

If Furth wants to explain Aristotle's claim that no universal is a substance in a way compatible with the traditional view, his best bet is to adopt the Woods-Code line, according to which species-forms are not universals, because they are predicated not of individuals but only of matter (which does not constitute any individual prior to form's being predicated of it).[27] This, however, will not solve the problem that in taking the *Metaphysics* to replace the subject criterion with a causal one, Furth overlooks not only the *Metaphysics*' repeated claim that substances are subjects, but also the way in which Z 13 appeals to the subject criterion in defending the claim that no universal is a substance.[28]

---

[25] On p. 247 Furth quotes Aristotle's claim [at 1038b14–15] that "things whose essence is one and whose substance is one are themselves one" and takes this to show that things whose substance and essence are one, are one only in *species* and *not* in number. But this does not show that things that are one in species do not have their own numerically distinct forms, as Aristotle's full statement of this view seems to require. Furth himself—*Aristotle: Metaphysics VII–X* (Indianapolis, IN: Hackett, 1985)—translates 1040b17 as saying, "the substance of what's one is one, and *things whose [substance] is one in number are one in number*." But Furth now ignores this passage in which Aristotle seems to be saying that it is a condition for the numerical distinctness of Socrates and Callias that their substances (i.e., their forms) be numerically distinct. The idea here seems to be that if the substance of Socrates were one in number (and not simply one in species) with that of Callias, then Socrates himself would be one in number with Callias. A less plausible alternative, given the context, is to take "one in number" as a one-place predicate and so to take Aristotle as saying that the substance of what is one in number must itself be one in number. This too might be taken to require individual forms, but one could attempt to avoid that conclusion by arguing (like Code, *Aporematic Approach*) that the species-form is one in number in the relevant sense.

[26] At *De Interpretatione* 17a38–b1 Aristotle says that a universal is what is "by nature such as to be predicated of many" [*ho epi pleionôn pephuke katêgoreisthai*] and then cites as his example Man, which is a specific (not a generic) kind. And at *Metaphysics* 1035b27–30, Aristotle takes Man and Horse (which are clearly species and not genera) to be over [*epi*] particulars, which is (according to *Met.* 999b35–1000a1) sufficient for their being universals.

[27] See note 4 above.

[28] See, e.g., Aristotle's reaffirmation of the claim that substance is subject at *Metaphysics* 1042a26. Note also that Z 13 argues that no universal is a substance on the grounds that "substance is what is not said of a subject, while the universal is always said of a subject" [1038b15–16].

On this point, Frede and Patzig rightly claim that the *Metaphysics* seeks to combine the subject criterion and the causal one so as to make primary substances *both* ultimate subjects *and* causes of being [Vol. 1, p. 37]. The key, of course, is to take the form of a compound as its essence (or formal cause) and so as the subject that persists through (and governs) any changes in its accidents [Vol. 1, pp. 40, 45–46]. But this threatens to lead to individual forms. For on this view, Socrates' form is *his* essence as well as *the subject* underlying changes in *his* matter and accidents. And it is a spatiotemporally unified individual that exists when and only when Socrates exists.[29]

5. MATTER AS SOURCE OF PLURALITY WITHIN SPECIES

Most of Furth's arguments against taking substantial forms to be individuals are at best inconclusive.[30] The strongest argument rests on the traditional view that Aristotle takes matter to be the source of plurality within species, something he would not have needed to do had he admitted a plurality of numerically distinct forms within each species. The idea here is that the only way to account for the distinction between two individuals that share the same species-form is by appeal to the numerical distinctness of their respective matters.[31] So if forms are immaterial, then there cannot be a plurality of forms within a species and any plurality within a species must be a plurality of compounds. On Furth's view, individuals come to be only when a species-form (which is not itself an individual) comes to be embodied in some matter, which again (being simply some stuff and not a countable thing) is not itself an individual. And the only

---

[29] Frede explains this view (in English) in "Substance in Aristotle's *Metaphysics*" (in his *Essays in Ancient Philosophy*, 73–80). I am not sure why Frede and Patzig [Vol. 1, p. 38] deny the claim (supported by *Generation and Corruption* 321b25–28 and 322a28–33) that form underlies matter, especially given their claim that the form "nimmt eine geeignete Materie an" [Vol. 1, p. 48]. But if they allowed form to include functional matter (in the way suggested in section 5 below) then it might be easier for them to view the form as a subject underlying the particular portions or quantities of stuff that constitute its functional matter at different times. Taking forms to include matter would thus assist them in explaining how Aristotle combines the subject and causal criteria.

[30] On pp. 193–94, Furth presents the following three arguments (in addition to the one discussed above) *against* individual forms: (1) Z 17 shows that Socrates' form, if it is to be the cause of Socrates' being, must be distinct from Socrates; (2) Z 8 [at 1033b29–1034a8, quoted and discussed here in section 5] shows that the form must *preexist* the compound and so "cannot temporarily coincide with it"; and (3) Z 8 and 15 show that "the form itself *cannot* either come-to-be or pass-away" and so (given Furth's argument on p. 194) that forms must be eternal.

Against (1), Z 6 argues that *some* things *must* (on pain of regress) be immediately identified with their essences and so with the causes of their being [1031b31–32]. The prime mover is, for example, *identical* with its form, which is not only the cause of its being but exhaustive of it; so (1) is false. Against (2), the form that preexists a compound may simply be the individual form *of its father*, which is the efficient cause of its *own* individual form coming to be embodied in the matter provided by its mother. This does not show that the compound cannot share its temporal boundaries with its own numerically distinct form. I discuss the inadequacy of (3) in section 7 below.

[31] But as I argue in "Form and Individuation in Aristotle" [Chapter 1, this volume], there is a problem here about how to account for the numerical distinctness of these individuals' respective matters without appealing to form.

proper individuals (besides necessarily unique immaterial substances like the Prime Mover) are compounds.

Frede and Patzig's translation of the locus classicus for this traditional view departs uncharacteristically (and unnecessarily for their purposes) from their practice of rendering Greek words uniformly whenever possible.[32] For as demonstrated by the translations of Ross and Bonitz, Frede and Patzig do not *need* to render '*eidos*' in three different ways in the course of the following paragraph (translated by Ross with all instances of 'form' rendering '*eidos*,' and with Frede and Patzig's alternative renditions enumerated in brackets):[33]

> In some cases it is even obvious that the producer is of the same kind as [*toiouton men hoion*] the produced (not, however, the same nor one in number, but in form [(1) *der Art nach*] as in the case of natural products (for man begets man).... Obviously, therefore, it is quite unnecessary to set up a form [(2) *Form*] as a pattern ... the begetter is adequate ... to the causing of the form [(2) *Form*] in the matter. And when we have the whole, such and such form [(2) *Form*] in these flesh and in these bones, this is Callias or Socrates; and they are different in virtue of their matter (for that is different), but the same in form [(3) *der Spezies nach*] (for the form [(3) *die Spezies*] is indivisible). [*Met.* 1033b29–1034a8][34]

Ross, of course, takes this passage to support the traditional view that Frede and Patzig are concerned to avoid. But Frede and Patzig argue (ad 1034a6) that the initial '*toiouton*' is intended to prevent the reader from mistakenly taking the relevant *eidos* to be one in number; and [ad 1034a7–8] that 1032a24's reference to the producer as *homoeidês* with

---

[32] Other less obviously motivated failures to render the same terms consistently wherever possible occur in Frede and Patzig at 1030a4–5 where '*hoper tode ti*' is rendered "was diese Sache eigentlich ist" (presumably justified by the controversial claim ad 1028a12 that '*tode ti*' is there epexegetic for '*ti esti*'); and at 1028b18 where '*para*'—which is usually rendered '*neben*' but sometimes rendered '*zusätzlich zu*' [1031b1 and b29] and once rendered '*ausser*' [1037a11]—is rendered '*über ... hinaus*.' This last departure is worrisome because '*über*' also renders '*epi*' as (at 1040b29) in the standard phrase used (except in the *Posterior Analytics*) to refer to Platonic forms (that is, '*hen epi pollôn*'). Note, however, that at 1035b27, where Aristotle is talking about "Man and Horse and the things that are in this way *epi* the particulars, but universally"—a passage often thought to be about Platonic forms—Frede and Patzig render '*epi tôn kath' hekasta*,' '*auf die Einzeldinge zutrifft*.' Perhaps Frede and Patzig would justify these departures by claiming that 1028b18 (where '*para*' is rendered '*über ... hinaus*') is about Platonic forms, while 1035b27 (where '*epi*' is rendered '*zutrifft auf*') is not. But it would be nice to have some note of this in the commentary, especially since many commentators have taken 1035b27 to be about Platonic forms.) Another such failure where the motivation is again clear is at 1040a3 where '*epistêmê*'—generally rendered '*Wissen*' [as at 1039b33]—is rendered '*die Kenntnis.*'

[33] Moreover, Aristotle could have varied his terminology along the lines suggested by Frede and Patzig, had he chosen to do so. For as alternatives to '*eidos*,' Aristotle often uses '*morphê*' to refer to form (as opposed to matter), and '*genos*' (especially in the biological works) to refer to species. So it may be significant that he chose to use '*eidos*' consistently throughout. (It is, however, probable that Aristotle would be reluctant to use '*genos*' for species *here*, given that the technical distinction between *eidos* and *genos* is just on the horizon.)

[34] Bonitz, like Ross, renders '*eidos*' with the same word ('*forma*') throughout.

the thing produced would be unintelligible if Aristotle thought that they had numerically the same form. This, if correct, would support reading this passage as requiring only that the numerically distinct forms of Socrates and Callias are *homoeidês* (or the same in species) with one another and it would do so even if we rendered '*eidos*' consistently as 'form' throughout. One might, however, wonder whether '*homoeidês*' must be taken as requiring numerically distinct forms: could not the producer and his product be *homoeidês* the sense that they share a unique form (whether or not Aristotle regards that form as one in number)?

There is, moreover, further apparent support for the traditional view in the following passage:

> For if there are more heavens <than one> just as there are men, the principle<s> for each will be one in *eidos* but many in number. But whatever <things> are many in number have matter (for one and the same *logos* is of many, e.g., of Man, while Socrates is one). But the *first* essence (*to ti ên einai . . . to prôton*) does not have matter, for it is actuality. So the first mover, being unmoved, is one both in logos and number. [*Met.* 1074a31–37][35]

Furth cites this passage (along with *De Caelo* I.9 and the locus classicus) in support of the traditional view, and it should be clear why.[36] For they seem to suggest that any plurality within a species must be a plurality of *compounds* (rather than forms) because only *matter* can distinguish one conspecific individual from another. But matters are not so simple.

Note first the implicit assumption (shared by Frede and Patzig) that forms, even if they must themselves be realized in a certain sort of matter, do not themselves contain any matter that might distinguish them from other, numerically distinct conspecific forms.[37] If we abandoned this assumption and allowed forms to contain matter, we could allow a plurality of forms within a species (though this would in some sense *also be* a plurality of *compounds*). So it is important to note in this connection Aristotle's claim [at 1074a35–36] that the *first* essence does *not* have matter. For there would be no point to this restriction if Aristotle did not allow *some* essences (or forms) to have matter. And this seems to suggest that Frede and Patzig should abandon their assumption of (4'). But this conclusion may be premature. For there are two different ways in which matter might account for the plurality of forms within a species, one of which takes forms to *include* matter and one of which does *not*.

First, the forms of perceptible substances may be (as Frede and Patzig argue) only *necessarily* (and not essentially) embodied in the sense that they *cannot exist* apart

---

[35] I accept Owens's arguments in *The Doctrine of Being in the Aristotelian Metaphysics*, 3rd edn. (Toronto: Pontifical Institute of Mediaeval Studies, 1978), 447–50, against the claim that this passage is an interpolation.
[36] On *De Caelo* I.9, see section 6 below and note 59.
[37] This is essentially (4'), attributed to Frede and Patzig at the outset.

from a certain sort of body.³⁸ In this case Aristotle may claim that the matter in which a form is *necessarily* embodied accounts for the numerical distinctness of that form from the forms of other conspecific individuals. This view differs from Furth's (which also takes the forms of perceptible substances to be necessarily enmattered) insofar as it allows material differences to yield the numerical distinctness of conspecific *forms* and not simply (as on Furth's view) the numerical distinctness of conspecific *compounds*.³⁹ But on this view, the numerical distinctness and individuality of forms is a *consequence* of their respective relations to matter, which is not itself a part of them. And this undermines Frede and Patzig's case for (2′). For this makes forms dependent for their individuality on matter, which is not itself a part of them, and so threatens the primacy of individual forms as such.

The second alternative is to take the forms of perceptible substances to be *essentially* embodied insofar as the matter in which they are embodied is in some sense part of the *essence* of these forms. This allows Aristotle to claim that the matter that plays a role in accounting for the plurality of forms within a species is itself part of the *essence* of these forms, with the result that conspecific forms can be essentially and non-derivatively numerically distinct from one another. On this account, individual forms are themselves compounds of a certain sort. So apparent evidence that any plurality within a species must be a plurality of compounds *need not* be taken as evidence against the view that there can be a plurality of individual forms within that species.

The second alternative better accounts for the view that individual forms are the primary substances of *Metaphysics* Z. For if (as the requirement that a substance be *tode ti* seems to suggest) a form qua primary substance must be *essentially tode ti* (and so *essentially individual*), then (as the requirement that substances be separable seems to suggest) a form should not depend for being individual or *tode ti* on its relation to any matter that is not in some sense a part of its being. And Aristotle can satisfy these requirements if he distinguishes the matter that belongs *essentially* to such forms (i.e., the functionally defined organic bodies and their parts) from the matter that belongs *only accidentally* to such forms (i.e., the particular portions or quantities of stuff that constitute the functionally defined bodies and their parts at particular times).⁴⁰ For he

---

³⁸ Aristotle explicitly recognizes the distinction between parts of the essence proper and necessary concomitants of a thing at *Metaphysics* 1025a30–34 and *De Anima* 402b16–25.

³⁹ This requires Furth to explain Aristotle's references to forms as (each) *tode ti* by saying that the species-form (qua cause of the matter's constituting an individual compound) is sometimes called *tode ti* derivatively from its relation to an individual compound that is strictly speaking *tode ti*. Although Furth's defense of this view by appeal to the *Generation of Animals* improves Ross's original suggestion, it does not avoid the problem that the best explanation of Aristotle's practice of calling the cause of something's being an individual *itself an individual* is his belief that the cause of something's having a certain property must itself have that property [*Met.* 993b34–38]. That is why Aristotle says both that if the principles of things were one only in form or species, then nothing would be one in number [1000b24–25]; and that the principles of particulars must themselves be particular [1071a20–21]. Frede and Patzig [Vol. 1, p. 52] rightly reject Ross's suggestion, but fail to see that they should for similar reasons reject this first alternative in favor of the second.

⁴⁰ I defend Aristotle's commitment to this distinction in my "Living Bodies," in M. Nussbaum and A. Rorty (eds.), *Essays on Aristotle's "De Anima"* (Oxford: Oxford University Press, 1992) [Chapter 3, this volume].

can then claim that any form the essence of which *includes* its belonging to such a body is *separable* (or self-contained) in a way in which any form the essence of which does not include its belonging to such a body is *not*.

Frede and Patzig's case for the primacy of individual forms would thus be strengthened by adopting the second alternative, and there seems to me to be nothing to prevent them from doing so. For as I shall now argue, their commitment to the first alternative rests on an unnecessary and unjustified reading of Z 10–11. I choose to discuss these chapters in detail both because of the importance traditionally attached to them and because I think Frede and Patzig's sophisticated and subtle account of these chapters one of the most interesting parts of their commentary.

6. FREDE, PATZIG, AND SOCRATES THE YOUNGER

Aristotle argues in Z 10 and 11 that not all the parts of a thing are mentioned in the definition of that thing: the definition is of the form alone, so it mentions only those parts that belong to a thing's form. Aristotle then asks in Z 11 what sorts of parts are parts of the form and what sorts of parts are parts not of the form but of the thing taken together with its matter. He asks in particular about parts like the flesh and bone in which the human form always appears, whether they too are parts of the form or whether they are rather matter that we are unable to distinguish from the form because the form does not also appear in different sorts of matter in the way in which the form of a circle appears in different sorts of matter—some in stone, some in bronze, and so on. Aristotle then objects to the practice of those philosophers (possibly Pythagoreans) who eliminated not only perceptible matter (like stone and bronze) but also intelligible matter (or extension) from the forms and definitions of geometrical objects: circles and lines are *essentially* extended and so cannot be *defined* without reference to intelligible matter (or extension), which must (given the requirement that only parts of the form appear in a definition) belong to the *forms* of geometrical objects. Aristotle then criticizes Socrates the Younger's definition of Man on what appear to be similar grounds: in reducing all things in this way [*houtô*] and eliminating matter (presumably perceptible) from the definition of Man, he

> leads away from the truth and makes us suppose that man can exist without his parts, just as the circle <can exist> without bronze. But the case is not similar. For an animal is presumably something capable of perception[41] and cannot be defined without change, and so, not without its parts being in a certain state. [*Met.* 1036b23–30]

---

[41] I have adopted Frede and Patzig's plausible suggestion (discussed below) that we read '*aisthêtikon*' ("capable of perception") rather than '*aisthêton*' ("perceptible"), so as to make my argument as acceptable as possible to them. This, however, raises a question about what in their view counts as an "acceptable" reading not to be departed from: for '*aisthêton*' is shared not only by EJ but by *all* available manuscripts.

Because Aristotle introduces his criticism of Socrates the Younger by saying that it is "going too far to reduce all things in this way and to eliminate matter, for some things are presumably this in this [*tod' en tô(i)d'*] or these <things> in this <state>," the most natural way to read Z 11—especially the claim that the case of man is "not similar" to that of the circle—is as parallel to E 1, where Aristotle distinguishes the objects of physics (which include souls) from the objects of mathematics by arguing that the essences of physical objects contain perceptible matter in a way in which the essences of mathematical objects do not. For Aristotle's standard example of a "this in this" is the one introduced in E 1—namely, that of *snubness* (i.e., concavity in a nose) or *the snub*. And the point there is that physical objects resemble *the snub* (the definition of which must refer to the subject to which it belongs—namely, a nose) while mathematical objects resemble concavity (the definition of which does *not* refer to the subject to which it belongs).[42] If we take Z 11 in this way, as parallel with E 1, its point is that the definition (and so also the form or essence) of Man contains perceptible (as opposed to intelligible) matter in a way in which the definition (and so also the form or essence) of Circle does not.

Frede and Patzig nevertheless resist this interpretation: they reject the parallel with E 1 on the grounds that E 1 admits a distinction between definitions of forms and definitions of compounds, while Z 11 admits no such distinction, because it allows that there are definitions of compounds only insofar as there are definitions of their respective forms.[43] Frede and Patzig argue that since Z 11 (unlike E 1) no longer admits definitions of compounds that include matter, we should interpret Z 11 as claiming *not* that Socrates the Younger is *mistaken* in eliminating perceptible matter from the definition of Man but *only* that his account is *misleading* insofar as it might lead someone to suppose that a man can *exist* without those parts without reference to which he can be *defined*. Since a definition refers only to parts of a thing's form or essence, the difference between Frede and Patzig's account and the preceding one is a difference (as described in section 5 above) between taking the forms of perceptible objects to be *only necessarily* embodied (in the sense that they *cannot exist apart* from a certain sort of body) and taking such forms to be *essentially* embodied in the sense that they *cannot be defined apart* from a certain sort of body).

There is, however, a slight complication here. Frede and Patzig take Z 11 to distinguish *three* sorts of cases in which a form always appears with certain parts (not necessarily its own): first, cases (like that in which all circles were as a matter of fact embodied in bronze) where it is difficult [*chalepon, Met.* 1036b2–3] but not impossible to separate the form of the circle from bronze in thought because the form of the circle

---

[42] For this view, see also *Physics* II.2.
[43] Frede and Patzig [ad 1036b29] allow that E 1 could be taken as compatible with their reading of Z 11 if we took 1026a2–3 with Ross, as saying only that natural things (as opposed to their definitions) have matter. They decline, however, to do so and stick with the more plausible reading of Kirwan, who takes this passage as asserting that the accounts themselves include matter. See C. Kirwan, *Aristotle's Metaphysics* (Oxford: Oxford University Press, 1971), 185–86.

is only "externally" related to bronze (which is clearly matter and no part of the form of a circle); second, cases where it is not just difficult but impossible for us [*adunatoumen*, 1036b7] to separate a form in thought from some part because that part is matter that is "internally" related to that form; and third, cases where it is again not just difficult but also impossible to separate a part in thought, but this time because that part is itself part of the form.

Frede and Patzig argue that confusion arises here because we possess no criterion for distinguishing cases of the second sort from those of the third. This leads to two kinds of mistake. We may mistake some part that is only matter (but matter internally related to a certain form) for part of the form. Or we may, conversely, mistake part of the form for matter that is only internally related to that form. Those who eliminate intelligible matter from the definitions of geometrical objects make the second sort of mistake. Frede and Patzig take Aristotle to be accusing Socrates the Younger of making the first sort of mistake—that of mistaking matter that is only internally related to the human form for part of that form.

Frede and Patzig's case for taking the human form to be internally related to a certain sort of matter is apparently related to their proposal to read '*aisthêtikon*' (i.e., capable of perception) rather than '*aisthêton*' (i.e., perceptible) at 1036b28.[44] For they defend this proposal on the grounds that without it we lose the fundamental Aristotelian thought that the relation between form and matter is so close in living things (as distinct from artifacts) that only an actually ensouled body can serve as the matter of a living thing. This suggests that we take Aristotle's view—that the organic body and its functionally defined parts cannot exist in the absence of soul—to capture the sense in which the matter of a man is internally related to its form in a way in which the matter of an ax is not.[45] But according to Frede and Patzig, it should *not* be taken to follow from this that the form or definition of a man *contains* matter in a way in which the form or definition of an ax does not. What follows is only that the definition of Man should *imply* (apparently in a way in which the definition of an ax does not) that the definiendum (which is a purely immaterial form) must be realized or embodied in a certain sort of matter.

There are, however, several problems with Frede and Patzig's account. Note first that after arguing (in Z 10) that definitions refer only to the parts of a thing's form, Aristotle goes on (in Z 11) to ask what sorts of things are parts of the form and what sorts of things are not, obviously with an eye to determining what is and is not mentioned in the definition of a thing. Now if in this context Aristotle had intended a distinction between what is explicitly mentioned in a definition and what is only implied by what is mentioned in that definition, one might expect him to make some attempt

---

[44] This reading is also adopted by Irwin in *Aristotle's First Principles*; see p. 569, n. 39.

[45] On Aristotle's view that the organic body and its functionally defined parts are *essentially* ensouled, see M. Burnyeat, "Is an Aristotelian Philosophy of Mind Still Credible?" and the discussions of it by Nussbaum and Putnam; Cohen; and Whiting [Chapter 3, this volume] all in the Nussbaum and Rorty volume cited in note 39 above.

to alert his reader (or auditor) to that fact, especially since it is fundamental to his argument and he has the resources with which to do so. For he claims elsewhere that having angles equal to two right angles is *not* part of the essence or definition of a triangle but rather something that is somehow implied by its essence or definition.[46] Moreover, Frede and Patzig's account requires Aristotle's criticism of Socrates the Younger to be misleading in precisely the way in which *it* accuses Socrates the Younger's account of being misleading. For as evidenced by centuries of commentary, Aristotle's criticism fails to make clear that the definitions of natural objects should imply matter without mentioning it.

More important, however, is the fact that Frede and Patzig do not provide adequate justification for rejecting the apparent parallel with E 1. For even if E 1 distinguishes definitions of forms from definitions of compounds and allows for definitions of compounds in a way in which Z 11 does not, this plays no role in these chapters' arguments, which are parallel in the relevant respects. The primary contrast in E 1, as in Z 10–11, is between two kinds of objects or essences and not between forms and compounds. Z 10 begins [at 1034b24–26] by distinguishing circles (which *do not* contain the segments into which they are divided) from syllables (which *do* contain the letters into which they are divided), but switches [at 1035a4–6] to E 1's distinction between concavity and snubness, and then [at 1035a9–10] back to that between circles and syllables again. And Z 11's claim [at 1037a22–24] to have explained "why in the case of some things the *account of the essence* [*ho logos tou ti ên einai*] has the parts of the thing being defined, while in the case of other things it <i.e., the account of the essence> does not" is matched by E 1's claim [at 1025b30–32] that there are two kinds of *definienda or essences*, some like the snub and some like the concave [*esti de tôn horizomenôn kai tôn ti esti ta men hôs to simon ta d' hôs to koilon*]. This explains why Aristotle says that the case of man and that of the circle are "not similar," and it removes the alleged puzzle about why Aristotle returns (immediately after criticizing Socrates the Younger) to the mathematical examples [at 1036b32–1037b5].

Why then do Frede and Patzig think it necessary to distinguish Z 11 from E 1? Perhaps because they take Z 10's conclusion that forms alone are the proper objects of definition to exclude the possibility that any proper definition should refer to matter, which is supposed to be unknowable and indefinable. Here, however, it is important to distinguish the organic body and its functionally defined parts, which can be known and defined in terms of their functions, from the various unknowable and indefinable portions of stuff that constitute these bodies and their functionally defined parts at different times. For if (as suggested above) the forms of some things are essentially (and not just necessarily) enmattered in the sense that these forms *include* functionally defined matter, then Aristotle can allow that the definitions of these things refer to matter without violating the requirement that forms and forms alone are the proper objects of definition. To assume otherwise is to beg the question. And Frede and Patzig

---

[46] See again *Metaphysics* 1025a30–34 and *De Anima* 402b16–25.

should by their own admission be less confident about their conclusion. For it requires them to distinguish things that (according to them) Aristotle says we have no criterion for distinguishing.[47]

This—in conjunction with the way in which allowing form to include functionally defined matter would strengthen their case for the primacy of individual forms—completes my argument that Frede and Patzig should abandon (4′) in favor of the view that the individual forms of natural objects are themselves material in the sense that they *essentially* include material parts.

7. THE GENERATION (AND DESTRUCTION) OF FORMS

Abandoning the generic premise of which (4′) is an instance—i.e., the premise that forms are themselves immaterial in the sense that they do not have any material parts—helps to explain not only how forms *can* be particulars (and hence individuals) but also how (pace both Furth and Frede-Patzig) forms can be generated and destroyed, as seems to be required by Aristotle's explicit references to perishable (and hence generable) forms at *Physics* 192b1 and *Metaphysics* 1060a22.[48] I introduce this issue briefly here for three reasons: (1) to provide an example (primarily for the lay reader) of how unwarranted the confidence with which Furth asserts some of his views may be;[49] (2) to illustrate how taking forms to include matter can remove certain exegetical difficulties (like the one raised by Aristotle's references to perishable forms); and (3) to prepare the way for the suggestion that we should give more consideration to the view (given short shrift by Frede-Patzig and Furth) that Aristotle recognizes *both* individual forms *and* (universal) species-forms (of which individual forms are instances).

---

[47] Here Frede and Patzig could perhaps profit from Furth's illustrative account (in sec. 23) of how solving the problem of the unity of substance requires Aristotle to redraw the form-matter (or actuality-potentiality) distinction *within* form (or actuality) itself.

[48] On the way in which particularity entails individuality and is associated with perishability, see note 4 above. If forms are particulars, they will be perishable (and hence generable). I want to *allow* that forms are particulars (without, however, building it into translations) insofar as the functional matter that belongs to their essence is at any given time necessarily constituted by some particular portion of perceptible matter, thus yielding a sense in which they are identified (or at least necessarily coincident) with particular compounds.

[49] Lay readers should also beware of various forms of slippage in Furth's translations. For example, Furth [p. 15] renders '*to ti leukon*' "the particular shade of light color," thus building into his translation a gratuitous reference to a *shade* (as opposed to a particular *occurrence* of that shade); the Greek itself is *indeterminate* on this point. Furth then renders the grammatically similar '*ton tina anthrôpon*' "the individual man," thus using 'individual' in the grammatical position where he had previously used 'particular shade of' [p. 29]; and he goes on [p. 44] to render other grammatically similar expressions (like 'F ti') sometimes as "a sort of F" and sometimes as "a particular sort of F." For another example, see p. 151, where Furth renders '*toiô(i)di*' as "this" (rather than "such") which—although it captures the sense of Aristotle's claim—does not faithfully represent Aristotle's use of his own technical terms. Since I discuss elsewhere what I take to be inaccuracies in Furth's account of Aristotle's biology, I shall not discuss these issues here. See my "Comment on Furth," *Proceedings of the Boston Area Colloquium of Ancient Philosophy* (1986): 268–73.

Furth's third argument against individual forms is roughly that Z 8 and 15, in showing that forms are not produced and cannot come to be or pass away, show that forms must be eternal and so that Aristotle is talking about species-forms (which are eternal) and not about individual forms (which exist when and only when their respective compounds exist). Z 8 is supposed to show that forms do not come to be because of its claim [at 1033b18–19] that "in everything generated, matter is present." But this argument fails if we abandon (4′) and allow some forms to include matter.

Furthermore, *even if* we retain (4′) and accept Furth's view that Z 8 and 15 rule out the generation and destruction of forms on the grounds that forms do not include matter, it does not follow that forms are eternal. For Aristotle allows in Z 15 that some things "are and are not without generation and perishing," and he clearly has forms in mind because he goes on (obviously referring back to Z 8) to say, "for it has been shown that no one generates or produces these" [1039b25–27; cf. 1033b5–8]. Frede and Patzig—presumably because of their commitment to (4′)—take this to show that individual forms, though not themselves subject to a *process* of coming to be or passing away, nevertheless are and are not when their respective compounds (which *are* subject to processes of coming to be and passing away) are and are not.

Furth "hopes that [Aristotle] is not trying to mean this because that is one of those things it is impossible to mean" [p. 194]. Furth's hope springs eternal at 1043b14–16, where Aristotle offers an alternative: *either* forms are perishable without perishing and have come to be without coming to be *or* they are eternal. Furth concludes, "I take Aristotle to be stating that the form is eternal because of the nonsensicality of the alternative. At least, the alternative really being nonsensical, the principle of charity recommends this reading" [p. 195].

There are, however, numerous passages (besides the one in Z 15) where Aristotle allows that some things are and are not without undergoing processes of generation and perishing—e.g., *Physics* 247b1–14; *De Caelo* 280b20–34; *PN* 446b4–5; *Metaphysics* 1044b21–26; and *Nicomachean Ethics* 1174b9–13. Aristotle even argues [at *Met.* 1027a29–32] that there *must* be principles that are and are not without generation and perishing since otherwise all things would be from necessity. Charity demands that we try to make sense of these passages.

Here, however, there are alternatives to Frede and Patzig's proposal that it is *individual* forms that are and are not without generation and perishing. One is to allow that Aristotle recognizes *both* individual forms *and* universal forms and to say that Aristotle takes individual forms to come to be and pass away in a way in which universal forms—which are and are not without generation and perishing in the sense that they are when they have instances and are not when they lack instances—do not. On this view, individual forms come to be and pass away insofar as the compounds with which they are identified come to be and pass away.[50] But universal forms "are and are

---

[50] This is suggested by Z 8's claim that one can produce a form accidentally [or coincidentally, *kata sumbebēkos*] because the bronze sphere (i.e., the compound) is a sphere (i.e., a form) and one makes that (i.e., the bronze sphere).

not without generation and perishing" insofar as they are simply instantiated at some times and not at others.⁵¹ There are several things to be said for this view.

First, it allows us to make sense of Aristotle's explicit references to perishable forms at *Physics* 192b1 and *Metaphysics* 1060a22. Second, it allows us to take the distinction [at *Met.* 1039b24–25) between *being-a-house* (which does not come to be or pass away) and *being-this-house* (which does come to be and pass away) quite naturally, as a distinction between a universal form (or essence) and an individual form (or essence), and not, as Frede and Patzig suggest, as one between an individual form and its respective compound. This is supported by the parallel in *De Caelo* I.9, where Aristotle characterizes the distinction between being-a-circle (or being-a-heaven) and being-this-circle (or being-this-heaven) as one between a circle (or heaven) *haplôs* and a particular [*kath' hekaston*] circle (or heaven). For it is clear from Z 10 and 11 that the distinction between the circle *haplôs* and the *kath' hekaston* circle is one between a universal and a particular.⁵² Furthermore, this alternative, in admitting universals, admits objects of knowledge in a way in which Frede and Patzig's view does not. I shall return to the importance of this in section 8. The important point here is simply that there is more than one sensible alternative to concluding that forms must be eternal.

8. TYPOLOGICAL ESSENTIALISM WITHOUT TYPES?

At this point, I should like to turn briefly to Aristotle's biological works, which are often thought to provide some of the strongest evidence not just for individual forms but for individual forms that include matter—albeit (according to some commentators) at the expense of the *Metaphysics*' alleged typological essentialism. Balme, for example, appeals to the priority Aristotle assigns to the particular in reproduction to argue that the species-form is not an efficient cause of individual development but rather a *consequence* of two facts: first, that our reproductive mechanisms are geared to produce offspring resembling their parents (principally their fathers) in as many details as possible; and second, that individuals in similar circumstances, being benefited by similar

---

⁵¹ See Irwin, *Aristotle's First Principles*, p. 266. I take Aristotle to distinguish species-forms (which are eternal insofar as they *always* have instances) from non-substance universals (which can be instantiated at some times and not at others). And I think that when Aristotle talks of what is and is not without generation and destruction, he tends to have the latter in mind [as at *Met.* 1044b21–24]—though he is sometimes thinking of both [as at 1039b20–27], this last passage being one in which Aristotle applies the same term both to a genus and (more strictly) to one of its species. Another possibility—suggested in section 8 below—is to distinguish biological kinds or species (as constituted by their extensions) from the universals actualized in thought and then to take the kinds to be eternal (insofar as they always have instances) while saying that the universals actualized in thought are and are not without generation and destruction because thought itself (being an *energeia*) is and is not without generation and destruction. Either account suggests that 1043b14–16 refers *not* to exclusive alternatives but to two kinds of forms—those which are eternal and those which are and are not without generation and perishing.

⁵² *Metaphysics* 1035a25–b2 distinguishes the particular circle from the circle *haplôs*, while 1036b32–1037a5 distinguishes the particular circle from the *katholou* circle.

features, will (given Aristotle's teleology) come to resemble one another.⁵³ On this view, similarities—and hence groups of individuals resembling one another—will be reproduced at practically all levels of generality from Socrates' family on up, with the members at each level resembling one another progressively less closely as the resemblances become more and more generic. So this view has been taken to undermine the privileged position traditionally accorded to species: they are simply one among other similarity classes resulting from the tendencies of offspring to resemble their parents and to develop in similar ways in similar circumstances.⁵⁴

Those (like Pellegrin) who study Aristotle's classifications of animals—particularly his flexible use of classificatory terms like '*genos*' and '*eidos*'—claim that their results confirm this conclusion.⁵⁵ It is thus somewhat surprising that Furth embraces the anti-essentialist views of Balme and Pellegrin in support of his view that Aristotle is a typological essentialist who not only privileges species-form but crowns it *primary substance*.⁵⁶ For such anti-essentialism seems more congenial to Frede and Patzig's nominalism, according to which Z rejects the existence of those universals that the *Categories* took to be secondary substances (i.e., species and genera in the category of substance). But it is not clear that Frede and Patzig can afford such nominalism without compromising their typological essentialism. For what, we might ask, is the force of '*ein dies von der Art*' supposed to be in the absence of the *kinds* in which the *thises* come? Given the absence of substantial kinds, would not "some this" provide a better rendering of '*tode ti*'?

Here, however, I think we must suppose that Frede and Patzig would distinguish substance species and genera conceived as *universals proper* from substance species and genera conceived roughly as *kinds* (i.e., as sets or classes of individual substances). For insofar as mere kinds are constituted by individual members each of which is itself a primary substance, the author of Z would (according to Frede and Patzig) have found them unproblematic in a way in which universals proper are not. The problem with species and genera conceived as universals proper is (according to Frede and Patzig) that the author of Z could not bring himself to put them either in the category of substance or in any non-substance category and so had to conclude that they did not

---

⁵³ D. Balme, "Aristotle's Biology Was Not Essentialist," in Gotthelf and Lennox (eds.), *Philosophical Issues in Aristotle's Biology*, 291–312. (On the priority of the particular in reproduction, see *Generation of Animals* IV.3, esp. 767b24–768aI 1.) Compare the way in which Frede and Patzig speak about a form's being aimed not simply to survive as *an object* of a certain kind but as *some particular object* of the relevant kind [Vol. 1, p. 45].

⁵⁴ P. Pellegrin, "Aristotle: A Biology without Species," in A. Gotthelf (ed.), *Aristotle on Nature and Living Things*, 95–115.

⁵⁵ P. Pellegrin, *Aristotle's Classification of Animals*, A. Preus (trans.) (Berkeley: University of California Press, 1982).

⁵⁶ I do not mean to suggest that the flexible use of terms like '*genos*' and '*eidos*' in the biological (or other) works is incompatible with typological essentialism. My point is only that Furth's conjunction of typological essentialism with the anti-essentialist reading of the biological works cries out for explanation of a sort that Furth does not provide.

exist [Vol. 2, p. 246].⁵⁷ But this does not require the author of Z to reject the existence of substantial kinds conceived roughly as sets or classes of individual substances grouped according to their similarities with one another.

This, however, leaves open the possibility of the endless variety of overlapping kinds at all levels of generality attested in Aristotle's biological works and no clear algorithm for determining the relative epistemological significance of these various kinds. It does not get us anything like the privilege that typological essentialism usually accords to *infimae species*, and this is a view for which the *Metaphysics* contains abundant evidence. So without disputing the richness and complexity of Aristotle' biological theory and practice, I want to suggest briefly that the *Metaphysics* contains *both* more evidence *and* less difficulty than Frede and Patzig allow for the reality of substance universals conceived as existing in a plurality of subjects.

First, the "more evidence" claim: Aristotle says at the end of *Metaphysics* M 9 that knowledge is not possible without universals [1086b5–6]. He then proceeds (in M 10) to solve the *aporia* according to which knowledge is impossible *both* if the principles of substance are particular (in the sense that they are *not* repeatable in form or kind) *and* if the principles of substance are universal (in the sense that they *are* repeatable in number) by arguing that the principles of substance must be *repeatable in form but not in number*: the aporia is resolved if they are individual (and non-repeatable) instances of a repeatable form or kind.⁵⁸ This, I take it, is part of the point of calling them '*tode ti*,' which Aristotle often uses to pick out an individual instance of some kind—for example, *this* (as opposed to *that*) *F*.⁵⁹ Moreover (as we saw at the end of section 7 above), *De Caelo* I.9 provides support for taking Z.15's distinction between being-a-house and being-this-house as a distinction between a universal form and an individual form. *De Caelo* I.9 also supports taking the universal form to be the essence and object of

---

⁵⁷ Frede and Patzig's argument moves too quickly here. They might consider an argument parallel to the one that they offer [Vol. 2, p. 48] about matter, which they claim is not as such (i.e., as matter) in any category, but which they do not therefore conclude does not (according to Aristotle) exist. Aristotle's references to matter as substance are presumably to be explained by appeal to the fact that matter constitutes items in the category of substance, and Aristotle might locate universals in the category of substance (or some other category) in a similar way: universals may appear both in substance and in non-substance categories insofar as they exist potentially in the substance and non-substance items that actually belong in those categories. This suggestion receives some support from Aristotle's association of universals with matter and potentiality at *Met.* 1087a16–17. [N.b., I speak here of the author of Z to refer to Aristotle at the time when he was writing Z, so as to allow that he may at some point(s) have held a different view.]

⁵⁸ The idea here is roughly that we must take the principles of substances to be *repeatable in kind* (in order to avoid the first arm of the dilemma) and *non-repeatable in number* (to avoid the second).

⁵⁹ See *De Caelo* I.8 where Aristotle argues that if there were a plurality of worlds the same in form, the elements in each would have to move to their own particular places—the water or air in this world to *this* (as opposed to some other) middle [*pros tode ti meson*] and the earth or fire in this world to *this* (as opposed to some other) extreme [*pros tode ti eschaton*]. This provides some support for rendering '*tode ti*' as "this something," which is compatible with the '*ti*' sometimes picking out a kind (as in "this animal, e.g., the Horse"). It is also compatible with there being a derivative use of '*tode ti*' to mean "some this."

definition, thus suggesting that Aristotle acknowledges *both* universal *and* individual forms and attaches epistemological importance to the former.⁶⁰

Now for the "less difficulty" claim, which I can at this point only sketch and not defend: if we take seriously Aristotle's claim that universals proper are somehow in the soul and actualized in thought and we distinguish these universals from the kinds to which the concrete individuals (in which these universals exist only potentially) belong, we can allow that Aristotle combines a realist account of biological kinds (the existence of which is mind-independent and determined by facts about reproduction) with a conceptualist account of universals (the actual existence of which is mind-dependent).⁶¹ The appropriate model here is perhaps the account of time that Aristotle presents in *Physics* IV.14, where time is said to be the number of motion and so to be incapable of existing in the absence of an enumerating soul *even though* what Aristotle calls the "substratum" of time—that is, the motions that are there to be enumerated—might exist in the absence of any such enumerator.⁶² On this account, universals proper (like time) would not exist in the absence of minds that are capable of actualizing them in thought, even though the substrata of these universals—that is, the biological kinds—might exist in the absence of any such minds.⁶³

This would allow us to explain how universals are necessary for *knowledge*—which is after all mind-dependent—without being necessary for the existence of those realities (or substances) that we take to be the ultimate objects of knowledge.⁶⁴ It may also help to answer the familiar question about why Z 15 appears where it does—i.e., after Z 13 and 14. The point may be to remind the reader that there is knowledge (or understanding) of individuals *only* insofar as they are instances of substantial kinds, so that

---

⁶⁰ *De Caelo* I.9 distinguishes *being-an-F* (which is the form itself in itself [*autê kath' hautên hê morphê*, 277b35] and the essence [*to ti ên einai*] and object of definition) from *being-this-F* (which is the form mixed with the matter [<*hê morphê*> *memigmenê meta tês hulês*, 277b35] and one of the particulars). Taking the former to be universal is supported by its association with *the F-haplôs*, which is here (as in Z 10) opposed to *the kath' hekaston* F; cf. note 51.

⁶¹ *De Anima* 417b23–24 says that universals (which it distinguishes from particulars) are '*pôs*' in the soul.

⁶² See *Physics* 223a25–28, which I take to suggest that even if time (qua number of motion) could not exist in the absence of soul (qua enumerator), the substratum [*ho pot' estin*] of time (i.e., motion) might nevertheless be able to exist in the absence of soul *qua enumerator* even if not in the absence of soul *qua mover*. There is a problem about how the counterfactual condition could be fulfilled, if one and the same thing (i.e., soul) is supposed to serve both as enumerator and as mover, but this need not prevent us from drawing the conceptual distinction that Aristotle attempts to draw in this passage. Moreover, it may be reasonable to assume that the unmoved mover cannot be an enumerator lest (in the process of enumerating) it itself be subject to change.

⁶³ Compare *Metaphysics* 1010b30–1011a2, where Aristotle allows that the substrata of perception (i.e., the objects perceived) might exist in the absence of perceiving subjects; and *De Anima* 426a15–25, where the actual (but not the potential) existence of sound and flavor are said to require the actual existence of hearing and taste.

⁶⁴ This is equally true if following Burnyeat—"Aristotle on Understanding Knowledge," in E. Berti (ed.), *Aristotelian Science: The Posterior Analytics* (Padua: Editrice Antenore, 1981), 97–139—we take '*epistêmê*' as 'understanding' (rather than 'knowledge').

we do not (like Frede and Patzig) mistakenly conclude from Z 13 and 14 that there are no universals corresponding to items in the category of substance.[65] Such universals are actualized in thought, where they represent the truth about individual forms qua members of their respective kinds. This explains the sense in which I take the truth to lie in a proper synthesis of the views of Frede-Patzig and Furth.[66]

---

[65] I say "corresponding to" since these universals need not themselves be in the category of substance. They may be in the category of quality (if thoughts are) or [as 1056b35–1057a1 suggests] in the category of relatives. If, however, we allow that the *Metaphysics* implicitly retains the distinction between primary and secondary substance—as suggested in note 9 above, point (2)—we may allow such universals to be in the category of substance in whatever way the secondary substances of the *Categories* are.

[66] I should like to thank Terry Irwin and Johanna Seibt for written comments on previous drafts of this notice. I am also grateful to Gisela Striker for her advice and—as usual—critical encouragement.

5

Locomotive Soul

THE PARTS OF SOUL IN ARISTOTLE'S SCIENTIFIC WORKS

ARISTOTLE MAKES A remarkable move in *De Anima* (*DA*) III.7: he suggests at 431a8–14 that the desiring part of soul [τὸ ὀρεκτικόν] is in some sense the same as the perceiving part of soul [τὸ αἰσθητικόν]. The idea seems to be that feeling the sort of pleasure and pain that Aristotle associates with desire and aversion is part of what is involved in perceiving things as good and bad, so that perceiving something as good or bad *involves* desire or aversion. This is remarkable insofar as it seems obvious that one can perceive something (e.g., giving up alcohol) as good without desiring to do it, and that one can perceive something (e.g., unsafe sex) as bad without having any aversion to it. Moreover, Aristotle himself—insofar as he recognizes the possibility of incontinence—must to some extent agree. So what is going on here?

One might seek to explain 431a8–14 by arguing that Aristotle is speaking here only of *non-rational* animals, who are blissfully ignorant of the phenomenon of incontinence, and that it is only in the next lines [*DA* 431a14–23] that he turns to the example of *rational* animals, who are all too familiar with this phenomenon. I doubt, however, that this is the best way to explain this passage.

For even if we take the next lines to focus on the case of rational animals and to state that imagination [φαντασία] plays for them the role played by perception in the case of non-rational animals, a similar problem still arises: it seems possible that a subject's imagination should represent something as good (perhaps even good all-things-considered) without her desiring to do it, and that a subject's imagination should represent something as bad (perhaps even bad all-things-considered) without her having any aversion to it. Moreover, other texts (to be examined below) provide a strong case for taking Aristotle in some sense to identify the desiring part of soul not only with the perceiving part but also with the imagining part.

I want in fact to argue that what we have here is ultimately a single unified part of soul, which (because it is the part responsible for moving the animal) I shall call the "locomotive" part, though Aristotle's canonical term for it is τὸ αἰσθητικόν. My thesis is that these capacities constitute a single, functionally integrated part of soul that has two aspects—one an internal, representational aspect and the other an external, behavioral aspect—each aspect being inseparable from the other insofar as an animal's behavior is for the most part an expression of its representational states (including perceptual appearances, beliefs, and desires). This perceptive/locomotive part differs from the nutritive part characteristic of plants, and probably also from the theoretical part characteristic of gods, these being the three canonical parts recognized in Aristotle's scientific account of soul. And though the perceptive/locomotive part is more complex in rational than in non-rational animals, it is still—even in the case of rational animals—a single unified part. Moreover, it is (in rational animals) the part in which phronêsis resides. Or so I shall argue.

1. PRELIMINARY POINTS

It is worth noting, before we proceed, that labels such as τὸ αἰσθητικόν, τὸ φανταστικόν, and τὸ ὀρεκτικόν are ambiguous. They might refer either to the *capacities* of soul in virtue of which an animal perceives, imagines, and desires. Or they might refer to the *parts* of soul with which an animal does these things. So in order not to build any prejudice into my translations, I shall translate the -ικόν forms with similarly ambiguous '-ive' forms (or with some equivalent such as "what is capable of . . . -ing"): τὸ αἰσθητικόν as "the perceptive" (or "what is capable of perceiving"), τὸ φανταστικόν as "the imaginative" (or "what is capable of imagining"), and τὸ ὀρεκτικόν as "the desiderative" (or "what is capable of desiring"). This practice is useful in that it leaves us open to the possibility that Aristotle may use the -ικόν forms to refer to different things in different passages, sometimes to capacities of soul and sometimes to the parts of soul in which these capacities reside. It thus leaves us open to the possibility that he assigns distinct *capacities* of soul to a single *part* of soul—the perceptive and desiderative capacities (for example) to the part that I call "locomotive."[1]

---

[1] Aristotle does not himself tend to speak of a locomotive capacity or part in a way parallel to that in which he speaks of these other capacities or parts—i.e., as τὸ κινητικόν. This may be because of the ambiguity of τὸ κινητικόν, which might refer either to what can move something else (in the way that the relevant part of soul might move the animal) or to what is itself capable of moving or being moved (in the way that the animal itself might be capable of moving or being moved). But it may also be—as I shall argue here—that Aristotle wants to avoid suggesting that the locomotive capacity or part is *a distinct* capacity or part *beyond* the capacities or parts just mentioned. On the view defended here, the locomotive part of soul is *constituted* by the desiderative, perceptive, and imaginative capacities *functioning together* in something like the way in which the various senses function together to constitute the common sense.

Another point worth noting before we proceed is that Aristotle recognizes different kinds of separability together with different kinds of separation. The kinds of separability relevant for present purposes are roughly as follows. First, there is the kind familiar from Plato's discussions of the soul and body in the *Phaedo* and elsewhere. Plato seems to think that the soul is separable from the body in the sense that it *can exist* apart from the body.[2] This kind of separability involves some sort of capacity for independent existence: *A* is separable in this way from *B* if and only if *A* can exist apart from *B* (which may or may not be able to exist apart from *A*). This corresponds to the sort of unqualified separability that Aristotle distinguishes from separability in account when he says [at *Metaphysics* (*Met.*) 1042a26–31] that the form of a thing is τῷ λόγῳ χωριστόν, while the compound (of form and matter) is χωριστὸν ἁπλῶς. The form is separable only in account because it cannot exist apart from some matter or other in which it is embodied; but the compound of form and matter is separable ἁπλῶς insofar as it contains everything required for its existence. Separability ἁπλῶς can thus be viewed as a kind of self-sufficiency. Aristotle believes that substances (from the prime mover on down to individual plants and animals) are separable in this sense, while their qualities and quantities (for example) are not: a quality is always the quality *of* some substance, so qualities lack the sort of unqualified separability—or self-sufficiency—characteristic of substances. The prime mover is of course maximally separable in this sense: it can exist apart from all other things, none of which can exist apart from it. But even individual animals are separable in this sense insofar as they can exist apart from one another: each is a self-sufficient whole capable of existing apart from other such wholes.

Aristotle's notion of separability ἁπλῶς seems to be similar to his notions of separability in magnitude [μεγέθει] and separability in place [τόπῳ]. For he seems to regard separability in magnitude and separability in place in much the same way, and he contrasts each with separability in account in much the same way that he contrasts separability ἁπλῶς with separability in account.[3] Still, however, I think we should distinguish separability ἁπλῶς from separability in magnitude and separability in place (which are intimately related to each other). For things can be separable in magnitude from one another—or separable in place from one another—without being separable ἁπλῶς: a hand, for example, may be separable both in magnitude and in place from a foot in the sense that each is composed of distinct and non-overlapping bits of matter, even though neither has the kind of self-sufficiency required for separability ἁπλῶς.

And the locomotive part is simply the same part—considered from a different point of view—as the perceiving part (which Aristotle identifies with the imagining and desiring part): talk of this part as "locomotive" simply emphasizes the external or behavioral aspects of the internal representational states that are emphasized in talk of it as "perceptive," "imaginative," and "desiderative."

[2] See, e.g., *Phaedo* 67 A, where Plato speaks of the soul after death as existing αὐτὴ καθ' αὑτήν . . . χωρὶς τοῦ σώματος.

[3] See, e.g., *DA* 413b14–15, in (2)(A) below, where Aristotle asks of various capacities of soul whether they are separable only in account or *also* in *place* (as if these were the two primary kinds of separability); and 432a18–20, in (9)(A) below, where he asks whether what moves the soul is separable either in *magnitude* or in account (as if *these* were the two primary kinds of separability).

As we have seen, Aristotle contrasts each of these kinds of separability with separability in account, which is a matter of *definitional* (as distinct from existential) independence. The idea seems to be that A is separable in account from B if and only if A can be *defined* without reference to B (whether or not B in turn can be defined without reference to A). Here, however, we should distinguish separability in account (or definition) from mere *difference* in account (or definition). X might be *different* in account from Y without being *separable* in account from Y. For what it is to be Y might be *different* from what it is to be X, even though what it is to be X cannot be defined without *reference* to Y. For example, what it is to be a color is different from what it is to be a surface, even if what it is to be a color cannot be defined without reference to surface. This distinction is important because it leaves open the possibility that Aristotle might say that desire and perception are different in being from one another even if he thinks that desire (for example) cannot be defined without reference to perception (specifically, to perception of something as good or pleasant). In this case, desire and perception would be more intimately related to one another than either is related to nutritive activity (assuming that nutritive activity can be defined without reference to desire or perception, and that desire and perception can be defined without reference to nutritive activity). And this, I think, is the sort of view that Aristotle ultimately adopts.

One last point about separability: things can be different (and perhaps even separable) in account from one another without being separable from one another in magnitude or place. For example, the white in this sugar cube and the sweet in this sugar cube are different (and presumably separable) in account from one another, since what it is to be white is different from what it is to be sweet. But they are inseparable from one another in magnitude and place insofar as each is the affection of one and the same portion of matter.

It will be useful, as we proceed, to keep in mind the way in which Aristotle would apply these various kinds of separability to the parts of an animal's body, both in relation to one another and in relation to the body as a whole. For I want to suggest that his conception of animal souls and their parts is modeled on his conception of animal bodies and their parts. The animal bodies in question here are *living* or *ensouled* bodies. For a corpse is only homonymously a body of the relevant sort: it is an animal body only in name and not in account.[4] An animal body is a self-sufficient whole capable of existing apart from other such bodies. Its parts are functionally defined and as such cannot exist apart from the whole, a detached eye or hand being only homonymously an eye or a hand. But the whole may exist apart from at least some of them: the whole can, for example, survive the loss of an eye or hand but not the loss of its heart. The important point here is that the parts are inseparable from the whole in the sense that they cannot exist apart from it. This means that they are to some extent inseparable from one another: no part can exist in the absence of there being enough of the right sort of parts

---

[4] See *DA* 412b18–27, where Aristotle applies to the body as a whole the homonymy principle that he elsewhere applies to bodily parts. (For the application to bodily parts see *Meteorologica* 390a10–12 and *Generation of Animals* 734b24–27.) I discuss this issue in my "Living Bodies," in M. Nussbaum and A. Rorty (eds.), *Essays on Aristotle's "De Anima"* (Oxford: Oxford University Press, 1992), 75–91 [Chapter 3, this volume].

to constitute a whole of the relevant kind. But the parts are generally separable both in account and in magnitude and place from one another. The functions of the stomach are different from the functions of the brain, so the account saying what it is to be a stomach is different from the account saying what it is to be a brain. And the stomach and the brain are realized in different bits of matter, as a result of which they are separable both in magnitude and in place from one another. Let us turn, then, keeping these examples in mind, to Aristotle's conception of an animal's *soul* and *its* parts.

2. THE UNITY OF SOUL IN GENERAL

Let me begin by noting that the *De Anima*'s positive account of soul is framed, from start to finish, as much by concerns about the separability of the capacities or parts of soul from one another as by Aristotle's more often discussed concerns about the separability of soul from body. At the end of Book I, after surveying the views of his predecessors and before embarking on his own positive account of soul, Aristotle says,

(1)(A) Since knowing and perceiving and believing belong to the soul, and, further, appetite and wishing and generally all desires [ἐπεὶ δὲ τὸ γινώσκειν τῆς ψυχῆς ἐστὶ καὶ τὸ αἰσθάνεσθαί τε καὶ τὸ δοξάζειν, ἔτι δὲ τὸ ἐπιθυμεῖν καὶ βούλεσθαι καὶ ὅλως αἱ ὀρέξεις]—and <since> locomotion [ἡ κατὰ τόπον κίνησις] and also growth and maturity and decay occur in animals by <means of> the soul—is it to the whole soul [ὅλῃ τῇ ψυχῇ] that each of these belongs? And is it with all <the soul> that we think and perceive and move and do and suffer each of the others [καὶ πάσῃ νοοῦμέν τε καὶ αἰσθανόμεθα καὶ κινούμεθα καὶ τῶν ἄλλων ἕκαστον ποιοῦμέν τε καὶ πάσχομεν]? Or is it with different parts <that we do> different things [ἢ μορίοις ἑτέροις ἕτερα]? And living [τὸ ζῆν]: is it in some one of these, or also in several or all <of them>? Or is there also some other cause of it? [*DA* 411a26–b5]

(B) Some say it <sc., the soul> is divisible into parts [μεριστήν], and that through one <part> it thinks and through another <part> it desires [ἄλλῳ μὲν νοεῖν ἄλλῳ δὲ ἐπιθυμεῖν]. What then holds the soul together if it is by nature divisible into parts [τί οὖν δή ποτε συνέχει τὴν ψυχήν, εἰ μεριστὴ πέφυκεν]? For it is not in any case the body. For, on the contrary, the soul seems rather to hold the body together: at any rate when it <sc., the soul> has gone out <of the body>, <the body> dissipates and rots. If then some other thing makes it <sc., the soul> one, that thing would be most of all soul [ἐκεῖνο μάλιστ' ἂν εἴη ψυχή]. And it will be necessary to enquire in turn into *that*, whether *it* is one or has many parts. For if *it* is one, then why is not it true straightaway [εὐθέως] that the soul too is one?[5] But if *it* is divisible into parts [μεριστόν], the argument will again

---

[5] I take this to be a rhetorical question, suggesting a way to block an alleged regress, like the one at *Metaphysics* 1031b31–32: 'Yet what prevents some things in fact being straight away (their own) essence, if [or: since] the essence is substance? [καίτοι τί κωλύει καὶ νῦν εἶναι ἔνια εὐθὺς τί ἦν εἶναι, εἴπερ οὐσία τὸ τί ἦν εἶναι;]'

inquire what it is that holds *that* together, and in this way <the argument> will proceed ad infinitum. [*DA* 411b5–14; cf. 402b9–13]

(C) <And if the soul is divisible into parts>, someone might also puzzle about the parts of it, what capacity each has [τίν' ἔχει δύναμιν ἕκαστον] in the body. For if the whole soul holds the whole body together, it is also appropriate for each of its parts to hold together some <part> of the body. But this seems impossible. For what sort of part intellect [ὁ νοῦς] will hold together, and how, is difficult even to imagine. And plants when divided appear to live, and even among animals some insects <do so>, as having <in each division> the same soul in form even if not in number <with the whole> [ὡς τὴν αὐτὴν ἔχοντα ψυχὴν τῷ εἴδει, εἰ καὶ μὴ ἀριθμῷ]. For each of the parts has perception and moves in place for some time. If they do not survive, this is nothing strange. For they do not have the <bodily> organs to preserve their nature. But nonetheless all of the parts of the soul belong in each of the parts <of the division> and they <sc., the parts of soul> are the same in form with one another and with the whole, since they <sc., the parts of soul> are not separable from one another, although the soul as a whole is divisible [ἀλλ' οὐδὲν ἧττον ἐν ἑκατέρῳ τῶν μορίων ἅπαντ' ἐνυπάρχει τὰ μόρια τῆς ψυχῆς, καὶ ὁμοειδῆ ἐστιν ἀλλήλοις καὶ τῇ ὅλῃ, ἀλλήλων μὲν ὡς οὐ χωριστὰ ὄντα, τῆς δ' ὅλης ψυχῆς ὡς διαιρετῆς οὔσης].[6] And even the principle <of life> in plants [καὶ ἡ ἐν τοῖς φυτοῖς ἀρχή] seems to be a kind of soul [ψυχή τις]. For animals and plants have this alone in common. And this can be separated from the perceptive principle [χωρίζεται τῆς αἰσθητικῆς ἀρχῆς], but nothing has perception without this [i.e., without the nutritive principle].[7] [*DA* 411b14–30; cf. 408a10–13, 412b23–25]

---

[6] I translate the Oxford Classical Text prepared by Ross, except where noted. See W. D. Ross, *Aristotelis De Anima* (Oxford: Clarendon Press, 1956). Ross reads τῆς δ' ὅλης ψυχῆς ὡς <u>οὐ</u> διαιρετῆς οὔσης here, thus departing from the manuscript tradition. I follow the tradition and omit 'οὐ.' This makes better (and perfectly good) sense of the genitive absolute, which Ross abandons in his later commentary in spite of the fact that it appears in all the manuscripts (W. D. Ross, *Aristotle De Anima* [Oxford: Clarendon Press, 1961]). The point of the genitive absolute is clearly concessive: *although the soul as a whole seems to be divisible in the sense that plants and even some insects can continue to live after being divided, nevertheless* (Aristotle here claims) the parts of the soul are not separable from one another.

[7] Aristotle is clearly referring here to the nutritive principle or capacity, which he identifies at *DA* 416a19 with the generative principle or capacity. He sometimes refers to this as the nutritive soul [ἡ θρεπτικὴ ψυχή], which he says at *DA* 415a23–25 is the "first and most common capacity [δύναμις] of soul, in virtue of which living belongs to all [living] things." Aristotle routinely contrasts this both with ἡ αἰσθητικὴ ψυχή and with ἡ νοητικὴ ψυχή (as at *Generation of Animals* (*GA*) 736b8–14 = passage (16) below). But he never, as far as I know, speaks of ἡ κινητικὴ ψυχή, ἡ ὀρεκτικὴ ψυχή, or ἡ φανταστικὴ ψυχή. I take this to provide some (admittedly inconclusive) support for my claim that he recognizes only three fundamental parts of soul, some of these parts, however, having multiple capacities. Just as ἡ θρεπτικὴ ψυχή has both nutritive and generative capacities, so too, I argue, ἡ αἰσθητικὴ ψυχή has both desiderative and imaginative capacities in addition to perceptive (and locomotive) ones.

The examples used in (1)(B)—namely, νοεῖν and ἐπιθυμεῖν—are of special interest here. For in using these examples Aristotle is explicitly raising the question whether one part of the soul thinks while another part (appetitively) desires. And he is indicating that the regress argument presented in (1)(B) is supposed to tell even against the apparently basic distinction between a part that thinks and a part that (appetitively) desires.

The regress argument appears of course to apply to any sort of division of the soul into parts. But we must keep in mind that this passage is aporetic: Aristotle has just set out the various *endoxa* and is now raising puzzles to be resolved later in the work. So we should not assume straightaway that he himself accepts the regress argument as it is presented here. As we shall soon see, his real target seems to be the division of soul into separable parts (in some yet to be specified sense or senses of 'separable'). This is foreshadowed in (1)(C), where he (apparently in his own voice) takes the phenomenon of divided insects to suggest not that the soul is not divisible into parts, but rather that the parts—or at least some of them—are inseparable from one another. The parts mentioned here are the parts responsible for perception and locomotion. And his choice of examples is once again significant: for insofar as locomotion involves desire, he is implicitly suggesting the inseparability of perception from desire (which fits with their apparent identification in the non-aporetic passage from *DA* III.7 with which I began).

The inseparability of perception from desire is explicit when he returns to the phenomenon of divided insects in his own positive account of soul in *De Anima* I.2:

> (2) (A) For now, let only this much be said, that the soul is the principle [ἀρχή] of the [activities] mentioned and is defined by <capacities for> these— by nutritive, perceptive, and cognitive <capacities> and by motion [θρεπτικῷ, αἰσθητικῷ, διανοητικῷ, κινήσει].[8] Whether each of these is <a> soul or <a> part of soul [ψυχὴ ἢ μόριον ψυχῆς], and if <a> part of soul, whether in such a way as to be separable in account only [χωριστὸν λόγῳ μόνον], or also in place [ἢ καὶ τόπῳ], is in some cases not difficult to see, while other cases are puzzling. For just as in the case of plants some evidently live when divided and separated from one another— the soul in these being one in actuality in each plant, but potentially

---

[8] It is worth noting the shift here from talk of capacities or of what has these capacities (i.e., the shift from θρεπτικῷ, αἰσθητικῷ, and διανοητικῷ) to talk of motion itself (i.e., to κινήσει) (on which see note 1 above). It is also worth noting here that the initial list of capacities by which the soul is determined contains no mention of τὸ ὀρεκτικόν as such (though Aristotle does mention it in a similar list at *DA* 414a31–32). This may be because Aristotle is assuming that τὸ ὀρεκτικόν is implicitly included here on account of its coincidence with τὸ αἰσθητικόν (asserted in *DA* III.7) or on account of its coincidence (argued in *DA* III.10) with what moves the animal—perhaps even (as I am arguing) on account of its coincidence with "both." A comparable point could be made about τὸ φανταστικόν, which is not only *not* mentioned here but is (unlike τὸ ὀρεκτικόν) *never* mentioned in any such list. What we have here are references to the three fundamental parts or capacities of soul mentioned in note 7 above, together with reference to an activity that (I argue) belongs to the so-called perceptive part. My suggestion is that Aristotle here omits reference to the desiderative and imaginative capacities as such because he thinks that they too belong to the perceptive part; and that he refers to motion itself, rather than to a locomotive part or capacity, so as not to suggest that the locomotive part or capacity is a distinct part or capacity.

more <than one> [ὡς οὔσης τῆς ἐν αὐτοῖς ψυχῆς ἐντελεχείᾳ μὲν μιᾶς ἐν ἑκάστῳ φυτῷ, δυνάμει δὲ πλειόνων]—similarly we see this happening in the case of other differentiae of soul [περὶ ἑτέρας διαφορὰς τῆς ψυχῆς] in the divisions of insects: for each of the parts has perception and movement according to place, and if perception also imagination and desire [εἰ δ'αἴσθησιν, καὶ φαντασίαν καὶ ὄρεξιν].[9] For where there is perception <there are> also pleasure and pain, and where these <are>, of necessity <there is> also appetite [ἐπιθυμία]. [DA 413b11–24]

(B) Concerning νοῦς and the theoretical capacity [περὶ δὲ τοῦ νοῦ καὶ τῆς θεωρητικῆς δυνάμεως] nothing is yet clear, but it seems to be a different kind of soul [ἀλλ' ἔοικε ψυχῆς γένος ἕτερον εἶναι], and this alone to be capable of being separate [καὶ τοῦτο μόνον ἐνδέχεσθαι χωρίζεσθαι][10] just as the eternal <is> from the perishable. That the remaining parts of soul [τὰ δὲ λοιπὰ μόρια τῆς ψυχῆς] are not separable [χωριστά] as some say <they are>[11] is plain from these <phenomena>.[12] But that they are different in account is plain [τῷ δὲ λόγῳ ὅτι ἕτερα, φανερόν]. For being capable of perception is different from being capable of believing, since perceiving <is different> from believing [αἰσθητικῷ γὰρ εἶναι καὶ δοξαστικῷ ἕτερον, εἴπερ καὶ τὸ αἰσθάνεσθαι τοῦ δοξάζειν]. And similarly also with each of the other <differentiae of soul> mentioned. [DA 413b24–32]

(2)(B) distinguishes the theoretical capacity from the capacities that are associated in (2)(A) with locomotion and action—i.e., the capacities (or perhaps the parts of soul in which they reside) responsible for perception, imagination, and desire. The point here is not primarily that the theoretical capacity is separable from the body in the sense that it can exist apart from the body (though it may well be). For this is not what the phenomenon of the divided insects makes "plain." The point is rather that the theoretical capacity seems to be separable from the other capacities

---

[9] There is controversy about this passage because Aristotle seems to be of two minds about whether having perception is sufficient for having imagination. DA 415a10–11 seems to allow that there are animals that have perception without imagination, as a result of which some commentators have suggested that we delete 'καὶ φαντασίαν', while others have suggested that we put the comma after 'καὶ φαντασίαν' (yielding "and if perception *and* imagination, then also desire"). But Aristotle goes on in DA 433b31–434a5 to suggest that animals having only touch may have an indeterminate sort of φαντασία corresponding to the indeterminate ways in which they move, and he connects this with the fact that they feel pleasure and pain, and so must have ἐπιθυμία. So I have adopted the traditional punctuation. But Aristotle may well think the reference to φαντασία dispensable, since he makes the point about the connection between perception and desire without any mention of φαντασία at De Somno 455b29–30. In any case, the textual issues are helpfully discussed by R. D. Hicks in his *Aristotle, De Anima* (Cambridge: Cambridge University Press, 1907), ad 413b22, 428a10ff., 433b31–434a5.

[10] Reading ἐνδέχεσθαι (following Simplicius) rather than ἐνδέχεται (with Ross).

[11] See Plato *Timaeus* 69 D ff.

[12] One reason for thinking that Aristotle's target is not the division of soul into *any* sort of parts but rather the division of the soul into *separable* parts is the fact that here (as elsewhere), where he is clearly speaking in his own voice, he speaks without hesitation of parts of soul.

(or parts) of soul in a way in which the other capacities (or parts)—at least those mentioned in (2)(A)—are *not* separable from one another: *it seems to be capable of existing apart from these other capacities in a way in which they are not capable of existing apart from one another.*

The fact that the nutritive capacity (or part) is not mentioned in (2)(A) raises a question about whether Aristotle takes it to be separable from the capacities (or parts) mentioned there in a way in which those capacities (or parts) are not separable from one another, or whether—as (2)(B)'s blanket reference to "the remaining parts of soul" may seem to suggest—the nutritive capacity (or part) is inseparable from the capacities (or parts) mentioned in (2A) in the same way that they are inseparable from one another. He clearly thinks that the nutritive capacity (or part) is separable from the others in the sense that it can exist in plants in the absence of the other capacities (or parts) [*DA* 413a31–b1]. So the question here is whether it is inseparable from the other capacities (or parts) in creatures that have *both* sorts of capacities (or parts).

One might argue that, even in creatures with both, the nutritive capacity (or part) is separable from the others in the sense that it can survive and function without the others in a creature with irreversible coma. But it is not clear that Aristotle would argue this way. For it seems plausible to suppose that he takes the relevant claim about separability to be one that applies "for the most part" [ὡς ἐπὶ τὸ πολύ] in the sense that it applies to *non-defective* members of the relevant kinds: otherwise his analogous claims about the inseparability of touch from the "higher" senses like sight and hearing might threaten to rule out the possibility of a blind or deaf animal that nevertheless retains its sense of touch. Here, however, Aristotle would presumably say that a blind man (for example) lacks *not* the relevant capacity or part of soul, but only the bodily conditions required for its exercise. For he suggests in (1)(C) that divided insects have *all* of the parts of soul in *each* of their divided parts and that the failure of the divided segments to survive is a matter *not* of their lacking the nutritive *capacity* but rather of their lacking the bodily organs required to *actualize* this capacity. And this fits what he says in *DA* I.4, where he suggests that the incapacities of perception and thought that are characteristic of old age are due not to the destruction of these capacities but rather to bodily impediments to their actualization: "If an old man were to receive the right sort of eye, he would see just as a young man does; so old age is due not to the soul's being affected in a certain way but rather to that in which [the soul resides being affected in a certain way], as in drunkenness and illnesses" [*DA* 408b21–9].[13] So even defective members of a kind may have all the capacities (or parts) of soul associated with membership in that kind.

My own view is that we should model Aristotle's way of distinguishing the various parts of soul and their fundamental capacities, however many they prove to be, on

---

[13] There is a serious question here, which I cannot now address, about the compatibility of this with Aristotle's hylomorphism. [On the sorts of explanatory asymmetries afforded by Aristotle's teleological framework, see Chapters 6, 7, and 9 of this volume, especially the discussion in Chapter 7, section 5.]

his way of distinguishing the various parts of an animal's body and their fundamental capacities, which is a strategy that makes prima facie sense, given his hylomorphism. This will allow us to say that one part of soul may house multiple capacities, just as the human tongue, for example, houses the capacities both to taste and to utter articulate sounds [*Parts of Animals* (*PA*) 660a18–25]. But more importantly for present purposes, it will allow us to say that just as the various parts of an animal's body cannot *exist* apart from one another even though they are *separable in magnitude or place* from one another in the sense that they are constituted by different portions of matter or located in different places, so too the various parts of an animal's soul cannot *exist* apart from one another even though they are *separable in magnitude or place* from one another in the sense that they are embodied in what we might call different "physiological systems"—i.e., physiological systems involving bodily organs that are constituted by distinct portions of matter and/or located in different places. The nutritive and reproductive capacities are embodied in one physiological system (for Aristotle takes what we should call the "digestive" and "reproductive" systems to form a single system), while the capacities of perception, imagination, and desire are (for the most part) embodied in a different physiological system from that in which nutrition and reproduction are embodied. Each of these physiological systems is centered in one and the same organ (namely, the heart), which helps to explain their unity with one another. But each can (at least in some circumstances) function relatively independently of the other. The nutritive system can function in comatose creatures and is (according to Aristotle) most active during sleep, when the other system is relatively inactive (though not altogether inactive given that dreams involve imagination) [*De Somno* 454b30–455a3]. And the other system—the 'perceptive' or 'locomotive' one, which is roughly equivalent to what we call the 'nervous' system, *functions* autonomously in divided insects (which lack the organs required for the functioning of the nutritive system but not the organs required for perception, desire, and locomotion).[14] But these systems cannot *exist* apart from one another: the loss or destruction of either spells the destruction of the whole.

This model allows us to say, as I think the texts suggest, that even if in animals the nutritive capacity (or part of soul) is inseparable from the capacities (or parts of soul) mentioned in (2)(A) in the sense that it and they cannot *exist* apart from one another, the nutritive capacity (or part) is nevertheless inseparable from these capacities (or parts) in a *different* way from that in which they are inseparable from one another: even if the nutritive capacity (or part) cannot in creatures with both *exist* apart from these capacities (or parts), it may nevertheless be separable in magnitude or place from them in the sense that it and they are realized in different physiological systems while they (all being realized in one and the same physiological system)

---

[14] One might object here that the perceptual system is a different system from the locomotive system, the organs of perception being different from the organs of locomotion. But we shall see from passage (8) both that and why Aristotle might regard the perceptual organs and the locomotive ones as constituting a single system. For their unity is in his view required to explain animal *motion* or *action*.

are not separable in magnitude or place from one another. This would explain why Aristotle explains *their* relationship to one another by saying that they are separable *only in account* from one another, but *never* says that the nutritive capacity (or part) is separable only in account from *them*.

For these reasons, I read passage (2) as claiming that the capacities of perception, imagination, and desire that constitute what I call "locomotive" soul are inseparable from one another not only in a way in which the theoretical capacity seems not to be inseparable from them but also in a way in which the nutritive capacity is not inseparable from them: the nutritive capacity is separable in magnitude or place from them, and the theoretical capacity (which cannot be separable in magnitude or place from them if it has neither magnitude or place) seems to be separable in the stronger sense that it is capable of *existing* apart from them. Here, however—as elsewhere—Aristotle remains agnostic about whether the theoretical capacity is in fact separable in this stronger sense. We shall return to this point. But we must now turn to Aristotle's reasons for taking the capacities mentioned in (2)(A)—the capacities that constitute locomotive soul—to be inseparable from one another in a *special* way, one in which the nutritive capacity (at least) is not inseparable from them. There are two sorts of reasons here: first, textual reasons that we might give for concluding that Aristotle did in fact take these capacities to be inseparable from one another in a special way; and second, philosophical reasons that Aristotle *himself* might have had for thinking that these capacities are inseparable in the relevant way.

3. EVIDENCE THAT ARISTOTLE IN FACT SEES A SPECIAL SORT OF UNITY AMONG THE CAPACITIES OF "LOCOMOTIVE" SOUL

Let me begin by citing some textual evidence that Aristotle did in fact take these capacities to be inseparable from one another in a special way. Consider first the passage mentioned at the outset:

(3) (A) Perceiving, then [τὸ μὲν οὖν αἰσθάνεσθαι], is like simply saying or thinking [ὅμοιον τῷ φάναι μόνον καὶ νοεῖν]. Whenever <the perceptible object> is pleasant or painful <the soul>, as if asserting or denying, pursues or flees <the perceptible object>.[15] And to feel pleasure or pain is to act with the perceptive mean toward the good or bad as such [καὶ ἔστι τὸ ἥδεσθαι καὶ λυπεῖσθαι τὸ ἐνεργεῖν τῇ αἰσθητικῇ μεσότητι πρὸς τὸ ἀγαθὸν ἢ κακόν, ᾗ τοιαῦτα].[16] And flight and desire, in actuality, are the same [καὶ ἡ φυγὴ δὲ καὶ ἡ ὄρεξις ταὐτό, ἡ κατ᾽ ἐνέργειαν].[17] And what is capable

---

[15] Cf. *Nicomachean Ethics* (*EN*) 1139a21ff.

[16] See also *Physics* 7. 3, esp. 247a16–17, where Aristotle says that pleasures and pains are alterations of τὸ αἰσθητικόν.

[17] As explained in the text below, I follow the manuscript tradition in reading ταὐτό rather than Bekker's (see note 18 below) τοῦτο.

of desiring and what is capable of fleeing are not different, either from one another or from what is capable of perceiving, but their being is different [καὶ οὐχ ἕτερον τὸ ὀρεκτικὸν καὶ τὸ φευκτικόν, οὔτ' ἀλλήλων οὔτε τοῦ αἰσθητικοῦ· ἀλλὰ τὸ εἶναι ἄλλο]. [DA 431a8–14]

(B) But to the thinking soul images are like perceptions [τῇ δὲ διανοητικῇ ψυχῇ τὰ φαντάσματα οἷον αἰσθήματα ὑπάρχει]. And whenever it [sc., the thinking soul] says or denies <that something is> good or bad, it pursues or avoids <that thing>; hence the soul never thinks without an image. And just as the air makes the pupil thus, and this [sc., the pupil] <affects> something different (and similarly in the case of hearing), the last thing is one, and one mean, but its being is more <than one> [τὸ δὲ ἔσχατον ἕν, καὶ μία μεσότης, τὸ δ' εἶναι αὐτῇ πλείω]. By what means it judges what is the difference between sweet and hot has been said earlier, but should be said also as follows. For it is some one thing, and <one> in the way a boundary [is] [ἔστι γὰρ ἕν, οὕτω δὲ ὡς ὁ ὅρος]. [DA 431a14–23]

This passage raises many questions, particularly concerning the applicability of the claims made in (A) to the thinking souls clearly in view in (B) (to which I shall return). And while I am at this point primarily concerned with sameness of τὸ ὀρεκτικόν and τὸ αἰσθητικόν asserted in (A), I have included (B) here because its implicit reference to the "common sense" will play an important role in the account I shall soon give of the probable reasons both for this identification of τὸ ὀρεκτικόν with τὸ αἰσθητικόν and for the identification of τὸ φανταστικόν with τὸ αἰσθητικόν that we find in the following passage:

(4) What is capable of imagining is the same as what is capable of perceiving, but what it is to be is different for what is capable of imagining and what is capable of perceiving [ἔστι μὲν τὸ αὐτὸ τῷ αἰσθητικῷ τὸ φανταστικόν, τὸ δ' εἶναι φανταστικῷ καὶ αἰσθητικῷ ἕτερον]. [De Insomn. 459a15–17][18]

It seems plausible to suppose, as I shall argue below, that the sort of sameness involved in the "sameness but difference in being" asserted in these passages is transitive. If this is right, then it follows from the conjunction of (3A) and (4) that τὸ ὀρεκτικόν, τὸ αἰσθητικόν, and τὸ φανταστικόν are (at least in non-rational animals) all the same in the relevant sense, though they clearly differ in being and account from one another (their accounts being accounts of what it is for each of them to *be*): what it is to be capable of desiring is not the same as what it is to be capable of perceiving, nor is what it is to be capable of perceiving the same as what it is to be capable of imagining. But what does it *mean* to say that A and B are "the same but different in being"? And *why* would Aristotle say that these capacities or parts of soul *are* "the same but different in being"?

---

[18] All translations from the *Parva Naturalia* are from the revised edition of the Loeb Classical Library text prepared by W. S. Hett (Cambridge, MA, 1957), which is based on Bekker's Berlin edition of 1831.

The first question here concerns the sort of *sameness* involved. For *Topics* I. 7 distinguishes three ways in which things are called the same. Things are called the same *in number* if there is one thing of which there are several names [ἀριθμῷ μὲν ὧν ὀνόματα πλείω τὸ δὲ πρᾶγμα ἕν], as in the case where we call one and the same thing a "mantle" and a "cloak." This is contrasted with cases where there are several things that are either the same in *form* (or in *species*) (e.g., several men or several horses) or the same in *genus* (e.g., several animals of different species). The sort of sameness involved in (3) and (4) is clearly sameness in number. For Aristotle's standard example of *designata* that are the same in number but different in being (or account) is that of the road-up and the road-down, where there is one subject—the road—which is called by different names.[19] But he draws further distinctions here in *Topics* I.7. Things are one in number in the primary and strictest sense when they are the same in name or definition [ὀνόματι ἢ ὅρῳ]—as in the case of the cloak and the mantle or that of man and biped animal. But things can also be one in number when one is a non-accidental property [τὸ ἴδιον] of the other, as in the case where what is capable of receiving knowledge is one in number with man (all and only men having this capacity); or when one is a (mere) accident [τὸ συμβεβηκός] of the other, as in the case where the seated thing or the musical thing is the same in number with Socrates. Moreover, as Aristotle elsewhere allows, the seated thing can also be the same in number with the musical thing because being seated and being musical both belong to the same subject (e.g., to Socrates).

There is some controversy here about which if any of these various sameness relations is what *we* call "identity," which is the equivalence relation that is distinguished from other equivalence relations (i.e., from other relations that are also reflexive, symmetrical, and transitive) by its conformity to Indiscernibility of Identicals (according to which if *a* is identical to *b*, then everything truly predicable of *a* is truly predicable of *b* and vice versa). For while it might seem that sameness in number (of whatever kind) corresponds to what we call "identity," Aristotle suggests [at *Physics* (*Ph.*) 202b14–16] that the Indiscernibility of Identicals is satisfied only by sameness in account, a cloak and a mantle having all the same properties while the road from Athens to Thebes and the road from Thebes to Athens (which are one in number but different in being) do not.[20] My own view is that Aristotle did not have precisely our notion of identity but that the notion of his that corresponds most closely to it is that of sameness in number, his notion of sameness in *both* number *and* being (or account) being *stronger* than our notion of identity. For *we* might well express the point he seeks to make at *Ph.* 202b14–16 by saying that although the road from Athens to Thebes is identical to—and thus has all and only the same properties as—the road from Thebes to

---

[19] Aristotle seems to use "same but different in being" interchangeably with "same but different in account." This makes sense given that the relevant account is a definition—i.e., an account of the being or essence of the *definiendum*.

[20] For some discussion of this issue see D. Charles, *Aristotle's Philosophy of Action* (London: Duckworth, 1984) [esp. chap. 1]; and T. H. Irwin's critical notice of it: "Aristotelian Actions," *Phronesis* 31 (1986): 68–89 [esp. 71–73].

Athens, still some of its properties belong to it qua running from Athens to Thebes (e.g., its being uphill and taking a relatively long time to traverse) while others belong to it qua running from Thebes to Athens (e.g., its being downhill and taking a relatively short time to traverse). But I cannot resolve this issue here. The important points for present purposes are (*a*) that the sort of sameness involved seems to be transitive; and (*b*) that in all the cases of sameness in number mentioned so far (whether involving sameness in being or not) there is a *single subject* that is called by multiple names, these names sometimes being the same in definition with one another, sometimes not. This suggests that Aristotle is saying of τὸ ὀρεκτικόν, τὸ αἰσθητικόν, and τὸ φανταστικόν that they are (or belong to) a single subject in the way that the road-up and the road-down are (or belong to) a single stretch of road.

Here, however, someone might object that Aristotle also presents a different sort of example of things that are the "same but different in being," an example involving two distinct subjects. For he says (in *Physics* III.3) that (actual) teaching and (actual) learning are the "same but different in being," and he explains this in terms of the existence of two distinct subjects, one of which has a capacity that is actualized *in* the other. The idea here is roughly that the actualization of the teacher's capacity to teach *just is* the bringing to actualization of the learner's capacity to learn, which is something that occurs in the learner (who is changed in this process in a way that the teacher is not).[21] And this, one might object, is a better model for the "sameness but difference in being" of τὸ ὀρεκτικόν and τὸ αἰσθητικόν: we might construe these things as distinct parts of soul one of which has a capacity that is actualized in the other in something like the way the teacher's capacity to teach is actualized in the learner. Just as the teacher teaches and as a (non-separable) result the learner learns, so too τὸ αἰσθητικόν perceives and as a (non-separable) result τὸ ὀρεκτικόν desires. By a "non-separable result," I mean—as Aristotle himself suggests in explaining the difference in being of teaching and learning—that one *just is* the actualization of the other [*Ph.* 208b8–10]. This suggests that teaching and learning are one in the way that a soul and its organic body are: teaching stands to learning as soul stands to the body whose essence or actualization it is. The proposal is thus that perceiving and desiring are one in a similar way: although each is the actualization of a distinct capacity, one stands to the other as form to functionally defined matter, the perception of something as pleasant or painful simply *constituting* a form of desire. This seems plausible at least in the case of non-rational animals, in whom perceiving something as pleasant seems inseparable from desiring it. It is of course less plausible in the case of rational animals, subject as they are to the phenomena of continence and incontinence, where the perception of something as *pleasant* may come apart from the perception of something as *good*.

I want, however, to bracket for the moment questions about rational animals and to ask whether Aristotle applies the proposed two-subject model to non-rational animals.

---

[21] This suggests—quite plausibly, I think—that 'to teach' is a success verb (however depressing some of us may find this).

For there seem to be good reasons for thinking he does not. First, there is the following obvious difference: in the teaching and learning case, he says of two apparently distinct *processes* that they are the "same but different in being" from each other. But in the cases of concern to us, he says of two apparently distinct *capacities* (or perhaps of the *subjects* to which they belong) that they are the "same but different in being" from each other. Had he wanted to say that one capacity was actualized in the other, he could have focused on the process of perceiving and the process of desiring and said of them that they are (or are constituted by) a single process that is the actualization of two distinct capacities, this not being a problem for the reasons explained in *Physics* III.3. But this is not what he does. Furthermore, even in the case of the teaching and learning, Aristotle identifies a single subject—namely, a κίνησις—to which both belong [*Ph*. 202b19–20].[22] So even in that case, there is something analogous to the stretch of road, namely, a single κίνησις that can be described in different (and definitionally non-equivalent) ways. So the teaching-learning example does not involve any departure from the general model according to which *A* and *B* are the same but different in being only if *A* and *B* are (or belong to) a single subject. The point is simply that the relevant subject need not be a substance. But that should have been clear from Aristotle's example of the sameness but difference in being of the interval from one to two and the interval from two to one.

It thus seems that Aristotle is in fact saying of τὸ ὀρεκτικόν, τὸ αἰσθητικόν, and τὸ φανταστικόν that they are (or belong to) a single subject, which can be described in different and definitionally nonequivalent ways. This raises two questions. First, is Aristotle *identifying* each of these things with a common subject? Or is he saying simply that each *belongs to* a common subject? And second, what is the relevant subject? Is it a part of soul? Or is it rather the whole soul?

The answers to these questions depend partly on how we resolve the ambiguity of τὸ ὀρεκτικόν, τὸ αἰσθητικόν, and τὸ φανταστικόν in interpreting Aristotle's claims that these things are "the same but different in being" from one another. And while he may sometimes use these terms to refer to the relevant capacities, I think it less likely that he means to identify these capacities with one another than that he means to ascribe them to a common subject. For even if the actualization of one (e.g., τὸ φανταστικόν) consists in the actualization of the other (e.g., τὸ αἰσθητικόν) the teaching and learning example shows that there being only one actualization is not sufficient for there being only one capacity: even if the actualization of τὸ φανταστικόν consists in a certain sort of actualization of τὸ αἰσθητικόν, we can still have two distinct capacities, one of which is actualized in the actualization of the other.

One reason for thinking that Aristotle would regard these capacities as distinct is that he seems to allow that they can—at least in some cases—be actualized independently

---

[22] We might put this point by saying that while this particular instance of teaching is identical to this particular instance of learning, still some of its properties (e.g., being an actualization of the teacher's capacity to teach) belong to it qua its being an instance of teaching while others (e.g., being an actualization of the learner's capacity to learn) belong to it qua being an instance of learning.

of one another. Even if actual perception involves the formation of images and so the actualization of the capacity of imagination, the actualization of this capacity does not always involve actual perception: the capacity of imagination is actualized in dreams when the capacity of perception is not. And this is true not only in the case of rational animals but also in the case of (at least some) non-rational ones. For it is clear [from *De Insomn.* 461a26-30] that Aristotle allows that some non-human animals dream and so (like humans) imagine that they are actually perceiving when they are not. Similarly also—though this applies only to rational animals—incontinence seems to involve cases in which the capacity of perceiving things *as good* may be actualized while the capacity of desire is not (or vice versa). But if A can be actualized while B is not, then A and B cannot be the *same* capacity. So when Aristotle says that these things are the "same but different in being" from one another, it seems plausible to suppose that he is *not* referring to the capacities themselves and identifying *them* with one another, but is instead referring to the *subjects* to which these capacities belong and ascribing these *capacities* to one and the same *subject*.[23] In other words, τὸ ὀρεκτικόν, τὸ αἰσθητικόν, and τὸ φανταστικόν seem to be functioning in these contexts as names or descriptions of the *subjects* of the relevant capacities. If this is right, then Aristotle's point is that there is a single subject with multiple capacities, and so a single subject that can be described in different (and definitionally non-equivalent) ways: i.e., as desiderative, as perceptive, and as imaginative.[24]

This leaves us with the question *what* the relevant subject *is*. Is it a part of soul? Or is it the whole soul? There is little reason for thinking that it is the whole soul, given that we never, as far as I know, find Aristotle claiming of any other capacity of soul, such as the nutritive capacity, that it is the "same but different in being" from any of these capacities, as it would be if what he meant by this sort of claim was simply that the *relata* belonged to the same *soul*. So in saying that τὸ ὀρεκτικόν and τὸ αἰσθητικόν are the "same but different in being" he seems to be saying of these capacities something more than that they belong to the same *soul:* he is, I shall argue, saying that they belong to the same *part* of soul, a part distinct from the nutritive part even though it may be incapable of existing apart from the nutritive part. The full argument for this will have to wait until we have asked why Aristotle should posit a special sort of unity among the capacities of what I call the "locomotive" soul.

---

[23] This argument is not conclusive. Aristotle could identify the relevant *capacities* (rather than the parts of soul in which they reside) and then say—along the lines of what he says at *De Memoria* (*De Mem.*) 459a21-23—that the unitary capacity is, in the sort of cases imagined, actualized qua *one* thing (e.g., qua αἰσθητικόν) but not qua *another* (e.g., qua ὀρεκτικόν). But I think it most natural to take the *De Memoria* passage as saying of one and the same part of soul that dreaming belongs to it insofar as it is exercising the capacity of imagination and not insofar as it is exercising the capacity of perception, these capacities themselves being distinct from each other although they belong to (or constitute) a single subject or part of soul.

[24] This does not mean that these terms, whose ambiguity I have pointed out, must *always* refer to the subjects to which the capacities belong rather than to the capacities themselves. So the fact that Aristotle sometimes uses these terms to refer to the capacities—as, for example, at *DA* 414a31ff.—is not a problem for this view.

But to anticipate a bit, I take the point of positing a distinct part here to be to capture the idea of a distinctive sort of subject, the sort of subject to which psychological states—such as pleasures and pains, beliefs, desires, and images—might belong. Although Aristotle recognizes that such a subject must be embodied, he wants, I think, to distinguish the sorts of states and changes that belong strictly speaking to its body as such (e.g., its size, its temperature, and even its more distinctively animal states such as its respiratory rate, its digestive states, etc.) from the sorts of states and changes that belong strictly speaking to *it*, states and changes that—however much they may depend on and affect its bodily states and changes—are nevertheless governed by their own autonomous (or at least semi-autonomous) principles. There is a kind of dualism here, but *not* the sort that allows for a *separately existing* psychological subject. It is a kind of dualism that applies to us not in virtue of our being rational animals or persons or anything highfalutin like that, but simply in virtue of our being *sentient* creatures whose sentience plays a distinctive sort of role in helping to explain our behavior: some of our behavior—like that of many other animals—can be explained only by presupposing the existence of a *psychological* subject, one that experiences pains and pleasures and can represent the causes and objects of its pains and pleasures in ways such that it can move to end or avoid the former and to sustain or bring about the latter.[25] And the movements involved here, while they may affect and be affected by the more or less autonomic functions of the body as such, are governed by their own internal—we might say "psychological"—principles. Similarly, the more or less autonomic functions are precisely that: *autonomic*. Though some of them can to some extent be brought under intentional control, they typically proceed more or less according to their own autonomous (or at least semiautonomous) principles. It is their relative independence that leads Aristotle—in spite of his tendency to think of the soul as a unitary entity—to speak here of two distinct parts of soul. But their distinctness does not imply separability: the perceptive/locomotive part of soul, although it is a distinct part, can neither exist nor function without the nutritive part. So even if Aristotle thinks that there are fewer parts of soul than many of his contemporaries think, his primary target is *not* the idea that there are *distinct* parts of soul; it is *rather* the idea of *separable* parts of soul (though he allows that he may need to make an exception for the theoretical part).

Before turning to the reasons Aristotle might have had for positing a special sort of unity among the capacities of locomotive soul, I want to mention one more textual reason for adopting a single-subject account (at least as applied to non-rational animals): namely, that the comparison in (3)(A) of the relationship between τὸ αἰσθητικόν and τὸ ὀρεκτικόν to the relationship between τὸ ὀρεκτικόν and τὸ φευκτικόν lends

---

[25] It is like what I call the "Lockean dualism" of person and animal, except that it does not require anything as complex as a person. See my "Personal Identity: The Non-Branching Form of What Matters," in R. Gale (ed.), *The Blackwell Guide to Metaphysics* (Oxford: Wiley-Blackwell, 2002), 190–218 [I.5]. This sort of view has been developed most explicitly by Sydney Shoemaker, especially in his "Self, Body, and Coincidence," *Proceedings of the Aristotelian Society*, suppl. 63 (1999): 286–307.

strong support to a single-subject account, which allows us to make the best sense of the manuscripts. For some commentators have been so puzzled about how to understand Aristotle's claim at *DA* 431a12, that the *contraries* (actual flight and actual desire) are the *same*, that they have proposed that we read τοῦτο instead of ταὐτό.[26] But this is unnecessary: ταὐτό makes perfect sense if Aristotle is thinking of actual desire for an object and actual flight from *its* contrary (e.g., of actual desire for health and actual flight from illness). Moreover, it seems reasonable to suppose that this is in fact what Aristotle has in mind when he characterizes the underlying capacities for desire and flight as the same but different in being. For he speaks elsewhere of the (actual) movement to health and the (actual) movement away from illness as the same but different in being: the idea seems to be that there is one actual κίνησις that can be described either as the generation of health or as the destruction of illness [*Ph.* 229a17–20]. Similarly here, we may have one part of soul that can be described either as the part responsible for flight or as the part responsible for desire. If this is right, then (3) (A)'s comparison of the relationship between τὸ ὀρεκτικόν and τὸ αἰσθητικόν to the relationship between τὸ ὀρεκτικόν and τὸ φευκτικόν suggests that τὸ ὀρεκτικόν and τὸ αἰσθητικόν are similarly one part of soul that can be described in different ways— either as the part responsible for desire or as the part responsible for perception (and ultimately of course as *both*). The same then would go for the relationship asserted in (4) between τὸ αἰσθητικόν and τὸ φανταστικόν, and ultimately (given the transitivity of the relevant sort of sameness) of the relationship between τὸ ὀρεκτικόν and τὸ φανταστικόν as well.

4. A HYPOTHESIS ABOUT WHY ARISTOTLE SEES A SPECIAL SORT OF UNITY AMONG THE CAPACITIES OF 'LOCOMOTIVE' SOUL

Why then should Aristotle want to say that what we have here is a single part of soul rather than (for example) several parts of soul that are perhaps inseparable from one another in something like the way in which this perceptive part of soul is supposed to be inseparable (in creatures with both) from the nutritive part?

My hypothesis is this: Aristotle worries that ascribing these capacities to distinct parts of soul gives rise to problems parallel to the problems of judgment that he associates with distinguishing the various senses too sharply from one another and that lead him ultimately to posit a single common sense with different (and definitionally non-equivalent) capacities. He thinks that if the various senses are distinct *subjects*—sight, for example, being *what sees* and taste being *what tastes*, etc.—then we shall be unable to explain how we manage to judge that the objects of different senses (e.g., the white and the sweet) are in fact different.[27] For if sight and taste are distinct *subjects*, then sight's perceiving

---

[26] See Hicks ad *DA* 431a12.

[27] It is worth thinking here about the criticisms in Plato's *Theaetetus* of treating the various senses (or sense organs) as if (like soldiers lodged in a wooden horse) they were themselves the proper subjects of

something white and taste's perceiving something sweet will no more make it clear to any individual subject that being white is different from being sweet than would *my* perceiving something white and *your* perceiving something sweet: there must be some *one subject* that can compare the two perceptibles and judge them different in kind; and insofar as the objects judged are perceptible, this one subject must be a perceiving subject. Similarly also if sight and taste are distinct subjects, the case in which *A*'s sight judges that *x* is white while *A*'s taste judges that *x* is sweet will be no different from the case in which *A* judges that *x* is white while *B* judges that *x* is sweet: in neither case would it be possible to establish that one and the same thing is both sweet and white. Aristotle concludes that there must be some one subject that is indivisible in number but divisible in actual operation and so in account or being. And in expressing this point, he uses not only the same locutions but also the same analogies as he uses in (3A) and (B): he speaks of something that is indivisible in number but divisible in being, and compares its divided operation to the way in which a single point or boundary can serve as two (i.e., as the end of one segment or field and the beginning of another). Aristotle calls this subject the "common sense" [ἡ κοινὴ αἴσθησις] and distinguishes it from each of the five individual senses, each defined by its proper objects (sight by colors, hearing by sounds, and so on).[28]

(5) (A) Each <proper> sense [ἑκάστη μὲν οὖν αἴσθησις], residing in its perceptual organ qua organ [ὑπάρχουσα ἐν τῷ αἰσθητηρίῳ ᾗ αἰσθητήριον], is of its underlying perceptible, and judges[29] the differentiae of its underlying perceptible. For example, sight <judges> light and dark, taste <judges> sweet and bitter, and similarly in the other cases. But since we judge white and sweet and each of the other perceptibles in relation to each <perceptual organ>,[30] by what do we also perceive that these things differ from one another? It must be by perception; for they are perceptibles [ἀνάγκη δὴ αἰσθήσει· αἰσθητὰ γάρ ἐστιν]. So it is clear that flesh is not the ultimate perceptual organ. For in that case it would be necessary for that which judges to judge by touching it. Nor is it possible for it to judge that the white and

---

various sorts of perception. For an excellent discussion of these criticisms see M. F. Burnyeat, "Plato on the Grammar of Perceiving," *Classical Quarterly* NS 26 (1976): 29–51.

[28] Please note that, although I generally use 'perception' and its cognates (e.g., 'perceptible' and 'capable of perceiving') for 'αἴσθησις' and its cognates, I shift here to using 'sense' for 'αἴσθησις' so as to indicate that Aristotle is not referring to the activity of perception but rather to the *faculties* of perception, including *both* the individual senses, which are defined by their proper objects (colors being the proper objects of sight, sounds of hearing, and so on) *and* what calls "the common sense" (whose objects include movement, magnitude, and number). But in speaking (and translating talk) about these objects, I continue using 'perceptible,' thus speaking of "perceptibles" where I could equally well speak of "sensibles."

[29] Or perhaps "discriminates" [κρίνει].

[30] There is some question, at various points throughout this passage, whether Aristotle is referring to the senses themselves (as "each sense" at the beginning of the passage might be taken to suggest) or to the perceptual organs (as his repeated use of masculine/neuter endings, together with the claim about flesh in lines 15–16, might be taken to suggest). I am generally inclined to think that he means to refer to the organs at least up until line 20, where the turn to "saying" and "thinking" makes it difficult not to assume that he is, at *least* from this point on, referring to a perceptual capacity or part of soul. But I have (at that point) invoked the neutral "thing," so as to leave the relevant questions open.

the sweet are different by means of separate <organs>, but it is necessary for both to be manifest to some one thing [οὔτε δὴ κεχωρισμένοις ἐνδέχεται κρίνειν ὅτι ἕτερον τὸ γλυκὺ τοῦ λευκοῦ, ἀλλὰ δεῖ ἑνί τινι ἄμφω δῆλα εἶναι]. Otherwise, if I perceived one thing and you perceived another, it should be manifest that they were different from one another. But it is necessary for the one <thing> to say that they are different. For the sweet is different from the white. The same <thing> therefore says <that they are different>. Hence just as it says, so also it thinks and perceives [ὥστε ὡς λέγει, οὕτω καὶ νοεῖ καὶ αἰσθάνεται].[31] That, then, it is not possible to judge separate <qualities> by separate <things> is clear [ὅτι μὲν οὖν οὐχ οἷόν τε κεχωρισμένοις κρίνειν τὰ κεχωρισμένα, δῆλον]. [DA 426b8–23]

(B) But surely it is impossible for the same <thing> insofar as it is indivisible [τὸ αὐτὸ ᾗ ἀδιαίρετον] to be moved simultaneously by opposite motions and in an undivided time. For if <the object is> sweet, it moves perception or thought in this way [ὡδὶ κινεῖ τὴν αἴσθησιν ἢ τὴν νόησιν], while the bitter <moves perception or thought> in the opposite way and the white <moves perception or thought> in a different way. Is then that which judges at the same time indivisible and inseparable in number but separate in being [ἆρ' οὖν ἅμα μὲν καὶ ἀριθμῷ ἀδιαίρετον καὶ ἀχώριστον τὸ κρῖνον, τῷ εἶναι δὲ κεχωρισμένον]? There is a sense in which it is what is divisible that perceives divided things, but there is another sense in which it <does this> qua indivisible [ἔστι δή πως ὡς τὸ διαιρετὸν τῶν διῃρημένων αἰσθάνεται, ἔστι δ' ὡς ᾗ ἀδιαίρετον]. For in being it is divisible, but in place and number it is indivisible [τῷ εἶναι μὲν γὰρ διαιρετόν, τόπῳ δὲ καὶ ἀριθμῷ ἀδιαίρετον]. [DA 426b29–427a5]

(C) Or is this impossible? For potentially the same indivisible thing can be in opposite states, but in <actual> being it cannot <be in opposite states at the same time>, but in its actual operation it is divisible [δυνάμει μὲν γὰρ τὸ αὐτὸ καὶ ἀδιαίρετον τἀναντία, τῷ δ' εἶναι οὔ, ἀλλὰ τῷ ἐνεργεῖσθαι διαιρετόν]. And it is not possible for it to be simultaneously white and dark, so that it cannot be affected <simultaneously> by the forms of these, if perception and thought are such <i.e., being affected by forms>. Rather like what some call a point, insofar as it is both one and two, it too is divisible in this way. So insofar as it is indivisible, what judges is one and <it judges things> together, while insofar as it is divisible, <what judges> uses the same mark in two ways at the same time [ἀλλ' ὥσπερ ἣν καλοῦσί τινες στιγμήν, ᾗ μία καὶ δύο, ταύτῃ (καὶ ἀδιαίρετος) καὶ διαιρετή. ᾗ μὲν οὖν ἀδιαίρετον, ἕν τὸ κρῖνόν ἐστι καὶ ἅμα· ᾗ δὲ διαιρετὸν ὑπάρχει, δὶς τῷ αὐτῷ χρῆται σημείῳ ἅμα].[32] Insofar as it uses the limit in two ways, it judges two

---

[31] Cf. DA 431a8–20.
[32] There may be a point to the shift here from στιγμή to σημεῖον—namely, that something essentially indivisible (e.g., the soul or a part of soul) is able, in virtue of being in some sense located in something divisible (i.e., some bodily part), to be divided in its actual operations.

things and is <judging> separately; but insofar <as it uses the limit> as one, it is one <and judges things> together [ᾗ μὲν οὖν δυσὶ χρῆται τῷ πέρατι, δύο κρίνει καὶ ἔστιν ὡς κεχωρισμένως· ᾗ δὲ ἑνί, ἓν καὶ ἅμα]. [*DA* 427a 5–14]

(6) (A) If the soul perceives sweet with one part and white with another [εἰ δὲ δὴ ἄλλῳ μὲν γλυκέος ἄλλῳ δὲ λευκοῦ αἰσθάνεται ἡ ψυχὴ μέρει], then what is composed of these <sweet and white> is either some one thing or it is not. But it must be one. For what can perceive is some one part [ἕν γάρ τι τὸ αἰσθητικόν ἐστι μέρος]. What one <object> then does that [sc., τὸ αἰσθητικόν] <perceive>? For there is no one <thing> composed of these <sweet and white>. It is necessary, then, that there is some one <part or capacity> of soul, by which it perceives all things, as has been said before, <each> different kind <of object> being perceived through a different <organ> [ἀνάγκη ἄρα ἕν τι εἶναι τῆς ψυχῆς, ᾧ ἅπαντα αἰσθάνεται, καθάπερ εἴρηται πρότερον, ἄλλο δὲ γένος δι' ἄλλου]. Then is what perceives <both> sweet and white some one thing insofar as it is undivided in its activity but different whenever it has come to be divided in its activity [ἆρ' οὖν ᾗ μὲν ἀδιαίρετόν ἐστι κατ' ἐνέργειαν, ἕν τί ἐστι τὸ αἰσθητικὸν γλυκέος καὶ λευκοῦ, ὅταν δὲ διαιρετὸν γένηται κατ' ἐνέργειαν, ἕτερον]? [*De Sensu* 449a5–13]

(B) Or <isn't it> rather that what is possible in the case of the <perceptible> objects themselves [ἐπὶ τῶν πραγμάτων αὐτῶν] is in the same way <possible> also in the case of the soul? For what is the same thing and one in number is white and sweet and many other things as well, if the qualities are not separable from one another but what it is to be for each <of them> is different [τὸ γὰρ αὐτὸ καὶ ἓν ἀριθμῷ λευκὸν καὶ γλυκύ ἐστι, καὶ ἄλλα πολλά, εἰ μὴ χωριστὰ τὰ πάθη ἀλλήλων, ἀλλὰ τὸ εἶναι ἕτερον ἑκάστῳ]. Similarly, then, it must also be supposed in the case of the soul that what perceives all things is the same thing and one in number but different in being, different in genus in the case of some <of its objects> and different in species in the case of others [ὁμοίως τοίνυν θετέον καὶ ἐπὶ τῆς ψυχῆς τὸ αὐτὸ καὶ ἓν εἶναι ἀριθμῷ τὸ αἰσθητικὸν πάντων, τῷ μέντοι εἶναι ἕτερον καὶ ἕτερον τῶν μὲν γένει τῶν δὲ εἴδει]. So it would be possible to perceive <different qualities> simultaneously with one and the same <part>, though not <with a part that is> the same in account [ὥστε καὶ αἰσθάνοιτ' ἂν ἅμα τῷ αὐτῷ καὶ ἑνί, λόγῳ δ' οὐ τῷ αὐτῷ]. [*De Sensu* 449a13–20]

My admittedly speculative suggestion is that Aristotle is worried for the same sort of reasons about treating the capacities of desire, perception, and imagination as belonging to distinct parts of soul. If these capacities were separate from one another in the sense that they functioned independently of one another in the way in which the nutritive capacity can function independently of them, then there would be a problem about how one part of *A*'s soul *desiring* good (or pleasant) things and another part of *A*'s soul *perceiving* things as good (or as pleasant) would result in action: just as *A*'s desiring good (or pleasant) things does not combine with *B*'s perceiving something as good (or as pleasant) to produce action, so too—if different parts of *A*'s soul are the proper subjects of, respectively, desire and perception—it is not clear how *A*'s desiring good (or pleasant) things will combine with *A*'s perceiving things as good (or as pleasant) to produce action. This suggestion seems plausible, given (3)(B)'s explicit reference to the sort of unity secured by the common sense: when Aristotle says that "the last thing is one and one mean, but its being is more than one," he is clearly referring to the common sense—either to the sense itself or perhaps to its organ (i.e., the heart, which is ultimately affected by the affections produced by perceptible objects in the eyes, ears, and other sense organs). And he seems to be suggesting that in the case of desire and imagination, as in the case of desire and perception, there must similarly be some one thing that can function in different ways—something like a boundary, which is in one sense indivisible but in another sense divisible because it can function both as the end of one area and the beginning of another.

It is worth noting in this connection what Aristotle says about the heart, which is the central organ not only of the perceptive/locomotive system but also of the nutritive/generative system. After explaining that animals must have both homoiomerous and anhomoiomerous parts—homoiomerous ones being necessary for perception and anhomoiomerous ones for action—Aristotle points out that the heart is *both*.

(7) Since the perceptive capacity and the one moving the animal and the nutritive capacity are in same part of the body [τῆς δ' αἰσθητικῆς δυνάμεως καὶ τῆς κινούσης τὸ ζῷον καὶ τῆς θρεπτικῆς ἐν ταὐτῷ μορίῳ τοῦ σώματος οὔσης] ... the primary part which has such principles must be (insofar as it is capable of receiving all the perceptibles) among the simple parts and also (insofar as it is locomotive and practical) among the anhomoiomerous parts. Hence in blooded animals the heart—and in bloodless animals its analogue—is such <a part>. For it is divisible into homoiomerous <bits>, just as each of the other visceral parts is, but it is anhomoiomerous on account of the form of its shape [διὰ δὲ τὴν τοῦ σχήματος μορφὴν ἀνομοιομερές]. And each of the other so-called viscera follows this, for they are composed of the same matter ... And the heart—because it is the source of the blood vessels and has in it the primary capacity that fabricates the blood—it is reasonable that it itself should be composed of the sort of nutriment of which it is the source. [*PA* 647a25–b8][33]

One might argue here that the dual function of the heart as central organ *both* of the nutritive/generative system *and* of the perceptive/locomotive system shows that the nutritive/generative part of soul and the perceptive/locomotive part of soul are also the same but different in being from one another. But this would, I think, be a mistake. Not only does Aristotle never say anything like this, but it is plausible to suppose that he would treat the heart as analogous to a point: just as a single point B can be both the center of a circle

---

[33] I translate from the revised edition of the Loeb Classical Library text prepared by E. S. Forster (Cambridge, MA, 1961), which is based on Bekker's Berlin edition of 1831.

and the mid-point of the segment of a line that bisects the circle *without* its being the case that the circle and the segment are the same but different in being from one another, so too the heart can be the central organ of two distinct physiological systems (and so of the parts of soul embodied in these systems) *without* these two systems (or parts of soul) being the same but different in being from one another. Let the circle stand for the nutritive/generative system (or part of soul) and the segment of the line bisecting it for the perceptive/locomotive system (or part of soul). Then note that point B can *also* function, with respect to the segment itself, both as the *end* of segment AB (representing perception) and as the *beginning* of segment BC (representing locomotion). It is on this *second* double function that passage (7) is primarily focused: the heart functions *both* as the final terminus of perception (qua which it must be composed of homoiomerous parts) *and* as the initial terminus of locomotion and action (qua which it must itself be anhomoiomerous). The additional function of the heart—as central locus of the nutritive-cum-generative system—means that the homoiomerous stuff of which it is composed must be stuff that is not only capable of receiving perceptibles but also capable of providing nutriment both for the body and for reproduction. But that is an additional claim.

We can best see the dual function of the heart, simply qua center of the perceptive/locomotive system, by turning to *De Motu Animalium,* whose picture of animal action is essentially the same as the one we shall find in *De Anima* III.9–11. The main difference is that *De Motu* is explicitly focused on the question how the soul moves *the body.* As we can see from the following passage, the principle of perception and the principle of locomotion must be located together in the center of the body, and the reason for this is clearly that their *coincidence* is required to explain locomotion.

(8) (A) Since <an animal> is similarly situated with respect to <movements> from its left and from its right, and it is possible for the opposite <sides> to move at the same time so that it is not possible for the left to be moved in virtue of the right resting, or for this <to move> in virtue of that <resting>, it is necessary for the principle of locomotive soul to be in the middle [ἀνάγκη ἐν τῷ μέσῳ εἶναι τὴν ἀρχὴν τῆς ψυχῆς κινούσης], the middle being an end point of both extremes.[34] And it [sc., the animal] is similarly related to the movements from above and below, such as those from the head, and to <the movements down> the spine in those <animals> having a spine. And it is reasonable that this should occur. For we say that τὸ αἰσθητικόν too is there, so that when the area around the principle is altered and changed on account of perception, the adjacent parts expanding and contracting change together with it, so that necessarily on account of these things, movement occurs in animals. [*De Motu* 702b12–25]

---

[34] It has been a guiding assumption of the entire work, from 698a16 on, that if one part of an animal moves, some other part must be at rest, which is why animals have joints (which remain at rest while their associated limbs move). The image of the joint is in fact the dominant image in this work. Note that Aristotle does not speak of τὸ κινητικόν, as he goes on to speak of τὸ αἰσθητικόν. Again, I think he wants to avoid suggesting that what moves the animal is a distinct capacity (or part) of soul.

(B) And the middle part of the body is potentially one, but in its activity it is necessary for it to become several [δυνάμει μὲν ἕν, ἐνεργείᾳ δ' ἀνάγκη γίνεσθαι πλείω]. For the limbs can be moved simultaneously from the origin, one [sc., the origin] resting while the other [sc., the limbs] are moved. I mean, for example, in the case of ABC, B is moved, while A moves it.[35] But it is necessary for something to be at rest, if the one is to be moved and the other is to move <it>. A, then, will be one in potentiality but two in actuality, so that it is necessary for it to be not a point but rather some magnitude. But surely it is possible for C to be moved simultaneously with B, so that it is necessary for both of the principles in A to move <something else> while <themselves> being moved. So there must be something different, besides these, which moves but is not <itself> moved. Otherwise the extremities and the origins in A would, when moving, support themselves against one another, just as if those leaning back to back were to move their legs. But the thing moving both must be (one), and this is the soul, being different from such a magnitude [sc., A] but being in this <magnitude>.[36] [*De Motu* 702b25–703a3]

(C) According, then, to the account giving the explanation of <animal> motion, desire [ἡ ὄρεξις] is the middle, which moves <the animal> while <itself> being moved. In ensouled bodies, there must be some such body [sc., one that moves while being itself moved].[37] What is moved but is not by nature such as to move <something else> can be affected by an alien power, but what moves <something else> must have some power and strength <of its own>. All animals clearly have connate *pneuma* and have strength on account of this . . . This [sc., *pneuma*] seems to be related to the psychic principle [sc., the heart or its analog] in a way similar to that in which the point in the joints which is both moving and being moved is related to what is unmoved [sc., to desire]. Since this principle is in some <animals> in the heart, and in other <animals> in the analogous <part>, it is clear that the connate *pneuma* is also there . . . The activities of motion

---

[35] Nussbaum (whose text I translate) interprets this, plausibly, as referring to an angle BAC, with A being the point common to segments BA and AC. See Martha Nussbaum, *Aristotle's De Motu Animalium* (Princeton, NJ: Princeton University Press, 1978).

[36] Nussbaum inserts ἕν, in accordance with the translation of Moerbeke and the paraphrase of Albertus Magnus. An alternative would be to follow the manuscripts and to translate, "it is necessary for the mover to be both." The task is then to determine what the "both" are. The most plausible candidates seem to me to be the δυνάμει μὲν ἕν, ἐνεργείᾳ δ'. . . πλείω back in lines 30–31, with the remainder of our sentence then explaining that this is possible because the soul, though not itself a magnitude, is *in* a magnitude and can thus be actually divided in its operations. But it does not matter, for present purposes, whether or not we follow Nussbaum: whichever way we go on that, the soul is clearly supposed to be one but divided in its operations.

[37] I take the point about desire being in the middle as a point about the capacity of soul, and the next point to be a point about the conditions of its embodiment: it must be embodied in some body that (like desire itself) moves while itself being moved (though it may undergo alteration).

are pushing and pulling, so the instrument of motion must be capable of expanding and contracting. And such is the nature of the *pneuma* . . . It is necessary for what is going to move ‹an animal› not by alteration [τὸ μέλλον κινεῖν μὴ ἀλλοιώσει] to be this sort of thing. [*De Motu* 703a4–26][38]

(C) seems to assume an analogy between that part of a bodily joint that moves the limb while itself being moved and that part of the soul that moves the animal while itself being moved (i.e., the desiderative part of soul). Like the part of the joint that moves ‹something else› while itself being moved, and like the common sense, the desiderative part of soul must be one thing, which is, however, capable of being divided in its actual operation: it must *perceive* (or *imagine*) things as pleasant and painful (or as good and bad), thus *moving* the animal to pursue and avoid the things so perceived (or imagined).

One might object here that there are *other* ways to secure the unity required for action than by positing a single part of soul with multiple capacities. One might, for example, seek to explain the requisite unity in the way that Irwin seeks to explain it—i.e., by suggesting that the desiring part of soul cooperates with the perceiving and other parts of soul to produce action insofar as each is part of one and the same teleological system. And one might support this view as Irwin supports it by appeal to the holism of belief/desire ascriptions or more generally of appearance/desire ascriptions.[39]

But it is difficult to explain the sort of unity that Aristotle ascribes to τὸ ὀρεκτικόν and τὸ αἰσθητικόν simply by assuming that they are parts of a single teleological system. For this would not distinguish the more intimate relationship he seems to posit between τὸ ὀρεκτικόν and τὸ αἰσθητικόν from the less intimate relation he seems to posit between these capacities and the nutritive-cum-generative capacities, which are *also* part of the same teleological system. For even though the processes involved in nutrition and growth, simply as such, do not require the operations of desire and perception, the latter operations do serve an animal's nutritive needs, desire and perception being at least partly *for* moving an animal in ways that enable it to eat.[40] And

---

[38] I follow Nussbaum's text and am influenced by her translation. But I disagree with her understanding of μὴ ἀλλοιώσει. She translates this "without undergoing alteration," which seems to me to conflict with the alleged difference (at 701b1ff.) between automatic puppets (in which the parts that move the puppet do *not themselves suffer alteration* but simply change place) and animals (in which the parts that move the animal *themselves suffer alteration*). So I think the point of μὴ ἀλλοιώσει is simply to indicate that the motions in question are not alterations but rather locomotions.

[39] See secs. 173–75 of T. Irwin, *Aristotle's First Principles* (Oxford: Oxford University Press, 1988). It is clear from the last paragraph of sec. 175 that Irwin (who stresses the *unity* of the desiring part) regards the desiring part of soul as distinct from the perceiving part (and from the nutritive, thinking, and deliberative parts).

[40] See *De Somno* 454b32ff., where Aristotle says that τὸ θρεπτικόν functions more effectively when an animal is asleep than when it is awake, because it does not need perception for processing nutriment or growth: τὸ ἔργον τὸ αὑτοῦ ποιεῖ τὸ θρεπτικὸν μόριον ἐν τῷ καθεύδειν μᾶλλον ἢ ἐν τῷ ἐγρηγορέναι· τρέφεται γὰρ καὶ αὐξάνεται τότε μᾶλλον, ὡς οὐδὲν προσδεόμενα πρὸς ταῦτα τῆς αἰσθήσεως.

the "lower" nutritive processes in turn serve the "higher" activities of the locomotive system, the "lower" activities generally being (according to Aristotle) at least partly for the sake of "'higher" ones: without proper nutrition an animal's perceptual and locomotive activities—and presumably also any theoretical activities in which it might engage—would suffer. Yet in spite of all this, Aristotle never says of τὸ ὀρεκτικόν or τὸ αἰσθητικόν that it is the same as τὸ θρεπτικόν though different in being from it. He seems to see a *tighter* connection within an animal between its perceptive and desiderative capacities than between these capacities on the one hand and its nutritive-cum-generative capacities on the other. In fact, his comparison of the relationship between τὸ ὀρεκτικόν and τὸ αἰσθητικόν to that between τὸ ὀρεκτικόν and τὸ φευκτικόν suggests that he views τὸ ὀρεκτικόν and τὸ αἰσθητικόν as one in the way that, for example, the road-up and the road-down are one. But taking these things simply as parts of a single teleological system would support only the conclusion that τὸ ὀρεκτικόν and τὸ αἰσθητικόν are two things, like a heart and a liver, each of whose functional existence requires and so entails the other's functional existence. So we cannot explain the degree of intimacy that Aristotle seems to see between the τὸ ὀρεκτικόν and τὸ αἰσθητικόν simply by appeal to their being parts of a single teleological system.

The more intimate relation between perception and desire is, I think, a function of their joint role in explaining intentional animal behavior: that, after all, is what perception and desire, along with imagination, are *for*. The same seems to be true, in the case of rational animals, of the intimate relationship between desire and practical νοῦς. But I want to bracket the issue of practical νοῦς for now. The point here is simply that Aristotle thinks that the activities of perception, desire, and imagination are activities of a single part of soul that I call "locomotive," a part of soul that is in important respects analogous to what Aristotle calls the "common sense."[41] Just as there are animals (or quasi-animals) that have touch but lack the other senses and thus lack the common sense, so too there are animals (or quasi-animals) that lack locomotive soul. (I call these "quasi-animals" because Aristotle suggests at History of Animals 588b11–18 that they are on the borderline between plants and animals.) And just as most animals have various senses besides touch, senses that *together constitute* the common sense, so too most animals have capacities besides that of elementary perception, capacities that *together constitute* what I call the "locomotive" part of soul. So the fact that not all animals have locomotive soul is not a problem for my central claim, which is that the locomotive part of soul is no more a distinct part of soul over and above the capacities of desire, perception, and imagination than the common sense is (in those animals that have it) a distinct sense over and above the five proper senses.

Taking these capacities to belong to a single part of soul allows us to explain Aristotle's otherwise odd view that perception—or at least perception together with the requisite sort of imagination—*entails* desire. For surely we can *conceive of* the

---

[41] On the common sense, and the way in which the combination of special senses is *for* perceiving the common perceptibles, see I. Vasiliou, "Perception, Knowledge, and the Sceptic in Aristotle," *Oxford Studies in Ancient Philosophy* 14 (1996): 83–131.

existence of creatures who perceive things without, however, having any desires. And Aristotle's attempt to explain the link between desire and perception through their connection with pleasure and pain does not entirely solve the problem. For even if we grant that being subject to pleasure and pain is sufficient for having desires, why should we grant that being a subject of *perception* entails being a subject of *pleasure and pain?* Why could animals not perceive things simply as *hot and cold*, as *wet and dry*, as *colored, odorous, shaped*, etc.?[42] The answer no doubt has to do with the fact that animals are not automatically nourished by things to which they are more or less permanently attached: unlike plants, most need *to move* in order to take in nourishment. So they need something to *motivate* them. This is the role played by pleasure and pain, which are essentially *motivational* states, states that simple animals are moved either to sustain or to end and that complex animals—capable of representing them in imagination—are also moved either to bring about or to avoid. This is itself a kind of desire, both in the case of the immediate perception of the pleasant or painful (i.e., what we might call immediate "sensations" of pleasure and pain) and in cases where imagination *represents* some object as pleasant (and so to be pursued) or as painful (and so to be avoided). Perception of something as pleasant (or painful) thus *involves* desire (or aversion).[43] Moreover, at least some of an animal's perceptions *must* be of things *as pleasant* or *painful;* otherwise perception would not play its primary teleological role in explaining an animal's movements.[44] For if perception were simply of things as *hot and cold*, as *wet and dry*, as *colored*, etc., and desire were simply for things *as pleasant*, it is not clear how perception and desire, even taken together, could explain the voluntary movements of animals. In order to explain that, one and the same subject must desire pleasant things and perceive things *as pleasant*. This subject must be one, but divided in its activity in something like the way in which the common sense is one but divided in *its* activity: just as common sense both sees and tastes, and is thus able to *judge* that one and the same thing is both white and sweet, so too the locomotive soul both perceives and desires, and is thus able to *move* the animal.

---

[42] The point here is not simply that the proper and improper functioning of the perceptual capacities are (respectively) pleasant and painful, as they presumably are. For that is presumably true of the proper and improper functioning of the nutritive and reproductive capacities as well. The point is that the *objects* of perception are perceived *as pleasant* or *painful*.

[43] There is room here for multiple kinds of relations between desire and the perception *of* something as pleasant—the latter often entailing the former and the former sometimes contributing to the latter. For example, Aristotle may think that it is *precisely because* animals are endowed with perception and desire that an animal's taking nourishment is pleasant in a way in which plant's taking in nourishment is not. The idea may be that at least some of the pleasures that animals take in nourishing themselves are at least partly *desire-dependent*—i.e., that *precisely because* animals *desire* their nutrition in a way in which plants do not some of an animal's nutritive activities are *pleasant* in ways in which a plant's are not. And there may be good teleological reasons for (most) animals to have such desires.

[44] This seems to be true even of stationary animals: although they do not change location, they are supposed (for example) to open and close in response to pleasant and painful stimuli.

5. ARISTOTLE'S OFFICIAL ACCOUNT OF WHAT MOVES THE ANIMAL: *DE ANIMA* III.9–10

The claim that what moves the animal is not an additional part of soul, distinct from the perceptive part, is confirmed by *De Anima* III.10's official account of what moves the animal. Aristotle introduces this discussion, at the start of III.9, by asking explicitly whether what moves the animal [τὸ κινοῦν τὸ ζῷον] is

(9) (A) some one part of it [sc., soul], which is separable either in magnitude or in account [ἕν τι μόριον αὐτῆς μόριον χωριστὸν ὂν ἢ μεγέθει ἢ λόγῳ], or the whole soul [ἢ πᾶσα ἡ ψυχή]; and if it is some ⟨one⟩ part, whether it is some distinctive ⟨part⟩ [ἴδιόν τι] beyond those commonly asserted and the ones mentioned above, or some one of these. [*DA* 432a18–22]

Aristotle then raises some puzzles about how (if at all) we should speak of parts of soul and about how many parts there are. These puzzles, which provide the context for his own positive account, are intended to cast doubt on two common ways (especially among Platonists) of dividing the soul into parts: one the standard tripartite division into a calculating part, an emotional part, and an appetitive part, and the other the standard bipartite division (which Aristotle himself seems to adopt in his ethical works) into a part having reason and a non-rational part.[45]

---

[45] Although the ethical works *seem* to treat the distinction between τὸ λόγον ἔχον and τὸ ἄλογον as fundamental, I do not think that this is their considered view. For not only does Aristotle suggest that the account of soul he adopts in his ethical and political works is a popular account that we can, however, use for ethical-cum-political purposes [*EN* 1102a23–28]; he also goes on to articulate the popular distinctions in a way that renders them fully compatible with the precise account offered in his scientific works. For the ethical works describe the practical (as opposed to the theoretical) part of τὸ λόγον ἔχον—somewhat surprisingly—in the same way that they describe the non-nutritive part of τὸ ἄλογον (i.e., as *obeying* reason) [*EN* 1103a1–3]. This suggests that Aristotle may view the practical part of τὸ λόγον ἔχον as standing to the part of τὸ ἄλογον that obeys reason in something like the way in which the convex stands to the concave (i.e., as two aspects of a single part) and that he may view this part as (9)(C), (D), and (E) view τὸ αἰσθητικόν, τὸ φανταστικόν, and τὸ ὀρεκτικόν: i.e., as neither purely rational nor purely non-rational but as rational in some respects and non-rational in others. This is in fact how I take Aristotle's claim at *EN* 1102a28–31: I take him to be saying that it will not matter if—as he thinks his scientific account requires—what we ordinarily think of as two distinct parts of soul turn out to be related to one another in something like the way in which the convex is related to the concave. For that is how—according to the scientific account developed in the *De Anima*—practical reason and the desiderative part turn out to be related: practical reason (to the extent that a subject has it) is simply a (formal) aspect of that subject's ὀρεκτικόν. So there is in the end no conflict between the threefold division of the scientific works and the apparently fourfold division of the ethical works: for two of the four parts identified in the ethical works prove to be the same. I develop this account of the ethical works more fully in my "Hylomorphic Virtue" [Chapter 6, this volume. [I discuss the argument of *EN* I.13 in more detail in "See the Right Thing: 'Paternal' Reason, Love, and *Phronêsis*," in Boyle and E. Mylonaki (eds.), *Reason and Nature: New Essays on Themes from John McDowell* (Cambridge, MA: Harvard University Press, 2021), 243–84.]

(9) (B) There is a puzzle straight away in what way we ought to speak about parts of the soul and how many <they are>. For in one way they appear to be countless [ἄπειρα], and not only those which some distinguish <as> calculating and emotional and appetitive <parts> [λογιστικὸν καὶ θυμικὸν καὶ ἐπιθυμητικόν] and others <distinguish> as the <part> having reason and the non-rational <part> [τὸ λόγον ἔχον καὶ τὸ ἄλογον]. [*DA* 432a22–26]

(C) For according to the differentiae by which they separate these, there will appear to be other parts, too, having greater distance <from one another> than <do> these about which we have just spoken: both τὸ θρεπτικόν, which belongs both to plants and to all animals, and τὸ αἰσθητικόν, which one could not easily posit either as non-rational [ὡς ἄλογον] or as having reason [ὡς λόγον ἔχον]. [*DA* 432a26–31]

(D) And further τὸ φανταστικόν, which is different in being from all these but raises much difficulty <concerning> which of these it is the same as or different from, if someone is going to posit separate parts of the soul [ὃ τῷ μὲν εἶναι πάντων ἕτερον, τίνι δὲ τούτων ταὐτὸν ἢ ἕτερον ἔχει πολλὴν ἀπορίαν, εἴ τις θήσει κεχωρισμένα μόρια τῆς ψυχῆς]. [*DA* 432a31–b3][46]

(E) And in addition to these, τὸ ὀρεκτικόν, which would seem to be different both in account and in capacity [καὶ λόγῳ καὶ δυνάμει ἕτερον] from all of these. And it is indeed strange to break this up [καὶ ἄτοπον δὴ τὸ τοῦτο διασπᾶν]. For wish comes to be in the calculating <part>, while appetite and emotion <come to be> in the non-rational <part> [ἔν τε τῷ λογιστικῷ γὰρ ἡ βούλησις γίνεται, καὶ ἐν τῷ ἀλόγῳ ἡ ἐπιθυμία καὶ ὁ θυμός]. And if the soul <has> three <parts>, there will be desire [ὄρεξις] in each <part>. [*DA* 432b3–7]

(9)(C) and (9)(E) explicitly raise parallel problems concerning τὸ αἰσθητικόν and τὸ ὀρεκτικόν, problems that cast doubt on taking the soul to be divided primarily into two parts, one having reason and the other lacking it. For neither of these capacities can be easily assigned either to the rational or to the non-rational part of soul. Moreover, it is plausible to suppose that (9)(D), sandwiched as it is between (9) (C) and (E), implicitly raises a similar problem concerning τὸ φανταστικόν, as suggested by the distinction Aristotle goes on to draw—at *DA* 433b29, in (10)(I) below—between the calculative form of imagination characteristic of rational animals and the (merely) perceptual form of imagination characteristic of non-rational animals.

The point here is not just that rational and non-rational animals alike share the relevant capacities of perception, desire, and imagination. For that is true of the nutritive capacity as well, but it belongs unambiguously to the non-rational part of soul. The

---

[46] I have italicized 'separate' here to emphasize that the target of Aristotle's criticism seems to be not simply dividing soul into parts, but rather dividing soul into parts that are supposed to be separate in certain ways (perhaps different ways in the case of different parts).

idea seems rather to be that each of the relevant capacities has—at least in rational animals—an ambiguous status: each seems in some ways to belong to the so-called rational part of soul and in other ways to belong to the so-called non-rational part. Desire, for example, includes βούλησις (which seems to belong to the so-called rational part) as well as ἐπιθυμία and θυμός (which seem to belong to the so-called non-rational part, though θυμός does not sit very happily there). Similarly, some perceptions (e.g., perceptions of things as good or as triangles) seem to belong to the so-called rational part, while others (e.g., perceptions of things as sensually pleasant) seem to belong to the so-called non-rational part. And some images (e.g., images of future goods or of triangles) seem to belong to the so-called rational part, while others (e.g., images of at least some present objects of appetite) seem to belong to the so-called non-rational part. But each of these appearances rests on the assumption that the soul is properly divided primarily along the rational/non-rational axis. And this is precisely the assumption that I take Aristotle to be challenging not simply in this passage but throughout the *De Anima* as a whole. His point is not (I think) that we cannot *characterize* at least some parts of soul as "rational" and "non-rational," but rather that we should not *define* various parts of soul in terms of their having or lacking *logos*. We should instead define parts of soul in terms of their functions and their respective objects. This will leave it open whether a part of soul is rational, non-rational, or somewhere in between, being rational in some respects and non-rational in others. And the important point here is that τὸ αἰσθητικόν, τὸ φανταστικόν, and τὸ ὀρεκτικόν all have the same ambiguous status, being neither purely rational nor purely non-rational. This is not surprising if—as I have been arguing—they all are (or belong to) one and the same part of soul.

Let us return, though, to the question what part or parts of soul move the animal κατὰ τόπον. The remainder of the chapter gives arguments, culminating in a puzzle, against taking what moves the animal to be any one of the parts either commonly asserted or already mentioned in Aristotle's own discussion. What moves the animal is not (i) the nutritive capacity (ἡ θρεπτικὴ δύναμις). For locomotion (unlike the nutritive process) is *both* for the sake of something *and* accompanied by imagination and desire. In other words, locomotion is *intentional* [*DA* 432b15–19].[47] Nor is what moves the animal (ii) τὸ αἰσθητικόν. For many animals have perception but are stationary throughout their lives (i.e., even in maturity) [432b19–26][48] Nor is what moves the animal (iii) what calculates or what is called νοῦς (τὸ λογιστικὸν καὶ ὁ καλούμενος νοῦς). For (*a*) theoretical νοῦς thinks nothing practical (or achievable in action), nor about what is to be avoided or pursued. And (*b*) it is not the case that, whenever νοῦς

---

[47] Nutritive processes are of course for something—i.e., the preservation of the animal. But they are not *intentional*: they do not work by means of *representations of* and *desires for* the ends for the sake of which they occur.

[48] On my account, this claim must ultimately be qualified: what moves the animal *is* τὸ αἰσθητικόν (where this refers to the relevant part of soul and not simply to the capacity to perceive). But what moves the animal is *not* τὸ αἰσθητικόν ᾗ αἰσθητικόν: it is τὸ αἰσθητικόν ᾗ ὀρεκτικόν. See the discussion of (10)(F) below; and note 61.

contemplates something that is to be pursued or avoided, it immediately commands one to pursue or avoid that thing. Often there is no command but some part of the body simply moves on its own—the heart, for example, in the case of fearful things, some other part in the case of pleasant things. And even when νοῦς does command and thought [διάνοια] says that one should pursue or avoid something, the animal is not always moved accordingly; sometimes (as in the case of the incontinent subject) the animal moves according to ἐπιθυμία [DA 432b19–433a6]. Nor, finally, is it (iv) desire that controls locomotion [οὐδ' ἡ ὄρεξις ταύτης κυρία τῆς κινήσεως].[49] For continent subjects do not do what they desire, but follow νοῦς [433a9–15].

Taken together, the phenomena of continence and incontinence suggest that none of the parts or capacities of soul thus far discussed can by itself account for all the kinds of movements of which animals (especially rational animals) are capable. So it is natural, especially in the light of points (iii) and (iv), to propose a disjunctive account according to which an animal may be moved by one or the other of *two* different things—νοῦς or ὄρεξις—different things moving the animal in different sorts of cases. This is the suggestion with which the next chapter begins.

(10) (A) It appears at any rate that these two are <the> movers—either ὄρεξις or νοῦς—if one were to posit imagination [φαντασία] as a kind of thinking [ὡς νόησίν τινα]. For many <people> follow their imaginations against knowledge [παρὰ τὴν ἐπιστήμην]; and in other animals, there is neither thought [νόησις] nor calculation [λογισμός], but <only> imagination. *Both* of these then—νοῦς and ὄρεξις—are movers according to place.[50] (That is, νοῦς that calculates for the sake of some <end>, which is practical <νοῦς> [νοῦς δὲ ὁ ἕνεκά του λογιζόμενος καὶ ὁ πρακτικός]. For this differs from theoretical <νοῦς> by its end [διαφέρει δὲ τοῦ θεωρητικοῦ τῷ τέλει].)[51] [DA 433a9–15]

(B) All ὄρεξις is for the sake of something [ἕνεκά του]. For the object of desire [οὗ γὰρ ὄρεξις] is the origin of practical νοῦς [ἀρχὴ τοῦ πρακτικοῦ νοῦ] and the last thing <in practical thought> is the origin of action. So it seems reasonable that these two are the movers, ὄρεξις and practical thought [διάνοια πρακτική]. For the object of desire moves <something>, and on account of this [sc., the object of desire's moving this

---

[49] Note the shift here from talk of the various capacities [ἡ θρεπτικὴ δύναμις, τὸ αἰσθητικόν, τὸ λογιστικὸν καὶ ὁ καλούμενος νοῦς] to what seems to be talk of the activity itself [ἡ ὄρεξις]. This may be significant. The point may be to allow that it is always τὸ ὀρεκτικὸν ἢ ὀρεκτικόν that moves the animal, while leaving it open that the animal is not always moved in accordance with an actual ὄρεξις. The ὀρεκτικόν of a merely continent subject might, for example, move the subject contrary to its actual ὄρεξις. But this would *not* be a case of something *other* than τὸ ὀρεκτικὸν moving the subject; it would simply be a case of τὸ ὀρεκτικὸν qua *practical* νοῦς moving the subject.

[50] Note the shift from ἢ ὄρεξις ἢ νοῦς in 433a9 to ἄμφω . . . νοῦς καὶ ὄρεξις in 433a13. I take this to be significant in the light of the subsequent argument, which—given its parity with (1B)—suggests that they work together as *one*.

[51] See *EN* 1139a5–15.

thing] thought moves <the animal>, because its [sc., thought's] origin is the object of desire [τὸ ὀρεκτὸν[52] γὰρ κινεῖ, καὶ διὰ τοῦτο ἡ διάνοια κινεῖ, ὅτι ἀρχὴ αὐτῆς ἐστι τὸ ὀρεκτόν].[53] [*DA* 433a15–20]

But the chapter proceeds quickly to an argument for the unity of practical νοῦς (including imagination) and τὸ ὀρεκτικόν with one another, an argument similar in form to the argument of (1)(B).

(C) And imagination, whenever it moves <an animal>, does not move <it> without desire ἄνευ ὀρέξεως.[54] Indeed, what moves <an animal> is some one thing, τὸ ὀρεκτικόν.[55] For if two things—νοῦς and ὄρεξις—moved <it>, they would move <it> according to some common form [εἰ γὰρ δύο, νοῦς καὶ ὄρεξις, ἐκίνουν, κατὰ κοινὸν ἄν τι ἐκίνουν εἶδος]. But in fact νοῦς evidently does not move <anything> without desire [νῦν δὲ ὁ μὲν νοῦς οὐ φαίνεται κινῶν ἄνευ ὀρέξεως]. For wish is desire [ἡ γὰρ βούλησις ὄρεξις].[56] And whenever one is

---

[52] Some manuscripts read τὸ ὀρεκτικόν, but lines 433b10–12, in (10)(F) below, make it clear that Aristotle takes τὸ ὀρεκτόν to be the first mover of the animal, the thing that moves the animal, without itself being moved, by being thought or imagined—imagination being, as (10)(A) suggests, a kind of thought. So it is pretty clear that he is relying throughout this chapter on the claim that τὸ ὀρεκτόν moves the animal by being in some way an object of thought. And this plays a crucial role in getting us to the conclusion sought here—namely, that thought moves (or at least helps to move) the animal. One might note—by way of further support for this reading that Aristotle expresses the same view—that τὸ ὀρεκτόν moves an animal by being on object of thought, at *Metaphysics* 1072a24–30, where he says that the primary objects of thought and desire, which move without themselves being moved, are the same, and explains this by saying that we desire things because we think them good more than (or rather than) thinking them good because we desire them. I prefer "more than" to "rather than" as a rendering of μᾶλλον ἤ because it leaves open something I think Aristotle wants to allow—namely, that some subjects may think things good at least partly because they desire them. This is one of the ways in which pleasure and pain (and so desire) can corrupt one's beliefs, as Aristotle indicates at *EN* 1140b11–19, in (13)(B) below. But even if we understand Aristotle to be saying "rather than," his claim is one about how things *should*—as a matter of teleological fact—be. There is nothing in principle that would prevent many people—perhaps even most people—departing from this norm.
[53] David Sedley has suggested that we take αὐτῆς (in ἀρχὴ αὐτῆς) to refer to ὄρεξις. I find this hard, not simply because of the immediate proximity of ἡ διάνοια, but also because it yields only a tautological premise (namely, that the origin of desire is the object of desire), which does not move us toward the desired conclusion (namely, that thought somehow moves or helps to move the animal). Obviously there is room for considerable controversy about how to read this sentence, but I think it makes the most argumentative sense if we take it to be saying that τὸ ὀρεκτόν moves practical intellect (to think, for example, about how to achieve τὸ ὀρεκτόν) and on account of τὸ ὀρεκτόν's moving practical intellect, thought can be said to move the animal. One might suppose that what τὸ ὀρεκτόν moves is τὸ ὀρεκτικόν, but the problem is then to get from this to the conclusion that διάνοια moves the animal.
[54] We must read what precedes this as having made a parallel point about thought. Cf. *EN* 6.1, especially 1139a5–6.
[55] Some manuscripts have τὸ ὀρεκτόν here. But it seems clear from the context that the point is about the desiderative capacity or part of soul, and not about its object.
[56] The idea here seems to be that βούλησις, which is a form of νοῦς, is *also* a form of ὄρεξις. There should be no problem with taking Aristotle to be saying this, given his willingness (mentioned below) to speak of προαίρεσις both as ὀρεκτικὸς νοῦς [at *EN* 1139b4–5] and as ὄρεξις διανοητική [at 1134b4–5] or ὄρεξις βουλευτική [at 1139a23 and 1113a10–11].

moved in accordance with calculation [κατὰ τὸν λογισμόν], one is moved also in accordance with wish [καὶ κατὰ βούλησιν]. But desire [ὄρεξις] also moves <some people> against calculation [παρὰ τὸν λογισμόν]. For appetite is a kind of desire [ἡ γὰρ ἐπιθυμία ὄρεξίς τίς ἐστιν]. [DA 433a20–26]

(D) All νοῦς, then, is correct. But ὄρεξις and φαντασία are both correct and incorrect. So the object of desire [τὸ ὀρεκτόν] always moves <the animal>, but this is either the good or the apparent good. And not every good, but <only> the practical good. And the practical is what is capable of being otherwise. [DA 433a26–30]

(E) That, then, such a capacity of soul moves <the animal> [ἡ τοιαύτη δύναμις κινεῖ τῆς ψυχῆς], the one called ὄρεξις, is clear. But to those who divide the parts of the soul, *if* they divide <it> and separate <the parts> *according to its capacities*, <the parts> prove to be very numerous—nutritive, perceptive, thinking, deliberative, and further desiderative [τοῖς δὲ διαιροῦσι τὰ μέρη τῆς ψυχῆς, ἐὰν κατὰ τὰς δυνάμεις διαιρῶσι καὶ χωρίζουσι, πάμπολλα γίνεται, θρεπτικόν, αἰσθητικόν, νοητικόν, βουλευτικόν, ἔτι ὀρεκτικόν]. For these differ more from one another than <do the> appetitive and spirited [ἐπιθυμητικὸν καὶ θυμικόν]. [DA 433a30–b5]

(F) Since desires [ὀρέξεις] come to be opposed to one another and this happens whenever reason [ὁ λόγος] and the appetites [αἱ ἐπιθυμίαι] are opposed,[57] and <this> comes to be in those <animals> having perception of time—for νοῦς orders <them> to hold back on account of the future, but ἐπιθυμία <orders them to proceed> on account of the present, for the present pleasure appears to be pleasant without qualification and good without qualification [ἁπλῶς ἡδὺ καὶ ἀγαθὸν ἁπλῶς] on account of <their> not seeing the future—the mover will be one in form—that is, the ὀρεκτικόν qua ὀρεκτικόν (the first <mover> of all <is of course> the object of desire, for this, without itself being moved, moves <the animal> by being thought or imagined)—but the movers will be more <than one> in number [εἴδει μὲν ἓν ἂν εἴη τὸ κινοῦν, τὸ ὀρεκτικόν, ἢ ὀρεκτικόν—πρῶτον δὲ πάντων τὸ ὀρεκτόν· τοῦτο γὰρ κινεῖ οὐ κινούμενον, τῷ νοηθῆναι ἢ φαντασθῆναι—ἀριθμῷ δὲ πλείω τὰ κινοῦντα]. [DA 433b5–12]

The remainder of the chapter then provides an account of the embodiment of desire and the movements it causes, one that is essentially the same as the one we found in *De Motu Animalium* (to which (H) seems to refer).

(G) Since there are three things, (*a*) the mover [τὸ κινοῦν], (*b*) that by which it moves [ᾧ κινεῖ], and (*c*) the thing being moved [τὸ κινούμενον]; and (*a*) the mover is twofold: (*a*1) the unmoved <mover> [τὸ μὲν ἀκίνητον] and (*a*2)

---

[57] Note that the opposition here is not just between λόγος and ἐπιθυμίαι. This opposition is said to involve—or at least to result in—ὀρέξεις themselves being opposed to one another, perhaps because (as I am claiming) the relevant states of λόγος are themselves ὀρέξεις. See the previous note.

what moves and is moved [τὸ δὲ κινοῦν καὶ κινούμενον]; (a1) the unmoved <mover> is the practical good, (a2) what moves and is moved is τὸ ὀρεκτικόν (for the thing being moved is moved insofar as it desires [ᾗ ὀρέγεται] and desire is some sort of movement or actuality), and (c) the thing moved is the animal. [DA 433b13–18]

(H) (b) The organ by which desire moves <the animal>, this is already bodily. So it is necessary to study it among the functions common to soul and body.⁵⁸ But to summarize <those studies> for present purposes, what moves <the animal> organically is where <the> origin [ἀρχή] and <the> end [τελευτή] are the same, like a hinge. For there the convex and the concave <serve> respectively as the end and the origin, on account of which the one rests while the other moves, being different in account but inseparable in magnitude [λόγῳ μὲν ἕτερα ὄντα, μεγέθει δ᾽ ἀχώριστα]. For all <animals> move by pushing and pulling. Hence it is necessary, as in a circle, for something to remain <at rest> and for the motion to begin from this. [DA 433b19–27]

(I) In general, then, as already said, insofar as the animal is capable of desire, in that respect it is capable of moving itself [ᾗ ὀρεκτικὸν τὸ ζῷον, ταύτῃ αὑτοῦ κινητικόν]. But it is capable of desire not without imagination, and all imagination is either calculative or perceptive [ὀρεκτικὸν δὲ οὐκ ἄνευ φαντασίας· φαντασία δὲ πᾶσα ἢ λογιστικὴ ἢ αἰσθητική]. Of this [sc., imagination], then, even the other animals partake. [DA 433b27–30]

It seems clear from this chapter that Aristotle takes practical νοῦς, broadly construed so as to include imagination, to be no less a mover of animals than ὄρεξις is. More importantly, he seems to think that *both* are required to explain animal movement in the sense that *both* are required to explain *any* movement of the relevant sort, and *not* in the sense that νοῦς is required to explain *some* movements, while ὄρεξις is required to explain *others*. For the point of (C) seems to be that it is never νοῦς *alone* (or imagination *alone*) that moves an animal. And the point of (I) is that it is never ὄρεξις *alone* that moves an animal: we must attribute νοῦς in the form of imagination even to non-rational animals in order to explain locomotion (which is always toward an end represented in imagination).⁵⁹

This leaves open the question whether νοῦς and ὄρεξις are *two* things that *cooperate* in moving the animal or whether they are *one* thing that can be described in different ways. And (C) can easily be read as suggesting the latter: the idea seems to be that neither νοῦς generally nor imagination in particular moves an animal without desire, but that we should not conclude from this that there are two independent things—i.e., νοῦς

---

⁵⁸ See passage (8) above, and *De Motu*, passim.
⁵⁹ This point seems to be confirmed by the fact that *De Anima* III.11 says that even incomplete animals, which have only the sense of touch, have an indefinite sort of φαντασία corresponding to the indefinite ways in which they move. [For detailed discussion of *De Anima* III.11, see "The Mover(s) of Rational Animals," Chap. 9, this volume.]

and ὄρεξις—that move the animal. For, as (C) says, if there were two distinct movers then they would move the animal according to some common form. The idea here seems to be similar to the idea in (1)(B) that if there is some further thing that holds the various capacities of soul together, then that further thing would be most of all [μάλιστα] the soul: in other words, if νοῦς and ὄρεξις were distinct capacities that together moved the animal, we should then have to identify the mover with the common form in virtue of which they *together* moved the animal, in which case *that* would be the true mover. So Aristotle's suggestion seems to be that what moves an animal must (like the common sense) be one in number but more than one in being or account. In other words, the suggestion seems to be that the mover is one thing that can be described either as νοῦς (construed broadly so as to include imagination) or as ὄρεξις, and ultimately as *both*.[60]

But if this suggestion is correct, then it may seem puzzling that Aristotle should say in (F) that the mover (i.e., τὸ ὀρεκτικόν, ᾗ ὀρεκτικόν) is one in form, while the movers are several in number. For since Aristotle seems [at *Ph.* 190b23–25] to use the label "one in number but two in form" as equivalent to "one in number but two in being or account," we might expect him to say that τὸ ὀρεκτικόν is one in number but several in being or account—i.e., one thing which can be described in various ways, not simply (as we have seen) as τὸ ὀρεκτικόν, τὸ αἰσθητικόν, and τὸ φανταστικόν, but also (as we now see) as νοῦς. But the puzzle disappears once we realize that (F) is making a very different sort of point. Consider (G)'s claim that we speak of the mover in two ways—i.e., both as (*a*1) the practical good (or object of desire), which moves the animal without itself being moved, and as (*a*2) τὸ ὀρεκτικόν, which itself being moved in turn moves the animal. This allows us to identify the several numerically distinct movers mentioned in (F) with (*a*1), the various objects of desire that serve as *unmoved* movers, while identifying the one mover in (F) with (*a*2), τὸ ὀρεκτικόν or *moved* mover. But that still leaves us with the question what (F) means in saying that this mover is one in form [εἴδει].

A plausible answer—suggested by the context provided by (10)(E)—is this: in saying that τὸ ὀρεκτικόν ᾗ ὀρεκτικόν is one in form though its objects are several in number, Aristotle means to warn us against supposing (with the Platonists) that there are distinct forms (or species) of desire in the sense that there are distinct *subjects* of desire, one part of soul (τὸ ἐπιθυμητικόν) desiring sensual pleasure, another (τὸ θυμικόν) desiring (for example) honor, and yet another (τὸ λογιστικόν) desiring something like an all-things-considered good. For (10)(E) clearly refers back to (9)'s criticisms of various ways of dividing the soul. And (9)(E) suggests that Aristotle is opposed to breaking up [διασπᾶν] desire and assigning different forms (or species) of it to different parts of soul, some to a part of soul having reason and some to a non-rational part. This is clear not only from (9)(E)'s claim that it is strange or absurd [ἄτοπον] to break up

---

[60] Insofar as Aristotle views φαντασία *as* a kind of νοῦς, the identification of φαντασία with αἴσθησις, taken together with the identification of αἴσθησις with ὄρεξις, would seem to confirm that νοῦς is a kind of ὄρεξις. This is also suggested in (10)(C), where βούλησις is an example of a kind of νοῦς that moves by being a kind of ὄρεξις.

desire in this way, but also from its use of διασπᾶν, which connotes a *violent* separation of the parts from one another.⁶¹ Moreover, Aristotle hints in (9)(D) that he is opposed to separating τὸ φανταστικόν from other parts of soul, presumably τὸ αἰσθητικόν and τὸ ὀρεκτικόν. For he says there—just after mentioning τὸ αἰσθητικόν in (C) and just before mentioning τὸ ὀρεκτικόν in (E)—that there is much difficulty about τὸ φανταστικόν, concerning which of the other capacities of soul it is the same as (or different from) "*if* someone is going to posit *separate* parts of soul." The implied solution is that we should not posit *separate* parts of soul, at least not separate parts for each of the capacities mentioned here and perhaps even no separate parts at all. This solution is once again implied in (10)(E), which is directed against those who propose to divide the soul according to its *capacities* and to posit *separate* parts (presumably for each capacity). This suggests that Aristotle wants at the very least to allow that one and the same part of soul can have multiple capacities. And it leaves open the more extreme possibility that he would reject *any* division whatsoever of the soul into parts.

But Aristotle's frequent references (even in non-aporetic contexts) to various "parts" of soul render it implausible to suppose that he objects to *any* division whatsoever of the soul into parts: it is more plausible to suppose that his objection is—as his own formulation suggests—to dividing the soul into *separate* parts. And the objection may take different forms in the case of different alleged parts. In the case of some allegedly distinct parts associated with different capacities, he may claim that there is in fact no distinction of parts at all, that there is simply one part with multiple capacities (e.g., one part with capacities of desire, perception, and imagination); while in the case of other allegedly distinct parts associated with different capacities, he may allow that there are in fact distinct parts that, however, are inseparable from one another in the sense that they cannot *exist* apart from one another. For he may think (as I have already suggested) that although the nutritive/generative part of an animal's soul is inseparable from its perceptive/locomotive part of soul in the sense that neither part can exist independently of the other, these are nevertheless two genuinely distinct parts of soul, each being embodied in a distinct physiological system that (although it shares its central organ with the other system) functions relatively independently of the other. And he may think this while denying that the capacities of perception, imagination, and desire each belong to a distinct part of soul: he may think (as I have been arguing) that they are inseparable from one another in a *stronger* way from that in which they together are inseparable from the nutritive/generative part. In other words, he may think that these capacities belong to—or constitute—a single part: i.e., what I have been calling the "locomotive" part.

It is perhaps significant that Aristotle elsewhere endorses an alternative to the principle of dividing the soul into parts according to its various capacities. In *Nicomachean*

---

⁶¹ Cf. *DA* 416a6–9: "What is τὸ συνέχον of fire and earth, tending as they do in opposite directions? For they will be torn apart [διασπασθήσεται] unless there is something preventing this. But if there is, then this is the soul and the cause of growth and nourishment."

Ethics VI.1, he identifies τὸ ἐπιστημονικόν (which contemplates necessary truths) and τὸ λογιστικόν (which contemplates variable things) with distinct parts of soul on the grounds that *objects* of knowledge that are different in *kind* must be grasped by *parts of soul* that are different in *kind* (the reason being that knowledge is supposed to belong to a subject on account of some sort of similarity or affinity with its object) [*EN* 1139a6–15]. This suggests that he might have an additional reason for assigning τὸ ὀρεκτικόν, τὸ φανταστικόν, and practical νοῦς to the *same* part of soul. For (10)(F) identifies the objects of desire with the objects of practical thought and imagination: the *object of desire* moves the animal by *being thought* or *imagined*. In other words, the *same* objects are both desired and practically thought or imagined.

This reason is not entirely distinct from the reasons offered above by parity with the argument for a common sense. It is because one and the same subject *both* desires objects as pleasant (or as good) *and* thinks or imagines objects as pleasant (or as good) that locomotion occurs. The *objects* of desire, practical thought, and imagination must—like their *subjects*—be the same. For if desire on the one hand and practical thought or imagination on the other hand had different objects, it is not clear how they would cooperate in the production of action. This would be no different from the case in which one and the same subject had both a desire for something achievable in action and theoretical thought of an eternal and invariable object: no action or locomotion would result.

The account proposed here will allow us to explain why (F) says not simply that τὸ ὀρεκτικόν moves the animal but that τὸ ὀρεκτικόν ᾗ ὀρεκτικόν moves the animal.[62] The answer to the question posed at the start of *De Anima* III.9 is that what moves the animal is *not* some distinctive part of soul beyond those mentioned: it is simply τὸ ὀρεκτικόν. But since the desiring part of soul is one and the same part of soul as the perceiving part, the imagining part, and the practically thinking part, the identification of the part that moves the animal with the *orectic* part demands clarification. It is not qua identified with a form of νοῦς that τὸ ὀρεκτικόν moves the animal, for there is another form of νοῦς (i.e., theoretical νοῦς) that does not move animals. Nor is it qua identified with τὸ φανταστικόν that τὸ ὀρεκτικόν moves the animal, for there is another form of φαντασία (namely, theoretical φαντασία) that does not move animals. Nor is it qua identified with τὸ αἰσθητικόν that τὸ ὀρεκτικόν moves the animal, for there are theoretical forms of perception that do not move animals. In other words, although τὸ ὀρεκτικόν is in some sense one with τὸ αἰσθητικόν and τὸ φανταστικόν, and also (in the case of rational animals) one with practical νοῦς, it is qua ὀρεκτικόν and not qua any of these things that τὸ ὀρεκτικόν moves the animal.[63]

---

[62] It is worth comparing this with *De Insomniis* 459a21–23, which says that dreaming belongs to τὸ αἰσθητικόν, but belongs to it ᾗ φανταστικόν.

[63] I do not say that it is qua κινητικόν that τὸ ὀρεκτικόν moves the animal, because this would be insufficiently explanatory, a kind of "dormitive virtue" explanation.

6. THE INCLUSION OF PRACTICAL νοῦς IN "LOCOMOTIVE SOUL" AND THE PROBLEM ABOUT THEORETICAL νοῦς

De Anima III.10—passage (10)—suggests that practical νοῦς stands to τὸ ὀρεκτικόν of a *rational* animal in something like the way τὸ φανταστικόν, which is the same but different in being from τὸ αἰσθητικόν, stands to τὸ ὀρεκτικόν in *any* animal. But I think it would be a mistake to see a mere analogy here. For (as we shall soon see) Aristotle seems to view practical νοῦς (and perhaps also theoretical νοῦς) as a kind of extension or development of τὸ αἰσθητικόν. This suggests that the unity of a rational animal's practical νοῦς with its ὀρεκτικόν is not simply analogous to the unity of non-rational animal's αἰσθητικόν with its ὀρεκτικόν, but rather a *special case* of the general unity found in *all* animals of τὸ αἰσθητικόν with τὸ ὀρεκτικόν. If this is right, then practical νοῦς is—like τὸ φανταστικόν—the same but different in being from τὸ αἰσθητικόν, and so the same but different in being from τὸ ὀρεκτικόν. What distinguishes rational animals from non-rational ones is simply that they have more complex forms of perception and so more complex forms of imagination—forms of perception and imagination so complex that they constitute a *form* of νοῦς (perhaps even a form of theoretical νοῦς). And with these more complex forms of perception and imagination come more complex forms of desire.

To see this, let us begin with the following passage from *De Anima* II.3 concerning the most elementary form of perception—namely, touch (with which taste is closely associated):

(11) (A) Of the capacities of soul [τῶν δὲ δυνάμεων τῆς ψυχῆς] mentioned above—to some <living things> all <these capacities> belong, just as we said, while to some <only> some of them <belong>, and to others one alone <belongs>. The capacities we mentioned are nutritive [θρεπτικόν], desiderative [ὀρεκτικόν], perceptive [αἰσθητικόν], locomotive [κινητικὸν κατὰ τόπον], and thinking [διανοητικόν]. To plants, τὸ θρεπτικόν alone belongs, but to other <living things> both this and τὸ αἰσθητικόν <belong>. [*DA* 414a29–b1]

(B) And if τὸ αἰσθητικόν, then also τὸ ὀρεκτικόν. For ὄρεξις <includes> appetite [ἐπιθυμία], spirit [θυμός], and wish [βούλησις]. And all animals have one of the perceptual capacities: namely, touch. And to that to which perception belongs, pleasure and pain and the pleasant and painful also <belong>, and to those to which these belong, ἐπιθυμία also <belongs>. For this [sc., ἐπιθυμία] is desire for what is pleasant. Further, they <creatures with touch> have perception of nourishment. For touch is perception of nourishment. For all living things are nourished by dry and wet things, and by hot and cold things, and touch is perception of these, and of the other perceptibles <only> coincidentally [κατὰ συμβεβηκός]. For sound, color, and smell contribute nothing to nourishment, and flavor is one of the objects of touch. And hunger and thirst are <forms of> ἐπιθυμία, hunger being of <what is> dry and

> hot, and thirst being of <what is> cold and wet. And flavor is like some sort of seasoning of these. It is necessary to speak more clearly about these things later on, but for now let so much be said, that to those of the animals having touch, desire [ὄρεξις] also belongs. [*DA* 414b1–16]

It is clear from this passage that Aristotle thinks that perception entails desire because the most fundamental form of perception entails ἐπιθυμία, which is a form of desire: because touch is prior to all other forms of perception, any creature endowed with touch will also be endowed with at least some appetitive desires (namely, those involved in hunger and thirst). What is less clear from this passage is whether he thinks that other forms of perception entail other forms of desire—either other forms of ἐπιθυμία or forms of θυμός or βούλησις.

It is worth noting here that Aristotle seems to think that animals endowed only with the sense of touch belong to imperfect species in which sexual division is absent and reproduction is nonsexual. This suggests that he would take additional and increasingly complex forms of desire—at least additional and increasingly complex forms of ἐπιθυμία—to accompany additional and increasingly complex forms of perception. Adding the sense of smell might, for example, contribute to the production of desires for certain tastes, so that taste, though associated primarily with touch, is no longer a matter of touch alone: taste, we might say, is altered by its association with smell in ways such that taste itself becomes (along with its possible objects) more complex. Similarly, sexual desire, which is also associated primarily with touch, might be very different among animals endowed with keener senses of smell and among animals endowed with keener senses of sight. Adding more discriminating forms of sight might, for example, contribute to the production of desires for voyeuristic pleasures, so that sexual desire, though associated primarily with touch, is no longer a matter of touch alone: sexual desire too might be altered by its association with sight in ways such that it too becomes (along with its possible objects) more complex. Think, for example, of poor Leontius at 439E in Plato's *Republic*.

It seems reasonable to suppose that Aristotle is well aware of this general phenomenon. For this would help to explain the distinctive pleasures of sight that he attributes to human animals at the beginning of the *Metaphysics*. The idea there is presumably that sight is altered by its association with intellect, so that sight itself—along with its possible objects and the pleasures of its exercise—is rendered more complex. Instead of seeing things as non-rational animals see them—simply, for example, as predators or prey and so as potential sources of pain or pleasure—rational animals, because of the ways in which their sight is informed by intellect, can see things as triangles, eclipses, and other objects of knowledge.[64] Sight is thus associated in rational animals with distinctive sorts of contemplative pleasures and with correspondingly distinctive sorts of contemplative desires.

---

[64] For an interesting discussion of some of the issues involved here, see Charles Brittain, "Non-Rational Perception in the Stoics and Augustine," *Oxford Studies in Ancient Philosophy* 22 (2002): 253–308.

Given that Aristotle allows this, it is not surprising that he seems also to allow that the emergence of *practical* intellect alters and informs sight in similar ways, yielding forms of perception complex enough to register what (for example) is noble or what justice requires here and now, forms of perception that go hand in hand with ethical forms of desire and the pleasures associated with their satisfaction.[65] This helps to explain why he seeks to elucidate φρόνησις in perceptual terms, and why he explicitly says that human beings have *perception* of what is *good and bad* and of what is *just and unjust*.

(12) Hence it is plain why man is more a political animal than any bee or any gregarious animal. For nature, as we say, makes nothing in vain. And humans alone among animals have speech. [Mere] voice [ἡ μὲν φωνή] is a sign of the painful and pleasant, on account of which it [sc., mere voice] belongs even to the other animals—for their nature extends up to this point, to having perception of the pleasant and painful and signifying these to one another; but speech [ὁ δὲ λόγος] is for revealing the advantageous and the harmful [τὸ συμφέρον καὶ τὸ βλαβερόν], and so also the just and the unjust. For this is peculiar to human beings in relation to the other animals, to alone have perception of good and bad, of just and unjust, and other such things [τοῦτο γὰρ πρὸς τὰ ἄλλα ζῷα τοῖς ἀνθρώποις ἴδιον, τὸ μόνον ἀγαθοῦ καὶ κακοῦ καὶ δικαίου καὶ ἀδίκου καὶ τῶν ἄλλων αἴσθησιν ἔχειν]. [*Politics* 1253a7–18][66]

This of course does not mean that all human beings accurately perceive what is in fact good and bad, or what is in fact just and unjust. For as Aristotle says in (13) (B) below, pleasure and pain can corrupt someone in ways such that what is really good fails to appear to her as such:

(13) (A) It remains then for it [sc., φρόνησις] to be a true state, involving reason, for action concerning things good and bad for a human being [ἕξιν ἀληθῆ μετὰ λόγου πρακτικὴν περὶ τὰ ἀνθρώπῳ ἀγαθὰ καὶ κακά]. For in the case of production [τῆς μὲν γὰρ ποιήσεως] the end is different [from the producing], but in the case of action [τῆς δὲ πράξεως] [the end] could not be [different from the acting]; for acting well itself [αὐτὴ ἡ εὐπραξία] is its end. On account of this, we believe Pericles and such men to be practically wise [φρονίμους], because they are able to contemplate the things that are good for themselves and for men in general. And we think that household managers and politicians are such people. [*EN* 1140b4–11]

---

[65] See the reference in passage (14) to the distinctive [ἴδια] sorts of pleasures associated with virtue. See also *EN* 1099a7–21.

[66] I translate the Oxford Classical Text prepared by W. D. Ross, *Aristotelis Politica* (Oxford: Oxford University Press, 1957).

(B) This is also why we call temperance [τὴν σωφροσύνην] by this name, on the grounds that it preserves φρόνησις. For it preserves this sort of supposition [σῴζει δὲ τὴν τοιαύτην ὑπόληψιν]. For it is not every <sort of> supposition that pleasure and pain corrupt and pervert—for example, not <the supposition> that the triangle has or does not have two right angles, but <rather> those <suppositions> concerning matters of action [τὰς περὶ τὸ πρακτόν]. For the origins of actions are that for the sake of which the actions <are done>. And to one who has been corrupted by pleasure or pain, straightaway <the> origin does not appear [εὐθὺς οὐ φαίνεται ἀρχή], nor <does it appear to him> that it is for the sake of this or on account of this that he ought to choose and to do all things. For vice is destructive of <the> origin. Hence it is necessary for φρόνησις to be a true state, involving reason, for action concerning human goods [ὥστ' ἀνάγκη τὴν φρόνησιν ἕξιν εἶναι μετὰ λόγου ἀληθῆ περὶ τὰ ἀνθρώπινα ἀγαθὰ πρακτικήν]. [EN 1140b11–21][67]

Similarly in *EN* III. 4, in discussing whether the object of wish (ἡ βούλησις) is the (genuine) good or only the apparent good (τὸ φαινόμενον ἀγαθόν), Aristotle says.

(14) Should we say then that, without qualification and in truth the good is <the> object of wish [ἁπλῶς μὲν καὶ κατ' ἀλήθειαν βουλητὸν εἶναι τἀγαθόν], but to each individual the apparent <good is the object of wish> [ἑκάστῳ δὲ τὸ φαινόμενον]? For to the excellent person <the object of wish is> what is truly <good> [τῷ μὲν οὖν σπουδαίῳ τὸ κατ' ἀλήθειαν εἶναι], but to the base person <the object of wish is> whatever happens <to seem good to him> [τῷ δὲ φαύλῳ τὸ τυχόν]. And just as with bodies, to those in a good condition what are healthy are the things that are truly such [τὰ κατ' ἀλήθειαν τοιαῦτα ὄντα], while to those that are ill different things <are healthy>, and similarly in the case of what is bitter, sweet, hot, heavy, and each of the others. For the excellent person judges each of these things correctly, and in each case what is true appears to him [ὁ σπουδαῖος γὰρ ἕκαστα κρίνει ὀρθῶς, καὶ ἐν ἑκάστοις τἀληθὲς αὐτῷ φαίνεται]. For to each state <of character> its own distinctive things are fine and pleasant [καθ' ἑκάστην γὰρ ἕξιν ἴδιά ἐστι καλὰ καὶ ἡδέα], and the excellent person excels perhaps most in seeing what is true in each case, being like a standard and measure of these [sc., of fine and truly pleasant things] [καὶ διαφέρει πλεῖστον ἴσως ὁ σπουδαῖος τῷ τἀληθὲς ἐν ἑκάστοις ὁρᾶν, ὥσπερ κανὼν καὶ μέτρον αὐτῶν ὤν]. Among the many, however, error seems to occur on account of pleasure. For not being good it [sc., pleasure] appears <good>. So they choose the pleasant as being good and avoid pain as being bad. [*EN* 1113a23–b2]

---

[67] Here and in what follows, I translate the Oxford Classical Text prepared by I. Bywater, *Aristotelis Ethica Nicomachea* (Oxford: Oxford University Press, 1894).

These passages suggest that there is an important sense in which the perceptual capacity involved in φρόνησις is one that is not shared equally by virtuous and non-virtuous agents alike. Although non-virtuous agents may, like virtuous agents, see things as good and bad, and perhaps even as just and unjust, only virtuous agents see these things truly: only virtuous agents have veridical perceptions of what is good and bad, just and unjust, etc. That is because their perception has been educated to see what is good and bad, just and unjust, and so on, through a kind of habituation not unlike the intellectual habituation involved in learning to see things as triangles, eclipses, and so on. The need for this sort of perceptual education is, I take it, part of the point of Aristotle's comparison of ethical perception to mathematical perception:

(15) It [sc., φρόνησις] is opposed to νοῦς. For νοῦς is of definitions, of which there is no account, but it [sc., φρόνησις] is of the last thing, of which there is not scientific knowledge [ἐπιστήμη] but ‹rather› perception [αἴσθησις]—not [perception] of proper perceptibles but like that by which we perceive that the last thing among mathematicals is a triangle. For it will stop there. But this is more perception than φρόνησις is, though a different form of it [sc., a different form of perception] [ἀλλ᾽ αὕτη μᾶλλον αἴσθησις ἢ φρόνησις, ἐκείνης δ᾽ ἄλλο εἶδος]. [EN 1142a25–30]

As Aristotle explains here, ethical perception is not of proper perceptibles, concerning which any normal perceiver is more or less infallible, but more like the sort of perception by means of which someone (and presumably *only* someone) with mathematical training is able to see that the last thing among mathematicals is a triangle. Similarly, someone (and presumably *only* someone) with the right sort of ethical education will be able to see the good and the bad, the just and the unjust, and so on. But it does not follow from the fact that perception must be ethically educated in order for someone to see what is good or just that she does not really *see* these things; this does not follow any more than it follows from the fact that perception must be mathematically educated in order for someone to see that the last thing is a triangle that the mathematician does not really *see* this. Even if mathematical perception is more perception—in the sense that it is closer to perception of proper perceptibles—than ethical perception is, ethical perception is still a form of perception (but a different form of it). And just as a mathematician's perceptions of mathematical facts are veridical, so too the practically wise person's perceptions of ethical facts can be veridical.

One might even be tempted to translate the occurrences of ἕξιν ἀληθῆ in (13) as "veridical state," and so to take Aristotle to identify φρόνησις with a "veridical and practical state, involving reason, concerned with human goods." And one might support this by appeal to the fact that Aristotle often uses φρόνησις interchangeably with νοῦς in the sense of practical νοῦς, which he says at *De Anima* 433a26 is always correct; see (10)(D). Moreover, we can explain why this sort of νοῦς is *practical* if we suppose, as I have been arguing, that it is not simply a form of perception but *also*—given the general coincidence of perception and desire—a form of ὄρεξις. And it is clear that Aristotle has no reservations about calling one and the same state *both* a form of νοῦς *and* a form of ὄρεξις. For he refers to προαίρεσις *both* as "desiderative thought" [ὀρεκτικὸς νοῦς, at *EN* 1139b4–5] *and* as "thinking desire" [ὄρεξις διανοητική, at 1134b4–5] *or* "deliberative desire" [ὄρεξις βουλευτική, at 1139a23 and 1113a10–11]. There are of course problems here about how τὸ ὀρεκτικόν is supposed to be related to τὸ αἰσθητικόν in incontinent and merely continent subjects.[68] But the important point is that Aristotle's general identification of τὸ αἰσθητικόν with τὸ ὀρεκτικόν allows him to view the complex forms of perception involved in φρόνησις (which yields correct προαίρεσις) as themselves involving complex forms of ὄρεξις.

If this is right, then we can read our focal passage (3) not as restricting the identification of τὸ ὀρεκτικόν with τὸ αἰσθητικόν to non-rational animals, but rather as making the point that the αἰσθητικόν-cum-ὀρεκτικόν is more complicated in thinking than in non-thinking animals. Instead of taking the contrast between (3)(A) and (3)(B) as one between the souls of animals that have only perception (along with the sort of desire that goes with it), and the souls of thinking animals, we can take (3)(B) as pointing to the way in which the emergence of thought alters and complexifies perception and desire.[69]

This way of reading (3) is especially plausible if Aristotle assigns the activities of thought and imagination mentioned in (B) to τὸ αἰσθητικόν, as suggested by passage (4)'s identification of τὸ φανταστικόν with τὸ αἰσθητικόν. But here again someone might object that (4)'s identification applies only to non-rational animals. And one might seek to support this objection by appeal to (10)(I)'s distinction between φαντασία λογιστική and φαντασία αἰσθητική, the idea being that τὸ φανταστικόν of a rational animal must be identified with its λογιστικόν rather than its αἰσθητικόν. But this would be a mistake. For passage (4) clearly applies to *rational* animals: Aristotle is concerned there—and throughout *De Insomniis*—primarily with *human* dreams. So we should not suppose that he intends to identify τὸ φανταστικόν with τὸ αἰσθητικόν only in the case of non-rational animals. We must instead see if we can explain the association of φαντασία with thought in a way that does not conflict with the identification of τὸ φανταστικόν with τὸ αἰσθητικόν.

It seems to me that the resources for some such explanation lie ready to hand in Aristotle's account of the emergence of knowledge (including, apparently, theoretical

---

[68] I discuss these in my "Hylomorphic Virtue" [Chapter 6, this volume].

[69] [I have in recent years been developing the views expressed here in the direction of what Matthew Boyle calls "transformative" (as opposed to "additive") conceptions of rationality. See M. Boyle, "Additive Theories of Rationality: A Critique," *European Journal of Philosophy* 24, no. 3 (2016): 527–55; and "Essentially Rational Animals," in G. Abel and J. Conant (eds.), *Rethinking Epistemology* (Berlin: Walter de Grutyer, 2012), 395–428. And while one might think that talk of rationality as "emergent" is in tension with the idea of rationality as "transformative," my aim is to show that Aristotle thinks *both* that human rationality emerges from capacities (such as perception and imagination) that we in some sense share with other animals *and* that the capacities in question are ones whose operations in human beings differ in kind from their homonymous counterparts in non-rational animals. I am very much indebted to Matt—and to John McDowell—for discussion of these issues over many years, and I hope to publish some of the fruits of these conversations sometime in the not too distant future.]

knowledge) from perception and memory. For it seems clear that he wants to ground our activities of thought, especially but not only practical thought, in the activities of perception and memory that we in some sense share with other animals. As he explains in *Metaphysics* I.1, all animals have perception, and from perception some develop memory while others do not. Those endowed with memory are more intelligent [φρονιμώτερα] than those without.[70] But even among animals endowed with memory, few are able to connect various memories of the same thing into a single body of what Aristotle calls "experience" [ἡ ἐμπειρία]. So most animals live by means of φαντασία (presumably perceptual) and memories (presumably less rather than more connected). But human animals are able to connect various memories of the same thing with one another, so from memory humans come to have experience. Experience differs from science [ἐπιστήμη] and craft [τέχνη] in that experience is a kind of knowledge [γνῶσις] of individuals, while science and craft are knowledge of universals. Experience is knowledge that Socrates, when ill in this way, responded to such and such a treatment; that Callias, when ill in a similar way, responded to a similar treatment; and so on. Science or craft is knowledge that *all* men suffering from one form of illness respond to a certain sort of treatment. Aristotle says that this sort of universal knowledge develops from experience. The idea is presumably that memory allows the subject to connect various bodies of experience with one another in much the same way that memory originally allows the subject to connect various perceptions with one another so as to form bodies of experience. There is no mention in this story of νοῦς or λόγος. This suggests that Aristotle may view νοῦς and λόγος as something like emergent capacities that do not so much explain our development as emerge in it: perhaps (at least in developmental contexts) he views νοῦς and λόγος as explananda rather than explanantia.

Michael Frede suggests something like this in his accounts both of *Metaphysics* I.1 and of *Posterior Analytics* II.19, where Aristotle gives a similar account of how we come to grasp universals:

> Aristotle in [*Posterior Analytics*] B 19 is quite specific as to what kind of abilities it takes to acquire reason. On his view (cf. 99b32ff) it primarily takes the ability to perceptually discriminate, but then also the ability to remember what we have perceived and to process what we remember in a certain way. His view quite definitely is not that it takes the ability to perceive, the ability to remember, and, in addition, potential reason. The view rather is that reason develops out of our ability to discriminate perceptually and remember. Given the way human beings perceive, given

---

[70] The frequency with which Aristotle speaks in the biological works (and elsewhere) of various animals as φρόνιμος, and of some as φρονιμώτερα than others, is an important but frequently neglected point (especially in the standard account of the distinction between us rational animals and all other ones). One person who has given this point the sort of attention it deserves is J. L. Labarrière. See his "De la phronesis animale," in D. Devereux and P. Pellegrin (eds.), *Biologie, logique, et métaphysique chez Aristote* (Paris, 1990), 405–28; and "Imagination humaine et imagination animale chez Aristote," *Phronesis* 29 (1984): 17–49.

their powerful memory, which allows them to develop a powerful experience, they come to form the right concepts and thus to acquire reason. Hence it seems that, if we want to talk about potential reason at all, it is not an ability which we have innately in addition to the specifically human forms of the abilities to perceive and to remember; to be potentially rational seems to consist in nothing else but the particular powerful way in which human beings can perceive and remember.[71]

The plausibility of some such account suggests that we need not take the association in rational animals of φαντασία with νοῦς to undermine Aristotle's identification of a rational animal's φανταστικόν with its αἰσθητικόν. Because rational animals have more sophisticated forms of perception and more powerful memories, rational animals have more sophisticated forms of φαντασία—φαντασία, for example, of absent and future objects. Furthermore, while it may be true that rational animals have a form of φαντασία that non-rational animals lack—namely, φαντασία λογιστική—we should not forget that φαντασία is not only present in non-rational animals but also necessary for adequate explanations of *their* intentional movements. So we should not take φαντασία to do for rational animals what perception alone does for non-rational ones: φαντασία (which is an activity of τὸ αἰσθητικόν) is required in *both* cases. It is just that in the case of rational animals the forms of φαντασία are more sophisticated *because* the forms of perception are more sophisticated (and probably also vice versa). The φανταστικόν of a rational animal is not limited to representing objects that are perceptually present to its subject; it can represent past and future objects, as well as absent and merely possible ones. Nor is it limited (as in the case of non-rational animals) to representing objects as pleasant or painful; it can also represent objects (including absent, future, and merely possible objects) as good and bad, just and unjust, etc. In other words, the activities *of* τὸ φανταστικόν are less closely tied in rational than in non-rational animals to the activities of perception as such. And the point of (3)(B) may be to call attention to this fact—i.e., to call attention to the way in which the emergence of νοῦς signals a complexification of the activities of τὸ φανταστικόν, and so also of the activities of the αἰσθητικόν-cum-ὀρεκτικόν with which τὸ φανταστικόν is identified not simply in the case of non-rational animals but in the case of rational ones as well.

Here, however, we must note that viewing intellect as an extension of τὸ αἰσθητικόν raises questions about the status of theoretical intellect, especially in relation to the capacities of locomotive soul. For the parallel passages in *Metaphysics* I.1 and *Posterior Analytics* II.19 suggest that theoretical intellect no less than practical intellect grows out of the capacities of perception and memory that we share with other animals, and so may (like practical intellect) belong to the locomotive part of soul. Indeed Aristotle suggests, consistently with this, that that with which we discriminate or judge the *essence* of a natural thing (like the snub) *may* stand to τὸ αἰσθητικόν (with which we discriminate or judge the thing itself) as what is bent stands to itself when it has been straightened: in other words, that that with which we discriminate or judge the

---

[71] M. Frede, "Aristotle's Rationalism," in M. Frede and G. Striker (eds.), *Rationality in Greek Thought* (Oxford: Oxford University Press, 1996), 157–73.

essences of natural things *may* be the same thing (only in a different condition) as τὸ αἰσθητικόν (with which we discriminate or judge the things themselves). Similarly, he suggests that that with which we discriminate or judge the *essence* of a mathematical entity like the straight *may* be the same thing—but in a different condition—as that with which we discriminate the mathematical entity itself [*DA* 429b10-22]. One way to explain this would be to suppose that that with which we discriminate the *essence* of a natural thing is τὸ φανταστικόν, which is (as we have seen) the same thing but different in being from τὸ αἰσθητικόν (with which we discriminate the thing itself) and might thus be said to stand to τὸ αἰσθητικόν as what is bent stands to itself when it has been straightened. Similarly, we might say that that with which we discriminate the *essence* of a mathematical entity is theoretical νοῦς, which may be the same but different in being from that with which we discriminate the mathematical entity itself (presumably τὸ φανταστικόν) and so might be said to stand to the latter as what is bent stands to itself when it has been straightened. This, however, is only a conjecture.

The important point here is that taking that with which we discriminate or judge essences as the same thing only in a different condition from that with which we discriminate or judge the things themselves is only one of two alternatives suggested here, hence my italicized 'may.' Aristotle says that that with which we discriminate or judge the essences of things is *either* a different thing *or* the same thing in a different condition—ἢ ἄλλῳ ἢ ἄλλως ἔχοντι at *DA* 429b13; and ἑτέρῳ ἢ ἑτέρως at 429b20-21—from that with which we discriminate or judge the things themselves. And he seems to me genuinely agnostic about the status of theoretical intellect in mortal subjects. Recall, for example, (2)(B), where he says that *theoretical* intellect seems to be a different kind of soul [ψυχῆς γένος ἕτερον], capable of existing apart from the remaining parts of soul (presumably in a way in which *they* are not capable of existing apart from *one another*) just as the eternal can exist apart from what is perishable. There is a similar suggestion in a famous passage of *De Generatione Animalium* (*GA*) II.3:

(16) (A) It is clear, then, that they [sc., the semen and the embryo of an animal] have the nutritive soul [τὴν θρεπτικὴν ψυχήν] ... and also, as they develop, the perceptive [soul] in virtue of which an animal <exists> [προϊόντα δὲ καὶ τὴν αἰσθητικὴν καθ' ἣν ζῷον]. For <an embryo> does not simultaneously come to be an animal and a man, or animal and horse, and the same goes for the other <kinds of> animals. For the end [τὸ τέλος] comes to be last, and the end of the generation of each <kind of animal> is what is distinctive [ἴδιον] <of its kind>. Hence there is greatest difficulty concerning νοῦς, when and how and from where those having a share of this principle receive it. [*GA* 736a35–b8]

(B) Clearly we must suppose that semen and the embryos that are not yet separate have nutritive soul potentially, but do not have it actually until (like embryos that have been separated) they draw nourishment and perform the function of this sort of soul. For at first all such things seem to live the life of a plant. [*GA* 736b8–13]

(C) It is plain that we must speak accordingly of the perceptive soul [περὶ τῆς αἰσθητικῆς ψυχῆς] and of the one that thinks [περὶ τῆς νοητικῆς]. For it is necessary to have all <of these> potentially before having them actually. And it is necessary either (1) that all come to be in it [sc., the embryo] not having existed previously or (2) that all existed previously or (3) that some <existed previously> but others did not. And <it is necessary that> that they come to be in <the embryo> either (4) not having entered the matter with the semen of the male or (5) having entered there from outside; and if they enter with the male <semen> or from outside [ἐν δὲ τῷ ἄρρενι ἢ θύραθεν ἐγγιγνομένας],[72] either (6) all must come to be in <the embryo> in this way or (7) none must or (8) some must <enter in this way> while others do not. [GA 736b13–20]

(D) That it is impossible for all to preexist is plain from the following sorts of considerations: in the case of all principles ὅσων γάρ ἐστιν ἀρχῶν ἡ ἐνέργεια σω-ματική whose actuality is bodily, it is clear that these cannot exist without a body: for example, walking [cannot exist] without feet. Thus it is also impossible [for these things] to enter from without. For being inseparable they cannot enter themselves by themselves; nor can they enter in a body. For the semen is a residue of the changing nutriment. So it remains [possible] for νοῦς alone to enter from outside and for it alone to be divine. For bodily activity has no share at all in the activity of it. [GA 736b21–29][73]

Here again Aristotle is tentative: the modal status of the early claims (that nutritive and perceptive soul *cannot* enter from without) makes it natural to read the final claim in a similar way (as a claim about what is *possible*). So it is difficult to resolve the question how exactly Aristotle takes the theoretical intellect of mortals to be related to perceptive or "locomotive'" soul—whether he thinks of the theoretical intellect of a human animal as a different part of its soul, capable of existing independently of the perceptive or "locomotive" part of its soul, or whether he identifies the theoretical intellect of a human animal with its perceptive or "locomotive" soul only in a different condition from that in which it perceives and locomotes. He seems on the whole to regard theoretical intellect as belonging to a distinct part of soul, partly because (as we have seen) he thinks its objects are different in kind from the objects of perception and practical intellect, and so must be grasped by a different kind of subject. But he is tentative in advancing this view.

---

[72] For the suggestion that we take ἢ θύραθεν, not as offering an alternative, but as a gloss on ἐν δὲ τῷ ἄρρενι, see W. Charlton, "Aristotle on the Place of Mind in Nature," in A. Gotthelf and J. G. Lennox (eds.), *Philosophical Issues in Aristotle's Biology* (Cambridge: Cambridge University Press, 1987), 408–23, esp. 415–16.

[73] I translate the Oxford Classical Text prepared by H. J. Drossaart Luloffs, *Aristotelis De Generatione Animalium* (Oxford: Oxford University Press, 1965).

One possible way to reconcile Aristotle's different claims would be to suppose that the theoretical intellect of a human animal emerges only gradually with the development of its perceptual and imaginative capacities, and so only in connection with certain bodily processes that are necessary conditions but not essential components of its activity, but that once it has come to be it can then exist and function apart from the body and its processes (a possibility that seems plausible, given that the theoretical intellect of a divine subject can presumably exist ab initio apart from any body). To the extent that the theoretical intellect of a human animal relies (at least in the early stages of its development) on the bodily processes involved in perception and imagination, these processes are *necessary* for its operations (at least early on). But these processes may belong—as Aristotle says of memory in general—only *accidentally* to the thinking part of soul, being essentially processes (like the capacities whose actualizations they are) of the perceptive part of soul [*De Mem.* 450a12–17].[74] Unfortunately, we cannot resolve this issue—which would require at least another treatise—here. The important point for present purposes is that *whatever* we say about *theoretical* intellect, it is pretty clear that *practical* intellect belongs to perceptive or "locomotive soul", which—although it cannot exist in animals independently of the nutritive-cum-generative part—is nevertheless a part of soul distinct from the nutritive-cum-generative part.

7. AFTERWORD

There is, obviously, much work that remains to be done here, particularly concerning the relationship between, on the one hand, theoretical intellect, and on the other hand, the perceptive and imaginative capacities that are here associated primarily with the locomotive part of soul; and also concerning the relationship between the threefold division of the soul that we find in Aristotle's scientific works and the fourfold division that we seem to find in his ethical works. But as I have indicated in note 44 above, I see no fundamental conflict between the division we find in the scientific works and the division we find in the ethical works. For I take the ethical works to view practical νοῦς as standing to the desiderative part of soul—i.e., to the part of soul that *can obey* practical νοῦς—in something like the way in which the convex stands to the

---

[74] I defend a view like this in "Human Nature and Intellectualism in Aristotle," *Archiv für Geschichte der Philosophie* 68 (1986): 70–95 [II.2] where I argue (1) that Aristotle views bodily activity as a necessary condition for theoretical thought, though not (as in the case of practical thought) part of its essence; and (2) that Aristotle does not identify theoretical intellect (at least in mortal subjects) with the active intellect of *De Anima* III.5 (the formidable difficulties of which I cannot now discuss). If one accepts this distinction between the theoretical intellect of a mortal subject and the active intellect of *De Anima* III.5, then one might suppose that (2)(B)'s reference to a different kind of soul, which alone is capable of being separate, is to active intellect and not to the theoretical intellect of a mortal subject. For a survey of the various accounts given of active intellect, see F. Brentano, *Die Psychologie des Aristoteles* (Mainz, 1866), translated into English by R. George as *The Psychology of Aristotle* (Berkeley: University of California Press, 1977).

concave. I say "something like" this because I think that the relationship is ultimately more like the relationship between a soul and its organic body, whose form or essence Aristotle says the soul is [*DA* 412b10–12].[75]

On this sort of account, first suggested by John McDowell, the relationship between practical νοῦς and the orectic part of soul is hylomorphic: practical νοῦς is the proper form (or actualization) of the orectic part of soul.[76] This is not to say that τὸ ὀρεκτικόν of every human being is fully actualized by *practical* νοῦς (which is, as we have seen, a developmental achievement). For Aristotle would clearly deny that, not just in the case of so-called natural slaves and women but also in the case of non-virtuous male adults. But this is not a problem for the hylomorphic account. For just as a living body can fail to be fully actualized by soul (as in the case of a blind or paralyzed subject), so too τὸ ὀρεκτικόν of a rational animal can fail to be fully actualized by practical νοῦς (as in the case of continent and incontinent subjects, whose wayward actions Aristotle explicitly compares to the wayward actions of defective limbs).

How exactly the hylomorphic account is supposed to work is a story for another occasion. But one advantage of telling a hylomorphic story is that it helps to explain some of the more puzzling features of Aristotle's ethical works—for example, his claim [at *EN* 1144a36–b1] that one cannot be φρόνιμος without being good. It also renders Aristotle's account of human behavior continuous with his general account of animal behavior: the unity of practical νοῦς with τὸ ὀρεκτικόν is on the hylomorphic account simply a special case of the general unity he sees among animals of τὸ αἰσθητικόν with τὸ ὀρεκτικόν. Nevertheless, I had always—prior to arriving at the views defended here—regarded McDowell's hylomorphic account as perverse: for it seemed to me obvious that Aristotle regards practical reason and desire as belonging to distinct parts of soul, one rational and the other not. But I have come, in the course of reading Aristotle's scientific works, to see the plausibility of McDowell's view. What impresses me now is the way in which the scientific works, which McDowell was surely not considering, provide such elegant support for his heterodox reading of the partitioning we find in the ethical works.[77]

---

[75] On this relationship see my "Living Bodies" [Chapter 3, this volume].

[76] My understanding of the ethical works is much indebted to the work of John McDowell, especially to sec. 11 of his "Some Issues in Aristotle's Moral Psychology," in S. Everson (ed.), *Ethics* (Cambridge: Cambridge University Press, 1998): 107–28; reprinted in McDowell's *Mind, Value, and Reality* (Cambridge, MA: Harvard, 1998), 23–49.

[77] This essay has evolved from the first half of my "Locomotive Soul and Hylomorphic Virtue," the second half of which was published separately under the title "Hylomorphic Virtue" [Chapter 6, this volume]. The longer paper was originally prepared for the Princeton Colloquium of Ancient Philosophy and later presented to audiences at UCLA and Syracuse University. I should like to thank the members of these audiences—especially Cass Weller, who was my commentator at Princeton—for much profitable discussion. I should also like to thank Terry Irwin, Sean Kelsey, and Susan Sauvé Meyer for comments on an early draft, and Chris Shields for comments on multiple drafts. I am, however, most indebted to David Sedley, whose probing comments—the most helpful I have ever had from the editor of a journal—led me to rethink my view in ways that have significantly improved its articulation.

6

Hylomorphic Virtue

COSMOLOGY, EMBRYOLOGY, AND MORAL DEVELOPMENT IN ARISTOTLE

MY AIM HERE is to develop the case for ascribing to Aristotle the hylomorphic conception of virtue sketched at the end of "Locomotive Soul" (Whiting, 2002 [Chapter 5, this volume]). That piece stems from a longer piece prepared for Princeton's Classical Philosophy Colloquium, where the "Locomotive Soul" part went over far better than the "Hylomorphic Virtue" one. The editor of *Oxford Studies* followed suit, but generously allowed me an "Afterword" in which to sketch the basic idea of the hylomorphic conception—namely, that Aristotle takes practical intellect [*nous*] to stand to the desiring part of soul in a way comparable to that in which he takes soul itself to stand to body—i.e., as form [*morphê*] to matter [*hulê*].

There is a version of this idea in the work of John McDowell, who argues that Aristotle regards *phronêsis* (which is the proper *virtue* of practical *nous*) as "the properly moulded state of the motivational propensities, in reflectively adjusted form" (1998). Much of the scholarly resistance to my view was clearly due to my assimilation of it to McDowell's. And I understood the resistance. For I myself had long resisted McDowell's identification of Aristotelian *phronêsis* with ethical virtue. Surely Aristotle meant to *disagree* with Socrates' identification of virtue with knowledge and with Socrates' corollary rejection of the possibility of *akrasia* (i.e., the possibility of acting against one's knowledge of what one ought to do). For Aristotle spends the better part of *Nicomachean Ethics* 7 seeking to give an account of akratic action. And he explicitly says things like "in saying that the virtues are all forms of knowledge [*phronêseis*], Socrates erred, but in saying that they are *not without* knowledge, he spoke well" [*EN*

1144b18–21]. So it had always seemed to me clear that Aristotle was committed only to the reciprocity—and not to the identity—of virtue and *phronêsis*.[1]

But when I started looking closely at Aristotle's various accounts of the "parts" of soul, I came to see flaws in the standard readings of these accounts. And I began to appreciate the extent to which resistance to McDowell's view rests on the standard readings, according to which practical *nous* is a part of soul distinct from the so-called desiring part [*to orektikon*]. For much of the resistance, my own included, simply assumed that the opposition between practical nous and *to oretikon* in an akratic agent presupposes the distinctness of practical *nous* from *to orektikon* in any and every agent. The turning point for me was coming to see that this assumption is false: Aristotle need not regard as distinct in the virtuous agent any and every psychic part that he regards as distinct in an akratic (or merely enkratic) one.

Independent study of the famous passage at the end of *Republic* IV—where Plato has Socrates speak of psychic elements that were "previously many" becoming "entirely one"—assisted me here (Whiting 2012a [I.8]; see also Korsgaard 1999). If Plato entertained the sort of contingency I see there, not just in relations among the so-called parts but in the number of parts involved, then Aristotle might easily have done the same. So we cannot simply assume that Aristotle treated as distinct in virtuous agents those parts he found it necessary to distinguish in order to account for the behavior of akratic agents. He may well have given different kinds of accounts of cases where things go as they *should* go and of cases where things go *wrong*. For this sort of explanatory asymmetry is, as I argue below, a feature, not a bug, of Aristotle's teleology.

My plan is thus to supplement the arguments of "Locomotive Soul" by situating the explanatory asymmetries I see in Aristotle's ethical works in a broader context. For recognizing the presence of such asymmetries in his cosmology and his embryology should make it easier for readers to recognize them in his moral psychology.

1. HYLOMORPHISM: THE PARADIGM CASE

The hylomorphic label was coined by commentators seeking to describe Aristotle's account of the relationship between soul and body as *special* sort of relationship between form and matter. So in order to appreciate the case for extending this label to the relationship between practical intellect and *to orektikon*, we must first grasp what is supposed to make the paradigm case special and not simply another example of the sort of relationship we find between the form and the matter of, say, an ax.

---

[1] Books 5–7 of the *Nicomachean Ethics* (*EN*) double as Books 4–6 of the *Eudemian Ethics* (*EE*). All quotations from here on out are from Aristotle and identified by Bekker numbers, which are used in most modern editions and translations. Translations are my own. With many terms, such as '*akrasia*' and '*enkrateia*' (most often rendered 'incontinence' and 'continence') there is no adequate translation, so I shall simply transliterate.

According to Aristotle, an ax has a form and essence that is defined by its end—namely, actual chopping. So too an eye has a form and essence defined by its end—namely, the *capacity to see* (which stands to *actual seeing* as what Aristotle calls "first" to "second" actuality). And what goes for the parts of an animal goes for its body as a whole. Aristotle's general (but not therefore exceptionless) account of soul is thus "the first actuality of a natural body having the power of life" [*De Anima* (*DA*) 412a27–b6]. The possible exception concerns intellect: though Aristotle tends to be unsure what to say about the capacity for thought, he thinks it obvious that the other capacities by which animal souls are defined—reproduction, perception, locomotion—are *essentially embodied*.[2]

The idea that most capacities of soul are essentially embodied is part, but only part, of Aristotle's hylomorphism. For the capacity of an ax to chop is no less essentially embodied than the capacity of a bird to fly. Yet Aristotle sees an important difference. He says that *if* an ax *were* a natural body, its essence (which is its capacity to chop) would be its soul. But an ax is just an ax: *its* matter is not a natural body having *in itself* a source of motion and rest [*DA* 412b10–17].

Aristotle recognizes compositional plasticity in the case of the ax and other artifacts, but he is not quite sure what to say in the case of an animal (which is part of what is at issue here).[3] The head of an ax must be made of some stuff or other capable both of holding a sharp edge and of withstanding the blows required if it is to chop, and the haft must be rigid but sufficiently light to allow a woodchopper to wield it. Such stuffs are, as Aristotle says, "hypothetically necessary" for the existence of an ax. But these conditions can be satisfied by any number of stuffs. The head could be made of stone, diamond, or one of the usual metallic suspects; the haft could be made of wood, plastic, or metal. Furthermore, which stuff is used in any given ax endows that ax with properties that are not themselves hypothetically necessary for the existence of an ax. The head may be made of stuff that is shiny, dull, or transparent; that is susceptible (or not) to rusting; and so on.

There are several points here crucial to what follows. First, none of these "piggyback" features belongs, in the way that sharpness does, to the essence of the ax-head: they are all accidents of it. Second, even though being sharp belongs to the essence of an ax-head, the head can (as Aristotle observes) be blunted by what it cuts [*Generation of Animals* (*GA*) IV.3, on which more below]. Moreover, since it is contingent whether any particular ax-head is sharp at any given time, it seems contingent whether the essence of any particular ax is realized at any given point in time; and when a particular ax fails to be sharp, being dull would seem to be an accident of it.

---

[2] For '*dunamis*' and its cognates, I use different terms and their cognates in different places, without intending any distinction: 'capacity,' 'potentiality,' even [in *DA* 412a27–b6] 'power,' so as to make it clear that the body in question is *actually* alive.

[3] For some expression of his uncertainty, see *Metaphysics* VII.11. For "hypothetical necessity" [foreshadowed in Plato's *Phaedo* 98b–99c], see *Physics* II.9 and *Parts of Animals* I.1.

Many commentators take Aristotle's hylomorphism to be aimed primarily against the sort of dualism often associated with the Socrates of Plato's *Phaedo:* dualism in which a human soul is an independent substance capable of existing apart from any body. But *DA* I.3's attack on the Pythagorean idea that an animal soul can migrate from one body to another, perhaps even to a body of another species, suggests that his hylomorphism is also motivated by his views about the importance of the "fit" between a soul and any body it animates. In fact, Aristotle takes this fit to be so tight that an animal body and its parts can no more exist or be understood apart from soul and the psychic capacities by which bodily parts are defined than a soul can exist or be understood apart from a body with the kinds of parts required for the exercise of the soul's constitutive capacities. This is why Aristotle speaks of the soul as the form *and the essence* [*to ti ên einai*] of the body that is supposed to stand to it as matter to form [*DA* 412b11–12].

Aristotle's talk of animal bodies as *essentially ensouled* has troubled countless commentators for various reasons, some endoxic (surely an animal body can become a corpse), some theoretical (matter, qua potentiality and substratum of change, is what can first acquire and then lose form, so it seems that any form it embodies should be an *accident* of it). But on the endoxic front, Aristotle's treatment of corpses and their so-called organs and limbs is subtle in ways that confirm his commitment to the idea of essentially ensouled animal bodies: he speaks of corpses and most of their parts as only "homonymously" bodies and parts of the relevant sorts, while allowing a sense in which *homoiomerous* parts such as flesh, which admit of compositional (as well as functional) definition, can persist, at least for a while, in rotting corpses.[4] On the theoretical front too, Aristotle's commitment is well grounded. One ground, among others, is this: essentially ensouled matter plays a crucial role in establishing the reality of generation and destruction *simpliciter* against materialist attempts to explain away their appearance by treating them simply as rearrangements of atoms or alterations of previously existing stuff. If the generation of animals is *really* generation, then an animal's form cannot be a mere accident of its matter (Whiting 1990 [Chapter 2, this volume]).

In sum, Aristotle is as clearly committed to the idea of essentially ensouled bodies as he is to the idea of essentially embodied souls. But not even the reciprocal nature of this relationship suffices to distinguish it from that between the form and the matter of an ax. For we could well speak of a very old ax and its parts—a wooden haft so rotted that it will disintegrate if lifted and a stone head so worn by use that it cannot cut—as only "homonymously" an ax, haft, or head. And we could analyze the phenomenon in the way Aristotle analyzes that of a corpse: the ax and its functional parts no longer exist, except in name, but the stuffs that once constituted them—the wood and the

---

[4] See n. 16 of Whiting 1992 [Chapter 3, this volume], which treats in detail these and other issues taken up below.

stone—persist in the way that Aristotle allows rotting flesh to persist in a corpse even as it wastes away.

For this reason, I take the crucial feature of Aristotle's hylomorphism to be the importance he attaches to the idea that the matter of a natural substance, unlike that of an artifact, "strives" [*ephiesthai*] to realize the relevant form [*Physics* (*Ph.*) 192a16–25]. I say "realize" rather than "embody" so as to cover two sorts of case. One is developmental, as when menstrual fluid "strives" to embody the form introduced by the movements in conspecific seminal fluid. The other involves a special kind of completion, as when an eye is actually seeing. In each case, Aristotle thinks that the matter is doing something that it is by its nature—and not simply accidentally—oriented to do. Here, however, it is important to keep in mind that matter's natural orientation toward form is compatible with matter's sometimes falling short, as the language of "striving" itself suggests and as Aristotle himself duly acknowledges. He allows both for eyes whose capacity for sight is partly impaired [*DA* 408b19–24] and for embryos that (as he puts it) get as far as being generically animal without, however, developing the traits characteristic of mature members of the relevant species [*GA* 769b1–13].

The contrast between the body of an animal and the body of an ax should now be clear. Though the materials of which an ax is composed must be capable of performing their functions, neither the stuff of the head nor the stuff of the haft "strives" to be or to become an ax. Steel, for example, is no more oriented to constituting the head of an axe than to constituting a statue, a bullet, or any other such thing. And even once the ax-head is formed and attached to a suitable haft, neither of these functionally defined parts "strives" to chop. Nor does the ax as a whole. It is the logger who does that, *with* the axe.

Aristotle's hylomorphism is thus tied closely to his natural teleology. He argues in detail that we cannot plausibly explain the sorts of regularities we see in the reproduction and maturation of living things without positing the existence of formal and final causes [*Ph.* II.8; *Parts of Animals* I.1]. Man begets man, dog begets dog, and so on. And embryos of each kind routinely develop parts that are not only like the parts developed by others of their kind and developed in the same order, but also suited to the survival and well-being of the kind and its individual members (thus evincing final as well as formal causation). Aristotle thinks that, in order to explain such phenomena, we must suppose that there is some force shaping the matter in ways *analogous* to those in which a craftsperson shapes matter so as to bring about a product of a certain kind: just as the craftsperson shapes the wood and bronze so as to produce an ax, there must be something shaping the menstrual fluid so as to produce another human being or another canine one and so on [*GA* I.22 and passim].

Note, however, that Aristotle seems to think that art imitates nature, not the other way around [*Ph.* 194a21–22]. So comparing the matter-form relationship in a natural body to the matter-form relationship in an artifact goes only, heuristically speaking, so far. Aristotle surely regards the relationship between an animal body and its soul as more like that between a heavenly body and its form, to which I now turn.

2. ASYMMETRIES: COSMOLOGICAL AND EMBRYOLOGICAL

Aristotle thinks that the cosmos and the order we find in it are eternal: they did not come to be and will not pass away. But he sees a fundamental distinction between the superlunary and sublunary worlds. The superlunary world is relatively simple. The bodies we find there—the sun, the moon, planets, and stars—are made of eternal, imperishable stuff, aether, whose natural motion is circular. Unlike sublunary bodies, whose natural motions are rectilinear, heavenly bodies do not have to stop and reverse their motions: they move continuously (and perpetually) along the same path [*De Caelo* I.2–3]. Heavenly bodies thus move as they do with exceptionless regularity and the superlunary world is governed by a kind of absolute necessity.

Aristotle seeks to explain the motions of the heavenly bodies without succumbing to the need for an infinite regress of "moved movers," each setting other things in motion while itself being set in motion by some prior moving thing. Since he thinks that such a regress is impossible but (unlike the Eleatics) accepts the evidence of his senses that there is in fact motion in the cosmos, he concludes that there must be at least one "unmoved mover"—that is, at least one being that sets material things in motion without itself moving. Aristotle hypothesizes that such a being moves things in something like the way in which an object of thought or desire can move an agent without itself moving.

His idea is roughly this: the first mover, which he calls God, is an absolutely perfect and self-sufficient being, not dependent for its existence or its activity on any other thing. Since Aristotle takes its self-sufficiency to be incompatible with its depending for its activity on anything (even an object of thought) other than itself, he describes it as "thought thinking itself" [*Metaphysics* (*Met.*) XII.7; Whiting 2012b]. Other things may imitate it, but it does not depend for its existence on their doing so: it is presumably even unaware of their existence. Think, for example, of movie stars and their fans. I used to say "rock stars" and was gratified to see a band called "The Prime Movers" performing in Berlin. But rock stars jump around too much.

Aristotle argues in *Metaphysics* XII.8 that there must in fact be multiple unmoved movers if we are to explain the panoply of superlunary motion. The exact number is not important: what matters is that an unmoved mover is supposed to move its heavenly body in something like the way in which objects of thought and desire move us: just as my thought of a perfect being—or my desire to be as much like a perfect being as possible—might cause me to move in various ways that do not presuppose any movement on the part of the perfect being itself, so too a heavenly body's thought of a perfect being may cause it to move as it does, in one continuous and eternal circular motion. This is its way of "imitating God."[5]

---

[5] Insofar as desire is associated with the lack of its object, Aristotle may think it inappropriate to speak of a heavenly body, which is *always actually* moving, as desiring to move in the relevant way. He may simply ascribe to it a kind of thought that moves its subject. Such thought is arguably the paradigm for human *prohairesis*, described in *EN* VI.2 as being "either desiderative thought [*orektikos nous*] or thinking desire [*orexis dianoêtikê*]." The idea here seems to be of *one* thing that can be described in two ways, *both* as a

This relationship between matter and form is so intimate that it seems odd to speak of the matter as "striving" to realize the form. For Aristotle, perhaps a bit too conveniently, takes heavenly bodies to be *entirely* composed of stuff that moves *naturally* in the relevant way and *only* in that way [*De Caelo* I.2–3]. There is no possible source of resistance to their doing what they think best. There is thus no basis in *them* for akratic action. None of them ever thinks anything like "I know it's just perfect to move eternally along this path, but it's so damned boring and I'd like to know what Mars is up to. So damn the consequences, I'll run over there and take a quick look, but just this once."

There are difficult questions here about how Aristotle's concepts of form, qua actuality, and matter, qua potentiality, are supposed to apply in the superlunary world, where there is no generation, and so no move from pure potentiality to first actuality. And even the distinction between first and second actuality is problematic insofar as heavenly bodies never move from first to second actuality but are *always actually* moving in the ways they do. Still, it seems reasonably safe to say (a) that what we find in a heavenly body is the highest possible sort of unity of form with matter (the next stop is surely immaterial substance); and (b) that such unity serves as the paradigm for the sort of unity in the sublunary world that the hylomorphic analysis is meant to capture. For as Aristotle says, after giving his general account of soul as the "first actuality of a natural organic body," "*hence* we ought not to inquire whether the soul and the body are one, just as we do not <inquire> whether the wax and the imprint <are one> or generally whether the matter and that of which it is the matter <are one>, *for* unity and being are said in many ways, but the strictest way involves the actualization <of some potentiality>" [*DA* 412b6–9].

Aristotle is speaking here of the sort of unity characteristic of animal bodies, which is the sort relevant to understanding the hylomorphic conception of virtue. An eye is not a piece of matter with a certain physical structure *plus* the capacity of sight: the capacity of sight is the *essence* of the eye. Similarly, an eye that is actually seeing is not an eye *plus* some activity: actual seeing is the *complete actualization* of the eye's essence. The same goes not only for other organs of perception and for organs of locomotion and reproduction, but also for the body as a whole. An animal is not a body with a particular structure *plus* a soul: the soul is the set of actual capacities that *constitute* its body as a body of the relevant kind—a canine one, for example, or a human one. Moreover, the actualizations of these capacities (in, for example, actual perceiving and locomoting) are not "extras": these activities are the complete realizations of the body's essence.

But the kind of matter involved here, unlike that in the superlunary world, is condemned to "strive" in ways such that it can fall short. That is because everything in the sublunary world is in some sense ultimately composed out of the four elements, each of which has its own distinctive "natural" motion: fire, left on its own, moves up;

---

kind of thought *and* as a kind of desire. And unity is vital to the hylomorphic nature of this idea. So it is misguided (not to mention tendentious) to translate this as "understanding *combined with* desire or desire *combined with* thought" (Irwin 1999).

earth, left on its own, moves down; air and water, left on their own, move up and down but not to such extremes. So if there were no forces in the sublunary world other than those associated with the natures of the four elements, the sublunary world would look like a sphere of Neapolitan ice cream: chocolate-brown sphere on the inside and a strawberry-red layer on the outside, with the bland stuffs, air and water, sorting themselves out in between.

Fortunately, there are other forces in the sublunary world, including formal causes and pneuma, a sublunary stuff comparable to the aether of which heavenly bodies are composed and carrying with it special sort of heat, the "psychic heat" found in all living things [GA 736b30ff, 762a20–21]. And formal causes work with pneuma to move and to hold the four elements, contrary to their natural tendencies, into various combinations suitable for forming the parts of plants and animals: for example, *homoiomerous* stuffs like flesh, blood, and bone. Such stuffs are hypothetically necessary for the formation of *anhomoiomerous* parts, such as the limbs and organs that are hypothetically necessary for the existence of animals capable of nourishing themselves and reproducing, as well as for perceiving and locomoting in ways characteristic of their kinds.

Primary among these formal causes are the souls of animals, which Aristotle explicitly describes as holding animal bodies and their parts together [DA 411b6–9]. This need to be held together stems from the fact that the four elements from which animal parts are ultimately constituted in some sense retain tendencies to move to their natural places even while they constitute flesh, blood, and bone. And the elements' expressions of these tendencies may interfere with the maintenance of those conditions hypothetically necessary for the proper functioning of the parts.

Take, for example, an eye. Given that an eye must be composed largely of transparent stuff and that the only transparent elements available are water and air, it is necessary that an eye be composed largely of water and/or air. And because water is more easily confined and condensed than air is, it is hypothetically necessary that an eye be composed largely of water [DA 438a12–16]. But certain features piggyback on its watery composition, among them a vulnerability to drying out. This vulnerability is not part of the form or essence of an eye, since (as *we* might say) there are other possible worlds in which eyes are made from different stuffs, perhaps from something more like the indestructible aether of Aristotle's superlunary realm. Many features of an organism will in fact be due not to its form but to the stuffs from which it must, given the elements available, be made: for example, the tendencies of my bones to degenerate and my teeth to get cavities.

Here, as elsewhere in the sublunary world, there is a struggle between form and matter that serves to account for the perishability of sublunary substances. Aristotle describes this in *De Caelo* II.6, which is primarily concerned with the absolute regularity of the movements of heavenly bodies. He introduces the decline of animal bodies by way of contrast, attributing aging and "natural" death to the tendency of the elements that constitute an animal's body to seek their natural places. As I age, the elements that constitute my bodily parts exert pressure (so to speak) on my soul, gradually weakening its ability to hold them together. Heat and moisture escape until the elements are no longer present in those proportions hypothetically necessary to sustain life. But even then, the elements keep on moving toward their natural places: the rotting of corpses is simply the continuation of this process [*Meteorologica* 390a14–24; Whiting 1992 [Chapter 3, this volume].

What this adds up to is an explanatory asymmetry between, on the one hand, the generation and maturation of an organism, and, on the other hand, its "natural" decline. The true causes of generation and maturation (on which more below) are largely formal. But "natural" decline is largely element driven: it results from the natural tendencies of the elements that constitute the animal parts to move to their (the elements') proper places, thus weakening and eventually destroying the organism's form. But this is *not* a teleological process: death is not a telos except in the chronological sense.

Moreover, although my organic body can be either healthy or diseased, Aristotle thinks it is potentially healthy in a way in which it is not potentially ill. For the relevant notion of potentiality is of a teleologically defined capacity. Health is the proper functioning of the organic (and so teleologically defined) parts, for which certain material conditions are of course necessary. But disease is a disturbance due to the absence or deterioration of these material conditions as such. Aristotle calls attention to such asymmetries in *Metaphysics* VIII.5, where he says that wine is no more potentially vinegar than a body is potentially a corpse, though vinegar can of course "come from" wine and corpses "from" animal bodies. In both cases, it is the matter that constitutes the *terminus ex quo* (the water in the wine or the elements in the animal body) that becomes the *terminus ad quem* (the vinegar or the corpse).

In sum, an animal's mortality is not due to its form: it is due to the fact that the only stuffs available for making the bodily parts of which its form is the first actuality are perishable stuffs. But animals compensate for their mortality by reproducing, which is a function of the so-called nutritive capacity. As Aristotle says in *DA* II.4, the most natural capacity of a living being to produce another "like itself." Though no animal can be eternal "in number" [*arithmô(i)*], each can achieve a kind of immortality "in form" or "species" [*eidei*], by reproducing *its* form in another, who will in turn reproduce *its* form in another, and so on *ad immortalitatem* [*DA* 415b2–7; *GA* 732a34–36]. This is an animal's way of "imitating God."[6]

This brings us to one of the oddest bits of Aristotle's corpus—namely, his tendency to explain the generation of female animals, in spite of their obvious teleological value, as involving deviation from the form toward which the matter provided by the mother is supposed to be "striving." Aristotle regards animal reproduction as a process in which the male principle imposes its form on the matter provided by the mother. He thinks that the result, in non-deviant cases, is a "reproduction" of the *father*, resembling him not only in species but also in various more particular respects, including (perhaps

---

[6] I prefer 'form' to 'species' here, since the idea seems to be that each man wants another little *himself*—for example, another "little Aristotle"—and not simply another member of the species (which other men will no doubt happily supply).

most importantly) his sex. So Aristotle needs to explain how it sometimes occurs not only that some offspring are female but also that some offspring (even male offspring) resemble the mother and her kin.

Aristotle speaks explicitly in GA IV.3 in terms of deviation: nature *parekbainei* from the relevant *genos* in ways that range from the first deviation (where the offspring is female) through deviations so extreme that the offspring does not even resemble its parents in form but is rather some monstrosity. He says that the original source of such deviations is the production of what is female rather than male, though this is (as Aristotle puts it) "necessary by nature," in order that the *genos* be preserved. I suspect that he is thinking of hypothetical necessity but I cannot defend that here. We must focus rather on the mechanisms he invokes to account for the generation of females and other deviations, ranging from male children who resemble their mothers to human offspring who (due to the disease "satyriasis") resemble satyrs. For Aristotle's discussion of these mechanisms reveals a form of explanatory asymmetry highly relevant to the hylomorphic conception of virtue.

The generic mechanism is reciprocal action: what acts is affected by that on which it acts. Aristotle's examples are of what is cutting itself being blunted by what it cuts and of what is heating itself being cooled by what it heats [GA 768b16–21]. He goes on to say that depending on the relative strengths of the agent and the patient, one can be more or less affected by the other, and that an agent can, in extreme cases, be affected more by the patient than the patient is by it. He then says,

> The patient [*to paschon*] departs <from the agent's type> and fails to be mastered [*ou krateitai*] either on account of a deficiency of power in the concocting and moving <principle> or on account of the magnitude and coldness of what is being concocted and determined. [GA 768b25–28]

Aristotle is referring to the way in which the seminal fluid may be deficient because it is not sufficiently endowed with vital heat or its movements are too weak, while the menstrual fluid is too great in quantity and/or too cold. In such cases, the male principle may succeed less in acting on the matter than in being acted on by it, at least with respect to some of its powers, such as the one that determines sex.

> The seed of the male differs because it has in itself a principle such as to move the animal [sc., the embryo] and to concoct [*diapeptein*] what serves ultimately as nutriment for it, while the seed of the female has matter alone. If then it <the male seed> masters <the matter of the female seed>, it draws the matter into itself [*kratêsan men eis hauto agei*], while if it is mastered <by the matter of the female seed>, it changes into its opposite [*kratêthen d' eis tounantion metaballei*] or is destroyed. [GA 766b12–18]

When things go as they should go, and the male principle prevails, it concocts the matter provided by the mother, and in prevailing *draws this matter into itself*; but when things go wrong and the male principle is defeated, the male principle is converted into its opposite or is destroyed. In cases of the latter sorts, the matter remains to some extent autonomous, working according to its own natural tendencies and not entirely in the ways the form seeks to impose on it. Think, by analogy, of complete versus partial cultural assimilation in cases of colonization. What results in successful cases is a kind of unity that is lacking in less successful ones, where the matter remains to some extent autonomous and continues to shape the product according to its own inherent tendencies.

There are problems with the overall coherence of Aristotle's views, in part no doubt because he grants too much influence to ideologically motivated endoxa—for example, the common (if not "reputable") opinion that 'female' designates not simply the contrary of 'male,' but a kind of *deficiency* of the capacity to generate (as distinct from nourish) another "like itself" [*GA* VI.1].[7] This makes it hard to treat the reproductive parts of female animals as being on a teleological par with those of male animals, and as involving anything like the sort of complete actualization of the creature's essence that Aristotle seems to see in male anatomy. And while he seeks at one point to preserve the unity of species by assigning the difference between male and female to matter in something like the way he assigns differences in skin color to matter[*Met*. X.9], the need to assign teleologically crucial differences to matter is theoretically awkward.

It is also awkward to treat being male as part of an animal's essence in a way that being female is not. But Aristotle seems to regard being male as part of the complete actualization of an animal's essence, which leaves an animal's being female like an eye's lacking the capacity to see. Insofar as this capacity is the essence of an eye, blindness is an accident of any would-be eye, to be explained largely by appeal to the ways the materials involved interfere with the eye's functioning in the way that it belongs to the essence of an eye to function. Similarly, insofar as the capacity to *generate* another "like itself" belongs the essence of an animal, being female seems to be an accident that comes about as a result of the ways in which the materials involved interfere with an embryo's developing as it should (i.e., into a female). Aristotle recognizes of course that an important function is served by the fact that a significant percentage of any given species is born female. But he may simply regard this as hypothetically necessary for the preservation of the species.

The crucial point is that Aristotle takes the defective parts of animals to be explained in ways different from those in which non-defective parts are to be explained. The genesis of defective parts is largely matter-driven and non-teleological, while the genesis of non-defective ones is largely form-driven and teleological. But we need not, in order to accept this, include female reproductive organs among defective parts: we can accept the general idea without having to accept Aristotle's most outrageous—even by his own teleological standards—application of it.

---

[7] The ideological nature of the idea should have been clear to Aristotle from the infamous speech in Aeschylus' *Eumenides* where Apollo defends the transition from "mother-right" to "father-right" [lines 657–74].

Moreover, when things go as they should, teleologically speaking, go, matter is subdued (so to speak) by form in a way such that the result enjoys a kind of unity that is lacking in cases where matter, acting to some extent in accordance with its own tendencies, prevents a form from being completely realized. In other words, when a form is only incompletely realized in some matter, there are two potentially competing elements in play, one acting in accordance with the form (to the extent that it is realized) the other acting in accordance with the matter (to the extent that it retains some degree of autonomy).

3. PARTS OF SOUL IN ARISTOTLE'S ETHICAL-POLITICAL WORKS

Let us turn, keeping these points in mind, to the hylomorphic conception of virtue. According to this conception, there are not two distinct things, one of which (practical *nous*) is added to the other (*to orektikon*): practical *nous* is the proper actualization of the orectic part of soul. In other words, practical *nous* constitutes the *orektikon* of a human being as the kind of *orektikon* it is—namely, *human* and so subject to distinctively human forms of desire, including (when all goes well) the forms of desire characteristic of a virtuous agent.

Aristotle argues [in *EN* VI.12–13] that ethical virtue in the strict or "authoritative" sense is achieved only when an agent achieves *phronêsis,* and that *phronêsis* itself presupposes "authoritative" virtue (Whiting 1996) [II.4]. But this leaves it open whether Aristotle regards *phronêsis* and ethical virtue as distinct states of soul, neither of which can exist apart from the other, or whether he sees here a single state of soul that can be described in either—and indeed in both—of two ways. McDowell reads Aristotle as committed to the latter, ultimately Socratic identification of ethical virtue with *phronêsis.* But most commentators read Aristotle as committed only to the reciprocity of *phronêsis* and ethical virtue. For most commentators read Aristotle's ethical works as dividing the human soul into four parts and assigning ethical virtue and *phronêsis* to distinct parts: *phronêsis* to the practical (as distinct from theoretical) subpart of the so-called rational part [*to logon echon*], and ethical virtue to the desiderative (as distinct from the nutritive) subpart of the so-called non-rational part [*to alogon*]. But it is far from clear that the locus classicus of this "canonical" division—namely, *EN* I.13—supports this reading.

We should keep in mind that Aristotle presents the account of the human soul in I.13 as having only as much precision as required for the purposes of the political scientist [*ho politikos*], further precision involving more work than required for these purposes [*EN* 1102a23–26]. But my argument does not depend mainly on that. Aristotle continues here as follows [*EN* 1102a26–b28]:

[1] [A] Some things are said about it [sc., the soul] adequately in the nonspecialist accounts, and we should make use of these [in doing political science]: for example, that one <part> of it is non-rational [*to men alogon autês einai*] while one <part> has reason [*to de logon echon*]. Whether

these <parts> are (a) distinguished in the way that parts of the body (or anything divisible into parts) are, or whether they are (b) two in account but by nature inseparable just as the convex and the concave in the periphery <of a circle> are, makes no difference for present purposes.

[B] Of the non-rational <part>, one <part> seems to be common and vegetative, I mean the one responsible for nutrition and growth ... But let us set *to threptikon* aside, since it is by nature without a share of <specifically> human virtue.

[C] There seems to be some other non-rational nature in the soul, which partakes in a way of *logos* [*metechousa mentoi pê(i) logou*]. For we praise the logos, and the part of soul having logos, of the *enkratês* and *akratês*. For it urges them correctly, toward the best things. It appears that in them [*en hautois*] there is also some other natural <element> in addition to logos, which fights against and opposes logos.[8] For as when someone decides to move to the right, paralyzed parts of the body simply go astray in the opposite direction, toward the left, so too in the case of the soul: for the impulses of akratic <souls> tend in opposite directions. But in bodies, we see the <part> that is going astray, while in the case of the soul we do not. Perhaps, however, we should suppose that in the case of the soul, too, there is some <part> in addition to reason [*para logon*] being opposed to this and resisting <it>.

[D] But how this <part> is different <from reason> makes no difference. And even this seems to partake of reason, as we have said. For in the *enkratês*, at any rate, it obeys reason [*peitharchei goun tô(i) logo(i)*]. And it is presumably even more ready to listen [*eti d' isôs euêkoôteron*] in the case of the temperate and courageous person; for <there> it agrees with reason in all things [*panta gar homophônei tô(i) logo(i)*].[9]

Please note the striking claim at the end of [1][A], echoed at the start of [D]: that it makes no difference for present purposes if what are called 'rational' and 'non-rational' parts of soul turn out to be distinguished only in the way that the convex and the concave in a circle are (i.e., are simply two aspects of a single thing, each of which entails the other). Since [D] is concerned with the relationship between reason (apparently practical) and what [E] calls the desiring part, I take the "no difference" claim in [A] to apply *at least* to that relation, which is arguably the focus of the overall passage. For the nutritive part is quickly set aside and the remainder is more or less silent about theoretical reason as such.

---

[8] The '*en hautois*' invites the thought that the additional element may not be present in the *phronimos* [or fully virtuous agent].

[9] The hylomorphic conception allows us to make good sense of the distinction between genuine virtue and mere *enkrateia*, which is (as McDowell 1979 stresses) no less problematic for Aristotle than *akrasia* is.

It is in fact surprisingly difficult, in spite of the canonical view's status as canonical, to find a neat distinction between the theoretical and practical subparts of *to logon echon* in *Nicomachean Ethics* I.13. Aristotle continues as follows [1102b28–1103a3]:

(E) And it does seem that the non-rational <part> is indeed twofold. For the vegetative <part> in no way shares in reason, but the appetitive and in general the desiring [*to d' epithemêtikon kai holôs orektikon*] <part> partakes <of reason> in a way, insofar as it is attentive to it and disposed to obey [*hê(i) katêkoon estin autou kai peitharchikon*]. In this way too we say that we possess <the> reason of our father or our loved ones but not <the reason> of the mathematicians [*houtô dê kai tou patros kai tôn philôn phamen echein logon, kai ouk hôsper tôn mathêmatikôn*].

[F] That the non-rational <part> is persuaded in a way by reason, admonishment and all criticism and encouragement bear witness. But if we must say that even this <part> has reason, then *to logon echon* will also be twofold, one <part having logos> strictly and in itself [*to men kuriôs kai in hautô(i)*] and the other <having logos> just as something such as to listen to his father does [*to d' hôsper tou patros akoustikon ti*].

It is far from obvious that [F] divides the part that has reason into theoretical and practical subparts. For the distinction between what has logos "strictly and in itself" and what has logos "in the way that something such as to listen to his father does" reads like a distinction between something that has reason in the sense that it can work things out for itself and something that has reason in the sense that it can follow or obey the reasoning of another, presumably another capable of working things out for itself. It seems to leave open whether what is being worked out—or being followed—is theoretical or practical.

We might attempt to map [F]'s ostensible division of *to logon echon* onto the distinction between theoretical and practical *nous* by tying the alleged division to [E]'s distinction between possessing reason in the way we possess the reason of a father or a loved one and possessing reason in the way we possess the reason of the mathematicians. For [E] might seem to involve a distinction between consulting someone for practical advice and seeking a tutor in some theoretical sphere. But this gambit not only leaves [F] describing practical *nous* as having reason in much the same way that [E] describes the desiring part as having reason; it also leaves [F] describing what is supposed to be practical *nous* in terms of the capacity to attend to and obey reason in something like the way we might attend to and obey the reason of a father or a loved one. And this is at least odd, especially given Aristotle's description of *phronêsis* (which is the proper virtue of practical intellect) as *epitaktikê* or "such as to give orders" [*EN* VI.10, 1143a8].

We could perhaps remove some of the oddity by noting two things: first, that the contrast in *Nicomachean Ethics* VI.10 is with *sunesis*, which is a kind of understanding that is concerned with the same objects as *phronêsis* is but is *kritikê monon* (i.e., "only such as to discern [or judge]") [*EN* 1143a6–10]; and second, that *sunesis*, being concerned with the same objects that *phronêsis* is, is presumably a virtue of practical rather than theoretical intellect. For where Aristotle *does* distinguish theoretical from practical *nous*, he argues that they must be distinct because their objects differ in kind [*EN* VI.1, 1139a3–18]: *to epistêmonikon* contemplates objects whose principles *cannot* be otherwise than they are, while *to logistikon* contemplates objects that *can* (or whose principles *can*) be otherwise than they are (as a result of which *to logistikon* also engages in deliberation and is sometimes called *to bouleutikon*). Taking *sunesis* to be a virtue of the practically oriented *logistikon* rather than the theoretically oriented *epistêmonikon* reduces somewhat the oddity of reading [F] as characterizing practical reason in terms of the capacity to listen and obey rather than the capacity to give orders. For *to logistikon* has both capacities, *sunesis* being especially associated with understanding where someone *else* is speaking [*allou legontos, EN* 1143a22].

Still, there remain problems with this way of taking *EN* I.13 to divide *to logon echon* into theoretical and practical subparts and thus to yield the sort of fourfold division presupposed in *Nicomachean Ethics* VI.12–13, where Aristotle refers to the nutritive part as the "fourth" part, then sets it aside (as in I.13) and moves on to identify the virtues of the three remaining parts as *sophia* (clearly theoretical wisdom), *phronêsis,* and ethical virtue. For this reading fails to do justice to the argument actually given in I.13 for dividing *to logon echon*. The argument does not appeal, as the argument in VI.1 appeals, to a difference in kind between the objects of its respective subparts. It appeals rather to the fact that *to alogon* has a subpart that can be described as having logos in the sense that it can be persuaded by logos. For, as [1][F] says with reference to this subpart,

> *if* we must say that *even this* has logos, *then* the <part> having *logos* will *also* be twofold, one <part having logos> strictly and in itself and the other < having *logos*> just as someone capable of listening to/obeying his father does.

In other words, the argument of *Nicomachean Ethics* I.13 is that taking desire to partake of reason in whatever way it does *entails* that *to logon echon itself* has two parts. And the easiest way to explain this is to assume that Aristotle takes a subpart's having logos in the relevant way to render that subpart sufficiently rational count as a citizen of *to logon echon.*

If this is right, then we can accommodate the oddity of Aristotle's speaking in the *same* terms of what is supposed to be a subpart of the *to logon echon* and of what is supposed to be a subpart of *to alogon* by taking him to be talking about one and the same part but referring to it in different ways in different contexts. And Aristotle might well be talking this way if he is thinking of a unitary part with two aspects, one rational and one non-rational, and taking the former to stand to the latter in a hylomorphic relationship like the one he sees between an animal's soul and its body. In other words, Aristotle might well be talking this way if he assumes a hylomorphic conception of virtue, which, however, leaves open the possibility that there is no such unitary part in the soul of a non-virtuous agent (whether enkratic, akratic, or vicious).[10]

---

[10] I am bracketing vice for present purposes. But it is clear from *EN* IX.4 (at least when read with *Republic* VIII–IX in mind) that Aristotle does not treat vice as a kind of mirror image of virtue, involving a comparable sort of unity.

On this reading, Aristotle recognizes a part that is so to speak "bi": it is neither purely rational, as the theoretical part is, nor purely non-rational, as the nutritive part is, but has both rational and non-rational aspects. Let's call this the "practical" part. In a fully virtuous agent, this part will be unified in the "strict" sense associated with hylomorphism at *DA* 412b6–9: that in virtue of which it is called "rational" stands to that in virtue of which it is called "non-rational" as form to matter. But in non-virtuous agents—for example, akratic ones—the practical part will lack such unity: desire will be only partially mastered by practical *nous*, so there will sometimes be conflict between what an agent most wants to do and what she thinks it best to do. In such cases, we should describe the agent's soul as having four, rather than three, parts.

This may explain the "no difference" claim in [1][A], to which commentators have not paid adequate attention. Most, I suspect, assume that Aristotle takes the relations among the various so-called parts of soul to be uniformly distinguished *either* as parts of the body are *or* as the convex and concave are. Few, I suspect, consider the possibility that he is leaving room for the kind of psychic contingency I see in Plato's *Republic*, where what are at early stages of development "many" can "become one" (in which case they are related like the convex and concave) but may, in cases where virtue fails to come about, remain distinct (in which case they are related in something like the way parts of the body are).

In sum, *EN* I.13 seems to divide the human soul into three basic parts, one of which is itself divided in some but not all agents: (1) the nutritive; (2) the practical; and (3) the part that "has logos strictly and in itself." Aristotle says little here about the third part, but I take him to be referring to theoretical intellect, whose virtue he distinguishes from the virtue of practical nous by saying that the latter—namely, *phronêsis*—is a *hexis* that does not involve logos alone [*oud' hexis meta logou monon*, *EN* 1140b25–30].

To see the plausibility of supposing I.13 divides human souls in this way, let us turn briefly to the scientific works, where Aristotle's treatment of souls and their parts is presumably "more precise."

4. PARTS OF SOUL IN ARISTOTLE'S SCIENTIFIC WORKS

The scientific works are useful here insofar as they reveal two things: first, the frequency with which Aristotle uses different terms in different contexts to refer to what he regards as a single unitary part of soul; and second, his reluctance to partition the human soul primarily along the rational/non-rational axis.

Aristotle tends in his scientific works to recognize three "kinds" (sometimes called "parts") of soul: the nutritive [*threptikê*], which belongs to all living things (at least all mortal ones, including embryos); perceptive [*aisthêtikê*], which distinguishes animals from plants; and thinking [*noêtikê*], which distinguishes human from other animals. See, for example, *Generation of Animals* II.3, where Aristotle explains the sequential formation of these in a human being and calls attention to the difficulties surrounding the origins of *nous*. In this passage, which wears its hylomorphism on its sleeve, Aristotle (a) distinguishes *nous* from other psychic capacities, on the grounds that no bodily activity [*energeia*] shares in its activity; and (b) concludes, in what appears to be an argument by elimination, that "it remains for *nous* alone to enter from outside [*thurathen*] and for it alone to be divine [*theion*]" [GA 736b27–29].[11]

Most commentators read this as indicating that even in a human being *nous* is an immaterial substance that can, unlike nutritive and perceptive soul, exist apart from a body. For, as Aristotle argues in *De Anima* III.4, there is no organ of thought comparable to the organs of seeing, hearing, and the other senses. This is why *nous*, unlike essentially embodied capacities of soul, seems not to come to be in a human being via the material (and essentially hylomorphic) processes characteristic of human reproduction. But it does not follow from this that *nous* must be an immaterial substance that is later injected in something like the way an immaterial pilot might be parachuted (so to speak) into a ship. There is another salient possibility—namely, learning, whether via induction, perception, habituation, or some other such process [*EN* 1098b3–4]. We shall return to this point.

Here we must inquire whether Aristotle does not in his scientific works recognize more than the three parts of soul mentioned in the *GA* passage. For he says explicitly in *DA* III.9 that there are puzzles not just about how we should speak of parts but also about how many there are. He explains this by citing two common ways of dividing the human soul—one into the three parts familiar from Plato's *Republic* (*to logistikon*, *to thumikon*, and *to epithumêtikon*), the other into the two parts from which we saw him starting in *Nicomachean Ethics* I.13—and then arguing as follows [*DA* 432a22–b7]:

[2] [A] For according to the differentiae by which they separate these, there will appear to be other parts too, having greater distance [from one another] than [do] these about which we have just spoken: both *to threptikon*, which belongs both to plants and to all animals, and *to aisthêtikon*, which one could not easily posit either as non-rational [*hôs alogon*] or as having reason [*hôs logon echon*].

[B] And further *to phantastikon*, which is different in being from all these but raises much difficulty [concerning] which of these it is the same as or different from *if* someone is going to posit separate parts of the soul.

[C] And in addition to these, *to orektikon*, which would seem to be different both in account and in capacity from all of these. And indeed it is strange to break this up.[12] For wish [*hê boulêsis*] comes to be in the *logistikon*

---

[11] Translated as passage [16] in Whiting 2002 ["Locomotive Soul" (Chapter 5, this volume)].

[12] Aristotle's reluctance to break this up is manifest in *EN* I.13. Because he does not want to assign one form of desire to the part that has reason "strictly and itself" while assigning the others to the non-rational part, he concludes that there must be at least one part of soul that is neither purely rational nor purely non-rational.

<part>, while *epithumia* and *thumos* come to be in the *alogon* <part>. And if the soul has three <parts>, there will be *orexis* in each of these.

But in spite of this argument, neither *to phantastikon* nor *to orektikon* appears in the scientific works' canonical division. For Aristotle ends up identifying each of these (i.e., *to phantastikon* and *to orektikon*) with *to aisthêtikon*. He says not only that *orexis*, *aisthêsis*, and *phantasia* are for the most part, if not always, found together [*DA* 413b22–23]; but also (1) that *to orektikon* and *to aisthêtikon* are "the same but different in being" [431a12–14], and (2) that *to aisthêtikon* and *to phantastikon* are "the same but different in being" [*De Insomniis* 459a15–17].[13]

It is clear that Aristotle is speaking here of the parts of soul that have the relevant capacities and not of the capacities [*dunameis*] themselves. (For a list of *dunameis*, see *DA* 414a29–32.) The capacity of desire is clearly distinct from the capacity of perception in the sense that one can be actualized while the other is not, and the same goes for the capacity of imagining and the capacity of perceiving.[14] So his points are (a) that the part of soul that is capable of desiring is one and the same as the part that is capable of perceiving and (b) that the part of soul that is capable of imagining is one and the same as the part of soul that is capable of perceiving. But *what it is* for this part to be capable of desiring, like *what it is* for it to be capable of imagining, is distinct from *what it is* for it to be capable of perceiving.

Aristotle is not explicit about his reasons for positing a single part here, but he uses the same sort of locutions ("same but different in being") and the same sorts of examples as he uses in arguing for the unity of the five canonical senses. In both cases, he compares the indivisible item in question to a point, the paradigm of something indivisible that can, however, function in multiple ways, both (for example) as the end of one segment and the beginning of another.[15] His idea seems to be that just as there must be a single, indivisible sense that can function in different ways (not only seeing, but also hearing, touching, etc.), so too there must be a single, indivisible part of soul that can function in different ways (not only perceiving, but also desiring and imagining).

In the case of the senses, Aristotle argues that their unity is required in order to explain how, for example, a subject can judge that one and the same object is both white and sweet. If sight and taste were distinct, one limited to seeing and the other to tasting, there would be no subject capable of judging that one and the same thing (such as a sugar cube) was both white and sweet. It would be just as if one person saw something white and another person tasted something sweet. In order for anything

---

[13] See passages [3] and [4] in Whiting 2002 ["Locomotive Soul" (Chapter 5, this volume)], where most of the claims made in this section are defended in detail.
[14] In non-rational animals and in fully virtuous rational ones—but not in akratic or enkratic ones—the actualization of the one capacity will coincide with the actualization of the other. So this coincidence holds "for the most part," with notable human exceptions.
[15] See passages [5] and [6] in Whiting 2002 ["Locomotive Soul" (Chapter 5, this volume)].

to judge of one and the same object that it is both white and sweet, the senses have to function together as a single subject.¹⁶

A parallel argument would explain Aristotle's commitment to the unity of perception and desire. If one part of soul desired sensual pleasure and another perceived things as opportunities for sensual pleasure, then no action would result: it would be just as if I desired my sensual pleasure and you perceived things as opportunities for me to achieve sensual pleasure. In order to generate action, there must be a single subject that both desires certain sorts of things and perceives situations as affording opportunities to achieve such things. Similar arguments apply to the relations between perception and imagination, and between imagination and desire, but I need not rehearse them here. They stem in part from the ways in which imagination can play a role analogous to that played by perception in the generation of action.

In sum, there are good reasons for supposing that Aristotle takes desire (on the one hand) and perception and imagination (on the other) to belong to a single, indivisible part of soul. The canonical label for this multifaceted part is '*hê aisthêtikê <psuchê>*.' But it may be more perspicuous to call it "locomotive," since locomotion is largely *what it is for:* to pursue nutriment and partners for reproduction and to avoid predators and other threats to life and limb.¹⁷

The upshot of [2] is that the locomotive part cannot be classified either as rational or as non-rational. For the difficulty in [2][A] about classifying *to aisthêtikon* as either rational or non-rational is *not* that some perceiving subjects are non-rational while others are rational. That point applies to nutritive subjects as well, but Aristotle does not hesitate to classify *to threptikon*, even in rational subjects, as purely non-rational. The point is rather that even in rational subjects, there are more and less "rational" forms of perception, ranging from perceiving something as a triangle (which may be purely rational) through perceiving something as pleasant or painful (which may be purely non-rational). Aristotle mentions in passing an unspecified difficulty in classifying *to phantastikon*, then moves on in [C] to make about *to orektikon* a version of the point made in [A] about *to aisthêtikon*: *to orektikon*, if there is such a part, is not easily classified either as rational or as non-rational, for there are both rational and non-rational forms of desire. It seems highly likely that he intends a parallel point in [B], sandwiched as it is between [A] and [C].

The basic idea seems to be that any division that takes the distinction between the rational and non-rational parts to be fundamental in a way such that any part must be assigned *exclusively either* to the rational part of soul *or* to the non-rational part will require us to do violence to what would seem—at least according to the functional criteria used to distinguish the nutritive part—to be single, unitary parts. Aristotle

---

¹⁶ See *De Sensu* VII, 449a5–19. Cf. *DA* III.2, 426b12ff.

¹⁷ Since Aristotle usually employs functional labels such as '*aisthêtikê*' and '*threptikê*,' I suspect he avoided '*hê kinêtikê <kata topon>*' lest readers infer that the soul itself moves, not in the transitive sense that it causes other things to move but in the sense it itself moves from one place to another. But there is no harm in our adopting the label "locomotive" in English.

seems to be suggesting not just that it is *possible* for there to be a part that is neither purely non-rational (as the nutritive part is) nor purely rational (as theoretical *nous* seems to be), but that the locomotive part is *precisely* such a part. If this is right, then the three parts found in the scientific works can be specified in a bit more detail as follows:

(1) the nutritive part, which is purely non-rational;
(2) the locomotive part, which is neither purely rational nor purely non-rational;
(3) the thinking part, which would seem to be purely rational.

There are daunting questions here about the thinking part, especially concerning its respective relations to theoretical and practical thought. The best I can do now is to suggest that Aristotle would surely take the genesis of human action to presuppose a unity of the cognitive and the desiderative that is either the same in kind as or at least analogous to the unity involved in the genesis of non-human animal action. In other words, he would surely take the reasons he sees for positing the unity of a non-rational animal's *aisthêtikon* with its *orektikon* as reasons for positing the unity of a rational animal's practical *nous* with its *orektikon*. If this is right, then practical *nous* belongs to locomotive rather than to thinking soul, and we end up with what appears to be a generic version of the division suggested at the end of section 3, with the part that has logos strictly and in itself corresponding to the (presumably theoretical) thinking part and the practical part corresponding to locomotive soul. On this account, a unitary practical part is the *norm* for a human being, with its unity being a special case of the sort of unity characteristic of locomotive soul as such.

Taking such unity to be the norm for a human being is of course compatible with allowing for a range of cases in which the norm fails to be fully actualized. But just as Aristotle does not take the possibility of an eye with defective vision as a reason for treating an eye with perfect vision as an eye *plus* vision, neither should he take the possibility of a partly defective *orektikon* as a reason for treating a perfectly formed *orektikon* as an *orektikon plus* reason. His embryology suggests that his view runs the other way around. Any defect in an eye is presumably due to its matter retaining some degree of autonomy and seeking (as it were) to do its own thing: it is thus matter's *lack* of unity with form that makes for a defective eye. Similarly, it will be the *orektikon's* lack of unity with practical *nous* that makes for a defective *orektikon*.

In most human souls, of course, practical *nous* will be incompletely actualized, so practical *nous* and *to orektikon* will remain at least to some extent distinct, capable of opposing one another. So in most human souls there will be four parts. But in the ideal case, where the "practical" part is unified, there will be only the three parts identified in the scientific works: the nutritive, the thinking, and the locomotive (or "practical") part. This renders the division in Aristotle's ethical works consistent with the division in his scientific works.

It should, moreover, be clear that we cannot read Aristotle as taking any and every human soul to have the same number of parts—at least not if we take what he says in

Politics I.13 at face value. For in this chapter, which refers explicitly to parts of soul [*ta moria tês psuchês*] Aristotle says that the deliberative part [*to bouleutikon*] is (a) generally missing in the slave (presumably the "natural" slave); (b) present but not in control [*akuron*] in the female; and (c) present but incomplete [*ateles*] in the child.

We are now in a position to see the plausibility of reading Aristotle as committed to the hylomorphic conception.

5. HYLOMORPHIC VIRTUE

My proposal assimilates Aristotle's account of moral development to his embryology. When all goes well, practical *nous* comes to be in stages not unlike those in which an animal's essentially embodied capacities come to be. Just as Aristotle takes the emergence of the heart to mark an embryological turning point, whence the embryo's own heart starts to guide its development, so too he may take the emergence of practical *nous* to mark an ethical turning point, whence the agent's own practical *nous* starts to guide her development. But we should not expect practical *nous* in its early stages to be anymore capable of doing everything it is the function of mature practical *nous* to do than we expect the heart of an embryo to do everything it is the function of a mature heart to do. Practical *nous* in an adolescent is at best incomplete, and Aristotle thinks that it remains incomplete in many (perhaps even most) adults.

When Aristotle says that *nous* comes from outside [*thurathen*], I suspect he is thinking of the need for learning: in the case of theoretical *nous*, learning that involves perception, memory, and induction, in the case of practical *nous*, learning that involves the habituation of desire. The importance of habituating desire explains why, after Aristotle describes *phronêsis* as a state of soul involving reason, he adds that it is "not a state involving reason alone" [*all' mên oud' hexis meta logou monon*] [*EN* VI.5, 1140b20–30].[18]

Practical *nous* enters not with the movements in the seminal fluid of the father, but only later with the kinds of advice the father gives and the examples he sets. Of course it is not just the father, as Aristotle himself acknowledges in [1][E], where he may intend *kai tôn philôn* to refer primarily to other relatives, including of course the mother. The idea is roughly as follows.

A human infant starts out with autonomous desires—for food, for drink, for warmth, for affection, etc., perhaps even for polymorphously perverse pleasures. But insofar as these initial desires are generally for objects that promote the infant's survival and well-being, these desires "strive" for the form that a proper upbringing allows them to take: they are the "matter" for moral development. As the infant matures, these autonomous desires get shaped in various ways, at first through directions from

---

[18] It follows from this that practical nous *cannot* be the virtue of a purely rational part of soul; hence Aristotle's need to recognize a part of soul that is neither (like theoretical *nous*) purely rational nor (like nutritive soul) purely non-rational.

the practical *nous* of her father and other loved ones (henceforth her "parents," broadly construed so as to include those responsible for her upbringing, whether or not they are blood kin.) Parental direction is initially analogous to the movements transmitted in the father's semen. But gradually the child acquires the ability to work things out for herself, at which point she begins to control her own development in something like the way the heart controls later stages in the development of an embryo.

The shaping here consists largely in the original desires being trained to take appropriate objects, in appropriate circumstances, to the appropriate degree and so on, in all the ways specified in Aristotle's doctrine of virtue. If all goes well, the child will grow up to be someone with a highly context-dependent sensitivity to whatever is required by the particular circumstances in which she finds herself, and she will then see particular things as good only when and to the extent that they are genuinely good. Insofar as her seeing is evaluatively loaded, it will be motivationally pregnant in the way required if her *perception* of what she should do is to coincide with what she *desires* to do. Deliberation may sometimes be involved in getting the agent to see something as "the thing to do," but once she sees a thing this way, straightaway she will act—unless, that is, something intervenes.[19]

That is a rough sketch of how, in the virtuous agent, the sort of perception with which Aristotle seems to identify *phronêsis* might come to coincide with desire. We should not suppose that there are two parts of soul there all along, practical intellect on the one hand and desire on the other. The infant simply starts out with a bundle of autonomous desires and it is the practical *nous* of her parents that shapes these desires in ways such that the child gradually internalizes at least some of her loved one's values. As a result of such internalization, practical intellect begins to emerge in her. At some point she internalizes enough of her parents' values to have moved beyond a mere desire to avoid punishment or to receive praise and other forms of reward: she may begin to experience within herself the sort of conflict characteristic of akratic or perhaps enkratic agents. We can perhaps view this as analogous to the stage in which the heart comes to be in an embryo: just as the heart then helps to regulate the embryo's further physical development, so here these internalized values help to regulate the child's—or by now the adolescent's—further development.

But just as things can still go wrong in embryological development, so too things can still go wrong in moral development. In each case, there are various ways in which things can go wrong. Just as the father's semen may be too cold, or the movements in it too weak, so too the parent's practical intellect may be weak. And an unruly child may, like the thing being cut that blunts the knife, further weaken her parent's practical intellect: think, for example, of the overindulgent parent, perhaps one whose own psychic needs interfere with his imposing on the child the sort of discipline she needs. Furthermore, just as the matter provided by the mother may be too cold or too great

---

[19] For this rider as expressing the sort of explanatory asymmetries operative in Aristotle's account of *akrasia*, see Pickavé and Whiting 2008 [Chapter 7, this volume]. For the idea (stressed by McDowell) of *phronêsis* as involving a kind of perception, see *EN* VI. 8.

in quantity, the autonomous desires of the child may be too weak or too strong—as, for example, in the case of congenitally lethargic or unresponsive child or the case of an excessively willful one.

Things can also go wrong due to the interference of outside forces: the embryo's further development may be impeded by its mother's excessive drinking, or by its father's beating of her, and an adolescent's further development may be impeded by peer pressure or too much drinking of her own, or by bad role models at home or at school. There is nothing really mysterious here. A child acquires practical wisdom by imitating the behavior of practically wise adults. But the sort of imitation involved is not mindless. The child must repeatedly ask himself not simply, "how would so and so *behave* in this situation?"; but "how would so and so *act* in this situation?" where the relevant sort of action includes the agent's reasons for acting as he does. In other words, the child must imitate the reason-engaging behavior and not simply the external behavior, of practically wise models.

All the mystery comes in trying to understand how anyone could ever become both so wise that she could always perceive what was required (or permitted) by the particular circumstances in which she finds herself and so well formed orectically that she would never desire to do anything other than what was required (or at least permitted) by those circumstances. But here it is appropriate to recall that Aristotle's conception of *phronêsis*—like the conception of ethical virtue whose flip side it is—is an *ideal*. Even if no one ever gets all the way there, that would not suffice to show that Aristotle does not conceive of the emergence of practical wisdom as the progressive shaping of autonomous desires toward an ideal limit that is characterized by the absence of any sort of psychic conflict.[20]

Note, however, that the sort of contingency we find in the extent to which practical *nous* actually informs the *orektikon* of any given human individual should no more count against crediting Aristotle with a hylomorphic conception of virtue than the occurrence of blind members of essentially sighted animal kinds counts against crediting him with a hylomorphic conception of the relation between an animal's body and the sensory and other capacities that constitute its soul. Scholars may be puzzled about how, given the apparent shortage of practical intellect in the day-to-day operations of human desire, Aristotle *could* treat practical intellect as the proper form of the human *orektikon*. But such puzzlement is on a par with puzzlement about how, given the number of bodies we encounter that lack properly functioning organs, Aristotle *could* treat an animal's soul as the form and essence of its body: the fact is that he does adopt a hylomorphic account of the relation between soul and body, however exactly we are to understand it. In other words, we should not expect commentators to find the hylomorphic conception of virtue any less puzzling than commentators have found his hylomorphic account of the relation between body and soul. Puzzlement is par for the hylomorphic course.

---

[20] For more on this, see Whiting (2021).

But puzzlement sometimes tampers with the evidence. Consider, for example, what we find in manuscripts P and C of the following passage from *Eudemian Ethics* VIII.2 [aka VII.14]:

> So it is clear that those *hexeis* of <the> other <part of soul> are simultaneously wise and good [*hama phronimai kai agathai ekeinai hai <tou> allou hexeis*] and the Socratic <argument> says correctly that nothing is stronger than *phronêsis*. But in saying that <*phronêsis*> is *epistêmê*, <the argument> is not correct, for it [sc., *phronêsis*] is virtue and not *epistêmê*, but a different kind of cognition [*alla genos allo gnôs<eôs>*]. [*EE* 1246b32–36]

The text is admittedly corrupt and various emendations have been suggested. But a few things seem clear. The context suggests a contrast between *to epistêmonikon* (which is featured in what precedes) and some "other" part of soul. And the passage seems to refer to a single part of soul and to say that *its hexeis* are simultaneously wise and good. But this puzzles commentators, who assume that 'wise' and 'good' must be predicated of states belonging to distinct parts of soul, 'wise' being predicated of the states of some thinking part and 'good' being predicated of the states of some desiring part.

Manuscript L avoids the problem. It has the masculine plural '*phronimoi*,' where P and C have the feminine plural '*phronimai*' (agreeing with '*hexeis*'). But '*phronimoi*' is grammatically awkward. It requires the interpolation of a grammatically masculine subject, as in Michael Woods's translation: "so it is clear that, at the same time, *men are wise* and their other states of soul are good" (Woods 1992). So I suspect that some scribe or commentator, not appreciating Aristotle's commitment to the hylomorphic conception of virtue, emended the grammatically smoother and better-attested reading of P and C, thus making it easier for subsequent readers (including Woods) to ignore apparent evidence of this commitment.

Insofar as the better-attested reading rests on the hylomorphic conception of virtue, it allows us to make better sense of the passage as a whole, especially its apparent commitment to Socrates' identification of virtue with *phronêsis*. For Aristotle seems here to be agreeing with Socrates that there is a form of cognition such that nothing can overpower it, but criticizing Socrates for (at least sometimes) calling such cognition '*epistêmê*,' since this fails to register the way in which such cognition does "not involve reason alone" but presupposes a properly formed *orektikon*.

A truly *phronimos* agent will neither act acratically nor suffer the sort of internal conflict that might plague a merely enkratic one. But it does not follow from this that someone whose *orektikon* is only partially actualized by practical nous cannot suffer the sort of conflict that might lead her to act against—or unhappily in accordance with—the commands of her partially actualized practical *nous*. So we can explain the fact that Aristotle attempts to account for the phenomena of *akrasia* without having to give up the idea that he identifies "authoritative" virtue with a kind of cognition such that its subject cannot act against it.

There is much more to say about the phenomenon of partial actualization and how it works, but no space for it here.[21] I want to conclude simply by noting the exceptional status of akratic and enkratic agents in Aristotle's cosmos. A fully virtuous agent, whose *orektikon* is so thoroughly actualized by practical *nous* that she never experiences any conflict between what appears good and what she wants to do, has attained a godlike state. But she has also become—indeed thereby become—like a non-rational animal, whose *aisthêtikon* is generally one with (though different in account from) its *orektikon*. In this sense akratic and enkratic agents are true anomalies in Aristotle's great chain of being. So we should not generalize the lack of unity we find in them and assume that it must be present in virtuous agents any more than it is present either in other animals or in the gods whose lives the virtuous agent seeks to imitate.[22]

BIBLIOGRAPHY

Irwin, T. 1999. *Aristotle: Nicomachean Ethics*, 2nd edn. Indianapolis, IN: Hackett.
Korsgaard, C. 1999. "Self-Constitution in the Ethics of Plato and Kant." *Journal of Ethics* 3: 1–29; reprinted in C. Korsgaard 2008. *The Constitution of Agency: Essays on Practical Reason and Moral Psychology*. Oxford: Oxford University Press, 100-126.
McDowell, J. 1979. "Virtue and Reason." *The Monist* 62: 331–50; reprinted in McDowell 1998b.
McDowell, J. 1998a. "Some Issues in Aristotle's Moral Psychology." In S. Everson (ed.), *Ethics*. Cambridge: Cambridge University Press, 107–28; reprinted in McDowell 1998b.
McDowell, J. 1998b. *Mind, Value, and Reality*. Cambridge, MA: Harvard University Press.
Pickavé, M. and Whiting, J. 2008. "*Nicomachean Ethics* 7.3 on Akratic Ignorance." *Oxford Studies in Ancient Philosophy* 34: 323–71. [Chapter 7, this volume]
Whiting, J. 1990. "Aristotle on Form and Generation." *Proceedings of the Boston Area Colloquium of Ancient Philosophy* 6: 35–63. [Chapter 2, this volume]
Whiting, J. 1992. "Living Bodies." In M. C. Nussbaum and A. Rorty (eds.), *Essays on Aristotle's "De Anima."* Oxford: Oxford University Press, 75–91. [Chapter 3, this volume]
Whiting, J. 1996. "Self-Love and Authoritative Virtue: Prolegomenon to a Kantian Reading of *Eudemian Ethics* VIII.3." In S. Engstrom and J. Whiting (eds.), *Aristotle, Kant, and the Stoics: Rethinking Happiness and Duty*. Cambridge: Cambridge University Press, 162–99. [II.4]
Whiting, J. 2002. "Locomotive Soul: The Parts of Soul in Aristotle's Scientific Works." *Oxford Studies in Ancient Philosophy* 22:141–200. [Chapter 5, this volume]
Whiting, J. 2012a. "Psychic Contingency in the *Republic*." In R. Barney, T. Brennan, and C. Brittain (eds.), *Plato on the Divided Self*. Cambridge: Cambridge University Press, 174–208. [I:8]

---

[21] Whiting 2012a ["Psychic Contingency in the *Republic*" (I.8)] goes into a bit more detail in connection with the unity of reason in Plato's *Republic*. Many of the points made there apply to the hylomorphic conception of virtue I see in Aristotle.

[22] I am grateful to members of audiences in Princeton, Stanford, Toronto, Leipzig, Emory, and Berkeley. I am especially indebted to Hendrik Lorenz for his comments in Toronto—and of course to John McDowell.

Whiting, J. 2012b. "The Pleasures of Thinking Together: Prolegomenon to a Complete Reading of EE VII.12." In F. Leigh (ed.), *The "Eudemian Ethics" on the Voluntary, Friendship, and Luck*. Leiden: Brill, 77–154. [II:7]

Whiting, J. 2021. "See the Right Thing: 'Paternal' Reason, Love, and Phronêsis." In M. Boyle and E. Mylonaki (eds.), *Reason in Nature: Essays in Honor of John McDowell*. Cambridge, MA: Harvard University Press, 243–84.

Woods, M. 1992. *Aristotle, Eudemian Ethics, Books I, II, and VIII*, 2nd edn. Oxford: Clarendon Press.

7

Nicomachean Ethics VII.3 on Akratic Ignorance

AKRATIC IGNORANCE EXPLAINED FROM THE POINT OF VIEW PROPER TO ITS NATURE

Co-authored with Martin Pickavé

NICOMACHEAN ETHICS (*EN*) VII.3 [= *Eudemian Ethics* (*EE*) VI.3] is generally agreed to be the foundational chapter in Aristotle's account of *akrasia*. It is also agreed to involve extreme difficulties, not only about how to interpret particular lines but even about what lines to read. Some difficulties are so great that commentators have proposed radical emendations without manuscript support, such as Ramsauer's proposal to read 'particular' for 'universal' in 1147a4. Others raise questions about the structure of the whole: there is enough at least apparent repetition that some commentators hypothesize that VII.3 is a patchwork containing redundant bits of what were originally two separate treatments. Cook Wilson, for example, takes the four central bits and treats the second and fourth more or less as alternative versions of the first and third.[1] But we believe that each bit introduces an important ingredient in Aristotle's eventual account, which is presented in stages: each seems to resolve an issue left unresolved in the earlier bits. We also believe that radical emendations are unnecessary and have been motivated largely by failure to appreciate the "progressive articulation" by which we think this chapter can

---

[1] On Ramsauer's proposal, see section 4 below. The idea of two redactions was suggested by H. Rassow in *Forschungen über die Nikomachische Ethik des Aristoteles* [*Forschungen*] (Weimar, 1874), 20ff.; and developed by J. Cook Wilson in *Aristotelian Studies I: On the Structure of the Seventh Book of the "Nicomachean Ethics" Chapter I–X* [*Aristotelian Studies*] (Oxford: Clarendon Press, 1879). For a modern commentator sympathetic to a double redaction view, see H. Lorenz, "Nicomachean Ethics 7.4: Plain and Qualified Lack of Control," in C. Natali (ed.), *Aristotle's Nicomachean Ethics Book VII: Symposium Aristotelicum* (Oxford: Oxford University Press, 2009), 72–102.

be read as a coherent whole. Our aim is thus to elucidate and defend this "progressive articulation," which, however, requires us to give up one assumption on which otherwise divergent commentators seem to agree—namely, that Aristotle seeks to explain akratic behavior by appeal to a failure either to have or to use knowledge of some *particular*.

1. PRELIMINARIES: THE VOLUNTARY BUT NON-VICIOUS CHARACTER OF AKRATIC BEHAVIOR

In interpreting VII.3, we take as our guide the general summary provided in VII.10:

[1] *EN* **VII.10: 1152a6–19**

(A) Nor is the same person able to be simultaneously *phronimos* and akratic. For character has been shown to be simultaneously *phronimos* and excellent. Further, <one is> *phronimos* not by knowing only but also by being *praktikos*; and the *akratês* is not *praktikos*. (But nothing prevents someone who is clever being akratic; whence it also seems that people are sometimes *phronimoi* but akratic, because cleverness differs from *phronêsis* in the way mentioned in the first arguments, being close <to *phronêsis*> with respect to the *logos* <involved> but different with respect to the *prohairesis* <involved>.)[2]

(B) Nor <is the *akratês*> like one knowing and contemplating, but rather like one asleep or drunk.

(C) And <the *akratês* acts> voluntarily (for he knows in some way both what he does and for the sake of what), but is not bad. For <his> *prohairesis* is decent with the result that he is <only> half-bad... One <sort of *akratês*> does not stick by the results of his deliberations, while the other, melancholic <sort> does not deliberate at all.

(A) alludes to the conclusion of *EN* VI.12–13 (namely, that one cannot be *phronimos* without being fully virtuous) and then states a corollary developed in *EN* VII (namely, that one cannot be simultaneously *phronimos* and akratic). (B) and (C) then explicate the condition of the *akratês*. According to (B), the *akratês* knows what she knows not in the way that someone contemplating what she knows knows it, but rather in something like the way in which someone who is asleep or drunk knows it. According to (C), she acts voluntarily in the sense that she in some sense knows what she is doing.

The requirement that the *akratês* act voluntarily plays a crucial role in our account, so it is worth noting how Aristotle explains it in *EN* III.1. An action will be voluntary only if it satisfies two conditions. The first, that the source be in the agent herself, is

---

[2] προαίρεσις is a technical term for Aristotle. It has become common to render it 'decision' (as distinct from 'choice,' which is used for the nontechnical αἵρεσις), but we shall simply transliterate so as to signal its technical status and to avoid taking a stand on how exactly Aristotle conceives of it. The same rationale applies to our transliteration of φρόνησις (often rendered 'practical wisdom') and its cognates.

irrelevant to the discussion of *akrasia*. What matters is the second condition—namely, that she act "knowing the particulars [εἰδότι τὰ καθ' ἕκαστα] involved in the action" [1111a22-23]. The following passage (whose references to drunkenness and madness show its relevance to VII.3) indicates the sort of particulars in question and reveals an important distinction between ignorance of *these*, which often constitutes a kind of excuse, and the sort of ignorance that is involved in vice and does not constitute any excuse—namely, ignorance in one's *prohairesis* or of some *universal*.

[2] *EN* III.1: 1110b24–1111a26

(A) Acting because of ignorance [δι' ἄγνοιαν] seems to be different from <acting> in ignorance [τοῦ ἀγνοοῦντα]; for the one drunk or angry seems to act not because of ignorance but because of some one of the things mentioned [e.g., drunkenness or anger], not <however> knowing but being ignorant. Every wicked agent is ignorant of the things that he ought to do and from which he ought to refrain, and because of such error <people> come to be unjust and generally vicious. But the <term> 'involuntary' [τὸ δ' ἀκούσιον] is not meant <to apply> if someone is ignorant of the sorts of things that are <generally> advantageous. For ignorance in the *prohairesis* is not the cause of the involuntary but of wickedness; nor is it <ignorance> of the universal <that is the cause of the involuntary> (for people are blamed because of this), but rather ignorance of the particulars in which and concerning which the action occurs . . .

(B) Perhaps then it is not a bad idea to define these, what and how many they are: who, what, concerning what, and in what someone acts, and sometimes also with what (for example, with <what> instrument) and for the sake of what (for example, <for the sake> of safety), and how (for example, gently or excessively). *No one could be ignorant of all of these unless he were mad.* It is plain that he could not be ignorant of the one acting. For how at any rate <could he fail to know that it is> himself? But one might be ignorant of *what* he does, as, for example, those saying that the things just slipped out while they were speaking . . . And someone might think his son to be an enemy (just as Merope <did>), or the pointed spear to be covered with a button, or the stone to be a pumice <stone> . . .

(C) Since what is involuntary is what is by force or because of ignorance, the voluntary would seem to be that of which the source is in the <agent> himself, knowing the particulars involved in the action. For things <done> because of *thumos* or *epithumia* are presumably not rightly called involuntary, first of all because <on this account> none of the other animals will act voluntarily; nor will children . . .

The reference to *thumos* or *epithumia* points to the distinction, articulated in *EN* VII.4–6, between the qualified forms of *akrasia* associated with *thumos* and the unqualified form associated with *epithumia*. And the passage reflects Aristotle's general view that, although the *akratês* is capable of *prohairesis*, she acts—like beasts and children—voluntarily but not from *prohairesis* [1148a13–17, 1150a19–31, 1151a1–14].[3]

Yet it is not to beasts or children that VII.3 compares the *akratês*: it is rather to those asleep, drunk, and mad. But assimilating the *akratês* to those who are mad, drunk, and asleep threatens the claim that the *akratês* acts voluntarily. For [2](B) explicitly associates madness with the sort of ignorance of particulars that renders an action involuntary. And [2](A) suggests that the ignorance *in* which (if not *because of* which) the drunk acts differs from the wicked agent's ignorance precisely in being ignorance of some particular rather than ignorance in the *prohairesis* or of some universal. This suggests that Aristotle takes drunken actions of the relevant sort to be *involuntary* (but still perhaps culpable). But he clearly takes akratic actions to be *voluntary*. So there remains a question about the point of [1](B)'s comparison between the *akratês* and those who are asleep or drunk.

Moreover, the more one takes the *akratês* to be characterized by ignorance of the relevant particulars, the less puzzling it becomes how she can act against her knowledge of what she ought or ought not do. It is only to the extent that the *akratês* acts knowing both what she does *and* that she ought not do it, that there is a real problem explaining how akratic action is possible. And Aristotle seems to share Socrates' sense that there *is* a real problem here, one associated with the idea that knowledge is especially powerful.

[3] *EN* VII.2: 1145b22–31

... some deny that it is *possible* for someone who knows <to act akratically>. For, as Socrates believed, it would be *deinon* if, when knowledge [ἐπιστήμη] is in <someone>, something else should rule and drag it about like a slave. For Socrates generally fought against the account <according to which knowledge is dragged about>, maintaining that there is no <such thing as> *akrasia*. For no one acts against what is best while supposing <that he does so>; but <it is only> because of ignorance <that such actions occur>. This [viz., Socrates'] argument, then, is clearly opposed to the phenomena, and it is necessary to inquire about the condition [τὸ πάθος] <of the *akratês*>: if it *is* because of ignorance, then what sort of ignorance does this turn out to be? For it is clear that the one who acts akratically does not think, before he comes to be in this condition, <that he should do what he actually does>.[4]

Given that Aristotle takes knowledge of particulars to be required for voluntary action, it is easy to conclude that the kind of ignorance involved in akratic action (if ignorance is involved) is ignorance of something universal. But this is problematic, given [2](A)'s association of such ignorance with vice. Although *Socrates* may diagnose so-called

---

[3] On beasts and children see *EN* 1111b6–10, 1149b31–1150a1.
[4] We choose 'condition,' which often connotes a temporary abnormality, to render πάθος, so as to reserve 'state,' which lacks this connotation, for ἕξις.

akratic behavior as due to ignorance about what in general ought to be done, Aristotle seems to rule this out: he thinks the *akratês* must know generally the sorts of things she ought and ought not do, and must in some sense reach the right *prohairesis* about what to do and yet act against her knowledge. So if Aristotle is to include ignorance among the causes or conditions of *akrasia*, he must toe a narrow line: he must avoid the kind of ignorance of universals that would render the agent vicious, without, however, appealing to the sort of ignorance of particulars that would undermine the claim that she acts voluntarily.

2. SETTING UP THE MAIN QUESTION OF VII.3

The question whether the *akratês* acts knowingly, and if so in what way she knows, heads the list of questions with which VII.3 opens, and it remains the focus throughout. The other questions are taken up in the chapters that follow.

[4] *EN* VII.3: 1146b8–24[5]

(A) First, then, we must inquire (1) whether <akratic agents act> knowing or not; and <if they know> in what way they know. Next we must set down (2) the sorts of things with which the *akratês* and the *enkratês* are concerned, I mean whether <they are> concerned with every pleasure and pain or with some definite ones [taken up in VII.4-6]; and (3) whether the *enkratês* and the tough are the same or different [taken up in VII.7]; and similarly (4) concerning the other <problems>, whatever ones are akin to this inquiry [presumably those discussed in VII.8–10].

(B) The starting point of our inquiry is whether the *enkratês* and the *akratês* are differentiated by the *things* with which <each is concerned> or by the *way* in which <each is concerned with the relevant things>. I mean, whether the *akratês* is *akratês* merely by being concerned with these things, or rather by the way <in which he is concerned with these> or not <simply by one> but by both. [And then whether *akrasia* is concerned with all things or not.] For the *haplôs akratês* is not concerned with all things, but with the things with which the intemperate agent [ὁ ἀκόλαστος] is concerned. Nor <is he *akratês*> simply by being concerned with these things—for then <*akrasia*> would be the same as intemperance—but <he is *akratês* by being concerned with them> in the following way: the one [viz., the *akolastos*] *prohairoumenos* is led <to act> thinking that he should always pursue the present pleasure; while the other [viz., the *akratês*] thinks he should not <pursue the present pleasure> but pursues it anyway.[6]

---

[5] Passages [4]–[10] provide a continuous translation of the whole of *EN* VII.3.
[6] For this construction of οὐκ οἴεται, see H. W. Smyth, *Greek Grammar* (Cambridge, MA: Harvard University Press, 1920), 2692a.

The point of (B) is that the intemperate agent and the *akratês* pursue the same object but in different ways: the intemperate agent thinks she *should* pursue the present pleasure, while the *akratês* thinks she *should not*. But many commentators are puzzled about how exactly (B) is supposed to follow on (A). Some worry because they think it obvious that (B) addresses question (2) and they take Aristotle to return to question (1) only in the lines immediately following this passage (viz., in passage [5] below).[7] Others have a more general worry about what they see as (B)'s repetition of points made in (A).[8] But both worries assume that the question bracketed in (B) corresponds to question (2). If, as some editors suggest, this question does not belong where it appears, there is no problem.[9] Aristotle *first asks* whether akratic agents in *general* are to be distinguished from others by the objects with which they are concerned, by their attitudes toward these objects, or by both. He *then explains* why this question arises in spite of what might seem to be the presumption in favor of distinguishing them by their objects—namely, because there is one sort of *akratês* who seems to be concerned with precisely the *same objects* with which the intemperate agent is concerned. So in order to explain how *this* sort of *akratês* differs from the *akolastos*, Aristotle must appeal to some difference in their *attitudes*.

Aristotle thus turns to an idea mentioned back in VII.2: the idea that the *akratês* does not *know but only believes* that she should not do what she does. He dismisses this quickly, apparently because it rests on the false assumption that belief tends to be associated with lesser confidence in its objects than knowledge is:

[5] *EN* VII.3: 1146b24-31

Concerning <the suggestion> that it is true belief and not knowledge by which people act akratically, this *makes no difference* [οὐδὲν διαφέρει] to the account. For some of those who <merely> believe are not at all divided <in their beliefs>

---

[7] Irwin reads (B) as taking up in chiastic order the questions raised in (A). See Irwin's *Aristotle: Nicomachean Ethics*, 2nd edn. [*Aristotle: Nic. Eth.*] (Indianapolis, IN: Hackett, 1999), 257. But this does not fully address the problem. For (B) does not address (2): it simply assumes, largely by way of returning to question (1), points made in later chapters.

[8] Cook Wilson suggests that (B) was originally an alternative version of the material covered in (A) and he proposes to bracket or excise one or the other of these paragraphs. See his *Aristotelian Studies*, 19. Broadie is sympathetic; see S. Broadie and C. Rowe, *Aristotle, Nicomachean Ethics* [*Aristotle, Nic. Eth.*] (Oxford: Oxford University Press, 2002), 388.

[9] See G. Ramsauer, *Aristotelis Ethica Nicomachea* [*Arist. Eth. Nic.*] (Leipzig, 1878) ad loc.; and R. A. Gauthier and J. Y. Jolif, *Aristote: L'Ethique à Nicomaque*, 2nd edn. [*Arist.: L'Ethique*] (Louvain and Paris: Peeters Publisher, 1970) ad loc. One can easily see how the bracketed question might have been introduced by an editor or copyist who had difficulty in its absence with understanding the connection between (i) the original question about how the *akratês* and *enkratês* differ from other characters and (ii) the γάρ that introduces the subsequent claim that the *haplôs akratês* is not concerned with all things but only with the things with which the intemperate agent is concerned. For this claim seems simply to answer the original question, while the γάρ suggests that something is being argued or explained. But this is perfectly intelligible once we see that the original question (like most of what precedes) speaks of the *akratês* in *general*, while the γάρ sentence refers to a *specific* sort of *akratês*, the *haplôs akratês*, whom Aristotle takes to be concerned with precisely those pleasures with which the *akolastos* is concerned. Given this shift, the paragraph makes perfect sense without the bracketed question, which was perhaps introduced by an editor or copyist who failed to appreciate the shift.

but take themselves to know exactly. If, then, it is because of their trusting only weakly <in what they believe> that those who believe act against their supposition more than those who know, knowledge will differ in no way from belief. For some are no less confident in the things they <merely> believe than others are in the things they know. Heraclitus makes this clear.

One might object that the difference between knowledge and belief is in fact relevant for reasons having nothing to do with any differences in degree of confidence. One might allow, for example, that knowers and mere believers may be equally confident, and then argue that knowers (unlike mere believers) can give proper accounts of what they know. But even if Aristotle *is* overlooking this possibility, that is irrelevant here: he clearly thinks, whether correctly or not, that this distinction makes "no difference."

3. THE GENERIC SOLUTION: THE FIRST STEP IN ARISTOTLE'S "PROGRESSIVE ARTICULATION"

Aristotle moves on immediately to a distinction that he says *"will* make a difference."

[6] *EN* VII.3: 1146b31–35

But since we speak of knowing [τὸ ἐπίστασθαι] in two ways—for both the one having but not using his knowledge and the one using it are said to know—it *will make a difference* [διοίσει] whether <we talk about> having but not contemplating, or about contemplating, the things one ought not do.[10] For this [viz., acting akratically while contemplating the things one ought not do] seems *deinon*, but <it does> not <seem *deinon* to act akratically> if one is not contemplating <these things>.

Here Aristotle invokes a distinction, familiar from Plato's *Theaetetus*, between the state of someone who has acquired knowledge but is not at the moment using it and the state of someone who is actively using previously acquired knowledge.[11] Aristotle treats this distinction, in *De Anima* II.1, as involving two kinds of actuality [ἐντελέχεια]: the kind involved when someone who has acquired knowledge is *not actively using* that knowledge and the kind involved when someone who has acquired knowledge *is actively using* her knowledge [*DA* 412b21–28]. Because Aristotle refers to the former as "first" actuality, commentators typically speak here of "first" and "second" actuality knowledge. First-actuality knowledge is itself a kind of potentiality or capacity [δύναμις], to be

---

[10] Following I. Bywater, *Aristotelis Ethica Nicomachea* (Oxford: Oxford University Press, 1894), we omit τοῦ ἔχοντα καὶ θεωροῦντα.

[11] The *Theaetetus* [see 197 B–98 D], however, puts the point somewhat differently, distinguishing τὸ κεκτῆσθαι (viz., having acquired and so possessing something) from τὸ ἔχειν (which is a stronger form of having, a kind of having something actually "in hand"). So Socrates uses τὸ ἔχειν to refer specifically to what Aristotle calls 'using' or 'contemplating' what one knows.

distinguished from the mere capacity to *acquire* knowledge that is characteristic of someone who has not yet learned some subject; it is a capacity to *use* (already acquired) knowledge in situations where such use is called for [see *DA* 417a21–b2].

Aristotle says that the distinction will make *some* difference to the account of *akrasia*. The question is *how far* it actually takes us. What is Aristotle's point when he says that it seems *deinon* if someone does what she ought not do while actively contemplating and so *using* her knowledge of what she ought not do, but not *deinon* if someone does what she ought not do while she is not actively contemplating but merely *has* (first actuality) knowledge of what she ought not do? Does '*deinon*' mean something like "absolutely amazing," in which case Aristotle would seem to be ruling out what is sometimes called "clear-eyed" *akrasia*—viz., cases where someone who knows she should not Φ nevertheless Φ-s while actively thinking she should not? Or does '*deinon*' mean simply "strange," in which case Aristotle may or may not be allowing that "clear-eyed" *akrasia* sometimes occurs? Is the idea that clear-eyed *akrasia* is, as we might say, "strange but true"?[12]

Note, however, that nothing much is to be gained by specifying the sense of '*deinon*', since even if we read Aristotle as rejecting "clear-eyed" *akrasia* there remain questions about the spirit in which he proceeds. He may be assuming that his readers will agree that there is nothing strange about acting against knowledge one is not actively using, and so simply trotting out standard distinctions that he takes to illuminate this phenomenon. But it is not clear that Aristotle would be entitled to this assumption. As he himself recognizes, those who *have* knowledge typically *use* it in situations in which it is called for [see *Physics* VIII.4, 255a33–b5]. So he himself should be puzzled by the idea that someone can act against knowledge she *has* provided only that she is not *using* this knowledge. Perhaps then we should read what follows as seeking to *justify* his claim that there is nothing strange in this.

What follows [6] are three bits of text each introduced by '*eti*,' which clearly signals some further point. There is, however, controversy about how each additional point is related to the preceding points. For example, does the first '*eti*' signal the first in a series of *mere additions* to the fundamental account, whose essentials are *already present* in [6]? Or does it perhaps signal the second in a series of steps that lead *only eventually* to an adequate characterization of akratic failure?

Some commentators speak of several different "solutions" to the problem of explaining how the *akratês* can act against her knowledge. Of these, some see the "real" solution as coming only in the fourth stage.[13] Others see the essence of Aristotle's solution as more or less fully present in [6], whose distinction between *merely having* and

---

[12] The same question arises in [3]. Because this recalls *Protagoras* 352 B–C, many commentators take its use of *deinon* to connote the sort of impossibility of *akrasia* defended by Socrates in the *Protagoras*. Note, however, that, although Plato sometimes uses '*deinon*' to refer to something especially paradoxical (as, for example, at *Hippias Minor* 375 D 3 and *Theaetetus* 203 D 6), this term does not appear in the *Protagoras* argument.

[13] See, for example, J. Burnet, *The Ethics of Aristotle* (London: Methuen, 1900), 299: "the first three are dialectical ... The fourth is the real *lusis* and is of a strictly psychological character. We need not expect to find the three first quite consistent with each other or with the fourth."

actively using reappears in somewhat different guises in each of the remaining "solutions."[14] But many commentators see each of the earlier stages as preparing in some way for the account reached in the last stage or stages. Some think we do not get a proper characterization of akratic failure—as distinct from examples of *other* sorts of failure that shed light on it—until the third or fourth stage. Irwin, for example, claims that in the first three stages Aristotle "discusses different cases that do not completely fit incontinents, but eventually help us to understand some aspects of incontinents' state of mind" (which Irwin takes to be characterized in the fourth stage).[15] Others see Aristotle as reaching one sort of *akratês* (namely, the impetuous) in the third stage, and another (namely, the weak) only in the fourth.[16]

We agree with those who see the earlier stages as preparing for the proper account, which is given only in the fourth stage. But we do not think the early stages introduce examples only of *other* sorts of failure that shed light on the failure of the *akratês*. We see instead a progression in which the first stage describes a generic sort of failure of which the *akratês'* failure is eventually shown to be a species. Each subsequent stage is required because the previous stage does not yet capture the sort of failure *distinctive* of the *akratês*. In this sense, each stage takes us "further" along a continuous route.

4. THE FIRST *ETI* PASSAGE (AND SECOND STEP): A DIFFERENCE IN THE UNIVERSAL

The progressive articulation is perhaps clearest in the transition from the first to the second stage—viz., from [6] to the first *eti* passage:

[7] *EN* VII.3: 1146b35–1147a10

(A) Further [ἔτι], since there are two *tropoi* of *protaseis*, nothing prevents someone who has both <*protaseis*> from acting against <his> knowledge if he is using the universal <*protasis*> but not the particular one [χρώμενον μέντοι τῇ καθόλου, ἀλλὰ μὴ τῇ κατὰ μέρος].[17] For it is the particulars [τὰ καθ' ἕκαστα] that are to be acted on.

---

[14] See, for example, R. Robinson, "Aristotle on Akrasia," ["Akrasia"], in Robinson, *Essays in Greek Philosophy* (Oxford: Clarendon Press, 1969), 139–60 (reference at 141). [Reprinted in J. Barnes, M. Schofield, and R. Sorabji (eds.), *Articles on Aristotle, vol. 2: Ethics and Politics* (New York: St. Martin's Press, 1977), 72–91.] "I hold that Aristotle accepts this solution"—viz., the one given in [6]—"and believes it to contain virtually everything necessary for the explanation of akrasia, since it shows how the akratic both knows and does not know that his act is wrong . . . However, Aristotle adds three more solutions."

[15] Irwin, *Aristotle: Nic. Eth.*, 258; and A. Kenny, "The Practical Syllogism and Incontinence" ["Practical Syllogism"], *Phronesis* 10 (1966), at 173–76.

[16] See, for example, Rassow, *Forschungen*, 128; J. A. Stewart, *Notes on the Nicomachean Ethics* [*Notes*] (Oxford, 1892), vol. II, 146; G. Hughes, *Aristotle on Ethics* (London: Routledge, 2001), 148–59.

[17] We render both κατὰ μέρος (in this line) and καθ' ἕκαστα (in what follows) as 'particular' because Aristotle often uses these terms interchangeably, as he seems to do here. (For the reverse move in another practical context, see *EN* 1107a28–32.) Either term can of course be applied both to a particular

(B) There is a difference *also* with respect to the universal [διαφέρει δὲ καὶ τὸ καθόλου]: for one <universal> applies to oneself and the other to the object. For example, that dry <foods> benefit every man, and that one is <oneself> a man or that such <food> is dry. But whether this <food> is such, either he does not have or does not exercise.

(C) With respect to *these tropoi* there will be an enormous difference [κατά τε δὴ τούτους διοίσει τοὺς τρόπους ἀμήχανον ὅσον], so that it seems that to know in this way <yet act against one's knowledge> is in no way strange, while <acting against one's knowledge> is otherwise amazing.

Aristotle builds here on the suggestion in [6] that the *akratês* might have knowledge without actively using it. But even if [6] provides a generic solution, its account is still incomplete. Since there are two kinds of proposition knowledge of which someone might have but fail to use, there is a further question about whether it is knowledge of one rather than the other kind of proposition that the *akratês* fails to use, and if so which one: knowledge of a *universal* proposition or knowledge of a *particular* one.[18]

Aristotle thinks this distinction important because he sees no difficulty—at least in the sense that there is no contradiction involved—in someone's acting against knowledge where it is only knowledge of a *universal* proposition that is active or "used." He elsewhere describes cases of theoretical knowledge in which someone has and uses only knowledge of a universal proposition—for example, the case in which someone knows that all triangles have angles equal to two right angles but does not recognize of some particular figure that is in fact a triangle that it has angles equal to two right angles, either because she is not (yet) aware of its existence or because she does not (yet) recognize it *as* a triangle [*Prior Analytics* II.21; *Posterior Analytics* I.1]. And just as he sees no contradiction in such theoretical cases, he may see no contradiction in practical ones.

We must, however, caution against assuming too quickly, as many commentators assume, that Aristotle's appeal to cases like those in the *Analytics* shows that he takes the failure of the *akratês* to lie likewise in a failure either to have or to use knowledge of some *particular*.[19] For it may be that we are intended to carry only some and not all of

---

kind (e.g., to chicken as a particular kind of dry food) and to a particular token of some kind (e.g., to a particular piece of chicken). Aristotle may use κατὰ μέρος here because he wants to allow [especially in 1147a4–7] that some universal terms such as 'dry food' (as compared with 'man') are applied in a series of steps, first from a whole kind (e.g., dry food) to a part of that kind (e.g., chicken), then to a particular instance of that part (e.g., this here piece of chicken). And καθ' ἕκαστα is perhaps more strongly associated than κατὰ μέρος with particular instances.

[18] We follow David Charles in taking '*protasis*' to mean 'proposition' while recognizing that Aristotle often uses it to refer specifically to premises in an argument. See D. Charles, *Aristotle's Philosophy of Action* [*Action*] (London: Duckworth Publishing, 1984), 120 n. 13; and "NE VII. 3: Varieties of Acrasia" ["Varieties"] in Natali, *Aristotle: Nic. Eth. VII*. We thus remain neutral on the question of whether Aristotle means to refer to the premises of some syllogism.

[19] Commentators who refer to the *Analytics* passages, and then proceed to identify the failure of the *akratês* as a failure to have or to use some *particular* proposition, include H. H. Joachim, *Aristotle: The Nicomachean Ethics* (Oxford, 1951), 223–29; Gauthier and Jolif, *Arist.: L'Ethique*, vol. II, 606; F. Grgić,

the features of theoretical cases over to the practical case. This is especially plausible, since theoretical knowledge is primarily of universals in a way that practical knowledge is not. Moreover, it is more obvious in theoretical than in practical contexts how one might use a universal without applying it to particulars: for this is how universals are in fact used in demonstrations. But the idea that one can actively use universal knowledge without applying it to particulars may not transfer readily to practical contexts, where competent use of a universal *consists* largely in applying it to particulars. In such contexts, there is a question how one *could* use a universal proposition without thereby (or at least also) using one's knowledge of particular propositions.

More importantly, there is a special problem with taking it to be knowledge of *particular* propositions that the *akratês* fails to use: this threatens the claim that she does *voluntarily* what she thinks she ought not do. For an action *must* be voluntary if it is to count as akratic; but according to Aristotle, ignorance of particulars renders actions involuntary (or at least non-voluntary) [see *EN* 1110b22–24]. This suggests that the practical case may differ from the theoretical one with respect to *which* sort of proposition fails to get used. If so, [7](A) may not diagnose the failure of the *akratês* as lying in her failure to use some *particular* proposition; it may seek to establish, by appeal to a familiar case, only that the *akratês* fails to use *one or the other* of these two sorts of proposition without yet telling us which.[20]

Indeed, the fact that Aristotle focuses in [7](B) on a "difference with respect to the *universal*" suggests that he may well be looking for a way to diagnose the *akratês*' failure at least partly in terms of her failure to use some universal proposition. But this possibility tends to be overlooked because most commentators focus primarily on Aristotle's claim that an agent might fail either to have or to use knowledge of the proposition "this food is such," but neglect to situate this claim in its proper context, which concerns a difference in the *universal*. Aristotle's point turns on the fact that universal propositions have two terms, either of which the *akratês* might fail to use properly. Some of these terms are such that their application is relatively straightforward in ways that the application of others is not. Consider Aristotle's example: "dry <foods>

"Aristotle on the Akratic's Knowledge," *Phronesis* 47 (2002): 344–55; A. W. Price, "Acrasia and Self-Control"' ["Acrasia"], in R. Kraut (ed.), *The Blackwell Guide to the Nicomachean Ethics* [*Guide*] (Oxford, 2006), 234–54.

[20] Sarah Broadie has objected (in discussion) that because *EN* III.1 (quoted in [2] above) has not yet introduced the distinction between merely having and actually using knowledge, it may claim only that voluntary action requires *having* knowledge of the relevant particulars, whereas our appeal to *EN* III.1 tends to assume that *actual use* is required. Note, however, that many of [2](B)'s examples of ignorance of particulars are of highly context-specific facts, such as whether the spear in one's hand at a particular place and time has a button on it, or whether the individual approaching at a particular place and time is one's son. With knowledge of such propositions, whose contents tend to be partly demonstrative, there is not generally the sort of dispositional knowledge, which might or might not be actualized in particular situations, that there is with knowledge of universal propositions. In other words, there seems to be less room here for the sort of gap required to make sense of the distinction between merely having and actually using the relevant knowledge. Moreover, as we shall see in [9](B), Aristotle's positive account explicitly says that the *akratês* actively uses knowledge of the relevant particular.

are good for every human." Any *practical* use of this universal requires the application of both of its terms: the agent must recognize *both* that she herself is human *and* that such and such food (viz., the kind before her) is dry. It goes without saying that the agent will use her knowledge that she herself is human, even if she does not stop to give it explicit thought.[21] So Aristotle points instead to the possibility that she either does not know or does not use her knowledge that *this* food (viz., the food before her) is such and such. And in this sense she fails to use her knowledge of various *universal* propositions, including the propositions that such and such food is dry, and that such and such food is beneficial for every human (herself included).

Reading Aristotle as shifting our attention to failure to use knowledge of a *universal* proposition suggests a way of explaining [7](C) that makes better sense than commentators usually make of what (B) is doing here in the first place. Commentators have been uniformly troubled by the question of how to take "these *tropoi*" in (C). For the only references to *tropoi* in the vicinity are to the two *tropoi* of *protasis* back in [7](A) and to "another *tropos* of having *epistēmē*" that Aristotle has yet to introduce in [8](A). It would be highly unnatural to take τούτους τοὺς τρόπους to refer forward. And while it might seem natural to connect the occurrence of τρόπους in (C) to its occurrence in (A), this too is problematic: for it renders (B) largely parenthetical and makes it hard to see why it is here at all. Moreover, the use of τούτους (rather than ἐκείνους) encourages us to seek a more immediate referent somewhere in (B).

Two possibilities are salient. One is to take τούτους τοὺς τρόπους to refer to the difference in (B) between *not having* the particular knowledge that this food is such and such and *having but not exercising* such knowledge.[22] The point of (C) would then be that there is so great a difference between merely having *particular* knowledge without exercising it and both having and exercising *particular* knowledge, that it would seem in no way strange for someone who has such knowledge without using it to act against that knowledge, while it would be absolutely amazing for someone who both has and uses such knowledge to act against it. But this makes the point of (C) virtually indistinguishable from the point of [6] and so makes it harder to see what [7] adds to [6].[23] It is

---

[21] As Aristotle notes in *De Motu Animalium* 7, some propositions are so obvious that thought does not stop to consider them; and his example is precisely that one is oneself human [701a26–29; see 701a13–16]. Moreover, in listing the particulars knowledge of which is required for voluntary action, Aristotle says in [2](B) that no sane agent could fail to know that she herself is the one acting.

[22] Commentators and translators tend, understandably, not to be explicit about what is going on here, so it is sometimes (as in Irwin's case) difficult to be sure how they take τούτους τοὺς τρόπους. For a relatively clear example of this first way of taking it, see Rowe's translation (in Broadie and Rowe) of 1147a7–8: "whether this is such-and-such—this is what the agent either does not 'have,' or does not activate; and which of *these ways* we mean will make an immense difference, with the result that his knowing seems, in one way, not at all strange, and in another way amazing." Note, however, that the scare-quotes with "have" seem to anticipate the different *tropoi* of having introduced in [8](A), so Rowe's position is not entirely clear.

[23] This might of course seem to be grist for Cook Wilson's mill. But if there is a way to interpret [7] as part of a coherent progression that adds to the point of [6], then we should reject his view. Still, the jury on our reading of [7] should be out until we show how it fits into the overall progression.

of course true that [7](A) focuses in a way that [6] does not on knowledge of particular propositions. Many take this to show that [7] *as a whole* diagnoses the *akratês*' failure as a failure to use knowledge of some particular proposition. But this makes it difficult not only (as we've seen) to claim that the *akratês* acts voluntarily but also (as we now maintain) to understand the point of [7](B).

There is, however, another way to take τούτους τοὺς τρόπους as referring to something in (B): we can take it as referring to the "difference with respect to the universal" introduced in (B). In this case, the point in (C) may be that there is so great a difference between failing to recognize that a term like 'human' applies to oneself and failing to recognize that a term like 'dry' applies to a certain sort of food, that it would be in no way strange for someone to act against her knowledge that "dry foods are good for every human" because she fails to apply a term like 'dry' to a certain sort of food (which happens to be in front of her), though it would be amazing for someone to act against this knowledge because she fails to apply a term like 'human' to herself.[24] This way of taking "these *tropoi*" allows us to explain why Aristotle introduces (B) in the first place. There would be little point to adding that there is difference *also* in the *universal* if his diagnosis of the *akratês*' failure rested entirely in her failure to have or to use knowledge of *particular* propositions. But introducing this difference makes good sense if Aristotle is seeking a way to trace the *akratês*' failure at least partly to her failure to use knowledge of some *universal* proposition.

It is worth pausing here to note that one commentator—namely, Ramsauer—was so puzzled by Aristotle's claim that "there is a difference also with respect to the universal" that he proposed to substitute κατὰ μέρος for καθόλου in 1147a4: he wanted to read "there is a difference also with respect to the *particular*"![25] But given the lack of any manuscript support, this is clearly the counsel of despair. So most commentators settle instead for reading Aristotle's remark about the "difference with respect to the universal" as merely parenthetical. But the weakness of this becomes clear when we consider two things: the emphatic position of διαφέρει and the overall context. Aristotle began, back in [5], by rejecting a distinction alleged to make a difference to the account of *akrasia*: he says in 1146b25 that this distinction will make *no difference* [οὐδὲν διαφέρει].

---

[24] It may be that Aristotle's main point is to distinguish terms whose application is obvious from terms whose application is not so obvious, and that the example he uses to illustrate this point simply happens to be one in which it is the *subject* term rather than the *object* term whose application is obvious. His way of putting the point admittedly suggests that he thinks that it is for "the most part" *subject* terms whose application is obvious. And he might have thought this (whether correctly or not) if he thought it difficult (though not perhaps impossible) to overlook the fact, *once one knows* it, that some relevant term (such as 'married' or 'diabetic') applies to oneself. See also note 46 below. The objection that one might easily fail to know that some practically relevant term (such as 'diabetic') applies to oneself is irrelevant here, since that would not yield a case in which the agent acts *voluntarily* against what she in some sense *knows*.

[25] Ramsauer, *Arist. Eth. Nic.*, ad loc. This is a far more radical emendation than the one proposed by Stewart, *Notes*, and discussed in section 8 below. But the stimulus is largely the same—namely, failure to understand how Aristotle could be tracing the failure of the *akratês* to some defect in her knowledge of *universals*.

He then turns in [6] to a distinction that he says *will* make a difference [διοίσει in b33] and follows up in [7] and in [8] with talk of further differences: the one in question here and the difference in *hexis* to be introduced in [8]. In this context, any talk of difference should be taken as talk of a difference that *matters*. And the position of διαφέρει in διαφέρει δὲ καὶ τὸ καθόλου is not just ordinarily emphatic: it is highly emphatic. The sentence it introduces would be extraordinary coming from someone who viewed his remark about the "difference with respect to the universal" as merely parenthetical.

Aristotle is no doubt concerned with the application of universals to particulars. For this plays a crucial role in the practical sphere, where, however, failure to have or to use knowledge of some particular proposition is not easily separated from failure to use knowledge of some universal proposition. In fact, an agent may sometimes fail to use knowledge of some universal proposition precisely because she either lacks or does not use knowledge of some particular proposition whose use would in fact *constitute* her use of the relevant universal. But given this, it might seem that the failure of those who act against knowledge can be described in *either* way—as failure to use knowledge of some particular *or* as failure to use knowledge of some universal. Why, then, should [7](B) flag a "difference with respect to the *universal*"?

Our hypothesis is that Aristotle redirects attention to a difference in the universal because he thinks this knowledge of the relevant universal is required in order for the akratic action to count as voluntary. In [7](B), he considers a case where an agent fails to use her knowledge of some universal *because* she fails either to have or to use knowledge of some particular. But in this case her action (or omission) is not voluntary. That is not a problem if (as we think) the point of [7](B) is not to capture the failure distinctive of the *akratēs*, but rather to redirect our attention generally to failures to use universal knowledge so as to prepare the way for the account of akratic failure to come in [9], where (as we'll see) failure to use knowledge of some universal proposition is explained by something other than the sort of ignorance of particulars that would undermine the claim that the agent acts voluntarily.

5. THE SECOND *ETI* PASSAGE (AND THIRD STEP): SLEEP, DRUNKNESS, AND MADNESS

Whichever sort of knowledge the *akratēs* is supposed to have but not use, Aristotle suggests that there is a *further* question about the sense in which the *akratēs has* this knowledge.

[8] *EN* VII.3: 1147a10–24

Further [ἔτι] "having knowledge" applies to human beings in another way [ἄλλον τρόπον] from those just mentioned.

(A) For <among cases of> having-but-not-using we see the *hexis* <itself> differing, with the result that <there is> also having in a way [πως] and not having <the

relevant knowledge>: for example, one sleeping or mad or drunk <both has in a way and does not have the relevant knowledge>. And surely those at any rate who are in passionate conditions [οἵ γε ἐν τοῖς πάθεσιν ὄντες] are so disposed. For *thumoi* and sexual appetites and some <other> such things clearly change the body, too, and in some folk even produce madness. It is plain then that we should say that akratic agents are disposed similarly to these <folk>.

(B) Uttering the formulae [τὸ δὲ λέγειν τοὺς λόγους] that stem from knowledge is no sign <of having knowledge>. For even those in such passionate conditions utter proofs and the verses of Empedocles, and those first learning string together the <relevant> formulae, but they do not yet know. For it is necessary for <the relevant contents> to become part of one's nature, and this takes time. So just as actors <utter the formulae>, we must suppose that akratic agents <do the same>.

Here Aristotle introduces a new sort of *hexis* to be included among the ways of having knowledge—viz., "having in a way [πως] and not having <it>." Talk of having knowledge has hitherto been talk of the sort of *dunamis* whose possession Aristotle takes to constitute first-actuality knowledge. And the subject of such a *dunamis* is ordinarily able to actualize it more or less at will—viz., to contemplate the relevant objects whenever she wishes, provided that nothing external is preventing her [see *DA* 417a27–28]. But if we take this ability as a *criterion* for having knowledge, then it may appear that those who are mad, drunk, or asleep do not even *have* the sorts of knowledge it seems clear (when they are sane, sober, and awake) they do have.

Aristotle, however, recognizes cases where a subject who clearly has a kind of knowledge is temporarily in a condition such that she is not able to exercise her knowledge at will—for example, the sleeping geometer mentioned at *Generation of Animals (GA)* 735a9–11. There is no suggestion here that the sleeping geometer *lacks* knowledge. And this makes sense because, as Aristotle explains at *Physics* 247b13–16, we would otherwise need to treat the geometer's waking as involving the reacquisition of knowledge. Moreover, Aristotle's general account of sleeping and waking helps to explain what is going on here. He regards sleep as a *pathos*, not itself involving any external impediment, in which its subject cannot activate or use her capacities in the ways she ordinarily can when she is awake.[26]

[8](A) compares the *akratês* not only to those who are asleep, but also to those who are mad and drunk. Note that this is the first place, since Aristotle started introducing distinctions that do "make a difference," where he explicitly likens the condition of the *akratês* to any of the states or conditions he describes. Though one might (and some commentators do) at various points take him to be assimilating the condition of the *akratês* to one of the states or conditions previously mentioned—for example, the

---

[26] For references to sleep as a *pathos* of the perceptive faculty, see *De Insomniis (De Insomn.)* 459a26 [see 460b31].

state of someone having but not using knowledge of *particular* propositions—Aristotle does not himself do so, at least not explicitly. So it is crucial to understand the point of these comparisons, especially since he returns in his summary in *EN* VII.10—i.e., in [1] (B) above—to the comparison with those who are asleep and drunk.

One common feature of these conditions is the fact that they (like madness) involve changes in the subject's body. Aristotle elsewhere explains some of these changes and the mechanisms underlying them in ways indicating that he thinks such changes can interfere with the normal functioning of perception and the other mechanisms that are involved in belief-formation. In the case of normal sleep, he thinks there are physical changes (associated with heating and cooling, and required for proper digestive functioning) that result in a seizing up of the primary sense organ so that it is not able to act—at least not in the ways it acts when the subject is awake [*On Sleeping and Waking* 458a28–29]. Similar changes occur in drunkenness, where heating and cooling may move the bodily elements around in similar ways [456b16–457a20]. Moreover, though Aristotle thinks we do not generally perceive during sleep, he allows that it is nevertheless possible for sight and the other senses to be affected [*De Insomn.* 459a1–9]. Dreams, for example, occur because one and the same faculty is involved both in normal perception and in the operations of imagination [459a15–23]; because the normal operations of the senses set up motions that can persist and cause other motions when the objects themselves are no longer present [459a23–b23]; and because some of these motions can be so like those caused by the actual presence of the relevant objects as to make it appear as if the objects were present when they are not.

Aristotle clearly allows that the doxastic faculty is at least sometimes active in sleep: "sometimes *doxa* says, as if the person were awake, that the thing seen <in a dream> is false; but sometimes <*doxa*> is taken in and follows the appearance" [459a6–8]. Aristotle makes the same point about the doxastic faculties of those who suffer various forms of illness. It may appear to those with fevers that there are animals dancing on the wall, and those whose fever is severe may be taken in by this appearance in ways that those whose fever is less severe are not: the latter may realize that the appearance is false and act accordingly, while the former act in ways suggesting that they take the appearance at face value [460b12–16]. We might, however, hesitate—and so might Aristotle—to say that the former *really believe* what their actions suggest they believe: for nothing prevents the contents of these appearances being such that the subject ordinarily denies them, in some cases denying even their possibility. Take, for example, a case where someone who would ordinarily deny the very existence of pink elephants is taken in by the appearance—in the sense that she *acts as if she accepted* the appearance—that pink elephants are dancing on barstools. Here we seem forced to choose between saying on the one hand that she *now* believes something that contradicts what she *ordinarily* believes, and saying on the other that she doesn't really believe what she now *appears* to believe even though she acts *as if* she did. If we say the former, the question then arises whether she now *also* believes what she ordinarily believes and so now has contradictory beliefs, or whether she has temporarily lost her ordinary belief. We cannot resolve these questions here. But Aristotle himself seems reluctant to ascribe pairs of contradictory beliefs to an agent, perhaps because he realizes that doing so threatens the coherence of ascribing *either* belief. So it seems likely that he takes the agent simply to act *as if* she believed something she does not really believe. Moreover, it seems open to him to do so, given the way in which he allows that *phantasia*, without belief in its contents, can sometimes (as in non-rational animals) play the role ordinarily played by belief in the generation of action.

We emphasize the ways in which the material and efficient causal conditions associated with sleep, drunkenness, and madness can interfere with the normal mechanisms of perception and belief-formation because Aristotle clearly sees similar conditions and disturbances accompanying the *pathê* characteristic of the *akratês*: for example, excessive anger and inordinate sexual desire. Such *pathê* are partly constituted by and can themselves give rise to bodily conditions like those associated with sleep, drunkenness, and certain forms of illness. Even thoughts can produce bodily changes, at least in cases where their objects are also objects of emotion. As Aristotle says in *De Anima* III.9, the thought of something fearful or pleasant, even when it does not lead to action, sometimes produces bodily changes: if the object is fearful, the heart is moved; if the object is pleasant, some other part [*DA* 432b29–433a1]. And such changes can interfere with the normal operations of perception and belief-formation. This is no surprise, since Aristotle takes perception itself to involve certain bodily conditions and perhaps also bodily changes.

Our account takes seriously Aristotle's explicit assimilation of the *akratês*' condition to the conditions of those asleep, mad, and drunk. And it takes the central paradigm to be that of the sleeping geometer. It is assumed that the *akratês generally has* the sort of knowledge she acts against (in the sense that she has *already acquired* first-actuality knowledge, which she can *ordinarily* actualize at will); but she is in a *temporary condition* that resembles sleep in that it prevents her from moving at will from first- to second-actuality knowledge. So, insofar as *having* knowledge involves the ability to actualize it at will, there is an important sense in which, when she is in this condition, she does *not have* the knowledge: that's why Aristotle says she both "has in a way and does not have <it>."

Here, however, one might wonder whether this *can* be what Aristotle has in mind, given that at least some akratics seem to be well aware of what they are doing. In fact, Aristotle himself seems to imagine someone asking how he can say this, given that some even say while they are acting that they should not be doing what they do. Aristotle accepts this appearance: he allows that some akratics "utter the formulae" that would normally indicate not only that they possess but are *in fact actualizing* the sort of knowledge they act against. Yet he denies that it follows from this that they are *really* actualizing the relevant knowledge. He cites three examples of people who may "utter the formulae that stem from knowledge" without, however, actualizing the knowledge that such formulae typically express: those who, in passionate conditions like anger and sexual desire, utter proofs and the verses of Empedocles; those first learning a subject; and actors. And while actors may or may not know whereof they speak, it is clear in the case of those "*first* learning" a subject that the agents do not yet possess the sort of knowledge their utterances ordinarily express. So *their* utterances *cannot* be taken as any sign that *they* are actualizing the relevant knowledge, which ex hypothesi they do not even possess.

The fact that some of the subjects mentioned do not even *have* the knowledge that their utterances seem to express is overlooked by those commentators who take Aristotle to assimilate the condition of the *akratês* to that of the learner.[27] Such commentators aim to explain the sense in which the *akratês* both "has in a way and does not have" the relevant knowledge by saying that she has only a *partial* grasp of it. And they seek to justify this partly by connecting [8](B) with passages where Aristotle emphasizes the crucial role played by experience of particulars in the acquisition of practical knowledge (as distinct from knowledge of subjects like mathematics). One such passage is indeed similar to [8](B): Aristotle says that in areas where experience of particulars is crucial, "young people lack conviction but simply speak" [*EN* 1142a19–20].

But if one assimilates akratic agents in general to learners, one moves away from the idea that the *akratês* is, like the sleeping geometer, someone who has already reached first-actuality knowledge but is in a condition such that she cannot, while in that condition, access it at will. Moreover, [8](B) does *not* say that the condition of the *akratês* is *generally* like that of the learner: it is aimed primarily at disarming the previously mentioned objection by showing that it does *not follow* from the fact that someone "utters the formulae that stem from knowledge" that she is *using* the relevant knowledge. Aristotle is not adding the learner to (A)'s list of paradigms. He simply appeals, in order to answer the objection, to a limited respect in which at least some akratic agents are like those first learning a subject.[28]

If one were to read [8](B) as adding to (A)'s list of paradigms, one should read it as adding the actor rather than the learner. For [8](B) concludes by saying that we should take the utterances of the *akratês* as we take those of actors. But here again the point of the comparison is limited. It concerns only what we can *infer* from the utterances of those *akrateis* who "utter the formulae that stem from knowledge"; it is not meant to provide a positive account of the disposition of such agents, let alone of akratic agents in general. Aristotle does not say here, as in [8](A), that akratic agents are in a condition similar to that of those to whom they are compared (in this case actors). His paradigm remains that of someone who has reached first actuality but is in a condition (like sleep, madness, and drunkenness) such that she cannot (or cannot readily) access it at will.

Some commentators may be reluctant to allow that this *is* Aristotle's paradigm because they underestimate the capacities of those asleep, mad, and drunk. They may worry that those who are asleep do not act at all, and that those who are mad and drunk do not know what they are doing in the way required for their actions to count

---

[27] See, e.g., N. O. Dahl, *Practical Reason, Aristotle, and Weakness of the Will* [*Practical Reason*] (Minneapolis: University of Minnesota Press, 1984), 208–10; Charles, "Varieties."

[28] See also G. Lawrence, "Akrasia and Clear-Eyed Akrasia," *Revue de philosophie ancienne* 6 (1988), at 90–101.

as voluntary. But Aristotle himself allows even to sleepers fairly sophisticated activities: some, for example, can answer questions when asked [see *On Dreams* 462a19–28]. Commentators who overlook this and, moreover, assimilate Aristotle's drunken subjects to those who are asleep are likely to take his drunken subjects, if not as literally passed out, at least as quite far gone. But drunkenness, as Aristotle himself would allow, "admits of the more and the less."[29] It is not every drunk who can recite the verses of Empedocles; it is only the drunk who already in some sense knows them. And while it seems possible for someone to memorize these verses without any comprehension of their contents, those who have some grasp of their contents are more likely to succeed in memorizing them. A similar point applies to the person who can utter proofs while in a condition of sexual passion: if you find yourself in bed with someone who does this, it is a good bet that she is someone who, when in her senses, actually has some understanding of these proofs. But the crucial point remains: it does *not follow* from this that her utterance of these proofs while she is in a passionate condition counts as an *expression* or *actualization* of that understanding. Even if her utterances of the very same formulae on *other* occasions are in fact expressions or actualizations of the relevant knowledge, we need not treat her utterances of these formulae while she is in a passionate condition as themselves expressions or actualizations of that knowledge.

This is important because one might be tempted in cases where the agent *does* have the relevant first-actuality knowledge to assume that the utterances that would normally express such knowledge must *always* involve the agent's moving from first to second actualization. But there is an important difference between an utterance being an *expression of* knowledge and an utterance being somehow *facilitated by* the subject's possession of the relevant knowledge. And the fact that only an agent with first-actuality knowledge of proofs is likely to be capable of uttering such proofs in passionate conditions does *not* show that any utterance of them in passionate conditions involves the sort of comprehension that is essential to the move from first to second actuality. This is the point of [8](B), whose examples include both those who have and those who do not even have the sort of knowledge their utterances might be taken to express: such utterances cannot be taken as any sign that the agent in question is in fact *actualizing* the relevant knowledge, not even in cases (like that of the sleeping geometer) where she in fact has the relevant (first actuality) knowledge.

---

[29] See, e.g., *Problemata* 3. 2: "Why is it that it is not those who are very drunk that are most troublesome in their cups, but those who are only half blotto? Is it because they have neither drunk so little that they still resemble the sober nor so much that they are in the incapacitated state of those who have drunk deep? Further, those who are sober have more power of judgment, while those who are very drunk make no attempt to exercise their judgment; but those who only half blotto can still exercise their judgment because they are not very drunk, but they exercise it badly . . ." [translation by E. S. Forster, in J. Barnes (ed.), *The Complete Works of Aristotle* [*Complete Works*] (Princeton, NJ: Princeton University Press, 1984)].

6. THE THIRD *ETI* PASSAGE (AND FOURTH STEP): THE FAILURE DISTINCTIVE OF THE *AKRATÊS*

One problem with assimilating the condition of the *akratês* to the conditions of those asleep, drunk, and mad is that these conditions involve relatively indiscriminate impairment of their subjects: they interfere not just with practical reasoning but also with theoretical reasoning and many other activities. This, we think, is why Aristotle adds the final *eti* section. Although this section is sometimes taken simply as explaining what he has already said, but from a different and more scientific point of view, we take this section to be crucial to completing Aristotle's account.[30] Its task is largely to identify and explain the relatively local impairment characteristic of the *akratês*, an impairment compatible with her being proficient, even during akratic episodes, in doing many things that those who are asleep or drunk are typically impaired in doing.

This, we think, is part of the point of examining the cause of the *akratês'* failure, as Aristotle puts it, *phusikôs*. He often distinguishes investigating something *phusikôs* from investigating it *logikôs* or *katholou*. The latter seem to involve examining something at a relatively high level of abstraction (often in a way to do with the meanings of terms), while the former seems to involve examining something according to principles proper to the specific nature of the phenomenon in question.[31] But the distinction is not always between investigations that appeal to principles within natural science and those that appeal to purely logical considerations. For, as *Generation of Animals* II.8 makes clear, there are more and less *logikê* proofs *within* natural science. Here, Aristotle criticizes the more *logikê* proof of those who seek to explain the sterility of mules by appeal to principles that apply to the products of *all* inter-species unions, because (as he says) their argument is "too universal and empty." He goes on to say that we are more likely to grasp the true cause of the mule's sterility if we start the investigation from specific facts about the horse and the ass [*GA* 747b27–748a16].

Though Aristotle tends to use '*phusikôs*' and its cognates primarily in connection with the objects of natural sciences, he draws similar distinctions in his ethical works between investigations that are carried out more and less *phusikôs*. But his usage is complicated, since what is more *phusikôs* is sometimes treated as being at what is in some sense a *higher* level of explanation than that to which is compared. Whether or not this is a good thing is determined by the primary consideration of whether the inquiry is at the level *appropriate* to the explanandum. So although Aristotle dismisses

---

[30] For a radical example of someone who fails to see any new point in the *phusikôs* passage, see Robinson, "Akrasia," who says on 151, "Aristotle adds a *phusikôs* explanation, not in order to get down at last to the question, but rather to set aside those unfortunate persons who cannot distinguish philosophy from psychology . . . Though Aristotle does not say so, I think I hear him adding under his breath: But this pretty psychological story has nothing to do with our question, the answer to which still resides in the logical distinctions I have drawn between the different kinds of knowing.' We note that a little later he refers us to 'the physiologers,' if we wish to know 'how the ignorance is dissipated and the acratic resumes his knowledge' [*EN* 1147b6–9]. That is physics, not ethics."

[31] See *De Caelo* 280a32–34 [φυσικῶς vs. καθόλου]; 283b17–18 [φυσικῶς δὲ καὶ μὴ καθόλου]; *Generation and Corruption* 316a5–14. For useful discussion of this contrast, see M. Burnyeat, *A Map of Metaphysics* Zeta (Pittsburgh: Mathesis Publications, 2001), 19–24.

the *phusikoteron* approach of those who seek to explain friendship by appeal to fundamental principles of matter on the grounds that this sort of approach is "higher" than it should be [ἀνώτερον, *EN* 1155b2] and "too universal" [λίαν καθόλου, *EE* 1235a29–31] he elsewhere rejects attempts to explain why benefactors love their beneficiaries more than their beneficiaries love them by appeal to the psychology of creditors and debtors, apparently because their explanation is *too specific*. In this case, Aristotle prefers what he calls the *phusikoteron* approach of those who appeal to general principles *of human nature* rather than principles peculiar to the psychologies of creditors and debtors [*EN* 1167b17–1168a9]. In sum, the issue is not so much level of specificity as whether the principles invoked are appropriate to the nature of the explanandum.[32]

So when the explanandum is *akratic* behavior, the move to considering the cause *phusikôs* must involve appeal to principles proper to the behavior of *rational* animals. It is a move to a distinctive kind of psychological investigation, one in which the explanation of behavior by appeal to interactions among the subject's beliefs (or belief-like states) and desires is complicated by the subject's degree of appreciation of logical relations, especially among the propositions that serve as both possible and actual contents of her beliefs. This is why, as we shall see, Aristotle takes the trouble in [9](B) to explain how the *akratês'* appetitive actions differ from the appetitive actions of *non-rational* animals. Aristotle attends here to the ways in which psychological states (such as beliefs and desires) tend to interact in *rational* animals, not just when things go right but also when things go wrong. And, as appropriate in a teleological framework, he begins in [9](A) with an account of "normal" or "default" cases, where things go as they are supposed to go; he then turns in (B) to cases where things go wrong, analyzing these by appeal to the ways in which they depart from the relevant norms.

[9] *EN* VII.3: 1147a24–b12

Further [ἔτι] one might also look at the cause <of the *akratês'* failure> in the following way, according to the point of view proper to its nature [φυσικῶς].

(A) For the one <?> is *katholou doxa*, while the other <?> is about the particulars, concerning which perception is in fact authoritative. And whenever one <?> comes to be from these, it is necessary with respect to what results [τὸ συμπερανθέν], in other cases [ἔνθα μέν] for the soul to affirm it, but in the productive cases [ἐν δὲ ταῖς ποιητικαῖς] <for the soul> to act <on it> straightaway.[33] For example, if one should taste everything sweet, and this is sweet <counts>

---

[32] On this use of '*phusikoteron*,' see J. Whiting, "The Nicomachean Account of *Philia*," in Kraut, *Guide*, 276–304 [II.6], especially 288. Note that we differ here from David Charles, who actually translates '*phusikôs*' as "more specifically" (see *Action*, 128).

[33] We stop short of introducing explicit reference to theoretical reasoning into our translation (as done both by Irwin and by Gauthier and Jolif); but we follow the common view that the contrast signaled in ἔνθα μὲν ... ἐν δὲ ταῖς ποιητικαῖς is one between theoretical reasoning and productive reasoning construed broadly enough to include the sort of *praxis* that Aristotle sometimes distinguishes from *poiêsis*. We are not persuaded by what we take to be the most plausible alternative—namely, John McDowell's suggestion that the clause is meant to contrast *praxis* proper with *poiêsis* proper. See his "Incontinence

as one of the particulars, it is necessary for one who is able and not prevented, at the same time as this [viz., τὸ συμπερανθέν] <comes to be>, also to act.

(B) Whenever then the universal <*doxa*> *preventing* tasting is present, <and also> the <universal *doxa*> that everything sweet is pleasant, and this is sweet[34] (and this <*doxa*> is active), and *epithumia* happens also to be present, then the one <*doxa*> says in fact to avoid this, but *epithumia* leads <the way>. For each of the parts <of soul> is able to move <the animal>.[35] So it happens by *logos* in a way and by *doxa* that he acts akratically, not <by *doxa*> opposed in itself to right reason but <*doxa* opposed only> coincidentally; for it is *epithumia* and not *doxa* that is opposed <to right reason>. And it is also because of this that beasts are not akratic, because they do not have universal supposition, but <only> *phantasia* and memory of particulars.

(C) How the ignorance [ἡ ἄγνοια] is dissolved, and the *akratês* again comes to be <in the condition of> one who knows, the same account <holds as> in the case of one who is drunk or asleep, and not <one> proper to this <particular sort of> *pathos*, <but> one we must hear from the *phusiologoi*. And since the last *protasis* is both a *doxa* about something perceptible and authoritative over actions,[36] it is this that <the *akratês*> either does not have while he is in this *pathos* or has <only> in the sense that he does not know but <simply> utters <the words>, like the drunk <uttering> the <verses> of Empedocles.[37]

There is some question straightaway what Aristotle takes himself to be talking about in the first sentence of (A). What are the unexpressed subjects that are said to be either "universal *doxa*" or "about the particulars," and from which something further is said to result? Aristotle's reference to what results as τὸ συμπερανθέν leads many commentators to read him as speaking here of syllogisms, in which some conclusion results in the sense that some proposition follows logically from a pair of premises [προτάσεις]— one a universal proposition and the other a proposition about particulars. And some

---

and Practical Wisdom in Aristotle" ["Incontinence"], in S. Lovibond and S. G. Williams (eds.), *Identity, Truth and Value: Essays for David Wiggins* (Oxford: Wiley-Blackwell, 1996), 95–112, especially 98–99.

[34] Although "this is sweet" might seem simply to report a fact and not actually to express the content of some further *doxa*, that would make it difficult to explain the agent's acting in accord with *either* universal. So we take "this is sweet," along with the immediately following claim that "this is active," to indicate that the agent actively thinks, of some particular, "*this* is sweet." See note 48 below.

[35] Most translators take this as making the point (similar to one made in *EN* 1110a15–17) that *epithumia* can move each of the parts of the body. But we follow David Charles ("Varieties") in thinking it more relevant here that each of the parts of soul can move the animal, than that *epithumia* can move each of the parts of the body. The idea here is pretty clearly that either reason or appetite might move the agent, one leading to enkratic and the other to akratic behavior. Ramsauer (*Arist. Eth. Nic.*, ad loc.) also adopts this view.

[36] On the proper way to read this, see section 7 below.

[37] The text continues with [10] below, which can be treated as completing the third *eti* passage. But it may simply clarify the relation between Aristotle's ultimate account (viz., the one culminating in the third *eti* passage) and the Socratic view with which Aristotle began. So we treat it separately in section 8.

translators actually supply *'protasis'* here in *EN* 1147a25 in spite of the fact that the term last appeared at 1147a1 (viz., twenty-five lines and two *'eti'*s ago): they read Aristotle as saying "since the one *protasis* is a universal *doxa* and the other *protasis* is about the particulars."[38]

It is, however, pretty clear from Aristotle's talk about what results when "nothing impedes" that he is thinking primarily about psychological states and not (or at least not primarily) about the contents of such states.[39] He is, for example, more concerned with actual states of belief than with the propositions that serve as their contents. The two are of course linked insofar as the psychological states of *rational* subjects tend to respect the logical relations among their contents. But the two need to be distinguished precisely in order to allow for cases where the subject's actual psychological states fail to mirror the logical relations—cases, for example, where a subject fails to draw from her actual beliefs logical consequences that would normally be transparent to her or fails to act in accordance with her beliefs and any consequences she draws (or at least seems to draw) from them. This appeal to beliefs and other psychological states is, in our view, part of what is involved in considering the matter *phusikôs*.[40]

Aristotle begins with normal or default cases: those in which someone has both a universal belief and a belief about particulars, as a result of which some further state comes about. He shows no signs here of thinking that he needs to explain how this further state comes about: when things are working as they should, it *just does*. That's part of what it *is* for their subject to be a *rational* animal. And this holds both in the theoretical sphere and in practical and productive spheres. Matters are of course more complicated in practical and productive spheres, where there is a potential gap between belief and action, and one might reach the proper conclusion (either about how one ought to act or about how to produce some result) but fail to act accordingly. Yet here, where Aristotle is discussing normal or default cases, he shows no sign of thinking he needs to introduce anything else, once the further state has resulted, to explain the action's occurrence. This may be because (as he elsewhere suggests) "what results" *is* the action. Or it may be simply that he treats "what results" as a belief in some proposition and thinks of the appropriate action as following with a kind of necessity from this belief, at least in cases in which things go as they are supposed to go.[41]

---

[38] See Rowe's translation; and D. Charles ("Varieties") who argues in detail for supplying *'protasis.'*

[39] This is also emphasized by J. Bogen and J. Moravcsik, "Aristotle's Forbidden Sweets" ["Forbidden Sweets"], *Journal of the History of Philosophy* 20 (1982), at 113–14.

[40] We offer the following hypothesis about why Aristotle does not supply a definite subject in (A): he lacks a term that would allow him to straddle, in the requisite way, the *contents* of the psychological states and the *states themselves*. In the case where things go right and these contents are affirmed, *doxa* is actually required to explain the agent's behavior. But in cases where things go wrong and the relevant beliefs do not result, *doxa* is neither appropriate nor explanatorily relevant. Nor is *protasis*, since the question is not primarily about logical relations but about the *actual* psychological states whose presence (or absence) explains what the agent does.

[41] Some commentators see here the view (explicitly expressed at *De Motu Animalium* 701a19–20) that the conclusion is an action. See, for example, G. E. M. Anscombe, *Intention* (Oxford: Blackwell, 1957), 60; and M. Nussbaum, *Aristotle's De Motu Animalium* (Princeton, NJ: Princeton University Press, 1978), 201–4 (see 184–86). Nussbaum seems to take the kind of necessity involved to be logical, but we want to leave

Aristotle turns in (B) to cases where things go wrong. Here again we lack an explicit subject. What is "the universal preventing tasting"? Is it (as some translations suggest) a universal *premise*? Or is it perhaps (taking '*protasis*' in its more general sense) a universal *proposition*? We take Aristotle's claim to consider the cause *phusikôs* to suggest that he means *neither*: here, where things go wrong, what matters is what the subject *actually* believes and desires, and how exactly she does so. Aristotle considers a case in which a subject has (in some sense of 'have') two universal *doxai*, one preventing tasting (presumably of sweet things) and the other affirming the proposition "everything sweet is pleasant."

Note that we differ here from those commentators who take the second *doxa* to be or to involve some *particular* proposition. We take it to be universal for two (related) reasons: first, it is natural to take the ἡ δέ clause that answers ἡ μὲν καθόλου as introducing another example of the sort of thing explicitly introduced in the ἡ μέν clause (viz., another universal *doxa*); and second, what follows the ἡ δέ (namely, "that everything sweet is pleasant") is as clearly universal as the next claim (namely, "that this is sweet") is particular. In this case, "this is active" seems to refer simply to the particular belief "this is sweet" and the immediately following reference to *epithumia* seems intended somehow to explain why the agent acts akratically in spite of the fact that the universal *doxa* preventing tasting is in some sense in the agent.[42]

Our account assumes what is in some sense uncontroversial—namely, that the universal *doxa* preventing tasting, however it is to be formulated, is *not used*. This is just the sort of diagnosis that our reading of the first *eti* passage led us to expect, one in which some failure to use knowledge of a *universal* is implicated. Note, however, that there is an important difference between the sort of case described in the first *eti* passage and the sort described here. In the first case, what explained an epistemic subject's failure to use a relevant bit of universal knowledge was the fact, cited in [7](B), that she either did not have or did not exercise some *particular* item of knowledge such as "*this* food is such." But in the present case, Aristotle goes out of his way to say that the analogous item—namely, "this is sweet"—*is active*.[43] If so, we cannot in *this* case appeal (as most commentators do) to the absence or inactivity of the *particular doxa* in order to explain why the relevant universal is not used. Nor would appealing to the absence or inactivity of the particular help, since that would (as we have

---

open the possibility that it is psychological, in which case the action may (when nothing impedes) follow necessarily without, however, being *identified* with the conclusion. So we propose to remain neutral on this issue. But for defense of the controversial view that the conclusion of practical reasoning is an action—though not of Aristotle's commitment to it—see P. Clark, "The Action as Conclusion," *Canadian Journal of Philosophy* 31 (2001): 481–506.

[42] Irwin (*Aristotle: Nic. Eth.*, 260) takes the second *doxa* to be the *conjunction* "everything sweet is pleasant *and* this is sweet," and he takes "this is active" to refer to this conjunctive belief. Price ("Acrasia and Self-Control," 237 and 241) and Kenny ("Practical Syllogism," 178–81) adopt a similar view.

[43] Note that even commentators who see the second belief or premise as conjunctive agree that "this is sweet" is (qua part of the conjunctive belief or premise) active. So they accept the difference, crucial to our account, between the case described here and the case described in the first *eti* passage.

seen) undermine the claim that the akratic agent acts voluntarily. So the present case requires a *different sort of explanation* (from the one given in the first *eti* passage) of why the relevant universal fails to get used.

Moreover, we take it to be part of the point of the second *eti* passage to prepare the way for the different sort of explanation, given here, of the *akratês'* failure to use her knowledge of the relevant universal. The second *eti* passage points to physical states, associated with conditions like sleep and drunkenness, that interfere with the mechanisms by which an agent normally moves from first- to second-actuality knowledge: when the agent is in one of these states, moves that are normally more or less automatic fail to occur and moves that are normally performed at will are no longer subject (or readily subject) to the agent's will. But conditions like sleep and drunkenness involve relatively *global* impairment, whereas the sort of impairment involved in akrasia seems *local*. The *akratês* may be able, while in the akratic condition, to move from first- to second-actuality knowledge in many domains, both theoretical and practical; her incapacity prevails primarily in areas where she is vulnerable to temptation.[44] We think it precisely in order to account for this that the third *eti* passage introduces *epithumia*, whose presence may help to explain why it is the *akratês'* knowledge only of certain universal propositions that fails to get actualized—why it tends to be only her knowledge of universals that *prohibit* pursuing the objects of *epithumia* that fails to get actualized and *not* her knowledge of universals that do *not* prohibit the pursuit of these objects.

The *akratês'* problem is that her *epithumia* encourages the "wrong" beliefs to be activated.[45] By "wrong" beliefs we do *not* mean *false* beliefs. Given the nature or strength of her desire, her perception of some particular as (for example) sweet leads her more or less immediately to think, truly enough, "this is pleasant,"[46] But whether or not she has previously deliberated and reached the conclusion that she should not taste this (or this sort of thing), it happens that when *epithumia* is active in the relevant way she thinks "this is pleasant" at the expense of thinking "this is fattening" or "this should not be tasted." And when this belief results, it is natural for her to act straightaway, provided she is able and nothing interferes. So what happens here is not unlike what happens in the normal case where things go as they are supposed to go. And here, as there, *epithumia* does not simply cooperate with belief to produce action; by facilitating the move from perception to some rather than other beliefs, *epithumia* actually helps to explain *which* universal beliefs get activated.[47]

---

[44] This point is emphasized by J. Gosling in "Mad, Drunk or Asleep?—Aristotle's Akratic," *Phronesis* 38 (1993): 98–104.

[45] Note that we generally oppose Irwin's view that deliberation itself excites the desire. See T. Irwin, "Some Rational Aspects of Incontinence" ["Rational Aspects"], *Southern Journal of Philosophy* 27 Supplement (1988): 70.

[46] Here we have an example of universal term whose application to a particular is so obvious that the agent can scarcely fail to apply it. This is like the case where she cannot fail to realize she is human; only here it is the *object* term in the universal, rather than the *subject* term, whose application is more or less automatic. See note 24 above.

[47] *Epithumia* can play other roles as well: it can color perception, sometimes even to the point of distorting it.

Note that the point here is simply that the *akratês* fails to actualize any universal that would prohibit her action, and not that there must be some universal that recommends or even prescribes her action. Though many commentators see two syllogisms here, one "good" and one "bad," and some even imagine that there must be a prescriptive major for the "bad" syllogism corresponding to the prohibitive major of the "good" one, Aristotle's example suggests that a merely descriptive universal, such as "everything sweet is pleasant," may be more or less automatically activated and acted on *before* the agent has a chance to activate any knowledge she might have of prohibiting universals.[48] The relatively automatic nature of the processes involved and the lack of any need for a prescriptive major are closely tied to the fundamentally animal nature of the *epithumiai* involved in "unqualified" *akrasia*, viz., the sort of *epithumiai* on which non-rational animals can act in the absence of *any* sort of belief (whether prescriptive or not). And while some commentators take the relatively automatic nature of these processes to show that Aristotle assimilates the *akratês*' behavior to that of non-rational animals, we would not ourselves go this far. We allow of course that in cases where *epithumia* is present, he takes akratic action to follow relatively automatically upon the perception of something as (for example) sweet. But we think that taking him to assimilate the *akratês*' behavior to that of non-rational animals fails to do justice to [9](B)'s claims that the *akratês* acts "by logos in a way and by *doxa*" and that she has a kind of universal *hupolêpsis* that non-rational animals lack.[49]

It is, however, important not to over-interpret Aristotle's claim that the *akratês* acts ὑπὸ λόγου by taking it to mean that she relies on some sort of prescriptive premise.[50] For this is neither necessary nor helpful. It is not necessary, since (as we have seen) his point is that a universal *doxa* such as "everything sweet is pleasant" can, together with the relevant desire, produce action in the absence of anything further.[51] Nor is

---

[48] Although some commentators who see two syllogisms here take the major of the "bad" syllogism to be prescriptive (e.g., Gauthier and Jolif, *Arist.: L'Ethique*, vol. II, 612; Broadie and Rowe, *Aristotle, Nic. Eth.*, 392), Irwin sees that this is not required and takes the two syllogisms to share a minor premise, such as "this is sweet." On his account, the agent has deliberated in a way such that she at some point connects "this is sweet" to the "good" major, which prohibits tasting such sweets, and so at some point draws the conclusion that she should not taste this; but the activity of the minor premise *later* leads (in conjunction with *epithumia*) to the minor premise becoming "detached" from the "good" major and being conjoined instead with the "bad" major (viz., with "everything sweet is pleasant") to produce action. See Irwin, *Aristotle: Nic. Eth.* 260–61 and "Rational Aspects," 67. For versions of the two-syllogism view that take each syllogism to have a different minor premise, see J. Cooper, *Reason and Human Good in Aristotle* (Cambridge, MA: Harvard University Press, 1975), 49–50, and Robinson, "Akrasia," 145.

[49] For a strong assimilation of akratic behavior to that of non-rational animals, see J. Müller, 'Tug of War: Aristotle on Akrasia' (unpublished paper) and H. Lorenz, *The Brute Within: Appetitive Desire in Plato and Aristotle* (Oxford: Oxford University Press, 2006), chap. 13, where Lorenz explicitly accepts in n. 27 (p. 197) the idea we reject, that Aristotle posits a global (albeit temporary) impairment of the *akratês*' reason. [A successor of Müller's paper has been published as "Aristotle on Actions from Lack of Control," *Philosophers Imprint* 15: 1–35.]

[50] It is important not to forget the πως in ὑπὸ λόγου πως.

[51] For this point, see *EN* 1149a32–35, where Aristotle is contrasting "qualified" *akrasia*, involving anger, with "unqualified" *akrasia*. He says "when on the one hand [μέν] *logos* or *phantasia* has revealed that there is hubris or a slight, the agent, as if having syllogized [ὥσπερ συλλογισάμενος] that it is necessary to fight such a thing, gets angry straightway. But when on the other hand [δ'] *logos* or *aisthêsis* simply

it helpful: for introducing a prescriptive universal would seem *either* to undermine the claim that the agent knows that she should not do what she does *or* to involve ascribing contradictory beliefs to her (which would itself undermine the claim that she *knows* the proper universal). This may be why Aristotle says that the relevant belief is not in itself *but only coincidentally* opposed to her admittedly correct reason: his point is that the relevant belief tends, when it coincides with certain *epithumiai*, to encourage *only action* (and not also *belief*) that is contrary to correct reason. For there is no *logical* conflict between the universal prohibiting tasting (however exactly it is to be formulated) and the merely descriptive universal "everything sweet is pleasant." So Aristotle can explain how the agent acts in a way that involves *doxa* (and not simply the sort of *phantasia* involved in the behavior of non-rational animals) *without*, however, having to introduce any beliefs that would conflict with the agent's knowledge of the "good" universal.

This is crucial because the *akratês must* in some sense share the virtuous agent's knowledge of what she ought to do. So she *cannot believe* when she acts that she *ought* to be doing what she is supposed to *know* she ought not do. For that would undermine her claim to *know* what she ought to do. It would also involve the sort of corruption of belief that Aristotle explicitly takes to characterize *vicious* as distinct from *akratic* agents. As he explains in *EN* VII.8, the *akratês* still in some sense has the right principle: her pathos masters her to the extent that she does not act in accordance with the right principle [ὥστε μὲν μὴ πράττειν κατὰ τὸν ὀρθὸν λόγον], but not to the extent that she becomes such as to be *persuaded* [τοιοῦτον οἷον πεπεῖσθαι] that she *ought* to act on some other principle [1151a11–26]. This, we argue, explains why Aristotle focuses on her failure to use or activate some sort of *universal* knowledge. Since her action must be voluntary, he cannot allow (as he did in the theoretical case) that she fails to use or activate her knowledge of the relevant *particular*. And since he cannot say that her belief in the relevant universal propositions is *corrupted*, he concludes that her access to these universal beliefs must be temporarily *impeded*.

The temporary impediment is of course due to *epithumia*, which renders the subject vulnerable to bodily disturbances like those involved in sleep and drunkenness. Like those who are drunk or asleep, the *akratês* is temporarily unable to actualize her knowledge in situations in which its use is called for. So it is not surprising that [9](C) refers to the temporary inability of the *akratês* as a kind of ignorance [ἄγνοια], and concludes with a few remarks about how "this ignorance is dissolved and the *akratês* comes again to be <in the condition of> one who knows." The point here is that there is no special sort of explanation peculiar to the recovery of the *akratês*; the same sort of explanation applies here as in the case of those asleep and drunk, the sort for which

---

says that something is pleasant, *epithumia* has an impulse [ὁρμᾷ] towards the enjoyment. So *thumos* follows reason in a way, but *epithumia* does not." The idea seems to be that *epithumia* does not require the sort of prescription that seems to be operative in the case of *thumos*, where the agent thinks "one must [or should, δεῖ] fight such a thing." And even in case of *thumos*, Aristotle says only that the agent becomes angry *"as if* having syllogized."

we must turn to the so-called *physiologoi*. Aristotle must have in mind the sort of explanation given in the his *Parva Naturalia*, where (for example) sleep is said to occur as a result of certain material and efficient causal processes (such as heating, evaporation, and settling) that are associated with the digestion of food, and waking is said to occur when these processes are complete and the heat that has been occupied in digestion returns to its normal position [*On Sleep and Waking* 457b20–58a26].[52] His idea seems to be that because the sort of desires and emotions involved in akratic episodes are associated with the body, and so with the sort of processes of heating and cooling that control bodily functions, akratic episodes too can pass as a result of similar material and efficient causal processes having run their course.

Aristotle's reference to the *phusiologoi* is sometimes read simply as a consequence of the *phusikôs* approach adopted in the third *eti* passage.[53] But we think this misguided. The point is clearly that the explanation of the *akratês*' recovery from her temporary ignorance is *not proper* to the *akratês*, but the same in kind as the explanation of the drunk's and the sleeper's recoveries from their temporary ignorance: when the body has returned to its "normal" state, the subject is in each case able once again to actualize her knowledge readily in situations where such actualization is called for. This is *not* a *phusikôs* explanation, which would be (as explained above) one *proper* to the nature of the phenomenon in question. Such an explanation would presumably mention psychological causes, such as satisfaction of the akratic desire or redirection of the agent's attention to other objects. It may of course be true that some such psychological causes supervene on some of the same sort of material and efficient causal processes as those involved in waking up. But it is one thing to explain the *akratês*' recovery of knowledge by appeal to such psychological causes and another to explain it by appeal to the sort of material and efficient causal processes mentioned (for example) in *De Somno*.

It is clear from the *Eudemian* discussion of friendship that Aristotle distinguishes the sort of explanations of friendship given by the *phusiologoi* from those "nearer and proper to the *phainomena*" in question: the *phusiologoi* tend to appeal to general principles such as "like to move toward like" or "opposites attract," rather than to

---

[52] The *Problemata*, which may or may not be by Aristotle, suggests (in Book 3) that drunkenness, which is also associated with processes of heating and cooling, subsides when the relevant processes have run their course. For, as Book 30 explains, those who are drunk are often temporarily in conditions (such as talkativeness or boldness) that are characteristic of the permanent character of others, which happens because wine and nature produce these characteristics by the same means (no doubt material and efficient causal ones), since "the whole body functions under the control of heat" [953a33–b23].

[53] Many translations do not signal the distinction between (a) φυσικῶς investigations and (b) investigations characteristic of τῶν φυσιολόγων: Irwin pairs (a) "referring to [human] nature" with (b) "the natural scientists"; Ross (in Barnes, *Complete Works, Volume 2*) is similar, pairing (a) "with reference to the facts of nature" with (b) "the students of natural science"; Rowe pairs (a) "scientifically" with (b) "natural scientists"; and Price ("Acrasia." 237) pairs (a) "scientifically" with (b) "scientists." Rackham (in the Loeb edition) signals a distinction and gets it nearly right with (a) "scientifically" (to which he adds the note "i.e., in this case, psychologically: literally with reference to its nature") and (b) "to physiology." The point is that Aristotle tends to associate the *phusiologoi* with explanations in terms of material principles. Such explanations will sometimes (viz., where they are in fact proper to the nature of the explananda) be *phusikôs*. But they should be conflated with *phusikôs* explanations as such.

principles specific to the behavior of animals, such as their tendency to love their own offspring [*EE* 1235a10–35]. It is also clear that Aristotle himself prefers to appeal to *phusikon* principles, such as the principle that those who have produced something (like a poem or child) tend to love it [1240b40–1241a9]. And however odd it may seem to *us* to explain the onset of the akratic episode by appeal to psychological mechanisms and the passing of the akratic episode by appeal to material and efficient causal ones, this does seem to be what *Aristotle* proposes, perhaps in part because of the sort of explanatory asymmetries afforded by his teleological framework. But we cannot discuss this here.[54] For present purposes, the lesson of (C) is simply that Aristotle takes some sort of ignorance—however it happens to be resolved—to be implicated in akratic behavior.

Aristotle speaks here of *agnoia* because he thinks the *akratês* is temporarily unable to make the sort of move from first to second actuality that is characteristic of those who have knowledge: her condition is thus a kind of temporary ignorance not unlike the temporary insanity of modern legal counsel. And it is, more specifically, knowledge of some *universal* that the *akratês* is temporarily unable to use. But this is not (as in the first *eti* passage) because she lacks the sort of knowledge of a particular that is required for the actualization of the universal. She has the requisite knowledge of particulars, but her *epithumia* somehow prevents her from applying her universal knowledge to the relevant particulars. In her present condition she does not actualize the universal she should actualize and would in fact actualize if the disturbances associated with *epithumia* did not prevail.

7. DIGRESSION ON THE DIFFERENT TYPES OF *AKRATÊS*: THE "WEAK" AND THE "IMPETUOUS"

Some commentators will object that our account cannot be right. For they take Aristotle's use of τοῦτο in [9](B)'s claim that "the one <*doxa*> says in fact to avoid *this*" to show that he thinks the *akratês does* reach the conclusion that follows from the prohibiting universal together with "this is sweet." Such commentators assume that Aristotle pictures the *akratês* as at some point thinking, with respect to some particular, "I should not taste *this*." They read Aristotle as concerned in this passage primarily (and perhaps even exclusively) with what he later calls the "weak"—as distinct from the "impetuous"—*akratês* [see *EN* 1150b20–28]. Their idea is that the paradigmatic *akratês* initially reaches the right conclusion but then manages to lose her grip on it at some point before the time when she acts against it.[55] Such commentators are likely to object to our account on the grounds that it applies primarily, and perhaps even

---

[54] For more on these explanatory asymmetries, see J. Whiting, "Hylomorphic Virtue: Cosmology, Embryology, and Moral Development in Aristotle" [Chapter 6, this volume].

[55] See, e.g., Irwin, *Aristotle: Nic. Eth.*, ad loc. and "Rational Aspects." 52–56 and 67–71; and Charles's account of the "weak" *akratês* (*Action*, 127–28).

exclusively, to the impetuous *akratês*. This will appear especially problematic if, as John McDowell suggests, the weak *akratês* is the only interesting variety.[56]

But given that Aristotle does not introduce the distinction between the impetuous and the weak *akratês* until VII.7, it seems preferable (if possible) to interpret VII.3 as giving a generic account meant to cover both. So just as we think it problematic for these commentators to claim that Aristotle means to speak here only about the weak *akratês*, we agree that it would be a problem for our interpretation *if* we had to read him as speaking here only about the impetuous.[57] But we do not think our interpretation requires this. Nor do we think it necessary to concede that [9](B) should be read as referring primarily, or even exclusively, to the weak *akratês*. Note in connection with this second point that Aristotle's use of τοῦτο does *not* require us to read him as taking the *akratês* to reach the conclusion "do not taste *this*" where "this" refers to some determinate particular. The point may simply be that the prohibiting *doxa* "says" that this should not be tasted *only* in the sense that the prohibiting *doxa* entails that this should not be tasted.[58] Note also how Aristotle formulates the particular proposition "this is sweet" in the immediately preceding line: he uses τουτί, presumably to indicate that he is talking about a concrete particular to which one can point here and now.[59] So he clearly *had*—and was even in the immediate context *using*—a device that would have allowed him to make it clear, had he wanted to, that what the agent was to avoid was not simply "this" as in this *sort* of thing, but *this here particular* thing.

The point about how to understand τοῦτο is closely connected to the vexed question of the meaning and reference of "the last *protasis*" [ἡ τελευταία πρότασις] in [9](C)'s claim that the last *protasis* is what the *akratês* "either does not have while he is in this *pathos* or has <only> in the sense that he does not know but <simply> utters <the words>." We take "the last *protasis*" to refer to the conclusion. But many commentators resist this on the grounds that in contexts where Aristotle is discussing arguments, he typically uses the term '*protasis*' to refer to a premise as distinct from the conclusion of an argument. This is one reason why so many commentators are convinced that the failure of the *akratês* must be the sort of failure (familiar from the *Analytics* examples) either to have or to use the *minor* (or some *particular*) premise. But saying this threatens, as we've seen, to compromise the claim that akratic action must be done voluntarily.

---

[56] McDowell, "Incontinence," 100.
[57] See D. Bostock, *Aristotle's Ethics* (Oxford: Oxford University Press, 2000), 133, who thinks the passage applies only to the impetuous *akratês*, and cannot accommodate the weak.
[58] For this way of taking λέγει, see W. F. R. Hardie, *Aristotle's Ethical Theory*, 2nd edn. (Oxford: Oxford University Press, 1980), 283; and Robinson, "Akrasia," 145. Note also that David Charles has suggested (in conversation) that οὖν in ἢ μὲν οὖν λέγει φεύγειν τοῦτο is a sign that some conclusion is being drawn. But even if οὖν signals a conclusion, it need not be the one reached by the *akratês*; it may be a conclusion Aristotle is priming his reader to draw. Moreover, οὖν need not be inferential; it may signal either a *new stage* in some non-inferential sequence or (as we render it) that something is *in fact* the case.
[59] We are indebted to Brad Inwood for calling our attention to the relevance of Aristotle's use of the deictic suffix '-ί.' See Smyth, *Greek Grammar*, 333g.

Fortunately, we need not take ἡ τελευταία πρότασις as referring to a premise as such.[60] Although Aristotle often uses πρότασις *specifically* (to refer to premises as such), nothing prevents us from taking it here in its *general* sense (to refer simply to some proposition)—not even its conjunction with τελευταία, which may indicate only that he is talking about the last in some series of propositions, possibly even (as we think) about a conclusion. In our view, Aristotle's point is that the *akratês either* lacks the conclusion "don't taste this" *or* has this conclusion only in the way in which the drunk uttering the verses of Empedocles may be said to have knowledge of what he utters: either way, of course, the *akratês* does not really have this conclusion.[61] Moreover, the fact that Aristotle mentions both possibilities here is probably intended (as many commentators think) to allow him to capture both the impetuous (who does not have it at all) and the weak (who has it only in the way the drunk who utters the verses of Empedocles "has" them).[62]

Note that the *akratês'* failure is supposed to be due to the fact that the physical changes associated with the presence of *epithumia* have put her in a condition such that she is temporarily prevented from actualizing her knowledge of the universal that prohibits tasting: for drawing the conclusion is precisely what would be involved in actualizing her knowledge of that universal in these circumstances. Our account can easily explain how this applies to the case of the impetuous *akratês*: she acts straightaway on the upshot of her perception of something as sweet and the "good" universal never gets properly activated. But more is required to explain how we can accommodate the case of the weak *akratês*, who has deliberated but fails (because of her *epithumia*) to abide by the results of her deliberation [*EN* 1150b19–21]. For this suggests that she reaches the right conclusion, and so that her knowledge of the universal premise *is* actualized.

The standard way of accommodating the weak *akratês* is to say that she reaches the right conclusion but then somehow loses it before the time when she fails to act accordingly. And there is nothing in our account that prevents us from adopting this line, provided we can read [9](B) as pointing to some mechanism capable of explaining not only how someone can be prevented from reaching the proper conclusion but also how someone might lose her grip on the proper conclusion after having reached it. And *epithumia* seems equally capable of playing both roles: even in cases where the agent has deliberated and reached the proper conclusion, the presence of *epithumia*—at least when it is strong—can lead an agent more or less automatically from her perception

---

[60] See note 18 above. The view that πρότασις here means 'proposition' rather than 'premise' has also been defended by Kenny, "Practical Syllogism," 183 n. 36, and Bogen and Moravcsik, "Forbidden Sweets," 125–26.

[61] Joseph Owens, somewhat surprisingly, takes "Don't taste this" as the *akratês'* τελευταία πρότασις but regards it as a *premise* (rather than a conclusion). See "The Acratic's 'Ultimate Premise' in Aristotle," in J. Wiesner (ed.), *Aristoteles: Werk und Wirkung*, Vol. 1 (Berlin: De Gruyter, 1985), 376–92.

[62] See, for example, Charles, *Action*, 127; Dahl, *Practical Reason*, 207; J. Timmermann, "Impulsivität und Schwäche: Die Argumentation des Abschnitts *Eth. Nic.* 1146b31–1147b19 im Lichte der beiden Formen des Phänomens 'Akrasia,'" *Zeitschrift für philosophische Forschung* 54 (2000): 47–66.

of something as sweet and therefore pleasant, to tasting that thing, in spite of the fact that she has previously deliberated and reached the conclusion that she should not taste sweets, perhaps even the conclusion that she should not taste this *particular* sweet. In such cases, she no longer properly grasps this conclusion at the time when she acts.[63]

The idea that the *akratês* lacks the conclusion when she acts, either because she never reached it or because she has lost her grip on it, may help to explain Aristotle's use of ἡ τελευταία πρότασις. He may be reluctant to use τὸ συμπέρασμα or any other term indicating a conclusion as such because his point is that the agent *lacks* the relevant conclusion in the sense that she does not believe it, at least not at the time when she acts. Similar reasoning might explain why Aristotle does not speak instead of "the last *doxa*": the *akratês* does not have the relevant *belief*, except in the sense that she believes things from which it follows—namely, the particular proposition "this is sweet" (which is currently active) and the universal proposition prohibiting tasting (which is not currently active and which something about her *epithumia* renders her temporarily unable to activate in the normal way). Note that ἡ τελευταία πρότασις is a hapax legomenon: Aristotle is apparently struggling for the right words to make his point. And neither τὸ συμπέρασμα nor ἡ τελευταία δόξα will do: either might mislead the reader into thinking that the akratic agent actively has the *particular belief* that she should not be doing what she now does.

One might object here that [9](C) explicitly refers to the last *protasis* as a *doxa*. But note what Aristotle says: "since the last *protasis* is both a *doxa* about something perceptible and authoritative [κυρία] over actions, it is this that <the *akratês*> either does not have ... or has <only> in the sense that he does not know but <simply> utters <the words> . . . ." Clearly Aristotle does *not* think that the *akratês acts* on the last *protasis*. So in this case, where things go wrong, he *cannot* be saying that the last *protasis* is *in fact kuria* over action. So he may not be saying that it is *in fact a doxa* either. This makes perfect sense if—as we maintain—Aristotle is contrasting the case of the *akratês* with normal cases like those discussed in (A). If this is right, then we should perhaps read the point in (C) as follows: since the last *protasis* is *normally* a *doxa* and *kuria* of actions, this (either the *protasis* or the corresponding *doxa*) is what the *akratês* either does not have or has only in the way the drunk uttering the verses of Empedocles might be said to have the propositions or beliefs those words normally express. Even if she "says the words" whatever they are—possibly even "I should not taste *this*"—she is not thereby expressing the *belief* those words normally express: at this point she grasps the relevant proposition (if at all) only in the way the drunk reciting the verses of Empedocles grasps the propositions these verses are normally taken to express.

---

[63] Aristotle may in fact think that the weak *akratês*, although she deliberates and *seems* to reach the right conclusion, does not *really* reach it. But our aim here is to show how we can handle what might seem the most difficult case for our view, the case in which Aristotle thinks that the weak *akratês* really draws the right conclusion.

This explains how we can take Aristotle to be giving a generic account, intended to cover both the weak and the impetuous *akratês*. Though neither strictly speaking *has* the conclusion she is said to act against, at least not when she acts, some weak akratics nevertheless *appear* to have this conclusion even when they act. They deliberate and can even when they act "say the words" normally used to express belief in this conclusion. But as we argued in our discussion of the second *eti* passage, the fact that someone "says the words" does not show that she is then actualizing the knowledge that utterances of those words ordinarily express—not even in cases where the speaker *has* the relevant (first-actuality) knowledge.

Some might worry that this way of accommodating the weak *akratês* does not leave room for the sort of struggle or psychic conflict that many commentators take to distinguish the weak from the impetuous *akratês*. Such commentators tend to emphasize passages like the following from *EN* I.13 [1102b12–25]:

> There seems to be also some other kind of non-rational soul, which, however, participates in a way in reason. For we praise the reason of the *enkratês* and *akratês*, and the <part> of <their> soul that has reason because it correctly exhorts <them> toward what is best. But there seems also to reside naturally in them something else besides reason, which fights and opposes reason [ὃ μάχεται καὶ ἀντιτείνει τῷ λόγῳ]. For just as when someone has decided to move the parts of the body affected by paralysis to the right, they are carried off to the left, something similar happens in the soul; for the impulses of akratic subjects are toward opposite things. But while we see the thing carried off in these bodies, we do not see <it> in the case of the soul. Nonetheless we should presumably say also that there is in the soul something besides reason, opposing this and resisting <it> [ἐναντιούμενον τούτῳ καὶ ἀντιβαῖνον].

Cook Wilson cites this passage, along with others, as evidence that Aristotle took "mental struggle" to characterize the *akratês* in a way such that Aristotle would have rejected any solution premised on a kind of ignorance (even temporary ignorance) that would obviate the element of struggle. Because he finds talk of such struggle prominent in other Aristotelian texts, Cook Wilson claims on the basis of VII.3's appeal to ignorance that

> [t]he theory [of VII.3] appears quite unworthy of Aristotle . . . Clearly the answer given in this chapter is worse than no answer: if in the *akratês*' knowledge of right and wrong is not realised but dormant [μὴ θεωροῦντα ἃ μὴ δεῖ πράττειν, 1146b33]; if, though he knows the general principle (the major premiss) which would condemn his action, he has not realised the particular circumstances (the minor premiss) in his act which make the principle applicable to it;—then he does not know that what he is doing is wrong, and therefore is not *akratês* at all. A mental struggle is impossible, since there is no actual

knowledge for appetite to struggle with. Aristotle could scarcely have acquiesced in a mistake like this.[64]

Cook Wilson concludes that VII.3 was probably not by Aristotle—nor by the author of the *Eudemian Ethics,* nor even the author of the most important parts of the rest of *EN* VII/*EE* VI.

Note that many of the problems Cook Wilson sees are eliminated by our interpretation, especially the problems posed by assuming ignorance of the minor premise. But what can we say about how much room is left for psychic struggle by the sort of appeal to ignorance we see in VII.3? Whether or not struggle is in fact excluded depends of course on what Aristotle takes to be involved in the relevant sort(s) of struggle. And the answer to this question seems to us to some extent indeterminate. First, the phenomenology of akratic experience seems to allow for a range of possibilities, running from the case of one who deliberates and later simply neglects her decision doing (without any struggle) something else instead, to the case of someone who is constantly vacillating and anguished over each of the alternatives from the point of view of the other. Second, Aristotle's texts do not make it clear what sorts of cases (if any) he takes to be paradigmatic: he himself seems to leave open a range of possibilities. Moreover, we need not take Aristotle's talk of ignorance as incompatible with the idea of struggle, for the *akratēs*' moments of ignorance may simply be phases of a cycle whose various stages together constitute a kind of struggle.[65] And though Aristotle often speaks as if the *akratēs* were simultaneously aware of (for example) the pleasures presently afforded by some pursuit and the prospective pains attendant on it, even his talk of such awareness need not indicate that he thinks of its subject as feeling especially torn at the time of action: she may happily pursue the present pleasure while giving lip service to the belief that she will regret it later. But in this sort of case, she must be saying what she says in something like the way in which the drunk recites the verses of Empedocles: her utterance is not at present a genuine expression of the relevant belief.[66]

---

[64] Cook Wilson, *Aristotelian Studies,* 48–49; he then refers (on 50) to *De Anima* 433a1–3 and 433b5–10 as further evidence of Aristotle's conception of the *akratēs* as characterized by "mental struggle."

[65] J. J. Walsh, in *Aristotle's Conception of Moral Weakness* (New York: Columbia University Press, 1963), 187, adopts something like this view when he suggests that the *akratēs*' ignorance is the "outcome of struggle" and says that "Aristotle might not have considered struggle and ignorance to be two contradictory descriptions of akrasia, but successive phases in it" [188].

[66] Note also that it does not follow from the fact that Aristotle speaks of the impulses of the *akratēs* as being opposed to one another, and of a part of the soul that opposes reason and resists it, that he thinks of the subject as necessarily *conscious* of the opposition. The claim in *EN* I.13 that "we do not see in the case of the soul" (as we do in the case of bodies) "the thing that is carried off" in the wrong direction suggests that he may even allow for a kind of unconscious opposition that counts as a form of struggle, but not a form that tells against our interpretation.

8. ARISTOTLE'S SOLUTION AND ITS RELATION TO SOCRATES' VIEW

Let us return to the remainder of VII.3. Aristotle concludes by explaining how his own view is related to the Socratic denial that required him, given his commitment to the endoxic method, to undertake the present investigation. And he allows that it follows from his own account that there is a sense in which Socrates was right.

[10] *EN* VII.3: 1147b13–19

And because <the proposition containing> the last *horos* does not seem to be universal, or scientifically knowable [ἐπιστημονικόν] in a way similar to the universal, what Socrates sought seems also to come about. For the *pathos* does not occur when what seems to be *epistêmê* in the strict sense is present [οὐ γὰρ τῆς κυρίως ἐπιστήμης εἶναι δοκούσης παρούσης γίνεται τὸ πάθος][67]—nor is this [αὕτη] dragged about because of the *pathos*—but <only when> perceptual <*epistêmê* is present>. Concerning, then, the one who knows and <the one who does> not, and how it is possible for one knowing to act akratically, let so much be said.

In saying that the *pathos* of *akrasia* occurs not when what seems to be *epistêmê* proper is present but when a kind of perceptual knowledge is present (by which he seems to mean 'active'), Aristotle seems to be saying that akratic behavior occurs when it is only the perceptual knowledge (which is of particulars), and not also the relevant universal knowledge, that gets used. In other words, he seems to be assuming that if the agent *did* use her universal knowledge by bringing her belief in the prohibiting universal to second actuality, then the proper conclusion *would* result and she *would* act more or less immediately in accordance with it. This makes good sense if (as we suggested in section 4 above) he takes using a *practical* universal to consist largely in applying it to the relevant particulars, which is scarcely distinguishable from reaching the proper conclusion. And given that Aristotle takes the conclusion to be either the action or something that leads (in the absence of preventing factors) to the action, his view looks highly Socratic.

Aristotle may, however, be reluctant to express his agreement with Socrates by speaking (as Socrates spoke) of a kind of *epistêmê* such that one *cannot* act against it. For at least some of the resistance to Socrates' view stems from a conception of *epistêmê* as purely theoretical and in itself inert. If one conceives of *epistêmê* in this way, then it will seem obvious that one *can* act against it and Socrates' view (at least as formulated in terms of *epistêmê*) will seem a complete nonstarter. This is presumably why Aristotle insists in *EE* VII.13 [aka VIII.1] that Socrates was right to say that nothing is stronger than *phronêsis*, but wrong to say that nothing is stronger than *epistêmê*, since *phronêsis* is not *epistêmê* but a different kind of cognition [ἀλλὰ γένος

---

[67] Stewart (*Notes*, vol. II, 163) mentions that a few manuscripts read τῆς κυρίως εἶναι δοκούσης ἐπιστήμης παρούσης, but this change in word order does not affect our interpretation.

ἄλλο γνώσ<εως>, 1246b34–36]. It may also explain why Aristotle speaks in [10] not simply of *epistêmê*, but of "what *seems* to be *epistêmê* in the strict sense" [τῆς κυρίως ἐπιστήμης εἶναι δοκούσης]. He is talking about what most people (including Socrates) would call *epistêmê*; but it is not *epistêmê* in the strict sense explained in *EN* VI, where he distinguishes *epistêmê* strictly so-called from various cognitive states (including *phronêsis*) that resemble it in certain ways.[68]

Many commentators miss this point and so are puzzled about why Aristotle speaks only of "what *seems* to be knowledge in the strict sense." Such commentators tend to assume that the object of the relevant knowledge is something like the prohibiting universal. And because they take *epistêmê* proper to be of universals, they think that knowledge of the prohibiting universal *is* a form of *epistêmê* proper. So they cannot understand what Aristotle seems to be saying here—namely, that akrasia does *not* occur in the presence of *epistêmê* proper. "The difficulty," as Broadie puts it, "is that nothing in the account so far suggests that the affective state [viz., *akrasia* or the affective state involved in it] does not occur *in the presence of* the universal."[69] But the difficulty appears largely because Broadie, like most commentators, identifies the *akratês*' failure as a failure to use knowledge of some *particular*. So in her view, which is shared by many, what Aristotle *should* be saying is that *akrasia* does not occur in presence of *particular* knowledge.

This explains why many, including Broadie and Rowe, adopt Stewart's proposal to emend the text by reading περιγίνεται in place of παρούσης γίνεται.[70] This allows them to read Aristotle as saying that it is not *epistêmê* proper, but only perceptual *epistêmê* (which is of particulars), that *pathos* overcomes.[71] But this emendation is not only (as Bostock admits) "paleographically improbable"; it is also unnecessary.[72] Moreover, the motivation for it is largely ideological, being grounded in the questionable (albeit common) view that it is *particular* (rather than universal) knowledge that the *akratês* fails to use. So if our account is right, much of the motivation for the emendation falls away.[73] We do not mean to say that the original text provides any *independent* argument for our thesis that it is knowledge of some *universal* that the *akratês* fails

---

[68] On the question whether Socrates himself conceived of what he called *epistêmê* as purely theoretical and so inert, on which we here remain neutral, see H. Segvic, "No One Errs Willingly: The Meaning of Socratic Intellectualism," *Oxford Studies in Ancient Philosophy* 19 (2000): 1–45.

[69] Broadie and Rowe, Aristotle, *Nic. Eth.*, 393. Robinson ("Akrasia," 152–53) is puzzled for similar reasons.

[70] See Stewart, *Notes*, vol. II, 161–64.

[71] Here is Rowe's translation: "For it is not what seems to be knowledge in the primary sense that the affective state in question overcomes (nor is it this kind of knowledge that is 'dragged about' because of the state), but the perceptual kind." Others who follow Stewart's proposal include Gauthier and Jolif and Ross (in Barnes, *Complete Works*). Note that Broadie herself suggests an alternative emendation in her *Ethics with Aristotle* (Oxford: Oxford University Press, 1991), 311 n. 38.

[72] Bostock, *Aristotle's Ethics*, 130 n. 21.

[73] Stewart offers an additional reason for emending the text: that the original requires us to take πάθος in two different senses (viz., as referring first to the pathos of ἀκρατεύεσθαι itself and then to the *epithumia* whose presence is responsible for the agent's ἀκρατεύεσθαι). But this is not obvious. If we are

to use. The argument for this thesis lies in our overall defense of the interpretation according to which Aristotle progressively articulates the failure of the *akratês* in the sequence discussed above. Given this interpretation, the original text makes perfectly good sense: if (as we suggest) Aristotle uses the phrase "what *seems* to be *epistêmê* in the strict sense" to indicate that he is referring to *phronêsis* and not to what he himself calls *epistêmê proper*, then the original text simply states a corollary of the view [defended in *EN* VI.13] that one cannot be *phronimos* without being fully virtuous, a corollary he spells out in *EN* VI.10, when he says in [1](A) "nor is the same person able to be simultaneously *phronimos* and *akratês*."

Aristotle's reasons for thinking that there is a form of practical cognition that cannot be overruled or dragged about like a slave are complicated and the interpretive issues involved in unpacking them are highly controversial. They are partly a function of his view that (correct) desire is involved in *phronêsis* itself.[74] This constitutes an important difference between *phronêsis* on the one hand and theoretical knowledge on the other, a difference explained in *EN* VI, which we take to set the stage for Book VII's discussion of *akrasia*. A proper study of the organizing role played in *EN* VI by the distinctions between theoretical and practical forms of cognition that are set up in *EN* VI would require at least another essay at least as long as this.[75] Obviously we can at present only recommend and not begin this eminently worthwhile project. Our point here is simply that the account of *phronêsis* presented in *EN* VI has remarkably Socratic implications to which Aristotle owns up in *EN* VII.3.[76]

---

right that "what seems to be *epistêmê* in the proper sense" refers to *phronêsis*, then Aristotle could well be using τὸ πάθος to refer to *epithumia* in both places: he could be saying that "it is not when *phronêsis* is present that the *pathos* [viz., the disruptive *epithumia*] comes about, nor is it *phronêsis* that is dragged about because of this *pathos*." And even if the first occurrence of τὸ πάθος does refer (as seems plausible) to the akratic condition itself, Aristotle might nevertheless proceed to use it to refer to the *epithumia* responsible for the agent's being in that condition: using τὸ πάθος in these two senses is not sufficiently problematic to warrant the emendation.

[74] It is clear from [1](A) that Aristotle takes *phronêsis* to involve *prohairesis*, which he describes in *EN* VI as "deliberative desire" [ὄρεξις βουλευτική, 1139a23; see 1113a9–11] and as (apparently indifferently) "either desiderative thought or thinking desire" [ἢ ὀρεκτικὸς νοῦς ἢ προαίρεσις ἢ ὄρεξις διανοητική, 1139b4–5].

[75] Commentators often often miss the organizing role played in the final chapters of *EN* VI by the distinction between theoretical and practical forms of cognition, as in the following passage where the fourth sentence is routinely misinterpreted as saying that *nous* is of last things "in both [viz., *both universal and particular*] directions": "All *ta pratka* are among the last and particular things. For it is necessary for the *phronimos* to recognize these things. And *sunesis* and *gnome* are about *ta prakta*, and these are last. *Nous* is of last things in both <viz., *theoretical and practical spheres*>" [1143a32–36; see 1142a23–30].

[76] We should like to thank David Sedley for the exemplary, but for him customary, editorial help he provided. We also want to thank those who participated in the workshop we held in Toronto in May 2006—especially Charles Brittain, David Bronstein, David Charles, Brad Inwood, Henrik Lorenz, Jessica Moss, and Jozef Müller. And we have benefited from comments by Myles Burnyeat and above all Sarah Broadie.

BIBLIOGRAPHY

Anscombe, G. E. M. 1957. *Intention*. Oxford: Blackwell.
Barnes, J. (ed.) 1984. *The Complete Works of Aristotle* [*Complete Works*, 2 volumes]. Princeton, NJ: Princeton University Press.
Bogen, J. and Moravcsik, J. 1982. "Aristotle's Forbidden Sweets" ["Forbidden Sweets"]. *Journal of the History of Philosophy* 20: 111–27.
Bostock, D. 2000. *Aristotle's Ethics*. Oxford: Oxford University Press.
Broadie, S. 1991. *Ethics with Aristotle*. Oxford: Oxford University Press.
Broadie, S. and Rowe, C. 2002. *Aristotle, Nicomachean Ethics* [*Aristotle, Nic. Eth.*]. Oxford: Oxford University Press.
Burnet, J. 1900. *The Ethics of Aristotle*. London: Methuen.
Burnyeat, M. 2001. *A Map of Metaphysics Zeta*. Pittsburgh: Mathesis Publications.
Bywater, I. 1894. *Aristotelis Ethica Nicomachea*. Oxford: Oxford University Press.
Charles, D. 2009. "NE VII.3: Varieties of Acrasia" ["Varieties"]. In Natali 2009, 41–71.
Charles, D. 1984. *Aristotle's Philosophy of Action* [*Action*]. London: Duckworth Publishing.
Clark, P. 2001. "The Action as Conclusion." *Canadian Journal of Philosophy* 31: 481–506.
Cook Wilson, J. 1879. *Aristotelian Studies I: On the Structure of the Seventh Book of the "Nicomachean Ethics" Chapter I–X* [*Aristotelian Studies*]. Oxford: Clarendon Press.
Cooper, J. 1975. *Reason and Human Good in Aristotle*. Cambridge, MA: Harvard University Press.
Dahl, N. O. 1984. *Practical Reason, Aristotle, and Weakness of the Will* [*Practical Reason*]. Minneapolis: University of Minnesota Press.
Gauthier, R. A. and Jolif, J. Y. 1970. *Aristote: L'Éthique à Nicomaque: Introduction, traduction, et commentaire*, 2nd edn. [*Arist.: L'Éthique*]. Louvain and Paris: Peeters Publisher.
Gosling, J. "Mad, Drunk or Asleep?—Aristotle's Akratic." *Phronesis* 38 (1993): 98–104.
Grgić, F. 2002. "Aristotle on the Akratic's Knowledge." *Phronesis* 47: 344–55.
Hardie, W. F. R. 1980. *Aristotle's Ethical Theory*, 2nd edn. Oxford: Oxford University Press.
Hughes, G. 2001. *Aristotle on Ethics*. London: Routledge.
Irwin, T. 1988. "Some Rational Aspects of Incontinence" ["Rational Aspects"]. *Southern Journal of Philosophy* 27 Supplement: 49–88.
Irwin, T. 1999. *Aristotle: Nicomachean Ethics*, 2nd edn. [*Aristotle: Nic. Eth.*]. Indianapolis, IN: Hackett.
Joachim, H. H. 1951. *Aristotle: The Nicomachean Ethics*. Oxford: Clarendon Press.
Kenny, A. 1966. "The Practical Syllogism and Incontinence" ["Practical Syllogism"]. *Phronesis* 10: 163–84.
Kraut, R. (ed.) 2006. *The Blackwell Guide to the Nicomachean Ethics* [*Guide*]. Oxford: Wiley-Blackwell.
Lawrence, G. 1988. "Akrasia and Clear-Eyed Akrasia." *Revue de philosophie ancienne* 6: 77–106.
Lorenz, H. 2006. *The Brute Within: Appetitive Desire in Plato and Aristotle*. Oxford: Oxford University Press.
Lorenz, H. 2009. "Nicomachean Ethics 7.4: Plain and Qualified Lack of Control." In Natali 2009.
McDowell, J. 1996. "Incontinence and Practical Wisdom in Aristotle" ["Incontinence"]. In S. Lovibond and S. G. Williams (eds.), *Identity, Truth and Value: Essays for David Wiggins*. Oxford: Wiley-Blackwell, 95–112.
Müller, J. "Tug of War: Aristotle on Akrasia." Unpublished paper.
Müller, J. 2015. "Aristotle on Actions from Lack of Control." *Philosopher's Imprint* 15: 1–35.

Natali, C. (ed.) 2009. *Aristotle's Nicomachean Ethics Book VII: Symposium Aristotelicum* [*Aristotle: Nic. Eth. VII*]. Oxford: Oxford University Press.

Nussbaum, M. 1978. *Aristotle's De Motu Animalium*. Princeton, NJ: Princeton University Press.

Owens, J. 1985. "The Acratic's 'Ultimate Premise' in Aristotle." In J. Wiesner (ed.), *Aristoteles: Werk und Wirkung*, Vol. 1. Berlin: De Gruyter, 376–92.

Price, A. W. 2006. "Acrasia and Self-Control" ["Acrasia"]. In Kraut 2006, 234–54.

Rackham, H. 1934. *Aristotle: Nicomachean Ethics*. Loeb Classical Library. Cambridge, MA: Harvard University Press.

Ramsauer, G. 1878. *Aristotelis Ethica Nicomachea* [*Arist. Eth. Nic.*]. Leipzig: Teubner.

Rassow, H. 1874. *Forschungen über die Nikomachische Ethik des Aristoteles* [*Forschungen*]. Weimar.

Robinson, R. 1969. "Aristotle on Akrasia" ["Akrasia"]. In Robinson, *Essays in Greek Philosophy*. Oxford: Clarendon Press, 139–60. Reprinted in J. Barnes, M. Schofield, and R. Sorabji (eds.) 1977. *Articles on Aristotle, Vol. 2: Ethics and Politics*. New York: St Martin's Press, 79–91.

Segvic, H. 2000. "No One Errs Willingly: The Meaning of Socratic Intellectualism." *Oxford Studies in Ancient Philosophy* 19: 1–45.

Smyth, H. W. 1920. *Greek Grammar*. Cambridge, MA: Harvard University Press.

Stewart, J. A. 1892. *Notes on the Nicomachean Ethics* [*Notes*]. Oxford.

Timmermann, J. 2000. "Impulsivität und Schwäche: Die Argumentation des Abschnitts *Eth. Nic.* 1146b31–1147b19 im Lichte der beiden Formen des Phänomens 'Akrasia.'" *Zeitschrift für philosophische Forschung* 54: 47–66.

Walsh, J. J. 1963. *Aristotle's Conception of Moral Weakness*. New York: Columbia University Press.

Whiting, J. 2019. "Hylomorphic Virtue: Cosmology, Embryology, and Moral Development in Aristotle." [Chapter 6, this volume]

Whiting, J. 2006. "The Nicomachean Account of *Philia*." In Kraut 2006, 276–304. [II:6]

8

The Lockeanism of Aristotle

MY TITLE IS fashioned after that of a famous paper by G. E. L. Owen, who once asked the obvious but rarely asked question just what was meant by 'Platonism' in debates about the Platonism of Aristotle.[1] Of course, debates about the Lockeanism of Aristotle do not rage in quite the way that debates about the Platonism of Aristotle once did. But debates about whether Aristotle and other ancient figures had anything like Locke's allegedly modern conception of the person or self do rage. 'Lockean' has become what Owen would have called a "familiar catchword" in contemporary debates about what constitutes a person's identity over time, a catchword for views that are supposed to be distinctively modern. And those who use this catchword—including some who apply it to their own views—tend to take it on trust, without attending carefully enough either to what Locke himself said or to the historical traditions within which he worked. This leads, I think, to two sorts of error. First, self-professed neo-Lockeans, like Derek Parfit and David Velleman, tend to develop their views in ways that seem to me unworthy of Locke's name. Second, historians asking whether ancient philosophers had anything like Locke's conception of the person or self are too quick to reach negative verdicts.

My primary concern here is with the second sort of error, but I shall comment toward the end on the first. I want to focus especially on the question whether Aristotle had anything like Locke's conception of the person or self.[2] For Aristotle is

---

[1] Owen 1956.
[2] It seems clear from sec. 26 of passage [R] below that Locke does not distinguish *persons* from *selves*: 'person' is simply the name used from the second- and third-person points of view for what from the first-person point of view each of us calls 'self.'

sometimes taken as an especially clear example of someone to whom Locke's allegedly modern conception is alien. Historians who posit fundamental differences between ancient and modern conceptions of the person or self tend to allow that their case is at least superficially more difficult when they consider later figures, like Epictetus and Plotinus; but they seem to think their case easily closed when it comes to Aristotle.

I am thinking especially of the widely cited work of Christopher Gill and of the philosophers whose lead Gill claims to follow—namely, Kathleen Wilkes in her book *Real People* and Peter Smith and O. R. Jones in their introduction to the philosophy of mind.[3] As Gill puts it,

> A key feature of the argument of these two books is that the understanding of consciousness presupposed in post-Cartesian thinking is both incoherent and untenable; in particular, the idea that we have *direct* and *incorrigible* access to *all* our mental states is one they present as vulnerable alike to common-sense objections and to scientific research.... If there is a good deal about my mind of which I am not directly aware, it is wrong to suppose that a first-personal view has the kind of authority often claimed for it in post-Cartesian thought. In any case, such a claim is incompatible with the empirical approach they regard as appropriate to the philosophy of mind, according to which the (third-personal) perspective of science is to be regarded as more authoritative than my (first-personal) view of myself. (Put more precisely, they think there is nothing about my *first*-personal view of myself which cannot be *more* effectively explained in *third*-personal terms.)
>
> ... both studies also suggest that their approach is close to that of Greek philosophers, especially Aristotle. Aristotle, they claim, instead of focusing on 'mind,' as conceived in Cartesian terms, as the locus of subjective or introspective experience, sets out to study the forms of life [*psuchê*] which actualise the essential capacities of complex natural kinds (human beings, beasts, etc.) Aristotle's approach in the psychological works is characteristically third-personal in the sense that he provides a 'map' of capacities (perception, memory, and so on) which are possessed by a number of natural kinds, not just by 'us.' Human psychological capacities are conceived as being more complex or sophisticated versions of capacities shared by other natural kinds, not as different in kind (that is, conscious rather than non-conscious) as they are in Cartesian theory. Their complexity can be described adequately in third-personal terms, without requiring us to adopt, or to posit, a distinctively first-personal view of ourselves.[4] In such a framework of thought, the misleading Cartesian underpinnings of the

---

[3] The argument of Gill 1996 is extended to Hellenistic and Roman philosophers in Gill 2006. The basic ideas are presented in Gill 1991, from which the passage quoted here (with my italics) is taken. The two books to which Gill refers are Wilkes 1988 and Smith and Jones 1986.

[4] Gill appends here the following note:

> Thus Wilkes draws attention to, e.g., Aristotle, *Nicomachean Ethics* (*EN*) VI, 2.1139b4–5: "choice is either desiderative reason or ratiocinative desire, *and such a source of action is a man*" (her translation and italics). She underlines, by contrast, the stress in modern discussions of personhood on

modern concept of the person do not appear; for Aristotle, the central notion is the human being, that is (as Wilkes sees it) the *real* person. [Gill 1991, 168–69]

It is clear that Gill takes Locke's account of consciousness to be fundamentally Cartesian, and so that Gill is pitting Locke's essentially *first*-personal concept of the *person* against what he takes to be Aristotle's exclusively *third*-personal concept of the *human being*. But there are multiple problems here.

First, Gill associates two importantly different sorts of claims with the post-Cartesian view: one is the *epistemological* claim that each us of has "direct and incorrigible access to all our mental states"; the other is what might be called the *ontological* claim that the first-person point of view is irreducible in the sense that there are features of it that cannot be fully explained in third-personal terms. Gill then moves very quickly from the fact that there is both scientific and common-sense evidence against the *epistemological* claim to a rejection of the *ontological* claim. But it is possible for an irreducibly first-person point of view to involve forms of epistemological privilege that fall short of *incorrigible* access to *all* of one's own mental states. There are indeed reasons for thinking that Descartes himself stopped short of that.[5] And even if one refrains from attaching strong forms of epistemological privilege to the first-person point of view, one might still think it necessary to assume the existence of irreducibly first-person points of view because there are subjects whose behaviors cannot be fully explained in third-person terms. Moreover, there is evidence (discussed in section 1 below) that Aristotle himself is committed to the existence of subjects whose behaviors cannot be adequately explained without assuming the existence of irreducibly first-person points of view that, however, involve only modest forms of epistemic privilege.

There are also problems with Gill's reading of Locke. It is clear that Gill takes Locke's account of personal identity to involve something distinctively modern because he both takes Locke's account of personal identity to presuppose a Cartesian account of consciousness and takes the Cartesian account of consciousness to be distinctively modern. So Gill's view can be challenged in either of two ways: we might deny that Locke's account of personal identity presupposes the Cartesian account of consciousness; or we might deny that the Cartesian account is distinctively modern. We might, in fact, deny both claims.

Of course, Descartes himself often encouraged us to think of his views as constituting a radical break from previous traditions. It is not just that he made a principle—or at least a show—of throwing out all of his beliefs and starting again from the

---

capacities such as sense-perception and pain, which are not distinctively human but which are given importance by the subjective perspective of post-Cartesian philosophy of mind.

The passage cited here plays an important role in what follows: 'choice' is Wilkes' rendering of '*prohairesis*,' Aristotle's account of which *both* assumes an irreducibly first-person point of view *and* plays a role in the evolution of Locke's own views (or so I argue in what follows).

[5] I am indebted here to discussion with Marleen Rozemond and to Rozemond 2004. See also Radner 1988.

foundations. He explicitly disavowed apparent connections between his views and those of his predecessors: for example, between his foundational cogito argument and the apparently similar argument advanced by Augustine. See, for example, his letter to Colvius:

> I am obliged to you for drawing my attention to the passage of St. Augustine relevant to my *I am thinking, therefore I exist*. I went today to the library of this town [viz., Leyden] and read it, and I find that he really does use it to prove our existence. He goes on to show that there is a certain likeness of the Trinity in us, in that we exist, we know that we exist, and we love the existence and knowledge we have. *I*, on the other hand, use the argument to show that this I which is thinking is an immaterial substance with no bodily element. In itself it is such a simple and natural thing to infer that one exists from the fact that one is doubting that it could have occurred to anyone. But I am very glad to find myself in agreement with St. Augustine, if only to hush the little minds that find fault with the principle.[6]

How honest this is, I cannot say. But even if we doubt that Descartes' views are always as novel as he pretends, it seems plausible to suppose that his explicit aims—not simply of showing that the thinking I "is an immaterial substance with no bodily element" but of using this claim to provide a secure foundation for his physics—set the epistemological bar higher than it had been set by his predecessors (including Augustine, who, although he invoked his cogito to answer a kind of skeptical doubt, did not doubt the truth of things perceived through the senses in anything like the way Descartes did).[7] And if Descartes' conception of consciousness does in fact involve stronger forms of epistemological privilege than we find in any earlier conception of consciousness, then it may well deserve to be called a new conception. But even if we assume for the sake of argument that there is something new in Descartes' conception and that what is new has something to do with the form or degree of epistemic privilege involved in it, it does not follow that when Locke speaks of consciousness he must be embracing a Cartesian conception of it—not even when he says Cartesian-sounding things. In fact Descartes himself seems—in his own remarks about the relation between his cogito and Augustine's—to warn precisely against jumping to such conclusions.

There are, moreover, good reasons (to be discussed in section 5) for doubting that Locke embraced a new and specifically Cartesian conception of consciousness. There are, for example, reasons for thinking that Locke's use of the term 'consciousness' owes

---

[6] Letter to Colvius, 14 November 1640 (Adam and Tannery edition: III.247–48). Translation by Anthony Kenny in Descartes 1991, 159–60. It is worth noting that the Augustinian arguments to which Descartes refers (*De Trinitate* XV.12 and X.10 and *De civitate Dei* XI.26) seem to be indebted to arguments presented by Aristotle in his discussion of friendship in *Nicomachean Ethics* IX.9 and perhaps also *Eudemian Ethics* VII.12. For more on the Aristotelian arguments, see Whiting 2006 [II.6] and 2013 [I.7].

[7] See *De Trinitate* XV.12.

less to the work of Descartes than to that of the Cambridge Platonist Ralph Cudworth, who was the first to make systematic use of this English noun.[8] But although Locke's relationship to Cudworth is often acknowledged, the significance of this relationship seems to me obscured by the common tendency to read Cudworth's conception of consciousness as itself Cartesian or at least as a Plotinian anticipation of Descartes. For I take the significance of any influence that Cudworth may have had on Locke to lie at least partly in the extent to which Cudworth's views had pre-Plotinian—especially Stoic and Aristotelian—roots.

Pre-Plotinian roots are important here insofar as Plotinus is sometimes viewed as anticipating Descartes and even as one of the possible sources of inspiration (if you want to call it that) for Descartes' conception of consciousness. So those who take Descartes to have seen something new that the ancients for the most part missed are unlikely to take evidence that Cudworth was borrowing from Plotinus as providing enough distance from the Cartesian conception to render the hypothesis of Cudworth's influence on Locke much help in rescuing Locke from the charge that his conception of consciousness is ultimately Cartesian. But in spite of the claim that Cudworth should have been called a "Plotinist" rather than a "Platonist," it is clear that Cudworth also borrowed heavily from Aristotle and the Stoics, and did so, moreover, in areas where his thinking seems most likely to have had some effect on Locke's—namely, in areas to do with the nature of freely willed action and the conditions of responsible agency.[9]

In section 3 below, we shall return to Cudworth's probable influence on Locke. If Locke did in fact inherit his conception of consciousness largely from Cudworth, then it will be even more difficult (than our reading of Aristotle alone suggests) to claim that Aristotle did not have or could not have had something like the Lockean conception of person. For (as I argue in section 5 below), Cudworth's conception of consciousness is largely Stoic, with roots in Aristotle's teleology.

Here, however, it is important to note that the hypothesis of Cudworth's influence on Locke is not strictly necessary to my overall line of argument. Locke was for a time Professor of Greek in Oxford and surely read and taught in the original many of the Stoic and Aristotelian texts whose views are employed by Cudworth. More importantly, the Stoic pedigree of Locke's conception is (as I argue in section 6 below) apparent even without the hypothesis of Cudworth's influence. It was in fact in testing my initial hypothesis of Stoic influence that I tripped over the signs of Cudworth's influence on Locke and came to worry, temporarily, that Locke's conception of consciousness might be more Plotinian than Stoic. But this worry is easily laid to rest once one appreciates the extent to which Plotinus himself was building on Stoic and ultimately Aristotelian

---

[8] See Theil 1991, whose claim that Cudworth's conception of consciousness is Plotinian is short sighted, not simply insofar as Plotinus is borrowing from even earlier sources but also insofar as Cudworth himself is borrowing directly (in ways we shall see below) from the relevant Stoic and ultimately Aristotelian sources.

[9] Coleridge's claim is reported in Passmore 1951, which seems to me to take Cudworth's conception of consciousness to be more Cartesian than it really is.

views. In sum, the case for taking Locke to be directly influenced by Stoic views is strong enough to render the hypothesis of Cudworth's influence on Locke unnecessary to my argument for taking Locke to adopt a kind of stoicized Aristotelianism, and so unnecessary to my argument for allowing that Aristotle himself had something like the Lockean conception. The hypothesis of Cudworth's influence merely strengthens these arguments.

1. ARISTOTLE AND THE FIRST PERSON: DELIBERATION, *PROHAIRESIS*, AND HUMAN BEINGS THEMSELVES AS *PROHAIRETIC* PRINCIPLES OF ACTION

Let us begin with some independent reasons for taking Aristotle to recognize the existence of subjects whose behavior cannot be fully explained unless we ascribe some irreducibly first-personal states or activities to them. Although it is true, as Gill claims, that Aristotle seeks to ground distinctively human capacities like the capacity for deliberation in capacities like memory that humans share with other animals, this does not prevent Aristotle from taking the sort of memory required for deliberation to be irreducibly first-personal in ways that involve modest forms of epistemic privilege. For it is clear from *De Memoria* that Aristotle takes the sort of remembering that is crucial to deliberation to involve more than a mere image of something previously encountered together with a sense of having previously encountered that of which it is an image. As Themistius explains in his commentary on *De Memoria*, even an ass can have that.

[A]   Memory then is neither perception [*aisthêsis*] nor imagination [*phantasia*] nor any other <kind of> thought [*tis hetera noêsis*], but some state or affection of these, whenever time is taken in . . . For perception is of what is present, anticipation of what is going to be, and memory of what has come to be, wherefore all memory is with time. Whence only those animals that perceive time remember, and <they do so> by no other part of the soul than that by which they perceive. For the ass that fell last year into this hole, seeing it today and retreating remembers that it first fell, but there is a difference. For the man, in addition to being aware [*pros tô(i)* **sunaisthanesthai**] when he saw or heard <something>, knows the difference between what is going to be and what has been; but non-rational creatures <know> this alone, that they now fall or fell before, and the <man> is aware of himself remembering [*ho men heautou* **sunaisthanetai** *mnêmeneuontos*], while the <non-rational creatures> are not [*ta de ou*]. [(Sophoniae) *in parva naturalia commentarium* 5, 6 (2), my bold][10]

---

[10] Themistius is commenting here on *De Memoria* 452b23–28 (quoted next in my main text). Here and elsewhere Themistius (like other commentators) uses the verb '*sunaisthanesthai*' in commenting on passages where Aristotle does not himself use the term, most notably passages concerning phenomena associated with the so-called common sense [*koinê aisthêsis*]. The verb Aristotle uses here is '*lanthanein*,' which is the verb Plato uses in the *Philebus*, whose discussion of *mnêmê, elpis,* and *nous* is clearly present

What is required for deliberation is not only awareness of time, but also knowing the difference between what has been and what will be—that is, having some sort of grasp of the future. One must also have some sort of awareness not only *of oneself* but also of oneself *as remembering*—rather than, for example, imagining or hallucinating. Aristotle explains this in *De Memoria*.[11] After discussing cases of lunatics taking themselves to be remembering when they are only imagining or hallucinating [451a2–13], he says the following:

> [B] Whenever the motion <corresponding to> the <past> event and the motion <corresponding to> the time <of that event> come to be together, then one actually remembers. And if someone not doing this supposes <he does>, then he *thinks* he remembers. For nothing prevents someone being deceived and seeming to remember while not <actually> remembering. But actually remembering while not believing <that one is remembering>, but <rather> failing to notice that one is remembering [*energounta de tê(i) mnêmê(i) mê oiesthai alla **lanthanein** memnêmenon*] is not possible. For this was not <what we said> remembering itself <is>. [*De Memoria* 452b23–28, my bold]

This makes it clear both (1) that Aristotle takes the sort of remembering necessary for deliberation to be *self-intimating* in the sense that one cannot be remembering in this sense without seeming to oneself to be doing so and (2) that he does *not* take the appearance that one is remembering to be *incorrigible* (since a subject can seem to herself to be remembering when she is, for example, hallucinating or merely imagining). In other words, the sort of remembering that is required for deliberation involves a modest form of first-person privilege: it involves a subject's having a kind of access to her own psychological states that others cannot have, but such access (though it is partly constitutive of her being in the relevant states) does *not* render her beliefs about the nature of the states she is in (let alone her beliefs about what the states themselves purport to represent) *infallible*. So insofar as Aristotle thinks there are forms of human behavior that cannot be adequately explained without appeal to our capacity for deliberation, he must think it necessary to introduce at least modest forms of first-person privilege in order to account for the full range of human behavior.

And Aristotle does indeed think that there are forms of human behavior that cannot be adequately explained without appeal to the capacity for deliberation. For he sees an important distinction between the sort of responsible agency characteristic of mature rational animals and the merely voluntary behavior of children and at least some non-rational animals. The latter can act voluntarily [*hekôn*] in the sense

---

in the background not only of *De Memoria* but also of the passages on friendship where Aristotle himself actually uses the verb '*sunaisthanesthai*' (typically in connection with one person perceiving and enjoying or suffering *together with* another). On these issues, see Whiting 2013 [II.7]. [For discussion of the role of the first-person point of view in Plato's *Philebus*, see Whiting 2014.]

[11] For the connection with deliberation, see Aristotle, *De Memoria* 453a13–14.

(roughly speaking) that (a) their actions stem from internal impulses (rather than external force or compulsion) and (b) they in some sense know what they are doing [*Nicomachean Ethics* (*EN*) III.1]. But this is compatible with their being dragged about (so to speak) by appearances, both in the sense that they are unable to do anything other than what appears best (that is, most pleasant or least painful) at the moment of action and in the sense that they are in no way responsible for how things appear to them in the first place. So even when they act voluntarily in the sense that they act on their own internal impulses, children and non-rational animals are not responsible for what they do in the way characteristic of a mature rational agent, who is, according to Aristotle, at least partly responsible for its character and so at least partly responsible for how things appear to it in the first place [*EN* III.5, especially 1114a31–b25]. But in order to account for this sort of responsibility, Aristotle thinks it necessary to ascribe to mature rational agents the capacity for what he calls '*prohairesis*,' a capacity intimately related to the capacity for deliberation, which is itself at least implicitly first-personal: an agent can deliberate only about things which it is up to *her* either to do or not to do [*Eudemian Ethics* (*EE*) 1226a27–28].

English translations tend nowadays to render '*prohairesis*' as "decision" rather than (as Ross had it) "choice," which is now reserved for the sort of mere *hairesis* (or selection) of which children and non-rational animals are capable.[12] The point of using 'decision' is largely to emphasize the status of '*prohairesis*' as a technical term referring to a *considered* choice—that is, to a preference in favor of [*pro*] one among other alternatives taken into consideration.[13] But 'decision' tends to favor the cognitive over the affective: we often speak of someone as *deciding* to do something she has *no desire* to do, as in Aristotle's example of someone doing something shameful that is commanded by a tyrant who threatens, if she does not do the shameful thing in question, to (for example) wipe out her family. In the case of such actions—actions that Aristotle calls 'mixed' because they in one sense voluntary and another sense not—Aristotle speaks only of *hairesis*, not of *prohairesis* [*EN* III.3].

This, I think, is because he treats *prohairesis* as a kind of *desire*: a "deliberative desire of things that are up to us" [*bouleutikê orexis tôn eph' hêmin*, *EN* 1113a10–11]. But it would be a mistake to think of *prohairesis* simply as a desire that comes about as a result of deliberation. For Aristotle claims that *prohairesis* is also a kind of *thought*. He says, in a passage that will play a crucial role in the story I aim to tell,

[C] **Of action, *prohairesis* is ⟨the⟩ principle [*archê*]** from which the movement ⟨arises⟩ and not ⟨the *archê*⟩for the sake of which ⟨the action is done⟩. **But of *prohairesis*, ⟨the principle⟩ is desire and reason that is for the sake of something.** Wherefore, *prohairesis* exists neither without

---

[12] Both Irwin 1999 and Rowe in Broadie and Rowe 2002 use 'decison' For 'choice' see the quotation from Gill in note 4 above; and Ross 1908. My own thoughts about *prohairesis* are much indebted to the unpublished work of Paul Matthewson.

[13] [The 'pro' is sometimes taken to have temporal force: see Inwood 1985, 240.]

intellect and thinking [*aneu nou kai dianoias*] nor without a state of character [*aneu êthikês hexeôs*]. For doing well [*eupraxia*] and its opposite in action are not possible without thought and character. But thought itself moves nothing [*dianoia d' autê outhen kinei*]; <only> the <thought that is> for the sake of something and practical <moves things>. For this <sort of thought> rules even in the case of production. For every maker makes for the sake of something; and it is not what is made that is an end without qualification (that is <an end only> in relation to something and of someone/something [*pros ti kai tinos*]) but rather what is done <that is an end without qualification>. For doing well [*hê eupraxia*] is an end <without qualification> and desire is of this [viz., of *eupraxia*]. **Wherefore *prohairesis* is either desiderative thought [*orektikos nous*] or thinking desire [*orexis dianoêtikê*], and a man is this sort of principle <of actions>.**
[*EN* VI.2, 1139a31–b5, my bold]

It is clear from the start of the chapter that Aristotle is talking about *praxis* in a special sense, a sense in which beasts are not capable of *praxis* [*EN* 1139a19–21]; and a sense in which *praxis* is (as here) contrasted with production, where some independent product comes about as a result of the relevant activity. Aristotle introduces production here, I submit, not simply to specify the sort of praxis of which *prohairesis* is the moving cause but also to make it clear that there are indeed forms of thought that *do* move their subjects. His point here is *not* the Humean point that thought by itself never moves its subject but can do so only when combined with some independently existing desire. His point is rather that thought *simply as such* (i.e., simply insofar as it is *thought*) does not move its subjects, since there is a form of thought (namely, theoretical thought) that does *not* move its subjects. But it does *not* follow from this that there are *no* forms of thought capable of moving their subjects: productive thought clearly moves its subjects and so too can what Aristotle calls "*prohairesis*." In other words, Aristotle introduces the example of productive thought partly to soften his readers up for the idea of a kind of *practical* thought, a kind of thought that is *itself* desiderative and so can equally well be called a kind of *desire*.[14]

The important point here is that the relevant sort of thought and desire are not independent of one another: *prohairesis* is not (as Irwin's translation has it) "thought *combined with* desire or desire *combined with* thought."[15] There is just *one* thing here that can be described in two different ways: as "desiderative thought" or as "thinking desire" (and ultimately as both). Moreover, a *prohairesis* is not just *any* desire that comes about as a result of deliberation. It is a desire that embodies the agent's *conception* of

---

[14] Another passage sometimes read in a Humean way is *De Anima* III.10. But I argue against the Humean reading of that passage in Whiting 2002a [Chapter 5, this volume]. So I do not take that passage to pose problems for my reading of [C].

[15] Irwin 1999 ad loc. I dwell on this point here because it is important when we come (in section 3 below) to Cudworth's rejection of faculty psychology and its possible influence on Locke.

the good and so her *understanding* of the sort of action in which living well consists. It is a desire that is, as Aristotle puts it, "more indicative of [the agent's] character than her actions are" [*EN* 1111b5–6]. For she can be compelled to *do* base things, but cannot be compelled to *prohairesthai* base things [*EE* 1228a14–15]. This is why Aristotle speaks only of *hairesis*, and not of *prohairesis*, in the case of mixed actions. The subject who *hairesthai*, even as a result of deliberation, to do the shameful thing that the tyrant demands of her, does not *prohairesthai* to do what she does; for she does what she does *against her will*.

This way of understanding *prohairesis* helps to explain Aristotle's suggestion, at the end of the passage quoted, that a human being *herself* is the sort of principle of action that *prohairesis* is. She is neither (as God is) a pure intellect nor (as a non-rational animal is) simply a subject of desires and perceptions in accordance with which she cannot help but act: she has what later came to be called 'the will.'

2. A BRIEF INTRODUCTION, VIA EPICTETUS, TO CUDWORTH'S STOICIZED ARISTOTELIANISM: THE *HÊGEMONIKON* AS *PROHAIROUMENON*

There is thus a significant continuity between Aristotle's conception of *prohairesis* and Epictetus' subsequent identification of a human being with her *prohairesis* [*Discourses* III.1.39].[16] For Epictetus identifies us with our *prohaireseis* on the grounds that our *prohaireseis* are the only things that are entirely (to use Aristotle's phrase) "up to us" [*eph' hêmin*]: nothing else—neither our bodies nor our possessions nor the fates of our parents and children—is up to us in the relevant way [*Discourses* I.22.10ff]. Epictetus thus associates *prohairesis* (in a way earlier Stoics did not) with the leading (or governing) principle of the human soul—that is, with what he (following earlier Stoics) calls "*to hêgemonikon*."

It is worth noting here that although the idea of *to hêgemonikon* is generally associated with the Stoics, it derives from Plato and Aristotle. We shall see it in Plato when we come to passage [O] below. And we can see it in the following passage of Aristotle, which points to a close connection—like the one found in Epictetus—between *prohairesis* and the leading principle.[17]

---

[16] For this point, see Inwood 1985, Appendix 2, 240–42. This is one of countless places where I am indebted to Inwood, not just for his published work but for his intellectual companionship both in the seminar in which I worked out the ideas presented here and in much else.

[17] See also *EN* X.7 on *nous* (or whatever is the best principle in us) as "by nature such as to rule [*archein*] and to lead [*hêgeisthai*] and to have a grasp of fine and divine ⟨things⟩" [1177a13–15]. This is relevant to my overall argument insofar as Aristotle explicitly says, in a context where he is clearly referring to *practical nous*, that each of us is most of all [*malista*] our *nous* [1169a2]. One of his arguments for this is that we call someone "*enkratês*" (or, as Rowe has it, "self-controlled") if she is controlled by her *nous*, and "*akratês*" (or, as Rowe has it, "un-self-controlled") if she is not. So his idea seems to be that a human being should be identified above all with her *nous*, where her *nous* is something like what the Stoics called "*to hêgemonikon*."

[D] It seems, as we have said, that man is <a> principle [*archê*] of the actions <he performs>. Deliberation is about the things he *himself* can do, and actions are for the sake of other things. For it is not the end [e.g., *eudaimonia* or health] but the things <that contribute> to the end that are subject to deliberation. . . . But if one deliberates always [viz., at every stage], one will go on ad infinitum. But what is subject to deliberation [*to bouleuton*] and what is *prohaireton* are the same, except that what is *prohaireton* is <something> already determinate. For what has been judged as a result of deliberation is *prohaireton*. For each stops inquiring about how he will act when he refers the principle <*archê*> back to himself [*eis hauton*] and to the leading <part> of himself [*kai hautou eis to hêgoumenon*]. For this is *to prohairoumenon* <part>. [*EN* 1112b31–1113a7]

Epictetus' account of our responsibility for what we do is focused less on the sort of deliberation of which Aristotle speaks and more on a rational creature's capacity to step back from the way things appear to it—that is, to step back from its sense-impressions and other *phantasiai*—so as to examine these *phantasiai*, and then either to assent to them or not, and so to act or not according to its own judgment.[18]

In a chapter called "How Reason is capable of contemplating itself" [*Peri tou logou pôs hautou theôretikos estin*], Epictetus describes the first task of the philosopher as that of testing the appearances, judging them, and applying none that has not survived the test [*Discourses*, II.18 and IV.1]. The primacy of this task stems from the fact that reason is itself a system [*sustêma*] of *phantasiai* [*Discourses*, I.20.5], which has two important consequences. The first is that reason is capable of contemplating itself in the sense that it can contemplate the individual *phantasiai* that constitute it. This is part of what makes a rational creature free and so responsible for its actions: a rational creature is not simply dragged about (as a non-rational animal is) by its impressions of things as good or bad, pleasant or painful. The second consequence of taking reason to be a system of *phantasiai* is that reason itself is corrupted when the *phantasiai* that constitute it are corrupted [*Discourses* II.18]. Hence the primacy of avoiding assent to false or corrupt *phantasiai*: it is a matter of keeping one's *hêgemonikon* pure [*Discourses* III.22.10]. And this is something that one can in principle do, given that one cannot be compelled to assent to false *phantasiai* [*Discourses* IV.1.69; cf. I.1.23–24]. For God has given us reason so as to free us from all constraint, even his own [*Discourses* I.VI.40].

Cudworth clearly adopts many of these views. He says in the first chapter of his *Treatise on Freewill* that "all men's words at least free God from the blame of wicked actions, pronouncing *ho theos anaitios* . . . and we cast the blame of them wholly on *the men themselves, as principles of action*." And he goes on (later in the same chapter) to

---

[18] See, for example, Epictetus' *Discourses* II.18 and IV.1.

endorse "the Stoical doctrine that the truest and greatest goods and evils of rational beings consist in *en tois prohairetikois* or *en tois eph' hêmin*, in their own free willed actions or things in their own power."[19]

Cudworth also identifies a mature human being with her *hêgemonikon* and takes this—given the *hêgemonikon's* capacity for self-examination—to play a crucial role in securing the sort of freedom required for responsible agency.

[E]   I say, therefore, that the *to hêgemonikon* in every man, and indeed that which is properly we ourselves (we rather having those other things of necessary nature than being them), is the soul as comprehending itself, all its concerns and interests, its abilities and capacities, and holding itself, as it were in its own hand, as it were redoubled upon itself, having a power of intending or exerting itself more or less in consideration or deliberation, in resisting the lower appetites that oppose it, both of utility, reason, and honesty; in self-recollection and attention, and vigilant circumspection, or standing upon our guard; in purposes and resolution, in diligence in carrying on steady designs and active endeavors—this in order, to self-improvement and the self-promoting of its own good, the fixing and conserving itself in the same. [*A Treatise on Freewill*, chap. X]

But we should not allow the Stoic branches of Cudworth's views to obscure their Aristotelian roots. For the strength of his Aristotelianism is clear not only in the following passage but also in passage [L] below.

[F]   Another argument used to prove that contingent freewill is a thing that cannot have existence in nature is because it is reasonable to think that all elections and volitions are determined by the reasons of good, and by the appearances of the greater good. Now the reasons and appearances of good are in the understanding only, and therefore are not arbitrary but necessary. Whence it will follow that all elections and volitions must needs be necessary. *But Aristotle himself long since made a question whether all appearances of the good were necessary or no. And it is most certain that they are not so. For as we do more or less intend ourselves in consideration and deliberation, and we do more or less fortify our resolutions to resist the lower appearances and passions, so will the appearances of good and our practical judgments be different to us accordingly.* Whence it comes to pass that the same motives and reasons

---

[19] This endorsement makes it more reasonable to associate Cudworth's talk of the "men themselves, as principles of action" with the views of Aristotle and the Stoics than with the views of Descartes that are cited by Hutton in her note on this passage in Cudworth 1996. Hutton's notes provide just one example of a widespread tendency to assimilate the views of Cudworth to those of Descartes when they are better assimilated to the views of the ancient sources that Cudworth himself cites in support of his views. This tendency is especially dangerous when Descartes' views are represented (often quite misleadingly) as distinctively modern and opposed to the ancient views in question.

have not the same effect upon different men, nor yet upon the same man at different times. *Wherefore this is but one of the vulgar errors; that men are merely passive to the appearances of good, and to their own practical judgments.* [*A Treatise of Freewill*, chap. XXI, my italics]

Here Cudworth is denying the premise on which the argument against the existence of freewill turns—i.e., the premise that the reasons and appearances of good are in the understanding only, and therefore are not arbitrary but necessary. His appeal to Aristotle is most plausibly taken as referring not (as Hutton suggests) to *Rhetoric* I.7 but to *EN* III.5, where Aristotle argues that *we ourselves* are partly responsible [*sunaitioi*] for the states [*hexeis*] that contribute to things appearing (or not appearing) good to us. The idea here is of the *man himself,* as distinct from some isolable part of him such as his understanding, being the origin or at least a partial cause of something—in this case of what does and does not appear good to him. And this idea stems—in ways we have seen in passages [C] and [D]—from Aristotle. So it seems appropriate to describe Cudworth's account of free will as involving a kind of stoicized Aristotelianism.

3. THE POSSIBLE INFLUENCE OF CUDWORTH'S STOICIZED ARISTOTELIANISM ON LOCKE'S ACCOUNT OF PERSONAL IDENTITY

Let us turn briefly, then, to the case for taking Locke's account of personal identity to show signs of Cudworth's influence. The case involves not simply the vague familiarity that Locke was generally influenced by Cudworth, but two more specific claims: first, that Locke's addition of the famous chapter on personal identity into the second edition of his *Essay* was connected to the extensive changes he made in the chapter on Power; and second, that the changes in the chapter on Power were made at least partly in response to problems raised by Cudworth.

Let us start with the second claim. In the chapters leading up to his explicitly Aristotelian defense of *to hêgemonikon* as the governing principle in us, Cudworth clearly distinguishes Aristotle's own view from the views of scholastic philosophers who treat the Understanding and the Will as distinct faculties one of which commands the other. Cudworth is attacking both intellectualist views (according to which Understanding determines the Will) and voluntarist views (according to which the Will determines Understanding): the very same pair of views that Aristotle himself rejects in passage [C], with his conception of *prohairesis* as something that can be described either as *orektikos nous* or as *orexis dianoêtikê*.

Cudworth speaks here of what he calls "the last practical judgement" as being "the same thing with *boulêsis,* the will, or volition." He seems to be thinking of a kind of judgment that is itself *practical* in the sense that it moves its subject to act in something like the way Aristotle's *prohairesis* is supposed to do. Cudworth then says at the start of the next chapter,

[G] But this scholastic philosophy[20] is manifestly absurd, and mere scholastic jargon. For to attribute the act of intellection or perception to the faculty of understanding, and acts of volition to the faculty of will, or to say that it is understanding that understandeth, and the will that willeth—this is all one as if one should say that the faculty of walking walketh, and the faculty of speaking speaketh, or that the musical faculty playeth a lesson on the lute, or sings this or that tune.

Moreover, since it is generally agreed upon by all philosophers, that *actiones sunt suppositorum,* who ever acts is a subsistent thing, therefore by this kind of language are these two faculties of understanding and will made to be two *supposita,* two subsistent things, two agents, and two persons, in the soul . . .

But all this while it is really the man or soul that understands, and the man or soul that wills, as it is the man that walks and the man that speaks or talks, and the musician that plays a lesson on the lute. That it is one and the same subsistent thing, one and the same soul that both understandeth and willeth, and the same agent only that acteth diversely. And thus it may well be conceived that one and the same reasonable soul in us may both will understandingly, or knowingly of what it will; and understand or think of this or that object willingly [*A Treatise on Freewill,* chap. VII].

It is worth comparing this with the following passage, which was already present in Locke's first-edition chapter on Power:

[H] . . . if it be reasonable to suppose and talk of *Faculties,* as distinct Beings, that can act, (as we do, when we say that the *Will* orders, and the *Will* is free,) 'tis fit that we should make a speaking *Faculty,* and a walking *Faculty,* and a dancing *Faculty,* by which those Actions are produced, which are but several Modes of Motion; as well as we make the *Will* and *Understanding* to be *Faculties,* by which the Actions of Chusing and Perceiving are produced, which are but several Modes of Thinking: And we may as properly say, that 'tis the singing *Faculty* sings, and the dancing *Faculty* dances; as that the *Will* chuses, or that the Understanding conceives; or, as is usual, that the *Will* directs the Understanding, or the Understanding obeys, or obeys not the *Will.* [*An Essay Concerning Human Understanding* II. XXI. 17]

It is true, as Stephen Darwall observes, that Hobbes makes similar points against scholastic views, and that the dancing example is to be found in his *Of Liberty and Necessity* [1646].[21] But the string of examples from Cudworth is remarkable. Even more

---

[20] It is important to keep in mind that Cudworth distinguishes "this *scholastic* philosophy" from Aristotle's own view.
[21] Darwall 1995, chap. 6, to which (together with chap. 5) I am much indebted throughout this section.

remarkable is the way in which Locke moves in the second edition's heavily revised and much expanded chapter on Power away from some of the Hobbesian views expressed in the first-edition chapter and toward something even closer to Cudworth's stoicized Aristotelianism than what we have already seen.

In the *first* edition [1690] Locke agreed with Hobbes in taking liberty to consist simply in the absence of obstacles to *acting* as one wills and not in any capacity to determine one's will in the first place; and he agreed with Hobbes in taking the will to be determined by "the appearance of Good, greater Good" [*An Essay Concerning Human Understanding* II. XXI. 33]. But Cudworth explicitly objected to the latter view on two grounds: first, an agent can sometimes fail to be moved by what appears to her to be the greater Good; second (and more importantly) this view leaves human beings (as Cudworth put it at the end of passage [E] above) "merely passive to the appearances of good, and to their own practical judgments." It is thus striking that Locke abandons this view in the second edition [1694] and puts in its place a view with clear affinities to Cudworth's own. As Locke explains,

[I]   It seems so establish'd and settled a maxim by the general consent of all Mankind, That good, the greater good, determines the will, that I do not at all wonder, that when I first publish'd my thoughts on this Subject, I took it for granted . . . But yet upon a stricter enquiry, I am forced to conclude that the *good*, the *greater good*, though apprehended and acknowledged to be so, does not determine the *will*, until our desire, raised proportionally to it, makes us *uneasy* in the want of it. [*An Essay Concerning Human Understanding* II. XXI. 35]

In speaking of our desire being "raised proportionally to" the greater good and making us "uneasy in the want of it," Locke appears to be speaking of the sort of explicitly Aristotelian mover of which Cudworth speaks in the chapter that follows passage [G]: that is, to what Cudworth describes as "a constant, *restless*, uninterrupted desire, or love of good as such, and happiness." The idea, I think, is of a kind of desire—or what Locke calls "uneasiness"—that helps to explain the ways in which an individual can fail to be satisfied with what merely appears at the moment to be her greater good and can thus be induced to suspend judgment and to examine the appearances in the ways recommended by Cudworth (who is of course following Epictetus and other Stoics). For Locke himself recommends something similar in the second-edition chapter on Power.

In the *second* edition Locke no longer regards liberty simply as the absence of obstacles to *acting* in accordance with what appears to the agent, at the time of action, as the greater good. He now regards liberty as the power to act or not "according as *the Mind* directs." For he now takes what determines the will in this or that particular direction to be *the Mind*, which he says (in a clearly Aristotelian vein) is "nothing but *the Agent it self* Exercising the power it has." [II. XXI. 29]. Locke summarizes his revised view as follows:

[J] *Liberty* is a power to act or not to act according as the Mind directs. A power to direct the operative faculties to motion or rest in particular instances, is that which we call the *Will*. That which in the train of our voluntary actions determines the *Will* to any change of operation, is some present uneasiness, which is, or at least is always accompanied with that of *Desire*. Desire is always moved by Evil, to fly from it: Because a total freedom from pain always makes a necessary part of our happiness: But every *Good*, nay every greater *Good* does not constantly move *Desire*, because it may not make, or may not be taken to make any necessary part of our Happiness. For all that we desire is only to be Happy. But though this general *Desire* of Happiness operates constantly and invariably yet the satisfaction of any particular *desire* can be suspended from determining the *will* to any subservient action, till we have maturely examin'd, whether the particular apparent good, which we then desire, makes a part of our real Happiness, or be consistent or inconsistent with it. The result of our judgment upon that Examination is what ultimately determines the Man, who could not be *free* if his *will* were determin'd by anything, but his own *desire* guided by his own Judgment. [*An Essay Concerning Human Understanding* II. XXI. 71]

Locke prefaces this summary by acknowledging the help of a "very judicious Friend" who prompted him to correct the errors in his first-edition account. It is often supposed that the friend in question was William Molyneaux, who had objected in a letter to Locke that Locke's first edition view seemed "to make all Sins to proceed from our Understandings, or to be against Conscience; and not at all from the Depravity of our Wills."[22] But, as Stephen Darwall has argued, it is difficult to see how Molyneaux's objection could have prompted the kind of changes actually made—changes that involved coming to treat the will as Cudworth treated it: that is, as a kind of self-conscious, self-directing power. It is thus worth considering the hypothesis of Cudworthian influence.

Locke was an intimate and lifelong friend of Cudworth's daughter, Damaris, herself a philosopher and correspondent of Leibniz. Locke in fact lived, starting about three years before the second edition of his *Essay* appeared until his death, in the home of Damaris and her husband, Sir Francis Masham. This was also at that time the home of the late Cudworth's library, including his unpublished manuscripts, to which Locke almost certainly had access. So it seems at least *possible* that the "judicious friend" whose influence Locke acknowledges in the revised chapter on Power was not, as often supposed, Molyneaux, but rather Damaris Cudworth, who may have been pressing Locke to answer her late father's objections. This seems in fact quite *plausible*, given that Locke did not elsewhere hesitate to mention Molyneaux by name, though he might well have thought it indiscreet to call public attention to his relation to Lady Masham (in whose arms some think Locke died).

---

[22] The letter, dated 22 December 1692, is printed in De Beer 1979, 600–601.

Let us turn then to the first of the two specific claims mentioned above. If the changes in the chapter on Power were in fact made partly in response to Cudworth, then there is reason to think that the chapter on personal identity was added partly in response to Cudworth. For Gideon Yaffe has argued quite effectively that the addition of the chapter on personal identity was related to the changes that Locke made in the chapter on Power. Yaffe's view is roughly that as Locke attempted to provide a more adequate account of the sort of volition required for free agency, he came to see that such volition could be ascribed only to a special sort of subject, a subject whose conditions for existence and persistence over time differ from those of a human animal as such.[23] On Yaffe's view, Locke came eventually to see that it is a necessary condition for the sort of volition associated with responsible agency that the subject of such volition *conceive* of the volition as being an exercise of one of its *own* capacities, as a result of which Locke came to see that only a subject with a *conception of itself and its own agentive capacities* is capable of the sort of volition associated with responsible agency. In other words, Locke came to see that only *persons* are capable of the sort of volition required for free agency and that a person is a *different kind of thing* both from the human animal whose body it (at least in this life) shares and from the sort of immaterial thinking substance with which Cartesians are supposed to identify it. As Locke himself explains,

> [K] ... we must consider what Person stands for; which, I think, is a thinking intelligent Being, that has reason and reflection, and can consider it self as it self, the same thinking thing in different times and places; which it does only by that consciousness, which is inseparable from thinking, and as it seems to me essential to it; It being impossible for anyone to perceive, without perceiving that he does perceive. When we see, hear, smell, taste, feel, meditate, or will anything, we know that we do so. Thus it is always as

---

[23] See Yaffe 2000, 120 (my bold):

> Locke tells us far less about the nature of "consciousness" than we would like. But this much is clear: For Locke, two person-stages are stages of the same person just in case the later of them is or can become "conscious" of the experiences of the earlier. **Further, to be "conscious" of a past action is to conceive of it as performed by oneself.** And, if I am right, for an appropriate mental act to be a volition, a choice, the agent must conceive of it as an exertion of one of her powers; she must conceive of it as arising in part from herself. It seems quite likely that the kind of awareness that an agent must have of a choice for it to count as a choice is very closely related to the kind of attitude that an agent must have toward a past action for it to have been performed by her. The capacities that are central to being a person are inextricably involved in the constitution of choice.

It is worth noting here that the view that Yaffe attributes to Locke is a version of the sort of neo-Lockean dualism that Sydney Shoemaker defends against the "Animalism" of Eric Olson 1999. For Shoemaker 1999 argues explicitly that there are internal relations between, on the one hand, different kinds of properties and activities and, on the other hand, the kinds of subjects to which different kinds of properties and activities can be ascribed, internal relations such that some of the properties and activities associated with personhood *cannot* be ascribed to human animals simply as such but *must* be ascribed to what Locke calls 'persons.'

to our present Sensations and Perceptions: And by this every one is to himself, that which he calls *self:* It not being considered in this case, whether the same *self* be continued in the same or diverse Substances. For since consciousness always accompanies thinking, and 'tis that, that makes every one to be, what he calls *self;* and thereby distinguishes himself from all other thinking beings, in this alone consists *Personal Identity,* i.e., the sameness of a rational Being; And as far as this consciousness can be extended backwards to any past Action or Thought, so far reaches the Identity of that *Person;* it is the same *self* now it was then; and 'tis by the same *self* with this present one that now reflects on it, that the Action was done. [*An Essay Concerning Human Understanding* II. XXVII. 9]

The fact that Locke distinguishes a person from the human animal with which it typically coincides, especially when taken together with the first-person orientation of his account of personal identity, can seem to leave a gulf between Lockean persons and Aristotelian human beings. But the gulf can perhaps be bridged, or at least narrowed, if we keep in mind the way in which Aristotle himself identifies a human being with the leading part of her soul, that is, with the part that *prohairesthai* and so has an irreducibly first-person point of view.[24]

4. PROHAIRESIS AND PRACTICAL KNOWLEDGE: A RATIONAL AGENT'S FUNDAMENTALLY ANIMAL BUT NEVERTHELESS SOPHISTICATED FORM OF NON-OBSERVATIONAL AWARENESS OF WHAT IT IS *DOING*

It is worth pausing here to note that Gill explicitly opposes taking Aristotle's conception of *prohairesis* to involve anything like what was later called the 'will,' which Gill associates with "conscious acts ... of a unitary 'I.'"[25] As Gill says,

> Although Aristotle takes the ability to make such choices [viz., *prohaireseis*] as the mark of developed human rationality, the form of explanation for action

---

[24] We should not be too troubled here by the fact that Locke thinks it possible that the first-person point of view with which I am identified should at some point part company with the human animal with which it so far coincides. For Aristotle himself does not rule out the possibility that my *nous* should some day part company with the body with which it so far coincides. So he too declines (in spite of his hylomorphism) to rule out the possibility that the locus of my responsible agency might in some circumstances come apart from the animal body to which it seems so closely wedded. What is not clear is whether Aristotle can (given his hylomorphism) allow that the locus of my responsible agency could continue as such (i.e., as a locus of responsible agency); for it is not clear that his hylomorphism leaves room for the *reincarnation* (so to speak) of *nous*, as distinct from its mere *disembodiment*. But even so, Locke and Aristotle seem to me to share a kind of *cautious* empiricism that renders each less dismissive than many empiricists are of the very *possibility* of realities neither readily accessible to experience nor readily falsifiable by it.

[25] Gill 1986, 44. The passage I go on to quote is from Gill 1986, 55–56.

provided is essentially the same as for simple human (and animal) responses. The action is explained by a more complex version of the belief-and-desire (or thought-and-desire) pattern displayed in the practical syllogism of Chapter 7 of *De Motu Animalium*. The resulting 'deliberate desire' (which is what 'choice' is) explains the action without any need to posit a further exercise of will by the agent.

The point of denying the need for a *further* exercise of will is unclear, given that Gill seems to deny the presence of *any* exercise of will. And the general denial is question-begging if *prohairesis just is* an exercise of the agent's will. But Gill resists understanding *prohairesis* in this way and cites in support of his resistance Elizabeth Anscombe's account of the practical syllogism as referring not to "actual mental processes" but rather to "an order which is there" in the behavior of any animal whose behavior can be explained and predicted by attributing beliefs (and desires) to it.[26]

Gill associates Anscombe's talk of "an order which is there" with the sort of interpretivism he finds in Davidson and Dennett, whose views he has in mind when he speaks (in the passage quoted at the outset) of the "third-personal perspective of science" that he sees not only in contemporary philosophy of mind but also in Aristotle's psychology.[27] Gill's idea seems to be that this perspective need *never* assume that the *subject* whose behavior is to be explained *herself* experiences or engages in any *actual* (by which Gill seems to mean *conscious*) mental processes of believing, desiring or deciding. So even when Gill insists (ostensibly against Anscombe) that human animals differ from other animals insofar as they are at least sometimes subject to such actual (or conscious) mental processes, he seems to treat this difference as relatively superficial. He speaks as if a human animal's *consciously* believing and desiring the things it believes and desires makes no real difference to what the animal actually *does* but simply allows it to *say* what it is doing and so perhaps to *understand* what it is doing in some way that a non-rational animal does not. But this is to treat the subject's knowledge of the beliefs and desires that are supposed to explain its actions as merely *theoretical* or *contemplative*: it is to speak as if what distinguishes human from other animals is primarily the fact that human animals merely happen to be aware "from the inside" of beliefs and desires that would be there *anyway*—and be what they are, explaining what they explain *anyway*—independently of the subject's having conscious access to them.

But this is precisely the sort of picture to which Anscombe herself objects when she complains about what she sees as the "incorrigibly contemplative conception of knowledge" characteristic of modern (by which she seems to mean Cartesian and post-Cartesian) philosophy and seeks to resurrect (alongside of the contemplative conception) a practical conception that she finds among ancient and medieval philosophers, including of course Aristotle.[28] Practical knowledge is, as she says, following Aquinas,

---

[26] Gill 2006, 42; Gill 1996, 44.
[27] See the essays in Davidson 1985 and Dennett 1987.
[28] Anscombe 1957, sec. 32.

"the cause of what it understands." It is a species of the sort of non-observational knowledge that vital subjects (that is perceiving-cum-desiring subjects) have, including the sort of non-observational knowledge such subjects typically have of the position of their bodily limbs.

Anscombe claims that we are entitled to speak here of knowledge insofar as non-observational deliverances as to the positions of our limbs can sometimes be mistaken and thus corrigible by appeal to observation, from which, however, it does *not* follow that we cannot *usually* tell, without looking, where our limbs are. And Anscombe would, I think, claim similarly that although the sort of observation of my own behavior that I might undertake with the help of my analyst can sometimes lead me to correct my conscious beliefs about what I am *really* aiming to do—when, for example, I tell myself that that I am doing research for my novel when what I am *really* doing is flirting night after night with my local bartender—it does *not* follow that I cannot *for the most part* tell, without engaging in such observation, what I am up to. For without the sort of non-observational knowledge of which Anscombe speaks, I would not be a genuine agent: I would not be capable of acting intentionally at all.[29]

Of course non-observational knowledge of the position of one's limbs is not always practical: I can know non-observationally where my limbs are even when someone else—for example, my doctor—is moving them about. But the relevance of this sort of non-observational awareness to our fundamentally animal capacities for action should be clear: without such awareness, we could not easily scratch where we itch, let alone do more complicated things like driving a car (which requires, for example, non-observational awareness of what our feet are doing). This sort of non-observational awareness goes hand in hand with the sort of non-observational awareness that we (like other animals) have of what we are doing when, for example, we move toward and reach for objects that appear to us pleasant or in some other way good; or move away from and repel objects that appear to us painful or in some other way bad. A non-rational animal's awareness of what it is doing when, for example, it moves toward the source of heat may be non-linguistic; but as long as the animal is responsive to changes in the location of the heat and is able to move its limbs in ways that allow it to engage in at least some tracking of the source of heat, there *is* an "order which is there" in its motivational structure, an order that makes it appropriate not only to speak of what the animal is doing as "seeking warmth," but also to speak of the animal as having some sort of non-observational awareness of what it is doing. And the same goes when the animal is doing something more complicated. If a squirrel is putting acorns in a secure place but the acorns keep disappearing, it will no doubt start putting its acorns somewhere else. For it is not simply putting the acorns wherever it is they are actually being put; it is storing them for winter.

---

[29] I am indebted here specifically to Moran 2004 and more generally to Moran 2001 and to conversations with the author over the years.

The point here is that the forms of non-observational knowledge of what one is doing that are available to a subject increase as the subject's practical and conceptual repertoires increase. And from the fact that non-rational animals have forms of non-observational awareness of what they are doing that does not involve anything irreducibly first-personal, it does *not* follow that *we* have no irreducibly first-personal forms of non-observational awareness of what *we* are doing. So even if Aristotle does seek to ground distinctively human capacities in capacities that we share with other animals—like, for example, the capacity for non-observational awareness of what one is doing—it does not follow that he recognizes no irreducibly first-personal forms of these capacities.

Consider the following example: I can know without observation that I am saving to buy a car rather than to pay for emergency medical care, even where paying for emergency medical care is what I end up *actually* doing with the money. In such a case we would not say that I had not really been saving to buy a car. Nor would we say—except as a kind of philosophical joke—that my seeming to myself that I was saving to buy a car was corrigible by appeal to observation in the sense that observation could ever reveal that what I had really been doing all along was saving for emergency medical care. And this is largely because when I am acting intentionally what I *take* myself to be doing is generally speaking partly constitutive of what I am *in fact* doing: this is what it means for me to be an *agent*—that is, a source of the sort of *praxis* of which (according to Aristotle) only mature rational agents are capable. It is also what it means for my knowledge of what I am doing to be "the cause of what it understands."

Practical knowledge is thus tied closely to an agent's capacity for *prohairesis*. For a *prohairesis* is the cause of what it understands in the sense that a *prohairesis* is the cause of the sort of *praxis* to whose intelligibility this *prohairesis* itself contains the key. *Prohairesis* thus yields a kind of knowledge of an action that only its *agent* can have—a kind of knowledge the agent has in virtue of the fact that she is the one whose conception of what she is doing *determines* (at least in cases where things go as they are supposed to go) *what* is being done. But this still leaves room for error: agents do not always succeed in doing what they are seeking to do and they may sometimes fail even to be clear about what it is they are seeking to do.

Third persons must observe my behavior and form hypotheses about what I am doing. Or they must *ask* me what I am doing, which works when it does only on the assumption that I myself tend *for the most part* to know, without observation, what I am doing. But from the fact that I *do* for the most part know without observation what I am doing, it does *not* follow that I am *always in fact* doing whatever I non-observationally take myself to be doing. I can sometimes observe patterns in my own behavior that are best explained by supposing that what I take myself to be doing is somehow deceptive—as in the example where I take myself to be doing research for my novel by spending every night in my local bar, flirting with the bartender while observing and eavesdropping on the patrons, the likes of whom figure prominently in my purported book. But the very possibility of such self-deception presupposes an irreducibly first-personal point of view: I must have the sort of conception of myself as temporally extended that is required of any subject who even purports to be writing a book, and I must in order to have such a conception have *for the most part* a kind of non-observational knowledge of what—at least at some fundamental level—I am up to: otherwise, I could not even make it, night after night, to the bar and home again (or wherever). So even the sort of corrigibility from the third-person point of view that Gill associates with contemporary philosophy of mind assumes an irreducibly first-person point of view involving at least *modest* forms of epistemic privilege.[30]

More importantly, even if an agent can *sometimes* act, and act rationally, without consciously applying to herself the descriptions under which she has reasons for acting in the way she does, it does *not* follow—nor does Anscombe herself think it follows—that we need *never* suppose, in explaining the behavior of a rational agent, that she consciously applies the relevant descriptions to herself. Aristotle himself recognizes that although agents must apply the relevant descriptions to themselves, they need not *always* do so consciously [*De Motu Animalium* 7]. And he is surely thinking here only of cases in which the application is obvious, as in his example "I am human."[31] For without the ability to reflect on the situations in which she finds herself, and on the opportunities afforded and demands posed to herself by these situations, an agent could not engage in the sort of deliberation called for in new and unusual (especially ethically problematic) situations. Nor could she achieve the sort of *prohairesis* that results from deliberation about what is *really* good, as distinct from what is *merely apparently* good (or even from what is merely the best one can achieve in bad circumstances). Such deliberation presupposes that the deliberator has some conception of herself as temporally extended: she must have some sense, presumably based on experience, of her own capacities, and she will ordinarily (that is, in circumstances that are not obviously fatal) have some sense of herself as likely to persist in the future and so as at least potentially subject to the future consequences of her present actions. This is no doubt facilitated by the kind of memory that Aristotle treats as distinctively human—the kind of memory treated in passage [B] as involving awareness not only *of oneself*, but of oneself *as remembering*.

Since animal action presumably involves some sort of indexical referencing facilitated by a kind of memory—as, for example, when an animal has a sense of *cold wet here, dry warm back there*—it may in fact be the lack of an explicit conception of *themselves* as existing in the future that helps to explain why Aristotle denies the capacity of deliberation even to those non-rational animals that (as he says) "evidently have a capacity of foresight concerning their own lives" [*hosa peri ton hautôn bion echonta phainetai dunamin pronoêtikên*] and are thus called *phronima* [*EN* 1141a26–28]. Aristotle may think that such animals have only an inarticulate sense of *their lives* as persisting into the relatively immediate future and not the sort of conception of *themselves* as temporally extended that is required for deliberation. This presumably differs from

---

[30] Here again I am indebted to Moran, especially Moran 1994.
[31] For more on this point, see M. Pickavé and J. Whiting, "*Nicomachean Ethics* VII.3 on Acratic Ignorance," *Oxford Studies in Ancient Philosophy* 34 (2008): 323–71 [chap. 7, this volume].

the sort of foresight that allows a squirrel, for example, to store nuts in anticipation of the winter cycle of *its life*. But however exactly he explains the distinction, Aristotle is clearly committed to the existence of a distinction between explanations of animal behavior that appeal simply to foresight and explanations that appeal to genuine deliberation. And he thinks (as we have seen) that in order to account for this distinction we must posit the existence of at least some irreducibly first-personal states or activities, including the sort of conception of herself that an agent must have if she is to be aware of herself as engaged in the sort of remembering that Aristotle takes to be required for deliberation.

5. CUDWORTH'S NON-CARTESIAN CONCEPTION OF CONSCIOUSNESS: ITS STOIC (AND ULTIMATELY ARISTOTELIAN) ROOTS

We are now in a position to see how Cudworth's conception of consciousness, which may well have influenced Locke's, is less Cartesian and more Aristotelian than often supposed. It will help if we start with a curious feature in Aristotle's account of voluntary action (of which actions that are *prohaireta* form a *species*). Aristotle says that an action is voluntary [*hekousion*] if and only if (1) its origin is in the agent (in, for example, some desire of hers) *and* (2) the agent acts knowing the relevant particulars [*EN* 1111a22–24]. These include "*who* <is acting>, *what* <she is doing>, in-*relation*-to-what or *in*-what . . ." [1111a3–5]. Aristotle goes on to say that "no one could fail to recognize *all* these things unless he were mad, nor plainly <could one fail to recognize> *who* is acting; for how at any rate <could one fail to recognize> *oneself* <acting>?" Aristotle goes on to illustrate ways in which one *could* fail to recognize *other* things, and then concludes by saying that "the most crucial [*kuriôtata*] things seem to be the *in what* and the *for the sake of what*" [*EN* III.1, especially 1110b31–1111a19].

I want to call attention here to three things. First, to the association between failing to recognize such things and *madness*, which places the agent, at least temporarily, outside the sphere of praise and blame (which is Aristotle's focus here).[32] Second, and more importantly, to Aristotle's use of the reflexive pronoun '*heauton*' in expressing the extreme difficulty, perhaps even impossibility, of failing to recognize that it is *oneself* acting. This signals a potential locus of something irreducibly first-personal. For I do not think, as someone once suggested to me, that Aristotle is speaking here of a case in which someone acts without knowing *who he is* in the sense in which Oedipus might be said to have acted without knowing who *he* was: Oedipus certainly knew it was he *himself* acting, even if he did not know various descriptions that applied to him, such as "son of the man I am striking" or "son of the woman I am marrying." Someone could fail to know these sorts of things without qualifying as mad. But when—as, for example, in cases of extreme dissociation—someone fails to experience actions performed by her as her *own*, then we are sure to speak of her as mad.

---

[32] This is also the focus of Locke's discussion of personal identity (on which more below).

Third, and most importantly for present purposes, note the curious suggestion that the agent might fail to recognize that *for the sake of which* she acts. For as we today might ask, especially in light of the conception of practical knowledge that Anscombe ascribes to Aristotle, isn't the *agent* the one whose conception of what she is doing in some sense *determines* the end for the sake of which she is said to act? How, if at all, could *she* fail to know *that*? Here again I think Aristotle takes it for granted that agents generally *do* know the ends for the sake of which they are acting, since they would not otherwise be agents in the relevant sense: they would not be performing voluntary actions (let alone the sort of *praxeis* that Aristotle associates with *prohairesis*). This is what makes it so curious that Aristotle bothers to make this point in the first place.

But the point makes perfect sense in a context where there are agents (in some sense) that do *not* recognize the ends of the sake of which they act. And Aristotle's natural teleology provides precisely this sort of context—one where parts of nature in some sense act without knowing the ends for the sake of which they act, as, for example, when an acorn grows into an oak or an embryo develops into an animal. This is clear from Cudworth's own (but ultimately Aristotelian) defense of natural teleology—including what Cudworth calls 'plastic nature'—against Cartesian mechanism in *The True Intellectual System of the Universe* Book I, chap. III:

[L] 14. Moreover, that something may act artificially and for ends, without comprehending the reason of what it doth, may be further evinced from those natural instincts that are in animals, which without knowledge direct them to act regularly, in order both to their own good, and the good of the universe. As for example: the bees in mellification, and in framing their combs and hexagonal cells, the spiders in spinning their webs, the birds in building their nests, and many other animals in such like actions of their's, which would seem to argue a great sagacity here, whereas, notwithstanding, **as Aristotle observes . . . they do these things, neither by art, nor by counsel, nor by any deliberation of their own; and therefore are not masters of that wisdom, according to which they act, but only passive to the instincts and impresses thereof . . .**

15. There is, in the next place, another imperfection to be observed in the **plastic nature**, that as it **doth not comprehend the reason of its own action, so neither is it clearly and expressly conscious of what it doth**; in which respect, it doth not only fall short of human art, but even of that very manner of acting, which is in brutes themselves, who, though they do not understand the reason of those actions, that their natural instincts lead them to, yet they are generally conceived to be conscious of them, and to do them by fancy; whereas, **the plastic nature in the formation of plants and animals seems to have no animal fancy, no express *sunaisthêsis*, con-sense, or consciousness of what it doth.** Thus the often commended philosopher: *Nature hath not so much as any fancy [phantasia] in it; as intellection and knowledge*

[*noêsis*] *is a superior thing to fancy, so fancy is superior to the impress of nature, for nature hath no apprehension* [*antilêpsis*] *nor conscious perception* [*sunesis*] *of any thing.*[33] **In a word, nature is a thing, that hath no such self-*perception* or self-*enjoyment* in it, as animals have.**

16. Now we are well aware, that this is a thing, which the narrow principles of some late philosophers [viz., Cartesian philosophers] will not admit of, that there should be any action distinct from local motion besides expressly conscious cogitation. For they making the first general heads of all entity to be extension and cogitation, or extended being and cogitative; and then supposing, that the essence of cogitation consists in express consciousness, must needs by this exclude such a plastic life of nature, as we speak of, that is supposed to act without animal fancy or express consciousness. Wherefore, we conceive, that the first heads of being ought to be expressed thus: [1] resisting or antitypous extension, and [2] life (i.e., internal energy and self-activity;) and then again, that **life or internal self-activity is to be divided into such as [2a] either acts with express consciousness and *synaesthesis*, or such as [2b] is without it;** the latter of which is the plastic life of nature; so that there may be an action distinct from local motion, or a vital energy, which is not accompanied by that fancy, or consciousness, that is in the energies of animal life; that is, there may be **a simple internal energy, or vital autokinesy, which is without that duplication, that is included in the nature of *sunaisthêsis*, con-sense, and consciousness**—which makes a being to be present to itself, attentive to its own actions, or animadversive of them, to perceive itself to do or suffer, and to have a fruition or enjoyment of itself... [my italics and bold]

The anti-Cartesian thrust of this should be clear, if only from Cudworth's talk of animal fancy and the sort of self-perception and self-enjoyment afforded by it—something that distinguishes animal action from the operations of plastic nature in (for example) the formation of animals and other living organisms.

In general, Cudworth rejects purely mechanistic explanations of non-cogitative nature and seeks to give an account of responsible agency that does *not* depend (as he thinks Descartes' account depends) on a sharp distinction between human and other animals. And Cudworth borrows heavily in doing so from Stoic and Aristotelian sources. Like

---

[33] Here Cudworth quotes (in translation) from Plotinus, *Ennead* IV.4.13. But Cudworth's emphasis in the very next sentence (and elsewhere) on the sort of *self-perception* and *self-enjoyment* that he associates with "animal fancy" points to the connection between his conception of *sunaisthêsis* and the Stoic conception of *oikeiôsis* (on which more below, where I argue that to the extent that Locke's emphasis on just such perception and enjoyment places his conception of consciousness closer to Cudworth's conception than to Descartes', Locke's conception of consciousness is at least as closely related to the Stoic conception of *oikeiôsis* as to anything that might more easily than the Stoic conception pass as an anticipation of Descartes' conception of consciousness).

Aristotle and the Stoics, Cudworth distinguishes cases in which parts of nature (such as plants) act for the sake of something *without recognizing* that this is what they are doing from cases in which parts of nature (such as ourselves) act for the sake of something *while recognizing* that this is what they are doing. This *recognizing what one is doing*, which is arguably the sort of non-observational knowledge of which Anscombe speaks, is what Cudworth calls "*sunaisthêsis*, con-sense, or consciousness."

Here, however, we should not allow the fact that Cudworth quotes Plotinus ("the often commended philosopher") to obscure the ways in which Cudworth's conception of consciousness derives largely from the conception of *sunaisthêsis* found in the Stoic doctrine of *oikeiôsis* (from which the eclectic Plotinus himself drew). This is the doctrine according to which all animals have, from birth, a kind of perception or awareness of themselves and a corresponding sense of what is *oikeion* (that is, proper or appropriate) to them, where this is largely a matter of what is required for their self-preservation. The Stoics take animals to aim primarily at self-preservation and not—as Epicureans claim—primarily at pleasure. And an animal aims at its self-preservation by aiming at things that are *oikeion* for it, given the kind of thing it is. The pursuit and especially the achievement of what is *oikeion* for an animal tend of course to produce pleasure in the animal, but this (as Aristotle suggests in *EN* X.4) is something that supervenes on their activity and not the primary goal of it.

That Cudworth is drawing on something that predates Plotinus should be clear from the following passage from the Stoic Hierocles, who flourished around 100 C.E. (well over a hundred years before Plotinus, who is said by Porphyry to have started writing in 253–254 C.E.).

> [M] ... as soon as an animal is born it perceives itself [*aisthanetai heatou*]. The first thing that animals perceive is their own parts ... both that they have them and for what purpose they have them, and we ourselves perceive our eyes and our ears and the rest. So whenever we want to see something we strain our eyes, but not our ears, towards the visible object ... Therefore, the first proof of every animal's perceiving itself is its consciousness [*sunaisthêsis*] of the parts and the functions for which they were given. The second proof is that animals are not unaware [*oude ... anaisthêtôs diakeitai*] of their equipment for self-defence. When bulls do battle with other bulls or animals of different species, they stick out their horns... Every other creature has the same disposition relative to its appropriate [*oikeion*] and, so to speak, congenital weapons.[34] [Hierocles I.51–57; 2.1–9; translation from Long and Sedley]

Sunaisthêsis is closely associated here (as elsewhere) with *aisthêsis*. And here at least the idea of the prefix 'sun-' seems to be that one thing is perceived *together with*

---

[34] For further discussion of the Hierocles, see Inwood 1984 and Long 1993. It should be clear from what follows that I see more signs in Plato and Aristotle than Long sees there of the sort of concept of self-perception that Long says the Stoics invented.

another: animals either perceive themselves and together with themselves their bodily parts and the functions for which these parts are given, or (perhaps) perceive their bodily parts and together with these parts the functions for which they were given. Other passages suggest that what is involved here is a kind of *comprehending* perception. The animal does not simply perceive its parts in the way one might perceive an unidentified flying object; in perceiving its parts it also *recognizes* them *as what they are*: it recognizes them, for example, *as weapons* or *as organs of perception*.[35] And the evidence that animals do so consists largely in their knowing how to make *appropriate* (that is, *oikeion*) use of these parts.

We get a fuller account of the Stoic doctrine in Diogenes Laertius' *Lives of the Philosophers* 7.85–86, which makes it clear that the Stoic doctrine was aimed primarily against Epicurean hedonists (in much the same way, I might add, that Cudworth's arguments were aimed against latter-day Epicureans like Thomas Hobbes):

> [N] (1) They [the Stoics] say that an animal has self-preservation as the object of its first impulse, since nature from the beginning appropriates it [*oikeiouseôs auto tês phuseôs ap' archês*] . . . (2) The first thing appropriate [*prôton oikeion*] for every animal, he says, is its own constitution and consciousness of this [*tên hautou sustasin kai tên tautês suneidêsin*].[36] For

---

[35] That the idea here is of a kind of *comprehending perception* receives support from the one passage where Aristotle uses the verb '*sunaisthanesthai*' in discussing something other than friendship, where he tends to use this verb to indicate some sort of perceiving *together with* one's friend. The anomalous passage is at *History of Animals* 534b15–21, where (in arguing that insects have all the senses) Aristotle says that insects "*sunaisthanetai* from a distance, as, for example, bees and cnipes <*sunaisthanetai*> honey <from a distance>" and then explains that "they recognize [*gignôskonta*] <the honey> by smell." The idea may be that these insects *aisthanetai* the smell, and *together* with this *sunaisthanetai* the honey as such. And Themistius (discussed briefly below) may even be channeling this example when in discussing Aristotle's common sense, he uses the example of someone seeing a yellow fluid and claiming that it is honey before having any perception of its sweetness [*In Aristotelis libros de anima paraphrasis* 81, 36–38].

If the comprehending perception account is on the right track, then it may be possible to read Aristotle's uses of '*sunaisthanesthai*' in the friendship passages in much the same way—that is, as pointing to the kind of *comprehending* perception of the experiences and activities of one's friend that is supposed to involve familiarity in something like the way recognizing honey from a distance does. The idea would then be that character-friends, in virtue of the similarity in character to one another, and perhaps also of their having perception of one another's *prohaireseis* [*EE* 1236b6], can achieve a kind of *comprehending* perception of one another's experiences and activities that is very much like the sort of (for the most part comprehending) perception each of them has of her *own* experiences and activities. And insofar as Aristotle seems to think it necessary to argue for comprehending perception of one's *friend's* experiences and activities in a way he does not seem to think it necessary to argue for comprehending perception of one's *own* experiences and activities, his discussions may presuppose a kind of first-person epistemic privilege. I discuss these issues in Whiting 2013 [II.7].

[36] Pohlenz 1940 proposed reading '*sunaisthêsin*' instead of '*suneidêsin*' here. But there is no manuscript support for this and the idea seems to be much the same whichever we read. For '*suneidêsin*', which Cicero (perhaps coining the Latin) rendered '*conscientia*,' need not be taken as morally charged in the way 'conscience' is in modern English; and '*suneidenai*' can be used in a relatively topic-neutral way, as when Socrates asks (in Plato's *Apology*) what the Oracle can mean in calling him wisest, when he is *not conscious to himself* of his being wise in anything either great or small [*egô gar dê oute mega oute smikron xunoida emautô(i) sophos ôn* (*Apology* 21b)]. This, I think, helps to explain Descartes' relatively

nature was not likely either to alienate the animal itself, or to make it and then neither alienate it or appropriate it. So it remains to say that in constituting the animal, nature appropriated it to itself. This is why the animal rejects what is harmful and accepts what is appropriate. (3) They [the Stoics] hold it false to say, as some people do, that pleasure is the object of animals' first impulse. For pleasure, they say, if it does occur, is a by-product which arises only when nature all by itself has searched out and adopted the proper requirements for a creature's constitution, just as animals [then] frolic and plants bloom. (4) Nature, they say, is no different in regard to plants and animals at the time when it directs animals as well as plants without impulse and sensation [*chôris hormês kai aisthêseôs*] and in us certain processes of a vegetative kind take place. But since animals have the additional faculty of impulse, through the use of which they go in search of what is appropriate to them, what is natural for them is to be administered in accordance with their impulse. (5) And since reason, by way of a more perfect management, has been bestowed on rational beings, to live correctly in accordance with reason comes to be natural for them; for reason supervenes as the craftsman of impulse. [*Lives of the Philosophers* 7.85–86, translation by Long and Sedley 1987]

Although the full-fledged doctrine of *oikeiôsis* seems to be Stoic, there are signs of it not only in Plato's *Republic* (on which more below) but also in Aristotle, at least in his discussions of friendship. Some early commentators even saw signs of the *oikeiôsis* doctrine in Aristotle's psychological works, but they may to some extent have been reading Aristotle through Stoic lenses.

Consider, for example, the following passage from Themistius' commentary on Aristotle's *De Anima*. Themistius seeks to elucidate the *De Anima's* account of animal motion and says repeatedly (1) that *aisthêsis* judges what is *oikeion* to a subject and what is *allotrion* to it; (2) that pleasure follows what is *oikeion* and pain follows what is *allotrion*; and (3) that desire and aversion follow pleasure and pain. And Themistius combines the talk of what is *oikeion* with talk of *sunaisthanesthai* in the following lines:

[O]   When they [zoophytes] touch dry, wet, hot, or cold objects, and not just as objects of touch but **sunaisthanomena** them as objects of taste too, they admit the ones that are *oikeia* and reject those that are *allotria*, so that they

---

topic-neutral use of 'conscientia' to refer to something like awareness of our own thoughts and perceptions. But I cannot enter into a proper discussion of these matters here. The point here is simply that the topic-neutral use of 'conscientia' is of ancient pedigree, so we should not be too quick to read 'conscientia' as strongly morally charged. Neither, however, should we be too quick to read the English 'consciousness' as merely a matter of awareness of (so to speak) the passing show. For (as I argue below) Locke's emphasis is firmly on the sort of consciousness and sameness of consciousness involved in *responsible agency*: and this sort of consciousness is at points close to (perhaps intertwined with) what we now (like Locke and his contemporaries) call "conscience." For further discussion of these issues, see Jung 1933; Gauthier and Jolif 1970, vol. 2, on the discussion of *sunesis* in *EN* VII.11; and Hennig 2004.

desire the former and avoid the latter, as far as possible, as is evident in the case of all testacea. [*In libros Aristotelis de anima paraphrasis* 47a23–25, translation from Todd 1987, slightly modified; **my bold**].

The idea here is that even very simple animals have a kind of awareness, not simply of proper sensibles like the hot, the cold, the wet, and the dry, but also of what is *oikeion* and what is *allotrion* to them. This seems to be the force of the 'sun-' in '*sunaisthanesthai*' as it is used here: these animals perceive [*aisthanesthai*] the hot, cold, wet, and dry, and they *co*-perceive [*sun-aisthanesthai*] (along with the hot, cold, wet, and dry) what is *oikeion* and what is *allotrion* to them.

The overall idea is that an animal tends (at least for the most part) to perceive things that are in fact *oikeion* to it as in some way pleasant and so to be pursued, while perceiving things that are in fact *allotrion* to it as in some way painful and so to be avoided, as a result of which it tends (at least for the most part) to pursue what is in fact *oikeion* to it and to avoid what is *allotrion* to it. But a non-rational animal does not realize that this—namely, pursuing the *oikeion* and avoiding the *allotrion*—is what it is doing, let alone the *reason for* its doing that. It simply has the sort of non-observational knowledge of what it is doing that allows it (at least for the most part) to move toward what is warm (or to take in more water) when *that* is what is *in fact oikeion* to it. In other words, a non-rational animal has no idea *why* it is moving toward what is warm (or taking in more water). So it cannot suspend its pursuit of these things in order to ask whether or not it *should* be pursuing them: it is, so to speak, dragged about by appearances (presumably the appearances of things that are in fact good for them *as pleasant*).

Rational animals, on the other hand, are able not just to do more complicated things but also to realize when they are doing these things both *what* they are doing and *why* they are doing them. They are thus able to realize *what* they are doing in a far richer sense than that in which a non-rational animal can realize what it is doing, a sense relevant to their capacity for responsible agency. For it is this richer sort of realization that enables a rational animal to ask of any apparent good whether it is *really* good and so *really* to be pursued. It is, in other words, what enables a rational animal (as Locke put it back in [J]) to "[suspend] the satisfaction of any particular desire . . . from determining the *will* to any subservient action, till [it has] maturely examin'd, whether the particular apparent good, which [it] then desire[s], makes a part of [its] real Happiness, or be consistent or inconsistent with it."

This is very close to the sort of stoicized Aristotelianism found in the work of Ralph Cudworth and perhaps also urged on Locke by Cudworth's daughter, Damaris. But as I said at the outset, the hypothesis of Cudworth's influence on Locke is not strictly necessary for my overall argument. For there are reasons independent of Locke's relationship to Cudworth for situating Locke in the largely Stoic (but not therefore non-Aristotelian) *oikeiôsis* tradition.[37] Let us turn then to these.

---

[37] For important work on this tradition, see Striker 1983 and 1991.

6. *SUNAISTHÊSIS* AND *OIKEIÔSIS*: FROM PLATO TO LOCKE

The seeds of the *oikeiôsis* tradition can be found in Plato's *Republic*, especially in the passage where Socrates argues for practices that will *unify* his ideal city, including both the abolition of private property and the community of women and children within the Guardian class, where no one is supposed to know who his or her biological parents or children are. His idea is that each member of the guardian class will regard everyone of the relevant age as his or her *own* mother or father, or his or her *own* son or daughter, or his or her *own* brother or sister. So *each* will regard every other member as *oikeion* to her in much the same way that Hierocles later argued each human being could come through similar practices (such as calling cousins "brothers" and aunts and uncles "mothers and fathers") to reduce her affective distance to every other.[38] On Socrates' view, the relevant practices are supposed to bring it about that each guardian feels pleasure when another feels pleasure and pain when another feels pain. And the abolition of private property has the same goal: that each member come to regard the common property as *oikeion* to her, so that all feel pleasure and pain together, according to the fortunes or misfortunes of their common property. The passage, with Socrates speaking and Glaucon replying, runs as follows:

> [P] Is there any greater evil we can mention for a city than that which tears it apart and makes it many instead of one? Or any greater good than that which binds it together and makes it one?
> —There isn't.
>
> And when, as far as possible, all the citizens rejoice and are pained by the same successes and failures, doesn't this *sharing of pleasures and pains bind the city together*?
> —It most certainly does.
>
> But when some suffer greatly, while others rejoice greatly, at the same things happening to the city or its people, doesn't this privatization [*idiôsis*] of pleasures and pains dissolve the city?
> —Of course.
>
> And isn't that what happens whenever such words as "mine" and "not mine" are used in unison? And similarly with "someone else's"?
> —Precisely.
>
> Then, is the best governed city the one in which most people say "mine" and "not mine" about the same things in the same way?
> —It is indeed.

---

[38] For this doctrine of Hierocles, see Stobaeus 4.671,7–673,11 (in Long and Sedley 1987).

> What about the city that is most like a single person? For example, when one of us hurts his finger, the entire association that organizes body and soul together into a single system under the ruling part within it [*pasa hê koinônia hê kata to soma pros tên psuchên tetamenê eis mian suntaxin tên tou archontos en autê(i)*] both perceives [*ê(i)stheto*] and feels (as a whole) pain together with [*hama sunêlgêsen*] the part that suffers. That's why we say that the *man* [*ho anthrôpos*] has a pain in his finger. And the same can be said about any part of a man, with regard either to the pain it suffers or the pleasure it experiences when it finds relief.
>
> —Certainly. And, as for your question, the city with the best government *is* most like such a person.
>
> Then, whenever anything good or bad happens to a single one of its citizens, such a city above all others will say that the affected part is its own [*heautês*] and will as a whole sense together and feel pain together <with the affected part> [*kai ê **sunêsthêsetai** hapasa ê sullupêsetai*]. [*Republic* 462a8–e1, Grube-Reeve translation, slightly modified]

There are many things to note here, starting with the talk in the final lines of the whole sensing or perceiving together with the affected part. Note especially the *objects* of this co-perception—namely, pleasure and pain, which are in this tradition the most fundamental forms of *aisthêsis*, the forms to which *all* animals are subject. Note also the way in which perception of a pleasure or pain in some sense binds the subject of the *perception* to the subject of the *original pleasure or pain*: that is, the way in which the relevant sort of perceiving of a pleasure or pain in some sense *makes* that pleasure or pain one's *own*. Note finally the talk of the system (or *suntaxis*, corresponding to Diogenes' *sustasis*) and of the ruling part of this system (*to archon*, which corresponds to the Stoics' *hêgemonikon*). There is no explicit reference here to what is *oikeion* to the subjects, but there is enough such talk (along with talk of what is *allotrion*, or foreign, to the subjects) in the surrounding context to place this passage squarely at the beginning of the *oikeiôsis* tradition.

It seems clear that Locke stands in this tradition.[39] Like Plato and the Stoics, he uses the language of appropriation both in *economic* contexts (where he is discussing the sort of appropriation involved in the acquisition of private property) and in *psychological* contexts (where he is discussing the sort of appropriation of actions and their merit involved in responsible agency), contexts that are not so obviously related to one another that we can easily chalk this up to mere coincidence.[40] This provides a strong prima facie case for taking Locke's thoughts, both about private property and about responsible agency, to have been influenced by the ideas expressed in the passage from Plato's *Republic* and/or by later Stoic developments of these ideas.

---

[39] Brandt 2003 argues along the same lines, without, however, tracing the tradition to Plato's *Republic* or developing the connection (developed below) with the Stoic *hêgemonikon*. But his emphasis on the importance of concern in Locke's account of personal identity seems to me just right.

[40] I was first encouraged to think of these things together in Locke's work by discussions with Tom Berry, from whom I have learned so much. See Berry 1998.

The more specific case for taking Locke's account of personal identity to have roots in the Stoic doctrine of *oikeiôsis* receives support from the account of *oikeiôsis* presented in Seneca's *Letter* 121, which was almost certainly known to Locke. Seneca's account is of course in Latin, so it will be useful to keep in mind the Greek terms for which he is providing Latin substitutes, to which end I have included notes from the following translation by Brad Inwood (2007):

[Q] 5. ... We were investigating whether all animals have an **awareness of their own constitution** [*constitutionis suae sensus*].[41] The main reason why it seems that they do have such an awareness is that they move their limbs easily and effectively just as if they had been trained for doing so. Each of them is nimble with regard to its own parts. An artisan handles his tools with ease, the helmsman of a ship directs the rudder with skill ... An animal is comparably agile in all the ways it makes use of itself ...

7. 'The reason,' he [the Epicurean opponent] replies, 'that animals move their parts appropriately is because if they moved them otherwise they would feel pain. So, as you yourselves say, they are compelled and it is fear rather than their wish which puts them on the right path.' But that is false. For things which are driven by necessity move slowly and what moves on its own has a certain nimbleness. Anyway, animals are so far from being driven to this action by pain that they strive for their natural motion even when pain impedes them.

8. Thus a baby who practices standing and getting used to moving around falls as soon as it begins to tax its strength. Over and over again it cries as it gets up again until despite the pain it works its way through to what nature asks of it ... An upside-down turtle feels no pain, yet it is disturbed by a desire for its natural position and will not give up struggling and flailing itself until it gets onto its feet ...

10. [The opponent] objects, 'according to you, **the constitution is the leading part of the soul in a certain disposition relative to the body** [*principale animi quodam modo se habens erga corpus*].[42] How can a baby comprehend this, which is so complicated and sophisticated that even you can scarcely explain it?'...

11. Your objection would be sound if I were saying that all animals understand the definition of their constitution rather than the constitution itself ... that baby does not know what a constitution is [*quid sit constitution non novit*]

---

[41] Inwood observes that we have in Diogenes Laertius 7.85 (quoted above) "a term for which Seneca's *constitutio* is an exact counterpart: *sustasis*."

[42] Inwood notes here, "the definition of 'constitution' is 'the mind in a certain disposition relative to the body,' which Seneca seems to translate literally here (the Greek, if it were attested, would be *hêgemonikon pôs echon pros to sôma*)." It is worth recalling here both the Aristotelian roots of the notion of *to hêgemonikon* (see passage [D] above) and the importance of this notion to Cudworth (as evidenced in passage [E] above).

yet knows its constitution [*constitutionem suam novit*]; and it does not know what an animal is yet is aware of being an animal [*animal esse se sentit*].

12. Moreover, it does have a crude, schematic and vague understanding of the constitution itself. We too know that we have a mind [*animus*]. But we do not know what the mind is, where it is, what it is like or where it comes from. Although we do not know its nature and its location, our awareness of our mind [*animi nostri sensus*] stands in the same relation to us as the awareness of their own constitution [*constitutionis suae sensus*] stands to all animals. For they must be aware of that through which they are aware of other things [*necesse est enim id sentient, per quod alia quoque sentient*]. They must be aware of that which they obey and by which they are governed.

. . . .

14. [The opponent] objects, 'you say that every animal has a primary attachment to its own constitution [*omne animal primum constitutioni suae conciliari*], but that a human being's constitution is rational and **so that a human being is attached to himself not** *qua* **animal but** *qua* **rational.** For a human is dear to himself with respect to that aspect of himself which makes him human. So how can a baby be attached to a rational constitution when it is not yet rational?'[43]

15. There is a constitution for every stage of life, one for a baby, another for a boy, <another for a teenager>, another for an old man. Everyone is attached to the constitution he is in . . .

16. A baby, a boy, a teenager, an old man: these are different stages of life. Yet *I* am the same [human][44] [*ego tamen idem sum*] as was also a baby and a boy and a teenager. Thus, **although everyone has one different constitution after another, the attachment to one's own constitution is the same.** For nature does not commend me to the boy or the youth or the old man, but to *myself*. [my bold]

Seneca goes on (in secs. 21 and 22) to provide further support for his view by mentioning the very examples Cudworth mentions in sec. 14 of passage [L]: namely, bees making honey and spiders spinning webs. And Seneca makes much the same point that Cudworth makes: the processes involved occur without any thought or deliberation [*sine ulla cogitatione . . . sine consilio*]. But we need not assume that Locke got the point from Cudworth: he probably read the Seneca long before he read the Cudworth.

---

[43] 'Primary attachment' is Inwood's rendering of '*conciliatio*,' which (as he points out) is Cicero's translation of the Greek '*oikeiôsis*.'
[44] I have bracketed this because there is nothing in the Latin corresponding to it: I discuss this point in what follows.

The central ideas in Seneca are in any case three. First, every animal has a kind of attachment [*conciliatio* or *oikeiôsis*] to its own constitution [*constitutio* or *sustasis*], an attachment that goes hand in hand with a certain kind of awareness [*sensus* or *aisthêsis*] of its own constitution. Second, the attachment itself persists throughout changes in the character of the constitution, changes that can sometimes be (as in the development of a rational animal) quite radical. Third, although the constitution of any given animal is the leading part of its soul in a certain (presumably leading) disposition in relation to its body, the leading part of a human soul stands in a different disposition in relation to its body from that in which the leading parts of other animal souls stand to their bodies: whereas the leading parts of non-rational animal souls lead *without* thought or deliberation, the leading parts of human souls lead *with* thought and deliberation. So a human animal—at least when it develops according to nature—ends up being attached to its reason insofar as its reason leads its body by means of thought and deliberation.

The idea that it is part of the natural (even if educationally facilitated) development of a human animal to come both to have and to be attached to a rational constitution is present in a passage in Plato's *Republic* where Socrates is arguing for the primary importance of education in music and poetry on the grounds that it prepares a child, before he is able to grasp the reasons why he should do so, to praise and enjoy fine things and to object to shameful things, so that "when reason comes [*elthontos de tou logou*], he will welcome it [*aspazoit' an auton*], recognizing [*gnôrizôn*] it on account of its kinship [*dia oikeiotêta*] <with himself>."⁴⁵ The crucial point here is that the kind of recognition involved in seeing something as akin to oneself is not *merely* epistemic. It is like the kind of recognition involved when we speak of someone's *recognizing* his child, not just in the sense that he can pick her out in a crowd but in the sense that he acknowledges his *relationship* to her and so begins to interact with her in ways *appropriate* to the relationship in question. It is both cognitive and affective in something like the way Aristotle's *prohairesis* is.

Like Plato, Seneca seems to think that when the rational constitution comes, the subject will be *attached* to it. The *object* of the attachment is clearly the rational constitution—i.e., the leading part of the soul in a certain relation to the body. But what is the *subject* of the relevant attachment? And how exactly does the *body* in question figure in its attachment?

Let us begin with the role played by the body in Seneca's account. The role is not such that the subject of the attachment to a rational constitution *must* be disposed to

---

⁴⁵ One could object here that Plato is talking not about the acquisition of *reason in general*, but rather about the acquisition of *specific reasons*, including both general reasons to (for example) return to others what belongs to them and *particular* reasons to (for example) refrain from returning a weapon to a madman. But even if that is what Plato is talking about here, that itself suggests that he takes the acquisition of reason in general to consist largely in coming to accept a web of such general and particular reasons (which fits Epictetus' idea, cited above, of reason as a system of *phantasiai*). So whichever way you read this particular passage, the *oikeiôsis* doctrine seems present at least in embryo: we find here the idea that a human being has a *sense of herself* and of what is *oikeion* to her, which leads her to be *attached* to reason as it comes to be present in her. [For more on the idea that Plato and Aristotle regard reason as a developmental achievement, see "Psychic Contingency in the *Republic*" (I.8); "Locomotive Soul" (Chapter 5, this volume) and "Hylomorphic Virtue" (Chapter 6, this volume).]

regard the object of that attachment as surviving in a case where the body in question ceases to be governed by the *hêgemonikon*. For in that case, the rational constitution as defined by Seneca would cease to exist. And even if the rational constitution *could* be succeeded by a constitution to which the relevant subject's attachment was *in fact* transferred, it is not clear that the subject's attachment *must* be transferred to any old constitution by which his rational constitution seems to be replaced. A subject that has come to *identify with* (in the sense that it is *attached to*) a certain sort of rational constitution might fail to see itself as continued in the absence of that sort of rational constitution. It is not necessary in a teleological framework to view departures from a natural *telos* in the same way that one views arrivals to it: so the replacement of a *more* rational constitution by a *less* rational one (or worse yet by a *non*-rational one) need not be viewed as a form of *self-preservation* in the way in which the normal developmental replacement of a *less* rational constitution by a *more* rational one tends to be viewed.

The most important point here is that there is nothing in the Latin of sec. 16 corresponding to Inwood's 'human,' which I have bracketed because I think its absence may be significant. Inwood says that although Seneca "has the resources to distinguish between a core 'self' and the varying constitution, this seems not to be his interest." But I think it would have been so easy and so natural for Seneca to say (if that is what he meant) that the *man* (or the *animal*) remains the same—or that he was the same *man* (or *animal*) that was the baby, the boy, and the teenager—that an argument ex silentio is not inappropriate here. Seneca may be trying to get at the idea of something like the *person* as distinct from the *human animal*, and at the way in which a subject's evolving attachment can help to *make* it the case that the different stages of the *animal's* life all belong to the life of the *person*—or, speaking from the first-person point of view, all belong to the life of one's *self*. In other words, Seneca's idea may be that the animal constitutions come and go—in something like the way Locke allows that animal bodies and/or Cartesian souls may come and go—while the attachment itself provides a kind of continuity: not the sort of continuity of *biological* life in which the persistence of a mere *animal* is supposed to consist, but rather continuity of the sort of *psychological* life in which the persistence of the *subject of the attachment* may be said to consist. For it is *this* subject that recognizes the boy, the youth, and the old man as belonging successively to *it: their* histories are part of *its* history.[46]

It is of course true—and Seneca surely recognizes—that there is an *animal* there of whose history the histories of the baby, the boy, and the old man are in some sense parts. But that truism does not seem enough to explain the conjunction of Seneca's next two *concessive* remarks: "Yet [or nevertheless, *tamen*] I am the same" and "*though* everyone has one different constitution after another, *the attachment . . . is the same.*" It seems natural here to wonder whether Seneca is not thinking of the *attachment itself* as part of what helps to bind the different stages together and to make them all stages

---

[46] [This is the backward-looking version of the point made about future-directed concern in "Friends and Future Selves" (I.1).]

of the same thing—not of course stages of the relevant human animal (since their all being stages of that is already provided for by the continuity of their biological life) but rather stages of what Seneca calls 'I' or 'myself.'

And even if that is not exactly what Seneca was thinking, it is easy enough to imagine someone else—for example, Locke—reading Seneca and thinking that. For this is just the sort of view that might lead someone to think—as Locke's famous thought experiment where we are supposed to imagine the consciousness of a Prince being transferred to the body of a Cobbler surely invites us to think—that the *subject* goes where the *attachment* goes. For it seems pretty clear that *we* are supposed to think that the Prince goes where his consciousness goes largely because this is where the *Prince himself* thinks he goes, partly no doubt on account of his attachment or (as Locke puts it) "concernment." In other words, Seneca's view is just the sort of view that might lead someone to conclude that the *subject* of the attachment in question *cannot* be the human animal but *must* be something with different conditions of existence and persistence over time: for example, something whose persistence over time is constituted by the continuity of its *psychological* life in a way analogous to that in which the persistence of an Aristotelian animal over time is constituted by the continuity of its *biological* life.

7. LOCKE AND SOME SO-CALLED NEO-LOCKEAN ACCOUNTS OF PERSONAL IDENTITY

We are now in a position to read Locke in historical context and so to see how some so-called neo-Lockean accounts of personal identity are not all that Lockean. One way to put the problem with these accounts is to say that they read Locke as having what we might, following Anscombe, call "an incorrigibly contemplative conception of *consciousness*."[47] This conception stems, I think, from their reading Locke as having a fundamentally Cartesian conception of consciousness instead of the sort of stoicized Aristotelian conception that I see in Cudworth. For these neo-Lockean accounts treat the sameness of consciousness of which Locke speaks primarily as a form of *epistemic access* to its subject's past and present *experiences*, a kind of access that gives rise in turn to certain expectations as to its future *experiences*. But the emphasis in Locke is clearly on consciousness of *actions*—and consciousness not simply of any old actions but of *one's own* actions *as such*. And Locke's claim is that such consciousness helps to *constitute* its subject *as a person*, which is something that such consciousness can do only insofar as it contains at least some of the sort of *practical* knowledge of which Anscombe speaks, knowledge that involves not just memory and expectation, but also (and more importantly) deliberation and decision: in other words, the sort of knowledge that is (at least where things go well) "the cause of what it understands."[48]

---

[47] Anscombe 1957, sec. 32.
[48] [I say "at least where things go well" to accommodate the sort of asymmetries afforded by a teleological world view that I discuss in "Locomotive Soul" (Chapter 5, this volume), "Hylomorphic Virtue"

I am objecting here to the recent trend toward deflationist readings of Locke, by which I mean readings that refuse to acknowledge Locke's commitment to a genuine dualism of Person and Animal. As Shoemaker 1984 has argued, this is *not* a dualism of soul and body and it does *not require* the existence of anything *non*-material: it is simply a view according to which 'Person' and 'Human Animal' are names of two *different kinds of things*, each with its own distinctive conditions for existence and persistence over time. I include among rejections of neo-Lockean dualism not only Derek Parfit's recent suggestion that "person" is simply a phase-sortal that (like 'adolescent' and 'husband') applies to a human animal only during a certain phase of its existence, but also David Velleman's attempt to distinguish, in a Lockean context, what he (Velleman) calls 'the self of personal identity' from what he (Velleman) calls 'the self of autonomous agency.'[49] I have already criticized Parfit elsewhere for his failure to appreciate what I call Locke's "constitutive move."[50] So I shall focus here on Velleman, who seems to me to be on the right track insofar as he takes the self to be "constituted by reflexive thought," but to err insofar as he seeks to separate the self of personal identity (which he describes as the self to which one has "reflexive *access*") from the self of autonomous agency (which he describes in more agentive terms).

The main problem with Velleman's view is that it fails to acknowledge Locke's fundamental concern with the conditions for responsible agency and the way in which it is this concern that leads Locke to distinguish Persons (or Selves) from the Human Animals with which they typically coincide. 'Person' is (as Locke says in sec. 26 below) "a forensic term appropriating actions and their merit."[51] So it is a term that applies

---

(Chapter 6, this volume), and "*Nicomachean Ethics* 7.3 on Akratic Ignorance" (with Martin Pickavé) (Chapter 7, this volume).] For an interesting attempt to read Descartes as having a practical conception of *conscientia* as "the cause of what it understands," see Hennig 2004, chaps. 6–7. If Hennig is right, then I am wrong to suggest that Locke differs from Descartes insofar as Locke has a more practical, and less "contemplative," conception of consciousness than Descartes does, though I admit there may be important differences between the views expressed by Descartes in the *Meditations* and the views he expresses elsewhere (especially in his *Passions of the Soul*). Still, Hennig's account treats Descartes as extending the traditional (and largely scholastic) sense of "*conscientia*" from actions to *thoughts*, and the result seems to me very different both from the sort of consciousness of *actions* of which Locke speaks and from the sort of consciousness of *what one is doing* of which Cudworth speaks. So I think it fair to describe Descartes' conception of consciousness as contemplative by comparison with the more practical conception of consciousness I see in Locke and Cudworth. But I hope to consider these questions more carefully in future work.

[49] Velleman 2006, especially 5–7.
[50] See Whiting 2002b [I.5] discussing Parfit 1999. Although I disagree with Parfit on this point, my work on these questions has been inspired from the start by his (1984) and by the lectures he gave in Oxford as he was preparing it for publication, lectures that first stimulated my interest in these questions. I have also benefited greatly over the years from conversation and correspondence with him.
[51] In saying that 'Person' is a "forensic term" Locke is not saying (as he is sometimes represented as saying) that claims about when we do and do not have the same person are largely *juridical*, a matter of our using the term 'person' in connection with certain contingent social practices the nature of which is largely constitutive of the conditions for its correct application. For in sec. 21 of this chapter, Locke more or less concedes that the difficulties of proving an accused man's lack of consciousness of his alleged crimes leave our courts with little alternative to working with the "same Man, same Person" principle, but then goes on to say in sec. 26 below, that "in the great Day, wherein the Secrets of all Hearts shall be laid open, it may be reasonable to think, no one shall be made to answer for what he knows nothing of." And this,

only to a subject that satisfies the conditions for responsible agency—that is, only to a subject that *rightly* imputes *actions* (roughly, Aristotelian *praxeis*) *to itself*, where this is not so much a matter of having a kind of special (but ultimately observational) access to the behavior of the animal body whose point of view the subject seems to occupy as of having the kind of control over the actions of that body that comes with the subject's capacity (as Locke put it back in [J]) to "[suspend] the satisfaction of any particular desire . . . from determining the *will* to any subservient action, till [it has] maturely examin'd, whether the particular apparent good, which [it] then desire[s], makes a part of [its] real Happiness, or be consistent or inconsistent with it." So 'Person' *cannot* be applied either to a mere Human Animal simply as such or to a bare Cartesian soul simply as such. This is why Locke thinks it necessary to distinguish Persons *both* from bare Cartesian souls *and* from the Human Animals with which Persons typically coincide, and to give an account of the conditions for the existence and persistence of Persons *as such*.

In other words, Locke's account of personal identity *just is*—pace Velleman—an account of the conditions for the existence and persistence of autonomous (and thus morally accountable) agents. This should be clear if we read the following passage in historical context.

[R]   17. **Self is that conscious thinking thing . . . which is sensible or conscious of pleasure and pain, capable of happiness or misery, and so is concerned for itself, as far as that consciousness extends.** Thus every one finds that, whilst comprehended under that consciousness, the little finger is as much a part of himself as what is most so. Upon separation of this little finger, should this consciousness go along with the little finger, and leave the rest of the body, it is evident the little finger would be the person, the same person; and self then would have nothing to do with the rest of the body. As in this case it is the consciousness that goes along with the substance, when one part is separate from another, which makes the same person, and constitutes this inseparable self: so it is in reference

---

given what Locke says in the rest of the chapter, is tantamount to saying that come Judgment Day, our practices will be set aside and the *true* criterion of personhood—that is, the *true* criterion of responsible agency—will be respected.

For this reason it is also wrong to read Locke's talk of 'Person' as a "forensic term" (as it is sometimes read) as showing that Locke is giving a "practical not metaphysical" account of personal identity: Locke is clearly interested in the *metaphysics* of responsible agency. The fact that he takes *psychological* states and relations to be partly constitutive of a person's identity over time is no reason for saying that his account of personal identity is practical *rather than* metaphysical: taking such states and relations to be constitutive of a *person's* identity over time is *no less* metaphysical than taking a certain kind of biological continuity (such as the continuity of a canine or a feline life) as a criterion for an *animal's* identity over time. It is perhaps salutary to keep in mind that on Locke's view persisting animals are no more substances, strictly so-called, than persisting persons are: the only genuine substances Locke recognizes are God, Finite Intelligences, and Bodies (apparently, in the end, only indivisible Particles of Matter) [*Essay* II. XXVII. 2]. So persons are—metaphysically speaking—on a par with persisting animals.

to substances remote in time. That with which the consciousness of this present thinking thing can join itself, makes the same person, and is one self with it, and with nothing else; and so attributes to itself, and owns all the actions of that thing, as its own, as far as that consciousness reaches, and no further; as every one who reflects will perceive.[52]

18. In this personal identity is founded all the right and justice of reward and punishment; happiness and misery being that for which every one is concerned for himself, and not mattering what becomes of any substance, not joined to, or affected with that consciousness. For, as it is evident in the instance I gave but now, if the consciousness went along with the little finger when it was cut off, that would be the same self which was concerned for the whole body yesterday, as making part of itself, whose actions then it cannot but admit as its own now. Though if the same Body should still live, and immediately from the separation of the little Finger have its own peculiar consciousness, whereof the little Finger knew nothing, it would not be at all concerned for it, as part of it *self*, or could own any of its Actions, or have any of them imputed to him. . . .

26. **Person, as I take it, is the name for this self.** Wherever a man finds what he calls himself, there, I think, another may say is the same person. **It is a forensic term,** appropriating actions and their merit; and so belongs only to intelligent agents, capable of a law, and happiness, and misery. **This personality extends itself beyond present existence to what is past, only by consciousness, whereby it becomes concerned and accountable; owns and imputes to itself past actions, just upon the same ground and for the same reason as it does the present.** All which is founded in a concern for happiness, the unavoidable concomitant of consciousness; that which is conscious of pleasure and pain, desiring that that self that is conscious should be happy. And therefore whatever past actions it cannot reconcile or appropriate to that present self by consciousness, it can be no more concerned in than if they had never been done: and to receive pleasure or pain, i.e. reward or punishment, on the account of any such action, is all one as to be made happy or miserable in its first being, without any demerit at all. For, supposing a man punished now for what he had done in another life, whereof he could be made to have no consciousness at all, what difference is there between that punishment and being created miserable? And therefore conformable to this, the Apostle tells us, that at the Great Day, when every one shall *receive according to his doings, the secrets of all Hearts shall be laid open.* The Sentence shall be justified by the consciousness all

---

[52] It would be a mistake to make too much of this, but Locke's choice of the finger as the locus of consciousness (which is continued in sec. 18) might well be an allusion (not necessarily conscious) to the *Republic*'s use of a finger in passage [P] above. This may have become a standard trope.

Persons have, that they *themselves*, in what Bodies soever they appear, or what Substances soever that consciousness adheres to, are the *same*, that committed those Actions, and deserve that Punishment for them. [*An Essay Concerning Human Understanding* II. XXVII; Locke's italics; my bold]

It should be clear that Locke's emphasis on sameness of consciousness is motivated primarily by his concern with the conditions for *just* reward and punishment, and so with the conditions for *responsible agency*. In this respect, Locke's affinity with Cudworth should be clear.

Locke's distance from Descartes will perhaps be clearest if we attend to his emphasis in sec. 17 on pleasure and pain, the capacity for happiness or misery, and the sort of concern that he takes to accompany these things. For commentators who assimilate Locke's conception of consciousness to Descartes' more contemplative conception do so largely (I submit) because they ignore the role played in Locke's conception by such factors, including especially *concern*. So it is worth keeping in mind that Locke himself goes so far as to say—in his earlier, clearly anti-Cartesian, and very Cudworthian chapter "Men think not always"—that "if we take away wholly all Consciousness of our Actions and Sensations, especially of Pleasure and Pain, and the *concernment* that accompanies it, it will be hard to know wherein to place personal Identity" (my italics). And the point reappears, in subtler guise, in the present chapter.[53]

Although Locke has already said sec. 9 of this chapter (i.e., in [K] above) that a Person is a "thinking, intelligent being," it is pretty clear—even apart from his argument that the substances that "think in us" could be replaced from one moment to the next without our knowing the difference—that he is *not* thinking of Persons in anything like the way in which Descartes thinks of his "thinking substances." Locke stresses the Person's susceptibility to pleasure and pain, and her capacities for happiness and misery, along with the sort of concern that accompanies these things. The capacities for happiness and misery are important here insofar as they distinguish the sort of agency of which persons are capable from the sort of agency of which non-rational animals are capable. For as we saw in [J], Locke thinks that a person is a free (and so responsible) agent because a person can escape her immediate susceptibility to pleasure and pain by suspending the satisfaction of the desires to which this immediate susceptibility gives rise until she has maturely examined whether the satisfaction of any given desire would *really* contribute to her happiness in the way it *appears* it would, and so until she can decide whether or not to follow any given appearance of a pleasure as good or a pain as bad. A person can do this because she has the sort of memory (roughly narrative memory) that gives rise not only to a conception of herself as temporally extended but also to a conception of her long-term satisfaction (or happiness), which is something that non-rational animals lack. This conception of herself

---

[53] For explicit discussion of the importance of concern to neo-Lockean accounts of personal identity, see Whiting 1986 [I.1] and 2002b [I.5].

and of her long-term happiness is part of what allows a person to escape being simply dragged about, in the way a non-rational animal is dragged about, by its appearances of the greater good.

Locke's idea in sec. 17 seems to be not simply that persons are conscious thinking things that *happen also* to be concerned about the hedonic quality of their experiences and their long-term happiness, *and are, moreover,* accountable for their actions. Locke seems to think of consciousness rather as a kind of *holistic package* whose components are functionally related to one another.[54] Consciousness in a normally embodied creature is (among other things) consciousness *of pleasure and pain*, the very *essence* of which engage their subject's *concern* in ways that lead their subject to *act* so as to increase the pleasures and diminish the pains of which it is (of course) conscious; and when a creature has the sort of memory of past pleasures and pains and the actions that gave rise to them, and can thus act in ways so as to increase future (and not simply immediate) pleasures and reduce future (and not simply immediate) pains, it is capable of a kind of action of which creatures moved simply by immediate appearances of pleasure and pain are not. It can perform actions that it expects to have desirable (but not necessarily immediate) natural and/or forensic consequences and it can abstain from actions that it expects to have undesirable (but not necessary immediate) natural and/or forensic consequences. And it can impute such actions *to itself* in a way that helps not only to make intelligible but also to justify the forensic practices of holding the subject responsible for these actions. It is this capacity to attribute past and present actions to itself, together with closely the related capacity to plan and execute future actions, that *makes* a responsible agent out of what starts off as a predominantly passive and reactive subject of phenomenal appearances. And these capacities are themselves arguably constituted by the entire package including immediate susceptibilities to pleasure and pain, the capacities for happiness and misery, and the sorts of concern that are built into these things.

It is important to note here how different the epistemological demands placed on Locke's conception of consciousness are likely to be, given the work he expects his conception to do, from the epistemological demands placed on Descartes' conception. Much more is required of a conception of consciousness that is supposed to provide a secure foundation for knowledge, one that is immune to radical doubt, than of a conception of consciousness that is supposed to serve as the basis for and perhaps even as constitutive of responsible agency. So taking personhood to involve something irreducibly first-personal in the way that Locke does leaves open what sort and what degree of epistemological privilege is involved in the requisite first-person point of view. And to the extent that Locke's primary concern is with the conditions for the existence and persistence of responsible agents, he may require no more than the modest forms of epistemic privilege I have argued Aristotle both needs and requires: that

---

[54] For a neo-Lockean (and in my view truly *Lockean*) defense of this conception, see Sydney Shoemaker 1984 and 1997 (where Shoemaker explains the difference he sees between the more Humean view he finds in Parfit 1984 and his own explicitly Lockean view). Here and elsewhere I am much indebted to Shoemaker, both for his written work and for many discussions over many years.

is, *no more than the sort of non-observational knowledge that a rational agent ordinarily has* (when she is not asleep, mad, feverish, drunk, etc.) *of what she herself is doing*, a kind of knowledge she ordinarily has in virtue of the fact that *she* is the one *doing* it.[55] So even when Locke says Cartesian-sounding things, we need to ask what exactly he is doing with them and what they must involve, given what they are supposed to be doing. That is the moral of Descartes' own remarks about Augustine.

Except in those rare cases where a philosopher (like, for example, Cudworth) cites or quotes the sources from which his own views are derived, it proves difficult at best to tell how a philosopher comes by any given view. And Locke is no exception here: we may never know to what extent his conception of consciousness was influenced either by Cudworth's conception or by Descartes' (or some other) conception. My aim here is largely to shift the burden of proof onto those who insist that Locke's account of personal identity involves a largely Cartesian and distinctively modern conception of consciousness, and thus to shift the burden of proof onto those who insist that Locke's conception of the person is something that Aristotle and ancients not only *did not* have but *could not* have had. And I rely here on the following master (but nevertheless modest) premise: namely, that anything Locke had such that he *could* have taken it from Aristotle and the Stoics—whether via Cudworth or not—is something Aristotle and the Stoics not only *could* have had but *did* have. So my title is to some extent misleading: the Lockeanism of Aristotle is ultimately the Aristotelianism—or more exactly the stoicized Aristotelianism—of Locke.[56]

BIBLIOGRAPHY

Anscombe, G. E. M. 1957. *Intention*. Oxford: Blackwell, 2nd edn.; Ithaca, NY: Cornell University Press, 1963; reprinted Cambridge, MA: Harvard University Press, 2000.

Berry, T. 1998. *Appropriating Persons: John Locke's Theory of Private Property*. Ph.D. dissertation: University of Pittsburgh.

Brandt, R. 2003. "Selbstbewusstsein und Selbstsorge: Zur Tradition der οἰκείωσις in der Neuzeit." *Archiv für Geschichte der Philosophie* 85: 179–97.

Broadie, S. and Rowe, C. 2002. *Aristotle: Nicomachean Ethics—Translation, Introduction and Commentary*. Oxford: Oxford University Press.

---

[55] [For discussion of those asleep, mad, drunk, etc. in connection with Aristotle's account of *akrasia*, see Pickavé and Whiting 2008 (Chapter 7, this volume).]

[56] I should like to thank the Alexander von Humboldt Stiftung for their support and Marta Jimenez for all her help during the period when I was preparing this essay for publication. I have also benefited significantly from discussions with audiences at the Pacific Division Meetings of the American Philosophical Association (especially my commentator Tad Brennan), the University of Toronto (especially my commentator Sarah Broadie), the Humboldt University, and the Universities of Basel and Göttingen. The extraordinary discussion with Sebastian Rödl's group in Basel (including Matt Boyle and Matthias Haase) raised difficult questions that I hope to grapple with in future work with my colleague Phil Clark (who also played a vital role in that discussion). Many thanks to all these folk and to those mentioned in the notes throughout. But thanks above all—for constant conversation and much else—to Tom Berry, whose own ideas about Locke played an important role in the development of the ideas expressed here.

Cooper, J. and Hutchinson, D. 1997. *Plato: The Complete Works*. Indianapolis, IN: Hackett.

Cudworth, R. 1648. *The True Intellectual System of the World, Wherein all the Reason and Philosophy of Atheism in Confuted and Its Impossibility Demonstrated*; a facsimile of the 1820 London edition was reprinted in 4 volumes by Elibron Classics in 2005.

Cudworth, R. *A Treatise Concerning Eternal and Immutable Morality*, with *A Treatise of Freewill*, Sarah Hutton (ed.) 1996. Cambridge: Cambridge University Press.

Darwall, S. 1995. *The British Moralists and the Internal "Ought": 1640–1740*. Cambridge: Cambridge University Press.

Davidson, D. 1985. *Inquiries into Truth and Interpretation*. Oxford: Clarendon Press.

De Beer, E. S. (ed.) 1979. *The Correspondence of John Locke, Vol. 4*. Oxford: Oxford University Press.

Dennett, D. 1987. *The Intentional Stance*. Cambridge, MA: MIT Press.

Descartes, R. *The Philosophical Writings of Descartes. Vol. 3: The Correspondence*. Anthony Kenny (trans.) 1991. Cambridge: Cambridge University Press.

Gauthier, R. A. and Jolif, J. Y. 1970. *L'Éthique à Nicomaque: Introduction, traduction, et commentaire*, 2nd edn. Louvain and Paris: Peeters Publisher.

Gill, C. 1991. "Is There a Concept of Person in Greek Philosophy?" In S. Everson (ed.), *Psychology: Companions to Ancient Thought, Vol. 2*. Cambridge: Cambridge University Press, 166–193.

Gill, C. 1996. *Personality in Greek Epic, Tragedy and Philosophy*. Oxford: Oxford University Press.

Gill, C. 2006. *The Structured Self in Hellenistic and Roman Thought*. Oxford: Oxford University Press.

Hennig, B. 2004. *"Conscientia" bei Descartes*. Alber: München.

Hobbes, T. 1646. *Of Liberty and Necessity*. [Cambridge University Press edition, edited by Vere Chappell, 1999.]

Inwood, B. 1984. "Hierocles: Theory and Argument in the Second Century A.D." *Oxford Studies in Ancient Philosophy* 2: 151–83.

Inwood, B. 1985. *Ethics and Human Action in Early Stoicism*. Oxford: Clarendon Press.

Inwood, B. 2007. *Seneca: Selected Philosophical Letters*. Oxford: Oxford University Press.

Irwin, T. 1999. *Aristotle: Nicomachean Ethics*, 2nd edn. Indianapolis, IN: Hackett.

Jung, G. 1933. "ΣΥΝΕΙΔΗΣΙΣ, Conscientia, Bewusstsein." *Archiv für Gesamte Psychologie* 89: 525–40.

Locke, John. *An Essay Concerning Human Understanding*. P. H. Nidditch (ed.) 1975. Oxford: Oxford University Press. [Originally published 1690; 2nd edn. 1694; 6th (and last) edn. 1710.]

Long, A. A. and Sedley, D. N. 1987. *The Hellenistic Philosophers*. 2 vols. Cambridge: Cambridge University Press.

Long, A. A. 1993. "Hierocles on *oikeiôsis* and Self-Perception." In C. Bouroudis (ed.), *Hellenistic Philosophy*. Athens, 93–104; reprinted in A. A. Long 1996. *Stoic Studies*. Cambridge: Cambridge University Press, 250–63.

Moran, R. 1994. "Interpretation Theory and the First Person." *Philosophical Quarterly* 44: 154–73.

Moran, R. 2001. *Authority and Estrangement: An Essay on Self-Knowledge*. Princeton. NJ: Princeton University Press.

Moran, R. 2004. "Anscombe on Practical Knowledge." In J. Hyman and H. Steward (eds.), *Agency and Action*. Cambridge: Cambridge University Press, 43–68.

Olson, E. 1999. *The Human Animal: Personal Identity without Psychology*. Oxford: Oxford University Press.
Owen, G. E. L. 1956. "The Platonism of Aristotle." *Proceedings of the British Academy* 51: 125–50; reprinted in G. E. L. Owen 1986. *Logic Science and Dialectic: Collected Papers in Greek Philosophy*. Ithaca, NY: Cornell University Press, 200–220.
Parfit, D. 1984. *Reasons and Persons*. Oxford: Oxford University Press.
Parfit, D. 1999. "Experiences, Subjects, and Conceptual Schemes." *Philosophical Topics* 26 (Special issue: *The Philosophy of Sydney Shoemaker*, edited by R. Moran, A. Sidelle, and J. Whiting), 217–70.
Passmore, J. A. 1951. *Ralph Cudworth: An Interpretation*. Cambridge: Cambridge University Press.
Pickavé, M. and Whiting, J. 2008. "*Nicomachean Ethics* 7.3: On Akratic Ignorance." *Oxford Studies in Ancient Philosophy* 34: 323–71. [Chapter 7, this volume]
Pohlenz, M. 1940. *Grundfragen der stoischen Philosophie*. Göttingen: Vandenhoeck & Ruprecht.
Plato. 1992. *Republic*, G. Grube (trans.), revised by C. Reeve. Indianapolis, IN: Hackett Publishing.
Radner, Daisie. 1988. "Thought and Consciousness in Descartes." *Journal of the History of Philosophy* 26: 439–52.
Ross, W. D. 1908. *Aristotle: Nicomachean Ethics*. Clarendon Press: Oxford; revised version by J. O. Urmson in J. Barnes (ed.) 1984. *The Complete Works of Aristotle*, 2 vols. Princeton, NJ: Princeton University Press.
Rozemond, M. 2004. "Critical Notice of Janet Broughton, *Descartes' Method of Doubt*." *Canadian Journal of Philosophy* 34: 591–614.
Shoemaker, S. 1984. "Personal Identity: A Materialist's Account." In S. Shoemaker and R. Swinburne (eds.), *Personal Identity*. Oxford: Oxford University Press, 67–129.
Shoemaker, S. 1997. "Self and Substance." *Philosophical Perspectives* 11: *Mind, Causation, and World*, 283–304.
Shoemaker, S. 1999. "Self, Body, and Coincidence" *Proceedings of the Aristotelian Society* Supp. vol. 73: 287–306.
Smith, P. and Jones, O. R. 1986. *The Philosophy of Mind: An Introduction*. Cambridge: Cambridge University Press.
Striker, G. 1983. "The Role of Oikeiosis in Stoic Ethics." *Oxford Studies in Ancient Philosophy* 1: 145–67. Reprinted in Striker 1996: 281–97.
Striker, G. 1991. "Following Nature: A Study in Stoic Ethics." *Oxford Studies in Ancient Philosophy* 9: 1–73. Reprinted in Striker 1996: 221–80.
Striker, G. 1996. *Essays on Hellenistic Epistemology and Ethics*. Cambridge: Cambridge University Press.
Theil, U. 1991. "Cudworth and Seventeenth-Century Theories of Consciousness." In S. Gaukgroger (ed.), *The Uses of Antiquity*. Dordrecht: Kluwer Academic Press, 79–99.
Todd, R. (ed.) 1996. *Themistius: On Aristotle's On the Soul*. Ithaca, NY: Cornell University Press.
Velleman, D. 2006. *Self to Self: Selected Essays*. Cambridge: Cambridge University Press.
Whiting, J. 1986. "Friends and Future Selves." *Philosophical Review* 95: 547–80. [I:1]
Whiting, J. 2002a. "Locomotive Soul: The Parts of Soul in Aristotle's Scientific Works." *Oxford Studies in Ancient Philosophy* 22: 141–200. [Chapter 5, this volume]
Whiting, J. 2002b. "Personal Identity: The Non-branching Form of 'What Matters.'" in R. Gale (ed.), *The Blackwell Guide to Metaphysics*. Oxford: Wiley-Blackwell, 190–218. [I:5]

Whiting, J. 2006. "The Nicomachean Account of Philia." In R. Kraut (ed.), *The Blackwell Guide to Aristotle's Nicomachean Ethics*. Oxford: Wiley-Blackwell: 277–304. [II:6]

Whiting, J. 2013. "The Pleasures of Thinking Together: Prolegomenon to a Complete Reading of *Eudemian Ethics* VII.12." In F. Leigh (ed.), *The "Eudemian Ethics" on the Voluntary, Friendship and Luck: The Sixth S. V. Keeling Colloquium in Ancient Philosophy*. Leiden: Brill, 77–154. [II:7]

Whiting, J. 2014. "Fools' Pleasures in Plato's *Philebus*." In M. Lee (ed.), *Strategies of Argument: Essays in Ancient Ethics, Epistemology and Logic*. Oxford: Oxford University Press, 21–59.

Wilkes, K. 1988. *Real People: Personal Identity without Thought Experiments*. Oxford: Oxford University Press.

Yaffe, G. 2000. *Liberty Worth the Name: Locke on Free Agency*. Princeton, NJ: Princeton University Press.

9

The Mover(s) of Rational Animals

DE ANIMA III.11 IN CONTEXT

ANY ATTEMPT TO understand *De Anima* III.11 as a self-contained unit—even one drawing on points previously established—is misguided. For the opening lines (= [1*]) are clearly parenthetical. And what follows them (= [2]) picks up where the final lines of III.10 (= [0*]) left off.[1]

> [0*] In general then, as previously said, insofar as an animal is capable of desire, it is on account of this capable of moving itself. But it is not capable of desire without *phantasia*. And all *phantasia* is either calculative [*logistikê*] or perceptual [*aisthêtikê*]. Of this, then, even the other animals have a share.
>
> ὅλως μὲν οὖν, ὥσπερ εἴρηται, ᾗ ὀρεκτικὸν τὸ ζῷον,
> ταύτῃ αὑτοῦ κινητικόν· ὀρεκτικὸν δὲ οὐκ ἄνευ φαντασίας·
> φαντασία δὲ πᾶσα ἢ λογιστικὴ ἢ αἰσθητική.
> ταύτης μὲν οὖν καὶ τὰ ἄλλα ζῷα μετέχει. [433b27–30]
>
> [1*] (We must inquire also about the imperfect <animals>, what is the mover of these, to whom only *aisthêsis* by means of touch belongs, and whether it is

---

[1] The translations are my own. Passages [1*] to [5*] provide a complete translation of *De Anima* 3.11. The asterisks indicate the final version of my translation; lack of an asterisk, as in [2] here, indicates an as yet incomplete translation with further decisions to be made and defended in what follows it.

I transliterate many Greek terms and their cognates both because they are difficult to render adequately in English and because they are familiar even to those without Greek, for whom I shall provide common renderings as I introduce the terms. The most important of these are φαντασία (commonly rendered 'imagination') and αἴσθησις (often rendered 'perception,' though 'sensation' is sometimes more appropriate). I shall use Greek font for *mention* (as here) and transliteration for *use* (as in [0*]).

possible for *phantasia* to belong to them or not, and also <whether it is possible for> appetite <to belong>. For pain and pleasure are evidently present in them. And if these <are present>, it is necessary that appetite is as well. But how could *phantasia* be present in them? Or is it the case that just as they move indeterminately, so too these are present in them, but indeterminately?)

(Σκεπτέον δὲ καὶ περὶ τῶν ἀτελῶν τί τὸ κινοῦν ἐστιν,
οἷς ἀφῇ μόνον ὑπάρχει αἴσθησις, πότερον ἐνδέχεται φαντασίαν
ὑπάρχειν τούτοις, ἢ οὔ, καὶ ἐπιθυμίαν. φαίνεται γὰρ λύπη καὶ
ἡδονὴ ἐνοῦσα, εἰ δὲ ταῦτα, καὶ ἐπιθυμίαν ἀνάγκη. φαντασία
δὲ πῶς ἂν ἐνείη; ἢ ὥσπερ καὶ κινεῖται ἀορίστως, καὶ ταῦτ᾽
ἔνεστι μέν, ἀορίστως δ᾽ ἔνεστιν.) [433b31–34a6]

[2] Perceptual *phantasia*, as previously said, belongs on the one hand [*men*] even among the other animals, whereas deliberative <*phantasia*> belongs on the other hand [*de*] among rational animals.[2] (For whether one will do this or that is already the work of calculation. And it is necessary <for ____ > to measure by one <____>, for <____> pursues the greater <good>; so <____> is able to make one <____> out of several *phantasmata*.)

ἡ μὲν οὖν αἰσθητικὴ φαντασία,
ὥσπερ εἴρηται, καὶ ἐν τοῖς ἄλλοις ζῴοις ὑπάρχει, ἡ δὲ βουλευτικὴ
ἐν τοῖς λογιστικοῖς. (πότερον γὰρ πράξει τόδε ἢ τόδε, λογισμοῦ
ἤδη ἐστὶν ἔργον· καὶ ἀνάγκη ἑνὶ μετρεῖν· τὸ μεῖζον γὰρ
διώκει· ὥστε δύναται ἓν ἐκ πλειόνων φαντασμάτων ποιεῖν). [434a6–10]

As [1*] indicates, Aristotle has been discussing what accounts for the self-generated movements of animals. He is specifically concerned to explain locomotion, as distinct from the sorts of movements in place to which the creatures mentioned in [1*] are limited. These creatures do *not locomote*. So whatever sort of *phantasia* might be required to explain their movements in place is not relevant here, where the question is what accounts for *locomotion*. Aristotle is thus content to toss off a few speculative and parenthetical remarks before returning to his official business.[3]

---

[2] Two points here. First, I use the awkward "on the one hand... on the other hand..." so as to flag the μέν/δέ structure for future reference. For I see in that structure the key to making sense of what follows, especially [3] and [4]. Second, I suspect that Aristotle uses ἐν τοῖς ἄλλοις ζῴοις and ἐν τοῖς λογιστικοῖς (rather than simple datives without ἐν) so as to signal that deliberative *phantasia* may not belong to all so-called rational animals and that even perceptual *phantasia* may not belong to all animals (which is precisely the possibility envisaged in [1*]). See *Politics* 1.13, with its rare use of τὸ βουλευτικόν (on which more below): "the slave is generally without the deliberative capacity, while the female has <this capacity> but it is not in control <in her>, and the child has it but it is <in him> incomplete." [1260a12–14]

[3] These speculative remarks are not especially germane to our topic, but I take the idea to be that stationary animals, in virtue of their limited sense of touch, experience pleasure and pain, and so a rudimentary form of desire, but not one that involves determinate representations of objects toward or away from which they might *locomote*. These creatures are affected by the tangibles associated with nutrition—hot, cold, wet, and dry, and perhaps also flavor (which Aristotle treats as a kind of tangible that supervenes on the former). So these creatures experience hunger (which is an *epithumia* for what is dry and hot) and thirst (which is an *epithumia* for what is wet and cold). But what they experience are

Seeing the parenthetical nature of [1*] might tempt us to read 3.11 as a relatively self-contained unit that starts with [0*] rather than [1*]. But that too would be misguided. For that would suggest that the chapter is mainly about the two forms of *phantasia* and their proper extensions. But (as I shall argue) 3.11 aims primarily to resolve an *aporia* that emerges towards the end of 3.9 and is articulated at the start of 3.10. This is an *aporia* about what "part" of soul is responsible for the second of the two capacities that are supposed to distinguish the souls of animals from those of plants—namely, the locomotive capacity.

The first of these capacities, the *kritikê*, or "cognitive" capacity, has been examined at length in 2.5–3.8, where Aristotle discusses *aisthêsis*, *phantasia*, and *nous* qua cognitive capacities.[4] *Nous* and *phantasia* figure again in the discussion of locomotion to which he turns at the start of 3.9, but they figure thenceforth only insofar as they play a role in accounting for locomotion. If there is any relatively self-contained unit here, it is what we now know—thanks to the editors who divided the *De Anima* into chapters—as III.9–11.[5]

I stress this point because I worry that taking III.11 to be concerned primarily with the two forms of *phantasia* and their proper extensions has led many readers, including prominent translators, to misread a key sentence. This is [3][a], which launches a highly compressed and anaphoric argument that I translate (with some gaps to be filled in as we proceed and some crucial bits in bold) as follows.

[3] [a] And this is the reason why _____ seems not to have/entail *doxa*—
[b] because _____ does not have/entail the <_____> that comes from reasoning,
[c] **but *this* has/entails *that*.**
[d] Whence *orexis* does not entail the deliberative capacity.[6]

---

more like mere sensations than representations of objects. So their survival depends not on the representation of perceptual *objects* as pleasant (and so to-be-pursued) or painful (and so to-be-avoided), but rather on pleasant and painful *sensations* together with rudimentary *epithumiai* for the persistence or cessation of these very *sensations*. Their movements are generally reactions to sensations, like scratching where there is an itch—for example, closing in response to noxious stimuli, opening to let warmth or moisture in, and so on. No determinate representations are required to explain such "indeterminate" movements.

[4] Aristotle uses νοῦς—which is typically rendered 'intellect' or 'thought'—sometimes to refer to the relevant *capacity* of thought and sometimes to refer to the *activity* of thought.

[5] The chapter divisions are not due to Aristotle but were established, in some cases following previous editions, in the Basle edition of 1531.

[6] Aristotle tends to use ὄρεξις as a generic term for desire, covering both *epithumia* (or "appetite," a form of non-rational desire) and *boulêsis* (or "wish," a form of rational desire associated with calculation). As he explains in *DA* III.10, in lines that are highly relevant to our topic (lines that follow immediately on [E] below):

And in fact, *nous* evidently does not move <an animal> without *orexis*, for *boulêsis* is *orexis*. And whenever an animal is moved in accordance with calculation [*logismos*], it is moved in accordance with *boulêsis*. But *orexis* also moves <animals> against calculation, for *epithumia* is a kind of *orexis*. [433a23–26]

This explains the point in [3][d]: because *epithumia* is a form of *orexis* that does not entail the presence of a deliberative capacity, *orexis* (simply as such) does not entail the presence of a deliberative capacity (or, as I suggest below, of deliberative *phantasia*).

[a] καὶ αἴτιον τοῦτο τοῦ δόξαν μὴ δοκεῖν ἔχειν,
[b] ὅτι τὴν ἐκ συλλογισμοῦ οὐκ ἔχει,
[c] **αὕτη δὲ ἐκείνην**,
[d] διὸ τὸ βουλευτικὸν οὐκ ἔχει ἡ ὄρεξις.[7] [434a10–12]

[4] [a] But sometimes _____ conquers and moves _____,
[b] **and sometimes *that* <conquers> *this*,**
[c] just as a sphere <conquers a sphere>,
[d] desire <conquers> desire whenever *akrasia* occurs.
[e] But *by nature*, the higher <*archê*> is always more of an *archê* and moves <the animal>.[8]
[f] So it [sc., the rational animal] is in fact moved with three different *phorai*.

[a] νικᾷ δ' ἐνίοτε καὶ κινεῖ [τὴν βούλησιν],
[b] **ὀτὲ δ' ἐκείνη ταύτην**,
[c] ὥσπερ σφαῖρα,
[d] ἡ ὄρεξις τὴν ὄρεξιν, ὅταν ἀκρασία γένηται·
[e] φύσει δὲ ἀεὶ ἡ ἄνω ἀρχικωτέρα καὶ κινεῖ
[f] ὥστε τρεῖς φορὰς ἤδη κινεῖσθαι. [434a13–16]

[5*] *To epistêmonikon*, however, is not moved, but remains <at rest>. But since the one <*doxa*> is a universal supposition or statement, while the other <*doxa*> is of the particular—for the one says that it is necessary for such <a person> to do such <an action>, while the other says that this <action> is such or that I am such <a person>—*either* this *doxa* [sc., the particular one] moves <the animal>, not the universal one, *or* both <move the animal> but the one is rather at rest, the other not.[9]

---

[7] Most editors place a semicolon here. But this simply encourages the standard (but in my view mistaken) reading of [4][a]. So I prefer a period (and, eventually, parentheses).

[8] Aristotle uses ἀρχή both in its specifically political sense (in which it refers to *governing* agents, such as monarchs and oligarchs) and in a more general sense (in which it refers to the principles or sources of phenomena such as motion or growth). In other words, not all principles in the general sense are *governing* principles. But (as I argue below) [4][e] is plausibly read as saying that higher principles are principles in a stricter sense than lower ones, by which I think he means that they are *governing* principles in a way that lower ones are not.

[9] In the official account of *phantasia* back in III.3, Aristotle uses ὑπόληψις (here rendered 'supposition') as a generic term that applies to *epistêmê*, *doxa*, and *phronêsis*, as well as their opposites. *Epistêmê* (generally 'scientific knowledge') and *phronêsis* (generally 'practical wisdom'), being forms of knowledge, cannot be false, but *doxa* ('belief') can be either true or false. I transliterate τὸ ἐπιστημονικόν, which refers to whatever part of soul has the relevant sort of *epistêmê*. Insofar as the *epistêmê* in question here seems to be practical rather than theoretical, Aristotle may be departing from the apparently canonical use at 1139a6–15, where *to epistêmonikon* is said to grasp things whose principles cannot be other than they are and is contrasted with *to logistikon* (which is explicitly associated with deliberation and said to be of things that are—or whose principles are—capable of being other than they are). And I think it worth exploring on some other occasion whether Aristotle speaks this way here because he thinks that at least some principles of the form "it is necessary for such <a person> to do such <an action>" are on a par with the necessary truths grasped in scientific inquiry.

> τὸ δ' ἐπιστημονικὸν οὐ κινεῖται, ἀλλὰ μένει.
> ἐπεὶ δ' ἡ μὲν καθόλου ὑπόληψις καὶ λόγος, ἡ δὲ τοῦ καθ'
> ἕκαστον (ἡ μὲν γὰρ λέγει ὅτι δεῖ τὸν τοιοῦτον τὸ τοιόνδε πράττειν,
> ἡ δὲ ὅτι τόδε τοιόνδε, κἀγὼ δὲ τοιόσδε), ἢ δὴ αὕτη κινεῖ ἡ δόξα,
> οὐχ ἡ καθόλου, ἢ ἄμφω, ἀλλ' ἡ μὲν ἠρεμοῦσα μᾶλλον,
> ἡ δ' οὔ. [434a16–21]

There is much here that remains to be resolved. But one point should be clear: if we do not understand [3], which introduces *doxa*, then we cannot easily understand how the argument is supposed to reach its conclusion in [5], which is about the role of *doxa* in moving rational animals. Our working hypothesis should thus be that *doxa*—or some item closely associated with it—functions here as a kind of "middle term" that connects [3] with [5].

But before we attempt to fill in the missing details, let us take a quick look at the general context in which the argument of III.11 appears.

1. THE GENERAL CONTEXT: *DE ANIMA* III.9–10

At the start of III.9, Aristotle explicitly sets aside the cognitive capacities by which the souls of animals are taken to differ from those of plants and turns to the locomotive capacities that are supposed to be distinctive of complete and non-mutilated animals. The official question is this: what in an animal soul is responsible for the animal's locomotion? Is it some one "part" that is separable either in magnitude or in account from other "parts" of soul? Or is it the whole soul? And if it is some one part, is it one proper to locomotion and additional to those previously mentioned? Or is it one of these—e.g., the *aisthêtikon*, the *orektikon*, or *nous*? In sum, what is the mover [*to kinoun*] of an animal?

It is clear by the end of III.9 that Aristotle's investigation is not simply about the movements of animals from one place to another simply as such. His references to *akrasia* and *enkrateia*, and to practical *nous*, reveal that his question extends to distinctively human forms of activity, including those in which virtues of character are exercised.[10] The conclusion of III.11, about the role of *doxa* in moving rational animals, is thus focused on a special case of the more general question raised at the start of III.9.

This conclusion is more specifically part of Aristotle's response to an *aporia*, articulated in III.10, about whether there is in the case of rational animals a single mover on a par with the one he sees in the souls of non-rational animals—namely, *to orektikon*. Let's take a closer look at how the *aporia* arises in III.9 and at how Aristotle approaches it in III.10.

---

[10] I transliterate ἀκρασία/ἀκρατής and ἐνκράτεια/ἐνκρατής because the standard translations are so inadequate. The idea, explained in passages [B] and [C] below, is of subjects who are either uncontrolled by reason or controlled by it. But there is, as we shall, an important difference between the sort of control exercised by reason in an enkratic agent and the sort of control exercised by reason in a genuinely virtuous agent.

Aristotle begins his search for the mover by eliminating possible candidates.

[A]   That it is not the nutritive capacity <that moves the animal> is plain, because this motion [sc., locomotion] is always both for the sake of something and together with *phantasia* and *orexis*.[11] [432b14–16]

Aristotle appeals here to the case of plants, which have the nutritive capacity but do not locomote—and not simply because they lack the requisite organs. For as he goes on to explain, if the nutritive capacity were a mover, then—given his views about how nature works—complete and non-mutilated plants would have locomotive organs. But the crucial point is that locomotion does not occur without *phantasia* and *orexis*. And for these *aisthêsis* is required.

One might thus suppose that *to aisthêtikon* is what moves the animal. But Aristotle makes a parallel move to eliminate *to aisthêtikon*. There exist complete and non-mutilated animals that have *aisthêsis* but are stationary: and given Aristotle's views about how nature works, these animals would have locomotive organs if *to aisthêtikon* were *for* locomotion.

Aristotle then turns to the calculating capacity or part [*to logistikon*] and, more generally, to *nous*. He quickly dismisses *theoretical nous* and then—after a famous remark aimed to answer an objection and/or raise a laugh—turns to cases where *nous* issues commands.

[B]   For theoretical *nous* contemplates nothing doable in action [*prakton*]; nor does it say anything about what is to be avoided or pursued, but the movement <of which we are speaking> always belongs to <someone> who is either fleeing or pursuing something. Nor, whenever it [sc., *nous*] contemplates some such thing, does it immediately [*hêdê*] command <its subject> to pursue or avoid <the thing>. For instance, it frequently thinks something fearful or pleasant but does not command fear (although the heart moves) or <pursuit> if <it thinks something> pleasant (although some other part <moves>).[12] [432b27–a1]

Further, even when *nous* commands and thought [*dianoia*] says one should avoid something or pursue <it>, <the subject> does not move [*ou kineitai*] but acts according to appetite [*kata tên epithumian*], as, for example, the *akratês* <acts>; and generally we see that the one who has

---

[11] ὅτι μὲν οὖν οὐχ ἡ θρεπτικὴ δύναμις, δῆλον· ἀεί τε γὰρ ἕνεκά του ἡ κίνησις αὕτη, καὶ μετὰ φαντασίας καὶ ὀρέξεώς ἐστιν.

[12] ὁ μὲν γὰρ θεωρητικὸς οὐθὲν θεωρεῖ πρακτόν, οὐδὲ λέγει περὶ φευκτοῦ καὶ διωκτοῦ οὐθέν, ἀεὶ δὲ ἡ κίνησις ἢ φεύγοντός τι ἢ διώκοντός τί ἐστιν. ἀλλ' οὐδ' ὅταν θεωρῇ τι τοιοῦτον, ἤδη κελεύει φεύγειν ἢ διώκειν, οἷον πολλάκις διανοεῖται φοβερόν τι ἢ ἡδύ, οὐ κελεύει δὲ φοβεῖσθαι, ἡ δὲ καρδία κινεῖται, ἂν δ' ἡδύ, ἕτερόν τι μόριον.

medical <knowledge> does not <always> cure, since something else—rather than the knowledge <itself>—is in control of his acting according to this knowledge [*kata tên epistêmên*].[13] [433a1–6][14]

We might be tempted to conclude that, at least in this sort of case, it is *orexis*—of which *epithumia* is a species—that moves the animal. But Aristotle problematizes this conclusion by turning to the converse case, that of the *enkratês*:

[C] But surely *orexis* is not in control [*kuria*] of the movement. For enkratic subjects, who desire and have appetites, do not do what they desire but follow *nous* <instead>.[15] [433a6–8]

Here ends III.9, in the midst of an emerging *aporia*, one due to the fact that rational animals are subject to the three kinds of movement [*phora*] to which [4][f] refers: the akratic, enkratic, and what I shall call the "normative" *phora* (on which more below).[16]

The *aporia* arises from a pair of appearances that seem to point to different answers to the question what moves a rational animal: whereas it is *orexis* (in the form of *epithumia*) that appears to move the *akratês* (who acts against *nous*), it is *nous* that appears to move the *enkratês* (who acts against *orexis*). And it may seem that Aristotle settles for a disjunctive conclusion according to which what moves the animal is in *some* cases *orexis* and in *other* cases *nous*. For as he says in the opening lines of III.10,

[D] It appears anyhow that these two are <the> movers either *orexis* or *nous*, if one counts *phantasia* as a sort of *nous*. For many <people> follow their *phantasiai* against *epistêmê*, and in other animals there is neither thinking [*noêsis*] nor calculation [*logismos*], but <only> *phantasia*.[17] [433a9–12][18]

---

[13] ἔτι καὶ ἐπιτάττοντος τοῦ νοῦ καὶ λεγούσης τῆς διανοίας φεύγειν τι ἢ διώκειν οὐ κινεῖται, ἀλλὰ κατὰ τὴν ἐπιθυμίαν πράττει, οἷον ὁ ἀκρατής. καὶ ὅλως δὲ ὁρῶμεν ὅτι ὁ ἔχων τὴν ἰατρικὴν οὐκ ἰᾶται, ὡς ἑτέρου τινὸς κυρίου ὄντος τοῦ ποιεῖν κατὰ τὴν ἐπιστήμην, ἀλλ' οὐ τῆς ἐπιστήμης.

[14] In *Metaphysics* 9.5, Aristotle claims that with rational capacities, which can produce contrary effects, it is *orexis* or *prohairesis* that determines what the agent does. In other words, it is *orexis* or *prohairesis* (which is a special kind of *orexis*) that will determine whether or not an agent uses her *epistêmê*. *Phronêsis*, however, is different: because it is inseparable from ethical virtue, its subject cannot fail to act on it. See *Nicomachean Ethics* VI/*Eudemian Ethics* VI, chaps. 12–13.

[15] ἀλλὰ μὴν οὐδ' ἡ ὄρεξις ταύτης κυρία τῆς κινήσεως· οἱ γὰρ ἐγκρατεῖς ὀρεγόμενοι καὶ ἐπιθυμοῦντες οὐ πράττουσιν ὧν ἔχουσι τὴν ὄρεξιν, ἀλλ' ἀκολουθοῦσι τῷ νῷ.

[16] Nothing in my argument depends on this, but I suspect that Aristotle uses the term φορά here (rather than κίνησις or even πρᾶξις) because there are (as *De Caelo* I.3 argues) three forms of φορά and because these three forms are appropriate metaphors for the forms of behavior with which *DA* III.11 is concerned. Circular motion, being perfect, corresponds to what I call the 'normative' *phora*; and the two forms of linear motion, one toward and one away from the center, correspond to *enkrateia* and *akrasia*, which are naturally represented as moving in opposite directions, one toward what *nous* commands and the other away from it.

[17] Φαίνεται δέ γε δύο ταῦτα κινοῦντα, ἢ ὄρεξις ἢ νοῦς, εἴ τις τὴν φαντασίαν τιθείη ὡς νόησίν τινα· πολλοὶ γὰρ παρὰ τὴν ἐπιστήμην ἀκολουθοῦσι ταῖς φαντασίαις, καὶ ἐν τοῖς ἄλλοις ζῴοις οὐ νόησις οὐδὲ λογισμὸς ἔστιν, ἀλλὰ φαντασία.

[18] The second conjunct ("and in other animals . . .") gives the reason for counting *phantasia* as a sort of nous [*hôs noêsin tina*]. But we need not read this as claiming that *phantasia* is strictly speaking a kind of

But it would be premature to take Aristotle's conclusion to be disjunctive. For that would not sit easily with the remainder of III.10, where Aristotle makes it clear that *nous* (construed broadly so as to include *phantasia*) can no more move the *enkratês* in the absence of *orexis* than *orexis* can move the *akratês* in the absence of *nous* (again construed broadly so as to include *phantasia*). Aristotle clearly thinks that *orexis* and *nous* must at least *cooperate*. But there are signs that he adopts a stronger view, at least in cases where the behavior of rational animals goes as it is supposed (teleologically speaking) to go. In these cases he seems to think that *nous* and *orexis* somehow *function as one*.

I have argued elsewhere that Aristotle treats τὸ ὀρεκτικόν and τὸ φανταστικόν (as well as τὸ αἰσθητικόν) as labels for one and the same "part" of soul, and that he uses different labels in different explanatory contexts.[19] When this part is functioning in a cognitive capacity, he tends to use τὸ αἰσθητικόν or τὸ φανταστικόν; when it is functioning in its locomotive capacity, he tends to use τὸ ὀρεκτικόν.[20]

I read Aristotle's argument for the unity of these so-called parts as parallel to his argument for the unity of the "common sense." If sight and taste, for example, did not function *as one* in perceiving honey, it would be as if one subject saw the gold color and another tasted the sweet flavor, and there would be no subject that perceived a single object as both gold and sweet. Similarly, if my *orexis* and my *aisthêsis* (or my *orexis* and my *phantasia*) did not function *as one*, it would be as if one subject desired honey and another saw (or remembered) some honey: no action to secure any honey would be taken.

Aristotle goes on in III.10 to make a parallel point about the need for *orexis* and practical *nous* to function *as one*.

[E] Both of these then—*nous* and *orexis*—are capable of moving <the animal> with respect to place. I mean the *nous* that is for the sake of calculating, i.e., practical *nous*. For it differs from theoretical *nous* by its end. And all *orexis* is for the sake of something. For that of which there is *orexis*, this is the starting point [*archê*] of practical *nous* [viz., of practical *reasoning*]. And the last

---

nous. This may be a *tis alienans*. On the minimalist reading that I prefer, the point is simply that *phantasia* plays in the behavior of non-rational animals the role that *nous* is supposed (teleologically speaking) to play in the behavior of rational animals. But the first conjunct ("many people follow their *phantasiai* against *epistêmê*") makes it clear that there are cases in which *phantasia* ends up playing in rational animals the role that *nous* should, teleologically speaking, play—namely, cases of *akrasia*. Aristotle says of course that the operations of *nous* will themselves involve *phantasmata* [431a16–17]. So what is envisioned here is presumably a case in which non-noetic or perceptual *phantasmata* dominate, perhaps occluding or overpowering the noetic *phantasmata* that should, teleologically speaking, determine the agent's behavior. This (as we shall see) is precisely the sort of conflict with which III.11 is concerned—namely, conflict between perceptual and deliberative *phantasia*.

[19] See Whiting 2002 [Chapter 5, this volume] for more detailed arguments for the views summarized in the next few paragraphs.

[20] I suspect that he avoids τὸ κινητικόν because he wants to avoid giving the impression that the "part" in question is itself a subject of locomotion.

thing [sc., the conclusion of practical reasoning] is the starting point [*archê*] of action.²¹ [433a13–17]

So it is reasonable that these two, *orexis* and practical thought [*dianoia praktikê*], appear to be the movers <of a rational animal>. For the object of desire [*to orekton*] moves <the animal> and on account of this thought moves <the animal>, because the starting point of this [sc., thought] is the object of desire. And *phantasia*, whenever it moves <the animal>, does not move it without orexis. **The mover [*to kinoun*] is indeed some one thing, *to orektikon*, since if two things**—*nous* and *orexis*—moved <the animal>, **they would move <it> according to some common *eidos*.**²² [433a17–22]²³

Aristotle's point here is that, just as in non-rational animals *aisthêsis* and *orexis* work together as one, so too in rational animals *nous* and *orexis* work together as one—at least when things go as they are supposed, teleologically speaking, to go. Akratic and enkratic behavior are of course all too common. But the unified operation of *nous* and *orexis* is nevertheless the *norm* for rational animals.²⁴

We can see what might be involved in *nous* and *orexis* working together as one if we consider how, in non-rational animals, *aisthêsis* and *orexis* work together as one. The idea is explained back in III.7, where Aristotle argues that the *aisthêtikon* and the *orektikon* are in some sense the same part or capacity of soul, even if they "differ in being" in the sense that the account of *what it is to perceive* is different from the account of *what it is to desire*. Aristotle's argument for the identity of these parts or capacities appeals to the fact, as he sees it, that whenever an object is perceived as pleasant or painful, the soul of the perceiver, "as if asserting or denying <something> pursues or flees" that object. The idea, I think, is that perceiving an object as pleasant *involves* desiring to pursue that object. In a non-rational animal, then, the perceptual appearance [*to aisthêma*] of an object as pleasant is inseparable from a desire to pursue that object, and whatever object appears perceptually most pleasant to the animal will be the object of the animal's strongest—and perhaps even its only—desire.

Matters are more complicated in the case of rational animals for whom at least some of the *phantasmata* employed in thought are no less separable from desires than the *aisthêmata* just mentioned are. For immediately upon concluding that the *aisthêtikon* and the *orektikon* are the same, Aristotle adds "to the thinking soul, *phantasmata*

---

²¹ ἄμφω ἄρα ταῦτα κινητικὰ κατὰ τόπον, νοῦς καὶ ὄρεξις, νοῦς δὲ ὁ ἕνεκά του λογιζόμενος καὶ ὁ πρακτικός· διαφέρει δὲ τοῦ θεωρητικοῦ τῷ τέλει. καὶ ἡ ὄρεξις <δ'> ἕνεκά του πᾶσα· οὗ γὰρ ἡ ὄρεξις, αὕτη ἀρχὴ τοῦ πρακτικοῦ νοῦ, τὸ δ' ἔσχατον ἀρχὴ τῆς πράξεως.

²² ὥστε εὐλόγως δύο ταῦτα φαίνεται τὰ κινοῦντα, ὄρεξις καὶ διάνοια πρακτική· τὸ ὀρεκτὸν γὰρ κινεῖ, καὶ διὰ τοῦτο ἡ διάνοια κινεῖ, ὅτι ἀρχὴ αὐτῆς ἐστι τὸ ὀρεκτόν. καὶ ἡ φαντασία δὲ ὅταν κινῇ, οὐ κινεῖ ἄνευ ὀρέξεως. ἓν δή τι τὸ κινοῦν, τὸ ὀρεκτικόν. εἰ γὰρ δύο, νοῦς καὶ ὄρεξις, ἐκίνουν, κατὰ κοινὸν ἄν τι ἐκίνουν εἶδος.

²³ As I explain in "Locomotive Soul," the argument here is similar in form to the argument at the end of De Anima 1.5 for the unity of the entire soul.

²⁴ It is what produces the third of the three kinds of *phora* mentioned in [4], the normative kind (as distinct from the akratic and enkratic kinds).

function like *aisthêmata,* and whenever <the thinking soul> says or denies <that something is> good or bad, it pursues or avoids <that thing>." The idea here seems to be that whenever the soul thinks of some x as good or bad, which it cannot do without having a *phantasma* of x as good or bad, the soul is disposed either to pursue x or to flee it. This suggests that having a *phantasma* of x as good can no more be separated from having a desire for x than having an *aisthêma* of y as pleasant can be separated from having a desire for y. And it is this inseparability that gives rise to the sort of conflict among *orexeis* that opens the door to the possibilities of *akrasia* and *enkrateia.*

These phenomena arise because the *phantasmata* that come about in perception may differ in content from the *phantasmata* that come about in thought, and each sort of *phantasma* is inseparable from its own *orexeis.* Perceptual *phantasia* may present x as pleasant and thus to-be-pursued, while deliberative *phantasia* presents x as unhealthy and thus to-be-avoided. So a creature with both forms of *phantasia* may end up being subject to conflicting *orexeis.*[25] For example, perceptual *phantasia* may dispose a subject to go for some object that deliberative *phantasia* disposes her to reject; or perceptual *phantasia* may dispose her to flee some object that deliberative *phantasia* disposes her to pursue.

Aristotle recognizes the seeds of such conflict in his official account of *phantasia* back in III.3, where the relation between *phantasia* and *doxa* is in question. As he says there, an object of which one has true *hupolêpsis* can appear falsely to some subject in the sense that the object can appear to that subject to be in some way other than it in fact is. For example, the sun may appear to a subject to be a foot across even though that subject is persuaded—i.e., *believes*—that the sun is larger than the inhabited world [428b2–4]. Similarly, one good (e.g., a pleasure) may appear to a subject be greater than another even though that subject *believes*—presumably as result of reasoning—that it is in fact smaller. In sum, the valence of an object's presentation in perceptual *phantasia* may differ from the valence of its presentation in deliberative *phantasia*; and if each presentation involves its own *orexis* the agent will be subject to conflicting *orexeis.*

III.11 is concerned with precisely this phenomenon. So let us return to it.

2. GETTING [2] AND [3] RIGHT

We left off approaching [3], with some pieces of [2] yet to be determined. One problem with [3] is that it is not clear what the subject of τοῦ δόξαν μὴ δοκεῖν ἔχειν is supposed to be. What is it that seems not to have or entail *doxa*?

There is also a question about what noun to understand with τὴν ἐκ συλλογισμοῦ in [b]. Is the point, as seems grammatically smoothest, about the kind of *doxa* that

---

[25] Deliberative *phantasia* may on its own generate conflicting *orexeis*, but this not the sort of case with which 3.11 is concerned. So I leave it aside.

comes from reasoning? Or is the point, as many translations have it, about the kind of *phantasia* that comes from reasoning?

Recent translations in English, French, and German take the subject of τοῦ δόξαν μὴ δοκεῖν ἔχειν to be τὰ ἄλλα ζῷα (from the end of [0], picked up again in [2][a]). This makes it difficult to understand δόξαν, as seems most natural, with τὴν ἐκ συλλογισμοῦ in [b]. For the claim would then be that the other animals seem not to have *doxa*, because they do not have the kind of *doxa* that comes from *sullogismos*. It would be odd for Aristotle to say this. Is lack of the kind of *doxa* that comes from *sullogismos* really what lies behind the common belief that the other animals lack *any* sort of *doxa*? Mightn't other animals have, as Aristotle thinks rational animals have, a form of *doxa* that comes simply from *aisthêsis*?

It is also unclear what this claim would contribute to the present argument. So translators who take τὰ ἄλλα ζῷα to be the initial subject tend to read Aristotle as saying that the other animals do not have the kind of *phantasia* that comes from reasoning.[26] These translators face two problems: first, to determine the referent of ἐκείνην ['that'] in [3][c]; and second, to show what role the resulting claim plays in the overall argument. Shields, in his new Clarendon translation, follows Bywater and solves both problems in one fell swoop: he excises the universally attested αὕτη δὲ ἐκείνην. Corcilius, in his new German translation, is more circumspect: he takes the point to be that the other animals seem to lack *doxa* because they lack deliberative *phantasia*, whereas deliberative *phantasia* entails perceptual *phantasia*.[27] But it is not clear what role the claim that deliberative *phantasia* entails perceptual *phantasia* would play in this context. For it is hard to see how this claim is supposed to be connected either with what precedes it (the claim that the other animals seem to lack *doxa* because they lack the kind of *phantasia* that comes from reasoning) or with the διό-claim that follows immediately upon it ("whence *orexis* does not entail the deliberative capacity").

But if, as I suggest, Aristotle is contrasting deliberative with perceptual *phantasia* and saying that perceptual *phantasia* does not entail the sort of *doxa* that comes from reasoning, then we can read the claim that perceptual *phantasia* does not entail the sort of *doxa* that comes from reasoning as explaining the διό-claim. We need only assume what Aristotle takes to be true of perceptual *phantasia* in non-rational animals—namely, that it can sometimes, by itself and without any help from *doxa*, produce *orexis*. From this it follows that *orexis* does not entail the presence of the deliberative capacity. For this reason, and others to be spelled out below, I take the initial subject of [3] to be ἡ αἰσθητικὴ φαντασία and I understand δόξα, as seems most natural, with τὴν ἐκ συλλογισμοῦ in [3][b].

---

[26] Corcilius 2017; Shields 2016; Barbotin 2009 (first edition 1966); Seidl (nach Theiler) 1995.

[27] "Dies ist auch die Ursache dafür, dass (die andere Lebewesen) keine Meinung zu haben scheinen, weil sie (nämlich) nicht die aus einer vergleichenden Überlegung hervorgegangene (Vorstellung) haben, diese aber jene (wahrnehmungsmässige Vorstellung hat)."

We can easily read [2] as setting up this reading of [3] if we read the remarks in [2] [c] and [d] as parenthetical remarks about deliberative *phantasia*.[28] We can thus read Aristotle as introducing the μέν/δέ pair in [2][a] and [b], and then making some parenthetical remarks about the δέ item before turning in [3] to compare the μέν item to the δέ item (and comparing them in a way that will help him to resolve the aporia with which he is concerned). And if this is what he is doing, then we can reasonably take the αὕτη ['this'] in [3][c] as referring to the proximate δέ-item, whose operations were described in the parenthetical remarks at the end of [2]. In other words, we can read the sequence as follows:

[2*] [a] Perceptual *phantasia* **[hê men aisthêtikê phantasia]**, as *previously said*, belongs even among the other animals,

[b] whereas deliberative <*phantasia*> **[hê de bouleutikê]** belongs among rational <animals>.

[c] (For whether one will do this or that is already the work of *logismos*.

[d] And it is necessary <for deliberative *phantasia*> to measure by one <measure>, for it [sc., deliberative *phantasia*] pursues the greater <good>; so *it* is able to make one <?>[29] out of several *phantasmata*.)

[3] [a] And this is the reason why it [sc., perceptual *phantasia*] seems not to involve *doxa*:

[b] <namely> because it does not involve the kind of *doxa* that comes from reasoning,

[c] **but this** <deliberative *phantasia*> **involves that** <the *doxa* that comes from reasoning>.

[d] (Whence orexis does not involve the deliberative capacity.) [my bold]

It might seem that I should, given my emphasis on the μέν/δέ structure, take ἡ αἰσθητικὴ φαντασία as the referent of ἐκείην ['that'] in [3][c]. But I do not think my emphasis on the μέν/δέ structure requires me to read ἐκείνην in this way. It would be natural for Aristotle to express the thought that the μέν-item seems not to entail some *x* that the δέ-item entails by saying that the μέν-item seems not to entail *x*, whereas the δέ-item does entail *that*. And reading [3][c] this way—i.e., as saying that deliberative *phantasia* (unlike perceptual *phantasia*) entails the sort of *doxa* that comes from reasoning—serves not only to license the διὸ-claim in [3][d]; it also allows us to make better sense of [4] than commentators have hitherto made of it. Or so I shall argue.

---

[28] Hicks parenthesizes in this way, but his motivation for doing so is misguided. He says that he puts the parentheses here in order to make it clear what he takes the antecedent of τοῦτο at the start of [3] to be—namely, the fact that the other animals have only perceptual *phantasia*. But the τοῦτο clearly looks forward to the ὅτι clause in [3][b]. So there is no need for parentheses to do the job that Hicks assigns to his. Still, someone who reads [2][c]–[d] as I propose—i.e., as making parenthetical remarks about deliberative *phantasia*—may for *that* reason adopt the parentheses proposed by Hicks.

[29] I find it difficult to suppress the thought that taking δόξα to be suggested by the context would render its introduction in the next line less abrupt. But the default here is φάντασμα.

But first let me propose a minor emendation of [3][d] that is not strictly necessary to my overall reading but attracts me for two reasons: it resolves a problem that many commentators have had and it makes the argument (at least as I read it) much smoother.

Commentators have been puzzled by the reference in [3][d] to the deliberative *capacity* [*to bouleutikon*]. For not only is the substantive τὸ βουλευτικόν comparatively rare in Aristotle's corpus; it is also unclear why Aristotle should speak of the capacity here. But there would be no puzzle if Aristotle had written τὴν βουλευτικήν instead of τὸ βουλευτικόν. Indeed τὴν βουλευτικήν, with φαντασίαν understood, is just what we might expect here, given that Aristotle is talking about *orexis* and *doxa*, not *to orektikon* and *to doxastikon*.[30]

I take the point here to be, as [5] suggests, about the roles played by token desires and beliefs in producing the behavior of rational animals. In other words, I read [3][d] as claiming that there can be individual *orexeis* even when deliberative *phantasia* is not in play. I also read [3][d] as parenthetical, since it contributes nothing to the argument, whose focus is *phantasia*, not *orexis*.[31]

If this is right, then we should not take ἡ ὄρεξις, as most translators do, as the subject of νικᾷ and κινεῖ in [4][a]. For there are plausible alternatives that allow us to make better sense of the overall argument. One is ἡ βουλευτικὴ φαντασία; the other, closely associated with the first, is ἡ ἐκ συλλογισμοῦ <δόξα>. The main advantage of the latter is that it keeps *doxa* explicitly in play, thus setting up the conclusion in [5]. But the idea is the same either way, since deliberative *phantasia* is now firmly associated with the kind of *doxa* that comes from reasoning. And my appeal to the μέν/δέ structure leads me to favor ἡ βουλευτικὴ φαντασία. Hence

[3*] [a] And this is the reason why perceptual *phantasia* seems not to entail *doxa*—
 [b] namely, because it does not entail the *doxa* that comes from reasoning.
 [c] But **this [sc. deliberative *phantasia*] entails that** [sc., the *doxa* that comes from reasoning],
 [d] (whence *orexis* does not entail deliberative <*phantasia*>)[32].
[4] [a] And sometimes it [sc., deliberative *phantasia*[33]] conquers and moves <the animal>. [my bold][34]

---

[30] Aristotle could easily have chosen to talk about these capacities had he wanted to. For the relevant substantives are (unlike τὸ βουλευτικόν) common in his corpus.
[31] Aristotle often does this: he will use a διό-claim to confirm a point he has just made, without taking the διό-claim itself as part of his argument.
[32] Please note that my argument for taking ἡ βουλευτικὴ φαντασία as subject in [4][a] does *not* depend on my proposal to read τὴν βουλευτικήν in place of τὸ βουλευτικόν in [3][d]. Because I am treating [3][d] as parenthetical, I am taking the subject of [3][c] as the default subject in [4][a].
[33] Alternatively: <the *doxa* that comes from reasoning>.
[34] Someone might object to the fact that my reading takes the first occurrence of νικᾷ as intransitive while taking the remaining occurrences as transitive. But I do not think it out of the question that Aristotle would do this. And one might, as an alternative, take the initial occurrence as transitive with something like πάντα as its implicit object.

There is no conclusive argument for this on purely grammatical grounds, so any decision in its favor must depend in part on the overall sense afforded by this reading as compared with other possible ones. Let me pause then to explain why I find the standard way of reading [4][a] unsatisfactory. Readers who are happy with the proposed reading of [4][a] and want simply to follow the argument as I interpret it to its conclusion may skip section 3. Anyone still tempted after reading section 4 to take ἡ ὄρεξις as subject of νικᾷ and κινεῖ can read section 3 later.

3. OPTIONAL DIGRESSION: PROBLEMS WITH THE STANDARD READING OF [4][A]

The main problem with taking ἡ ὄρεξις as subject of νικᾷ and κινεῖ is that doing so makes it difficult to align the elements of [4][a]–[e] with the three *phorai* mentioned in [4][f]. To see this, we should note that there are, schematically speaking, three ways to read [4]. The differences between them turn on where in [a]–[e] each of the three *phorai* mentioned in [f] makes its appearance.

The *phorai* are, as I have said, the enkratic, the akratic, and the "normative." The normative *phora* involves some analog of the unity of *orexis* and *phantasia* that characterizes the behavior of non-rational animals. I call it "normative" because it is the kind of *phora* we find when things go as they are supposed, teleologically speaking, to go. But things do not always go as they are supposed, teleologically speaking, to go: rational animals sometimes engage in both enkratic and akratic behavior. Still, we must keep in mind that these forms of behavior are anomalies in Aristotle's cosmos: neither beasts nor heavenly bodies are subject to such vagaries. The norm, as we have seen, is the unity of *nous* (broadly conceived so as to include *phantasia*) and *orexis*. Let us return then to [4], keeping this norm in mind.

It is clear that two of the three forms of *phora*—the enkratic and akratic—are introduced in [a]–[e]. But it is an open question where (if it all) the normative form is introduced: it is possible that it is not explicitly mentioned here but simply in the background provided by III.10, where the relevant form of unity is discussed at length. This possibility yields the first of the three schematic ways to read [4], which involves seeing in [4][a]–[e] *only* the akratic and enkratic *phorai*. Let's call this the "anomalous cases" schema.

The other ways of reading [4] are, by contrast, "exhaustive": they include the normative form along with the two anomalous forms. One locates each of the three *phorai* in [a]–[d] and then takes [e] to make either a meta-point or parenthetical remarks about what happens *phusei:* let's call this the "independent [e]" schema. The other locates the normative case in [e] and the anomalous cases in [a]–[d]: let's call this the "normative [e]" schema.

The anomalous/exhaustive choice-point has not been explicitly articulated in any place I know. I assume that most commentators unreflectively adopt some version of the exhaustive reading. This, I suspect, is why so many end up proposing to alter the received text: they have difficulty lining [4][a]–[e] up with each of the three *phorai* mentioned in [f], so they feel the need to *add* something.

Trendelenburg conjectures a δέ at the start of [d]—yielding ἡ δ' ὄρεξις τὴν ὄρεξιν—because this would allow us to locate the third form of *phora* in [d], which is explicitly concerned with the akratic *phora*. How exactly the rest should be sorted will depend on whether or not we follow the manuscript tradition in which τὴν βούλησιν follows νικᾷ δ' ἐνίοτε καὶ κινεῖ in [4][a]. If we read τὴν βούλησιν, [a] would introduce the akratic *phora* and so overlap with [d], in which case we would need either to locate the normative case in [e] or to read [4] as covering only the anomalous cases. But either way, the case for adding δέ is undermined. If we locate the normative case in [e], the relevant δέ awaits us there; if we read [4] as covering only the anomalous cases, then there is no need for another δέ. Either way, we should leave the text alone.

It should be noted that τὴν βούλησιν is independently awkward—and not just because of the word order. There is no parallel for κινεῖν τὴν βούλησιν elsewhere in Aristotle's corpus. And perhaps more importantly, the object of κινεῖ in III.9–11 is generally (though sometimes only implicitly) τὸ ζῷον, as in [5] (toward which [4] is working). So it is tempting to follow the manuscripts in which τὴν βούλησιν does not appear and to take τὸ ζῷον to be the implicit object of κινεῖ. This is the reading I prefer.

But some commentators think Aristotle *must* have written τὴν βούλησιν in [a] because they think it required in order to make sense of ὁτὲ δ' ἐκείνη ταύτην in [b]. Their reading runs as follows:

[4] [a$_{O/B}$] sometimes *orexis* <sc., a lower form of *orexis*> conquers *boulêsis* <i.e., a higher form of *orexis*>
  [b$_{O/B}$] but sometimes *this* <*boulêsis*> conquers *that* <the lower form of *orexis*>.

On this reading, [a] introduces the akratic *phora* while [b] introduces the enkratic one. But since [d] is explicitly concerned with the akratic phora, [a] and [d] once again overlap, and Aristotle seems to be jumping around. Hicks 1907 (ad loc) cites Simplicius 310, 28 in support of reading [d] as using ἀκρασία in a broad sense that includes *enkrateia* as well as *akrasia*, and so as providing a résumé of the enkratic and akratic cases. This would remove the appearance of jumping about. But I think we can do better.

I do not agree with Hicks that τὴν βούλησιν is required in order to make sense of ὁτὲ δ' ἐκείνη ταύτην in [b]. But I can easily imagine an early editor or scribe adding it because he (like Hicks) thought it (or something like it) required in order to make sense of [b]. For other changes have been proposed by commentators struggling to make sense of [b], some indeed quite radical. Cornford proposed to read ὁτὲ δὲ κινεῖ γ' αὐτήν in place of [b]'s ὁτὲ δ' ἐκείνη ταύτην; and Bywater, citing αὕτη δὲ ἐκείνην back in [3], proposed to add ὁτὲ μὲν αὕτη ἐκείνην before ὁτὲ δ' ἐκείνη ταύτην.

I suspect that there lies behind Bywater's radical proposal a knee-jerk tendency to assume that any ἐκείνη ταύτην requires a reciprocal αὕτη ἐκείνην.[35] But I think we can make good sense of [4] as it stands if we give up the idea that ἡ ὄρεξις from [3][d] is the subject of νικᾷ δ' ἐνίοτε καὶ κινεῖ in [4][a].

I cannot discuss in further detail what I find unsatisfactory with each of the various ways in which I have tried to make sense of III.11 while understanding ἡ ὄρεξις as the subject of [4][a]. So let me simply spell out what seems to me the best way to go *if* we take ἡ ὄρεξις as subject, and then explain how I think we can do better.

If we go with the manuscripts in which τὴν βούλησιν does not appear, then we can achieve a moderately satisfactory result provided we are willing read ἐκείνη in [b] as referring back (as ἐκείνη often does) to something in the preceding bit of text. My preferred candidate is ἡ φαντασία βουλευτική because I think that most natural, given the μέν/δέ structure of the passage. But I am willing to allow that ἐκείνη might refer back to ἡ ἐκ συλλογισμοῦ <δόξα>, which is associated with deliberative *phantasia*. Either way, the idea is the same: sometimes deliberative *phantasia*—or the *doxa* that results from it—conquers an opposed *orexis*.

Here, then, is the best sense I can make of the passage with ἡ ὄρεξις as subject:

[4$_{OR}$] [a] Sometimes <*orexis*> conquers and moves <the animal>
[b] but sometimes that [sc., deliberative *phantasia*[36]] conquers this [sc., *orexis*]
[c] just as a <higher> sphere <conquers a lower one>
[d] and *orexis* <conquers> *orexis* whenever *akrasia* occurs.
[e] But *by nature*, the higher <*archê*> is always more of an *archê* and moves <the rational animal>.
[f] So it [sc., the rational animal] is moved with three different *phorai*.

This allows us to read [a] as introducing the normative case, [b] as introducing the enkratic case, and [d] (with the conjectured δέ in Trendelenburg 1838) as introducing the akratic case. We can then read [e] as making a meta-point or simply a parenthetical remark about what happens *phusei*.

In this case, we should probably read the enigmatic reference to the operations of some sort of sphere as applying only to the enkratic *phora*, and we should probably read Aristotle as referring to a heavenly sphere rather than a ball in some game. If this is right, then Aristotle is comparing the operations of deliberative *phantasia* on *orexis* to the ways in which he takes higher heavenly spheres to control the movements of lower

---

[35] I suspect that assumption also drives the queer translation of 433a12–13 in Seidl (1995). Though Seidl renders ἐκείνη appropriately as 'jener,' he interprets it as referring to the immediately preceding τὴν βούλησιν, for which Aristotle would surely have used αὕτη (as in Bywater's proposal to add ὀτὲ μὲν αὕτη ἐκείνην before ὀτὲ δ' ἐκείνη ταύτην).

[36] Alternatively: <the *doxa* from comes from reasoning>.

ones.[37] But that raises the question why, given [4][e], the control of the higher spheres over the lower ones is not invoked in the normative case. And while we might answer that there are in the normative case no opposed movements to be controlled from above, I think we can do better—and without having to insert so much as a single δέ.

4. GETTING [4] RIGHT

The key is to read [4] as turning—after [3*]'s comments about perceptual *phantasia*—to deliberative *phantasia*, which is introduced in [3][c]. Hence

[4*] [a] And sometimes it [sc., deliberative *phantasia*] conquers and moves <the animal>[38]
   [b] but sometimes that [sc., perceptual *phantasia*] conquers this [sc., deliberative *phantasia*]
   [c] just as a sphere <conquers a sphere>
   [d] desire <conquers> desire whenever *akrasia* occurs.
   [e] But *by nature*, the higher <*archê*> is always more of an *archê* and moves <the animal>.
   [f] So it [sc., the rational animal] is moved with three different forms of movement [*phorai*].

One immediate advantage of [4*] is that it treats [4][b]–[d] as a coherent unit focused on *akrasia*, which allows us to make decent sense of the remark about the sphere along the lines suggested by Simplicius: the idea is that in all cases of *akrasia* the strongest desire defeats the weaker in something like the way in which the larger of two balls in some game—or the ball moving with greater force—knocks the other out of the way or at least off its course.

The idea, I think, is roughly as follows. The subject reasons her way to some belief—for example, that she should not consume alcohol when she is caring for children—and thus comes to have a rational desire (i.e., a *boulêsis* or *prohairesis*) never to drink when children are in her care. We must suppose here that the subject does not simply come

---

[37] On the ancient controversy about how to interpret ὥσπερ σφαῖρα, see Hicks 1907 ad 434a13. Commentators tend to take σφαῖρα to refer either (as Themistius took it) to a heavenly sphere or (as Simplicius took it) to a ball in some game. Hutchinson 1990 argues, quite plausibly, for a third view—namely, that Aristotle is adopting something like the account of orderly and disorderly motions found in Plato's *Timaeus* 43–44. It is difficult to be sure what Aristotle has in mind, but I am inclined at present to side with Simplicius both because Aristotle seems to restrict the comparison to the case of *akrasia* and because he does not mention the sphere in connection with the normative case. But this issue deserves more attention than I give it here.

[38] Someone might object to the fact that my reading takes the first occurrence of νικᾷ as intransitive while taking the remaining occurrences as transitive. But I do not think it out of the question that Aristotle would do this. One might, as an alternative, take the initial occurrence as transitive with something like πάντα as its implicit object.

to have an idle belief, without any connection to desire. The akratic case is, by hypothesis, one in which the subject's coming to have a belief involves or is at least associated with her coming to have a corresponding *boulêsis*. She may frequently—perhaps even for the most part—abstain from alcohol when she is caring for children. Yet on some occasions when children are in her care, the opportunity to have a drink presents itself and *appears* so attractive that she simply helps herself without attending to (let alone changing) her belief that she should not be doing so.

In this case, we should imagine that having the drink appears to the subject so pleasant that it dominates her practical outlook in something like the way in which certain objects can dominate her visual field, not necessarily by occluding other objects but simply by standing out for some reason—by being, for example, so bright in color that she does not notice other, less brightly colored objects in her visual field. In such cases, she may see the surrounding objects without really attending to them or recognizing the sort of import they normally have for her. So she simply acts on what is, at present, her strongest desire, which operates here like a larger ball (or one moving with greater force), mechanically knocking a smaller ball (or one moving with lesser force) out of its way.

But why should Aristotle restrict this simile to the case of *akrasia*? Why would he not treat *enkrateia* in the same way?

The answer, I think, is that *enkrateia* involves operations of reason in a way that *akrasia* does not. And the relevant operations of reason involve activities of deliberative *phantasia*. For, as Aristotle says at 1150b21ff, there are some people who, because they foresee [*proaisthomenoi kai proïdontes*] what is to come and prepare themselves in accordance with their reasoning [*proegeirantes heautous kata ton logismon*], are not overcome by their passion (whether it be pleasant or painful). The idea, I think, is that *enkrateia* involves some form of deliberate and conscious resistance in the face of whatever desires are opposed to the agent's *boulêsis*. We might thus contrast enkratic behavior with akratic behavior by saying that whereas reason goes on holiday in *akrasia*, reason works overtime in *enkrateia*.

If this is right, then enkratic behavior does not necessarily involve the stronger desire overpowering the weaker: *boulêsis* may be weaker than *epithumia* in a phenomenological sense but able to resist the force of *epithumia* because *boulêsis* is reinforced by the operations of deliberative *phantasia*. There is nothing outré here: visualizing the future benefits of resisting present temptation is a common strategy for resisting strong desires that tempt us to act against our *boulêseis*. But for this, the image of one moving ball knocking another out of the way is not quite right. We need something other than a moving ball, something capable of keeping a forcefully moving ball from reaching its destination: something like a goalie's mitt moving *in anticipation* of what is to come.

What is crucial here is the element of anticipation. *Enkrateia* is not simply a matter of one desire, a *boulêsis*, overpowering another in a mechanistic way, as one moving ball might overpower another. If *boulêsis* is to win out over opposed desires, *boulêsis* must rely on cognitive powers such as those involved in visualization: the subject must both imagine what is likely to come about and picture appropriate ways of responding to it, perhaps in conjunction with the probable rewards of responding in the appropriate ways. This, I submit, is why it is only *akrasia* that [4*] assimilates to one ball conquering another.

So I propose to read [4*], schematically speaking, as follows. First, [a] is about *enkrateia*, where deliberative *phantasia* is victorious over some wayward *orexis* (which cannot, of course, be *boulêsis*). Then [b] introduces *akrasia* by pointing out that the previously discussed form of *phantasia* [ἐκείνη = perceptual *phantasia*] sometimes conquers this [ταύτην = deliberative *phantasia*]; in this case, [b] explains, we find one *orexis* conquering another. This leaves [e] to cover the normative case. In other words, I propose to go with a "normative [e]" schema.

I read φύσει δὲ ἀεὶ in [e] as introducing a different *kind* of principle, one that does not involve knocking things about in something like the way one ball knocks another about. When this sort of principle is effective there is no opposition of the sort involved in *enkrateia*, so there is no need to rely on the sort of reinforcement that deliberative *phantasia* is capable of providing. This sort of principle *governs* the movements of the rational animal in a way comparable to that in which the unified principle responsible for the behavior of non-rational animals governs their movements. There is no conflict of principles requiring one to overpower another.

That is why Aristotle calls this sort of principle *archikôtera*. It does not simply *overpower* other movers like itself, as one ball overpowers another in a game or one desire overpowers another in cases of *akrasia*. Rather, this sort of principle *governs* the behavior of a rational animal in something like the way in which a wise ruler governs the behavior of willing subjects (i.e., subjects whose will is shaped by their *appreciation* of the contents of the ruler's wisdom, as distinct from merely trusting in the wisdom of whatever the ruler prescribes). In this case, the animal is moved *by practical nous*, though not, of course, in the absence of *orexis*. What we have here is what Aristotle elsewhere calls προαίρεσις and characterizes as either ὀρεκτικὸς νοῦς or ὄρεξις διανοητική.[39] These are not genuine alternatives, but rather two different ways of describing the same state of soul, a state that can be characterized equally well as a kind of thought *and* as a kind of desire: neither characterization is privileged.

The idea here is that in the normative case—the case of the *phronimos* or practically wise agent—the subject's *orektikon* is *shaped* by the principles that inhabit her practical *nous*. One might even say that the subject's *orektikon* is *en-formed* by the principles that *constitute* its practical *nous*. This is the hylomorphic conception of *phronêsis* that I, following John McDowell, elsewhere attribute to Aristotle. *Phronêsis* stands to the properly formed *orektikon* as Aristotle takes the soul to stand to the organic body; and just as the capacities that constitute the soul (e.g., capacities to reproduce, perceive, and locomote) cannot exist apart from a body with properly formed organs, so too

---

[39] 1139b4–5: διὸ ἢ ὀρεκτικὸς νοῦς ἡ προαίρεσις ἢ ὄρεξις διανοητική, καὶ ἡ τοιαύτη ἀρχὴ ἄνθρωπος.

phronêsis cannot exist apart from properly formed desires. It is, as John McDowell puts it, "the properly moulded state of the motivational propensities in reflectively adjusted form."[40]

5. CONCLUSION

This brings us to [5], which I read as completing the discussion of the normative case that is introduced in [4][e]. On this account, the *aporia* articulated at the start of III.10 is resolved in [4][a]–[d], where Aristotle indicates (very roughly) how conjunctions of perceptual and deliberative *phantasia* give rise to the possibilities of enkratic and akratic behavior, and then turns in [4][e] and [5] to what he sees as the norm in the animal world, i.e., the unified operation of *nous* (broadly construed so as to include *phantasia*) and *orexis*.

For rational animals, the norm involves *doxa* (both universal and particular) moving the animal. Universal *doxai* arise from reasoning; particular *doxai* arise sometimes from reasoning, sometimes directly from perception. When there is no conflict between deliberative and perceptual *phantasia*, the universal and particular *doxai* work together automatically, in ways that Aristotle describes in chaps. 7 and 8 of *De Motu Animalium*. For example, when the subject thinks the universal (that *every* man ought to walk) along with the particular (that *he himself* is a man), straightaway he walks—provided nothing interferes.[41]

The proviso is Aristotle's signal that he means to be describing the normative case: it tacitly acknowledges the existence of the deviant forms of *phora* to which [4][f] refers. The form of the proviso suggests that there is an explanatory asymmetry between the normative *phora* and its deviant counterparts. When things go as they are supposed (teleologically speaking) to go, the subject makes the relevant inferences more or less automatically and acts straightaway (again more or less automatically). But things do not always go as they are supposed (teleologically speaking) to go.

In some cases, the presence of a strong appetite, for example, an appetite to φ, can result in a *phantasma* of φ-ing as so pleasant that the subject acts straightaway, before her standing belief that she ought not φ in situations of the present sort is activated—that is, before any *phantasma* of φ-ing in that situation as harmful (or in some other

---

[40] I take the idea of hylomorphic *phronêsis*, or hylomorphic virtue, from John McDowell 1998. See Whiting 2016 [Chapter 6, this volume] and (2021).

[41] Aristotle's use of δόξα is like our use of 'belief': sometimes it refers to a propositional attitude (e.g., my belief that P), sometimes it refers to the propositional content of such an attitude (i.e., what it is that I believe—namely, P). The present question is whether (as in the normative case) a propositional attitude with the appropriate content both actually comes about and is effective, or whether (as in the other *phorai*) the propositional attitude either fails to come about or comes about but fails to produce the appropriate action because something else prevents it from operating as it is supposed (teleologically speaking) to do. For more on this issue, and the issues that arise in the next few paragraphs, see sections 6–8 of Pickavé and Whiting 2008 [Chapter 7, this volume].

way inappropriate) is formed. This is the form of *akrasia* that Aristotle calls "impetuous" [*propetês*] and opposes to the "weak" [*asthenês*] form.

In other cases, a *phantasma* of φ-ing in that situation as in some way inappropriate may be formed, with the result that there is conflict between the perceptual *phantasma* of φ-ing as pleasant (and so to-be-pursued) and the doxastic *phantasma* of φ-ing as in some way appropriate (and so to-be-avoided). How the conflict is resolved will presumably depend on the strength of the sort of reinforcements afforded by the subject's powers of deliberative *phantasia*. If they are sufficiently strong, her action will count as enkratic; otherwise, her action will presumably exemplify "weak" *akrasia*.[42]

In a subject with practical *epistêmê*—or what Aristotle usually calls φρόνησις—the universal *doxai* are stable and not subject to being dislodged either by perceptual *phantasiai* or by particular *doxai* arrived at by means of corrupt reasoning.[43] This explains why [5] describes *to epistêmonikon* as remaining at rest.[44] In the *phronimos*, the universal *doxai* remain constant while the particular *doxai* vary from one situation to another. And when, via either reasoning or perception, the *phronimos* comes to have some particular *doxa* that instantiates (so to speak) one of her universal *doxai*, then straightaway she acts—though not of course without *orexis*. For the *doxai* in question involve *phantasiai* that are themselves inseparable from *orexeis*.[45] In this (the normative) case,

---

[42] The passage in which Aristotle distinguishes "impetuous" from "weak" *akrasia* is the one (mentioned above) where he speaks of subjects who, because they foresee what is coming and prepare for it in accordance with reasoning, are not overcome by their passion: *EN* 1150b19–29. See also, *De Anima* III.7, where Aristotle allows that

[s]*ometimes*, by means of the *phantasmata* and *noêmata* in the soul, <the soul>, as if seeing, calculates and deliberates [*logizetai kai bouleuetai*] in relation to the things that are present what things are going to come about. And whenever it says that there <in the future> will be the pleasant or painful, here <in the present> it flees or pursues—and <so> generally in action.

But this is only *sometimes*. No such calculation or deliberation occurs in cases of "weak" *akrasia*.

[43] Aristotle's use of τὸ δ' ἐπιστημονικόν in this context is admittedly odd. See 1142a23ff: ὅτι δ' ἡ φρόνησις οὐκ ἐπιστήμη, φανερόν ... But it is not without parallel: see the translation of 1145b22–31 in sec. 1 of Pickavé and Whiting along with the discussion in section 8 of that essay [Chapter 7, this volume].

We might also deal with the oddity by taking Aristotle to be thinking, along the lines suggested in note 9 above, that the *hexis* (or condition) of someone who grasps the reasons for universals of the form "it is necessary for such <a person> to do such <an action>" is comparable to that of someone who grasps the principles involved in the sort of demonstrative reasoning characteristic of theoretical sciences, both natural and mathematical. In other words, he may be thinking of *epistêmê* in a generic way.

[44] I suspect that he is also alluding to the idea, prominent throughout *De Motu* (and elsewhere in his work), that movement generally involves both something that remains at rest and something that itself moves. But I do have not the space to pursue this point here.

[45] We might wonder here whether Aristotle thinks of vicious subjects as analogous to virtuous ones in having universal *doxai* that remain constant while their particular *doxai* vary from one situation to another. Aristotle may allow that at least some vicious agents achieve such stability, but his general view seems to be that vicious agents lack the sort of stability that he takes to characterize virtuous agents. Even so, it is hard to be sure what he would say here, since his discussions of this issue—see especially *Nicomachean Ethics* 9.4—do not clearly distinguish universal from particular *doxai*.

We might also wonder why Aristotle does not speak in [4][f] of *four phorai*. For I think it quite probable that he would, if he were explicitly considering the question of vice, treat vicious behavior as involving a fourth kind of *phora*. But I cannot pursue this question here.

nous and *orexis* work together as they do in other animals: they work together *as one*.[46] The other *phorai*—the enkratic and akratic—are the peculiar province of so-called rational animals.

WORKS CITED

Corcilius, K. 2107. *Aristoteles: Über die Seele/De Anima*. Hamburg: Felix Meiner Verlag.

Hicks, R. D. 1907. *Aristotle: De Anima*, with translation, introduction, and notes. Cambridge: Cambridge University Press.

Hutchinson, D. 1990. "Aristotle and the Spheres of Motivation: *De Anima* III.11." *Dialogue* 29: 7–20.

Jannone, A. (text) and Barbotin, E. (translation) 2009; 1st edn. 1966. *Aristote: De l'âme*. Paris: Les Belles Lettres.

McDowell, J. 1998. "Some Issues in Aristotle's Moral Psychology." In S. Everson (ed.), *Companions to Ancient Thought 4: Ethics*. Cambridge: Cambridge University Press, 107–28. Reprinted in McDowell, *Mind, Value, and Reality*. Cambridge, MA: Harvard University Press, 1998: 23–49.

Pickavé, M. and J. Whiting 2008. "*Nicomachean Ethics* 7.3 on Akratic Ignorance." *Oxford Studies in Ancient Philosophy* 34: 323–71.

Ross, W. D. 1956. *Aristotelis De Anima*. Oxford: Clarendon Press.

Theiler, W. and H. Seidl 1995. *Aristoteles: Über die Seele* (with the Greek text of Wilhelm Biehl and Otto Apelt). Hamburg: Felix Meiner Verlag.

Shields, C. 2016. *Aristotle: De Anima*, translation with introduction and commentary. Oxford: Clarendon Press.

Trendelenberg, F. A. 1833. *Aristotelis: De Anima Libri Tres*. Jena: Walzer.

Whiting, J. 2002. "Locomotive Soul: The Parts of Soul in Aristotle's Scientific Works." *Oxford Studies in Ancient Philosophy* 22: 141–200. [Chapter 5, this volume]

Whiting, J. 2016. "Hylomorphic Virtue: Cosmology, Embryology, and Moral Development in Aristotle." *Philosophical Explorations* 22, no. 2: 222–42. [Chapter 6, this volume]

Whiting, J. 2021. "See the Right Thing: 'Paternal' Reason, Love, and *Phronêsis*." In M. Boyle and E. Mylonaki (eds.), *Reason in Nature: Essays in Honor of John McDowell*. Cambridge, MA: Harvard University Press, 243–84.

---

[46] I was honored to be included in the Lille conference celebrating the career of Michel Crubellier, with whom I once had the pleasure of co-teaching in Berlin and from whom I have continued to learn since that time. I am thus pleased to contribute this essay in honor of him. I would like to thank Christian Wildberg and members of the Lille audience, especially David Charles and Robert Howton, for helpful discussion of these issues. Charles Brittian, as usual, deserves mega-thanks.

REPRINT INFORMATION

1. "Form and Individuation in Aristotle." *History of Philosophy Quarterly* 3 (1986): 359–77. All rights reserved. Reprinted by permission of the present editor.
2. "Aristotle on Form and Generation." *Proceedings of the Boston Area Colloquium of Ancient Philosophy* 6 (1990): 35–63. All rights reserved. Reprinted by permission of *Brill*.
3. "Living Bodies." In *Essays on Aristotle's "De Anima,"* edited by Martha C. Nussbaum and Amelie Oksenberg Rorty (1992): 75–91. (Oxford: Oxford University Press).
4. "Metasubstance: Critical Notice of Frede-Patzig and Furth." *The Philosophical Review* 95, no. 4 (1986): 607–39. Copyright Cornell University. All rights reserved. Reprinted by permission of the present publisher, *Duke University Press*. www.dukeupress.edu
5. "Locomotive Soul: The Parts of Soul in Aristotle's Scientific Works." *Oxford Studies in Ancient Philosophy* 22: 141–200. All rights reserved. Reprinted with permission of the present publisher, *Oxford University Press*.
6. "Hylomorphic Virtue: Cosmology, Embryology, and Moral Development in Aristotle." *Philosophical Explorations* 22, no. 2 (2019): 222–42. All rights reserved. Reprinted with permission of the present publisher, *Taylor & Francis*. www.tandfonline.com
7. "Nicomachean Ethics VII.3 on Acratic Ignorance," co-authored with Martin Pickavé. *Oxford Studies in Ancient Philosophy* 34 (2008): 323–71. All rights reserved. Reprinted with permission of the present publisher, *Oxford University Press*.

8. "The Lockeanism of Aristotle." *Antiquorum philosophia* 2 (2008): 1–36. All rights reserved. Reprinted with permission of the present editor.
9. "The Mover(s) of Rational Animals: *De Anima* III.11 in Context." In *Aristote et l'âme humaine: Lectures de "De anima" III offertes à Michel Crubellier*, edited by G. Guyomarc'h, C. Louguet, and C. Murgier. Leuven: Peeters Publishers. Reprinted with the permission of the present publisher, *Peeters*.

INDEX LOCORUM

For the benefit of digital users, indexed terms that span two pages (e.g., 52–53) may, on occasion, appear on only one of those pages

This index includes citations from this and its companion volume (see Preface)

LT for *Living Together*

BS for *Body and Soul*

PLATO
Apology
21b **BS:** 242–43
Phaedo
67a **BS:** 104
98b–99c **BS:** 153
Theaetetus
197b–98d **BS:** 183
203d6 **BS:** 184
Philebus
11b **LT:** 20
20b–22d **LT:** 15–16
20b–d **LT:** 254
20d **LT:** 226
20dff. **LT:** 226
20d–e **LT:** 20
20e5 **LT:** 238

21a–d, **LT:** 248
21c **LT:** 20; 215
22c–d **LT:** 20–21
31b–c **LT:** 227
31c–d **LT:** 20–21
32b–39e **LT:** 228
33a–b. **LT:** 227
33b2 **LT:** 226
51b **LT:** 227
52 **LT:** 265
55dff **LT:** 257
60a–c **LT:** 248
60b10 **LT:** 252
Symposium
192c1–2 **LT:** 271
192e1 **LT:** 271
193a5 **LT:** 271
208e **LT:** 151

PLATO (cont.)
210a8–b6 **LT**: 150
210b6–7 **LT**: 150
210c1–6 **LT**: 150

Phaedrus
252d–253c **LT**: 269
253d **LT**: 127

Alcibiades I
132d–133b, **LT**: 269

Lysis
215a–b **LT**: 193–94
216C **LT**: 194
217–19 **LT**: 147
220c–d **LT**: 147
222b–c **LT**: 194

Euthydemus
279b5 **BS**: 80
279–81 **LT**: 101
280b–281b **LT**: 102
281c **BS**: 80

Gorgias
466b–468e **LT**: 195

Meno
87–88 **LT**: 101

Hippias minor
375d3 **BS**: 184
376 **LT**: 204

Republic
II–IV **BS**: 3
IV **BS**: 152
439e **LT**: 127; **BS**: 140
V
462a8–e1 **BS**: 246
VI
490a **LT**: 112
VIII–IX **BS**: 3; 165
IX
591d **LT**: 121

Timaeus
43–44 **BS**: 277
69dff **BS**: 109

Laws
III
714a **LT**: 121
V
731d–2b **LT**: 158

ARISTOTLE
Protrepticus
B62 **LT**: 71

Categories
Chap. 1
1a1–4 **BS**: 60–61
Chap. 5
2a29–37 **BS**: 46
2b8–19 **BS**: 20
3b10–14 **BS**: 47
3b10–18 **BS**: 46–47, 82
3b11 **BS**: 84–85; 85
3b13–18 **BS**: 17–18
4b10 **BS**: 45

De Interpretatione
Chap. 7
17a38–b1 **BS**: 36
17a38–40 **BS**: 31
17a39–40 **BS**: 20

Prior analytics
I.27
43a27 **BS**: 79
II.21 **BS**: 186

Posterior Analytics BS: 48–49
I.1 **BS**: 186
I.4
73b8–9 **BS**: 47
I.18 **LT**: 67–68; 67–68
I.22
83b20–22 **BS**: 45
I.31
87b28–33 **BS**: 82, 146–47
II.19 **BS**: 145; 145–46; 146–47
99b32ff **BS**: 145–46

Topics
I.4 **BS**: 24
101b26–30 **LT**: 10–11; 39
I.5
101b37–102a2 **LT**: 66
102b4–10 **BS**: 51
I.7 **BS**: 114
103a7–25 **BS**: 18
IV.5
125b25–30 **BS**: 20
125b37–40 **BS**: 46

V.5
134b6–8 **BS:** 81

Sophistical Refutations
Chap. 22
178b38–179a10 **BS:** 47

Physics
I.7
190b23–25 **BS:** 136
I.9
192a16–25 **BS:** 155
192b1 **BS:** 95; 97
II.1
192b8–15 **BS:** 74
II.2 **BS:** 92
194a21–22 **BS:** 155
II.7
198b4–9 **LT:** 43–44
II.8 **BS:** 49, 155
II.9 **BS:** 153
III.3 **LT:** 9; **BS:** 115
202a19–21 **BS:** 54
202b5–22 **LT:** 96
202b14–16 **BS:** 114–15
202b19–20 **BS:** 115–16
IV.1
208b8–10 **BS:** 115
IV.11 **BS:** 8–9
IV.12
220b9–10 **BS:** 264
IV.14 **BS:** 100
223a25–28 **BS:** 100
V.1
224b25 **BS:** 32
V.4 **BS:** 25
V.5 **BS:** 25
229a17–20 **BS:** 90–91
VII.3 **BS:** 112
245b7–17 **BS:** 67
247a16–17 **BS:** 112
247b1–14 **BS:** 96
247b13–16 **BS:** 191
VIII.4
255a33–b5 **BS:** 184

De Caelo
I.2–3 **BS:** 156; 157
I.3 **BS:** 267
270a28 **BS:** 45
I.8 **BS:** 99

I.9 **BS:** 79, 80–81, 89; 89, 97; 99–100; 100
278a10 **BS:** 36, 79
I.10
280a32–34 **BS:** 196
I.11
280b20–34 **BS:** 96
I.12
283b17–18 **BS:** 196
II.6 **BS:** 158–59
288b15–19 **BS:** 66–67

Generation and Corruption
I.1
314a8–11 **BS:** 37, 69
314a13–15 **BS:** 38
I.2
316a5–14 **BS:** 196
317a20–22 **BS:** 45
317a20–27 **BS:** 44; 44; 53
I.3
318b32 **BS:** 17–18
I.4
319b6–31 **BS:** 44
319b10–16 **BS:** 42–43; 43
320a1–2 **BS:** 69
320a1–4 **BS:** 58
320a2–5 **BS:** 51
I.5
321b19–22 **BS:** 64
321b22–32 **BS:** 64
321b23–322a4 **BS:** 69
321b25–28 **BS:** 42, 87
322a28–33 **BS:** 42, 52; 69; 87
322a28–34 **BS:** 69
I.10
327b22–31 **BS:** 66

Meteorologica
IV.1
379a17–26 **BS:** 63–64
IV.12 **BS:** 62
390a10–12 **BS:** 60; 105
390a10–13 **LT:** 36
390a14–24 **BS:** 62; 63, 158–59
390b2–10 **BS:** 63–64

De Anima
I.1
402b16–25 **BS:** 90, 94
403a8–10 **LT:** 65
403a16–24 **LT:** 68–69

ARISTOTLE (cont.)
403a24–27 **LT**: 66
403a25–b9 **LT**: 66
I.3
406a4–6 **BS**: 32
I.4 **BS**: 110
408a29–31 **BS**: 32
408a30–35 **BS**: 32
408b19–24 **BS**: 155
408b21–9 **BS**: 110
408b30–32 **BS**: 32
I.5 **BS**: 269
411a26–b5 **BS**: 106
411b5–14 **BS**: 106–7
411b6–9 **BS**: 158
411b14–30 **BS**: 107
II.1 **BS**: 1; 74; 183–84
412a7–8 **BS**: 22
412a8–9 **BS**: 55
412a19–21 **BS**: 71–72
412a22–26 **LT**: 91
412a27–28 **BS**: 72
412a27–b6 **BS**: 153; 153
412a29–b1 **BS**: 60
412b6–9 **BS**: 157; 166
412b10–12 **BS**: 54; 149–50
412b10–17 **BS**: 178–79
412b11 **BS**: 28; 52–53
412b11–12 **BS**: 60; 154
412b14–15 **LT**: 65–66
412b18–27 **BS**: 62; 105
412b21–23 **LT**: 65–66 **BS**: 61
412b21–28 **BS**: 183–84
412b22–23 **BS**: 61
II.1–3 **BS**: 42
II.2
413a31–b1 **BS**: 110
413b11–24 **BS**: 108–9
413b22–23 **BS**: 168
413b24–32 **BS**: 109
413b25–27 **LT**: 64; 65, 66
414a20–22 **BS**: 32
II.3 **BS**: 139
414a29–32 **BS**: 168
414a29–b1 **BS**: 139
414a31ff **BS**: 117
414a31–32 **BS**: 108
414b1–16 **BS**: 139–40
415a10–11 **BS**: 109

II.4 **LT**: 43
415a23–25 **BS**: 107
415b2–7 **BS**: 159
415b8–28 **BS**: 74
415b11 **BS**: 28
415b18–19 **BS**: 61
415b20–21 **LT**: 38
415b28–416a8 **BS**: 66
416a6–9 **BS**: 137
416a19 **BS**: 107
II.5
417a21–b2 **BS**: 183–84
417a23–24 **BS**: 100
417a27–28 **BS**: 191
II.6
418b4–6 **BS**: 43
II.11
422b25–27 **BS**: 43
III.2
426a15–25 **BS**: 100
426b8–23 **BS**: 120–21
426b12ff **BS**: 169
426b29–427a5 **BS**: 121
427a5–14 **BS**: 121–22
III.3
428b2–4 **BS**: 270
III.4 **BS**: 167
429a25–27 **LT**: 66; 67; 67
429b4–5 **LT**: 65; 65–66
429b10–22 **BS**: 146–47
429b13 **BS**: 147
429b20–21 **BS**: 147
III.7 **BS**: 9; 281
431a8–14 **BS**: 102; 102; 112–13
431a8–20 **BS**: 121
431a12 **BS**: 118–19; 119
431a12–14 **BS**: 9–10; 168
431a14–17 **LT**: 65; 65–66, 67–68
431a14–23 **BS**: 102; 113
431a16–17 **BS**: 267–68
431b14–15 **BS**: 104
III.7–11 **BS**: 9
III.8
432a8–9 **LT**: 65; 65–66, 67–68; 68
III.9 **BS**: 138; 193
432a18–20 **BS**: 104
432a18–22 **BS**: 129
432a22–26 **BS**: 130
432a22–b7 **BS**: 167

Index Locorum

432a26–31 **BS:** 130
432a31–b3 **BS:** 130
432b3–7 **BS:** 130
432b14–16 **BS:** 266
432b15–19 **BS:** 131–32
432b19–26 **BS:** 131–32
432b19–433a6 **BS:** 131–32
432b27–433a1 **BS:** 266
432b29–433a1 **BS:** 193
433a1–3 **BS:** 210
433a1–6 **BS:** 266–67
433a6–8 **BS:** 267
III.9–10 **BS:** 265–70
III.9–11 **BS:** 9; 124; 129–38
III.10 **BS:** 224
433a9–12 **BS:** 267
433a9–15 **BS:** 131–32; 132
433a13–17 **BS:** 268–69
433a15–20 **BS:** 132–33
433a17–22 **BS:** 269
433a20–26 **BS:** 133–34
433a23–26 **BS:** 263
433a26 **BS:** 143–44
433a26–30 **BS:** 134
III.11 **BS:** 261–82
433a30–b5 **BS:** 134
433b5–10 **BS:** 210
433b5–12 **BS:** 134
433b13–18 **BS:** 134–35
433b19–27 **BS:** 135
433b27–30 **BS:** 135; 261
433b29 **BS:** 130
433b31–434a5 **BS:** 109
433b31–433a6 **BS:** 261–62
434a6–10 **BS:** 262
434a10–12 **BS:** 263–64
434a13–16 **BS:** 264
434a16–21 **BS:** 264–65

De Sensu
Chap. 2
438a12–16 **BS:** 158
Chap. 7
449a5–13 **BS:** 122
449a5–19 **BS:** 169
449a13–20 **BS:** 122

De Memoria
Chap. 1
449b30 **LT:** 68

451a2–13 **BS:** 222
Chap. 2
452b23–28 **BS:** 221–22
453a13–14 **BS:** 222

De somno BS: 204
Chap. 1
454b30–455a3 **BS:** 110–11
454b32ff **BS:** 126
Chap. 2
455b29–30 **BS:** 109
Chap. 3
456b16–457a20 **BS:** 192
457b20–458a26 **BS:** 203–4
458a28–29 **BS:** 192

De Insomniis BS: 144
Chap. 1
459a1–9 **BS:** 192
459a6–8 **BS:** 192–93
459a15–17 **BS:** 9–10; 113; 168
459a15–23 **BS:** 192
459a21–23 **BS:** 117, 138
Chap. 2
459a23–b23 **BS:** 192
459a26 **BS:** 191
460b12–16 **BS:** 192–93
Chap. 3
460b31 **BS:** 191
461a26–30 **BS:** 116–17

De Juventute
Chap. 3
469a7–22 **BS:** 63
Chap. 2
469b1–20 **BS:** 63

History of Animals
I.1
486a5–9 **BS:** 61
I.2 **LT:** 28–29
IV.8
534b15–21 **BS:** 242
VIII.1
588b11–18 **BS:** 127
IX.40 **LT:** 28–29

Parts of Animals
I.1 **BS:** 153, 155
640b34 – 641a8 **LT:** 65–66
640b34–641a34 **BS:** 60–61

ARISTOTLE (*cont.*)
II.3
647a25–b8 **BS:** 123
649b14–19 **BS:** 66; 72
II.4 **BS:** 66–67
655b12–13 **BS:** 66–67
656a5–10 **LT:** 46
660a18–25 **BS:** 110–11

De Motu Animalium
Chap. 6
700b32–35 **BS:** 286
Chap. 7 **BS:** 188, 237
701a13–16 **BS:** 188
701a19–20 **BS:** 199–200
701a26–29 **BS:** 188
Chap. 7–8 **BS:** 280
Chap. 9
702b12–25 **BS:** 124
702b25–703a3 **BS:** 125
Chap. 10
703a4–26 **BS:** 125–26

Generation of Animals
I.22 **BS:** 155
II.1
732a34–36 **BS:** 159
734b24–27 **BS:** 60; 105
734b24–735a9 **BS:** 60–61
735a9–11 **BS:** 191
II.3 **BS:** 166–67
736a35–b8 **BS:** 147
736b8–13 **BS:** 147
736b8–14 **BS:** 107
736b13–20 **BS:** 148
736b21–29 **BS:** 148
736b27–29 **BS:** 166–67
736b30ff **BS:** 158
II.4
738b27–30 **BS:** 49
II.6
745a15–20 **BS:** 66–67
II.7
746a29–b11 **BS:** 49
II.8 **BS:** 196
747b27–748a16 **BS:** 196
III.11
762a20–21 **BS:** 158
IV.1 **BS:** 161
766b12–18 **BS:** 160

IV.3 **BS:** 98, 153
767b24–768a1 **BS:** 98
768b16–21 **BS:** 160
768b25–28 **BS:** 160
769b1–13 **BS:** 155
IV.4 **BS:** 23
773a1–12 **BS:** 7

Metaphysics
I.1 **LT:** 27; **BS:** 144–45; 145; 146–47
I.3
983a30–b1 **LT:** 43–44
983b6–18 **BS:** 37, 69
I.9 **BS:** 49
II.1
993b24–26 **BS:** 55
993b34–38 **BS:** 90
III **LT:** 142
III.4
999b24–25 **BS:** 54–55
999b24–28 **BS:** 17–18
999b33–34 **BS:** 79
999b33–1000a1 **BS:** 36
999b34–35 **BS:** 17–18
999b35–1000a1 **BS:** 86
999b34–1000a1 **BS:** 78
IV.4 **LT:** 45; **BS:** 48–49
1007b2–5 **BS:** 45, 67–68
IV.5
1010b30–1011a2 **BS:** 100
V.2
1013b25–27 **LT:** 43–44
V.6
1016b31–32 **BS:** 22
V.8
1017b24–25 **BS:** 17–18
1017b24–26 **BS:** 17–18
V.30 **BS:** 51
1025a30–34 **LT:** 66 **BS:** 90, 94
VI.1 **BS:** 94
1025b30–32 **BS:** 94
1025b34–1026a6 **LT:** 66
VI.2
1027a13–15 **BS:** 52–53
VI.3
1027a29–32 **BS:** 96
VII.1 **BS:** 4; 8; 77–101; 77; 90–91
1028a36–1028b2 **BS:** 82

Index Locorum 291

VII.3
1029a20–21 **BS**: 22
VII.4
1030a2–14 **BS**: 46–47
1030a3–6 **BS**: 47
VII.6
1031b19–20 **BS**: 54
1031b31–32 **BS**: 106
1032b1–2 **BS**: 17–18, 42–43
1033a5–23 **BS**: 67
VII.8
1033b17 **BS**: 17–18
1033b29–1034a8 **BS**: 88
1034a5–8 **BS**: 17
VII.10
1034b24–26 **BS**: 94
1035a4–6 **BS**: 94
1035a17–22 **BS**: 63
1035a18–19 **BS**: 54
1035a31–34 **BS**: 63
1035a11–14 **BS**: 73
1035a25–b2 **BS**: 97n.51
1035b23–25 **LT**: 65–66
1035b24 **BS**: 61
1035b27–30 **BS**: 86
VII.10–11 **BS**: 8; 9; 54; 27
VII.11 **BS**: 94; 153
1036a31–34 **BS**: 42
1036b2–3 **BS**: 92–93
1036b21–32 **LT**: 66
1036b32–1037b5 **BS**: 94
1036b23–30 **BS**: 91
1037a22–24 **BS**: 94
1037a28–29 **BS**: 17–18
VII.13 **BS**: 20, 42, 78, 83, 86
1038b11–12 **BS**: 36
1038b15–16 **BS**: 42
1038b35–1039a1 **BS**: 17–18
1039a9–10 **BS**: 94
1039a19–20 **LT**: 71
VII.15 **BS**: 82, 99–100; 100–1
1039b24–25 **BS**: 97
1039b30–31 **BS**: 36, 79
VII.16
1040b5–10 **BS**: 28
1040b17 **BS**: 54–55
VII.17 **BS**: 55
1041b4–9 **BS**: 22

1041b7–9 **BS**: 17–18
VIII.1
1042a25–26 **BS**: 32
1042a26 **BS**: 86
1042a26–31 **BS**: 104
1042a27–28 **BS**: 22
1042a28–20 **BS**: 17–18
VIII.4 **BS**: 65
1044b1–2 **BS**: 65
VIII.5 **BS**: 159
1044b21–24 **BS**: 97
1044b21–26 **BS**: 96
VIII.6
1045b18–19 **BS**: 33; 73
IX.5 **BS**: 267
IX.6
1048a25–b9 **BS**: 72
1048b6–7 **BS**: 74
1048b26–27 **BS**: 73
1048b28–35 **BS**: 72
IX.7 **BS**: 65
1049a1–3 **BS**: 65; 65
1049a5–12 **BS**: 74
1049a13–14 **BS**: 74
1049a17–18 **BS**: 74
1049a35–36 **BS**: 17–18
IX.8
1049b36–37 **BS**: 52–53
1050b1–2 **BS**: 17–18
X.1 **BS**: 22
1052a19–20 **BS**: 22–23
1052a25 **BS**: 23
1052a25–26 **BS**: 31
1052a25–27 **BS**: 23
X.6
1056b35–1057a1 **BS**: 101
X.9 **LT**: 28; **BS**: 26–27; 31, 161
1058b23–24 **BS**: 49
XI.2
1060a22 **BS**: 95; 97
XI.9
1066a2–3 **BS**: 72–73
XI.12
1068b26 **LT**: 263
XII.3
1070a11–12 **BS**: 17–18
XII.5
1071a18–29 **BS**: 17–18

ARISTOTLE (cont.)
1071a20–21 **BS:** 17–18, 54–55
1071a26–29 **BS:** 31
XII.6 **LT:** 226
XII.7 **LT:** 23; 228, 229, 252, 256; 231; 264
   BS: 156
1072a28–29 **LT:** 100
1072a24–30 **BS:** 133
1072a29–b1 **LT:** 256
1072b14–28 **LT:** 227–28
1072b18–28 **LT:** 256–57
XII.8 **BS:** 156; 196–205
1073a14–16 **LT:** 21
1074a31–37 **BS:** 89
1074a36–37 **BS:** 36, 79
XII.9 **LT:** 226; 228, 229; 230–31; 232; 235; 252–62; 255; 256; 257; 257, 274
1074b17–18 **LT:** 231
1074b23–36 **LT:** 231–32
1074b23–27 **LT:** 231
1074b28–35 **LT:** 231–32
1074b35–36 **LT:** 232
1075a1–5 **LT:** 257
XIII.3
1078a23–26 **LT:** 72
XIII.9 **BS:** 99–100
1086b5–6 **BS:** 99–100
XIII.10
1087a16–17 **BS:** 99
XIV.5
1092a18–20 **BS:** 36, 79

Nicomachean Ethics
I **BS:** 52
I.1–2 **LT:** 79
I.3
1095a2–11 **LT:** 135; 137
I.4 **LT:** 79
1095a14–20 **LT:** 34
1095a16–17 **LT:** 76–77
1095a20–28 **LT:** 34
1095b2–8 **LT:** 141
1095b4–6 **LT:** 137
1095b4–8 **LT:** 135
I.5 **LT:** 8; 10; 23; 24; **BS:** 2
1095b19–22 **LT:** 10–11
1095b22–26 **LT:** 11; 211
1095b24–26 **LT:** 132
1095b31–1096a2 **LT:** 8

I.7 **LT:** 13–14; 23; 30; 63–64
1097a22–b21 **LT:** 226
1097a25–b6 **LT:** 60, 63–64
1097a30–31 **LT:** 63–64
1097a30–b6 **LT:** 34
1097a33–34 **LT:** 7; 14
1097a34–b1 **LT:** 63–64
1097b1ff **LT:** 94
1097b1–5 **LT:** 90
1097b8–11 **LT:** 16; 30; 52
1097b14–15 **LT:** 7
1097b14–16 **LT:** 60–61
1097b16–20 **LT:** 95–96
1097b16–21 **LT:** 16
1097b17–19 **LT:** 60–61
1097b23–35 **LT:** 35
1097b33–1098a7 **LT:** 138
1098a3–4 **LT:** 62, 71–72
1098a8–16 **LT:** 238
1098a12–18 **LT:** 35
1098a16–18 **LT:** 62, 80; 90; 192
1098b3–4 **LT:** 152 **BS:** 167
I.8 **LT:** 7; 27
1098b14–15 **LT:** 7; 193
1099a15 **LT:** 238
1099a34–b1 **LT:** 7
1099b7–8 **LT:** 7
I.9
1099b18–25 **LT:** 49
I.10
1100a14–21 **LT:** 8–9
1100a14–30 **LT:** 96–97
1100a21–31 **LT:** 9
1100b34–35 **LT:** 75–76, 77
I.10–11 **LT:** 8–9
I.12 **LT:** 131
1102a1–4 **LT:** 34
I.13 **BS:** 3, 13–14; 162; 164; 165; 165; 166; 167; 167, 210
1102a23–26 **BS:** 162
1102a23–28 **BS:** 129
1102a26–b28 **BS:** 162; 162–63
1102a28–32 **LT:** 70
1102b2–25 **BS:** 209; 209
1102b28–1103a3 **BS:** 164
1103a1–3 **BS:** 129

Index Locorum

II.1
1103a23–26 **LT:** 165–66
1103b4–21 **LT:** 123–24
II.2
1103b22 **LT:** 167–68
1103b26–30 **LT:** 1–2
II.3
1104b13–14 **LT:** 68–69
1104b30–31 **LT:** 194
II.4 **BS:** 162
1105a26–b10 **LT:** 85–86
1105a28–34 **LT:** 59–60
1105a30–34 **LT:** 104–5
1105a31–32 **LT:** 146
1105a32 **LT:** 80; 82–83
1105b5–9 **LT:** 74
II.7
1107a28–32 **BS:** 185–86
1107a33 **LT:** 68–69
III.1 **BS:** 178–79; 178–79; 187, 222–23; 238
1110a15–17 **BS:** 198
1110a25–29 **LT:** 255–56
1110b22–24 **BS:** 187
1110b24–1111a26 **BS:** 179
1110b31–1111a19 **BS:** 238
1111a3–5 **BS:** 238
1111a22–23 **BS:** 178–79
1111a22–24 **BS:** 238
III.2
1111b5–6 **BS:** 224–25
1111b6–10 **BS:** 180
III.3 **BS:** 223
1112b27–28 **LT:** 96
1112b31–1113a7 **BS:** 226
1113a9–11 **BS:** 213
1113a10–11 **BS:** 133, 143–44; 223
III.4 **BS:** 142
1113a23–b2 **BS:** 142
III.5 **BS:** 222–23; 228
1114a3–13 **LT:** 123–24
1114a31–b25 **BS:** 222–23
III.6
1115a5–6 **LT:** 108:
III.7
1115b10–13 **LT:** 59, 149
1115b21–22 **LT:** 89
1115b22–24 **LT:** 59
III.8 **LT:** 88, 127

1116a15–b3 **LT:** 88
1116b6–9 **LT:** 59–60
1116b24–1117a6 **LT:** 127
III.9
1117b6–9 **LT:** 59–60
1117b9–11 **LT:** 95 BS:
1117b15–16 **LT:** 95
III.10
1117b24–25 **LT:** 68–69
1118a1–3 **LT:** 68–69
III.11
1119a16 **LT:** 87–88
IV.1 **LT:** 86
1119b23 **LT:** 108
1120a8–9 **LT:** 108
1120a8–12 **LT:** 86
1120a21–23 **LT:** 86
1120a23–24 **LT:** 108
1120a31–b2 **LT:** 108
1120a34–b1 **LT:** 59
1120b20–24 **LT:** 86
1120b27–28 **LT:** 70
IV.2
1122b6–7 **LT:** 59–60; 59, 149
IV.3 **LT:** 106; 115; 115–16
1123b20–21 **LT:** 128
1123b21–22 **LT:** 108
1124a3–4 **LT:** 107
1124b8–9 **LT:** 111
1125a25–27 **LT:** 109
IV.7
1127a27–30 **LT:** 59–60
V.1
1129b1–6 **LT:** 18
1129b4–6 **LT:** 51
1129b5–6 **LT:** 195
1129b25–27 **LT:** 118–19
1129b30 **LT:** 117
1130a9 **LT:** 117
V.3
1131a24ff **LT:** 117
V.5
1132b31–1133a2 **LT:** 87
V.6
1134a35–b8 **LT:** 121
1134b4–5 **BS:** 133, 143–44
V.8 **LT:** 84
VI **BS:** 211–12; 213

ARISTOTLE (cont.)
VI.1 **BS:** 13; 13, 133, 137–38
1139a3–18 **BS:** 164–65
1139a5–6 **BS:** 133
1139a5–15 **BS:** 132
1139a6–8 **LT:** 68
1139a6–15 **BS:** 137–38; 264
1139a8–11 **LT:** 68
1139a11–15 **LT:** 68
VI.2 **BS:** 156–57
1139a19–21 **BS:** 224
1139a21ff **BS:** 112
1139a23 **BS:** 133, 143–44; 213
1139a31–b5 **BS:** 15; 223–24
1139b4–5 **BS:** 14–15; 133, 143–44; 213, 279
VI.5
1140a25–28 **LT:** 59–60; 69
1140a30–33 **LT:** 69
1140b3–4 **LT:** 80
1140b4–11 **BS:** 141
1140b6–7 **LT:** 81
1140b7 **LT:** 59–60
1140b11–19 **BS:** 133
1140b11–21 **BS:** 142
1140b20–21 **LT:** 68–69
1140b20–30 **BS:** 171
1140b25–30 **BS:** 166
1140b27 **BS:** 15
VI.7
1141a26–28 **BS:** 237–38
VI.8 **BS:** 172
1142a19–20 **BS:** 194
VI.9
1142a23ff **BS:** 281
1142a23–30 **BS:** 213
1142a25–30 **BS:** 143
VI.10 **BS:** 164–65; 212–13
1143a6–10 **BS:** 164–65
1143a8 **BS:** 164
VI.11
1143a22 **BS:** 164–65
1143a32–36 **BS:** 213
VI.12 **LT:** 31; **BS:** 14
1143b19–23 **LT:** 68–69
1144a9–10 **BS:** 14
1144a36–37 **LT:** 59–60
1144a36–b1 **BS:** 150
VI.12–13 **LT:** 31; **BS:** 162; 165; 178; 267
VI.13 **BS:** 212–13; 125

1144b2–14 **LT:** 125–26
1144b4–14 **LT:** 101–2
1144b14–17 **LT:** 138
1144b18–21 **BS:** 151–52
1145a7–14 **LT:** 70
VII **BS:** 151–52; 178
VII.1 **LT:** 27
1145a15–20 **LT:** 27
1145a29–33 **LT:** 27
1145b2–7 **LT:** 134
VII.2
1145b22–31 **BS:** 180; 281
VII.3 **BS:** 1–2; 11–12; 13; 177–215; 180; 181–83; 181
1146b8–24 **BS:** 181
1146b24–31 **BS:** 182–83
1146b25 **BS:** 189–90
1146b31–35 **BS:** 183
1146b34–1147a10 **BS:** 185–86
1147a1 **BS:** 198–99
1147a4 **BS:** 177–78; 189–90
1147a4–7 **BS:** 185–86
1147a7–8 **BS:** 188
1147a10–24 **BS:** 190–91
1147a24–b12 **BS:** 197–98
1147a25 **BS:** 198–99
1147b6–9 **BS:** 196
1147b13–19 **BS:** 211
VII.4
1147b23–31 **LT:** 59
1148a13–17 **BS:** 179–80
VII.4–6 **BS:** 179–80; 181
VII.5
1148b15–19 **LT:** 39, 40
VII.6
1149a32–35 **BS:** 202–3
1149b31–1150a1 **BS:** 180
VII.7 **BS:** 181
1150a19–31 **BS:** 179–80
1150b19–21 **BS:** 207
1150b19–29 **BS:** 281
1150b20–28 **BS:** 205–6
1150b21ff **BS:** 278
VII.8 **BS:** 203
1151a1–14 **BS:** 179–80
1151a11–26 **BS:** 203
VII.8–10 **BS:** 181
VII.10 **BS:** 191–92
1152a6–19 **BS:** 178

1152a32 **LT**: 167–68
VII.11 **BS**: 242–43
VII.12
1152b26–27 **LT**: 39
1152b36ff **LT**: 228
VII.13 **BS**: 23
1153b7–25 **LT**: 7
1153b9–12 **LT**: 228
1153b9–25 **LT**: 95–96
VII.14
1154b20–26 **LT**: 21
1154b20–31 **LT**: 62
VIII.1 **LT**: 193; 193–94
1155a3–6 **LT**: 193
1155a14–22 **LT**: 206
1155a26–28 **LT**: 238
1155a28 **LT**: 119
1155a28–29 **LT**: 59
1155b2 **BS**: 196–97
1155b9–13 **LT**: 193–94
VIII.2 **LT**: 194
1155b18–19 **LT**: 194
1155b19–21 **LT**: 194
1155b21–23 **LT**: 195
1155b23–27 **LT**: 39
1155b25–26 **LT**: 195
1155b27–1156a3 **LT**: 195
1155b29–31 **LT**: 38
1155b31–34 **LT**: 196
1155b34–1156a5 **LT**: 195
VIII.3 **LT**: 196
1156a10–16 **LT**: 201–2
1156a10–19 **LT**: 40; 50; 83–84
1156a31 **LT**: 201
1156a31–35 **LT**: 201; 283
1156b7–11 **LT**: 83–84
1156b7–24 **LT**: 40; 50
1156b10 **LT**: 83–84
1156b12–13 **LT**: 195
1156b12–17 **LT**: 207
1156b17–21 **LT**: 197
VIII.3–4 **LT**: 196–98
VIII.4 **LT**: 196; 198; 284
1157a7–12 **LT**: 201
1157a10–12 **LT**: 238
1157a20–33 **LT**: 197
VIII.5
1157b26–28 **LT**: 39
VIII.6 **LT**: 199

1158a2–4 **LT**: 199
VIII.7
1159a5–12 **LT**: 69
1159a8–12 **LT**: 42
VIII.8 **LT**: 202–5
1159a15–27 **LT**: 261
1159a16–34 **LT**: 203–4
1159a27–33 **LT**: 261
1159a27–34 **LT**: 9
1159b13ff **LT**: 263
VIII.9 **LT**: 119
VIII.11
1161b5–6 **LT**: 72
VIII.12 **LT**: 202–5
1161b18–29 **LT**: 204
1162a9–15 **LT**: 205
1162a25–27 **LT**: 35
IX.1
1164a13–16 **LT**: 51
IX.4 **LT**: 199; 206–7; 208; **BS**: 165; 281
1166a1–2 **LT**: 198
1166a10–23 **LT**: 74
1166a14–23 **LT**: 83–84
1166a20–24 **LT**: 42
1166a32 **LT**: 266
IX.4–6 **LT**: 198–99; 198
IX.5 **LT**: 199
1166b34–1169a3 **LT**: 83–84
1167a2–3 **LT**: 199
1167a14–17 **LT**: 195–96
1167a18–20 **LT**: 195–96
IX.7 **LT**: 9; 202–5
1167b17–1168a9 **BS**: 196–97
1167b25–27 **LT**: 218–19
1167b28–33 **LT**: 202–3
1167b33–1168a8 **LT**: 203
1168a3–8 **LT**: 96
1168a9 **BS**: 196–97
1168a9–12 **LT**: 203
1168a21–23 **LT**: 203
1168a23–27 **LT**: 203–4
IX.8 **LT**: 110; 110; 111; 112; 116; 117; 121; 193; 208
1168b3–4 **LT**: 119
1168b25–29 **LT**: 114
1168b25–1169a6 **LT**: 50
1168b26 **LT**: 111
1168b28–1169a3 **LT**: 74
1168b34–1169a3 **LT**: 83–84

ARISTOTLE (cont.)
1169a2 **BS:** 225
1169a8–10 **LT:** 114–15
1169a8–11 **LT:** 111
1169a8–31 **LT:** 59–60
1169a16–34 **LT:** 113
IX.9 **LT:** 209–13; 209; 209–13; 217; 217; 221; 226; 242; 252, 279–80; **BS:** 219
1169b3–20 **LT:** 210
1169b5–6 **LT:** 61
1169b8–10 **LT:** 59–60; 237
1169b17–25 **LT:** 9
1169b18–19 **LT:** 52
1169b18–1170a4 **LT:** 210–11
1169b23–28 **LT:** 210
1169b33 **LT:** 210–11
1170a1–3 **LT:** 211
1170a2 **LT:** 210–11
1170a4–11 **LT:** 211–12
1170a16–24 **LT:** 253–54
1170a20–21 **LT:** 252
1170a25–b8 **LT:** 214
1170b5–8 **LT:** 214
1170b7–14 **LT:** 279–80
1170b8 **LT:** 252
1170b10 **LT:** 215
IX.10 **LT:** 18
1170b26–27 **LT:** 18
1170b28–1171a16 **LT:** 18
IX.12
1171b35–1172a1 **LT:** 259
X.2 **LT:** 22; 23
1172b21 **LT:** 200
1172b26–33 **LT:** 22–23
X.3 **LT:** 215
X.4 **BS:** 241
1174b9–13 **BS:** 96
1174b14–33 **LT:** 95–96
X.6
1176a3–4 **LT:** 72–73
1176a30–32 **LT:** 72–73
1176b1–9 **LT:** 59
1177a8–9 **LT:** 49
X.7 **LT:** 2; 11; 12; 14; 21; 26; 30–31; 192; 173–74; **BS:** 225
1177a13–15 **BS:** 267
1177a28–29 **LT:** 69–70
1177b4–6 **LT:** 30–31
1177b19–21 **LT:** 68
1177b24–25 **LT:** 62
1177b24–1178a22 **LT:** 192
1177b27–28 **LT:** 73
1177b31–34 **LT:** 173–74
1177b31–1178a1 **LT:** 57–58; 77
1178a2 **LT:** 64
1178a6–8 **LT:** 71
1178a8 **LT:** 57–58
X.7–8 **LT:** 10–13; 28; 64
X.8 **LT:** 11; 12; 26; 119
1178a9 **LT:** 64; 71
1178a9–10 **LT:** 72–73
1178a14–23 **LT:** 64
1178a22 **LT:** 64
1178a25–26 **LT:** 69–70
1178b3–4 **LT:** 70; 74–75
1178b3–5 **LT:** 74–75
1178b3–7 **LT:** 12
1178b5–7 **LT:** 74–75
1178b5–8 **LT:** 71
1178b25–32 **LT:** 29; 31
X.9 **LT:** 123; 127
1178b33–35 **LT:** 69–70
1179b5–16 **LT:** 168–69
1179b20–23 **LT:** 123
1179b23–30 **LT:** 137
1179b23–31 **LT:** 168–69
1179b24–1180a18 **LT:** 135
1179b34–1180a4 **LT:** 123–24
1180a4–11 **LT:** 168–69

Magna Moralia
I.2
1183b20–30 **LT:** 131
1184a34–38 **LT:** 61
II.8
1207a4–6 **LT:** 126
II.13
1212a37–40 **LT:** 117–18
II.14
1212b15–20 **LT:** 115–16, 119
1212b18–20 **LT:** 206–7
II.15 **LT:** 260–61; 269
1213a7–26 **LT:** 210–11
1213a10ff **LT:** 270
1213a16 **LT:** 210–11

Eudemian Ethics
I.1 **LT:** 79
I.2
1214b6–28 **LT:** 34, 57

I.3
1215a13–19 **LT**: 123
I.5 **LT**: 2; 10;, 242
1216a10–27 **LT**: 242
1216a11–14 **LT**: 1–2
1216a12–14 **LT**: 29
I.6
1216b26–32 **LT**: 54; 134
II.1 **LT**: 62
1219a1–5 **LT**: 35
1219a12–1220a6 **LT**: 62
1219b8–16 **LT**: 131
II.2
1219b40–1220a2 **LT**: 69
II.10
1226a27–28 **BS**: 222–23
II.11
1228a14–15 **BS**: 224–25
III.1
1228b18–22 **LT**: 39
III.5 **LT**: 106
1233a22–25 **LT**: 107
VII.1
1235a10–35 **BS**: 204–5
1235a18–19 **LT**: 208
1235a29–31 **BS**: 196–97
1235a30 **LT**: 193–94
VII.2 **LT**: 240
1235b13–18 **LT**: 193
1235b30–34 **LT**: 39
1235b30–1236a7 **LT**: 195
1236a23–32 **LT**: 196–97; 239
1236b2–6 **LT**: 273
1236b6 **BS**: 242
1237a23ff **LT**: 225
VII.4
1239a34–39 **LT**: 34, 57
VII.5
1239b10–29 **LT**: 238
VII.6
1240a29–30 **LT**: 266–67
1240a33–b1 **LT**: 238, 267
1240a33–b37 **LT**: 267–68
1240b3–11 **LT**: 267
1240b11–20 **LT**: 267–68
1240b27–37 **LT**: 268
1240b40–1241a9 **BS**: 204–5
VII.6 **LT**: 270; 271–72; 272–73

VII.9
1241b11–22 **LT**: 238
1241b11–24 **LT**: 238
1241b17–22 **LT**: 246–47, 272
VII.10
1242a26–35 **LT**: 238
VII.12 **LT**: xi; 2–3; 221; 221–89
1244b1–4 **LT**: 237
1244b1–21 **LT**: 237–40
1244b1–1245b19 **LT**: 230
1244b4–7 **LT**: 238
1244b7–10 **LT**: 238
1244b10–15 **LT**: 239
1244b15–21 **LT**: 239–40
1244b21–26 **LT**: 240
1244b21–22 **LT**: 240
1244b22–26 **LT**: 240
1244b26–29 **LT**: 242
1244b26–33 **LT**: 242–43
1244b26–33 **LT**: 242–43
1244b33–1245a1 **LT**: 252
1244b33–1245a10 **LT**: 252
1245a1–5 **LT**: 257
1245a2 **LT**: 258
1245a5–10 **LT**: 258
1245a11–16 **LT**: 262
1245a11–29 **LT**: 262–64
1245a16–18 **LT**: 263
1245a18–26 **LT**: 263
1245a26–29 **LT**: 264
1245a29–30 **LT**: 32
1245a29–35 **LT**: 269–70
1245a29–b9 **LT**: 269–
1245a35–37 **LT**: 223
1245a35–39 **LT**: 274–75
1245a38 **LT**: 280
1245a39–b9 **LT**: 275–76
1245b1 **LT**: 281
1245b6–7 **LT**: 282–83
1245b9–14 **LT**: 285
1245b9–19 **LT**: 285–86
1245b14–19 **LT**: 285–86
VIII.1
1246b32–36 **BS**: 174
VIII.2 **LT**: 126
VIII.3 **LT**: 32–33; 99–133
1248b8–16 **LT**: 117
1248b26–30 **LT**: 101

ARISTOTLE (cont.)
1249a5–7 **LT:** 104
1249a12–b23 **LT:** 238
1249a15–16 **LT:** 84
1249a21–b23 **LT:** 70
1249b16–23 **LT:** 31–32; 103

Politics
I.2 **LT:** 26; 28–29; 201
1252b29–30 **LT:** 201
1253a1–4 **LT:** 26
1253a4–6 **LT:** 26–27
1253a8–9 **LT:** 52
1253a19–25 **BS:** 60–61
1253a20ff **BS:** 71
1253a21–24 **LT:** 65–66
1253a27–29 **LT:** 26–27
I.5
1254b25–30 **LT:** 28
I.8 **LT:** 28–29
I.13 **BS:** 170–71; 262
1260a12–14 **LT:** 49; **BS:** 262
II.2
1261a16–22 **LT:** 272
II.4
1262b10–14 **LT:** 272
II.9 **LT:** 105–6; 127–28
1271b7–10 **LT:** 109–10
III.3
1276b1–9 **BS:** 41
III.6 **LT:** 21–22

1278b20–21 **LT:** 21–22
III.9
1280a31–34 **LT:** 46
1280a31–35 **LT:** 49
III.16 **LT:** 120–21
1287a28–32 **LT:** 121
IV.11
1296a16–20 **LT:** 121
V.1
1301b30ff **LT:** 117
VI.1 **LT:** 124
VI.14 **LT:** 120
VII.1
1323b7–29 **LT:** 124–25
1323b24–29 **LT:** 49
VII.8
1328a21–b4 **LT:** 34, 57
1328a38–40 **LT:** 76–77
VII.13
1332b6–8 **LT:** 137

Rhetoric
I.2
1356b29–33 **BS:** 82
I.7 **BS:** 228
II.8
1386a10 **LT:** 269
II.12–13 **BS:** 164; 283

Poetics
Chap. 4
1448b5–17 **LT:** 209

GENERAL INDEX

For the benefit of digital users, indexed terms that span two pages (e.g., 52–53) may, on occasion, appear on only one of those pages

This index includes citations from this and its companion volume (see Preface)

LT for *Living Together*
BS for *Body and Soul*

accident, accidental [(kata) sumbêbêkos] **LT:** 39; 41; 69; 83–84; 104; 202; 207–8; **BS:** 2; 27–28; 27; 43–45; 44; 48–49; 50–51; 96; 114; 153–54
   accidental unity *see* **unity**
   change, substantial and non-substantial *see under kinêsis*
   see also essence, essential
Ackrill, J. L. **LT:** 15–17; 60; **BS:** 5–6; 8; 51; 58; 58–76 **passim**
action [praxis/poiêsis] **LT:** 34; 47; 51–52; 135–36; 222–23; 223–24; 273; 276–77; 279
   rational/non-rational **BS:** 124; 170
   voluntary/involuntary **BS:** 178–81; 180; 180–81; 187; 196; 190; 203; 222–23; 231; 238–39

virtuous **LT:** 24–26; 27–28; 30–31; 68–69; 75–76; 208; 209; 210–11; 213–14; 217–18; 242; 250–51; 258
   chosen for themselves or for their own sakes 3; 5; 12–13; 25; 59; 74–75; 79–98 **passim**, 99–133 **passim**, 134–89 **passim**, 203; **BS:** 4; 4
   vs. production [poiêsis] **LT:** 80–81; 81; 82–83; **BS:** 197–98; 224
Aeschylus **LT:** 1–2; 8; 29; 242; **BS:** 161
affection [philêsis/philein] **LT:** 3; 9; 149; 151; 192; 194; 195; 204; 205; 211
   see also reciprocity [antiphilêsis/antiphilein]
affections, attributes [pathê] **LT:** 87–88; 88; 137; 137–38; **BS:** 42–44; 43; 44; 45; 48–49
   of soul **LT:** 50; 66

affections, attributes [pathê] (cont.)
  of body
    psychophysical **LT:** 47–48; 68–69; 69
agent and patient
  reciprocal action **BS:** 160–16
Agency **BS:** 232
  rational, non-rational **LT:** 47–48; 49; 49; 52; 135; 146; 163; 164–65; **BS:** 255–56
  Responsible **LT:** 234–35; 251; **BS:** 220; 222–23; 227; 232; 233; 240–41; 242–43; 244; 246; 252–53; 256–57
akrasia / enkrateia **LT:** 27; 27; 48; 125; 137–38; 164–65; **BS:** 11–12; 102; 115; 116–17; 131–32; 132; 143–44; 150; 151–52; 152; 174; 177–215 **passim**, 264; 265; 267; 267–68; 269–70; 275; 276–77; 277; 277–80; 280–81; 281
Anaxagoras **LT:** 1–2; 29; 242; **BS:** 38
Annas **LT:** 102; 111; 112
aporia **LT:** 110; 115; 221–22; 230–31; 230; 233; 237; 237–40; 248; 262–64; 286; **BS:** 99–100; 263; 265; 267; 272
Aristophanes (in Plato's *Symposium*) **LT:** 222; 223; 271–72
artifact **LT:** 35; **BS:** 42; 46; 74; 93; 153; 155; 155
attachment [concern(ment)] [oikeiôsis or conciliatio] **LT:** 206; 278; **BS:** 240; 241; 243; 244; 245–51 **passim**
autonomy / autonomous **LT:** 49; 122; 124; **BS:** 46–47; 110–11; 118; 160–61; 162; 170
  agency *see* agency
  desires **BS:** 3–4; 171–72; 172–73
  movements **BS:** 9–10
  of ethical reasons **LT:** 146; 178–79; 184

Barnes, J. **LT:** 134; **BS:** 38
Bekker, I. **BS:** 152
benefactor, beneficiary **LT:** 9; 96; 119; 202–5 **passim**, 218–19; **BS:** 196–97
benefits **LT:** 3; 5; 25; 38; 39; 45; 47; 49; 86–87; 96; 112; 115; 117–18; 167–68; 171; 200; 202–3; 239; 271; 283; 287; **BS:** 4; 278
Bobonich, C. **LT:** 101; 216; 286
body
  indivisible **BS:** 6
  Lockean **BS:** 25; 26
  organic (functionally defined) **BS:** 2; 5–6; 6; 7; 51; 51; 52–54; 53; 59; 61; 64–65;

66–67; 67–68; 70–71; 71–72; 73; 93; 94–95; 149–50; 159; 279–80
Bonitz, H. **LT:** 242; **BS:** 77; 77; 88
Brittain, C. **BS:** 140
Broadie, S. **LT:** 105–6; 194; **BS:** 182; 187; 212; 212
Broadie and Rowe **BS:** 188; 202; 212; 212–13; 223
Buddhist views **BS:** 2
Burnyeat, M. F. **LT:** 33; 152; 155; 184–85; 186; **BS:** 10–11; 58–59; 60; 62; 68; 71; 93; 100; 119–20; 196
Butler, Bishop Joseph **LT:** 21; 110

Cairns, D **LT:** 121
Callicles **LT:** 52; 141; 142–43; 186–87
Casaubon, I. **LT:** 263–64
causes **LT:** 43; 43
  efficient (or moving) **LT:** 231; **BS:** 2; 4; 23; 74–75; 87; 97–98; 160; 193; 203–5; 224
  final **LT:** 13; 26; 31; 34; 43–44; 92; 104; 191–92; 199–200; 200; 242; 257; **BS:** 49–50; 74; 155
  formal **LT:** 27; 43–44; **BS:** 2; 11–12; 23; 34; 158
  material **BS:** 12; 65; 193; 203–5
change *see kinêsis*
Charles, D. **LT:** 81; 85; 94; **BS:** 11–12; 15–16; 114; 177–215 **passim**
choice [hairesis]
  haireton [choiceworthy/such-as-to-be-chosen] **LT:** 7; 103; 193; 203; 226; 234–35; 236; 241–42; 242–43; 244; 246; 246; 247; 248; 249–52; 252; 252; 253–55; 253–54; 255; 255–56; 257–58; 259; 260–61; 261; 263–64; 278–79; 279–80; 285; 286–87
  vs. decision [prohairesis] **BS:** 178; 223; 223; 224–25
Cicero **LT:** 23; 24; 28; 30; 89; **BS:** 242–43; 248
Clark, S. L. R. **LT:** 37; 61
Cognition **LT:** 232; 236; 256–57; **BS:** 174; 211–12; 213; 213
  cognitive hexeis / virtues
    see epistême
    see doxa
    see hupolêpsis
    see phronêsis
  cognitive capacities *see* perception; phantasia; **nous**

coincident, coincidental *see* accident, accidental
Collingwood, R.G. **LT:** 280; 282; 283
coming-to-be and passing-away see under *kinêsis*
community [koinônia] **LT:** 21–22; 26; 201; 246–47; 262; 272; 275–76; 283; **BS:** 246
complete *see* teleion
compound *see* form; matter **BS:** 29–30; 50; 52–55; 55; 69
  accidental **BS:** 47–48
  hylomorphic **BS:** 2
  psychophysical **LT:** 64; 65; 67–69; 69
conceptualism *see* realism
conditionality thesis **LT:** 13–20; 29–33; 101–2; 104–5; 118–19; 121; 129–30
  See also under Socrates
consciousness, self-consciousness **LT:** 91–92; 222–23; 223; 247; 248; 248; 222–23; 278–79; **BS:** 216-60 **passim**
consequentialism **LT:** 77–78; 148–49
contemplation [theôria] **LT:** 1–2; 3; 11–13; 15; 17; 19; 21; 23; 23–24; 24; 28; 31; 31–32; 33; 34–35; 41–42; 42; 44; 44; 47–48; 50; 51–52; 57–78 **passim**, 80; 90; 98; 98; 103; 106; 109–10; 112–13; 115; 128–29; 132; 209; 211–12; 213–18 **passim**, 226–29; 232–33; 258; 263; 265–66; 278; 280; 285; 286
continence/incontinence see *akrasia / enkrateia*
contingency **BS:** 13
  psychic **BS:** 2–3; 9; 12–13; 14; 15; 151–76; 166; 177–215
  see also necessary
continuity
  biological **BS:** 252–53
  psychological **LT:** 4
  spatio-temporal **BS:** 22; 32–33; 85
  simple, natural, artificial **BS:** 22–24; 22; 22
convex / concave **LT:** 70; **BS:** 129; 135; 149–50; 162–63; 163; 166
  see also snub, snubness
  see also unity
Cooper, John **LT:** 2; 3; 6–7; 12; 24–25; 35; 39; 46; 57–78 **passim**, 79; 97; 101; 119n.35, 190–91–191n.2, 194; 196; 200; 201; 209; 210–13; 218; 224; 248

craft [technê] **LT:** 23; **BS:** 2; 15; 144–45; 155
  see also **artifact**
Cynics **LT:** 7–8; 10; 23–24

Davidson, D. **LT:** 276
Décarie, V. **LT:** 238n.35, 252–53; 270; 274; 275
decision see *prohairesis*
deducibility / deductivism **LT:** 144; 144; 157–58; 158; 182–83; 183
defect, deficiency **LT:** 26; 27; 28; 40; 146; 169; 195; 195; 228; 231; **BS:** 81; 110; 150; 161; 170
definitions **LT:** 64; 66; 66n.27, 150; **BS:** 8–9; 122–25 **passim**, 100
  functional vs. compositional **BS:** 60–61; 64–65; 154
  see also separability
deliberation [bouleusis] **LT:** 48–49; 51; 59–60; 69; 93–94; 128–29; 135–36; 149–50; 163–64; **BS:** 221–25 **passim**, 226; 237–38
deliberative desire [bouleutikê orexis]: see under *prohairesis*
deliberative *phantasia*, see under *phantasia*
  of the akratic **BS:** 178; 201; 201; 207–9; 208; 281
  see also **parts**
Democritus **LT:** 121; 139–40; **BS:** 6; 38; 58
Denniston, J.D. **LT:** 252
desire [orexis] **BS:** 10–11; 106; 130; 167–68; 263; 266; 267–69; 270; 271; 272; 273; 274; 275–77; 279–82
  boulêsis [wish] **BS:** 142; 191; 228; 263; 275; 277–79
  in friendship **LT:** 40; 42; 50; 69; 83–84; 190–220 **passim**, 222; 266–67; 267–68; 269–71; 272–74; 285
  to perceive or to know oneself **LT:** 257; 257; 258; 258; 260
  epithumia [appetite] **LT:** 47; 53; 75–76; 110; 121; 138; 228; 268; **BS:** 179–80
  first/second-order **LT:** 48–49; 105
  thumos [spirit] **LT:** 110; 121; 127; **BS:** 130; 130–31; 139–40; 167–68; 179–80; 202–3
  see also prohairesis
determinacy/indeterminacy **LT:** 215; **BS:** 63
determinable, determination **BS:** 84

development
  embryological **BS:** 4; 149; 151–76 **passim**, 172–73
  moral **LT:** 123–24; 155; **BS:** 151–76 **passim**, 171–75
dialectic / dialectical argument **LT:** 45; **BS:** 48–49
  strong **LT:** 134–89 **passim**
dianoia see intellect and thought
Dirlmeier, F. **LT:** 119; 125; 246; 252–53; 269; 270; 270; 272–73; 274; 275; 280; 281; 282–83; 286
distribution of benefits and burdens/harms **LT:** 3; 5; 25; 87; 96; 112
  kat' axian [in accordance to merit] **LT:** 117–18; 118; 129–30
divinity see God
divisibility of self see indivisiblity
dominant end conceptions of eudaimonia see *under* eudaimonia
Dostoevsky, F. **LT:** 174
doxa **LT:** 215; 232; **BS:** 192–93; 265; 265; 270; 270–71; 272; 272; 273; 273; 276
  universal vs. particular **BS:** 197–99; 200–1; 202–3; 205–6; 208; 264; 280; 281–82; 281
  see also **parts**
  see *hupolêpsis*

ego, egoism
  colonizing ego **LT:** 4; 192; 224
  egoism, rational **LT:** 4; 5–6; 177–78; 178; 186–87; 191–92; 218–19
  egocentrism and ethnocentrism vs. ethocentrism **LT:** 4; 205; 205–9; 206
ethnocentrism see *under* ego
ethocentrism see *under* ego
elements [*stoicheia*] **BS:** 2; 6; 6; 28; 38; 41; 43; 59; 61–62; 64–65; 65–67; 68; 68–69; 99; 157–59; 192
elenchus, elenctic reasoning **LT:** 147; 149; 150; 150–51; 151–52; 158–59; 159–60
end [*telos*] see *under* teleology
endoxon, endoxic **LT:** 32–33; 54; 81; 139; 193; 196; 206; **BS:** 108; 154; 161; 211
Engstrom, S. **LT:** 102; 130; 133
epistêmê [knowledge] **LT:** 102–3; 122; 215; 232; **BS:** 11–12; 11–12; 36; 48–49; 79; 82; 82; 97; 99–101; 132; 132; 137–38; 140; 143; 144–45; 266–67; 281

and *akrasia* **BS:** 177–215 **passim**
  see also *akrasia / enkrateia*
equality [to ison], proportional vs. numerical **LT:** 117–18; 120
ergon [function, work] **LT:** 2–3; 10–11; 35; 46; 61–62; 96; 138; 171; 203; **BS:** 60; 60–61; 61; 62–65; 105–6; 110; 130–31; 137; 147; 155; 159
erga [facts] vs. *logoi* [arguments] **LT:** 233; 237; 264
idion **LT:** 10–11
erôs **LT:** 149; 190–91; 199; 263; 263–64
essence [to ti ên einai] **LT:** 26; 41; 66; 67; 68; 71; 71–72; 98; 142–43; 202; **BS:** 1; 4; 5; 6; 8–9; 20; 28; 34; 42–43; 44–45; 46; 49–50; 50; 52–53; 53; 54; 60; 64–65; 69–70; 73; 80–81; 81; 83–84; 85–86; 89; 90–91; 92–122; 93–94; 95; 97; 100; 106; 114; 146–47; 149–50; 153–54; 157; 161; 173
  as nature **BS:** 4; 9; 66–67
  human essence **LT:** 10–11; 21; 41–42; 43–45; 46–48; 51; 58; 72; 73; 90; 144; 166–85 **passim**, 186
  see also essentialism
essentialism **BS:** 20; 50; 81–83; 85; 97–101
ethocentric (vs. ethnocentric) reasons see **ego, egoism**
eudaimonia **LT:** 16; 281; **BS:** 226
  as an activity of the soul **LT:** 5; 7; 9; 48–49; 62; 80; 90; 95–97
  dominant end conceptions of **LT:** 14–15; 29; 50; 71; 71; 77–78; 80; 135–36
  eudaimonism / eudaimonist axiom **LT:** 3–4; 4–5; 5; 13; 25–26; 79–80; 79n.2, 80; 81; 82; 89–90; 91–92; 191–92; 191; 218–19
  inclusivist vs. exclusivist conceptions of **LT:** 2; 12; 13; 14–16; 18; 18–19; 19–20; 23; 25; 29; 50; 57–78 **passim**
eunoia [good will], *homonoia* **LT:** 195–96; 199; 207
eupraxia **LT:** 81; 88–89
eu zên [living well] see eudaimonia

families
  parents and offspring **LT:** 16; 30; 39; 96; 123–24; 190–91; 204; 204n.16, 205–6; **BS:** 97–98; 160; 171–72; 204–5; 225; 245

resemblance between **BS:** 2; 97–98; 159–60
mothers **LT:** 9; 127–28; 198–99; 203–4; 204; 211; 261; 267; **BS:** 37; 159–60; 171; 245
    matter provided by **BS:** 78; 87; 159–60; 160–61; 172–73
fathers **LT:** 128; 203–4; 204; 266–67; **BS:** 1; 13; 14–15; 164; 165; 245
    form provided by **BS:** 1; 2; 3–4; 78; 87; 172–73
female *see* reproduction
"for the most part" *see hôs epi to polu*
form [morphê, eidos] **LT:** 227; 26; 64; 66; 197; 227; **BS:** 31; 77–101 **passim**
    see also essence
    see also hylomorphism
    provided by the father
        see under parents
individual **BS:** 7–9; 17–34 **passim**, 36–37; 36n.6, 50–55; 70; 77–101 **passim**
    as principle of individuation **BS:** 17–19; 17–18
    Platonic **BS:** 88
    species form **BS:** 20; 26–27; 35–36; 78; 83–84
Frede, D. **LT:** 215; 248
Frede, M. **BS:** 8–9; 77–101 **passim**, 145
friendship *see philia*
Fritzsche, A.T.H. **LT:** 283
Function [ergon] *see ergon*

Gauthier, R.A. **BS:** 182; 186–87; 197–98; 202; 212; 242–43
Glassen, P. **LT:** 37
God [theos]—divine/godlike [theion] **LT:** 2–3; 10; 21; 23; 26–27; 31; 32; 41–42; 47–48; 68–69; 69; 83–84; 116; 121; 123–24; 132; 192; 221–89 **passim**; **BS:** 149; 156; 159; 166–67; 175; 225
goods
    bodily and psychic **LT:** 7; 59–60; 124–25
    categorical [haplôs] vs. "for someone" [tini] **LT:** 38–39; 39–41; 40; 41; 42–43; 51; **BS:** 134
    external **LT:** 7–8; 12; 59–60; 69–70; 74–75; 76; 84; 97–98; 100–1; 101; 104; 106; 107; 109–10; 113; 114–15; 116–17; 117–18; 118–19; 120; 124–25; 128–29; 130; 132; 132–33; 210; 237

instrumental vs. final **LT:** 15; 38; 40; 40–64; 50; 82; 90; 97–98; 211–12; 223; 274; 281; 282
natural vs. of fortune and contested **LT:** 18; 19; 31–32; 32–33; 101–2; 102–6; 109–10; 110; 112–13; 113–14; 115; 117; 118; 124; 126–27; 129–30; 130
the good [to agathon] **BS:** 112–13; 143
vs. the apparent good **BS:** 11; 134; 142
the highest (human) good
    see eudaimonia
unconditional [haplôs] vs. conditional **LT:** 18; 38–39; 101–2; 129–30
see also kalon
Greenwood, L.H.G. **LT:** 34; 57

habit [hexis] and habituation [ethismos] **LT:** 126; 93; 123–24; 123–24; 132; 141; 152; 152; 154–56; 164; 165; 166–68; 167–68; 169; 170–71; **BS:** 143; 167
haireton see under Choice
Hardie, W. F. R. **LT:** 37; 61; 215; **BS:** 206
Harlfinger, D. **LT:** 225
heart, as principle of animal **BS:** 7; 23; 63; 105–6; 110–11; 122–24; 171–72
hedonism, hedonic value **LT:** 35; 44; 148–49; 255–56; **BS:** 256
Heinaman, R. **LT:** 53–54; 86; **BS:** 37; 78–79; 79
homonoia see eunoia [good will]
homonymy, homonymy principle **LT:** 65–66; **BS:** 35; 60–61; 61; 61–62; 105
honor [timê]/honorable or to-be-honored [timion] **LT:** 10–11; 18; 24; 34–35; 50; 60; 66; 75; 87–88; 100–1; 101; 106–7; 108–10 **passim**, 110; 112–13; 113; 116–17; 117–18; 118–19; 121; 127–28; 128–29; 131–33; 150; 151-**C**; **BS:** 4
hope/expectation [elpis] *see under phantasia*
horos, standard **LT:** 31–32; 103; 132
hôs epi to polu [for the most part, usual] **LT:** 217; **BS:** 49; 110
hou heneka see end
Hume, D. **LT:** 85–86; 180–81
    see also **Humean**
Humean **LT:** 180–81 **BS:** 224; 224; 256
    quasi-Humean **LT:** 156–57
hupolêpsis **BS:** 202; 270
Hurka, T. **LT:** 97

hylomorphism **LT:** 53–54; **BS:** 58–76 **passim**, 151–76 **passim**
see also matter; form

identity **LT:** 63
see also **unity**
personal **LT:** 4; 58–59; 62; 63 **BS:** 216–60 **passim**
indexical(ity) **LT:** 69; **BS:** 237–38
individual see particular(s); form
individuation **BS:** 17–34 **passim**
synchronic and diachronic **BS:** 20
see also identity, unity
Indivisible
in number **BS:** 10; 47; 82; 119–20; 121
see also **individual**
in species [infima species] **BS:** 84–85
magnitudes **BS:** 40
Inwood, B. **LT:** 119; 225; 269; 270; 274; **BS:** 206; 225; 247–48n.43, 250
images [phantasmata] see under *phantasia*
imagination see *phantasia*
impartiality **LT:** 119; 120–21; 121; 163–64; 208–9
impediment, external interference **LT:** 18; 32; **BS:** 74; 110; 191; 199; 199–200; 203–4
to contemplation **LT:** 12; 74–20; 77
inclusivist vs. exclusivist readings see under eudaimonia
instrumental, non–instrumental see under **goods**
intellect and thought [nous, dianoia] **LT:** 2; **BS:** 263
practical **LT:** 47–48; 58; 62; 67; 68–69; 72; 156–57; **BS:** 3–4; 14; 14–15; 151; 164–65; 172–73
theoretical **LT:** 12; 21; 51; 52; 58; 57–58; 61; 62; 65; 67; 67; 68; 69; 71; 71–72; 73–74; 192; **BS:** 7; 146–47; 148–50
"from outside" [thurathen] **BS:** 148; 166–67; 171
intellectualism
"intellectualist" conceptions of eudaimonia **LT:** 2; 3; 33; 57–78 **passim**
Socratic intellectualism (in moral psychology) see Socrates

interpersonal comparison **LT:** 112; 115
Irwin, T. H. **LT:** 14; 15–16; 17; 36–37; 40; 45; 58; 79; 81; 95; 101; 111; 111; 113; 114; 119; 134–89 **passim**, 191–92; 192; 196; 196; 197–98; 199–200; 200; 201–2; 204; 204; 206; 208; 212; 212; 213; 214; **BS:** 15; 36; 38n.13, 49; 60–61; 65; 70; 78–79; 79; 93; 97; 114; 126; 126; 156–57; 182; 184–85; 188; 197–98; 200; 201; 202; 204; 205; 223; 224–25

Joachim, H. H. **LT:** 73; **BS:** 38; 43; 186–87
justice / injustice **LT:** 4; 19; 37; 52–54; 70; 102n.9, 103–4; 105–6; 116; 116–20 **passim**, 120; 129; 130; 138; 157; 165–66; 180–81; 183; 186; 197–98; 218; 222; 223–24; 260–61; **BS:** 141; 254

kalokagathia [fine–and–goodness], kaloskagathos [the fine–and–good person] · **LT:** 99–133 **passim**
kalon [fine] **LT:** 89; 99–133 **passim**, 135; 149; 152; 168–69; 169; 194; 201; 203; 209; 231; 231; 255–56; 256; 257; 257; 260; 261–62; 278
Kant, I. **LT:** 82–83; 82–83; 99–133 **passim**, 178–79
Kenny, A. **LT:** 17; 61; 105; 225; 270 **BS:** 185; 200; 207
Keyt, D **LT:** 44; 57; 77
kinds
natural (vs. artificial?) **LT:** 39–40; 40; 40–41; 42; 42–43; 44–45; **BS:** 217–18
kinêsis
alteration **LT:** 45; **BS:** 6; 124; 35–57 **passim**, 112
change, substantial and non–substantial **BS:** 35–57 **passim**, 58–60; 60; 67; 67; 68–71
generation and corruption/coming-to-be and passing-away **LT:** 45; **BS:** 5; 17–18; 35–57 **passim**, 58; 59; 60; 67; 67; 68–69; 70–71; 73; 95–97; 96; 96–97; 97; 118–19; 154; 157
growth and decay **BS:** 35–57 **passim**, 69; 70; 106

locomotion **BS:** 5; 106–8; 123–24; 131–32; 138; 262–63; 265–66
   locomotive *see under* **parts**
   vs. *energeia* **BS:** 72–73; 73
koinônia see Community
Konstan, D. **LT:** 191
Korsgaard, C **LT:** 82–83; 83; 100; 105; **BS:** 152
Kosman, A **LT:** 221–89 **passim**
Kraut, R. **LT:** 2; 3; 6; 13; 17; 22–23; 23; 34, 41; 73; 79–80; 83; 111n.21, 112; 120; 192

law [nomos] **LT:** 120–22 **passim**, 132 **BS:** 6
life [bios/zoê] **BS:** 250–51
   emergence of **BS:** 58–59; 59–60; 60; 68–71
lives [bioi]
   active or political **LT:** 1; 11–12; 26; 29–30; 30–31; 57–58
   choice between **LT:** 1–2; 76–77
   contemplative **LT:** 2–3; 11–12; 25–26; 28–31; 32–33; 57–58; 71; 73; 106
   mixed **LT:** 2; 15–16; 19–20; 22; 57–58; 73
Locke, J. **LT:** 35; 224 **BS:** 7; 15–16; 118; 216–60 **passim**
   Lockean body *see under* **body**
logikôs vs. *phusikôs* **LT:** 214; **BS:** 196–97
logos
   account or definition **LT:** 66n.27; **BS:** 8–9; 44–45; 60–61; 62–63; 94; 105–6; 153
   see also under separability
   argument **LT:** 2–3; 243; 246–47; 249–50; 259–60; **BS:** 191
   Reason **BS:** 129; 130; 134; 141; 144–45; 163; 164; 165
   see also universal
love/loving *see* affection [philêsis/philein]
Lorenz, H. **LT:** 125; 225; **BS:** 177; 202; 213
luck [tuchê] **LT:** 26; 26
   fortune (good vs. bad) **LT:** 6; 7; 8–9; 18; 101; 102–3; 124–25; 126; 129–30; 132
   constitutive **LT:** 100–1; 122–25 **passim**, 128; 128; 132–33

male *see* **reproduction**
matter **LT:** 144; **BS:** 1–9; 17–34 **passim**, 50–54; 58–60; 61–62; 67–75
   functional vs. compositional **BS:** 6–7; 45; 49; 51–53; 53; 54; 63; 64–65; 69; 70; 71; 87; 95

perceptible vs. intelligible **LT:** 66; **BS:** 8; 91–93; 95
proximate vs. non-proximate **BS:** 27; 28; 33–34; 54; 65; 65
McCabe, M. M. **LT:** 221–23; 222–23n.3, 224; 230; 239; 271; 272
McDowell, J **LT:** 19; 52; 53–54; 103; 134–89 **passim**; **BS:** 3; 12; 150; 151–52; 162; 163; 172; 197–98; 205–6; 206; 279–80
mechanical, mechanism **LT:** 159; 173–74
megalopsuchia **LT:** 106–10 **passim**, 111; 113; 115–50; 115–16; 116–17; 120; 128–29
memory *see phantasia*
Menn, S. **LT:** 111; 124
Meno **LT:** 18; 101; 102; 260–61
menstrual fluid [katamenia] **BS:** 1; 2; 3–4; 78; 155; 160
merit, reward, punishment **LT:** 85; 88; 117–18; **BS:** 172; 254; 254–55; 278–79
   see also distribution of benefits and burdens / harms
Meyer, S. **LT:** 122; 123–24
Mill, J. S. **LT:** 265
Miller, F. **LT:** 73
Moody-Adams, M. **LT:** 122
monists vs. pluralists [Presocratic] **BS:** 37–38; 38; 38–39; 39–42; 44–45; 50; 53
mothers / fathers *see* family
motive/motivation *see* desire
movers **BS:** 102–50 **passim**, 261–82 **passim**
   moved/moving **BS:** 125–26; 125; 136; 156
   prime (first) **LT:** 227–28; **BS:** 36; 81–82; 87; 89; 104; 156
   of the animal **BS:** 133; 134; 134–35
   unmoved **LT:** 284; **BS:** 100; 136; 156

Nagel, T. **LT:** 49; 122
nature [phusis] **BS:** 2
   first vs. second **LT:** 165–66; 166; 166–67; 167–68; 173–74; 175–77; 179–80; 180–81; 183
   human vs. animal **LT:** 57–78 **passim**
   see also essence
phusiologoi vs. *phusikoi* **BS:** 204
   by nature [phusei] **LT:** 2–3; 11; 16; 21–22; 26; 26–28; 30; 31; 41; 52; 101; 268; 269; **BS:** 264; 274; 276

necessity, necessities [to anankaion, ta anankaia] **LT:** 180–81; 282–83; 283
  absolute / unconditional [haplôs] **BS:** 156
  hypothetical or conditional [ex hupotheseôs] **LT:** 59; **BS:** 64–65; 153; 153; 158–59; 160; 161
Nietzsche, F. **LT:** 173–74
nominalism [nominalist] **BS:** 78–179; 84; 98
normativity **LT:** 28–29; 37–38; 43; 43–44; 45; 45; 144; 192; 194; **BS:** 267; 267; 269; 274–77 **passim**, 279; 279–80; 281–82
  norms **LT:** 150; 159–60; **BS:** 3; 197
nous see Intellect
Nozick, R. **LT:** 37
Nussbaum, M. **LT:** 156; 286; **BS:** 38; 59; 125n.36, 126; 199–200

objectivist (vs. subjectivist) **LT:** 6–7 **BS:** 240; 241
  conceptions of good **LT:** 34–35; 35; 36–37; 44; 44
oikeiôsis, to oikeion see Attachment [concern(ment)] [oikeiôsis or conciliatio]
  more and less *oikeion* explanation see *phusikôs* vs. *logikôs*
one see **Identity**; **unity**
Osborne, C, **LT:** 242; 244; 270; 274; 283

Parents – offspring *see* family
particular, particulars [kath' hekaston/kath' hekasta] **LT:** 160; **BS:** 17–34 **passim**, 36; 45; 80–81; 88; 97; 178–79; 185; 185–86; 198–99
  Individual substance **BS:** 5–6; 8; 38; 45–46; 46; 47–48; 48; 81; 83–85; 98–99
  vs. individuals **BS:** 79
  see also universal
  see also form
parts
  of animals [homoiomerous, anhomoirmerous] **BS:** 1–2; 61–62; 61; 62–64; 66–68; 110–11; 123–24; 154; 158
  of soul **LT:** 68; 111; 138; **BS:** 3; 9–10; 12; 13; 103; 105–12; 169–70; 265; 266; 269
    aisthêtikon [perceptive] **BS:** 9–11; 14; 91; 93; 167; 168; 169; 170; 175

    bouleutikon [deliberative] **LT:** 41; 68; 70
    epistêmonikon [scientific] **BS:** 164–65; 174; 264; 264; 281–82
    epithumêtikon [appetitive] **BS:** 3; 167
    "locomotive" **BS:** 10; 14; 103; 103–4; 118; 123–24; 127; 137; 139; 146–47; 148; 149–50; 169–70
    logistikon [rational] or *doxastikon* [opinative] **BS:** 13; 165; 167; 264; 273
    noêtikê [intellective] or *dianoêtikon* [thinking] **LT:** 83–84; **BS:** 166–67
    orektikon [desiderative] **BS:** 1–2; 3; 9–11; 13–15; 152; 152; 162; 164; 167–68; 169; 170; 173; 174–75; 265; 269–70; 273; 279–80
    phantastikon [imaginative] **BS:** 9–26; 14; 167; 168; 169
    threptikon [nutritive] **BS:** 13–14; 103; 105; 107; 108–12; 117–20; 122–24; 126–27; 128n.43, 130–32; 134; 137; 147; 148–49; 159; 162; 163; 165; 166; 166–67; 169; 241; 243; 266
    see also separability
Pears, D. **LT:** 87–88; 87
perception **LT:** 67–68; 67–68; 135–36; 152; 204
  joint perception or co-perception see *sunaisthêsis*
  aisthêtikon [perceptive] see under **parts**
perishability **BS:** 32; 95; 158–59
perishable vs. imperishable **BS:** 36; 79; 95; 95; 96; 97; 109; 147; 156; 159
phainomena [appearances] **BS:** 204–5
phantasia **LT:** 65–66; 67–68; 67–68
  hope/expectation **LT:** 128; 227–28; 228; 284; **BS:** 221–22
  images [phantasmata] **LT:** 65; 67–68; 67–68; **BS:** 10–11; 262; 267–68; 269–70; 281
  perceptual vs. deliberative **BS:** 10–11; 168; 192–93; 198; 202–3; 221; 226; 239–40; 261–82 **passim**
  memory **LT:** 20; 215; 217; 228; 228; 284; **BS:** 144–45; 145–46; 146–47; 149; 171; 198; 217–18; 221; 237–38; 251; 255–56
phantastikon [imaginative] see under **parts**
phantasmata [images] see under *phantasia*

philia **LT:** 4–5; 13; 14; 21–22; 25–26; 32; 38; 40; 40; 50; 52; 61; 75; 83–84; 90–91; 99; 119; 121; 125; 190–220 **passim**, 221–89 **passim**; **BS:** 196–97; 204–5; 242; 243
   on account of pleasure [dia hêdonên] **LT:** 3; 196–97; 199–200; 202; 224–25; 238; 240; 283
   on account of advantage or utility [dia to chresimon] [aka "utility friendship"] **LT:** 18; 83–84; 84; 194; 194; 196; 197–98; 199–200; 201–2; 205; 283
   on account of virtue [di' aretên] [aka "character friendship"] **LT:** 3; 4; 35; 194; 194n.8, 195–96; 196–97; 198; 199; 200; 202; 205; 206; 207; 213; 218; 224; 224–25; 238; 239; 239; 240–41
   kath' hauton vs. *kata sumbebêkos* **LT:** 83–84; 83–84; 196–98
philêsis, philein see affection [philêsis/philein]
phronêsis [practical wisdom], *phronimos* [practically wise] **LT:** 31; 47–48; 51; 59–60; 64; 65; 68–69; 101–2; 102–3; 103; 124–25; 125–26; **BS:** 1; 3; 4; 12; 14–16; 103; 151–52; 162; 163; 164–65; 166; 171; 172; 173; 174; 178; 211–13; 212–13; 213; 237–38; 264; 263; 279–80; 281–82
   see also virtue
phusis see nature
plasticity, compositional **BS:** 64–65; 153
   plastic nature (Cudworth) **BS:** 239–40; 240
Plato **LT:** 1–2; 104n.71; 112; 127–28; 146–21; 157–25; 161; 184–85; 196; 232; 260–61; **BS:** 3; 17–18; 104; 152; 166; 184; 225; 241; 245–46; 249; 249
platonism, anti-platonism **BS:** 31; 58–59; 83; 84; 129; 136–37; 216; 220
pleasure(s) **LT:** 2–3; 7; 8–9; 20–26; **passim**; **BS:** 11; 102; 108–9; 109; 112–13; 118; 165; 133; 134; 136–37; 139–41; 141; 142; 181–82; 210; 241; 242–43; 245–46; 253–56; 262–63
   as alterations see under *kinêsis*
   life filled with **LT:** 10–11; 15–16; 20–22; 51; 171; 215

sensual **LT:** 2; 50; 51; 51; 87–88; 135–36; 242; **BS:** 169
   of virtue **LT:** 68–69; 84; 96
   noetic **LT:** 221–89 **passim**
Plutarch **LT:** 270
polis [city] **LT:** 1; 26–27; 53; 81–82; 87–88; 90; 96; 108; 111; 172; 201; 272
political **BS:** 3; 41; 162–63
   Animal **LT:** 2–3; 11–12; 14; 16; 21–22; 26; 27; 28–29; 36–37; 52; 53; **BS:** 141
   life see under lives
praise [epainos] **LT:** 130–33 **passim**, 206
   praiseworthy [epaineton] **LT:** 103–4; 103; 106; 113; 129; 131; 131; 131n.50, 132
   praise vs. blame **LT:** 122; 130; 251
praxis
   vs. *poiêsis* see under action
   eupraxia **LT:** 81; 88–89; **BS:** 223–24
   see also action
predication, predicates see properties
premises see under propositions
Price, A. W. **LT:** 61; **BS:** 186–87; 200; 204
prime mover see under mover
Principle of Non-Contradiction (PNC) **LT:** 142–43; 142; 145; 166; **BS:** 48–49
prohairesis [decision] **LT:** 127; 135; 146; 251; 268; 273; **BS:** 15–16; 156–57; 178–79; 179; 179–80; 213; 217–18; 223; 221–28 **passim**, 228; 233–34; 236–37; 249; 267; 277–78
   as a deliberative desire [bouleutikê orexis] **LT:** 10; **BS:** 11; 143–44; 213; 223
   as *orexis dianoêtikê* or *orektikos nous* **BS:** 14–15; 156–57; 223–24; 228
properties [affections, attributes]
   coincidental/accidental **LT:** 39; 83–84; 84; **BS:** 52–53; 67; 67–68; 68–69; 69; 153
   essential / non-essential **LT:** 39–40; 40; 41–42; 66; **BS:** 20; 39; 42–43; 44–45; 48–49; 53
   necessary **LT:** 42; 66
   see also affections
propositions [protaseis] **BS:** 197; 199
   premises **BS:** 207; 208
   Major, minor **LT:** 159; 160
   of good, possible,
   universal vs. particular **LT:** 160; **BS:** 185; 186–89; 187; 188; 191–92; 198–99; 200; 201; 203

hê teleutaia protasis [last proposition] **BS:** 198; 206; 208
Protagoras **LT:** 6–7; 34–35
Putnam, H. **LT:** 86; **BS:** 59; 93
Pythagoras, Pythagorean **LT:** 23; 29; 224–25; **BS:** 154
quantity (or portion) of stuff **BS:** 6; 6; 7; 18; 40; 40; 42; 42; 51; 52–53; 59; 64–65n.20, 68; 69; 70–71; 87; 90–91; 94–95; 110–11

Rackham, H. **LT:** 238; 239; 245; 269; 270; 274; 283; 286; **BS:** 204
rationalist, non-rationalist, anti-rationalist readings **LT:** 134–89 **passim**
realism about kinds / universals **BS:** 78–79
  vs. nominalism see nominalism
Reason see *logos*
reasons
  internal vs. external **LT:** 155–56; 159
  motivating vs. justifying **LT:** 154
reciprocity
  of goodwill [*eunoia*], see *eunoia* [good will], *homonoia*
  antiphilêsis **LT:** 195
reductionism **BS:** 49–50
  Materialist **BS:** 154
reflective reassurance **LT:** 53; 145; 172n.49, 175–76; 176–77; 179; 179–80; 182–83; 184; 185; 186
reproduction
  female **BS:** 161
  Male **BS:** 159–60
  reproductive isolation **BS:** 49
  sexual vs. nonsexual **BS:** 140
Richards, H. **LT:** 243; 269
Rieckher, J. **LT:** 285; 286
Robinson, D. B. **LT:** 239; 275
Robinson, R. **BS:** 185; 202; 206; 212
Ross, W.D. **LT:** 71; 197; 204; 204; 206; 208; 214; 238; **BS:** 36; 36; 77; 80–82; 80–81; 88; 88–89; 88; 90; 92; 107; 109; 204; 212; 223; 275
Rowe, C. **LT:** 194; 197; 206; 208; 214; 225; **BS:** 182; 188; 199; 202; 204; 212; 212–13; 223; 225

scholastics, scholasticism **BS:** 34; 228; 229; 229–30
seed – male, female, **BS:** 160–61
  see also **reproduction**

self
self-deception **LT:** 218; 273
self-determination **LT:** 126–27
self-knowledge **LT:** 107; 109; 120; 120; 210–11; 212; 215; 218; 223; 224; 252; 260–61; 265; 269; 278
self-love **LT:** 50–51; 99; 110–20; 129; 193; 199; 206–7; 208–9
  proper vs. improper **LT:** 110; 111; 111; 114; 116; 115–16; 117–19; 121; 208–9
self-sacrifice **LT:** 115
self-sufficiency [autarkeia] **LT:** 7; 10; 16–17; 21; 23; 26; 28; 30; 60–61; 75–76; 76–77; 183; 192–93; 201; 209–10; 212–13; 221–89 **passim**
separability **LT:** 64; **BS:** 103–6 **passim**
  actual **LT:** 64; 64; 65–67; 69; 70–71
  in account or definition [logôi] or thought **LT:** 64; 66; 70; **BS:** 5; 104; 105–6; 108–9; 135
  in magnitude and place [megethei and topôi] **BS:** 104; 104; 105–6; 110–12; 265
  of substance **BS:** 17–18; 54; 69–70; 90–91
  unqualified [haplôs] **BS:** 104
sets [kinds] **BS:** 98–99
Siegler, F. **LT:** 37
silencing **LT:** 19; 136
similarity in character **LT:** 207; **BS:** 242
Smyth, H.W. **LT:** 58; 254; **BS:** 181; 206
snub, snubness **BS:** 8; 92; 94; 129; 135; 146–47; 149–50; 162–63; 163; 166
  see also Concave vs. convex
Socrates **LT:** 2; 7–8; 10; 15–16; 23; 102; 146–49; 150; 153–54; 157; 160–61; 161; 184–85; 186–87; 193–94; 200; 207; 213; 215–16; 272; **BS:** 2–3; 14; 152; 154; 245–46
  conditionality thesis **LT:** 18; 101–2; 130
  identification of virtue with knowledge **LT:** 101; 102–3; 103; **BS:** 14; 151–52; 174
  on the types of life and goods **LT:** 20–21; 226–27; 238; 248
    self-awareness and value 248n.54, 250–51; 254–55; 265
  views on akrasia **BS:** 151–52; 180–81; 184; 211–13 **passim**
Solomon, J. **LT:** 239; 245; 246; 252–53; 253; 270; 274

Sorabji, R. **LT:** 44; 230; 243; 270
soul **LT:** 4–5; 41–42; 43; 62; 151; **BS:** 102–50 **passim**
 activity of: see under eudaimonia
 beauty of **LT:** 150; 151–52; 152–53; 159–60
 goods of: see under **goods**
 parts of, see **parts**
 vs. body **LT:** 7; 64; 70; 269; 271; 272; **BS:** 1; 3; 4–6; 6; 28; 32; 34; 42; 51; 52–54; 53; 54; 58–76 **passim**, 93; 104; 105–6; 125–26; 149–50; 151; 152–53; 154–55; 157; 158–59
 virtues of: see virtues
 see also form
Spartans **LT:** 99–133 **passim**
Spengel, L. **LT:** 239
Stern-Gillet **LT:** 224
Stoics **LT:** 5; 7–8; 19; 23; 24–25; 30; 31; 88–89; 94–95; 102; 102; 206; 278; **BS:** 216–60 **passim**
Striker, G. **BS:** 244
Susemihl, F. **LT:** 283
Suits, B. **LT:** 37
subject, substratum [hupokeimenon] **BS:** 6; 35–57 **passim**, 58; 60; 67–71; 85–87; 96; 154
substance [ousia] **LT:** 142–43; 144; 181–82; 256
 immaterial or non-sensible **BS:** 17; 87–88; 157; 167; 219
 material, sensible, or natural **BS:** 8; 9; 17; 36; 38; 79; 80; 82; 89–90
 primary **BS:** 17–18; 42; 46–47n.31; 78–80; 82; 83–84; 85–86; 87; 90–91
 secondary **BS:** 80–81; 82; 83; 98–99; 101
sublunary, superlunary **LT:** 251–52; 256; **BS:** 36; 49; 81; 156–59 **passim**
sumpheron, to [advantage] **LT:** 119; 194; **BS:** 141; 179
sunaisthêsis **LT:** 211; 215; **BS:** 221; 221–22; 238–51 **passim**, 246
superstructure view **LT:** 32–33; 77
sustoichia [column] **LT:** 256
suzên [living together] **LT:** 3; 5; 21–22; 25; 210; 215; 222–23; 238; 238; 239–40; 239; 241–42; 259; 261; 263–64; 265–66; 267; 274–76; 276–77; 280–81; 279–80; 283–84; 284–85

technê see Craft; artifacts
teleology **LT:** 40; 43; 49; 52; 89; 91–92; 122; 123–24; 180; 180; **BS:** 2; 11–12; 14; 97–98; 110; 126–27; 151–76 **passim**, 197; 220; 239
 end [telos] **LT:** 142–43; 180; **BS:** 147; 153; 223–24; 249–50; 268–69
 of action **LT:** 118; 184; 194
 final cause *see under* **causes**
 see also eudaimonia
 explanatory asymmetry **BS:** 1–2; 11–12; 20; 110; 152; 156–62; 172; 204–5
teleion, teleioteron, teleiotata **LT:** 5; 7; 13–15; 16; 60; 60; 62; 62–63; 63–64; 72–73; 80; 95–97; 97; 117; 215; 226
 final vs. complete **LT:** 14–15
 perfect **LT:** 14; 60; 62; 63; 96–97
time
 number of motion **BS:** 100; 100
 perception of **BS:** 134
twins, conjoined **BS:** 7; 9; 23

unity
 accidental/coincidental vs. intrinsic **BS:** 4–5; 6; 39; 47–48; 50; 52; 53–54; 69–70; 69
 numerical **BS:** 10; 47; 47; 55
 psychic contingency *see under* **contingency**
universal [to katholou] **LT:** 193–94; 196–97; **BS:** 19–20; 20; 26–27; 27; 33; 35–36; 36; 37; 42; 78; 78; 78–79; 79; 79; 79; 80; 80–81; 82; 82; 83; 83; 83; 83–84; 86; 86; 83–84; 86; 88; 95; 96–97; 97; 97; 97–101 **passim**, 144–45; 145; 177–78; 178–79; 179; 180; 180–81; 185–90 **passim**, 196–205 **passim**, 211–13 **passim**, 264; 280; 281–82; 281; 281
 vs. individuals or particulars **BS:** 20; 27; 38
 see under doxa; proposition
 see also particulars
"up to us" [eph' hêmin] or "up to agent" **LT:** 103–4; 123; 129; **BS:** 223; 225; 226–27
utility [to chresimon] see *philia*

vice [kakia] or wickedness [mochthêria] **LT:** 27; 104–5; 108; 109–10; 137; 164–65; 184–85; 253–54; **BS:** 4; 142; 165; 178–79; 180–81; 281; 179; 180; 226–27

virtue [aretê]:
    complete see under *teleion*
    ethical or moral **LT:** 4–5; 7–8; 11–13; 16;
        18–19; 21–22; 23; 24–26; 27; 28–33;
        35; 35; 36; 37; 37–38; 42; 42; 47;
        48–49; 49; 49; 51; 52; 50; 54; 57–78
        passim, 80; 90–92; 177; 180
    hexis prohairetikê **BS:** 4
    intellectual vs. ethical   **LT:** 11–12; 64; 62;
        190; 202–3; 212
    natural vs. "authoritative"   **BS:** 4; 14; 162; 174
    politikê [civic] or natural   **LT:** 128; 132–33
    sovereignty / supremacy of   **LT:** 8; 8
    see also Socrates

Walzer and Mingay   **LT:** 134; 244; 275; 275
White, N.   **LT:** 111; 114
White, S.   **LT:** 105
Wilkes, K.   **LT:** 37; **BS:** 217; 217–18n.4
Will   **LT:** 101–2; 174; 174–81; **BS:** 225; 228–29;
    187–231; 244; 252–53
    weakness and strength of see *akrasia / enkrateia*
    goodwill see *eunoia*
Williams, B.   **LT:** 86; 87; 94; 94
Wittgenstein, L.   **LT:** 179
Wood, A.   **LT:** 99–100; 100; 111; 111; 116; 118;
    120
Woolf, R.   **LT:** 225; 270; 274